NO LONGER PROPERTY OF
SEATTLE PUBLIC LIBRARY

D0557912

# GREAT MUSLIMS OF THE WEST

*Makers of Western Islam*

MUHAMMAD MOJLUM KHAN

*Great Muslims of the West: Makers of Western Islam*

First published in England by

Kube Publishing Ltd
Markfield Conference Centre
Ratby lane
Markfield
Leicestershire LE67 9SY
United Kingdom

Tel: +44 (0) 1530 249230
Fax: +44 (0) 1530 249656

Website: www.kubepublishing.com
Email: info@kubepublishing.com

© Muhammad Mojlum Khan, 2017 All rights reserved

The right of Muhammad Mojlum Khan to be identified as the author of this work has been asserted by him in accordance with the Copyright, Designs and Patents act, 1988.

Cataloguing-in-Publication Data is available from the British library

ISBN 978-1-84774-113-4 casebound
ISBN 978-1-84774-112-7 paperback
ISBN 978-1-84774-114-1 ebook
Book Design: © Fatima Jamadar
Cover Design: Inspiral Design
Typesetting: Nasir Cadir

Printed by: IMAK Ofset, Turkey

This book is dedicated to:

MRS FULESA KHANUM
*my mother, for her love and sacrifices.*

FAHMIDA KHAN AND MUHAMMAD ABDUL WAHID
*for their kindness and encouragement.*

ASEFA AND MOHAMMAD ALI QAYYUM
*for their support and co-operation.*

*May the Islamic world and the West
continue to learn and promote knowledge,
understanding and co-operation
for the benefit of the whole of humanity!*

# CONTENTS

# INTRODUCTION

The study of history can be traced back to the origin of humanity because, ultimately, it is the study of the record or recollection of man's actions, deeds, misdeeds and endeavours since the beginning of his journey on earth. That is why humanity has always been preoccupied in the study of history since the beginning of time. Indeed, man's longing for immortality is clearly reflected in his efforts to undertake positive and, at times, negative actions so as to leave his indelible mark; to stand out from the rest of the crowd, so to speak. However, it is equally true that the study of history requires sound knowledge and an understanding of a wide range of subjects and disciplines including relevant linguistic skills. That explains why most of the world's greatest philosophers, thinkers and writers have also been prominent historians because our present condition can only be properly understood and appreciated when it is explored and analysed in the light of our past.

But what actually is history? In his classic study, also entitled *What is History?* (1961), the British historian Edward H. Carr (1892–1982) wrote, 'History consists of a corpus of ascertained facts. The facts are available to the historian in documents, inscriptions and so on, like fish on the fishmonger's slab. The historian collects them, takes them home and cooks and serves them in whatever style appeals to him.'[1] This raises another question: who decides what is 'fact' or 'fiction'? Again, Carr argued that the 'facts do not, as is sometimes said, speak for themselves, or if they do, it is the historian who decides which facts shall speak – he cannot give the floor to them all.'[2] Why?

Simply because there is no such thing as pure objectivity in the study and exploration of the past, present and the future. In other words, the historian's experiences, background, education, approach and personal biases often play a far greater role in the formulation of their point of view than is generally appreciated. That is why – in addition to a sound knowledge of the 'past' – an awareness and understanding of the 'self' and its place in relation to the whole is essential for developing a rounded view of history and its relevance to the present and future. Indeed, the philosopher and historian, Robin G. Collingwood (1889–1943), argued in his *Idea of History* (1946) that, 'Knowing yourself means knowing what you can do; and since nobody knows what he can do until he tries, the only clue to what man can do is what man has done.'[3]

However, according to other historians, history is nothing more than a story of the development of humanity through the passage of time, taking note of their rise and decline, achievements and failures, deeds and misdeeds. To them, 'history', or the 'past', is a sequence of events that have unfolded one after another, whilst the professional historians, unlike the annalists, are more interested in the 'why' and 'how' of history rather than only the 'what' and 'when'. Although Sir Isaiah Berlin (1909–1997), the Russian-British intellectual historian and author of *The Proper Study of Mankind: An Anthology of Essays* (1997), was of the opinion that humans possessed a unique capacity for moral choice, which enabled them to maintain some independence from impersonal forces. However, Edward Carr argued that 'while historical events were of course set in motion by the individual wills, whether of great men or of ordinary people, the historian must go behind the individual wills and inquire into the reasons which made the individuals will and act as they did, and study the factors or forces which explain individual behaviour.'[4]

Moving away from individual action to collective behaviour, the celebrated fourteenth century historian, Abd al-Rahman ibn Khaldun (1332–1406), explained in his pioneering *Muqaddimah fi Ta'rikh* (Introduction to History) that cultures and civilisations rise and decline based on a number of factors including the political, economic, social, spiritual and moral condition of that society. His cyclical theory of history later inspired Sir Arnold Joseph Toynbee (1889–1975) to argue in his *A Study of History* (1934) and *Civilisation on Trial* (1948) that civilisations do not emerge in a vacuum; rather, a civilisation arises and flourishes only after coming in contact with another decaying or extinct one, which, in turn, leads to a new impetus or renaissance. In other words, according to Toynbee, the rise and development of Western civilisation took place as a result of its contact and encounters with other living civilisations, albeit weaker and decaying ones.

By comparison, in *The Rise of the West*, William Hardy McNeill (1917–2016) attempted to transcend both Oswald Spengler's (1880–1936) historical pessimism (see his *The Decline of the West*, 1918) as well as Toynbee's cyclical approach (see his *A Study of History*, 1934–1961), by formulating a more integrated and nuanced approach to the study of history. Based on the concept of cultural diffusion, he argued that civilisations emerge through the diffusion of cultural ideas and values that are common to humanity as a whole. Such an integrated approach enabled McNeill to explain the rise of the

West as a convergence rather than the culmination of Eurocentrism. That is to say, McNeill's work shifted our attention away from European or Western exceptionalism to multicultural encounter and civilisational interdependence.

Deploying a similar approach to Islamic culture and civilisation, in *The Venture of Islam: Conscience and History in a World Civilization* (1975), the celebrated American historian, Marshall G. S. Hodgson (1922–1968), situated Islam in its global context rather than projecting it essentially as a Middle Eastern phenomenon. In his *Rethinking World History: Essays on Europe, Islam, and World History* (published posthumously in 1993), Hodgson went further and challenged both Eurocentrists and Multiculturalists to rethink their views on Western history in the global context. Simply tracing the origins of Western civilisation from the ancient Greeks to the Renaissance was nothing short of an 'optical illusion' without reference to other global cultures and histories, he argued.

Despite McNeill and Hodgson's efforts to move away from an exceptionalist, essentialist or Eurocentrist approach to history, most European or Western historians have continued to explain the development of Western civilisation from an entirely exceptionalist perspective without giving due consideration to other cultural and civilisational influences. Despite Norman Davies' contention that Eurocentrism is a matter of attitude rather than content, the majority of Western historians, both of the past and present, have interpreted the 'rise of the West' as the culmination of human civilisation and, in so doing, they have blurred the line between individual attitude and the interpretation of historical facts.

For example, in his *Civilisation: A Personal View* (1969), Kenneth Clark (1903–1983) had traced the origins of Western civilisation to its ancient Greek and Roman roots, completely overlooking the political, economic, cultural, intellectual and literary contributions of the Muslims of medieval Spain, Granada, Sicily, Italy and North Africa. His efforts to connect ancient Greek times to the modern history of Europe without accounting for the so-called European Dark Ages were not only conceptually blinkered, but also factually inaccurate. How, then, are we to account for what was happening in Europe during the Dark Ages?

In the development of Western thought and culture, the historian Philip K. Hitti (1886–1978) argued that 'Spain and Sicily served as bridges over which Arab cultural elements were transmitted into Europe to vitalize its culture and awaken it from its so-called Dark Ages. Of the bridges the Spanish was, of course, the wider, busier and more enduring. Syria in the period of the Crusades...was the third bridge. Turkey, which provided the fourth bridge, had little to offer. Moslem Spain wrote a brilliant chapter in the intellectual life of medieval Europe. For centuries it lifted high the torch of science lit in Baghdad and now rendered more bright in Cordova, Seville, Granada and particularly Toledo. Toledo had flourishing schools, some of which were continued under Christian rule.'[5]

Even so, probably influenced by Kenneth Clark, the historian John Morris Roberts (1928–2003) went on to explain the 'rise of the West' from an entirely exceptionalist, if not essentialist, perspective in his *The Triumph of the West: The Origin, Rise, and Legacy of Western Civilization* (1985), with utter disdain for other cultures and civilisations. As far as Roberts was concerned, the 'triumph of the West' was a purely Western phenomenon as he considered other cultures and civilisations (with the exception of Japan) to be backward and uncivilised. In his own words – and it is worth quoting him at some length:

> Western civilisation had come to birth and matured in Europe, before spreading across the seas to other continents settled by Europeans. By 1900, North and South America, Australia, New Zealand and South Africa were its overseas centres and strongholds. Not all of those continents and countries reached the same levels of civilised achievements in all sides of their life. But that was true in Europe, too; it was freely admitted that in some parts of Europe – Russia, for instance, or parts of the Balkans – the process of civilisation had not gone as far as it ought to have done and that you could reasonably argue about whether they ought to be regarded as 'civilised' or not. Nor was western civilisation outside Europe confined to lands settled by Europeans, for the men of the West had been for a long time civilising the whole world in their own image by means other than migration. As their ideas and institution spread round the globe, some of them were prepared to concede that there were westernised Indians, Chinese, [and] Africans, who could be counted as 'civilised' men. In the last two or three decades of the nineteenth century, indeed, one wholly non-western country, Japan, appeared to be joining the civilised world, accepting its standards, ideas and many of its ways. Nevertheless, around 1900 most thinking people would have broadly agreed that it was only in a 'western' world, however you might precisely define it, that true civilisation was to be found.[6]

Like Roberts, Niall Ferguson recently argued in his *Civilization: The West and the Rest* (2011), that the modern West is the creation of six 'killer applications' that are uniquely Western in their origins, namely competition, science, democracy, medicine, consumerism and the notion of work ethic.[7] Needless to say, both Roberts and Ferguson's accounts of the rise and development of Western culture and civilisation are not only exceptionalist, but also factually inaccurate.

Unfortunately, such skewed and slanted views are also reflected in the writings of many Western intellectual historians. For example, in his acclaimed book, *A History of Western Philosophy* (1946), Bertrand Russell (1872–1970) devoted fewer than nine pages to the Muslim contribution to philosophy in a book consisting of more than 800 pages. Indeed, the obscure 'Franciscan Schoolmen' received more attention from Russell than did Abulcasis, Ibn Hazm, Avenzoar, Avempace, Dreses, Abubacer, Averroes and Bitar combined, who, by all accounts, were medieval Europe's foremost intellectual trail-blazers. Likewise, Raymond Williams' popular work, *Keywords: A Vocabulary of Culture and Society* (1976) provides a detailed exploration of more than 130 key terms or words that have today come to define our language, thought and culture. And whilst terms like 'Anarchism' , 'Evolution', 'Naturalism', 'Positivism' and 'Utilitarian' are covered in considerable detail in his book, other significant and enduring cultural terms like 'Arabic Numerals', 'Algorithm' and 'Algebra' are conspicuous by their absence. How does one account for this?

In his *Islam and the West: A Historical Cultural Survey* (1962), Philip K. Hitti argued that it was the European people's memories of the past (especially that of the Crusades) – and the lingering fear of a powerful and encroaching Middle Eastern enemy, threatening to overwhelm the whole of Western Christendom – that has continued to perpetuate such bias and negativity towards Islam, despite the West having benefited greatly from its pioneering cultural contributions and achievements.

As it happened, Norman Daniel (1919–1992), a renowned medievalist and author of the acclaimed book, *Islam and the West: The Making of an Image* (1960) went even further in his assessment. 'Summing up the Western view of Islam', he argued, 'we can say that it was based in the crucial period on a good deal of sound knowledge, but it also accepted a great deal that is now seen, and was seen by many then too, to be nonsense. Nonsense was accepted, and sound sense was distorted, because whatever seemed useful to faith was thought likely to be true, a failure of logic, and indeed of faith as well, which is not peculiar to this subject or these people...It was not only among Christians that mediaeval concepts proved astonishingly durable; they or their reflections are still a part of the whole cultural inheritance of the West today.' [8]

That raises a number of important questions, namely, how are we to define 'Europe' or the 'West'? And what is 'Islam'? If 'Christianity' – despite being born in the Middle East – has always been considered to be a Western faith, why is Islam deemed to be an alien intrusion into the Western hemisphere?

Although Europe is the world's sixth largest continent located in the northern hemisphere – bordering the Arctic Ocean to the north, the Atlantic Ocean to the west and the Mediterranean to the south, with a population of around 750 million people – according to the historian Norman Davies, the 'idea of Europe' is relatively new. In his acclaimed book, *Europe: A History* (1997), he argued that 'Europe' came to replace the medieval concept of Western Christendom over a period of 400 years. Indeed, it was during the Enlightenment period that the search for a secular (as opposed to a religious) designation for that part of the world gave birth to the concept of Europe.

Unsurprisingly, prominent enlightenment thinkers like Francois-Marie Arouet, better known as Voltaire (1694–1778), Jean-Jacques Rousseau (1712–1778) and Edmund Burke (1729–1797), among others, became vociferous champions of the 'idea of Europe' during the eighteenth century, although the precise geographical, political, economic and cultural parameters of the continent has remained a matter of debate and discussion to this day.[9] So much so that, even a fiercely Eurocentric historian like John Morris Roberts is forced to concede that, 'We still do not easily agree even on who are Europeans or (if we think we can answer the question) what it is that they share. The answer must always be different things at different times, and such questions demand historical answers. History settled much of the way most Europeans see themselves (though they may not know it), and it is worthwhile to try to discern what it was that left many of them with a shared experience.'[10]

However, in his *Europe: A Cultural History* (1998), the Dutch historian Peter Rietbergen argued that, 'Europe is a political and cultural concept, invented and experienced by an intellectual elite more specifically whenever there was cause to give a more precise definition of what can pragmatically yet simply be described as the western edge of Eurasia, the earth's largest land mass. When was there cause to give such definitions? Often, in a moment or period of crisis, of confrontation. After all, it is only when self-definition is necessary that people become self-reflective, and describe their own identity.'[11] Rietbergen also pointed out how Europe existed by contrast with the opposite, that is to say, the European man, more often than not, defined himself in opposition or confrontation with the 'Other'. Not surprisingly, if defining 'Europe' is fraught with insurmountable difficulties and challenges, then making sense of the terms 'West' and 'Western' are even more challenging and complex.

Indeed, the general understanding of the word 'West' (Latin *Occidens* and Arabic *Gharb* or the 'sunset') refers to the present-day territories of North America and Western Europe. However, from a cultural and sociological perspective, the term 'Western' is defined as the cultures that have been derived from, or influenced by, Europe, particularly Western Europe (such as France, United Kingdom, Ireland and Belgium). That is why the terms 'West' and 'Western' amount to nothing but rather vague definitions for North America and Western Europe because they exclude Eastern Europe, the Balkans, Crimea and Russia.

This realisation forced Norman Davies to concede that, 'Whatever Western civilization is, therefore, it does not involve an honest attempt to summarize European history. Whatever 'the West' is, it is not just a synonym for Western Europe. This is a very strange phenomenon. It seems to assume that historians of Europe can conduct themselves like the cheese-makers of Gruyere, whose product contains as many holes as cheese.'[12] Despite that, the majority of North American and Western European historians, of both the past and present, have completely monopolised the terms 'West' and 'Western' by not only excluding other parts of Europe from their parameters, but also by their failure to acknowledge the presence of other cultural and civilisational influences in the formation of 'Western' culture and thought.

For example, referring to the emergence of historical thinking and reflection, John Harold Plumb (1911–2001), a renowned British historian, argued in his *The Death of the Past* (1969) that historiography as a science is essentially 'a Western development.'[13] Plumb was either unaware of Ibn Khaldun's pioneering contribution to the subject, or he had deliberately ignored the great North African Muslim historian because the latter was not a European or Westerner.

Indeed, according to Norman Davies, such highly selective and idealised accounts of Western thought and history represents nothing short of falsification of the past because 'they extract everything that might be judged genial or impressive; and filter out anything that might appear mundane or repulsive. It is bad enough that they attribute all the positive things to the West, and denigrate the East. But they do not even give an honest account of the West: judging from some of the textbooks, one gets the distinct impression that everyone in the West was a genius, a philosopher, a pioneer, a democrat, or a saint, that it was a world inhabited exclusively by Platos and Marie Curies. Such hagiography is no longer credible. Overblown talk about Western civilization threatens to render the European legacy, which has much to be said in its favour, disreputable.'[14]

Not surprisingly, the great French historian Fernand Braudel (1902–1985) argued in his *A History of Civilisations* (1995), that cultures and civilisations are essentially the products of intercultural exchange that take place through a continuous process of learning, adaptation, assimilation and transmission across time and space. That is to say, the history of civilisations are, in his opinion, the history of our shared and collective humanity.

It is clear from the above discussion that it is not easy to provide a precise or universally accepted definition of what constitutes 'Europe' or the 'West', and much less explain who is a 'European' or 'Westerner' due to a combination of political, economic, cultural, geographical and religious reasons. However, for the purpose of this book, the term 'West' includes both Western and Eastern Europe, including the Balkans, Russia, Tatarstan, Crimea as well as Ottoman Turkey, in addition to North America and Canada. The islands of the Caribbean, Central and South Americas, as well as parts of North Africa have not been included within the broad definition of the 'West' for the sake of brevity and simplicity.

Another important question that we need to consider here is: where do 'Islam' and 'Muslims' fit into such a complex and contentious 'European' or 'Western' historical and cultural matrix?

'Surrender to the Will of God' is the name of Islam, which, according to the Qur'an, was preached by all Divinely-inspired Prophets and Messengers including Adam, the first human being and Prophet, and Noah, Abraham, Moses, David, Solomon, John the Baptist and Jesus (peace be on them all). This message was completed with the advent of Prophet Muhammad (peace be on him) in Arabia in the seventh century who, for the very last time in human history, invited humanity to the worship of One God. Within two decades of his death in 632, the message of Islam spread across Arabia before reaching the Indus Valley in the east and the coasts of the Atlantic in the west. The emergence and expansion of Islam was not only sudden and unexpected, but it was also truly explosive and unprecedented in history. How are we to account for the rise and spread of Islam?

According to Fazlur Rahman (1919–1988), a renowned American-Pakistani academic and Islamic scholar, 'The real explanation lies in the very structure of Islam as a religious and political complex. Whereas the Muslims did not spread their faith through the sword, it is, nevertheless, true that Islam insisted on the assumption of political power since it regarded itself as the repository of the Will of God which had to be worked on earth through a political order…To deny this fact would be both to violate history and to deny justice to Islam itself. To us there is little doubt that this fact, coupled with the inherent Islamic features of egalitarianism and broad humanitarianism, hastened the process of Islamization among the conquered people.'[15]

Although it is widely known that Islam first made in-roads into Europe during the early part of the eighth century under the inspirational leadership of Tariq ibn Ziyad (b.ca. 650–.ca.728), however, according to the renowned medieval historian Ibn al-Athir (1160–1233), Muslims first launched a raid against Constantinople (present-day Istanbul), the bastion of Byzantine Christendom, as early as the mid-seventh century (in 652–653).[16] This account is not only corroborated by the early Muslim chroniclers (such as Ahmad ibn Yahya al-Baladhuri and Ibn Jarir al-Tabari), but also confirmed by Sebeos, a seventh century Armenian bishop and historian, who stated that the raid took place around 653–654.[17]

It was also during this period that Muslims first launched a naval incursion against the Byzantine island of Sicily. According to the historian Aziz Ahmad (1914–1978), this took place in 652 when Mu'awiyah ibn Abi Sufyan (602–680), the governor (*wali*) of Syria, sent Mu'awiyah ibn Khudayj, who was one of his naval commanders, to raid Sicily. Despite their bravery, the Muslims failed to breach the Byzantine defences and were forced to return to Syria with some booty and captives.[18]

According to other historians, Muslims first launched an expedition to Cyprus as early as 648/28 AH when Mu'awiyah was the governor of Syria during the Caliphate of Uthman ibn Affan (r. 644–656).[19] This proves that Islam first came into contact with the West within a few decades after the death of the Prophet rather than during the early part of the eighth century. However, it is equally true that it was Tariq ibn Ziyad's incursion into Gibraltar (derived from the Arabic *Jabal al-Tariq* or 'Tariq's Mount') that firmly established Muslim presence in the West for the first time in 711. From their base in North Africa and the Straits of Gibraltar, the Muslims rapidly moved into southern Spain and parts of Portugal and Italy before crossing the Pyrenees to make their way into Merovingian (fl. 450–750) and Carolingian (fl. 750–887) France.

Indeed, excavations recently carried out at Nimes, a city in the Languedoc-Roussillon region of southern France, have led to the discovery of three early medieval Muslim graves. Led by a team of archaeologists, anthropologists and geneticists, the discovery of the graves and analysis of the skeletons has confirmed that two of the three were males and their age range was from 25 to 35, while the third was around 50 years old. Analysis of their DNA has also proved that they were of North African background, perhaps of Berber origin. Most interestingly, in the three graves the bodies were placed on their right-side facing towards the south-east, namely in the direction of the *Qibla* (the Grand Mosque in Makkah, located in the present-day Kingdom of Saudi Arabia), thus confirming the fact that the Muslims had made their way into southern France during the early part of the eighth century.

It is worth pointing out that Nimes formed a part of the Visigothic Kingdom which, at the time, consisted of Spain, Portugal and parts of southern France. In other words, after their raid on Gibraltar, the Muslims not only went on to conquer Spain, having defeated King Roderick (Rodrigo) in the battlefield, they also swiftly moved into southern France where they eventually settled and died. That explains the presence of Muslim graves in Nimes dating back to the early eighth century.[20]

Needless to say, the arrival of the early Muslims into mainland Europe led to a period of remarkable political and cultural transformation which, substantially, changed relations between European societies and the expanding Muslim world in the wake of the collapse of the Western Roman Empire. This encounter had a transforming impact on both the West as well as the Islamic world. Indeed, with no clear precedents for an Islamic government other than the example of the early four rightly-guided Caliphs (*al-Khulafa al-Rashidun*), the Muslim rulers and governors of the time exercised their political and military authority over vast territories consisting of people from diverse cultures, faiths and ethnic backgrounds, which often forced them to find new solutions to emerging problems. They achieved this through a combination of innovation, adaptation and assimilation of policies and practices derived from not only Islamic sources, but also from Byzantine, Greek and Persian methods of diplomacy, governance and administration.

In other words, defining the relations between Islam and Western Christendom purely in terms of conflict and confrontation only provides a partial and incomplete account of more than fourteen centuries of their intercultural and intercivilisational history and encounter.

The fact that interaction between the Islamic world and Western Christendom transcended politics, conflict and geographical boundaries is most evident from the presence of Muslims in thirteenth century Lucera. In this Italian colony, around 20,000 Muslims lived in relative peace and harmony under a Christian monarch and they worked as farmers, craftsmen, tailors, leopard-keepers and doctors, in addition to being appointed as notaries and military officers. 'Muslim Lucera is of historic importance', wrote Julie Anne Taylor, 'because of its very creation. The colony's history is also significant because it expands and enriches our understanding of Muslim-Christian relations during the Middle Ages, particularly in Europe.'²¹ That is to say, Lucera provides a shining example of Muslim-Christian co-operation and co-existence in the heart of medieval Europe, especially at a time when the Spanish Muslims were being actively persecuted and expelled from the Iberian Peninsula in the wake of the *Reconquista*.

According to the historian Richard W. Bulliet (b. 1940), relations between Islam and Western Christendom 'denotes a prolonged and fateful intertwining of sibling societies enjoying sovereignty in neighbouring geographical regions and following parallel historical trajectories. Neither the Muslim nor Christian historical path can be fully understood without relation to the other. While "Judeo-Christian civilization" has specific historical roots within Europe and in response to the catastrophes of the past two centuries, "Islamo-Christian" involves different historical and geographical roots and has different implications for our contemporary civilizational anxieties.'²²

As it happens, I would go further and argue that, historically speaking, Islam and Western Christendom were not only neighbouring civilisations, but they were also actively engaged in political, economic, cultural, intellectual and literary interaction and exchange. In the process they borrowed, shared and exchanged services, goods and even people. That is clearly reflected in the biographies of their pre-eminent personalities who, despite being Muslims and Christians by faith, were ethnically, linguistically and culturally Westerners.

As such, Islam is as much a Western faith and culture as Christianity, and therefore the attempt to project the former as an 'alien' and 'foreign' intrusion into the Western hemisphere is not only historically, culturally and geographically questionable, but also factually inaccurate. Just as the case for American exceptionalism is misplaced, the idea of European universalism is equally factually inaccurate because Islam did not disappear from the West after the defeat of Muslim Spain. On the contrary, it became more widespread and entrenched in Europe, especially in parts of Eastern Europe and the Balkans during the heyday of the Ottoman Empire.

Spain and Sicily aside, the development of a large Muslim community in medieval Hungary over a period of four hundred years (from 1000 to 1400) is, strangely enough, not widely known today. Indeed, more than 1000 years of Islamic presence in Eastern Europe and the Balkans deserves more attention from Muslim and non-Muslim historians and researchers alike. Likewise, relations between the Islamic world and Elizabethan England were at its peak during the sixteenth century. According to the British historian Jerry Brotton,

> Tudor fascination with the Islamic world went back at least as far as the reign of Elizabeth's father, Henry VIII. He and his court enjoyed wearing Ottoman clothing, with the king often described as appearing at festivities 'apparelled after Turkey fashion', dressed in silk and velvet, and sporting a turban and a scimitar, adopting an Ottoman style that is now regarded as characteristically

'Tudor'. As well as rich silk, velvet and other fabrics, Tudor merchants imported exotic commodities from Islamic lands that included cotton, rhubarb, currants, sweet wines and intricate textiles, as well as the Moroccan sugar that Elizabeth consumed in such copious quantities. As early as the 1550s Englishmen were doing business in Muslim countries as far apart as Morocco and Syria, travelling by land and sea, exchanging ideas and beliefs with Muslims from different social groups and religious denominations.[23]

In other words, Islam has always been a Western faith and culture despite the fact that, like Christianity, it originated in the East. As such, if the case for Judeo-Christian roots of Western civilisation is a strong one, then the exclusion of Islam from that matrix is certainly baffling and inexplicable. The Prophet of Islam was born barely 500 years after Jesus, who, although rejected by the Jews, was always revered in Islam as the 'Spirit of God' (*ruh Allah*) and as a mighty Messenger of the Almighty (*rasul Allah*). Muslims also accept and revere Noah, Abraham, Jacob, Moses, David, Solomon and John the Baptist as Divinely-inspired emissaries (*anbiya*), although the Jews have always denied the message of the Arabian Prophet. Of the three Abrahamic religions, only Islam unconditionally accepts and reveres the seminal figures of both Judaism and Christianity. The latter not only reject each other, they have also repudiated the claims of Islam and its Prophet.

Accordingly, the claim of Islam to be the most open, inclusive and unifying of the three Abrahamic religions is more than credible. Likewise, historically speaking, Christianity found acceptance in the Western world incrementally and, of course, Judaism was always reviled across Europe up to the modern period, whilst Islam became an integral part of the European landscape from the early part of the eighth century. Yet the case for the Judeo-Christian roots of Western civilisation is frequently invoked at the exclusion of Islam. That never really made any sense to me – historically, culturally and geographically.

For that reason, in this book, an attempt has been made to highlight the lives, thoughts and achievements of fifty historically significant and geographically representative Western Muslims, both men and women, whose contributions to the development and progress of Western Islam was nothing short of unique and unprecedented. However, selecting fifty personalities from hundreds, if not thousands, of outstanding and influential Western Muslims was never going to be an easy and straight-forward task. That is why the last chapter of the book is titled 'honourable mentions', wherein twenty-five additional personalities have been highlighted for the benefit of the present and future generations. That is to say, I have deliberately focused on those individuals who, one way or another, have contributed substantially to the development and progress of Western Islam. But that raises another interesting question: what is Western Islam?

Islam at its core consists of a set of fundamental beliefs, principles and values that are at once eternal and temporal, local and universal, and rigid and flexible. Those who willingly accept and live by Islam are called 'Muslims' (those who have surrendered their will to the Will of God). Western Islam shares its fundamental Islamic beliefs, principles and values with Eastern Islam, but it has its own distinct history, culture and geography. In this book I hope to trace the origin, identity and formation of Western Islam spanning over fourteen centuries through the lives of some of its significant and enduring figures. In other words, by exploring the lives, thoughts and contribution of the fifty personalities featured in this book, I hope to show that Western Islam is as geographically widespread and culturally vibrant as Eastern Islam, if not more so. But I will leave it to my wise and discerning readers to decide whether I have succeeded in my task or not.

Due to historical, geographical, cultural and intellectual overlap, it was not possible to avoid some repetition. I hope the readers will understand this as they go through the book. All the entries are in chronological order and each biography begins with an introductory statement for the purpose of contextualisation. All the dates in the book are according to the Gregorian calendar for the sake of simplicity and brevity, but the Hijri (Islamic) dates have been included in the chronology for reference purposes. The main entries of the book are roughly of equal length but the entries in the last chapter are much shorter due to limitation of space and time. Again, I have avoided diacritics except for common words like the Qur'an and Shari'ah.

However, I have included a detailed chronology of Western Islam to enable the readers to develop a deeper understanding and awareness of the social, political and cultural context in which the personalities featured in this book lived and made their contributions. Likewise, I have minimised the number of footnotes at the end of each chapter, but the select bibliography is comprehensive enough to enable the readers to locate most of the references with relative ease or pursue further study and research. As with my other books, I have deliberately avoided jargon and technical terms as this work is aimed at the general readers, although the scholars and academics will, no doubt, find it interesting and informative.

However, some critics may argue that I have not been inclusive enough because only seven women have been featured in a book of more than fifty personalities. I agree that Muslim women have played a proactive and pivotal role in the development and progress of Islamic thought, culture and civilisation, although it is equally true that they more often than not preferred to make their contributions from behind the scenes. Due to their humility and humbleness, they often avoided the limelight and, for that reason, their contribution and achievements were not always recorded and acknowledged. Absence of reliable data and information about their lives, thoughts and achievements therefore presents an on-going challenge to all historians and researchers. I hope the readers will appreciate the difficulties and challenges I had faced as they go through the biographies of the seven women covered in this book.

When I was recently asked why some writers are more productive than others, my response was that some writers are fortunate to have more supportive wives (or husbands) than others. It would not have been possible for me to research and write this book without the unstinting support and co-operation of my wife who gracefully tolerated my excesses and absent-mindedness over a period of more than three years. To repay my debt to her, I have partly dedicated this book to her and my father-in-law, who never fails to remind me that there is no better wealth than knowledge and wisdom. Muhtadi and Mustafa, my two sons, also reluctantly accepted that their father had to confine himself to his study in the evenings, weekends and school holidays in order to complete this book. I pray for their success and prosperity, both here and in the hereafter.

Many other people have provided much-needed help and support whilst I was busy planning, researching and writing this book: Yahya Birt, formerly Commissioning Editor at Kube Publishing, contributed to the initial plans for this book before moving onto pastures new. Haris Ahmad, Director of Kube Publishing, agreed with our plans and thereafter enthusiastically supported the project. He also arranged for me and my family to stay at the Islamic Foundation premises in Leicestershire for a few days where I was able to undertake valuable research at the IF library. Asefa and Mohammad Ali Qayyum provided generous support throughout this project. Thanks to their kindness, generosity and hospitality, I was not only able to visit several institutions in London (including the British Library, the Senate House Library, the School of Oriental and African Studies Library and the Royal Asiatic Society Library), but Mohammad Ali Qayyum also went out of his way to locate and procure many important sources of references, without which, this book would have been much poorer.

Dr Enes Karic, professor of Islamic Studies at the University of Sarajevo and a prominent Bosnian scholar and historian, became an enthusiastic supporter of this project as soon as I had contacted him. He not only sent me copies of his books and articles, but also agreed to read parts of the book and provide constructive feedback. Dr Halit Eren, the Director-General of the International Research Centre for Islamic History, Art and Culture (IRCICA) in Istanbul, Turkey, swiftly dispatched a large box of books and research papers on aspects of Islamic history, culture and civilisation in the Balkans which proved to be invaluable.

Dr Imre Bangha of Oxford University's Faculty of Oriental Studies also sent me an electronic copy of his book covering Julius Germanus's time in Calcutta, India. Likewise, Anthony Cobbold of the famous Suffolk Cobbold family not only shared his knowledge of Lady Zainab (Evelyn) Cobbold's life, but also facilitated access to the original copies of her books. I am grateful to Aled Korca for supplying original information about Hafiz Ali Korca's life and works; Aled currently lives in Tirana, Albania and is a great-grandson of Ali Korca.

Furthermore, Dr Irena Nikaj, professor of Sociology at the Fan Noli University in Korca, Albania sent me a copy of her essay on Hafiz Ali Korca. Christine Watson of Kilwinning Heritage, North Ayrshire, Scotland, deserves appreciation for sending me one of John Yahya Parkinson's rare books. Likewise, Abdul Hayee, chief librarian at the Islamic Foundation Library, Leicestershire, was very helpful and supportive, as were Usaama al-Azami and Yosef Smyth, both Editors at Kube Publishing. Dr A. K. M. Yaqub Ali, professor emeritus of Islamic History and Culture at the University of Rajshahi, Bangladesh has been a source of inspiration for nearly a decade now, and I am grateful for his encouragement and on-going support. Over the years, I have had many discussions with Dr Abdul Mu'min Chowdhury, formerly of the universities of Dhaka, Exeter and London, about the nature and purpose of history, historiography and epistemology. Needless to say, his extensive knowledge and understanding has helped clarify my ideas and thoughts on these and related subjects.

Likewise, Dr Syed Mahmudul Hasan, a senior Bangladeshi academic, author and historian, continues to encourage and support my humble efforts. The passing away of Dr Muhammad Abdul Jabbar Beg in Cambridge in 2014 was an irreparable loss for me. A former professor of Islamic History and Civilisation at the National University of Malaysia, Dr Beg was a Cambridge University-trained historian who actively supported my research and literary activities; may the Almighty grant him the highest of stations in the hereafter. I am also happy to say that Mahdiya Khan, who is my niece and currently studying English Language and Linguistics at Kings College London, agreed to meticulously read and improve the whole manuscript; she also did most of the work on the chronology. I am most grateful for her support and co-operation.

Ultimately, all praise and glory is due to Him, both in the beginning and in the end, Who made my task easy for me and removed all the difficulties and obstacles from my path. Salutations (*salawat*) upon the beloved one (*al-Habib al-Mustafa*) who invited us to the One (*al-Ahad*). There is none but the One, the Manifest and Hidden, the all-Hearing and all-Wise, and the Most Merciful and Mercy-giving, who grants knowledge and wisdom to whom He wishes, *bi-ghayri hisab*.

1.  Edward H. Carr, *What is History?*

2.  Ibid.

3.  R. G. Collingwood, *The Idea of History.*

4.  Edward H. Carr, 'History and Morals', *Times Literary Supplement*, 17 December 1954.

5.  Philip K. Hitti, *Islam and the West: A Historical Cultural Survey.*

6. J. M. Roberts, *The Triumph of the West: The Origin, Rise, and Legacy of Western Civilization.*

7. Niall Ferguson, *Civilisation: The West and the Rest.*

8. Norman Daniel, *Islam and the West: The Making of an Image.*

9. Norman Davies, *Europe: A History.*

10. J. M. Roberts, *A History of Europe.*

11. Peter Rietbergen, *Europe: A Cultural History.*

12. Norman Davies, op. cit.

13. J. H. Plumb, *The Death of the Past.*

14. Norman Davies, op. cit.

15. Fazlur Rahman, *Islam.*

16. See Ibn al-Athir, *al-Kamil fi Ta'rikh*; al-Baladhuri, *Futuh al-Buldan.*

17. R. W. Thompson (ed.), *The Armenian History Attributed to Sebeos.*

18. Aziz Ahmad, *A History of Islamic Sicily.*

19. See Josef W. Meri (ed.), *Medieval Islamic Civilization: An Encyclopaedia.*

20. Gleize Y, and Mendisco F, et al., 'Early Medieval Muslim Graves in France: First Archaeological, Anthropological and Palaeogenomic Evidence', *PLOS ONE*, vol. 11, no. 2.

22. Julie Anne Taylor, *Muslims in Medieval Italy: The Colony at Lucera.*

22. Richard Bulliet, *The Case for Islamo-Christian Civilization.*

23. Jerry Brotton, *This Orient Isle: Elizabethan England and the Islamic World.*

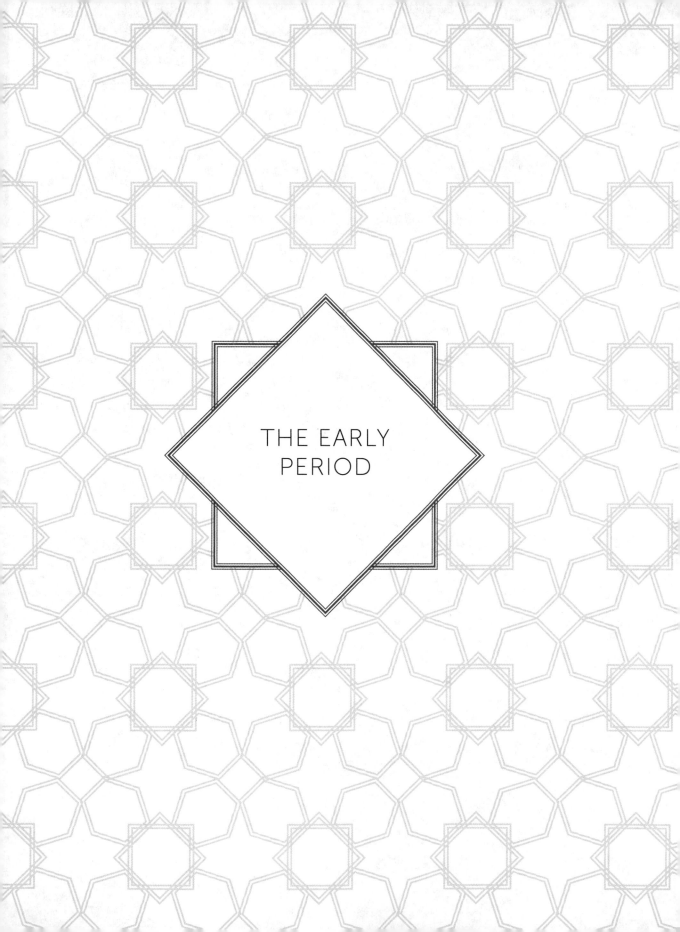

THE EARLY
PERIOD

# ABD AL-RAHMAN I

B. 729 – D. 788

SPAIN

Andalus is the Arabic name for Muslim Spain, derived from *bilad al-Andalish* or 'land of Vandals', who were eastern Germanic tribesmen that invaded Iberia. There, they established their hegemony until the Visigoths, who were western Germanic nomads, replaced them as rulers of Spain. After the arrival of the Muslims in the beginning of the eighth century, the Umayyad rulers of Andalusia established themselves in Cordova, the capital of Islamic Spain, and consolidated their rule. This rule was destined to continue for nearly three centuries before several other dynasties continued to rule parts of Andalusia for another five centuries, until eventually the Muslims were ousted from the Nasrid kingdom of Granada by Isabella and Ferdinand in 1492.

Abd al-Rahman ibn Mu'awiyah ibn Hisham ibn Abd al-Malik ibn Marwan ibn Hakam, better known as Abd al-Rahman I, was to be the first Muslim ruler of a European country as the founder of the Umayyad dynasty of Spain in the eighth century. The rule of Abd al-Rahman and his descendants lasted for nearly three centuries, and they became renowned for their patronage of learning, scholarship, arts and architecture in medieval Spain and across the rest of Europe.

Born into the famous Umayyad royal family of Damascus; Abd al-Rahman's father, Mu'awiyah (fl. 725–737), was the son of Caliph Hisham (691–743), and his mother Raha, hailed from the Berber tribe of Saba in present-day Morocco. His parents ensured he received a good education during his early years. It was a challenging and difficult period in the history of the Umayyad dynasty (r. 661–750) because their Abbasid rivals (r. 750–1258), encouraged by Umayyad family feuds and political waywardness, were busy planning their downfall. At the time, the Umayyad dynasty extended all the way from Yemen in the south to Morocco in the west, and from Uzbekistan in the north to the Indus Valley in the east. During the time when Marwan II was assassinated by Abbasid agents, in the summer of 750, young Abd al-Rahman was living in the peaceful surroundings of Zaytun in Aleppo. As the House of Umayyah (*Banu Umayyah*) began to crumble in the face of internal rivalry and external pressure, the ruthless and uncompromising Abbasids went in for the kill, massacring around seventy members of the Umayyad family in the notorious Banquet of Jaffa.[1] This horrific event sent a chill down the spine of young Abd al-Rahman before he bid farewell to the Islamic East and set off in the direction of North Africa (*al-Ifriqiya*) to carve out another remarkable chapter in the history of the Umayyad dynasty: this time in the Islamic West.

Flame-haired, tall and handsome, Prince Abd al-Rahman looked more European in his culture, mannerism and appearance than an Arab.[2] He was barely 20 when he had reached north-western Africa (or the Maghreb). The journey from Damascus to the Berber tribe of Nafza was, as expected, fraught with danger, uncertainty and suspense. But young Abd al-Rahman was relieved to have reached the ancestral home of his mother in one-piece, unlike his younger brother Yahya, who was captured on the banks of the Euphrates by their Abbasid pursuers and brutally put to death. Having witnessed many horrors, the Umayyad prince was determined not to become a victim himself. Despite repeated Abbasid attempts to assassinate Abd al-Rahman, he escaped unscathed against all odds and lived to tell the tale, much to the disgust and dismay of the former. That is why historians have often referred to him as the ultimate survivor, one who had defied and disrupted destiny, to keep the Umayyad flag flying in the Islamic West for almost 300 years!

After living in exile in North Africa for nearly five years; in 755, while Abd al-Rahman was in his mid-twenties, he, accompanied by his loyal guide and supporter, Badr, reached the Berber tribe of Mughila which was located close to the Moroccan coast. From there, the prince and his aide planned their next move, having closely observed the deteriorating political and economic situation that prevailed in Andalusia at the time. However, it was easy to assess the political situation in North Africa because as the Abbasid's grip on power weakened, the local rulers began to rebel and some even openly asserted their independence, leading to much tension, uncertainty and upheaval.

The governor of Ifriqiya (or North Africa) at the time was Abd al-Rahman ibn Habib al-Fihri (r. 745–755), who was a great-grandson of Uqba ibn Nafi (622–683), the Muslim conqueror of North Africa. He was originally appointed governor by the Umayyads, but after the latter's overthrow in 750, he fell out with the Abbasids, and became an autonomous ruler in all but name. Ibn Habib was initially sympathetic towards the Umayyad prince, but in due course, he became afraid of the latter's growing popularity, thus eventually leading to their fall out. Prince Abd al-Rahman made a lucky escape, only to find the political situation across the Straits in Andalus to be equally chaotic and confusing. Amir Yusuf ibn Abd al-Rahman al-Fihri (r. 747–756), a member of the Fihrid family of South Arabian (Yemeni) origin, was the de facto ruler of Andalus at the time.

However, Yusuf's authority was challenged by his son-in-law, Sumayl ibn Hatim, who hailed from the North Arabian Qaysi tribe. As the two men fought each other for political supremacy, the Umayyad prince sent Badr, his aide, to go and assess first-hand the political, economic and social conditions and, in the process, he established links with the opponents of Yusuf, including his rebellious son-in-law. This was a shrewd political move because linking up with various dissident groups, who now pledged to support the prince on his arrival there, paved the way for the 'young pretender' to make his move and carve out a unique place for himself in the history of Europe as *Sahib al-Andalus* or the 'Lord of Spain'.[3]

Prince Abd al-Rahman departed from the North African port of Ghazah having paid a fee to his Berber hosts. Finally on 13 September, 755 the prince set foot on the shores of Almunecar, located between present-day Malaga and Almeria, where he was met by two Umayyad officials; Ubaidullah Abu Uthman and Abdullah ibn Khalid. They not only received prince Abd al-Rahman warmly, but also gifted him with Spanish wines and a beautiful slave-girl. He reportedly turned down both; being a devout Muslim, he avoided alcoholic beverages and, as for the slave girl, his sight was firmly fixed on a much bigger prize: his burning desire to establish an Umayyad rule in Spain.

From his base in the heavily fortified village of Torrox, located between Iznajar and Loja, the prince swiftly made contact with, and won over, senior local Umayyad and Yemenite leaders. In a matter of days, Abd al-Rahman had secured the support of around 20,000 men who were ready to fight for him. As he toured other local towns and villages, his name and fame now began to spread like wildfire, earning the 26 year old prince more support and recognition. The governor of Elvira was then resounding defeat by the forces of Abd al-Rahman which, in turn, forced Amir Yusuf and his son-in-law to enter into negotiations with the former. Keen to win over the increasingly powerful prince, Yusuf offered him many gifts including a large estate in Cordova, his daughter in marriage, 500 gold pieces, expensive costumes and even the governorship of Elvira and Malaga. Unmoved, Abd al-Rahman proceeded to Seville, securing it in March 756 without the spilling of any blood. He achieved this whilst Yusuf and his son-in-law were busy suppressing a serious rebellion in the important commercial city of Zaragoza, located in the north of Andalusia.

Upon his triumphant entry into Seville, Prince Abd al-Rahman met Countess Sara the Goth and became an ardent admirer of her beauty and intelligence. Due to her nobility and high standing in society, her descendants, both Muslims and Christians, subsequently became known as Ibn al-Qutiyyah (son of the Gothic woman) and they continued to live in Seville, Niebla and southern Portugal for many generations. It is worth highlighting here that Mary, the Christian mother of Caliph Abd al-Rahman III of Spain (891–961), was in fact, a direct descendant of Countess Sara of Seville. So, if history is anything to go by, the life and works of Prince Abd al-Rahman on the one hand, and that of Countess Sara on the other – and that of their descendants – does indeed provide a compelling case for an Islamo-Christian culture and civilisation, whose pioneers were of course the Muslims and Christians of medieval Europe and Andalusia in particular.[4]

After successfully securing Seville, Abd al-Rahman turned his attention towards Cordova (*al-Qurtuba*), the biggest prize of all, but Amir Yusuf was, as expected, ever determined to defend his realm. Soon after receiving news of the Basque uprising in Pamplona, Abd al-Rahman dispatched a contingent of his army to suppress the revolt but unfortunately, they were soundly defeated. This forced Yusuf to turn his full attention to defending Cordova against the forces of Abd al-Rahman. The battle and fight to rule Andalus was now looming on the horizon as the two armies marched towards River Guadalquivir (*Wadi al-Kabir* in Arabic) and encamped on opposite ends of the plains of Musarah, located to the east of Cordova. Abd al-Rahman tried to out-smart his opponent by leaving the camp-fires burning at night as his forces moved into the territory of the enemies. However, Yusuf and his troops remained vigilant, until around 3,500 of his supporters – mainly of Yemenite origin and Umayyad sympathisers – deserted him and joined the enemy camp. This was a real blow for Yusuf, thus shattering the morale and confidence of his remaining troops.

To add to his woes, the waters of the Guadalquivir began to subside and Abd al-Rahman responded by calling a Council of War where he discussed various options with his advisors, before marching into the battlefield on Friday 15 May, 756. Led by the prince himself, the two armies clashed and a fierce battle ensued in which the forces of the former, supported by his Yemenite and Umayyad sympathisers, played a decisive role by tipping the balance in favour of the prince. Seeing his army in disarray, Yusuf and Sumayl fled the battlefield as Abd al-Rahman marched into Cordova virtually unopposed. Keen to avert any form of disorder or rioting, he pacified the disgruntled Yemenite leaders and swiftly won over the other local dissident groups to his side. Yusuf was eventually captured in Toledo, the Visigothic capital, as was Sumayl, who was strangled to death in Cordova's central jail, presumably to put an end to any further rebellions.

After removing his opponents, Abd al-Rahman proclaimed himself *Amir* (leader) of Andalus, although at the time he was only in control of southern Spain, with much of the central and northern provinces (such as Toledo, Zaragoza and Barcelona) being firmly in the hands of supporters of the former ruling family. Keen to take stock and strengthen his powerbase in southern Spain, the new Amir established an efficient and effective political and administrative system, ensuring the safety of his people and vigorously promoting economic activity. This important task occupied him from 756 to 763, until a large Abbasid contingent led by al-Ala ibn Mughith, the Abbasid governor of North Africa, landed in Andalus in a location close to modern Beja. The Abbasid Caliph, Abu Ja'far al-Mansur, wanted to oust Abd al-Rahman from power and, as such, he authorised al-Ala to lead the expedition. The Amir of Andalus on the other hand, was determined as ever to stay put. Although the Abbasid contingent consisted of 7000 professional and well-equipped troops, Abd al-Rahman went to meet them with only 700 hand-picked infantry. In the ensuing battle, the Abbasids were routed and this resounding victory helped the Amir to consolidate his position further.

During the next quarter of a century, Abd al-Rahman faced many rebellions from various groups; from Arab tribal chiefs to Berber tribes and even his own family members; but he successfully crushed all subversive activities and, in doing so, gradually expanded and strengthened his rule. During this period, he initiated and completed a series of projects, including the construction of the famous Great Mosque of Cordova, whilst also recruiting tens of thousands of Berbers from North Africa to join his army. He also established a functioning political and civil service in order to provide for his people as best he could.

It is also worth highlighting here that Abd al-Rahman became the first European ruler to offer official recognition to his minority subjects, including Jews and Christians. As a result, they played a proactive part in the political, social, economic and cultural life of Andalus and did so without having to dilute or renounce their faith and culture. Thus the credit for initiating a culture of tolerance and co-existence, the Spanish *convivencia*, must go to none other than Abd al-Rahman, who is known in the classical Islamic historical sources as *Sahib al-Andalus* (Lord of Spain), *Saqr Quraysh* (Falcon of the Quraysh), *al-Dhakil* (the Immigrant) and *Saqr al-Andalus* (Falcon of Spain).[5]

On a personal level, Abd al-Rahman was a learned, sagacious and devout Muslim. He was well-versed in the Qur'an, Arabic literature, traditional Islamic sciences and poetry. He fathered twenty children; eleven sons and nine daughters; with several wives of European, Berber and Arab descent. As expected, his children went on to rule Andalusia and their policies and practices, too, reflected their multicultural background, being both European and Muslim. Abd al-Rahman also constructed and patronised many mosques, schools, colleges and cultural institutions, and towards the end of his life, began to oversee the affairs of the Great Mosque of Cordova. Then in 787, he nominated his son, Hisham (757–796), as his *Wali al-Huda* (deputy), thus adding Hisham's name to that of Abd al-Rahman's in the weekly Friday prayer (*Salat al-Jumu'ah*) invocation.[6] This, of course, was an indication of his choice of Hisham as his political successor.

By all accounts, Abd al-Rahman was a great statesman, strategist, military commander and political administrator who single-handedly defied the might of the Abbasids, Charlemagne (d. 814), the Berbers and other factions, in order to establish himself in Spain and rule it for more than thirty years with remarkable tact, wisdom and tremendous success. The founder of Andalus eventually died peacefully in Cordova on 30 September, 788 at the age of 59, but his contributions, achievements and legacy continue to be a great source of inspiration for Western Muslims to this day. John (Yahya en-Nasr) Parkinson (see chapter 32), a prominent Scottish Muslim writer and poet of the twentieth century, paid Abd al-Rahman this glowing tribute:

*In the time of great en-Nasir, Cordova's enlightened age;*
*In the palmy days of Islam, chivalry became the rage.*
*And her scions in the tourney sought to win undying fame,*
*From the lowest to the highest, prince and chevalier and page.*
*And the fairest knew the bravest by the colours that he wore*
*And she knew to keep her favour he would desperate battle wage.*
*Not alone in camp or tourney, nor in court or courtly grace*
*Was the reign of Nasir storied by the poet's heritage;*
*Not alone in feats of knighthood or in deeds of bravery,*
*Nor in jousts for love and honour did the Moorish lord engage;*
*All around the lakes of learning overran the verdured banks*
*And the land was full of music and the wisdom of the sage;*
*For the sovereign was a scholar, one of nature's noblest sons,*
*Literature and science flourished underneath his patronage;*
*Every hill and every palace in beloved Andaloos*
*Was the meeting place of scholars and of birth and lineage.*[7]

**N**

1. T. B. Irving, *The Falcon of Spain: A Study of Eighth Century Spain.*

2. Ibid.

3. Stanley Lane-Poole, *The Muslims in Spain.*

4. Richard W. Bulliet, *The Case for Islamo-Christian Civilization.*

5. See Ibn al-Athir, *al-Kamil fi Ta'rikh.*

6. Reinhart Dozy, *Spanish Islam: A History of the Muslims in Spain.*

7. Yehya-en-Nasr Parkinson, *Muslim Chivalry.*

2

# ZIRYAB

B. 789 – D. 857

SPAIN

The dictionary meaning of the word 'culture' is 'activities that are related to art, music and literature' or 'the beliefs, way of life, art, and customs that are shared and accepted by people in a particular society'. Similarly, according to social scientists, it is not possible to imagine a nation, civilisation or even a society without referencing their attitudes, views and beliefs about something that they share or have in common as a group or organisation. The ancient people had minimal exposure to cultures other than their own, though this was transformed during the medieval period by many pioneering figures. Through travel, communication and dissemination of learning from India to China, from Arabia to Persia, and from there to the Islamic West, such cultural disseminators left their indelible marks on global cultural history. Ziryab was one such pioneer who assimilated diverse cultures, arts and entertainment, and was able to successfully popularise them in medieval Spain at a time when the Europeans rarely ventured beyond their immediate localities.

Abul Hasan Ali ibn Nafi, better known as Ziryab or the 'Blackbird', was born in present-day Iraq, which was then the seat of the Abbasid Empire. However, there has been disagreement among historians with regards to Ziryab's ancestry and early life. Some say he was of African origin, while others have suggested that he was of Persian or Kurdish extraction.[1] Although his real name was Ali, he became known as Ziryab due to his melodious voice and dark complexion. Some writers have pointed out that he was a freed slave who achieved a higher position in life as a result of his dedication, hard work and natural talent.

However, this view is far from conclusive given the fact that Ziryab was a polymath who had acquired mastery of many different subjects including astronomy, botany, geography, meteorology, music, cultural entertainment, cookery and fashion. It is more likely that he had hailed from an educated and cultured middle-class Muslim family. According to yet another account, which appears to be the most authentic, he was born in northern Iraq, possibly in the Kurdish city of Mosul, and became interested in music and poetry from an early age.

Ziryab grew up at a challenging time in the history of Islam. The once-powerful Umayyad dynasty (r. 661–750) was overthrown by their Abbasid rivals in 750, inevitably leading to considerable socio-political upheaval and uncertainty as the latter went out of their way to politically wipe out the former. Although Baghdad was the main centre of political tension at the time, Ziryab most likely spent his early years in northern Iraq before moving to the Abbasid capital in search of knowledge and employment opportunities.

To his credit, after commissioning the construction of the city of Baghdad in July 762, Caliph Abu Ja'far al-Mansur (714–775) and his successors soon transformed it into a centre of learning, culture, scholarship and entertainment, thus attracting people from across the Muslim world.[2] Like other talented and ambitious people of the time, Ziryab moved to Baghdad where he studied astronomy, geography, music and poetry, among other subjects, and soon became well-known for his knowledge and expertise in music and literature. According to historians, most of the Abbasid Caliphs, particularly al-Mahdi (r. 775–785), were great admirers of music and poetry. As a result, they offered handsome rewards to erudite performers to compete with one another for the biggest prize.

Likewise, Caliph Harun al-Rashid (763–809) was a generous patron of learning, scholarship and cultural pursuits, and Ziryab had access to many prominent scholars and tutors who lived in and around Baghdad. This included Ishaq ibn Ibrahim al-Mawsili (767–850), who was a prominent musician and the Caliph's favourite entertainer. Ishaq inherited his talent for music from his renowned father, Ibrahim al-Mawsili (742–804), who, as the Caliph's favourite performer, 'received the munificent regular monthly salary of 10,000 silver dirhams, plus monetary bonuses for excellence…Ibrahim's annual income was 24 million dirhams, counting bonuses routinely added to his salary for singing.'[3]

This clearly inspired Ziryab, who was no less ambitious, to polish his knowledge of music, poetry and cultural entertainment under the tutelage of the talented and wealthy Ishaq. In doing so, both the teacher and student soon went on to dominate the cultural scene at the Caliph's court. This naturally brought Ziryab closer to the city's elite and earned him considerable standing within the Caliph's inner circle of advisors, supporters and entertainers, so much so that the Caliph soon became a big fan of Ziryab and his remarkable talents and musical abilities. Indeed, this was a stunning achievement for someone who was still in his early twenties at the time.

After the death of Harun al-Rashid in 809, his son, Muhammad (787–813), succeeded him, taking the title of *al-Amin* or 'the Trustworthy'. During the reign of the latter, the political and cultural scene in Baghdad was not as vibrant as before. However, Ziryab continued to enjoy the patronage of the new Caliph and the Abbasid elite, until al-Amin decided not to honour his pledge to hand power over to his half-brother, Abdullah al-Ma'mun. Instead, he nominated his son, Musa, as his heir apparent. This set the two brothers on a collision course as they fought each other to secure the Abbasid throne.

During this tumultuous period in Abbasid history, Baghdad and its surrounding cities and provinces became a battleground which, as expected, led to a considerable loss of life and livelihood. The whole episode ended in tragedy as Caliph al-Amin was soon captured and put to death by the supporters of Abdullah, who went on to become Caliph al-Ma'mun (786–833). However, unlike the former, the latter was of an intellectual persuasion and preferred to patronise literary and scholarly endeavours rather than musical and cultural activities.

Fearing that he may not enjoy the same level of prestige and standing in the court of Caliph al-Ma'mun, Ziryab actively looked for new opportunities elsewhere. However, according to other scholars, there was an on-going rivalry between Ziryab and Ishaq al-Mawsili, his erstwhile mentor and guide, that eventually led to his departure from the Caliphal court in Baghdad. But rivalry over what?

There was no doubt that Ziryab was an immensely talented musician and entertainer, otherwise someone of al-Mawsili's reputation and standing would not have agreed to instruct him in music and drama in the first place. It seems that disagreements and rivalry between the two musicians erupted once it became obvious that Ziryab was naturally more talented than his tutor. Some scholars have even suggested that the former accused the latter of concealing his skills and abilities from him. Convinced that his pupil had deceived him, al-Mawsili then summoned Ziryab and offered him two clear choices: either to leave Baghdad at once or he would be removed from the scene permanently. Being the wise man that he was, Ziryab decided to leave Baghdad immediately.

Taking whatever money that al-Mawsili had offered him, Ziryab moved to Syria and from there to Egypt. Thereafter, he set-off for North Africa and settled in the historic city of Qayrawan in modern Tunisia, which at the time was the capital of the Aghlabid dynasty (r. 800–909) which ruled *Ifriqiyah* (or North Africa) on behalf of the Abbasids for more than a century. When Ziryab moved to Qayrawan, the Aghlabid ruler Abu Muhammad Ziyadat Allah I (d. 838) reigned supremely. Here, Ziryab received a warm welcome in the royal court and very quickly became known for his artistic talent. However, Ziryab soon fell out with Amir Ziyadat Allah and this, in turn, forced him to move to Cordova, the seat of the Umayyad dynasty of Spain.

At the time, the Arabs referred to the Iberian Peninsula as Andalus, or the land of the Vandals. The Vandals had held control of this territory since the fifth century until the

Muslims appeared on the scene during the early part of the eighth century and ousted them from power. Since then, southern Spain became known as Andalus. Under its Umayyad rulers, Andalus became a prominent centre of Islamic learning, education, culture and arts. This naturally attracted Ziryab's attention and on the invitation of al-Hakam I (r. 796–822), he moved to Cordova, the capital of Andalus.

However, on his arrival, Ziryab discovered that al-Hakam had died. Even so, al-Hakam's successor, Abd al-Rahman II (788–852), invited Ziryab, who was only aged 33 at the time, into his Caliphal court and offered him the post of 'Minister for Culture' with a monthly salary of 200 gold dinars, in addition to regular bonuses.[4] Like his father, Abd al-Rahman II was a renowned patron of learning, culture and arts. He is said to have established the first schools of music in Cordova under the stewardship of Ziryab, whereby the latter trained both male and female students in the art of music, singing, drama and other cultural performances and activities.

Under the patronage of Abd al-Rahman II, Ziryab went on to become a pioneering cultural figure initiating new trends in music, food, fashion and entertainment. At a time when most of Europe was lingering in the Dark Ages, Andalusia became a shining light, thanks to its Muslim rulers, scholars, writers, poets, artists and entertainers! Occupying a leading position in the Caliphal court, Ziryab not only improved but also invented many musical instruments, he not only used them in musical performances, but continued to experiment with them to enhance their capacity. He added a fifth pair of strings to the lute to improve its performance, fluency and range thus giving it a soul and making it more vibrant and sensitive. He also introduced the practice of playing this instrument with an eagle's talon rather than a wooden pick, and soon this became the norm across Andalusia and North Africa. In doing so, Ziryab laid the foundation for classical Spanish music and musical techniques which continue to this day.

As an innovator of cultural practices, Ziryab had no equal during his lifetime. He was a man of great creativity, diverse tastes and practices. Unsurprisingly, he became a pioneer in fashion, hairstyles, food and hygiene, among other things. He introduced different styles of dress to not only match the weather and season, but also different times of the day. This practice eventually spread across Andalusia, North Africa and the rest of the Muslim world, not to mention continental Europe. The historian, Ahmad ibn Muhammad al-Maqqari (d. 1632), wrote that the people of Cordova wore indistinguishable styles of clothing and kept their hair in a similar fashion until Ziryab introduced new, shorter hairstyles and designer dresses to suit diverse tastes.[5]

He is also credited with having introduced a series of innovative hygienic practices including taking baths in the mornings and evenings, and the use of toothpaste which he invented for the first time. He popularised shaving among men, and introduced a new deodorant to neutralise bodily odours. Although these practices were first introduced in Islamic Spain, subsequently they became the norm across Europe, North Africa and the rest of the Muslim world.

As a man of diverse tastes and practices, Ziryab also left his mark on culinary fashion and stylish dining by developing and popularising the idea of a three-course meal consisting of soup, main course and dessert. This innovative approach enabled food to be eaten by diners in an orderly fashion, beginning with starters and ending with desserts, and drinks. He introduced the idea of dining at a table covered with cloth and designed wooden cutlery to improve and enhance the eating experience. Needless to say, this style of dining also became popular in Muslim Spain and subsequently spread to the rest of Europe and beyond. He combined fruit and vegetable options with meat and fish to promote healthy living, and replaced metal cups with large crystal cups for serving drinks. Although many of these practices are taken for granted today, very few people are aware that the credit for introducing these and other similar cultural practices goes to none other than Ziryab who was, by all accounts, one of the most influential innovators, musicians, entertainers and multicultural icons of all time.

Known for his prodigious memory, having memorised thousands of songs, he was also a noted poet, scholar and great conversationalist. He lived in Cordova for nearly a quarter of a century and served Abd al-Rahman II and his successor with dedication and loyalty and, they in turn, rewarded him handsomely. He came from North Africa with virtually nothing but, over time, Ziryab became incredibly wealthy and influential due to his natural talents, abilities and his close relationship with the Caliph. This of course made other courtiers jealous of Ziryab but that did not deter him. He lived in a beautiful mansion in Cordova with his wife, eight sons and two daughters, whilst only leaving the city during holiday seasons to spend quality time with the family in his secluded villas located on the outskirts of Cordova. Following in the footsteps of their illustrious father, five of his children became well-known musicians and artists, thus keeping their father's legacy alive for generations.

Five years after the death of Caliph Abd al-Rahman II in 852, Ziryab passed away at the age of 67. Thanks to his contributions and achievements, Cordova became the most renowned centre of cultural innovation and artistic performance in medieval Europe. This was destined to last for many centuries, thus inspiring scholars, writers, poets, travellers and traders from across Europe to go and see for themselves the wonder that was Andalusia at the time. Many others flocked to Cordova from across Europe to study, explore and exchange ideas and thoughts in the city's leading institutions of learning and education and, in doing so, they expanded their intellectual and cultural horizons.[6]

In short, Cordova had something to offer to everyone at the time. There is no doubt that Ziryab's input and accomplishments transformed Muslim Spain into an interesting, vibrant and exciting place. For this reason alone, posterity will, without a doubt, fondly remember this great European Muslim musician and cultural icon for years to come.

Ⓝ

1. S. M. Imamuddin, *A Political History of Muslim Spain*.

2. Hugh Kennedy, *When Baghdad Ruled the Muslim World*.

3. Madeline P. Cosman and Linda G. Jones, *Handbook to Life in the Medieval World*.

4. Salim T. H. Al-Hassani, *1001 Inventions: Muslim Heritage in Our World*.

5. See al-Maqqari (Makkari), *Nafh al-Tib min Ghusni Andalus al-Ratib*.

6. Stanley Lane-Poole, *The Muslims in Spain*

3

# IBN FIRNAS

B. 810 – D. 887

SPAIN

The history of scientific invention and aviation is littered with many amazing and courageous efforts made by human beings to defy the laws of physics and gravity. Although these individuals have hailed from different cultures and backgrounds, they were all united in their effort and determination to succeed in their intellectual endeavours. As with science, philosophy, mathematics and technological innovations, the development and progress of the science of aviation was ultimately a collective and combined contribution made by people from diverse backgrounds, thus not allowing one individual or nation to claim sole credit.

From kite flying in ancient China to early Greek, Persian and Indian efforts to fly like birds, the development of the science of aviation undoubtedly received a major boost in medieval Andalusia (Islamic Spain) where, back in the ninth century, Ibn Firnas, an ingenious inventor, became one of the first people in history to make a scientific attempt at flying using devices he had invented to stay airborne and descend smoothly without crashing to the ground.[1] His efforts are considered by historians to be the first serious attempt at flying which subsequently inspired others to improve their methods and techniques and, in doing so, they laid the foundation of the modern science of aviation.

Abul Qasim Abbas ibn Firnas ibn Wardus al-Takaroni, better known as Ibn Firnas, was born in the city of Ronda in medieval Spain (Andalusia). Now located in the Spanish province of Malaga, it is today a bustling centre attracting thousands of tourists from across Europe and beyond every year. After the Muslim conquest of southern Spain in

711, this region became a prominent centre for trade, commerce and learning under its Umayyad rulers and their provincial governors.

Very little is known about Ibn Firnas's family background and education, although some scholars have suggested that he was of North African Berber origin. However, Andalusia during its formative period, was a very diverse place consisting of Visigoths, Arabs, North Africans and Persians, who were of Christian, Muslim and Jewish faiths, and inter-marriage and multicultural interaction was the order of the day. As such, it is highly likely that Ibn Firnas had hailed from a culturally diverse family.

After completing his early education in Ronda, Ibn Firnas moved to Cordova, the capital of Andalusia, to pursue further and higher education. This was inevitable given the fact that some of the leading institutions of higher education were located in the capital where the leading teachers and scholars of the day taught the Arabic language, literature, poetry, aspects of science and philosophy. They also taught traditional Islamic sciences such as Qur'anic exegesis (*tafsir*), Prophetic traditions (*hadith*), Islamic jurisprudence (*fiqh*) and Islamic history (*ta'rikh*), among other subjects.

After completing his higher education, Ibn Firnas opted to travel in search of knowledge. He left Andalusia and moved to Baghdad in order to pursue advance training in religious and scientific subjects. At the time, Baghdad was the foremost centre of learning in the world, attracting the best and brightest religious scholars, philosophers, scientists, mathematicians, historians and geographers, thanks to the generous patronage of the Abbasid Caliphs like Abu Ja'far al-Mansur (r. 754–775), al-Mahdi bi-'llah (r. 775–785), Harun al-Rashid (r. 786–809) and Abdullah al-Ma'mun (r. 813–833).

Indeed, the *Bayt al-Hikmah* (House of Wisdom) institute that was originally founded by Caliph Harun al-Rashid and subsequently expanded and transformed into *Dar al-Hikmah* (Abode of Wisdom) by his son and successor Caliph al-Ma'mun, became a thriving research centre and academy. The institute attracted renowned scholars, scientists and thinkers of the time, including Muhammad ibn Musa al-Khwarizmi (780–850), the founder of Arabic numerals and algebra; Abu Yusuf Yaqub ibn Ishaq al-Kindi (801–873), the pioneer of Islamic philosophy; and Abul Wafa al-Bujazani (940–997), a renowned astronomer and scientist. Being the young and ambitious man he was, Ibn Firnas soon moved to Baghdad to join the Dar al-Hikmah to study both religious and scientific subjects under the tutelage of its leading scholars. Ibn Firnas specialised in Arabic language, literature, astronomy, music and engineering.

It is not clear how long he stayed in Baghdad or whether he had visited other prominent centres of learning in Egypt, Syria and Persia before returning back to Cordova to join the Caliphal court as a poet laureate. Though he became famous for his engineering skills – and as a pioneer of aviation – Ibn Firnas was an equally impressive poet who could compose elegant Arabic verses at the drop of a hat. This endeared him to successive rulers of Andalusia, including Caliphs al-Hakam I (r. 796–822), Abd al-

Rahman II (r. 822–852), Muhammad I (r. 853–886) and al-Mundhir (r. 886–888), whose generous patronage he enjoyed throughout his career.[2]

Ibn Firnas lived and worked in the Caliphal court. However, this was by no means easy for him due to the incessant jealousy and rivalry that prevailed amongst the officials, especially during times of transition from one ruler to another. The unease was further compounded by the tension that existed between the Arab, North African, Berber and Spanish courtiers who were always vying for more influence, power and wealth. This, coupled with the political upheaval, economic uncertainties and cultural conflux of the time, forced scholars, intellectuals and scientific innovators like Ibn Firnas to not only maintain their political neutrality, but also to remain constantly vigilant. However, Ibn Firnas's prodigious talent and creativity always impressed his patrons. In addition to being an expert in medicine and serving at court as a physician to the Caliph, Ibn Firnas was a highly skilled inventor who had developed his own laboratory in the basement of his house in Cordova, where he engaged in scientific experiments and, in the process, invented many instruments and devices.[3]

Indeed, Ibn Firnas successfully designed a water clock, perhaps the first person to do so, even though the art of water clock-making was later perfected and popularised by Abul Izz ibn Ismail ibn al-Razaz al-Jazari (1136–1206) in the twelfth century. In al-Jazari's *Kitab al-Jami bayn al-Ilm wa'l Amal al-Nafi fi Sinat al-Hiyal* (The Book of Knowledge of Amazing Mechanical Devices), which he completed just before his death in 1206, he explained the meaning, purpose and function of around 100 mechanical devices including the water clock. Furthermore, Ibn Firnas was one of the first to invent crystal using sand and rocks. During his experiments, he manufactured glass using rocks procured from the mines of Patlios, which were subsequently used to make drinking glasses and to decorate the churches. This of course required Ibn Firnas to develop a process for cutting rock crystal which, in turn, helped Spain to end their exportation of quartz to be cut in Egypt and elsewhere. As if that was not enough, he also designed and built a multi-coloured planetarium using glass, much to the delight, wonder and amusement of the locals.

Ibn Firnas was an equally dedicated observer of nature and the celestial bodies. His formal education in astronomy in Baghdad enabled him to observe the sun, the moon, the stars, planets and other heavenly bodies, and he gained considerable insight and knowledge in this subject. His interests went further to the extent that he even had a room set aside in his house where people could visit to learn about and observe natural phenomena like lightning, thunder and clouds. Many locals did just that to satisfy their curiosity and they were often inspired by what they would see.

As a devout Muslim, he was encouraged to study astronomy by the Holy Qur'an which, in fact, encourages humanity to observe and admire the beauty and wonders of God's creation: 'Blessed is He in Whose hand is the Dominion, and He is able to do all things. Who has created death and life that He may try you, which of you is best in conduct; and He is Mighty, the Forgiving, Who has created seven heavens in harmony. You can see no fault in the Merciful One's creation; then look again; can you see any rifts? Then look again and yet again, your sight will return unto you weakened and made dim.'[4]

Nevertheless, Ibn Firnas is today best known for his pioneering contribution in aviation. Flying from one country to another, or even sending a rocket into space to explore the moon, the stars and other planets, is taken for granted these days. However, back in the ninth century, such scientific activities would have been considered to be completely beyond human capability, if not pure magic. At a time when myth and fantasy was more prevalent than empirical research, it was Ibn Firnas, a largely forgotten European Muslim polymath and scientist, who made the first scientific attempt at flying and, in doing so, he became the pioneer of aviation.

Although some historians have stated that the first person to make a successful attempt at flying was Armen Firman, other scholars have argued that this was the Latinised name of none other than Ibn Firnas, thus concluding that the two were in fact the same person. Indeed, the names of other medieval Muslim philosophers and scientists who became famous in the Western world were Latinised too, including Jabir ibn Hayyan (Geber in Latin), al-Khwarizmi (Algorithm), al-Ghazali (Algazel), Ibn Sina (Avicenna), Ibn Rushd (Averroes) and al-Farabi (Alpharabius), among others.

Ibn Firnas is important because he was the first man to invent a device that enabled him to fly. As a keen observer of nature, he was not only impressed by birds' ability to fly uninterrupted, but also their sheer strength, tack, vision and agility in the air. After closely studying them for years, he designed and developed a device using silk and feathers taken from an eagle. This device was strapped onto his body before he took off from a high place. It allowed him to control his descent using flaps fastened to his hands and body, thus enabling him to land without crashing to the ground. Although Ibn Firnas was in his late fifties at the time, he continued to improve the device and repeatedly experimented with it before finally making a successful flight in around 875. This, in turn, enabled him to fly from one place to another covering short distances. During this period of repeated tests and trials, he was supported by his close students and fellow enthusiasts and, at the same time, he was derided and ridiculed by others who considered him to be eccentric, if not deluded. But his efforts were amply rewarded when he made his first successful flight after many years of persistence, dedication and hard work.

Once Ibn Firnas was confident that he had perfected his flying device, he invited the locals to a display. He flew from Jabal al-Arus in Rusafa, located on the outskirts of Cordova. Gliding up and down, controlling his descent using the flaps fastened to his hands and body in the same way that birds utilise their wings to control their speed and movement, Ibn Firnas remained airborne for about ten minutes before he landed rather awkwardly. As a result of which, he suffered some minor injuries and his device was badly damaged.[5]

Considering that he was in his mid-sixties at the time, this accident ruled out any further flying experimentations on Ibn Firnas's part, but it was very clear to him that the tail-end of the device played a critical role when it came to achieving a smooth landing. He pinpointed that the tail-end of the device helped to reduce speed during the landing. Subsequently, this part was referred to as an 'ornithopter' by Leonardo Da Vinci, nearly seven hundred years after Ibn Firnas identified the concept in medieval Spain. As expected, all modern aeroplanes, helicopters and even space shuttles, land using their rear wheels or rear-end.

In other words, in his efforts to fly like the birds, Ibn Firnas became a pioneering figure in the field of aviation, paving the way for others to make their contribution in this field, including Leonardo Da Vinci (1452–1519), a famous Italian polymath and artist; Hazarfen Ahmed Celebi (1609–1640), a Turkish engineer and inventor; and Roger Bacon (1214–1292), an English scientist who studied in Cordova and authored *On the Marvellous Powers of Art and Nature* (1260). By comparison, Otto Lilienthal (1848–1896) and the Wright Brothers (Orville and Wilbur) made their contributions during the nineteenth and twentieth centuries, although the credit for laying the foundation of the science of aviation must go to none other than the ingenious Ibn Firnas.

Despite being a noted writer and well-known poet, unfortunately none of Ibn Firnas's literary works have survived other than a few verses here and there. Based on these limited sources and other secondary information, modern historians have reconstructed his life for the benefit of posterity. In addition to pursuing knowledge and scientific research, Ibn Firnas was a popular tutor who guided many students in astronomy and inventing new instruments, devices and objects. According to Ahmad ibn Muhammad al-Maqqari (1578–1632), a noted Moroccan historian, Abul Qasim Abbas ibn Firnas eventually died and was laid to rest in Cordova at the age of 76.[6]

1. S. M. Imamuddin, *A Political History of Muslim Spain*.

2. Salim T. H. Al-Hassani, *1001 Inventions: Muslim Heritage in Our World*.

3. Ezad Azraai Jamsari et al., 'Ibn Firnas and His Contribution to the Aviation Technology of the World', *Advances in Natural and Applies Sciences*.

4. See Surah [chapter] 67: verses 1–4.

5. Ezad Azraai Jamsari et al., op. cit.

6. See al-Maqqari (Makkari), *Nafh al-Tib min Ghusni Andalus al-Ratib*.

4

# ABD AL-RAHMAN III

B. 891 – D. 961

SPAIN

Thomas B. Irving (see chapter 46), a leading Canadian scholar of Spanish history, language and culture, once observed that,

> It was from the Spanish Arabs and their pupils like Roger Bacon, Michael Scott, William Ockham and Peter Abelard, that Europe received the spirit which has enabled man to dominate the world and utilise it to his own ends. It is worthwhile to point out that these thinkers were not exclusively Muslim; many Jews were included among their number, especially in the medical profession…And most remarkable of all, these investigators communicated to Europe that intellectual curiosity and restlessness which is so characteristic of the free mind of today.[1]

The seeds of political stability, economic prosperity, social progress, scientific outlook and literary creativity that were planted in medieval Spain during the reign of Abd al-Rahman I, subsequently led to the flowering of a unique and unprecedented multicultural civilisation in the heart of medieval Europe. This is a period that is otherwise known as the 'Dark Ages'. That was far from being the case in Muslim Spain which, at the time, became a beacon of light during the long and glorious reign of Caliph Abd al-Rahman III, the seventh Umayyad ruler of Andalusia, and which became the envy of Europe as a whole.

Historians have described Abd al-Rahman as having a fair complexion with blue eyes, good-looking face and short in stature, although he looked much taller than his height. He was of solid build, handsome appearance, with a thick black beard. By all accounts, Abd al-Rahman looked more European in appearance than an Arab or a North African. This was not surprising considering the fact that Abd al-Rahman's father, Muhammad, was of both European and Arab parentage, while his mother, Muzna, was a proud European of Christian heritage. In other words, his diverse family background had a positive impact on young Abd al-Rahman as he grew up and later went on to rule a country that became the harbinger of a diverse culture and civilisation in the heart of medieval Europe.[2]

Abd al-Rahman's early years were not as happy as they could have been due to incessant internal family feuds and political wrangling. According to one account, it was his uncle, al-Mutarrif, who allegedly conspired to remove his brother, Muhammad, from his path so he could succeed as the ruler of Andalus after the death of Abdullah. According to another less credible account, it was Amir Abdullah who was responsible for the demise of his sons so that his favourite grandson could succeed him as the sovereign of Muslim Spain. Either way, he ensured young Abd al-Rahman received a thorough education as he grew up in the safety and security of his mother's private quarters.

In addition to acquiring a sound knowledge of Islam, his awareness and understanding of politics, economic affairs and military tactics soon attracted his grandfather's attention. Impressed by his grandson's individual qualities and attributes, coupled with his all-round knowledge and skills, the ailing ruler formally nominated Abd al-Rahman as his successor, overlooking his own sons in the process.

In October 912, Amir Abdullah died at the age of 71 and, as expected, Abd al-Rahman succeeded his grandfather as the undisputed sovereign of Andalusia at the age of only 22 years. The transition itself was in fact smooth, but he inherited a divided and discordant nation that was on the verge of total collapse, compounded by internal family feuds and political dissensions. Not to mention open rebellion too, from provincial governors and persistent political plots and intrigues from neighbouring Christian rulers. Without a doubt, Abd al-Rahman's first priority was to establish his own political authority by fostering understanding between the rival factions within Cordova. Thus by doing so, Abd al-Rahman was able to establish internal peace and stability at home before focusing his attention on external threats. He achieved this by making peace between the Arab and Berber communities who were, at the time, at loggerheads as they competed for political influence and economic gain.

After winning over the Arab and Berber chiefs, Abd al-Rahman turned his attention to consolidating his army. He did this by diversifying its members, thus recruiting Berbers, Christians and Slavs into his fighting force. They were carefully chosen, provided with good training and offered military equipment. Furthermore, they were paid handsomely to fight for their chief and benefactor. Abd al-Rahman's army consisted of more than 13,000 men who became well-known for their fighting power and discipline in the battlefield, thus being seen as one of the best armies in Europe at the time. He deployed this formidable force with remarkable skill and tactical ability which enabled him to soon subdue the neighbouring towns and cities before Seville, Tolox, Bobastro, Ecija, Jaen and Elvira also succumbed one by one.

After subjugating much of southern Spain in 928, Abd al-Rahman turned his attention to other parts of the country including the provinces of Algarve, Toledo, Leon and Zaragoza, and began establishing his political authority in these places. Thereafter, he moved in the direction of the north where the Basques, the Aragonese and Castilians were constantly busy stirring up trouble and mischief. His firm and uncompromising actions against them kept them at bay and this, in turn, ushered in a period of peace.

In so doing, Abd al-Rahman was able to establish his political suzerainty across much of the country. He was not only a successful military leader, but also an effective political administrator. Soon after subduing a city or province, he would appoint a governor to ensure the place was administered efficiently and effectively. His choice of governors were unusually diverse and included Arabs, Berbers, Slavs and Christians, thus reflecting the make-up of the local population. This was indeed an achievement for a young man who had inherited a tiny kingdom which, at the time, consisted of no more than Cordova, but soon extended his rule all the way from Tarragona to the Atlantic Coast, and from Ebro to the Straits of Gibraltar. Undoubtedly, Abd al-Rahman's political awareness, tactical ability and individual bravery enabled him to win over much of the Iberian Peninsula and thereby allowed him to become the undisputed ruler of Andalusia.

As expected, Abd al-Rahman combined his internal policy of expansion with his foreign policy of countering growing Fatimid (fl. 909–1171) influence in North Africa and the Mediterranean. His initiatives in that direction enabled him to establish much-needed barriers and security against Fatimid encroachment and, in the process, allowed him to secure Tangier and Ceuta as a buffer zone. In addition, he took measures to forge closer relations with other leading European powers at the time, including France and Germany, and received officials from Emperor Constantine VII (r. 913–959) in 947.

Likewise, King Otto I of Germany (r. 936–973) entered into formal diplomatic relations with Abd al-Rahman by sending John, who was the monk of Gorze, as an ambassador to the Muslim ruler. The King of Italy followed suit and established friendly relations with Muslim Spain as a bulwark against Fatimid encroachment. Abd al-Rahman's senior officials, including Rabi ibn Zayd al-Qurtubi (d. cir. 1010), who was a Christian, and Hasdai ibn Shaprut (910–970), a leading Jewish scholar and diplomat, played key roles in promoting their interests abroad, thanks to his knowledge and understanding of different European languages, such as Latin, French, German and Arabic.

For example, with regards to Rabi ibn Zayd, the historian Richard Hitchcock wrote, 'He was an Arabic speaker, without being regarded within a Christian context as being "contaminated" by Islam. His origin as a member of the indigenous community of al-Andalus affirms that he was a Latin speaker, and it was, presumably, in this language that he communicated with Otto.'³ In short, Abd al-Rahman employed officials from different backgrounds to accomplish his political, military and diplomatic objectives, and his achievements were nothing short of impressive for his time.

However, his contributions and achievements in other areas were no less important and impressive. After assuming the title of Caliph in 929, he adopted the titles of *Amir al-Mu'minin* (Commander of the Faithful) and *al-Nasir li Din Allah* (Supporter of the Religion of God). Therefore, Abd al-Rahman symbolically rivalled the other two claimants to the Caliphate in the Muslim world at the time, namely the Fatimid and Abbasid Caliphs. Abd al-Rahman initiated a series of economic measures to develop and strengthen his kingdom. He actively promoted agriculture and farming, in addition to lowering taxes. He also provided incentives to farmers to increase food production. He did this by introducing new methods of irrigation, horticulture and farming which, as expected, soon paid dividends as food shortages, poverty and begging reduced substantially. This, in turn, improved people's quality of life and established peace across the country. The population of Spain also increased to around 30 million at the time, with more than a million people living in peace and security in Cordova alone.

Under Abd al-Rahman's rule, Spain soon became a bustling centre for trade and commerce leading to considerable economic prosperity and increased living standards. So much so that, according to the Fatimid geographer, Abul Qasim ibn Hawqal (d. cir. 978), the majority of the population of Andalusia, especially that of Cordova, travelled on mules and horses, and there was no shortage of money in the State Treasury.⁴ Not surprisingly, the remarkable success and prosperity that prevailed in Andalusia at the time soon attracted the admiration and envy of the rest of Europe.

Furthermore, the establishment of political stability, the pursuit of economic prosperity and patronage of intercultural co-operation, paved the way for scientific progress, cultural advancement and literary activities. As a result, Spain became a beacon of light for not only Europe, but also the Western world as a whole. Prominent scholars, thinkers and literary figures like Ibn Masarrah (d. 931), Ibn al-Ahmar (d. 969), Ahmad ibn Nasr (d. 944), Maslamah ibn al-Qasim (d. 964), Arib ibn Sa'id (d. 980), Ibn Abd Rabbihi (d. 940) and Ibn Hani al-Andalusi (d. 973), otherwise known as the al-Mutannabi of the West, lived during this period and thrived in Andalusia's new culture of learning and tolerance.

Ibn Masarrah, for example, is widely regarded as one of the first philosophers in Muslim Spain. He was also an ascetic Sufi who was censored for his supposedly unorthodox teachings in the Islamic East. However, Ibn Masarrah was given a warm welcome in Andalusia during the reign of Abd al-Rahman, where he continued to teach in his mountain retreat until his death. Likewise, prominent Muslim and Jewish physicians such as Hasdai ibn Shaprut, Arib ibn Sa'id and Yahya ibn Ishaq, were patronised and elevated to the positions of personal aides to the Caliph. Other outstanding literary figures that lived during the reign of Abd al-Rahman include Ibn Abd Rabbihi, who composed *Iqd al-Farid* (The Unique Necklace) wherein he vividly described Abd al-Rahman's remarkable military exploits, while Ibn al-Ahmar, who was another notable literary figure, served in his capacity as a Court librarian and authored a biographical account of the Caliph.

Furthermore, under Abd al-Rahman's generous patronage, science, mathematics and astronomy were also actively cultivated in medieval Spain. Scientists like Ahmad ibn Nasr and Maslamah ibn al-Qasim thrived during his reign and, in doing so, they laid the foundation for scientific research and enquiry in the heart of Europe. This was particularly notable as it was a time when the rest of the continent was buried up to their necks in myth-making and superstition. Scientists and scholars like Ibn Nasr and Ibn al-Qasim specialised in a wide range of subjects including mathematics, astronomy and medicine. The Caliph established many libraries and institutes of higher education including the famous Academy in Cordova, and provided generous funding to support research and scholarship. As a result, scholars and scientists, both Muslims and non-Muslims, flocked to Andalusia from many parts of the world, such as Ibn Hawqal, Ibn Shaprut and Nicolas, among others.

In addition to being an active patron of learning and scholarship, Caliph Abd al-Rahman was a very ambitious builder. He was renowned for constructing many palaces and mosques, not to mention markets, shops, roads, public baths, streets, bridges and other similar projects. Perhaps the Caliph's most ambitious project was Madinat al-Zahra. Located three miles to the north-east of Cordova, it took fifteen years to construct the main palace and another twenty-five years to complete the whole project. The design and construction of this new city was initiated by Abd al-Rahman in memory of his beloved wife, al-Zahra. Work started on this project in 936 and it was completed by al-Hakam II, his son and successor, in 975.

The project was spread over 280 acres and fortified by a thick wall with 5000 gates. Around 10,000 labourers worked on this project round the clock and nearly 200,000 dinars were spent annually in order to complete it. The centre piece of the project was the Palace and the Great Mosque. This was an impressive edifice which accommodated a large congregation with streams, rest rooms, shaded trees and other similar luxuries. The Palace consisted of 750 doors and 4316 pillars, and it was made of special materials obtained from places as far as Byzantium, Rome, Constantinople and Africa. A statue of al-Zahra, the Caliph's wife, was carved and placed over the main gateway to the Palace. Running water was made available to all the residents of Madinat al-Zahra, being the first city to have such a facility installed in medieval Europe.

It was also during the reign of Caliph Abd al-Rahman that the streets of Cordova were first lit with lamps at night; this was something that was completely unheard of anywhere else in Europe. At a time when the Cordovans could travel from one part of the city to another in the middle of the night without having to carry a lantern, the rest of Europe was engulfed in pitch darkness and gloom. Likewise, it was a feature of daily life in Cordova to have a regular wash with running water in public baths while, in the rest of Europe, people did not have access to such facilities, thus being forced to go without a wash for weeks, if not longer.

Caliph Abd al-Rahman's Cordova was a truly cosmopolitan city, reflecting his own blend of European, Christian, Arab and Muslim background and heritage. Divided into five districts with twenty-five suburbs, Cordova was not only multicultural but also multi-religious with its impressive mosques, churches and synagogues as well as schools, colleges, markets, shops, gardens, reservoirs and fortresses. The city's population was equally diverse and consisted of Arabs, Jews, Christians, Muslims, Berbers, Spaniards, scholars, teachers, writers, poets, entertainers, government officials, ambassadors, merchants, traders, cleaners and even slaves who hailed from Africa, Persia and parts of Europe.[5]

On a personal level, the Caliph was known for his polite and mild character, but he was also a determined and uncompromising individual. He was dedicated and hard-working with an eye for detail and was especially known for his sense of justice and fair-play. His tolerance, inclusive and accommodating leadership engendered a culture of understanding and co-operation that was very rare during those days.

However, towards the end of his long and remarkable reign of fifty years, he became somewhat autocratic and unpredictable, perhaps due to a combination of old age and poor health. He died at the age of around 70 and, as expected, he was succeeded by al-Hakam II, his favourite son and deputy whom he had carefully groomed for leadership. As a result, political stability was assured and Andalusia continued to march forward based on the solid foundation laid by the indomitable Caliph Abd al-Rahman III. In the words of the historian Stanley Lane-Poole (1854–1931):

> To Cordova belong all the beauty and ornaments that delight the eye or dazzle the sight. Her long line of Sultans form her crown of glory; her necklace is strung with the pearls which her poets have gathered from the ocean of language; her dress is of the banners of learning, well-knit together by her men of science; and the masters of every art and industry are the hem of her garments. Art, literature and science prospered as they then prospered nowhere else in Europe… Mathematics, astronomy, botany, history, philosophy and jurisprudence were to be mastered in Spain, and Spain alone. Whatever makes a kingdom great prosperous, whatever tends to refinement and civilization, was found in Muslim Spain.[6]

Likewise, John Yahya Parkinson (see chapter 32), a prominent Scottish Muslim writer and poet, paid Abd al-Rahman this fitting tribute:

No more glorious dynasty ever held sway in Europe than that of the Spanish Omeyyads. They were on the whole just rulers, generous both to friend and foe, their clemency to rebels being exceptional. On the whole they were beloved by their subjects and treated on equal terms with the Emperor of Germany and the Kings of France and Italy and Greece. In so much respect was Abd-er-Rahman III held by the European potentates for his learning and justice, that they called upon him to adjust disputes that had arisen between themselves in regard to boundary lines and other complications. The time of Spain's greatest prosperity was during the reigns of Abd-er-Rahman III, Hakeem II and Hisham II.[7]

1. T. B. Irving, *The Falcon of Spain: A Study of Eighth Century Spain.*

2. Maribel Fierro, *Abd al-Rahman III of Cordoba.*

3. Richard Hitchcock, *Mozarabs in Medieval and Early Modern Spain: Identities and Influences.*

4. S. M. Imamuddin, *A Political History of Muslim Spain.*

5. Maria Rosa Menocal, *The Ornament of the World: How Muslims, Jews and Christians Created a Culture of Tolerance in Medieval Spain.*

6. Stanley Lane-Poole, *The Muslims in Spain.*

7. Yehya-en-Nasr Parkinson, *Muslim Chivalry.*

5

# ABULCASIS

B. 936 – D. 1013

SPAIN

In a book of pioneering Muslims of the West, it should not come as a surprise if the leading political and scholarly personalities from medieval Muslim Spain are to feature prominently. By virtue of being the first country in Europe to be ruled by Muslims for nearly eight centuries – initially by the Umayyad's up until 1031, and subsequently by other emerging North African powers – Andalusia was destined to produce some of Europe's foremost and influential Muslim scholars and thinkers.

Many of these individuals went on to leave their indelible marks on the history of the Western world. The contributions made by the Spanish Muslims in subjects, including science, mathematics, philosophy, literature, poetry, arts and architecture, were so valuable and enduring that medieval Cordova, the capital of Islamic Spain, rivalled Baghdad and Cairo at the time, as one of the leading centres of learning and literature in the world. Abul Qasim Khalaf ibn Abbas al-Zahrawi, who became famous in the Latin West as Abulcasis, was one such scholar, physician and writer whose contributions to the development and dissemination of the science of medicine and surgery were second to none.

Abulcasis was born in Cordova during the long and glorious reign of Caliph Abd al-Rahman III, the seventh Umayyad ruler of Andalusia who had played a pivotal role in establishing peace and prosperity across Spain. Most of Abulcasis's biographers claim that he was born and brought up in the royal city of al-Zahra, located three miles towards the north-east of Cordova. However, this can be questioned when considering the fact that Caliph Abd al-Rahman had only just initiated the construction for al-Zahra in the year that Abulcasis was born.[1]

He was perhaps born in Cordova itself, which at the time was a bustling centre of learning, trade and cultural activities. Much of the credit for this goes to the tolerant and peaceful ambience that had been created as a result of the Caliph's sense of justice, fair-play and openness. Referring to the Cordova of the time, the historian Philip K. Hitti wrote:

> The city was peopled reportedly with half a million who worshipped in 700 mosques, patronized 70 libraries, used 300 public baths, and walked on paved streets at a time when Parisians and Londoners trudged in dark muddy alleys and when Oxford scholars looked upon bathing as a heathen custom. The display of splendour dazzled the eyes and stirred the imagination not only of Arab but of Latin writers. A Saxon nun in distant Germany styled the Moslem capital an "ornament" in the western parts of the globe.[2]

Young Abulcasis was fortunate to have been brought up and educated in such an enlightened and forward-looking city, where education and learning was actively promoted by its ruler. As expected, Abulcasis's family members – who claimed to be Arabs from Madinah, the City of the Prophet (located in present-day Saudi Arabia) – encouraged him to learn Arabic, the Qur'an and aspects of traditional Islamic subjects before he opted to specialise in science and mathematics.

Thanks to Caliph Abd al-Rahman's generous patronage, scholars initially moved to Cordova and subsequently to other Spanish cities and provinces in order to teach, pursue and advance research and propagate knowledge across Andalusia. Prominent scholars, physicians and scientists like Ibn Firnas (see chapter 3), Ziryab (see chapter 2), Ahmad ibn Nasr (d. 944), Maslamah ibn al-Qasim (d. 964), Arib ibn Sa'id (d. 980) and Hasdai ibn Shaprut (d. 970), among others, helped transform Cordova into a centre of excellence for science, medicine and mathematics. Abulcasis was fully aware that by opting to pursue science and medicine, he was not treading on unknown territory but, on the contrary, he was following in the footsteps of many scientific pioneers who had lived and contributed to the development of the subjects from native Cordova. Like his predecessors and contemporaries, Abulcasis was very studious, diligent, ambitious, and ever so keen to excel in his chosen field.

After successfully completing his formal studies at the famous Academy of Cordova, Abulcasis was recruited into the service of Caliph Abd al-Rahman. He was appointed as the Caliph's personal physician, though he was only in his early twenties at the time. Although Abd al-Rahman died when Abulcasis was 25, the Caliph was succeeded by his son, al-Hakam II, who swiftly promoted Abulcasis as his chief physician after the death of Hasdai ibn Shaprut, who died in 970. There is no doubt that Abulcasis was a highly respected professional who in fact received a generous salary of 5 million dirhams per year, even when people of the time could live comfortably on a salary of 1000 dirhams per annum.

Thus, under al-Hakam's generous patronage, Abulcasis not only thrived, but he also became the most prominent scientist and physician of his generation, overshadowing his contemporaries like Ali ibn Husayn ibn al-Wafid (d. 1074) and Abul Qasim Maslamah ibn Ahmad al-Majriti (d. 1008), who are also known in the Latin West as Abenguefit and Methilem. As it happened, Caliph al-Hakam was very fond of Abulcasis due to his dedication, loyalty and love for learning and education. Like his father, the Caliph actively promoted learning and scholarship but, unlike his father, he was a distinguished scholar in his own right. According to Philip K. Hitti:

> Intellectual progress kept pace with material progress. Abd al-Rahman's son and successor, al-Hakam (r. 961–976), himself a bibliophile, and perhaps the greatest scholar among all caliphs, established twenty-seven free schools in his capital, enlarged the school connected with its mosque into a university, invited professors from abroad and made it attractive to a cosmopolitan body of students. His agents ransacked bookshops in Alexandria, Cairo, Damascus and Baghdad in quest of books for its library, whose contents were estimated at 400,000 volumes. The caliph himself must have used certain manuscripts, for his marginal notes appeared on a few of them.[3]

To put things in historical context, it is worth mentioning here that the total population of Rome at the time was about 50,000 and that of London was only 18,000. Likewise, the largest library in Europe at the time was at St. Gall's monastery in Switzerland which contained only thirty-five books and manuscripts! This explains why the Islamic Kingdom of Andalusia was so widely admired and envied across medieval Europe and beyond. Indeed, Abulcasis saw Caliph al-Hakam as a very benevolent and enlightened ruler. However, what benefitted him the most was that he had direct access to the Caliph's vast library, which included an extensive list of books and manuscripts on aspects of Greek and Arabic medicine. This, undoubtedly, fired Abulcasis's imagination as he proceeded to read, analyse and evaluate existing literature on medicine before making his own contributions.

In addition to being thoroughly familiar with the works of Galen (d. cir. 210 CE) and Hippocrates (d. 370 BCE), he must have had access to the writings of early Muslim scholars and scientists such as Jabir ibn Hayyan (Latin Geber, d. 813), al-Khwarizmi (Algorithm, d. 847), al-Kindi (Alkindus, d. 873) and of course Abu Bakr al-Razi (d. 925), who became famous in the West as Rhazes. By contrast, trailblazers like Ibn al-Haytham (Alhazen, d. 1039) and Ibn Sina (Avicenna, d. 1037) were his contemporaries. Whilst these scholars were busy making their ground-breaking contributions in the fields of science, philosophy, mathematics and medicine in the Islamic East, Abulcasis became the standard-bearer of scientific innovation and progress in the Islamic West, thus paving the way for his successors.

If Jabir ibn Hayyan was the father of alchemy and chemistry and al-Khwarizmi the originator of Arabic algebra; if al-Kindi was the founder of Islamic philosophy and Abu Bakr al-Razi, a clinician and medical administrator *par excellence*; and if Ibn al-Haytham was a pioneering physicist and Ibn Sina the most gifted polymath of all time, then Abulcasis deserves to be recognised as the father of scientific surgery. He worked during the day as a royal physician, but devoted the rest of his time and efforts to pursuing research in all aspects of medicine. In doing so, Abulcasis authored his celebrated multi-volume medical encyclopaedia which was entitled *Kitab al-Tasrif Liman Ajaz an-il Ta'alif* (Concession to Those Who Lack the Capacity to Read Large Books).

Divided into thirty volumes, this work was completed in the year 1000, after forty years of dedicated research and writing, being the first fully illustrated medical encyclopaedia in the history of medicine. This monumental work covered all aspects of medicine, focusing particularly on surgery, diagnostics, orthopaedics, obstetrics, gynaecology, ophthalmology, pharmacology and general health and nutrition. In his own words,

> Whatever I know, I owe solely to my assiduous reading of books of the ancients, and to my desire to understand and appropriate this science. To this I have added the observations and experience of my whole life.[4]

Abulcasis repeatedly emphasised the importance of good doctor–patient relationships for effective diagnosis, treatment, care and recovery from illnesses and diseases. He was of the opinion that all doctors should have thorough education, training and practical experience in order to provide the highest quality of treatment, care and service to their patients, regardless of age, gender, race, creed, colour or social status. He wrote:

> Before practicing, one should be familiar with the science of anatomy and the functions of organs so that he will understand their connections, and know their borders. Also he should know the bones, nerves, and muscles, their numbers, their origins and insertions, the arteries and the veins, their start and end. These anatomical and physiological bases are important, and as said by Hippocrates: 'there are many physicians by title and a few by practice.'[5]

Reminding doctors to maintain good relations with their patients, Abulcasis went on to say that: 'Only by repeated visits to the patient's bedside can the physician follow the progress of the medical treatment.'[6] There is no doubt that Abulcasis advocated the need for adopting a holistic approach to the study, practice and development of medical science. Perhaps that is not surprising considering the fact that he was a practising Muslim who believed that the whole of creation was the handiwork of God, the One and All-Encompassing Creator, while humans were the 'cream of His creation'.

That is why he recommended remedies for ailments only after undertaking a proper examination and diagnosis, thus taking into consideration both the physical and psychological factors that make us humans who we are. Like Abu Bakr al-Razi and Ibn Sina, he felt surgery should always be the last resort to solving medical problems, but unlike them, he never hesitated to deploy his surgical skills once all other options were exhausted. In doing so, he became a pioneer of the science of surgery.

Abulcasis not only designed, developed and provided detailed descriptions of more than 200 surgical tools for the first time; he also used many of them to carry out numerous surgical procedures. Such procedures include caesarean section, eye operations, the removal of teeth and unwanted body tissues, among other things. As if this was not enough, he then described how such procedures should be undertaken and even offered advice on how to recover from the operations as quickly as possible. He developed and communicated such advanced, innovative principles and practices in medical science, at a time when people across Europe were resorting to witchcraft, magic and sorcery to cure common illnesses and diseases.

Unfortunately, the majority of European historians of the past and present, wittingly or unwittingly, have failed to acknowledge the contributions made by the Spanish Muslims to the development and progress of Western civilisation in general and Europe in particular. So much so that even books on the history of medicine and surgery often fail to take note of the contributions and achievements of a remarkable physician and scientist of Abulcasis's calibre.

On 30 September 976, the wise and benevolent Caliph al-Hakam died at the age of 61. Hisham, the son and successor of al-Hakam, was a minor aged 12 at the time, thus being incapable of asserting personal and political authority. This inevitably would have been a concern for Abulcasis, particularly because it led to a short period of political confusion and instability in Andalusia. Accordingly, the *Hajib* (Chief Minister) al-Mansur (r. 976–1002) assumed power and became a very capable ruler renowned for his military and administrative abilities, among other things (see next chapter for more information).

However, al-Mansur's death paved the way for another long period of socio-political turmoil in Islamic Spain, otherwise known as *muluk al-tawa'if* (reign of petty rulers). During this period, Abulcasis maintained a low profile whilst focusing his attention on his studies and research. His hard work and dedication bore fruit with the completion of *Kitab al-Tasrif*; he was in his mid-sixties at the time. It was hailed as a remarkable contribution during his own lifetime, although its full impact did not become clear until well after his death. According to Seyyed Hossein Nasr (b. 1933), a prominent historian of Islamic Science, Abulcasis 'was the greatest of Muslim surgeons and the thirtieth section of his *Kitab al-tasrif…*was the definitive guide for surgeons over the centuries.'[7]

In fact, Abulcasis's work became so well-known that it was translated from Arabic into Latin in 1178 by Gerard of Cremona (Latin Gerardus Cremonensis, 1114–1187), who was a prolific Italian scholar and translator. Thereafter, it was translated into Hebrew, French and English for promulgation across the Western world, with different editions being published in Venice in 1497, Strasbourg in 1532, Basel in 1541 and Oxford in 1778. As a result, it became a standard work on surgery for medical students in Europe, so much so that the renowned French surgeon, Guy de Chauliac (d. 1368), incorporated its Latin version into his own book titled *The Great Surgery* and published it in 1363.

For more than five centuries, Abulcasis's book was used as a standard textbook on surgery at universities across Europe, including the University of Salerno in Italy and the University of Montpellier in France. Hieronymus Fabricius of Aquapendente (d. 1619), who was the teacher of the famous English physician William Harvey (1578–1657), was also very fond of the book. In the words of the historian Donald Campbell:

> The chief influence of Abulcasis on the medical system in Europe was that his lucidity and method of presentation awakened a prepossession in favour of Arabic literature among the scholars of the West: the methods of Abulcasis eclipsed those of Galen and maintained a dominant position in medical Europe for five hundred years…[8]

Thanks to Abulcasis's expertise and influence, Cordova became the foremost centre of medicine and surgery in Europe during the latter part of the tenth and early half of the eleventh century. Hailed as the 'father of surgery' in medieval Europe, unfortunately Abulcasis did not receive similar recognition in the Islamic East where Ibn Sina (Avicenna), his contemporary and author of the famous *al-Qanun fi al-Tibb* (The Canon of Medicine), dominated the field. After a lifetime devoted to the study and dissemination of the science of medicine and surgery, Abulcasis died at the age of 77 and was laid to rest in his native Cordova.

Ⓝ

1.  S. M. Imamuddin, *A Political History of Muslim Spain*.

2.  Philip K. Hitti, *Islam and the West: A Historical Cultural Survey*.

3.  Ibid.

4.  See al-Zahrawi, *Kitab al-Tasrif*.

5.  Ibid.

6.  Ibid.

7.  Seyy ed Hossein Nasr, *Islamic Science: An Illustrated Study*.

8.  Donald Campbell, *Arabian Medicine and Its Influence on the Middle Ages*.

# ALMANZOR

b. 938 – d. 1002

SPAIN

Prior to his death in 976, Caliph al-Hakam II nominated his son, Hisham, as his successor. Only a minor aged 12 at the time, Caliph Hisham II was far too young and inexperienced to be able to assert his own authority. As a result, the Caliph's death led to considerable political infighting and intrigue within the highest echelons of power. Indeed, Hisham's accession to power was opposed by the Slavs from the outset because his mother, Sultana Subh, was a Basque by birth and as such, they feared being side-lined in the new political dispensation.

Consequently, the Slavs actively supported al-Mughirah, the uncle of Hisham II, as the most suitable candidate to succeed Caliph al-Hakam, thus overlooking Hisham's claim to succeed his father. But, al-Mughirah and his prominent Slav supporters were soon removed from the scene by Ja'far ibn Uthman al-Mushafi, who was the Chief Minister of Andalusia at the time. In due course, al-Mushafi himself and his close aides were out-manoeuvred by Abu Amir Muhammad ibn Abdullah, better known as al-Mansur ibn Abi Amir or Almanzor, who subsequently went on to become one of the most powerful rulers of Islamic Spain.

Almanzor hailed from an Arab family of Yemeni origin. According to the historian al-Maqqari (d. 1632), his great-great-grandfather, Abd al-Malik al-Ma'afiri, came to Spain during the time of Tariq ibn Ziyad in the beginning of the eighth century, and settled at Torrox in the province of Algeciras. There, the family soon became known for their learning and piety. His father, Abu Hafs Abdullah ibn Muhammad, was a noted Islamic scholar and jurist who died in Tripoli in North Africa on his way back from his pilgrimage to Makkah. His mother, Burayha bint Yahya, also hailed from a learned family. Her father, Yahya ibn Zakariya ibn Bartal al-Tamimi, was an Islamic scholar and judge, and was also noted for his learning and piety.[1]

Growing up in such a humble and learned family enabled young Almanzor to complete his early and intermediate education with success, before moving to Cordova to seek other opportunities. He must have been in his early twenties at the time although, according to another account, he was born in 942 and, therefore, would have been a teenager at the time.

Soon after his arrival, Almanzor joined the Academy in Cordova to study law, hoping perhaps to follow in the footsteps of his father and grandfather and become a qualified lawyer and jurist. A few years later, he passed his law examination with flying colours and was recruited into the service of Muhammad al-Salim, the Chief Justice of Cordova, as a copy-writer of petitions. Through the office of the Chief Justice, Almanzor came in contact with many powerful and wealthy personalities of Cordova, and it was this which inspired him to seek a suitable political appointment.

By all accounts, Almanzor was a highly ambitious young man who wanted to become powerful and wealthy like the elite of Cordova. Accordingly, he was introduced to Sultana Subh, the mother of Hisham II, by one of her aides and she duly appointed him manager of her elder son Abd al-Rahman's estate. The latter had a large estate and the Sultana felt that someone of Almanzor's proven legal and administrative skills and ability would be the ideal candidate to manage the entire estate. He was offered a monthly salary of 15 dinars with free lodging. To put things into historical context, a family during this time would have needed 20 dinars to live comfortably for a whole year in Mosul, not far from Abbasid Baghdad.[2] Clearly this was an attractive package and Almanzor was only too happy to accept the post, not least because it also brought him very close to one of the most powerful ruling families in Europe. He was in his late twenties at the time.

In due course, Almanzor proved his worth and the Sultana was more than happy to hand over the responsibility of all her estates to him. As a result, Almanzor now had direct access to the most powerful person in the royal family. Impressed with her protégé, a few years later, Sultana Subh promoted him again, but this time he was appointed the chief of the mint at Cordova. His swift promotion to one of the most important posts in the land did not go down too well with everyone. It was not long before his rivals accused him of political bias and financial corruption, but he successfully defended himself against all such charges. Then, in 972, Almanzor was appointed the chief of police (*sahib al-shurtah*) and was responsible for law and order in Cordova. Yet again, Almanzor was able to impress friend and foe alike by fairly and equitably policing the large capital city. By now, Almanzor had occupied several important government posts and on each occasion, had enhanced his reputation as a loyal, efficient and effective officer. He was now in his mid-thirties.

Having proved himself at home, Almanzor was subsequently posted to Mauritania in Africa as its Chief Justice and Treasurer. There, he worked closely with General Ghalib, who was in charge of the military and administrative affairs at the time. During this period, Almanzor became thoroughly familiar with aspects of military strategies and political administration. Impressed with his skills and abilities, General Ghalib immediately married his daughter, Asma bint Ghalib, to Almanzor. Their family alliance subsequently proved to be decisive in shaping the political future of Andalusia.[3]

This opportunity came soon after the death of Caliph al-Hakam II on 30 September 976. Hisham, his son and nominated successor, was only a minor aged 12. Hisham's lack of authority, thus the country's lack of stability, prompted the powerful courtiers at the Caliphal Palace to engage in bitter rivalry and in-fighting to preserve their own positions and wealth. Observing the political chaos that ensued in the heart of the Government in Cordova, the subversive neighbouring Christian leaders were encouraged to take steps to exploit the situation to their advantage. This prompted Almanzor, who was now actively supported by General Ghalib al-Nasiri, his father-in-law, to march out of Cordova and take action against the Christians. After subduing the enemies, he returned home with a huge amount of booty and this substantially enhanced Almanzor's reputation as the defender of the realm, thus winning him many influential supporters within the Government and across Cordova.

Emboldened by his newfound reputation, Almanzor now moved swiftly to remove Ja'far ibn Uthman al-Mushafi, the Chief Minister, and his other opponents, from his path to political power and leadership in Andalusia. In due course, General Ghalib also died fighting the Christian rebels. With all his potential rivals now removed from his path, Almanzor confined the young Caliph Hisham to his palace, while the former became the undisputed leader of Muslim Spain. By all accounts, this was a truly remarkable achievement, considering the number of obstacles Almanzor had to negotiate and overcome along the way to achieve the highest position in the land. Being a canny political operator, Almanzor continued to print the name of Caliph Hisham on the coins.

However, all political, military, economic, administrative, legal and religious decisions and orders were issued by him alone, with the exception of the Friday sermon (kutbah), which was read jointly in his name and that of the young Caliph. He could have gone a step further and claimed the title of Caliph for himself but, being a wise and clever politician, he opted to rule while maintaining some continuity with the past in the form of a ceremonial Caliphate. Even so, he lived and ruled in an age of pomp and pageantry, and not to have a grand title before his name was almost unthinkable. Thus, in keeping with the spirit of the age, Almanzor adopted the title of *al-Mansur bi-llah* (Victorious by God), and subsequently became known in Christian Europe as Almanzor.[4]

After installing himself as the ruler of Spain, Almanzor initiated a number of steps that further consolidated his position and power. He began by reorganising the military through the introduction of new personnel, equipment and training for his armed forces. For example, he actively recruited Berbers and Slavs into his army and rewarded them handsomely for their loyalty and hard work. He purchased eight thousand horses every year and on one occasion, obtained three thousand mules in just one week to strengthen his fighting capability. He also initiated a program of breeding horses to support his military expeditions. This enabled him to repeatedly march out of Cordova and suppress the subversive Christians of the north, often returning to the capital laden with booty. He paid his troops well and treated them fairly, so long as they were loyal and dedicated. However, he never hesitated to demote or even dismiss those who showed any sign of indiscipline. According to the historian S. M. Imamuddin,

> The total strength of his army was six hundred thousand as was found on the occasion of an expedition into the North…Mansur's army was well-disciplined because he was strict and an offence always met with condign punishment.[5]

With an army of more than half a million troops, consisting of both regular soldiers as well as mercenaries, Almanzor initiated several expeditions against Navarre and eventually subdued the Castilian army at the Battle of Cervera. He also marched in the direction of Catalonia and secured Barcelona in 985. Leon came under his tutelage three years later before heading to Galicia in 997, and he also annexed Santiago de Campostella. However, Almanzor did in fact spare the shrine of St James where he found a monk engrossed in his prayers. Prayer was more powerful than political and military power and no one recognised and respected that more than Almanzor. Unlike his father-in-law, Almanzor was not a trained soldier or military general. But circumstances, coupled with his burning desire and ambition to unify his people and strengthen his realm, compelled him to assume that role. He was brave, resolute and invincible, having fought more than fifty-five times against the Christians of the north whilst never losing a battle. In the words of the historian Stanley Lane-Poole (1854–1931),

> Once, when he sat in camp and saw his men in panic, running in, with the Christians at their heels, he threw himself from the throne, flung his helmet away, and sat down in the dust. The soldiers understood the despairing gesture of their general, and, suddenly turning about, fell upon the Christians, routed them, and pursued them even into the streets of Leon.[6]

He combined his role as a military general with that of a politician, statesman and patron of learning, very successfully. In addition to expanding and securing the borders of Andalusia, Almanzor transformed Cordova into a cosmopolitan capital city with

Arabs, Berbers, Christians, Jews and those of other faiths and backgrounds, living side-by-side in peace. He established a Council of Advisors and often consulted them on political, military, administrative, legal and religious issues of the day, but did not always follow their guidance or suggestions. Like Caliph Abd al-Rahman III, he built a separate city called Madinat al-Zahira, located towards the east of Cordova.

Unfortunately, similarly to Abd al-Rahman's Madinat al-Zahra, this palatine city was also destroyed during the upheaval that took place during the beginning of the eleventh century. He also expanded several mosques such as the Great Mosque of Cordova, in order to accommodate increasing numbers of worshippers. At the time, the population of the capital was more than one million and, thanks to Almanzor's policy of openness, toleration, active support for educational institutions and patronage of learning and scholarship, people flocked to Cordova from many parts of Europe and the Islamic East, to advance their careers or pursue higher education.

Almanzor provided generous funding for research in both religious and scientific subjects, and enjoyed the company of the *ulama* (Islamic scholars), scientists, writers, poets and entertainers. Some of the prominent scholars and scientists who thrived under his patronage include Abul Qasim Maslamah al-Majriti (d.1008), who specialised in astronomy, astrology and mathematics, and authored books on the astrolabe, improved al-Khwarizmi's mathematical tables and became a leading scientific figure at the Academy in Cordova. Abd al-Rahman Ishaq ibn Haytham was another prominent scientist and physician of the time. He served Almanzor as his personal physician and wrote a book on medicine. Likewise, Abul Walid ibn Ma'mar was a notable historian and bibliophile who was employed to catalogue all the books and manuscripts in Almanzor's library and write a history of his family, namely the Banu Amir. Almanzor was equally generous towards writers and poets, and on one occasion offered 1000 dinars to Sa'id al-Baghdadi who had dedicated his book, *Kitab al-Fusus,* to him.

He was a learned and tolerant ruler who encouraged interaction between Muslims, Christians and Jews. Almanzor's tolerance is evident from the intermarriages between people of different faiths and racial backgrounds, which became the norm. The ruler, a devout Muslim himself, married Abda, the daughter of Sancho Garces III (r. 1004–1035), also known as Sancho III of Pamplona, the Christian King of Navarre. Also, Almanzor's soldiers of Christian faith were not required to work on Sundays. For someone of such tolerance and understanding, he was surprisingly, very intolerant of philosophers and freethinkers. So much so that Almanzor ordered a large number of books and manuscripts on philosophy that were kept in the library of Caliph al-Hakam, to be thrown into the fire. He did so with the support and backing of many influential *ulama* of Cordova. Perhaps he agreed to carry out the wishes of the religious scholars because most of the *ulama* in Cordova, at the time, were literalists who considered philosophy and rationalism to be heretical. Almanzor, of course, did not want to upset them in anyway. That aside, according to the historian S. M. Imamuddin,

Al-Mansur was the most remarkable man of his age. After Abd al-Rahman III, he was the greatest warrior and statesman in Europe in the tenth century. He rose to power from obscurity mainly by dint of his own effort, intelligence, sagacity and diplomacy…Never, except under Abd al-Rahman III, had the star of Muslim Spain shone with such brilliance…Spain reached its height of glory and world power and Cordova became the envy of the whole Christian world.[7]

Almanzor died on 10 August, 1002 whilst on his way back from a military expedition; he was 61 at the time and was laid to rest in Madinat al-Salim, otherwise known as Medinaceli. Today, a statue of Almanzor stands proudly on display in the Spanish municipality of Calatanazor in memory of the great European Muslim ruler. Also, the 'Pico Almanzor', the highest mountain in the province of Avila located in central Spain, is also named after him. John Yahya Parkinson (see chapter 32), a leading Scottish Muslim poet of the twentieth century, eulogised this great ruler of Islamic Spain in the following words:

O'er the hills of Andalusia
Rings the Arab battle-cry,
Fast Islamic spearmen gather,
There Omeya's banners fly;
Great Almansur leads to battle
Cordova's effulgent shields;
Victor o'er his Christian foemen
On a hundred tented fields.
Never did a doughter leader
Guard the sacred law Kuran;
O'er the Muslim spears in battle
Eagle-eyed the conflict scan;
Where the sunshine it was sparkling
On the point of steeled lance;
With the sternest legions pressing
'Gainst the knights of Spain and France.
Thro' the heart of the Asturias,
Thro' the mountains of Navarre,
In a hurricane of fury
Swept the hero's helms afar;
Shrieked the north in sudden anguish
Where the warrior turned his course;
Desolation, desolation,
Trodden by the Moorish horse.

Fifty-two campaigns the chieftain
'Gainst his northern foemen led;
And his spearmen rode to conquest,
Trampling every pathway red,
In the dust Navarre is lying,
Bleeds Castile at every pore,
For Abdallah's mighty scion
Islam's colours proudly bore;
With the swordsmen of Elvira,
Cordova's renowned lance;
Where Toledo's troops are dashing,
Saragossa's Emirs prance,
O'er the wreck of wild Comarcas
Line on line the Muslims sped;
Not a foe dare stand for battle.
Not a Christian raise his head;
For the Eastern turbans glittered,
And the clarion tekbir ran;
When the lance of great Almansur
Led the Moorish battle-van.[8]

1.  S. M. Imamuddin, *A Political History of Muslim Spain*

2.  Ibid.

3.  Reinhart Dozy, *Spanish Islam: A History of the Muslims in Spain*

4.  Stanley Lane-Poole, *The Muslims in Spain*.

5.  S. M. Imamuddin, op. cit.

6.  Stanley Lane-Poole, op. cit.

7.  S. M. Imamuddin, op. cit.

8.  Yehya-en-Nasr Parkinson, *Muslim Chivalry*.

# IBN HAZM

B. 994 – D. 1064

SPAIN

Referring to the state of affairs in the Islamic East during the eleventh century, Marshall G. H. Hodgson wrote:

> The culture of the High Caliphate gradually became classical, an inherited model to look back to. The great schools of fiqh which it had developed became accepted as the only possible ones; the Shari'ah was no longer an adventure but a heritage. The canons of Arabic literary criticism and of grammar, which the scholars of Kufah and Basrah and Baghdad had quarrelled about, came to be semi-sacred inheritance, to be learned and believed; and the top literature of that older time was held unsurpassable in its kind, particularly in those countries where Arabic continued to be the chief cultural language. Formal political theory never abandoned its attachment to the caliph, not only after the end of the actual caliphal state, but after there was no longer even the title of caliph in Baghdad. [1]

During this period of social, political, economic and cultural stagnation in the Islamic East, a remarkable Muslim scholar and intellectual emerged in the Islamic West. He was never afraid to question received wisdom and, in the process, became an unsurpassed champion of creativity in Islamic thought and scholarship. He was none other than Ibn Hazm al-Andalusi.

Abu Muhammad Ali ibn Ahmad ibn Sa'id ibn Hazm, better known as Ibn Hazm al-Andalusi, was born into a wealthy and influential Muslim family in Cordova, the capital of Islamic Spain. According to some historians (such as al-Marrakushi), Ibn Hazm's family originated from the Islamic East and had links with the Umayyad royal family of Damascus.

However, others (like Ghulam Haider Aasi) suggest that they were of Persian origin and yet others, including Ibn Hayyan (see chapter 51) and Reinhart Dozy (1820–1883), claim that Ibn Hazm's ancestors were Christians from Algarve, located in present-day Portugal. The family subsequently converted to Islam and it was Sa'id, the grandfather of Ibn Hazm, who moved to Cordova perhaps during the mid-tenth century. His son, Ahmad, the father of Ibn Hazm, grew up and was educated in the capital of Andalusia. After completing his education in Arabic and aspects of Islamic sciences, Ibn Hazm became a highly respected figure in Cordova, known especially for his mastery of the Arabic language and literature. This endeared him to the ruling classes and thus, he occupied prominent positions in government during the reigns of Hisham II and al-Mansur (Almanzor), and even served as the latter's deputy on several occasions.

Ibn Hazm grew up in a distinguished family that wielded considerable political and economic power and influence in Muslim Spain. He spent his early years in his father's luxurious palace, surrounded almost entirely by women. He also had very little contact, if any at all, with the learned scholars, literary figures and visiting politicians that his father was required to interact with on a daily basis. By his own account, Ibn Hazm was a weak and frail child, yet one of his father's favourites. He received his early education in languages, calligraphy and poetry from the women who lived in the family palace, before pursuing traditional Islamic sciences which became his lifelong preoccupation. Nothing is known about his mother, although some of his biographers have suggested that she may have been blonde-haired, of Spanish or European origin.[2]

Thereafter, Ibn Hazm's father entrusted his education to several prominent scholars of the time, including Abd al-Rahman ibn Abi Yazid al-Misri, Abu Ali al-Husayn al-Fasi, Ahmad ibn al-Jassur, Abu Bakr Muhammad ibn Ishaq al-Hamadhani, Abdullah ibn Dahhun and Abdullah ibn Muhammad ibn al-Faradi, among others. He studied Qur'anic exegesis, Prophetic traditions, Islamic theology, jurisprudence, philosophy and logic from many prominent scholars of the time. He was particularly influenced by Baqi ibn Makhlad ibn Umayyah al-Shafi'i and Mundhir ibn Sa'id al-Dawudi al-Zahiri in his religious and legal thinking.[3]

Even so, Ibn Hazm was an independent-minded student who was prepared to question, delve deeper and explore not only the wider, but also the inner meaning of both the religious and philosophical sciences. He sought to understand and evaluate the true nature of knowledge, interpretation of religious scriptures and their implication in practice. Pursuing such an approach to learning and education set him apart from his peers, and his teachers expected him to become an outstanding scholar.

Ibn Hazm lived during unpredictable times and was barely in his teens when Andalusia was rocked by socio-political strife, leading to considerable loss of lives and livelihood. Such issues were inevitable given the sudden rise of the powerful politician and military leader, Almanzor, and the subsequent social, political and economic reforms he ushered in. Ibn Hazm's family were, at first, caught up in the political strife due to their loyalty to the Umayyad Caliphate of Spain. However, his father was quick to readjust his political position and was swiftly promoted by Almanzor to occupy an influential position in government, thus continuing to serve in this capacity with loyalty and dedication.

After Almanzor's death in 1002, Ahmad continued to serve al-Muzaffar (r. 1002–1008), the son and successor of Almanzor. But, the state of affairs changed in 1009 when the Cordovans had had enough of the Amirids and openly revolted, leading to the installation of Muhammad al-Mahdi as the new Umayyad Caliph. Unfortunately, al-Mahdi proved to be weak and incapable of restoring peace and security. During the next two decades, the political situation in Andalusia remained volatile and unpredictable, and Ibn Hazm's family were forced to endure considerable suffering and hardship.

As a result, in 1013, Ibn Hazm was forced to leave Cordova and move to Almeria where the local ruler continued to maintain some semblance of peace and normality. Here in Almeria, Ibn Hazm was initially received well. But, as time went on, Ibn Hazm fell out with Almeria's ruler due to political and religious differences, thus leading to his imprisonment. After spending nearly six years travelling in different parts of Andalusia, he eventually returned to Cordova in 1019, only to be forced into exile in 1025 to Jativa (Shatiba). During his stay there, he composed his celebrated *Tawq al-Hamamah* (The Dove's Necklace). He then returned to Cordova yet again but was forced out once more, although this time he lived in Valencia, Denia and Mallorca until 1048.

During this period, Ibn Hazm met many prominent scholars, including Ibn Sidah (1007–1066) and Ibn Abd al-Barr (978–1071), who he later praised for their learning and scholarship. From Mallorca, Ibn Hazm – now in his sixties – moved to Seville, before finally moving to his family estate at Manta Lisham where he spent his final years in relative peace, keeping himself fully occupied with research and writing.

Needless to say, Ibn Hazm lived during a highly unpredictable and tumultuous period in the history of medieval Spain. As a consequence of such turmoil, he was forced to move from one place to another to escape persecution and hardship. In his *Tawq al-Hamamah*, he explained the difficulties and challenges he faced:

After all the things that have happened to me and fallen upon my shoulders, it is a wonder that a state of mind like mine could have recalled anything, preserved any trace, or invoked the past. For you know quite well that my memory is unsteady, my state of mind is shattered because of the situation in which I find myself: exiled from home; harassed by fate, the tyranny of rulers, disloyalty of friends, adverse conditions, change of fortune, deprivations from inherited and acquired wealth, disposition of what parents and ancestors had left me, preoccupation from protecting my family and children, longing in despair to returning home, being the toy of fate, and awaiting for determination of God's decree.[4]

Despite suffering so much pain and hardship, it is quite remarkable that Ibn Hazm never abandoned his studies and research. Indeed, his thirst for knowledge and learning was truly unrelenting and, in the process, he became one of the foremost scholars in the history of Islam. Arguably, Ibn Hazm was the most prolific writer of medieval Europe. Spanning a period of more than forty years, he not only immersed himself in profound study and research, he also authored hundreds of books and treatises on all aspects of Islamic sciences, history, comparative religion, Arabic literature, poetry, philosophy, medicine, human psychology, logic and jurisprudence. How did he manage such tasks?

By all accounts, Ibn Hazm was an unusually gifted scholar and writer who pursued an analytical and systematic approach to Islamic sciences; he was dedicated, industrious and equally innovative in his thinking and observations, never shying away from questioning received wisdom. In the process, he pleased many people, just as he also annoyed and offended others, leading to considerable uncertainty, difficulties and challenges for himself and his family members. Yet, despite troubles, he never compromised his beliefs, principles and practices. Referring to his society, he remarked, 'Our al-Andalus is more envious of its good scholars than anywhere else in the world. If a scholar is good, they would say that he is an arrogant plagiarist; and if he is mediocre, they would say, "Could this be otherwise? Where did he study and what did he read?"'

With that said, Ibn Hazm's comment needs to be contextualised: the Muslims of Andalusia were much more discerning and inquisitive than their brethren in other parts of the Muslim world. This was mainly due to their peculiar social, political and intellectual conditions. Spain was also a multicultural society and the *ulama* (religious scholars) were fewer in numbers and more elitist than in the Maghreb or the Islamic East. This perhaps explains why the masses developed a questioning attitude towards all things religious in order to avoid being misled or misguided. The majority of the Andalusian's were strictly conservative Malikis, unlike Ibn Hazm, who was an adherent of the Zahiri methodology in *fiqh* (Islamic jurisprudence).

Thus understandably, the people were very uncomfortable with Ibn Hazm's literalist approach to the Qur'an and Prophetic traditions, not to mention his repudiation of *qiyas* (analogical deduction), *istihsan* (juristic preference) and *ra'y* (rational opinion) as sources of Islamic law. Likewise, he criticised the ideas and thought of revered early Muslim scholars (such as Abul Hasan al-Ashari, Abu Hanifah and Malik ibn Anas), and that offended the local religious authorities to the extent that they openly burnt his books. However, he stuck to his principles and directed his pen against those who criticised his ideas and thought. Even Ibn Hazm's opponents admitted that his pen was sharper than Hajjaj ibn Yusuf's sword.[5]

Ibn Hazm was tall, slim, of white complexion, but he also suffered from multiple health problems throughout his life. Nevertheless, he was a great European Muslim scholar, thinker, polemicist and writer who became surprisingly well known in the Islamic East. Although at the same time, Ibn Hazm was virtually unknown in the Western world. This was because he wrote almost entirely in Arabic and his works soon found a following in the Maghreb and subsequently in the Islamic East, but unfortunately they were not translated into Latin or other European languages until relatively recently. According to his sons, Fadl and Abu Sulayman, he authored 400 books and treatises consisting of more than 80,000 pages in total. In doing so, Ibn Hazm became one of the most prolific writers in the history of Islam after Ibn Jarir al-Tabari, the famous author of *Kitab Ta'rikh al-Rusul wa'l Muluk* (The Book of History of Prophets and Kings).

Although Ibn Hazm wrote on all branches of Islamic sciences, Arabic literature, poetry, philosophy, ethics, history and comparative religion; he is today best known for his following books: *Tawq al-Hamamah fi'l Ulfah wa'l Ullaf* (Doves Necklace concerning Love and Lovers); *Kitab al-Fasl fi'l Milal wa'l Ahwa wa'l Nihal* (Decisive Treatise on Religions, Sects and Denominations); *Kitab al-Muhalla bi'l Athar fi Sharh al-Mujalla bi'l Ikhtisar* (Book of Gems concerning Extant Information Expanding in a Summary Form on the Book 'The Adorned'); *al-Ihkam fi Usul al-Ahkam* (Judgement on Fundamental Legal Principles); *Maratib al-Ulum* (Categories of Sciences); *al-Taqrib li Hudud al-Mantiq wa Madkhaluh* (Facilitating Understanding between the Rules of Logic and its Comprehension); and *Kitab Akhlaq wa'l Siyar* (Book of Ethics and Morality).

*Tawq al-Hamamah* was one of Ibn Hazm's earliest works and is considered to be a masterpiece of medieval Arabic poetry. As the title indicates, the poetry deals with the subject of love and lovers. Growing up in his father's imposing palace in Cordova, surrounded by women, courtiers, intense rivalry, jealousy, intrigue and even plotting, he became a perceptive observer of human behaviour, its ups and downs, and captured the mood and swings of different characters and personalities. Ibn Hazm displayed all of this in a remarkable fashion in the book consisting of thirty chapters and an afterword. Ibn Hazm focuses on the subject of love and provides a multi-layered interpretation and understanding of the meaning, purpose and signs of love, longing, secrets of lovers, test of love, trials of separation and tribulations faced by the lover and the loved. He presents these from worldly, spiritual, ascetic and religious perspectives. Far from being a systematic study of the subject, this book represents one of the finest expositions of courtly love to have been produced in medieval Europe.[6]

By contrast, his *Kitab al-Fasl* was a pioneering work on comparative religion, although it remains unclear when the book was written. According to some of his biographers, he composed this book in around 1030 when he was in his mid-thirties. It is a voluminous work where Ibn Hazm provides a detailed study of world religions by combining the dialectic methodology of the theologians with the ecumenical approach of the interfaith practitioners. As a result, he rigorously analysed many religions, sects and denominations including Judaism, Christianity, Zoroastrianism and Manichaeanism. In the process, he attempted to separate the truth from falsehood, facts from fiction and myth from reality, and presented his findings in this book for the benefit of posterity. To Ibn Hazm, the main purpose of studying world religions, or comparative religion, was to arrive at the truth rather than regurgitate religious history for the sake of it. Consisting of five bulky volumes and translated into Spanish by Miguel Asin Palacios from 1927 to 1932, this book has established Ibn Hazm's reputation as the pioneer of comparative religion.

Ibn Hazm's *Kitab al-Muhalla*, *al-Ihkam* and *Kitab al-Akhlaq* are important contributions to aspects of traditional Islamic sciences, while his *Maratib al-Ulum* and *Taqrib* focus on the hierarchy, status, purpose and function of different branches of sciences, both religious and philosophical. He considered religious sciences to be the most virtuous, and therefore it was essential (*fard ayn*) to pursue them. Such religious sciences included the study of the Qur'an, Prophetic traditions, Islamic theology and jurisprudence. Simultaneously, Ibn Hazm argued that the pursuit of philosophical sciences was a collective obligation (*fard al-kifayah*) too.

Indeed, he divided philosophical sciences into two categories: demonstrative sciences, consisting of logic, mathematics, medicine and astronomy, while the other category was the spurious sciences, including alchemy, astrology, music and magic. His *Taqrib* is an important work on the subject of logic, which was praised by some for its lucidity and insight, but also strongly disapproved by the traditionalist scholars for espousing a logical approach to both the religious and philosophical sciences.

Undeterred, Ibn Hazm continued to write books and treatises, both complex and simple, large and shorter works, on a wide range of subjects. This earned him a lofty position in the history of Islamic thought, and certainly as one of medieval Europe's most original Islamic scholars and thinkers. In the words of Ibn Bashkuwal (d. 1183), '

Of all the natives of Spain, Ibn Hazm was the most eminent by the universality and the depth of his learning in the sciences cultivated by the Muslims; add to this his profound acquaintance with the Arabic tongue, and his vast abilities as an elegant writer, a poet, a biographer, and an historian...'[7]

After a lifetime devoted to research and writing, this great Spanish Muslim scholar and author died in virtual obscurity at the age of around 70. He was buried in Manta Lisham in the district of Niebla, located in the Spanish province of Seville, and in 1963, a statue of Ibn Hazm was unveiled in his birthplace. His contribution and achievements are more widely known today, thanks to the efforts of many prominent modern scholars and academics like Miguel Asin Palacios, Garcia Gomez, Ihsan Abbas, Abu Zahrah, A. G. Chejne and Ghulam Haider Aasi.

N

1. Marshall G. S. Hodgson, *The Venture of Islam*, volume 2.

2. A. G. Chejne, *Ibn Hazm*.

3. Ghulam H. Aasi, *Muslim Understanding of Other Religions*.

4. Ibn Hazm, *Tawq al-Hamamah* (translated by A. G. Chejne).

5. H. A. R. Gibb et al. (ed.), *Shorter Encyclopaedia of Islam*.

6. Philip K. Hitti, *History of the Arabs*.

7. Ibn Bashkuwal, *Kitab al-Sila fi Akhbar A'immat al-Andalus* (quoted by R. A. Nicholson, *A Literary History of the Arabs*).

8

# WALLADA BINT AL-MUSTAKFI

B. 1001 – D. 1091

SPAIN

The picture of Oriental women in general, especially that of Muslim women being presented as shy, secluded and submissive, clearly dominated both factual and fictional narratives about them both in the West and the East until relatively recently. The image of Muslim women was all too often associated with exotic, sensual and mysterious surroundings of a harem (women's quarter). This was where scores of women resided in total seclusion, only to be of service to the all-powerful and wealthy Oriental Caliph or Sultan. Although, contemporary scholarship, spearheaded by several Muslim women, has helped to break-down stereotypes and entrenched barriers. However, medieval Muslim women have continued to be portrayed as backward thinking, exotic and gullible up to this day.[1] Like so many other notable medieval Muslim women, the life, thoughts and achievements of Wallada bint al-Mustakfi, the celebrated eleventh century Andalusian poet and literary figure, clearly defies such generalisation and misrepresentation.

Born into the ruling Umayyad family of Spain, Wallada was the daughter of Caliph Muhammad III al-Mustakfi who ruled Andalusia from 1024 to 1025. As with many other medieval figures featured in this book, Wallada's date of birth is hotly contested among scholars. With some scholars suggesting she was born in 994, others have argued that she was born in Cordova in 1001. As most scholars agree she died when she was around ninety, the suggestion that she was born in 1001 appears most accurate. By all accounts, Wallada was born during a politically turbulent and unpredictable period in the history of Andalusia. It was a time when the Amirids were quickly losing their influence, leading to the rise and demise of successive claimants to power. Eventually, there came an end to the Umayyad Caliphate in 1031.

Muhammad al-Mustakfi, the father of Wallada, was himself an Umayyad prince who assumed power after ousting the incumbent Caliph Abd al-Rahman V al-Mustazhir in January 1024. At the time, Wallada was in her early twenties, having already completed her formal education in Arabic, the Qur'an, aspects of religious sciences and poetry. Nothing is known about her teachers other than the fact that she grew up in her father's palace in Cordova and therefore, most, if not all, her teachers would have been women who resided there at the time.

Needless to say, in those days the main interest and preoccupation of men and women in both the Caliphal palaces and courts, whether in Baghdad or Cordova, was literature and poetry. Referring to the Andalusia of that time, the historian Philip K. Hitti (1886–1978) wrote:

> Wherever and whenever the Arabic language was used there the passion for poetical composition was intense. Verses countless in number passed from mouth to mouth and were admired by high and low, not so much perhaps for their contents as for their music and exquisite diction. This sheer joy in the beauty and euphony of words, a characteristic of Arabic-speaking peoples, manifested itself on Spanish soil…Most of the sovereigns had laureates attached to their courts and took them along on their travels and wars. Seville boasted the largest number of graceful and inspired poets, but the flame had been kindled long before in Cordova and later shone brilliantly at Granada as long as that city remained the bulwark of Islam.[2]

Blue-eyed, blonde hair and fair-skinned, Wallada looked more European in appearance than Arab, yet she was an equally proud Arabic-speaking Spanish Muslim. She was also very beautiful and an unusually attractive young lady who, having fully absorbed the Arabic culture, ethos and mannerism of the Cordovan elite, subsequently went on to establish her reputation as a prominent composer of Arabic poetry and literature. In the meantime, her family were forced to endure considerable difficulties and hardship following the assassination of her father, Caliph Muhammad III al-Mustakfi, barely a year after his enthronement.

In the ensuing chaos and confusion, the political, economic and civic situation in Cordova became dire, which forced some of its citizens to invite Yahya of Malaga, a local ruler, to come and restore peace and security. Unfortunately, he also failed. This led to the formation of the Council of State, consisting of leading personalities of

Cordova. However, such a solution was not ideal, given the jealousy and rivalry that existed between the different members of the Council. Tired of constant changes to government and its negative impact on the people of Andalusia, coupled with the rising price of basic commodities and increasing unemployment in Cordova; Ibn Jawhar, the president of the Council of State, was prompted to assume power, even if his authority was recognised only in and around Cordova.

Following the assassination of her father, Wallada, being her father's heir apparent, inherited the family properties and wealth, and continued to live in the family palace in Cordova. Here, she devoted all her talents, energy and wealth to promoting learning and literary activities. As a result, she befriended many prominent scholars and literary figures of the time and, they in turn, admired the Umayyad princess for her beauty, independence and poetic talents. As a younger contemporary of Ibn Hazm, she must have been aware of his political and literary activities. Having served as the prime minister for Caliph Abd al-Rahman V al-Mustazhir, Ibn Hazm was not only a leading politician, but also a prominent literary figure of the time.

Despite being subsequently arrested and exiled by her father, Caliph Muhammad III, Ibn Hazm may have been one of Wallada's admirers due to her love for learning and poetry.

Although Wallada belonged to the most famous family of Cordova, she was very down-to-earth and everyone – high born or of lowly origin – felt equally comfortable in her presence, as long as they had some interest in literature, poetry or the arts. For a female member of a generally conservative ruling family, she was remarkably unconventional in her dress and habits. Refusing to wear the traditional veil, she mingled freely with both men and women, but never compromised her principles, values and morals. It was not long before her palace became one of the major centres of literary activities in Cordova attracting poets, scholars and artists alike. She was widely recognised and respected for her patronage of poetry and literature in Cordova's literary circles and beyond. So much so that Reinhart Dozy (1820–1883) hailed her as the 'Sappho of Spain'.[3]

Never married, Wallada lived the life of a spinster yet she was a true romantic at heart. Unsurprisingly, when Abul Walid Ahmad ibn Zaydun al-Makhzumi, better known as Ibn Zaydun, the leading politician and renowned poet of Andalusia, first attended one of her literary sessions, she was bowled over by his dashing looks, charming personality and literary abilities. Born in Cordova in 1003, Ibn Zaydun belonged to a prominent Arab family of the Makhzum tribe and subsequently established his reputation as a gifted poet and writer. Wallada and Ibn Zaydun, whilst still in their early twenties, fell in love and both expressed their affection for each other through beautiful and exquisite Arabic verses. Ibn Zaydun admired her so much that even after their separation, he lamented:

Yes, I have remembered you with longing, at al-Zahra, when the horizon was bright and face of the earth gave pleasure, and the breeze was soft in the late afternoon, as if it had pity on me. The garden was shining with its waters of silver, as if necklaces had been cast into its breasts. It was a day like the days of our pleasures which have now left us. We passed the night like thieves stealing that pleasure while fortune slept…A rose shone in its bed exposed to the sun, and the noonday grew more radiant at the sight of it; a water-lily passed, spreading its fragrance, a sleeper whose eyes had been opened by the dawn…My most precious, most brilliant, most beloved possession – if lovers can have possessions – would not compensate for the purity of our love, in the time we wondered free in the garden of love. Now I thank God for my time with you; you have found consolation for it, but I have remained a lover.[4]

Historians have advanced conflicting explanations for their separation. Some say Ibn Zaydun's links with anti-Umayyad political groups, such as Banu Jahwar, led to their parting of ways, while others suggest the main reason for their split was unfaithfulness on the part of Ibn Zaydun. However, if he had indeed been unfaithful to her, it would have been inappropriate for him to claim that he had 'remained a lover' but, as it happened, eleventh century Cordova was one of the most culturally tolerant, morally lax and politically unpredictable capitals in medieval Europe. Unsurprisingly, the conflict and contradictions of the time are also reflected in the 'love' and 'separation' experienced by Wallada and Ibn Zaydun.

In other words, there was more than one contributing factor that led to their parting of ways. It is obvious that Wallada was not a typical Cordovan woman; rather, she personified the morals and values of her society's elite and was fiercely independent-minded, economically affluent and always ready to push the moral boundaries of the time, often walking a tight rope between what was approved and disapproved. Her brave and libertarian attitude, and by extension, single-handed protest against the seclusion of women from the social, political and cultural spheres of her society, was best exemplified by her choice and design of dress. On the right side of her outer garments, she had the following words inscribed in gold: 'By Allah, I am apt for high deed, and I go my way and wander at will!' And on the left side of her robe, it stated: 'I yield to my lover the round of my cheek, and I give my kiss on him who desires it.'(5)

Needless to say, Wallada was not the first Muslim woman to become a champion of female liberty and empowerment. She followed in the footsteps of other prominent early Muslim women, including Aishah bint Talha, a cousin of Aishah (612–678), the wife of the Prophet; Princess Ulayya, the daughter of Caliph Mahdi (r. 775–785); and Zubaydah, the wife of Caliph Harun al-Rashid (r. 786–809), among others, who refused to wear the veil and became active members of their respective communities.

However, unlike her predecessors, Wallada hailed from one of Europe's most influential Muslim families. Living as she did, in a cosmopolitan society, enabled her to transcend barriers that other women could not overcome at the time. Indeed, following her separation from Ibn Zaydun, she befriended Abu Amir ibn Abdus, who was a powerful government minister in the service of Ibn Jahwar, though arch-rival of Ibn Zaydun. Thereafter, she moved into the minister's palace and lived there with him, while Ibn Zaydun's love and longing for her was expressed in beautiful and exquisite Arabic verses that have immortalised him. In the words of Philip K. Hitti,

> Aside from Ibn 'Abd Rabbih, Ibn Hazm and Ibn al-Khatib, Spain produced a number of poets whose compositions are still considered standard. Such a one was Abu al-Walid Ahmad ibn Zaydun (1003–1071), reckoned by some as the greatest poet of al-Andalus.[6]

Ibn Zaydun's efforts to regain his lost love were in vain, as Wallada shunned his overtures and Ibn Abdus, in turn, made sure that their separation became permanent. He did this by confiscating his rival's properties and possessions in Cordova, and eventually forced him to leave the capital and settle in Seville where he continued to serve the local ruler. Wallada's relationship with Ibn Zaydun was both close and distant, and her concept of love was platonic and practical, and equally complex and contradictory. Ibn Zaydun was her perfect lover in the garden of bliss, unimpeded by the march of time and untouched by the vicissitudes of daily life, but that was, it seems, always meant to be immature, emotional and idealistic rather than realistic and practical.

Her separation from Ibn Zaydun marked the end of 'idealism' and the beginning of 'realism' in her understanding and appreciation of love and affection as she experienced with Ibn Abdus, which was both mature and practical. When Ibn Zaydun accused her of betrayal, she defended herself poetically: 'Ibn Zaydun slanders me unjustly, in spite of his excellence, and in me is no fault. He looks askance at me when I come along; it is as if I have come to castrate Ali.'[7]

Wallada was unconventional not only in her behaviour, but also her dress and attitude to love and relationships, and was equally gifted as a poet and literary figure. Most of her writings are not extant and, accordingly, it is not possible to fully assess the overall quality and quantity of her poetic output. For example, only eight out of nine poems written by Wallada about her relationship with Ibn Zaydun have been preserved. Yet, they only provide a partial picture of her poetic skills, insight and abilities.

Even so, as the historian Ahmad ibn Muhammad al-Maqqari rightly pointed out, she was one of the foremost amongst medieval Spanish Muslim women who became renowned for their eloquence, wit and creativity. Some of her students later became prominent literary figures in their own right, such as Muhya bint al-Tayyani. According to some scholars, they collectively contributed to the development of romantic lyrics in medieval Europe, thus linking classical Arabic love poetry of the Umayyad and Abbasid eras, to their European equivalent during the Middle Ages, perhaps inspiring the composers of *Tristan and Iseult*, *Canterbury Tales* and the *Divine Comedy*. If that be true, then Wallada's contribution, achievements and legacy is certainly as pertinent today as it was during her own lifetime.

Wallada died on the day the al-Murabitun (Almoravids) of North Africa marched into Cordova on 26 March, 1091. She had outlived both Ibn Zaydun and Ibn Abdus, and was around 90 at the time.

Ⓝ

1.  See Rana Kabbani's *Europe's Myths of Orient*; Fatima Mernissi's *Beyond the Veil*; Amina Wadud's *Qur'an and Women*, and *Inside the Gender Jihad*.

2.  Philip K. Hitti, *History of the Arabs*.

3.  Reinhart Dozy, *Spanish Islam: A History of the Muslims in Spain*.

4.  Ibn Khaqan, *Qala'id al-'Iqyan* (quoted by A. Hourani, *A History of the Arab Peoples*).

5.  D. M. Dunlop, *Arab Civilization to AD 1500*.

6.  Hitti, op. cit.

7.  Abdullah al-Udhari, *Classical Poems by Arab Women*.

9

# AVENZOAR

B. 1094 – D. 1161

SPAIN

During the Umayyad reign of almost three centuries, Islamic Spain and especially its pre-eminent capital, Cordova, rivalled Damascus, Baghdad, Cairo and Bukhara as a major intellectual centre for the Muslim world. Writers, scholars, philosophers, physicians, mathematicians and scientists, both Muslims and non-Muslims, flocked to Cordova from different parts of Europe and the Islamic world to pursue advance study and research in medicine, philosophy, science, mathematics and literature. In the process, Cordova became – in the words of Hroswitha of Gandersheim, a tenth century Saxon nun – 'the Ornament of the World'.[1] It was Cordova that produced Abulcasis (see chapter 5) and Averroes (see chapter 13), who were two of the foremost physicians of medieval Europe. But Avenzoar, who was undoubtedly the third most influential Muslim physician of the era, was actually a native of Seville, which at the time rivalled Cordova as an outstanding centre of learning, education and scholarship in Europe.

Abu Marwan Abd al-Malik ibn Abu al-'Ala ibn Zuhr, better known as Avenzoar or Abumeron in the Latin West, was born into a foremost Muslim family, made up of physicians, scholars, writers and poets in the southern Spanish province of Seville, otherwise known as the Banu Zuhr family. They traced their origin back to the Arabian tribe of Iyad, who lived in a region located towards the north of Yemen. One of Avenzoar's ancestors by the name of Zuhr al-Iyad, left Arabia and eventually settled in Shatiba (Jativa), a town that is today located in the Spanish city of Valencia. He became the founder of the Banu Zuhr family that subsequently went on to produce prominent personalities like Abu Marwan Abd al-Malik ibn Muhammad (d. 1078), who was the grandfather of Avenzoar, while Abu al-ʿAla Zuhr (d. 1130) was his father and teacher, and Abu Bakr al-Hafid (d. 1199), in turn, was his son and successor. All three men were eminent physicians and literary figures in their own right.

However, the first person in the family to specialise in medicine was Abu Marwan Abd al-Malik, the grandfather of Avenzoar, who was a contemporary of the great physician and philosopher Abu Ali ibn Sina (980–1037), better known in the West as Avicenna. He travelled extensively in pursuit of knowledge, including to parts of North Africa and the Islamic East. After completing his formal education, he returned home to Denia, located towards the south of Valencia, and there he became renowned as a physician, jurist (*faqih*) and Qur'anic scholar (*mufassir*), in addition to serving Muhajid (d. 1045), the local ruler, as an advisor and physician. After the death of his patron, he moved to Seville where his son, Abu al-ʿAla Zuhr, studied Arabic literature, Islamic sciences and medicine under his tutelage.

Abu al-ʿAla Zuhr, the father of Avenzoar, soon established his reputation as a gifted physician and literary figure. He first served as the court physician of al-Muʿtamid ibn al-ʿAbbad (r. 1069–1091). He then became an influential figure in the administration of Yusuf ibn Tashifin (1019–1106), the puritanical founder of the North African al-Murabitun (Almoravid) dynasty that extended its rule into Andalusia.

In the process, they repeatedly hammered the Christian armies of Alfonso VI (r. 1077–1109), the King of Castile-Leon, who had taken Toledo in 1085. Additionally, they continuously threatened Seville and Granada, as well as other Muslim fiefdoms (*taʿifa*) that had emerged following the demise of the Umayyad rule in 1031.[2] Ibn Tashifin not only checked the *Reconquista*, but he also secured Valencia and Toledo and, in doing so, carved himself a noteworthy position in the history of Islamic Spain. Although the Banu Zuhr family rose to prominence under the leadership of Abu al-ʿAla during the al-Murabitun reign, they soon fell from grace after clashing with Ali ibn Yusuf (r. 1107–1143), the son and successor of Ibn Tashifin. This was perhaps on account of Abu al-ʿAla's rivalry with Abu Hasan Sufyan, another leading physician who was in the service of the al-Murabitun at the time.

Needless to say, Avenzoar was born and brought up during a politically charged and turbulent period in the history of Andalusia. However, he was fortunate to have received a thorough education in Arabic language, literature, Islamic sciences and medicine under the guidance of his renowned father. He was a bright student who, after completing his formal literary and religious education, went on to specialise in medicine and, in doing so, continued the family tradition of becoming a physician. During his early years, Avenzoar practised medicine under the watchful gaze of his father who was not only a diligent and dedicated physician, but also a meticulous teacher and guide. He later recalled,

I saw this condition, when I was young, in a villager who had drunk some very cold water when the weather was very hot. His stools could not come out and he felt a strong pain he could not bear. The condition baffled me and I discussed it with physicians who were there at the time. None of them provided me with a satisfactory answer; they even added to my confusion. I walked to my father, who was then at the land he owned, and I informed him about my quandary, asking him to advise me. He moved his hand to a book and took from it an excerpt of Galen that he passed to me, telling me to go without adding more. Each time I would ask him to teach me, he would say: 'Memorize this page. Be happy if you succeed in his treatment. And if were to treat him differently than this, be careful about undertaking anything that touches you on medical practice.' I left him and read that excerpt, repeating it to myself. What I memorized became suddenly clear. I undertook to treat the patient accordingly and he was cured. After a while, I saw my father (God have mercy on him). He interrogated me [about the patient] and I answered him. He was satisfied and stopped being angry with me.[3]

His father passed away when he was in his mid-thirties. He had already become well-known for his medical knowledge and expertise by that time. Subsequently, Avenzoar was requested to go to Cordova in order to treat Ali ibn Yusuf, the incumbent ruler, who was at the time suffering from a serious ear infection. Despite his personal dislike of the ruler, he treated and cured him. In his own words,

I remember, when I was young, I was summoned by the tyrant 'Ali ibn Yusuf to Cordoba because of a swelling inside his ear. I reached him at dusk as the pain had become sharp. I found him wishing himself to be dead, even slain. Such was his pain. This was because the swelling was undoubtedly deep at the end of the ear canal next to the junction to the nerve that carries the sense of hearing. He started displaying a faint spasm. I decided to fill his ear with tepid egg yolk, leaving this for a long hour. The pain eased. After two or three hours the swelling ruptured and pus ran out. I continued to clean [the ear] with honey water in which water was steamed, before mixing it with honey, with acorn and horsetail. His ear was then cleaned with soft feathers of chicken tails that were twirled in it. What was in his ear was drained out once or twice. The pus stopped after four days and it was possible to cure him.[4]

As expected, Ali ibn Yusuf was profoundly impressed by Avenzoar's medical knowledge and skills, and rewarded him handsomely for his successful diagnosis and treatment. However, Ali ibn Yusuf was an unpredictable individual and equally ruthless as a ruler, and Avenzoar was far from impressed by him. As expected, the former imprisoned Avenzoar in Marrakesh, although the reasoning for such drastic action remains unclear. It may have happened as a result of rivalry and intrigue in the court of the al-Murabitun ruler. Another reason could have been the emergence of the al-Muwahhidun (Almohad), another North African dynasty that subsequently went on to oust the former from power and, in doing so, they established their sway across the region, including Andalusia. Since Avenzoar personally detested the al-Murabitun dynasty and was more sympathetic towards their rivals, this may have contributed to his trials and tribulation. However, after the eighth and last Murabitun ruler, Ishaq ibn Ali was captured and put to death by the Muwahhidun in 1147, Avenzoar expressed his delight in these words:

> Thanks to God, redeemer of souls, our rescuer from nothingness, our guide from the darkness of tyranny to light, the one who inspired us to follow Muhammad, may God pray for him and grant him peace, and select us to follow the mission of the pure, intelligent, mighty, *Qurayshi*, Imam and Mahdi Muhammad ben 'Abd Allah al-'Alawi al-Fatimi,…and I thank Him the Almighty and ask Him to grant His grace and bounty by maintaining him for Islam and perpetuating the rule of the Caliph, Prince of the Believers, the most just Imam, Abd al-Mu'min ben 'Ali ben al-'Adl al-Zaki, may God maintain his rule and make the inhabited earth his dominion.[5]

Having suffered a long incarceration under the al-Murabitun rule, Avenzoar was not only happy and relieved to have been freed by the new ruler, he also went on to serve as the personal physician of Caliph Abdul Mu'min (r. 1147–1163), the ruler of the al-Muwahhidun dynasty - a dynasty destined to exercise power until 1269. However, unlike his father, Abu al-'Ala, and his own son, Abu Bakr al-Hafid, Avenzoar refrained from politics and was only too happy to practice medicine. It was also during this time that he met his younger contemporary, Abul Walid Muhammad ibn Rushd (1126–1198), better known as Averroes in the Latin West, in Seville.

Despite his seniority and disdain for philosophy and politics, he received the young philosopher, jurist and physician warmly, and clearly both men were impressed by each other's learning and acumen. Both also wrote extensively on aspects of medicine. Avenzoar may have written around half a dozen books, though his most prominent contributions include *Kitab al-Iqtisad fi Islah al-Anfus wa'l Ajsad* (The Book of Moderation for the Refinement of the Mind and Body), *Kitab al-Aghdhiya* (The Book of Foods) and *Kitab al-Taysir fi al-Mudawat wa'l Tadbir* (The Book of Facilitation on Therapeutics and Management).

The first book was written during his early years, perhaps when he was working as an assistant to his father, and it consists of seven parts focusing on medicine (*tibb*) as a source of cure and prevention, both to the mind and body. This book is based on Galenic medicine and it is not considered by the earlier and modern scholars to be an original contribution on the subject. However, it does prove that the young Avenzoar had acquired more than a cursory knowledge and understanding of Greek medicine as practiced by Galen of Pergamon (d. cir. 217).

By comparison, Avenzoar's *Kitab al-Aghdhiya* was a more refined piece of work. It was completed after his incarceration, perhaps on the recommendation of his new patron and supporter, Caliph Abd al-Mu'min, as the book was in fact dedicated to the latter. If his *Kitab al-Iqtisad* was a manual of Galenic medicine, this book could not have been more different: being a work on healthy food and diet, in this book he produced a list of items that promoted good health and wellbeing with virtually no reference to Galen or his own father. Even if it was composed at a time when Avenzoar had no access to other books or manuscripts, this book is today considered to be one of his most lucid and readable contributions on the subject.

However, the *Kitab al-Taysir* was undoubtedly his *magnum opus*. According to Averroes, this encyclopaedia was written at his own request. It may have been completed towards the final years of his life, but that is because it is a detailed, refined and systematic contribution on medicine that could only have been produced by someone possessing mastery of his subject. Consisting of two parts which, in turn, are divided into smaller sections; in this work, the author identifies, explains and offers remedies for the common illnesses and diseases of the time. His sources of reference included Galen, Hippocrates, Aristotle, Ptolemy and Abu al-'Ala Zuhr, his father, and other Andalusian physicians. Although Avenzoar rated Galen highly, he did not follow him or any other physicians blindly. He considered the application of rational faculty, circumstantial evidence and observational skills to be critical in the diagnosis and effectiveness of treating diseases and ailments. This clearly differed from the approach adopted by Averroes who successfully philosophised medicine in his *Kitab al-Kulliyyat fi al-Tibb* (The Book of Universal Rules of Medicine), which of course would not have pleased Avenzoar, not least because the latter was in favour of keeping the two subjects separate.

In addition to the above, Avenzoar authored several other works including *Kitab al-Qanun* (The Canon) and *Risalah* (Treatise). Two other works that are often attributed to him, namely *Kitab al-Zina* (The Book of Cosmetics) and *Kitab al-Tadhkira* (The Memo) are subject to disagreement and controversy. The former is regarded by some of his biographers to be a part of his *Kitab al-Iqtisad*, if not a different name for the same text, while the latter is said to have been authored by his illustrious father. What is undeniable, however, is that his medical contributions and achievements exercised considerable influence across medieval Europe, thus inspiring Muslim, Christian and Jewish physicians alike.[6]

As soon as Avenzoar's medical works, especially his *Kitab al-Taysir* (Latin *Liber teisir*), were introduced to the scholars and physicians who were based at the universities of Padua (in present-day Italy) and Montpellier (in southern France) back in the thirteenth century, they swiftly translated them into Latin for the benefit of their students. Averroes (see chapter 13), Moses Maimonides, known in Arabic as Musa ibn Maimun (1135–1204), John of Capua, otherwise known as Johannes de Capua (fl. 1262–1269) and William of Brescia (fl. 1280–1320), among others, played their part in the popularisation of Avenzoar across Europe at the time.

It was during this period that the scientific and medical works of medieval Muslim scholars and thinkers were translated into Latin, Hebrew, Italian, French and Catalan languages, and widely used in European medical schools including at Padua, Bologna, Montpellier and Paris. In the process, prominent European scholars and physicians like Peter of Abano (1257–1316), Arnald of Villanova (1235–1311), Bernard of Gordon (b. cir. 1260-1313), Guido de Vigevano (1280-1349) and Guy de Chauliac (1300–1368), among others, became familiar with Avenzoar's medical ideas and thought.

Likewise, the renowned Jewish philosopher and physician, Moses Maimonides, who was the personal physician of the famous Sultan Salah al-Din (1138–1193), better known in the West as Saladin, also rated Avenzoar very highly, as did Giovanni Battista Morgagni (1682–1771), who is today considered to be the father of the modern science of pathology. Indeed, Avenzoar's life and medical legacy continues to attract scholarly attention to this day. However, credit for this must be given to the efforts of several modern European and Middle Eastern historians, including Ernest Renan, Gabriel Colin, Abd al-Malik Faraj, Rosa K. Brabant, E. G. Sanchez and Henry Azar.

Unfortunately, very little is known about Avenzoar's personal and family life, other than the fact that he was a devout Muslim who undertook his research and writing as if it was his religious duty. He went out of his way to help and support the poor, regularly providing medical care and treatment to them free of charge. He had fathered several children by at least two women. We know more about Abu Bakr al-Hafid, his son and successor, than any other child or family member of his. Abu Bakr was born in Seville when his father was around 17 years of age. And, like his father, he went on to become a prominent Qur'anic scholar and physician, thus continuing the family medical tradition into the sixth generation.

However, unlike his father, Abu Bakr was also a gifted poet, very much like his grandfather, and became famous on account of his beautiful and exquisite Arabic verses rather than his medical output. His own son, Abdullah ibn al-Hafid (b. 1182), was destined to continue the family tradition until he was reportedly poisoned at the age of 25, which ended the Banu Zuhr medical dynasty. As for Avenzoar, he spent the last years of his life in his native Seville, where he eventually passed away at the age of around 67. According to Abd al-Rahman ibn Khaldun (1332–1406), the celebrated historian and father of the science of sociology, Avenzoar was one of the foremost physicians of Islamic Spain and medieval Europe as a whole. In his own words,

There have been leading physicians in Islam of surpassing skill, such as, for instance, ar-Razi [al-Razi or Rhazes, AH 251/865 – AH 313/925], al- Majusi

['Ali ibn 'Abbas or Haly Abbas, d. AH 342/994] and Avicenna [Ibn Sina, AH 370/980 – AH 428/1037]. There have also been many Spanish physicians. Most famous among them was Ibn Zuhr.[7]

1. Maria Rosa Menocal's *The Ornament of the World: How Muslims, Jews and the Christians Created a Culture of Tolerance in Medieval Spain.*

2. Abdul Ali, *Eminent Arab-Muslim Medical Scientists.*

3. Quoted by Henry Azar, *The Sage of Seville: Ibn Zuhr, His Time, and His Medical Legacy.*

4. Ibid.

5. Ibid.

6. Abdul Ali, op.cit.

7. Quoted by Henry Azar, op. cit.

10

# AVEMPACE

B. 1095 – D. 1139

SPAIN

Early Islamic thought was dominated by the traditional Islamic sciences. This was the case until during the Abbasid period, when ancient Greek thought and philosophy was translated and popularised in the Muslim world in the eighth and ninth centuries. This led to the development of the science of *ilm al-kalam* (dialectic theology) and *falsafah* (Islamic philosophy), thanks to the efforts of renowned Muslim scholars and philosophers like Yaqub ibn Ishaq al-Kindi and Abul Hasan Ali al-Ashari. The dissemination of ancient Greek ideas and thought presented many challenges to the traditional Islamic worldviews and, this in turn, forced the *ulama* (religious scholars) to learn more about philosophy in order to defend traditional Islam from the influx of Hellenistic thought.

As such, influential Muslim scholars like Abu Hamid al-Ghazali not only successfully repudiated Greek philosophy, but they also reinvigorated traditional Islamic thought. At a time when philosophy was in full retreat in the Islamic East, partly due to the Islamic traditionalists' onslaught on Neoplatonism, it found a warm welcome in the Islamic West. One of the first and most original Western Muslim philosophers was Avempace.

Abu Bakr Muhammad ibn Yahya al-Sa'igh al-Tujibi, better known as Avempace in the Latin West, was born into a notable Muslim family of Zaragoza, the present-day Spanish region of Aragon. Very little is known about his early life although, according to some scholars, his family may have been Jewish converts to Islam who established themselves in the province of Zaragoza and became known for their learning and education. Others have argued that he hailed from a prominent Muslim family of rulers of Arabian descent.

As things stand, information about Avempace's life, career and contributions is riddled with contradiction and speculation, partly due to the absence of primary sources, but also due to the lack of serious research undertaken on the subject by modern scholars. For example, we know substantially more about the philosophers Avicenna (Ibn Sina) and Alpharabius (al-Farabi), both of whom hailed from the Islamic East, and also Abubacer (Ibn Tufayl) and Averroes (Ibn Rushd), who belonged to the Islamic West, than we do about Avempace. That explains why he is not as widely known today as his aforementioned predecessors or as well as his successors.

By all accounts, Avempace was born and brought up during a politically volatile and unpredictable time in the history of Islamic Spain, as the disintegration of the Umayyad dynasty paved the way for the chaotic period of the *muluk al-tawa'if,* also known as the period of petty rulers. The demise of a central government created a political vacuum where governors of different regions of Andalusia became de facto rulers, thus leading to considerable tension, rivalry and volatility across the country. In the words of the historian S. M. Imamuddin:

The provinces began to secede from the centre and the centre of gravity started shifting from the capital to the provincial headquarters. The Arab monarchy withdrew from the scene and the chieftains created their own domain taking advantage of the political situation and physical features of the country...Political units existed with their capitals at Badjoz, Toledo and Saragossa in the Lower, Middle and Upper Marches respectively. The rest of the Muslim territories in Spain were split up into thirty smaller units. Some did not survive long the intrigues within and outside and ceaseless fighting for existence or extension. The political events of the period are thus confused.[1]

The period of the petty rulers came to an end with the triumphant entry of the al-Murabitun (Almoravids) of North Africa to Cordova in 1091. Within a short period of time, they established their hegemony in Spain, except Zaragoza which continued to be ruled by the Banu Hud family. Yusuf al-Mu'tamid ibn Hud reigned from 1081 to 1085 and was succeeded by al-Musta'in until the Almoravids secured the province in 1110. However, the descendants of Amir al-Mu'minin Yusuf ibn Tashifin, the founder of the Almoravids, soon became politically lax and complacent leading to considerable challenges and difficulties. To their credit, during their rule they actively promoted learning and scholarship, thus the pursuit of intellectual activities flourished in Spain at the time.

Avempace grew up, completed his formal education in Arabic, memorisation of the Qur'an and traditional Islamic sciences, before specialising in medicine, philosophy, logic, science, mathematics and literature during this period. Though he received a thorough and in-depth education in all the sciences of the time, very little is known of his teachers and mentors. However, what is known is that some of his predecessors and contemporaries include prominent scholars and thinkers like Sa'id ibn Fathun, Ibn Hazm, Ibn al-Kattani, Ibn al-Imam, Yusuf ibn Hasdai and Ibn Judi. Abu Uthman Sa'id ibn Fathun ibn Mukram hailed from Zaragoza and was well-known for his expertise in the philosophical sciences, grammar and philology, and was a notable predecessor of Avempace, while Ibn Hazm and Ibn al-Kattani were from Cordova and were both renowned scholars of their time (for further information about Ibn Hazm, see chapter 7).

Muhammad ibn al-Hasan Abu Abdullah al-Madhhiji, better known as Ibn al-Kattani, was an expert in medicine, logic and other sciences of the time. Ibn Hazm and al-Mushafi, among others, benefited from his writings and scholarship. He died in 1029 at the age of around 80. During his student days, Avempace must have studied and benefited from the writings of his aforementioned predecessors. By contrast, Ibn al-Imam, Yusuf ibn Hasdai and Ibn Judi were his prominent contemporaries.

Abul Hasan Ali ibn Abd al-Aziz ibn al-Imam al-Ansari, better known as Ibn al-Imam, hailed from Zaragoza but spent much of his career in Granada in the service of Tamim ibn Yusuf ibn Tashifin and his brother, Ali ibn Yusuf ibn Tashifin, who reigned from 1106 to 1143. Avempace and Ibn al-Imam not only came from the same city, they also knew each other very well and, thanks to the latter, we today know more about the former than we would have otherwise. Ibn al-Imam was a leading scholar and literary figure of the time and he had worked under Avempace for a while which enabled him to acquaint himself with the latter's philosophical ideas and thought. So much so that during his stay with Avempace in Seville in 1135, Ibn al-Imam transcribed some of his teacher's writings for the benefit of posterity. He took the manuscripts with him when he moved to Qus in Egypt and thereby, introduced Avempace's philosophy in the Islamic East, perhaps for the first time.

The other notable contemporary of Avempace was Abu Ja'far Yusuf ibn Hasdai, the great-grandson of Hasdai ibn Shaprut (d. 970), a renowned Jewish scholar and political figure. Supposedly, both men may have known each other during their early years in Zaragoza. Yusuf went on to become a notable astronomer and subsequently travelled to the East and served the Fatimids in his capacity as an astronomer and scientist. From Cairo, he continued to correspond regularly with Avempace and, during this period, the latter may have sent him some of his writings. The other notable personality worth highlighting here was Abul Hasan Ali ibn Abd al-Rahman ibn Musa ibn Judi al-Qaisi, otherwise known as Ibn Judi, who was a direct student of Avempace and he became thoroughly familiar with the literary and philosophical sciences of the time. A great admirer of his teacher, Ibn Judi also went on to serve as a political secretary and promoter of his mentor's philosophical ideas and thought.

One of Avempace's renowned successors was Abubacer (Abu Bakr ibn Tufayl), the author of *Hayy ibn Yaqzan* (Living Son of the Vigilant), a celebrated philosophic romance (see chapter 11 for more information). Referring to his illustrious predecessor, Abubacer wrote:

> Those who grew up in Spain endowed with superior intelligence, before the spread of logic and philosophy there, spent their lives in the study of mathematics, in which they made great advances, but were incapable of anything more. Then there grew up after them a generation which surpassed them by knowing something of logic. They investigated this science, but it did not bring them to the true perfection…Then there grew up after them another generation, possessing greater insight and nearer to the truth. There was none among them of more penetrating intelligence, sounder in investigation or with truer views than Abu Bakr b. as-Sa'igh (i.e. Avempace), except that worldly affairs engaged him, so that death cut him off before the appearing of the treasures of his knowledge and the divulging of the secrets of his wisdom.[2]

It is clear from Abubacer's statement that he considered Avempace to be a remarkable, if not one of the first and foremost philosophers, of medieval Muslim Spain. His efforts, however, did not reach their full potential. This is mainly because soon after completing his formal education and training – having already benefited from the learning and scholarship of his prominent predecessors – Avempace began practising medicine. This was before he joined the service of Abu Bakr ibn Ibrahim al-Sahrawi (also known as al-Tifalwit), the then governor of Zaragoza. Therefore, it left Avempace very little time to pursue his philosophical and literary activities.

Living during a politically unpredictable and confusing time, it is not surprising that Avempace's short career as a physician, political administrator and philosopher was marred by uncertainty, surprise and suspense. Indeed, in the wake of the Christian invasion of the city of Zaragoza in 1118, he moved to Seville and from there proceeded to Granada before settling in Shatiba (Xativa). Here he was arrested and put behind bars for supposedly espousing philosophical ideas and beliefs which the traditionalist *ulama* considered to be heretical. He was subsequently released, thanks to the intervention of the local judge, who apparently understood and appreciated Avempace's ideas and thought better than his fellow religious scholars. According to some writers, this judge was none other than the father of Ibn Rushd, the great Andalusian philosopher, commentator on Aristotle and successor of Avempace (see chapter 13 for more details). Although Avempace had served the Almoravids for almost twenty years, very little is known about his career from 1118 to 1136, other than the fact that he was in Seville in 1136 in the company of Ibn al-Imam, his student.[3]

Being too preoccupied with his worldly activities, Avempace experienced considerable difficulties, hardship and displacement throughout his short life and career. Like Avicenna, he led the life of a troubled philosopher who was always on the go, valiantly marching against the tide of political upheaval and uncertainty. It is this which explains why, despite being a highly gifted thinker, he never really found the time or opportunity to systematically develop his philosophy in the form of books and manuscripts. As it happened, it was Ibn al-Imam, a disciple of Avempace, who made a list of the writings of his master. Ibn Abu Usaybi'a did the same, as did Abubacer, who made references to several of his works.

However, thanks to the efforts of the Moroccan philosopher Jamal al-Din al-Alawi (1945–1992), we now have a better knowledge and understanding of Avempace's contribution and achievements. Al-Alawi carried out a detailed study of the writings of this great European Muslim philosopher. He not only explained the chronology of his literary output, but also identified three key stages of his intellectual development.[4]

During the first phase, Avempace was preoccupied with the study of mathematics, music, astronomy and logic. These subjects were very popular which meant there was no shortage of mathematicians, musicians and astronomers in Andalusia at the time. For logic, he would have had to study the writings of Alpharabius (al-Farabi) whose works on the subject were, according to Musa ibn Maimun (Moses Maimonides), 'finer than flour'. During this period, Avempace not only read the writings of Alpharabius, but also wrote notes and short commentaries on the latter's books, some of which are still extant.

In the next phase of his intellectual development, Avempace studied and wrote on natural philosophy. This subject was also popular and very wide in scope in those days, ranging from physics, mechanics, optics, philosophy of nature, as well as the study of void and motion. This is why Avempace considered natural philosophy to be a theoretical science dealing with concepts (*tasawwur*), problems (*masa'il*) and assents (*tasdiq*), and to be able to study this subject, a thorough knowledge of other sciences was essential. His *Kitab al-Nabat* (Book of Plants), *Kitab al-Hayawan* (Book of Animals), *Kitab an-Nafs* (Book on the Soul) and many commentaries on the works of Aristotle and Alpharabius, belong to this period.

During the last phase of his intellectual development, Avempace composed his most important contributions, including *Tadbir al-Mutawahhid* (Rule of the Solitary), *Risalah fi Ittisal al-Aql bi'l Insan* (Treatise on Union of the Intellect with Man) and *Risalat al-Wada* (Farewell Message). In the first two phases of his intellectual career, Avempace studied and explained how knowledge of the natural world is to be organised and structured. While in the final years of his life, Avempace wrote on the sciences that deal with human beings and their exercise of free will, choice and responsibilities including metaphysics, ethics and political philosophy. According to Avempace, human reason or ability to think and reflect is the most important faculty that man possesses. He then divided actions into human and animal. To achieve Divine proximity, he felt that the following three steps were essential:

1) Charge our tongues to remember God and glorify Him, and
2) charge our organs to act in accordance with the insight of the heart, and

3) avoid that [which] makes us indifferent to the remembrance of God or turns our hearts away from Him. These have to be followed continuously for the whole of one's life.[5]

In other words, according to Avempace, the main purpose of knowledge and philosophy is to inculcate noble qualities in human beings that endear them to the Truth, the Origin of all things. Although the pursuit of material comfort and joys are common to man and animals, it is only through the attainment of spiritual knowledge that humanity can then be truly rational, free and exemplary both in their thoughts and actions, individually and collectively. He emphasised this point to varying degrees in both *Tadbir* and *Ittisal*, and therefore the idea of attaining gradual perfection through union with the Divine is central to Avempace's philosophical thought. His ideas and thought later inspired Abubacer, his philosophical successor, to compose his *Hayy ibn Yaqzan*, showing how one can attain the summit of knowledge and spirituality through the proper use of his rational faculties. Although Avempace did not write as prolifically as Avicenna or Averroes, his mastery of philosophy and his originality earned him the respect of both his friends and foes alike. In the words of the historian Douglas M. Dunlop (1909–1987):

Avempace must rank with the greatest of the Arabic philosophers, though hitherto his work has been less known in the West than that of his compeers. He seems never to have been translated into Latin, unlike the others, in the Middle Ages.[6]

Indeed, like Aristotle and Alpharabius, Avempace was a rational philosopher, but unlike them, his ideas and thought were easy to understand and appreciate. As a result, he quickly acquired a considerable following in medieval Spain and elsewhere, thus exerting considerable influence over his successors, both Muslims and non-Muslims, including Abubacer (see chapter 12), Averroes (see chapter 13), the Latin Averroists, Maimonides (1135–1204), Ibn Khaldun (1332-1406), Ibn al-Khatib (see chapter 51) and Albertus Magnus (d. 1280), among others. Maimonides, in particular, recommended his work to others without any reservation along with that of Alpharabius, saying Avempace's books are 'plain to him that understandeth, and right to them that find knowledge.' It is unfortunate that this great European Muslim philosopher died at the young age of around 44 in rather mysterious circumstances. Although, according to some scholars, he was actually poisoned by his political or intellectual rivals.

Thanks to the efforts of scholars like Miguel Asin Palacios, Douglas Morton Dunlop, Jamal al-Din al-Alawi and Muhammad Saghir Hasan al-Ma'sumi, the life, work and legacy of Avempace is today more widely known than before.

Ⓝ

1. S. M. Imamuddin, *A Political History of Muslim Spain*.

2. D. M. Dunlop, 'Philosophical Predecessors and Contemporaries of Ibn Bajjah', *The Islamic Quarterly*, volume 2, pp100–116, 1955.

3. D. M. Dunlop, *Arab Civilization to AD 1500*.

4. Jamal al-Din al-Alawi, *Mu'allafat Ibn Bajjah*.

5. M. S. H. al-Ma'sumi, in *A History of Muslim Philosophy*, volume 1.

6. D. M. Dunlop, op. cit.

# DRESES

B. 1099 – D. 1161

SPAIN

Maps are used by geographers to describe the earth and its physical features, climates and political boundaries. Physical maps, for instance, show the earth's formation, seas and oceans, and vegetation including the rainforests, mountains and deserts. The thematic maps focus on specific themes or topics such as population make-up and climatic zones, while political maps show the landscape as carved by humans to form countries, cities and towns. Although maps are not perfect, they do provide valuable information about different parts of the earth with relatively accurate sizes, locations and climatic conditions. There is no doubt that today we have a far better knowledge and understanding of the earth's geography than our ancestors did during the ancient and medieval times.

Based on the works of the ancient Greeks, prominent Muslim scientists and scholars developed the science of geography considerably during the early Abbasid period. Hisham ibn Muhammad al-Kalbi (d. 820) was one of the first Muslims to write on the history and geography of pre-Islamic Arabia. However, it was Muhammad ibn Musa al-Khwarizmi's (d. 847) *Kitab Surat al-Ard* (The Shape of the Earth) that laid the foundation of Muslim contribution to the study of geography during the early part of the ninth century. Many others were, directly or indirectly, inspired by his work including Abu Yusuf Yaqub ibn Ishaq al-Kindi (d. 873), better known as a philosopher who authored *Rasm al-Maʿmur min al-Ard* (Description of the Populated Part of the Earth), while Ahmad ibn Muhammad al-Tayyib, also known as al-Sarakhsi (d. 899), composed two books titled *Kitab al-Masalik waʾl Mamalik* (Book of Routes and Kingdoms) and *Risalah fiʾl Bahr waʾl Miyah waʾl Jibal* (Treatises on Seas, Waters and Mountains).

Another distinguished early Muslim geographer was Abul Qasim Ubaidullah ibn Abdullah, better known as Ibn Khurdadhbih (d. 912), whose *Kitab al-Masalik wa'l Mamalik* (Routes and Kingdoms) was one of the best of its kind. Abul Hasan Ali ibn Husayn al-Mas'udi's (d. 957) *Muruj al-Dhahab wa Ma'adin al-Jawahir* (Meadows of Gold and Mines of Jewels) was an encyclopaedia of history and geography. Two other renowned early Muslim travellers and geographers include Abu Abdullah Muhammad ibn Ahmad Shams al-Din al-Maqdisi (d. 991) and Abu Raihan Muhammad ibn Ahmad al-Biruni (d. 1051). Al-Maqdisi, also known as al-Muqqaddasi, travelled extensively around the Muslim world and authored the famous book *Ahsan al-Taqasim fi Ma'rifat al-Aqalim* (The Best Divisions in the Knowledge of the Climes) at the age of 40. Like al-Maqdisi, al-Biruni was a gifted scholar whose *Kitab Ta'rikh al-Hind* (History of India) is today considered to be a pioneering work on regional geography.[1] However, the most celebrated Muslim geographer of the Middle Ages, who also became widely recognised in the Western world, was none other than Dreses.

Abu Abdullah Muhammad ibn Muhammad ibn Abdullah ibn Ash Sharif al-Idris al-Qurtubi al-Hasani al-Sabti, better known in the Muslim world as al-Idrisi and in the Latin West as Dreses, was born into a notable Muslim family in the present-day city of Ceuta in Spain. Information about his ancestry and early life is scarce, and the little that is known is hotly contested by his biographers.

According to one view, Dreses hailed from an educated Hispano-Arab family of Andalusia. Others, however, claim that he was the great-grandson of Idris II, the prince of the Spanish province of Malaga. The prince's grandson, Muhammad ibn Abdullah, was forced to leave Spain in 1058 after being ousted from power and thus settled in Sicily where Count Roger and other ruling elite received him warmly. The proponents of this view claim that Dreses was therefore born in Sicily rather than in Ceuta, a claim that has not been conclusively established.

However, the majority of scholars are of the opinion that his forefathers belonged to the Hammudid ruling family of Malaga and Algeciras (r. 1010–1058), being an offshoot of the Idrisid dynasty of Morocco that ruled from 789 to 985. It is they who claimed to have been the descendants of Hasan ibn Ali (625–670), the grandson of the Prophet and elder son of Ali ibn Abi Talib (599–661), the fourth Caliph of Islam.[2]

With that said, there is no disagreement over the fact that Dreses was born and brought up at a time when, after almost eighty years of non-stop political instability and upheaval across Spain, the al-Murabitun (Almoravids) of North Africa marched into Andalusia and united the warring factions. Being very strict and puritanical in their understanding and interpretation of Islam, they soon lost the support and goodwill of the masses and scholars across the land. In the words of the historian S. M. Imamuddin:

At the beginning of the Murabitin rule (*sic*), taxes were collected unhindered, agriculture improved, industry and trade developed. But the study of poetry and philosophy was not encouraged. Ibn Baki, one of the best poets of Andalucia, wandered hungry from town to town. Malik ibn Wuhayb of Seville intended to study philosophy but finding his life in danger gave it up and devoted himself to the study of theology. The Qadi of Cordova, Ibn Hamdun, condemned, *The Revival of Religious Science* as well as the study of the philosophical works of Ghazzali. He had the approval of Ali ibn Yusuf for the destruction of all copies of Ghazzali's book. Further, the Murabitin (*sic*) were less interested in art and culture than in preaching and conquest.[3]

Dreses' early years in Spain and North Africa consisted of him, undoubtedly, studying aspects of the Arabic language, literature, Qur'an and the religious sciences. Thereafter, he proceeded to Cordova where he studied under the guidance of prominent Muslim scholars and scientists who lived there at the time. Though the Academy of Cordova had by now lost much of its prestige and standing, it was still the foremost centre for the study and research in science, philosophy and mathematics in Europe at the time. Dreses' stay there enabled him to become familiar with the sciences of the time before resuming his travels and, in the process, visiting many countries, including northern Spain, Portugal, France, England, Scotland, Morocco, Algeria, Syria and even Asia Minor, among other places. Still in his twenties at the time, he was very fond of poetry and apparently entertained the masses with his literary talent wherever he went, thus attracting attention from the locals who, in turn, provided him with generous care and hospitality.

Needless to say, travelling in those days was risky, mainly because it was the time of the Crusades, when the Christians (mainly Catholics) from Europe were locked in a gladiatorial battle against the Muslims and other non-Christians in the Holy Land and elsewhere, with no end in sight. It is an irony of history that during the same period, trade and commercial activity between Europe and the Islamic East was thriving, thus facilitating travel and exchange of knowledge, goods and services like never before. Taking advantage of the favourable conditions of the time, Dreses travelled extensively not only in pursuit of knowledge, but also in search of fame and fortune. This naturally increased his curiosity and interest in people and their cultures, climes and locations. Thus everywhere he went, he closely observed and studied the customs, traditions and behaviours of the natives as well as the climate and geography of the places. Here is how he described the British Isles:

The first part of the seventh climate consists entirely of the ocean and its islands are deserted and uninhabited...The second section of the seventh climate contains a part of the ocean in which is the island of l'Angleterre [England]. This is a great island, shaped like the head of an ostrich; in it are populous cities, high mountains, flowing streams, and level ground. It has great fertility and its people are hardy, resolute, and vigorous. The winter there is permanent. The nearest land to it is Wissant in the land of France, and between this island and the continent there is a strait twelve miles wide…[4]

Dreses then briefly described many British cities and towns including Dover, Dartmouth, Cornwall, Southampton, Hastings, London, Lincoln and Durham, before describing Scotland as a '…island of England and is a long peninsula to the north of the larger island. It is uninhabited and has neither town nor village. Its length is 150 miles…' Though his description of England and Scotland is very brief, Dreses' knowledge and understanding of continental Europe was unusually detailed and accurate for that time.

He also described other prominent European cities with remarkable accuracy including Paris and Rome. He considered the former to be 'of mediocre size, surrounded by vineyard and forests, situated on an island in the Seine, which surrounds it on all sides…[and] it is extremely agreeable, strong, and susceptible of defense.' By contrast, Rome was more Oriental in its appearance, with its ships, merchants, commercial goods, hundreds of churches, shops and marbled streets. Dreses even went on to describe the ruler as a Pope. Indeed, he not only relied on local informants for his information, but he also visited and observed the places first-hand. This explains why he rarely made references to earlier Muslim and Western geographers and their works.

By the time Dreses had completed his *wanderjahren*, he was in his late thirties and was living in North Africa. But by now, his name and fame had already begun to spread far and wide. This prompted the Norman King of Sicily, Roger II (r. 1130–1154), to invite him to his court in Palermo where he offered Dreses generous patronage and requested him to compile a comprehensive book on geography, and to also produce the first scientific map of the world.[5] The court of Roger II was an unusual place for a European Christian King because his administration was dominated by Arabised officials, both Muslims and Christians, who conducted their business in Arabic. The other European monarchs, on the other hand, were busy supporting the Crusaders. According to the historian Jeremy Johns:

> Whereas in England, Henry I replaced Anglo-Saxon social mechanisms with a series of innovations amounting to the rapid expansion of the early state and the administrative machinery through which it was thenceforth to be governed, Roger II and his officers sought to preserve and to restore the ruined edifice inherited from Muslim Sicily by importing administrative practices, institutions, and personnel wholesale from the contemporary Islamic world, so that the Arabic administration of Sicily in the mid-12th century more closely approached the classical Islamic system, as exemplified in contemporary Fatimid Egypt, than had the Kalbid emirs before the Norman conquest.[6]

Settling into an Arabised politico-administrative system was not an issue for Dreses, and with the full backing of his patron, he devoted all his time and effort to composing his geographical masterpiece, *Kitab Nuzhat al-Mushtaq fi Ikhtiraq al-Afaq* (Entertainment for One Desiring to Travel Far), better known as *Kitab al-Rujari* (The Book of Roger), on which he worked on for more than a decade. Based on his extensive travel, wide reading and interaction with people of different countries and cultures, he developed a synthesis between European and Muslim understanding of human, cultural, thematic and political geography. He presented his findings in the form of a book, which is today considered to be one of the greatest cultural monuments of the Middle Ages.

Although Dreses' work is essentially a compilation of geographical information with its share of factual inconsistencies, the novelty of his *Kitab al-Rujari*, however, lies in the fact that the descriptive geography is accompanied by many original maps, both of the globe as a whole and the regions. Subsequently, Dreses' work inspired his successors, Muslims and non-Muslims alike. Indeed, he produced more regional maps than any other medieval cartographer, and his description of many parts of the world, such as northern Europe, were remarkably accurate and precise. This book was completed in January 1154, just before his patron died a month later; the author was in his mid-fifties at the time.

During his service to Roger II, Dreses also produced two other important works for his patron: namely a silver disc which depicted the map of the world and also a separate map of the globe, which in turn was divided into seven climatic zones and seventy sub-sections of equal length according to longitude. His identification and measurements of different zones and countries, all highlighted with colour coding, was considered to be unusually innovative and accurate for his time. In so doing, Dreses established his reputation as one of the greatest cartographers of the medieval period.

The other important point that needs to be made here is that the contribution of this great geographer led to a synthesis between the ancient Greek notion of astronomical (that is, essentially theoretical) and descriptive geography, thanks to his mastery of both. However, his critics have argued that his knowledge of astronomical geography was weaker on account of his poor knowledge of physical and mathematical geography. Unfortunately, the silver disc depicting the globe that he created has been lost, but the book and its maps have survived, still awaiting to be critically edited and published in its entirety.

After the death of Roger II in February 1154, Dreses continued to serve William I (r. 1154–1166), his son and successor, and during this period he produced several recensions and abridgements for him. Some scholars have attributed several other works to Dreses (such as *Kitab al-Adwiyah al-Mufradah* on medicine), but it appears that most of them were not original or popular. Although parts of his *Kitab al-Rujari* were first published in Rome in 1592, followed by a Latin translation entitled *Geographia Nubiensis*, and another two-volume translation undertaken by P. A. Jaubert between 1836 and 1840; none of these efforts were free from blemishes or error. His maps of the globe were also reproduced many times (for example, by Petrus Bertius in Paris in the 1620s) and became very popular across Europe.

Despite being a devout Muslim, Dreses lived in Palermo and was only too happy to serve a highly cultured and wise Christian King. This could potentially explain why Dreses did not receive much attention or suitable entries in the well-known Islamic biographical works or dictionaries. Even so, his contribution and legacy inspired many other notable scholars and explorers including Ibn Abd al-Mun'im, Ibn Sa'id (d. 1274), Ibn Khaldun (d. 1406) and Christopher Columbus (d. 1506), among others. He died in Sicily at the age of around 62.

George Alfred Leon Sarton (1884–1956), the renowned historian of science and author of the celebrated *Introduction to the History of Science* (1927) hailed him as 'the greatest geographer and cartographer of the Middle Ages'. Referring to Dreses' *Kitab al-Rujari*, the historian Douglas M. Dunlop also wrote:

> It is certainly a great monument of Arabic and Muslim geography and the measure of al-Idrisi's achievement can perhaps best be conveyed not by comparing him with his predecessors or contemporaries in the East, but rather by giving him his place simply as a geographer among geographers. Here he stands with Ptolemy, and if again we refrain from pressing the comparison, there is no doubt that, as far as cartography is concerned, the maps of the 'Book of Roger' were superior to anything produced in Europe or in the Muslim East (let him who doubts this last compare Ibn Hawqal's Mediterranean with al-Idrisi's) between Ptolemy and Matthew Paris.[7]

Finally, the renowned historian Philip K. Hitti paid him this fitting tribute: 'The most brilliant geographical author and cartographer of the twelfth century, indeed of all medieval time, was al-Idrisi, a descendant of a royal Spanish Arab family who got his education in Spain.'[8]

Ⓝ

1. Nafis Ahmad, *Muslim Contribution to Geography*.

2. Jeremy Johns, *Arabic Administration in Norman Sicily*.

3. S. M. Imamuddin, *A Political History of Muslim Spain*.

4. Bernard Lewis, *The Muslim Discovery of Europe*.

5. See *Baptised Sultans: The Contribution of Frederick II of Sicily in the transfer and adaption of Oriental ideas to the West*, published by ICR, London.

6. Jeremy Johns, op. cit.

7. D. M. Dunlop, *Arab Civilization to AD 1500*.

8. Philip K. Hitti, *The History of the Arabs*.

# 12

# ABUBACER

B. 1101 – D. 1185

SPAIN

Referring to the origins and development of Western thought and culture, Richard Tarnas (b. 1950), a notable American philosopher and historian, once wrote:

> Endowed with seemingly primeval clarity and creativity, the ancient Greeks provided the Western mind with what has proved to be a perennial source of insight, inspiration, and renewal. Modern science, medieval theology, classical humanism – all stand deeply in their debt. Greek thought was as fundamental for Copernicus and Kepler, and Augustine and Aquinas, as for Cicero and Petrarch. Our way of thinking is still profoundly Greek in its underlying logic, so much so that before we can begin to grasp the character of our own thought, we must first look closely at that of the Greeks.[1]

Consisting of more than 500 pages, Richard Tarnas's book provides a highly readable, though historically incomplete, if not inaccurate, overview of the history and development of Western thought. He traced the origin of Western intellectual history from the pre-Socratic period to modern times, as if ancient Greek ideas and thought were always known and widely studied in the Western world. Nothing could have been further from the truth. Indeed, there is an entire chapter missing in his book; a chapter that should have covered the contribution of medieval European Muslim philosophers and thinkers.

They, along with the *falasifah* in the Islamic East, not only played an instrumental role in rescuing the ancient Greek intellectual heritage from the vacuum of history by translating and expanding their works into Arabic, but subsequently transmitting such rich legacy to the Western world through Islamic Spain, Sicily and Granada. One medieval European thinker who wrestled with the ideas and thought of both ancient Greek thinkers and medieval Islamic philosophers and, in so doing, synthesised and popularised philosophical thinking in medieval Europe, was Abubacer of Islamic Granada.

Abu Bakr Muhammad ibn Abd al-Malik ibn Muhammad ibn Muhammad ibn Tufayl al-Qaysi, better known in medieval Europe as Abubacer, was born into a notable Muslim family of Arabian origin at Guadix (present-day Wadi Ash or Cadiz) in north-eastern Granada. At the time, Granada, and indeed Andalusia as a whole, was passing through considerable political upheaval as al-Murabitun's (Almoravid) hold on power was challenged by al-Muwahhidun (Almohad), a rival North African movement. It was this which led to further tension and uncertainty. The two rival Muslim powers vied for supremacy and that 'provided the Christians with good opportunities of ravaging the Muslim territories in Spain and committing atrocities on the Muslims.'[2]

Being aware of the chaos and disorder that prevailed in much of Spain at the time, the Christian rulers of Venice, Genoa, Castile and Barcelona attacked Muslim territories of Almeria, Seville, Carmona, Cadiz and Jaen. Many other cities and provinces suffered the same fate, so much so that even Cordova was not spared. Although Almoravid's hold on Spanish power came to an end in 1145, the vacuum left by them was not filled for another quarter of a century, until the Almohad's marched into Spain and restored some semblance of order and security. During this period, Abubacer completed his formal education and training, initially in Granada and subsequently in Cordova, which was the pre-eminent seat of learning at the time in Muslim Spain. Prominent scholars, scientists, philosophers and literary figures lived and taught in the capital of Andalusia. Subsequently, young Abubacer chose to study in the capital under their guidance, specialising in Arabic, religious sciences, philosophy and medicine.

Some scholars, such as Abd al-Wahid al-Marrakushi (b. 1185), have argued that Abubacer studied under the guidance of Avempace. However, such a claim is unfounded as Abubacer stated in the introduction to his *Hayy ibn Yaqzan* that he had not met the former, let alone study under his guidance.[3] After completing his formal education, Abubacer must have returned to Granada where he began practising medicine and, in due course, became well-known as a physician. His medical knowledge and expertise soon attracted the attention of the local ruler who, as a result, appointed Abubacer as his personal secretary and physician.

His learning, dedication and loyalty led to his swift promotion as Private Secretary to one of the sons of Abd al-Mu'min, the first Almohad ruler of Spain. At the time, his son was the governor of Ceuta and Tangier. The founder of this dynasty was Abu Abdullah Muhammad ibn Abdullah ibn Tumart (d. 1130) who espoused a worldview that was similar to the one developed by Abu Hamid al-Ghazali (d. 1111), the celebrated Islamic theologian of the Seljuk era, better known in medieval Europe as Algazel. Unlike the Almoravids who openly burnt the former's works, the Almohads were Ghazalian through-and-through.

However, the Almoravids were strict Malikites in jurisprudence (*fiqh*), while the Almohads championed the Zahiri (literalist) approach to interpreting Islamic law and jurisprudence. They were both North African Islamic reform movements that tried to assert their authority in Spain and the Maghreb and were successful to some extent. In the case of the Almohads, they began to establish their authority during the time of Abd al-Mu'min who captured Tlemcen, Fez and Ceuta, among other territories, and became the first ruler of the Almohad dynasty in Morocco in 1147. Abubacer was recruited into the service of the Almohads on account of his knowledge and skills as a physician.

He soon established himself as an acclaimed political administrator and advisor to governors and rulers. For most of his political career, Abubacer served as a *Qadi* (judge) and minister in the administration of al-Muwahhid Caliph, Abu Yaqub Yusuf, the third son of Abd al-Mu'min who reigned from 1163 to 1184. The ruler was renowned for his patronage of learning and scholarship and, as a result, the leading scientists, philosophers, religious scholars, writers, poets, musicians and artists of the time flocked to his Caliphal Court, initially in Seville and later in North Africa.

However, according to some scholars, Abubacer served the Almohads as a judge and there is no evidence to suggest that he was a government minister at all.[4] This view is only partially correct, as the position of a senior judge was, in those days, often a dual role, namely being responsible for administration of law and justice as well as serving as an advisor to the Caliph. In the case of Abubacer, he was more of a cultural advisor to the Caliph rather than a political guide or military strategist. He fulfilled his dual roles effectively and exercised considerable influence within the Caliph's inner circle of courtiers and advisors. Abu Yaqub Yusuf not only trusted him but also shared with him his passion for philosophy, science and arts.

With nearly two decades of working in government service, Abubacer began to establish his reputation as a writer and philosopher. Despite being very busy with his day job, in his spare time he pursued research in science and philosophy. As a physician and scientist, he was an innovative thinker who embraced solutions to problems that later became widely accepted in astronomy and medicine. Such solutions included the need for dissection and autopsy to explain the causes of diseases; removal of harmful objects from the body; and, he also critically reviewed Ptolemy's contribution to astronomy.

Although most of his research and writings on these subjects are no longer extant, his scholarly efforts were subsequently taken forward by his famous successors, including Abu Ishaq Nur al-Din al-Bitruji (Alpetragius, d. 1204) and Abul Walid Muhammad ibn Rushd (Averroes, see chapter 13). Building on the ideas and thought of Abubacer, Alpetragius became the first European astronomer to formulate and present a non-

Ptolemaic approach to astronomy during the latter part of the twelfth century. Alpetragius acknowledged this, thus showed his gratitude to Abubacer in the preface of his scientific works like *Kitab al-Hai'ah*.

As a physician and astronomer, Abubacer enjoyed considerable respect and standing during his lifetime. However, it was his contributions as a philosopher in particular that made him famous across medieval Europe and the Muslim world. He inherited the philosophical legacy of Avempace (who was a fiercely rationalistic thinker) and the traditionalist worldview of the Muslim theologians (such as Ibn Hazm and Algazel). He attempted to reconcile this with the puritanical religious views of the Almohads who were his political masters and patrons at the time.

In other words, being strict Ghazalians in their theology, Almohads repudiated any anthropomorphic notions of God; they were uncompromising in their belief in the absolute Unity and Oneness of Divinity. Likewise, inspired by Ibn Tumart, their founding preceptor, they strictly observed Islamic practices in their daily affairs and, at the same time, they were adherents of the Avempacian approach to philosophy. It championed the notion that the highest form of esoteric truth was reserved only for the elite, while the Zahiri (literalist) interpretation of law (*fiqh*) was enforced by the State.

Living in an age of contradictions and extremes, it was far from being an easy task to strike a balance between the competing religious and ideological approaches. However, being a gifted scholar and innovative thinker in his own right, Abubacer was more than capable of reconciling the conflicting philosophies and worldviews that prevailed at the time. Accordingly, he summarised his ideas and thoughts on philosophy and theology in the form of a novel or philosophic romance, which has ever since immortalised him, namely *Hayy ibn Yaqzan fi Asrar al-Hikmat al-Mashriqiyyah* (Living Son of the Vigilant in the Secrets of Eastern Wisdom). Writing a work of philosophical fiction was a shrewd move on his part because conveying his ideas through fictional characters, located in a desert island in the Indian Ocean, was less likely to offend his political masters or antagonise the powerful *ulama* (religious scholars) of the time, than if he had written a dry theological treatise or a mind-bending philosophical track.

As it happened, *Hayy ibn Yaqzan* was not only fictional, philosophical and mystical, but equally inspirational in its exposition of fundamental truths about human life and nature, also their meaning and purpose in the overall scheme of things. The novel revolves around three characters, namely Hayy, Asal and Salaman who, philosophically speaking, represent nature, contemplation and tradition. Hayy is a child of the natural world and gradually becomes knowledgeable through observation and experimentation. Asal on the other hand, is a contemplative individual who acquires knowledge of God, prophecy, revelation and life after death through curiosity, power of reason and rationality, and individual questioning and inquiry. Hayy's encounter with Asal proves to be highly enlightening for him until they visit another island ruled by Salaman, where the inhabitants live by fixed cultural and traditional practices.

Despite his efforts to explain the meaning and purpose underlying their practices using rationalistic concepts, he discovers to his surprise, that they cannot understand and make sense of such theoretical notions. This convinces him that one particular approach to understanding the truth cannot be comprehensive enough, much less suitable for people in a given society because all individuals, by their very nature, are different in their educational, intellectual, and cultural awareness, understanding and capabilities. Being familiar with the writings of the Muslim Neo-Platonists such as Avicenna and Alpharabius, as well as the ideas and thought of Avempace and Algazel, Abubacer endeavoured to develop a new and innovative, but equally coherent, Islamic philosophic-theological narrative that would make sense to both the scholars and the general public. In other words,

> Philosophically speaking, the treatise is a brilliant exposition of ibn Tufail's theory of knowledge, which seeks to harmonize Aristotle with the Neo-Platonists on the one hand, and al-Ghazali with Avempace on the other. Al-Ghazali was dogmatically critical of Aristotelian rationalism, but Avempace was Aristotelian through and through. Ibn Tufail, following the middle course, bridged the gulf between the two. As a rationalist he sides with Avempace against al-Ghazali and qualifies mysticism with rationalism; as a mystic he sides with al-Ghazali against Avempace and qualifies rationalism with mysticism. Ecstasy is the highest form of knowledge, but the path leading to such knowledge is paved with the improvement of reason, followed by the purification of the soul through ascetic practices...Al-Ghazali, true to his theologico-mystical position, takes ecstasy as the means to see God, but to ibn Tufail, the philosopher, the beatific vision reveals the active intellect and the Neo-Platonic chain of causes reaching down to the elements and back to itself.[5]

Unsurprisingly, Abubacer's views on God, creation, epistemology, ethics, philosophy and religion are at one level very traditional and conciliatory, and at another level, unconventional and uncompromising. It seems that, despite his efforts to break free from the religious and philosophical dogmatism of the time, he only succeeded in boxing himself into yet another corner of his own making. That is to say, in seeking to reconcile the prevailing conflicting philosophical, theological and mystical approaches to Islam, he only succeeded in oversimplifying many complex issues.

Nevertheless, thanks to the unexpected success of his philosophical romance, his ideas and thought soon spread across Europe and the Islamic East and, in the process, he inspired generations of scholars, thinkers and philosophers – Muslims and non-Muslims alike. Likewise, he was responsible for recruiting Averroes into the Almohad administration. Like him, his young protégé was a skilled physician, jurist and philosopher but, unlike Abubacer, Averroes subsequently went on to become the most perceptive and prolific commentator on the works of Aristotle that ever lived (see the next chapter for more information). He also patronised many other young scholars, thinkers and scientists of the time, including Alpetragius, who went on to become an outstanding astronomer and cosmologist.

After serving Abu Yaqub Yusuf for nearly two decades, Abubacer's patron died in 1184. His death occurred, perhaps, was a result of wounds that he had sustained during his battles against the encroaching Christians. Consequently, he was succeeded by his son, Abu Yusuf Yaqub (r. 1184–1199), otherwise known as 'al-Mansur bi-llah' (the Victory of God). By all accounts, Abu Yusuf was the greatest ruler of this dynasty and was known to have been a wise, generous, just and an equally pious individual in his personal life, as well as in his dealings with his subjects. As expected, he retained Abubacer as his personal physician and advisor until the latter retired in 1182 and was succeeded by Averroes. Three years later, this great European Muslim philosopher died at the age of around 84 and was buried in Marrakesh, in present-day Morocco.

However, his ideas and thought exerted considerable influence across Europe, thanks to the popularity of his *Hayy ibn Yaqzan* which, according to the *Encyclopaedia of Islam* (1954–2005) became recognised as 'one of the most remarkable books of the Middle Ages'.[6] According to some scholars, it was one of the most important books that inspired the Scientific Revolution and the European Enlightenment.[7] It was translated into Hebrew, Latin, Dutch, French, Spanish, German, English, Russian, Persian and Urdu, and continues to be read widely to this day. After its Latin translation, undertaken by Edward Pococke Jr., first appearing in 1671 under the title of *Philosophus Autodidactus*, Simon Ockley went on to produce the first English rendering in 1708.

As a result, it exercised considerable influence on scores of European Enlightenment thinkers, including John Locke (1632–1704), Francois-Marie Arouet (better known as Voltaire, 1694–1778), Thomas Hobbes (1588–1679), Jean-Jacques Rousseau (1712–1778), Isaac Newton (1643–1727), George Berkeley (1685–1753), David Hume (1711–1776) and Immanuel Kant (1724–1804), among others. It is widely believed that Abubacer's treatise also inspired Daniel Defoe to pen his *Robinson Crusoe* (1719) and John Locke to write his *An Essay Concerning Human Understanding* (1690), his most important intellectual contribution, having studied with Edward Pococke Jr. (1604–1691) at the University of Oxford, even if that is not so widely known today.

N

1. Richard Tarnas, *The Passion of the Western Mind*.

2. S. M. Imamuddin, *A Political History of Muslim Spain*.

3. Ibn Tufayl (Abubacer), *Hayy ibn Yaqzan*.

4. M. M. Sharif (ed.), *A History of Muslim Philosophy*, volume 1.

5. M. M. Sharif, op. cit.

6. See *Encyclopaedia of Islam*, vol. 2.

7. Samar Attar, *The Vital Roots of European Enlightenment: Ibn Tufayl's Influence on Modern Western Thought*.

# 13

# AVERROES

B. 1126 – D. 1198

SPAIN

In his well-known book, *A History of Western Philosophy* (1946), Bertrand Russell (1872–1970), a prominent British philosopher of the twentieth century, devoted no less than five separate chapters on different aspects of Aristotle's philosophical output. This included his output on metaphysics, ethics, politics, logic and physics. However, he covered the life, work and contributions of Aristotle's most famous medieval European commentator and populariser in less than two pages. In a chapter consisting of just over eight pages, titled 'Mohammedan Culture and Philosophy', Sir Bertrand wrongly stated that 'Arabic philosophy is not important as originally thought. Men like Avicenna and Averroes are essentially commentators'. It is surprising that a philosopher and intellectual historian of Sir Bertrand's stature and learning would make such a sweeping generalisation and inaccurate statement.

At a time when the philosophical ideas and thought of Plato and Aristotle were barely known in the Western world, the early Muslim scholars and translators not only preserved their works in Arabic, but they also systematically developed and refined ancient Greek contributions to philosophy. In so doing, they bequeathed to posterity a remarkable philosophical heritage that was second to none. One great European Muslim philosopher contributed more to the revival and resurgence of the ideas and thought of Aristotle in the Western world than anyone else; he was none other than Averroes.

Abul Walid Muhammad ibn Ahmad ibn Muhammad ibn Rushd, better known in the Latin West as Averroes, was born into a distinguished Muslim family of jurists in Cordova in present-day Spain. His grandfather, Abul Walid Muhammad, was a prominent Islamic jurist (*Qadi*), who served the al-Murabitun (Almoravids) as a chief judge, just as his father, Abul Qasim Ahmad ibn Muhammad, subsequently went on to train as a jurist and served the same dynasty that ruled much of Muslim Spain at the time.

Brought up and educated in such a learned family enabled young Averroes to swiftly learn Arabic, the Qur'an, Prophetic traditions (*hadith*), theology (*ilm al-kalam*) and aspects of Islamic jurisprudence (*fiqh*) during his early years. Keen to follow the family tradition and pursue a legal career, he went on to specialise in Maliki *fiqh* which was then prevalent in Spain and was being actively promoted by the Almoravids. During this period, he not only memorised *Kitab al-Muwatta* (Book of the Beaten Path) of Malik ibn Anas (d. 795) under the guidance of his father, but also revised and annotated the entire text to prove the fact that he had completely mastered it.

By all accounts, Averroes was a gifted student who soon completed his Arabic and Islamic education before going on to study medicine, mathematics and philosophy under the tutelage of prestigious local Muslim scholars and physicians. Some of his biographers have suggested that he studied philosophy under the guidance of Avempace, but that is very unlikely as Averroes was still a youngster when the former had died in 1139. However, it is true that he subsequently became familiar with Avempace's philosophical ideas and thought, and was deeply influenced by the latter's rationalistic approach to philosophy. Averroes may have also studied medicine under the tutelage of Abu Marwan ibn Zuhr in Seville, one of the leading Muslim physicians of the time, who had authored several books on aspects of medicine which exerted considerable influence. Ibn Zuhr had served the Almohads as a physician before he died in Seville in 1162 (see chapter 9 for more information).

Averroes grew up at a time when the Almoravids reigned supremely in many parts of Spain and North Africa. However, the political situation was transformed with the arrival of the al-Muwahhidun (Almohads) which was a rival North African power. It was established by Abd al-Mu'min in Morocco in 1147 and, subsequently, they established their authority in southern Spain. After the death of the latter, Abu Yaqub Yusuf, his third son and successor, became the Caliph in 1163 and he actively encouraged education, learning and scholarship. During this period of political upheaval and uncertainty in both Spain and North Africa, Averroes practised medicine in Seville and, like Ibn Zuhr, went on to serve the Almohads as a physician and jurist, while in his spare time he pursued his passion for philosophy. He was introduced to the Almohad ruler by none other than the philosopher Abubacer (Ibn Tufayl), who was then serving Abu Yaqub Yusuf as his chief physician and cultural advisor. In the words of Averroes himself:

Abu Bakr ibn Tufayl summoned me one day and told me that he had heard the Commander of the Faithful complaining about the disjointedness of Aristotle's mode of expression – or that of the translators – and the resultant obscurity of his intentions. He said that if someone took on these books who could summarize them and clarify their aims, after first thoroughly understanding them himself, people would have an easier time comprehending them. 'If you have the energy', Ibn Tufayl told me, 'you do it. I'm confident you can, because I know what a good mind and devoted character you have, and how dedicated you are to the art. You understand that only my great age, the cares of my office – and my commitment to another task that I think even more vital – keep me from doing it myself.'[1]

At the time, Averroes was better known for his expertise in medicine and Islamic jurisprudence than as a philosopher. But, Abubacer was sufficiently familiar with his breadth of learning and intellectual abilities, so much so that he recruited him into the service of the Almohads, despite the latter's theological puritanism. Indeed, they were strict adherents of Ghazalian theology and worldview, championing a strict and uncompromising concept of Divine Unity and, in so doing, repudiating any anthropomorphic beliefs or notions. Although Caliph Abu Yaqub Yusuf was happy to have someone of Averroes' calibre in his service, the latter had to tread carefully because his philosophical rationalism and theological censure of Algazel (al-Ghazali) would not have been tolerated. Serving initially as a physician to the Caliph, it seemed, would have been a far safer option for Averroes than engaging in controversial philosophical and theological discourse. He was fully aware of this. Again, in Averroes own words:

> When I entered into the presence of the Prince of the Faithful Abu Ya'qub, I found him with Abu Bakr ibn Tufail alone. Abu Ya'qub began praising me, mentioning my family and ancestors. The first thing the Prince of the Believers said to me was, 'What is their opinion about the heavens?' referring to the philosophers. 'Are they eternal or created?' Confusion and fear took hold of me…But the Prince of the Believers understood my fear and confusion, and turned to ibn Tufail and began talking about the questions he had asked me, mentioning what Aristotle, Plato, and all the philosophers had said…[2]

Averroes hesitated to answer the Caliph's question because he knew that the Muslim Neo-Platonists and dialectical theologians, such as Avicenna and Algazel, had clashed over this question. Given that Almohads openly championed the views of the latter on this and other philosophical and theological issues, it was prudent not to answer the question. Luckily, the Caliph did not press him on this matter and instead turned to the more experienced Abubacer who, no doubt, gave his political master a philosophically neutral answer to save the day for young Averroes. Even so, the Caliph was very impressed by the young scholar's all-round education and scholarship.

As it happened, Averroes went on to serve Abu Yaqub as a judge twice in Seville and once in Cordova until the latter's death in 1184, then serving his successor, Abu Yusuf

Yaqub, whose reign continued until 1199. The latter, in turn, became an admirer and supporter of Averroes and regularly consulted him on legal, medical and philosophical topics. As expected, his good working relationship with the Caliph eventually made the other senior courtiers and officials very jealous and antagonistic towards him which, most probably, led to his humiliation and forced exile to Lucena, a predominantly Jewish town located towards the south of Cordova. This happened during the last years of his life but, thankfully, Abu Yusuf eventually took him back into his patronage and Averroes spent the last year or so of his life in relative peace and comfort in Marrakesh (in present-day Morocco).[3]

Averroes was a prolific writer, having authored more than a hundred books and treatises on a wide range of subjects including astronomy, medicine, Islamic law, jurisprudence, literary criticism, philosophy, theology, history and countless commentaries on the works of ancient Greek thinkers (especially Aristotle). All his writings were completed over the forty years of his professional career; thus, unsurprisingly, his biographers have struggled to produce a comprehensive and accurate chronology of his approximately 20,000 pages of writing. Nevertheless, several scholars, including Jamal al-Din al-Alawi (1945–1992) and Manuel Alonso, endeavoured to produce chronological accounts of his literary output but, they were forced to admit that their efforts were far from being exhaustive or complete.[4] That is because Averroes was in the habit of writing books and treatises, and continuously revising and expanding them. As a result, it complicated matters for his biographers as most of his works were not dated.

Having said that, it is true that during the early part of his career, Averroes wrote shorter books and treatises mainly on Islamic law, jurisprudence and medicine; he was in his early thirties at the time. These included summaries or short commentaries on the writings of Alpharabius (al-Farabi), Avempace (Ibn Bajjah), Avicenna (Ibn Sina), Galen and Ptolemy, among others. Heavily influenced by the rationalistic philosophy of Avempace, who was the first Muslim philosopher to engage with the philosophy of Aristotle in the Islamic West, Averroes also mastered Greek and Islamic medicine, as developed by Galen and Avicenna, under the guidance of eminent physicians like Abu Ja'far Ali ibn Harun of Trujillo (Tarragona) and Ibn Zuhr of Seville (see chapter 9). The convergence of Greek and Islamic medicine led to the formation of a Graco-Islamic medical tradition of which Averroes was a notable practitioner and populariser.

Although he wrote several works on scientific subjects, especially astronomy and medicine, his most recognised contribution on the subject was *Kitab Kulliyat fi al-Tibb* (General Points in Medicine). It was most probably written between 1153 and 1169, and this established his reputation as a master of Graco-Islamic medicine, creating a synthesis between the medical thoughts of Galen, Hippocrates and Avicenna. Divided into seven sections (namely anatomy of organs, health, symptoms, sickness, drugs, food and treatment), the main objective of this book was to provide an overview of medicine, summarising, delineating and correcting the ideas of his predecessors on the subject.

With his *Kulliyat* and Ibn Zuhr's *al-Taysir al-Muddawat wa'l Tadbir* (Aid to Treatment and Recovery), Andalusia's contribution to medicine reached its peak. Both books were used as standard works of reference in medicine for centuries, though Avicenna's *al-Qanun fi al-Tibb* (The Canon of Medicine) was not received well in Spain. Translated initially into Latin under the title of *Colliget* in 1255 and then into Hebrew, it was repeatedly reprinted in Padua, Venice and Beziers, among other places.

Being a gifted jurist, who also served as a judge (*Qadi*) for a long time in Seville and Cordova, it is not surprising that Averroes wrote extensively on Islamic law and jurisprudence. As an adherent of Maliki *fiqh*, he is regarded as one of its greatest exponents. Though he authored many shorter works on aspects of Islamic law, his *Bidayat al-Mujtahid wa Nihayat al-Muqtasid* (Beginning for the Expert and the End for the Contented) is a monumental contribution to the comparative study of Islamic jurisprudence. It may have been written after 1169, as he was serving as a judge at the time and travelled regularly between Seville, Cordova and Marrakesh. Focusing on the topic of diversity of interpretation (*ikhtilaf*) in Islamic law; in this voluminous treatise, he attempted to transcend legal differences that existed between the various *madhahib* (schools of *fiqh*) and concentrated on the fundamentals that united them.[5]

As a devout Muslim, he felt that the law was sound but it was not always understood, interpreted and applied with the care, attention and scholarly depth that was needed, leading to considerable misunderstanding, partisanship and rivalry. His legal methodology was very much underpinned by his philosophical approach of moving from the specific problems and claims to universal remedies and solutions. His legal thinking was equally innovative and received widespread acclaim, both during his lifetime and subsequently. It is to his credit that the *Bidayat* continues to be regarded as a standard work of reference in Islamic jurisprudence to this day. So much so, that some scholars have considered it to be one of the best books on comparative *fiqh* to ever be written.

With his expertise in medicine and law aside, Averroes became famous across medieval Europe for his contribution to philosophy. Hailed as 'The Commentator' by none other than Dante Alighieri (d. 1321), author of *The Divine Comedy*, his three levels or categories of commentaries on the works of Aristotle ensured that the Greek philosopher's legacy became widely known for the first time in the history of the Western world. This raises an interesting question: was Averroes essentially a commentator on Aristotle, or did he make any original contributions himself? There is no doubt that Averroes was much more than a commentator. In addition to authoring shorter, intermediate and longer commentaries on the philosophical works of Aristotle; first in Arabic which, in turn, were then translated into Hebrew, Latin and other European languages, soon attracting the attention of scholars and thinkers across Europe; he became the most outstanding and widely read exponent of rationalistic thought and philosophy during the whole of the Middle Ages.

Clearly Averroes was a great admirer of Aristotle and, like the latter, he was fiercely rationalistic. But, unlike Aristotle, his philosophy and rationalism was firmly rooted in the Qur'anic worldview. No other Muslim thinker had succeeded in interpreting Islam so authentically while, at the same time, thoroughly mastering and assimilating Aristotelian philosophy and, doing so without undermining or diluting either of them, other than Averroes.

His critique of both Algazel (al-Ghazali) and Avicenna (Ibn Sina) demonstrated what an extraordinary mind he possessed as he subjected both to critical analysis, correcting the former's misconceptions about philosophy, while at the same time, pointing out the excesses of the latter. No one, not even his detractors, doubted his genius and originality as a Muslim thinker and philosopher *par excellence*. Even so, he was widely misunderstood, misinterpreted and even reviled in parts of the Islamic West and East, but his ideas and thought soon gave birth to a prominent new school of thought in the West, known as 'Averroism'. His followers fell into two schools: namely 'Jewish Averroists' and 'Christian Averroists'. In the words of the historian Philip K. Hitti:

> From the end of the twelfth to the end of the sixteenth century Averroism remained the dominant school of thought, and that in spite of the orthodox reaction it created first among the Moslems in Spain, then among the Talmudists and finally among the Christian clergy. Ibn-Rushd was a rationalist and claimed the right to submit everything save the revealed dogmas of faith to the judgement of reason, but he was not a free-thinker or unbeliever. His view of creation by God was evolutionary: not a matter of days but of eternity. Earlier Moslem Aristotelians had taken for genuine a number of apocryphal works, including some of Neo-Platonic character; ibn-Rushd's philosophy involved a return to purer and more scientific Aristotelianism. After being purged of objectionable matter by ecclesiastical authorities, his writings became prescribed studies in the University of Paris and other institution of higher learning. With all its excellences and all the misconceptions collected under one name, the intellectual movement initiated by ibn-Rushd continued to be a living factor in European thought until the birth of modern experimental science.[6]

In addition to Aristotle, Averroes engaged with the ideas and opinions of many other ancient Greek thinkers such as Plato, Porphyry, Ptolemy, Alexandra of Aphrodisias and Nicolaus of Damascus. Hailed as the founding father of European philosophical thought and thinking, Averroes' ideas and conceptualisations inspired generations of scholars, thinkers and writers across Europe, both Christian and Jewish. This includes William of Ockham, Michael Scott, Albertus Magnus, Thomas Acquinas, Siger of Brabant, Boetius of Dacia, Moses Maimonides, Giordano Bruno, Pico della Mirandola, Cesare Cremonini, Nicoleto Vernias, Agostino Nifo (Niphus), Alessandro Achillini,

Marco Antonio Zimara, Dante Alighieri, Rene Descartes, Baruch Spinoza, and too many others to name.

Indeed, Maimonides' *Dalalat al-Ha'irin* (Guide to the Perplexed), which is a foundational text of Jewish philosophy and theology, was originally written in Judeo-Arabic and was heavily influenced by the ideas of Averroes, while Scholasticism also emerged in Europe at the time as a Christian school of thought that engaged with Christianity and its beliefs, doctrines and practices from a rationalistic and critical point of view, again influenced by Averroes. In the words of the historian Douglas M. Dunlop:

> The Arabist legacy appears to have been two-fold…To take philosophy first, it may be summed up in a single name – Averroes. Averroism, which had become fashionable in Paris during the 13th century, had soon ceased to be influential there. But in north Italy and especially at Padua a rather special type of scholasticism gradually developed, in which Averroes rather than Aristotle was the great authority…The above-mentioned philosophers were all influenced positively or negatively by Averroes. The fate of Averroes is indeed singular. Almost entirely disregarded until the most recent times by his fellow countrymen and co-religionists, his writings became as it were naturalised during the 14th and 15th centuries of our era in what might have seemed the alien soil of Italy, and here Averroism flourished as nowhere else, before or since. A new and more potent intellectual movement – the Renaissance – took place, which should at once have outmoded the Averroism of Padua. Nothing of the kind happened. The school of Padua, supported by the republic of Venice, continued to flourish. It is a tribute no doubt to the merits of the philosophy of Averroes.[7]

In addition to being an influential philosopher, Averroes must be considered one of the most sophisticated Islamic theologians of all time. It was during his spell as a judge in Seville around 1178, that he composed three of his most important theological works, namely: *Fasl al-Maqal* (The Decisive Treatise), *Kashf an Manahij al-Adillah fi Aqa'id al-Milla* (Unveiling the Methods of Proof about the Beliefs of the Community) and *Kitab Tahafut al-Tahafut* (Treatise on the Incoherence of the Incoherence). If his critics thought that he was unduly influenced by the ancient Greek thinkers, then in these books, he repudiated such notions by subjecting Avicenna, Alpharabius (al-Farabi), Avempace (Ibn Bajjah) and Algazel, among others, to critical assessment and scrutiny like never before.[8]

As a devout student of the Qur'an, Averroes argued that reason and revelation were not contradictory but complementary, and therefore religion and philosophy were two paths leading to the same destination. He not only vigorously defended the philosophers, but he also argued that pursuing philosophy was highly beneficial from a religious and Islamic legal perspective. Although he made very good use of the Qur'an in his defence of philosophy – especially in the wake of Algazel's critique of the *falasifah* – his arguments were equally penetrating, cogent and successful. However, over time, and certainly in the case of the Islamic East, his voice was overshadowed by the ever growing protagonists of the Ghazalian worldview in that part of the world. Nonetheless, it is true that Averroes found peace and solace in philosophy, unlike Algazel, his philosophical opponent, who became a Sufi mystic. As such, Averroes was more successful as a philosopher, jurist and physician than as a theologian.

At a personal level, Averroes was known to have been very pious, well-mannered, fair and just in his dealings with others, and unusually modest and humble. He regularly delivered sermons in his local mosques and also led Friday prayers. Even his philosophical detractors acknowledged his superior qualities as a person, as well as a government official because, in an age of widespread cronyism, corruption and malpractice, no one was able to point a single finger at him.

He died in Marrakesh at the age of 72 and was laid to rest there. Abu Yusuf Yaqub, his patron and supporter, also died a few months after him.[9] Subsequently, his remains were transferred to his native Cordova where he was reburied with due respect and honour. His legacy, however, continues to exert a considerable influence on Western thought, philosophy and science to this day, even if it is not always acknowledged.

Ⓝ

1.  Abd al-Wahid al-Marrakushi quoted in *History of Islamic Philosophy*, volume 1, (ed.) S. H. Nasr and O. Leaman.

2.  Abd al-Wahid al-Marrakushi quoted in *A History of Muslim Philosophy*, volume 1, (ed.) M. M. Sharif.

3.  Majid Fakhry, *A History of Islamic Philosophy*.

4.  See Jamal al-Din al-Alawi's *Matn al-Rushdi*.

5.  Averroes (Ibn Rushd), *Bidayat al-Mujtahid wa Nihayat al-Muqtasid*.

6.  Philip K. Hitti, *History of the Arabs*.

7.  D. M. Dunlop, *Arabic Science in the West*.

8.  Jamal al-Din al-Alawi, op. cit.

9.  Majid Fakhry, *Averroes: His Life, Work and Influence*.

# IBN JUBAYR

B. 1145 – D. 1217

SPAIN

Marco Polo was born in Venice, Italy on 15 September, 1254. He grew up to be a trader like his father, Niccolo Polo, and uncle, Maffeo Polo, who travelled widely and established businesses in Constantinople, Crimea and as far as the Mongol Empire in Asia. Niccolo and Maffeo's extensive travel and trade inspired the young Marco to follow in their footsteps and become an international trader, travelling with his father and uncle to distant lands, including parts of Asia, to pursue business. His travels to distant lands subsequently became the subject of a travelogue titled *The Travels of Marco Polo*. After a long sojourn, when Marco eventually returned home to Venice, he was imprisoned and it was during his incarceration that he dictated his travel accounts to a fellow prisoner.[1]

After his release from prison, he went on to become a wealthy merchant and eventually died in 1324 at the age of 69, but it was his travelogue that made him famous in Europe and elsewhere. Although Marco Polo is today widely known across the Western world as a globetrotter and travel-writer, the name of Ibn Jubayr is hardly known, even though he was a European who travelled across the Middle East and Europe during the twelfth century. He left behind a pioneering account of his journeys long before Marco Polo was born.

Abul Husayn Muhammad ibn Ahmad ibn Jubayr al-Kinani, better known as Ibn Jubayr, was born into a notable Muslim family of Valencia, Islamic Spain. Little is known about his immediate family members, other than the fact that he descended from an Arab family that traced their origin to the tribe of Banu Kinanah, located close to Makkah in present-day Saudi Arabia. According to Roland Broadhurst, the translator of Ibn Jubayr into English, he was a descendant of Abd al-Salam ibn Jubayr who moved to Andalusia during the eighth century, joining an Umayyad army that was dispatched in 740 from Damascus to quell the unrest that was taking place in Spain at the time.[2]

Although the gist of the story is accurate enough, given the dating of the event, the expedition must have in fact been authorised by Caliph Hisham ibn Abd al-Malik, who reigned from 724 to 743. But that also raises another question: if there was political unrest in Spain, why would the Caliph send an expedition all the way from Damascus rather than sending reinforcements from the Maghreb? As it happens, linking Ibn Jubayr to his ancestor Abd al-Salam through the aforementioned story raises more questions than can be answered here. Suffice it to say that Ibn Jubayr was born into a notable Muslim family who lived in Valencia, and they served the North African al-Muwahhidun (Almohad) dynasty that ruled much of Islamic Spain at the time.

Ibn Jubayr's father was a civil servant and he ensured young Ibn Jubayr received a good education during his early years. A contemporary of Andalusian luminaries like Ibn Rushd (Averroes), Muhyi al-Din ibn al-Arabi (see chapter 51) and Moses Maimonides; Ibn Jubayr completed his early and higher education in the Arabic language, literature, poetry and traditional Islamic sciences in Jativa (Shatiba), where his father was posted at the time, and he also joined the Almohad administration.

By all accounts, Ibn Jubayr was a devout Muslim who was not only well versed in his faith and its sciences, but also endeavoured to live by the dictates of its teachings. He not only became thoroughly familiar with Arabic literature, poetry and Islamic sciences, he was widely recognised as a scholar and poet by the time he had reached his mid-twenties. It was perhaps due to his loyalty and superior education that he was subsequently promoted as an advisor and secretary to Abu Sa'id Uthman, the son of the Almohad ruler Abd al-Mu'min, who was then serving as governor of Granada. The Almohads ruled North Africa from 1130 to 1269, but they made in-roads into Spain after the decline of al-Murabitun's (Almoravid) hold on the country. That power vacuum was filled by this dynasty following Abd al-Mu'min's intervention in 1145, the same year in which Ibn Jubayr was born, and they swiftly went on to establish their rule across much of Andalusia. In the words of the historian Clifford E. Bosworth (1928–2015):

A powerful Almohad kingdom, with its capital at Seville, was now constituted on both sides of the Straits of Gibraltar. The countryside of the central and eastern Maghrib had become economically disrupted, and socially and politically disturbed, by influxes of nomadic Arabs from the East, and the coastlands were being harried by Norman Christian raiders. With his highly effective military and naval forces, Abd al-Mu'min conquered as far as Tunis and Tripoli, thus uniting the whole of North Africa under Almohad rule; the Ayyubid sultan Salah al-Din...sought – in vain, as it proved – Almohad ships for his war against the

Frankish Crusaders. The Almohad rulers now assumed the lofty titles of caliph and 'Commander of the Faithful'.[3]

Ibn Jubayr was in his mid-thirties when he was appointed a secretary to the governor of Granada. Under Abu Sa'id's tutelage, this city had been transformed into a politically stable, economically prosperous and culturally vibrant place, being perhaps one of the most peaceful and wealthiest places in Europe at the time. But the governor also had another side to him: despite being the son of the ruler of one of the most puritanical religious and political dynasties in the history of Islam, he was a very lax and easy-going Muslim who was very fond of wine, singing girls and extravagant parties. Unlike Abu Sa'id, Ibn Jubayr was a strict and observant Muslim who had no time for such frivolous activities and merry-making. That became evident as soon as the governor summoned Ibn Jubayr to his court for the first time and asked him whether he had tasted wine, to which – as one would expect – the former responded in the negative. According to Roland Broadhurst,

> The unregenerate prince, wishful of repairing this strange neglect, and with tones and gestures that allowed of no dispute, had thereupon cried: 'Seven cups, by Allah, shalt thou drink'; and the trembling scholar, his apprehensions of the wrath to come obscured by present terrors, had been fain to swallow the forbidden draughts. Yet no sooner had he done so than the prince was seized with sudden pity, and in remorse had seven times filled the cup with golden dinars and poured them into the bosom of his servant's gown.[4]

No doubt, this experience must have been a rude awakening for the young scholar and civil servant who had left his native city in pursuit of a promising career in government, only to find himself exposed to such hedonistic tendencies. However, Ibn Jubayr was realistic enough to know that the world he inhabited was far from being a perfect place. That is why he continued to serve the Almohad prince for about a year before the hajj season arrived, when Muslims from around the world set out in the direction of Arabia for the annual pilgrimage to Makkah.

Perhaps to expiate for the ungodly act of drinking liquor, the devout scholar requested the governor for permission to perform the hajj which was duly granted, and he made preparation for the long and arduous journey to the sacred city of Islam. It was in February, 1183 when he was around 37, that Ibn Jubayr joined the company of many other citizens of Granada, including Abu Ja'far Ahmad ibn Hasan, a local physician, and set off for the sacred pilgrimage. Making long distant journeys in those days were never easy; being fraught with danger, difficulties and uncertainty. That explains why it was a standard practice to travel in large groups or join caravans heading for Makkah, which often took months to reach their destination. The other alternative was to travel by ship, but that too was fraught with considerable dangers and uncertainty due to widespread piracy and unpredictable weather at sea. Ibn Jubayr opted to take the sea route, although it was more expensive than travelling by caravan, but it was a much safer and quicker route to Makkah from Granada in those days.

From Granada, he set off for Ceuta (Sabtah) which, at the time, was still under Muslim rule. The journey was longer than expected, but he and his fellow travellers finally reached their destination just in time to be able to board a Genoese ship on 24 February, 1183 heading for al-Iskandariyah, the Egyptian city of Alexandria. It was a rough journey at sea as Ibn Jubayr later recalled, ...the wind blew with violence upon us, throwing the sea into turmoil and bringing rain and driving it with such force that it was like a shower of arrows. The affair became serious and our distress increased. Waves like mountains came upon us from every side. Thus we passed the night, filled with despair, but hoping yet for relief in the morning to lighten something of what fallen on us. But day came...with increasing dread and anguish. The sea raged more, the horizon blackened, and the wind and rain rose to a tumult so that the sails of the ship could not withstand it and recourse was had to the small sails. The wind caught one of these and tore it, and broke the spar to which the sails are fixed...Despair then overcame our spirits and the hands of the Muslims were raised in supplication to Great and Glorious God. We remained in this state all that day, and only when night had fallen did there come some abatement, so that we moved throughout it with great speed under bare masts, and came that day opposite the island of Sicily.[5]

Passing the coasts of Sardinia and Sicily, the ship moved in the direction of the island of Crete (*Aqritish*) which, at the time, was under the suzerainty of the Emperor who ruled from Constantinople (present-day Istanbul). The journey continued across the coast of North Africa until they were able to see the lighthouse of Alexandria. Having travelled thirty days by sea, they finally arrived in Alexandria on 26 March, praising and thanking the Almighty for His benefactions, and booked into an Inn. The Ayyubids ruled Egypt at the time and Ibn Jubayr was impressed with Sultan Salah al-Din ibn Ayyub (Saladin) not only as a ruler, but also for his patronage of learning and education, as well as his kindness and generosity. However, it was Salah al-Din's uncompromising defence of the Islamic East against the European Crusaders that immortalised him in the East and the West alike.

After travelling around Egypt and visiting many mosques and historic sites where the Prophet's Companions were buried, Ibn Jubayr took a boat journey down the Nile to Qus before riding to the port of Aydhab to board a ship destined for Jeddah in present-day Saudi Arabia. He arrived in the sacred city of Makkah on 4 August, 1183 in time for the pilgrimage. He stayed here for more than eight months and successfully completed the hajj, devoting the rest of his time to worship, study and visiting sacred sites. He then set out in the direction of Madinat al-Nabi, the city of the Prophet, located towards the north of Arabia. He provided a detailed and meticulous description of the Prophet's mosque, tomb and pulpit, and also witnessed, to his utter disgust and disapproval, practices that he considered to be blameworthy innovations that had crept into the habits of local people.

From Madinah, Ibn Jubayr set out into the deserts of Arabia heading for Baghdad, the capital of the once mighty Abbasid Empire (r. 750–1258), visiting Qadisiyyah, Najaf, Kufah and Hillah on the way. Ibn Jubayr found Baghdad to be a shadow of its former self, with '…no beauty that attracts the eye, or calls him who is restless to depart to neglect his business and to gaze', but he did take notice of the fact that '…the beauty of its women, wrought between its waters and its air, is celebrated and talked of through the lands, so that if God does not give protection, there are the dangers of love's seductions.'[6]

Little did he know that around seventy years after his visit, the decaying Abbasid capital would be invaded and completely ransacked by the Mongol hordes. From Baghdad, he continued his journey towards the north, passing Mosul and Syrian Aleppo before reaching Damascus, which he found to be an impressive and dazzling city with its rich Islamic history and heritage. In Egypt, he also visited the prominent local mosques, tombs of the Prophet's Companions and other sites, providing a detailed and vivid description. From here, he proceeded to the port of Acre (Akka), which at the time was under the occupation of the Crusaders. In his own words,

> Acre is the capital of the Frankish cities in Syria…and a port of call for all ships. In its greatness it resembles Constantinople. It is the focus of ships and caravans, and the meeting-place of Muslim and Christian merchants from all regions. Its roads and streets are choked by the press of men, so that it is hard to put foot to ground. Unbelief and impiousness there burn fiercely, and pigs [Christian] and crosses abound. It stinks and is filthy, being full of refuse and excrement. The Franks ravished it from Muslim hands in the first [last] decade of the sixth [fifth] century, and the eyes of Islam were swollen with weeping for it; it was one of its griefs. Mosques became churches and minarets bell-towers, but God kept undefiled one part of the principal mosque, which remained in the hands of the Muslims as a small mosque where strangers could congregate to offer the obligatory prayers.[7]

At Acre, Ibn Jubayr boarded a ship destined for the Islamic West but, due to strong winds and rising tide, he suffered shipwreck close to Sicily which, at the time, was being ruled by the Arabised Christian ruler, King William II (r. 1166–1189), the grandson of Roger II of Sicily. He found the King and his officials to be tolerant and welcoming, and Arabic was the language of learning, scholarship and official transactions there at the time. As with Roger II, King William was also fluent in Arabic, and like his grandfather, he welcomed and patronised Muslim scholars and literary figures within his realm, to

Ibn Jubayr's surprise. His detailed description of Sicily, and in particular the city of Palermo, is not only revealing but also powerful evidence of, and argument for, the fact that Christians and Muslims can live side-by-side today as they had done in the past. From Sicily, Ibn Jubayr boarded a ship that took him back to his native Andalusia, arriving home to Granada in April 1185; he was 40 at the time.

Little is known about the rest of his life, other than the fact that he returned to the Islamic East twice: once when he was in his mid-forties, perhaps prompted by the news of Salah al-Din's capture of Jerusalem from the Crusaders, and again towards the end of his life, and died in Alexandria, Egypt at the age of 72. There is no record of the last two journeys he made, although his detailed account of his first trip was written down soon after returning to Granada, which luckily survived, along with a few of his poems. It is also worth stating that, as a scholar and noted poet, who was equally versed in Prophetic traditions (*ahadith al-nabawi*), Ibn Jubayr earned considerable respect and standing during his lifetime and subsequently. He lived in Malaga, Ceuta and Fez, Morocco until the death of his wife in 1217, whereupon he made his last trip to the Islamic East.

However, it was his travelogue, entitled *Rihla* (Travel Account), which became the first of its kind, predating the travel accounts left by both Marco Polo and Ibn Battutah by more than half a century in the case of the former, and over a century in the case of the latter. In other words, Ibn Jubayr deserves to be recognised as the originator of the genre of literature that is today known as *Rihla* or travelogue. As expected, his travel account earned him widespread acclaim, both in the Islamic East and the Western world, as a pioneering traveller, critical observer and gifted writer. The well-known historian and literary critic Lisan al-Din ibn al-Khatib (see chapter 51) paid Ibn Jubayr this glowing tribute:

Clear in doctrine, and an illustrious poet distinguished above all others, sound in reason, generous-spirited, and of noble character and exemplary conduct. He was a man of remarkable goodness, and his piety confirms the truth of his works...His correspondence with contemporary scholars reveals his merits and excellence, his superiority in poetry, his originality in rhymed prose, and his ease and elegance in free prose. His reputation was immense, his good deeds many, and his fame widespread; and the incomparable story of his journey is everywhere related. God's mercy upon him.[8]

Ⓝ

1.  See Marco Polo, *The Travels of Marco Polo*.
2.  Ibn Jubayr, *The Travels of Ibn Jubayr* (translated by Roland Broadhurst).
3.  C. E. Bosworth, *The New Islamic Dynasties*.
4.  Ibn Jubayr, op.cit.
5.  Ibid.
6.  Ibid.
7.  Ibid.
8.  Lisan al-Din ibn al-Khatib, *Kitab al-Ihatah fi Akhbar Ghranata* (quoted by R. Broadhurst).

15

# BITAR

B. 1197 – D. 1248

SPAIN

The remarkable scientific input and accomplishments of Geber (Jabir ibn Hayyan, d. 813), Algorithm (al-Khwarizi, d. 847), Rhazes (Abu Bakr al-Razi, d. 925) and Avicenna (Ibn Sina, d. 1037) are today recognised and acknowledged both in the East and the West. However, very few Westerners are aware of the fact that all of these scientists lived in the Islamic East and made their contributions during the medieval period. Indeed, scientific research and scholarship thrived in the Islamic West during this period, particularly in Andalusia, and Spain produced some of Europe's foremost scientists, mathematicians and philosophers of the time.

However, this important chapter in the intellectual history of medieval Europe has not been fully acknowledged or documented. Unfortunately, the scientific legacy of medieval European Muslims like Ibn Juljul (Gilgil, d. 994), Maslama al-Majriti (Methilem, d. 1008), al-Zahrawi (Abulcasis, d. 1013), al-Zarqali (Arzachel, d. 1087), Ibn Zuhr (Avenzoar, d. 1162), Ibn Rushd (Averroes, d. 1198), al-Bitruji (Alpetragius, d. 1204) and Ibn al-Khatib (see chapter 51), among others, not only appears to have been erased from modern European history books, but the same is also true in the Muslim world, where the contributions of these luminaries are equally neglected, if not ignored.

Abu Dawud Sulaiman ibn Hasan ibn Juljul, better known in the Latin West as Gilgil, was born in Cordova during the early part of the tenth century and became a renowned scientist specialising in medicine and pharmacology. He wrote many books and treatises on aspects of medicine which were later translated into Latin and read widely during the tenth, eleventh and twelfth centuries. Like Ibn Juljul, Abul Qasim Maslama al-Majriti (known as Methilem in medieval Europe) was born in the mid-tenth century, but unlike the former, he hailed – as his name suggests – from Madrid. He went on to become an outstanding scientist and polymath, known particularly for his expertise in astronomy, mathematics, chemistry and economics, and authored and translated many books. He died in Cordova at the age of around 60.

Abu Ishaq Ibrahim al-Zarqali, also known as Arzachel or Arsechieles in the Latin West, was born near Toledo during the mid-eleventh century. He subsequently moved to Cordova and became a renowned astronomer, astrologer and inventor. His writings on a range of subjects inspired generations of scientists, thinkers and scholars including Jacob Ziegler (d. 1549) and Nicolaus Copernicus (d. 1543), who made direct references to al-Zarqali's works. A crater on the moon has been named after him in recognition of his outstanding contribution to science. By contrast, Abu Marwan Abd al-Malik ibn Zuhr, known in medieval Europe as Avenzoar, was born in Seville towards the end of the eleventh century. A contemporary of Abubacer and Averroes, he hailed from the famous Banu Zuhr family that produced generations of well-known physicians.[1]

By all accounts, Avenzoar was a highly gifted physician who became widely known for his expertise in medicine. As a result, Avenzoar went on to author several important treatises on the subject which were later translated into Hebrew and Latin. He died in his native Seville while he was in his late sixties. Unlike Ibn Zuhr, Nur al-Din ibn Ishaq al-Bitruji, whose Latinized name was Alpetragius, hailed from the outskirts of Cordova and went on to become a renowned astronomer and jurist, having known Averroes and having studied under the tutelage of the philosopher Abubacer. He is best known for his theory of planetary motion and he also critically reviewed and improved Ptolemy's *Almagest*. His writings were later translated into Latin and Hebrew by Michael Scott in 1217 and Moses ibn Tibbon in 1259, respectively. He died during the beginning of the thirteenth century. By contrast, the contributions made by Abulcasis and Averroes have been covered separately in this book (see chapters 5 and 13 for more information).

Last but not least, Muhammad ibn Abdullah ibn Sa'id ibn Ali, better known as Lisan al-Din ibn al-Khatib, was born near Granada during the second decade of the fourteenth century. He is regarded as one of the gifted scholars and polymaths of his generation. An outstanding historian, poet and literary figure, he was equally known for his expertise in philosophy and medicine. He was one of the first physicians to formulate the idea of contagion, nearly four hundred years before Louis Pasteur (d. 1895), the French chemist and microbiologist who went on to propose the germ theory. After a lifetime devoted to research and writing, Ibn al-Khatib died in Fez, Morocco in 1374 (see chapter 51 for more information).[2] However, the rich and remarkable scientific legacy of the medieval Islamic West cannot be considered to be adequate or complete without paying attention to the life, contribution and achievements of Ibn al-Baytar who was, arguably, the greatest botanist and pharmacist to have lived during the European Middle Ages.

Abu Muhammad Diya al-Din Abdullah ibn Ahmad ibn al-Baytar al-Malaqi, better known in the Latin West as Bitar, was born into a notable Muslim family in Malaga, a southern coastal Spanish city. During this time, Malaga was an important centre for trade and learning, and was equally renowned for its ship-building centre known as *Dar al-Sana*. Though located far away from Cordova, Seville and Toledo, Malaga came under Muslim rule very early on, but it was in 1026 that it became the capital of the petty rulers (*ta'ifa*) of Malaga. Namely, the Hammudid dynasty and their rule continued on and off until around 1229, when the city was finally conquered by the Nasrids of Granada.

Although Bitar grew up at a politically tumultuous time in the history of Andalusia in general and of course, Malaga in particular, he was fortunate to have received his early education in a city that was home to many prominent religious scholars and scientists. After completing his early education in the standard curriculum of the day that consisted of Arabic, poetry and traditional Islamic sciences, he went on to specialise in science, mathematics and medicine. One of his most notable teachers was Abul Abbas al-Nabati who instructed him in medicine, botany and pharmacology, in which Bitar subsequently excelled and established his reputation as a gifted physician, pharmacist and botanist.

Bitar lived during a remarkable period of scientific advancement and progress in Andalusia, the foundation of which was of course laid much earlier by successive Umayyad Caliphs of Spain, including Abd al-Rahman III and al-Hakam II. In the words of the American scholar and writer, Michael Wolfe (b. 1945):

> It is rare when we can pin-point where one civilization went onto learn from another, but Muslim Spain provides a clear-cut case. It became the site for the most prolonged and intimate encounter in Europe among Judaism, Christianity, and Islam. In the explosion of philosophical thought triggered during this period, most of the 'lost' works of Aristotle, Plato, Hippocrates, Galen, Ptolemy, and Euclid were reintroduced into Europe through Arabic translations and the commentaries of Muslim philosophers and scholars. The full extent of this wealth of translations may never be uncovered, but on two points modern scholarship agrees: the works revived in Muslim Spain fuelled Europe's renaissance, and the flow of information was all one way, from the libraries of Cairo and Baghdad to the libraries of Spain and thence toward the rest of Europe. Christian scholars travelled south in numbers…at Toledo alone, the Englishman Robert of Ketton, the Italian Gerard of Cremona, and the Austrian Hermann of Carinthia could all be found actively translating hundreds of Greek classics from Arabic to Latin for European scholars.[3]

Although scientists like Bitar and his contemporaries were inspired by their illustrious predecessors, it is important to remember that they also made their own important contributions. In so doing, they left their indelible marks on the history of European thought and culture. Indeed, Bitar's burning desire to master science and pursue advanced research in this subject not only fired his imagination, but also drove him to act on a practical level. He was only in his early twenties when he left his native Andalusia and moved to the Maghreb in search of plants, herbs and scrubs to prescribe for various illnesses and ailments. As a physician, he was acutely aware that there were many diseases for which there was no cure or medication available at the time, other than what the previous physicians, both ancient Greek and Muslim had prescribed.

Though he was thoroughly familiar with the works of Hippocrates (d. 370 BC), Dioscorides (d. 90), Galen (d. 216), Abu Bakr al-Razi (Rhazes, d. 925), Abu Ja'far al-Ghafiqi (d. 1165), Ibn Sina (Avicenna, d. 1037) and Ibn Rushd (Averroes, d. 1198), among others, he was clearly not satisfied with their knowledge and understanding of various drugs and remedies for ailments. He was determined to push the boundaries of medicine by mastering botany, pharmacology and other related subjects, and, in the process, he hoped to discover new plants, herbs and scrubs as cures for diseases and illnesses.

After leaving Malaga in 1219, Bitar travelled extensively across North Africa, including Fez, Algiers, Tripoli and Tunis, before proceeding to Constantinople, Anatolia, Palestine and Arabia. His main intention in visiting these places was to collect samples of different plants, herbs and scrubs as possible medical remedies. He not only collected the samples, but he also made extensive notes about each item, their origin and availability, and their possible use for medicine and as cures for ailments. As Bitar continued his survey, his notebook became rather full and bulky, but that did not deter him in the least. Once the news of his expertise in medicine and herbal treatment reached the corridors of power, the fourth Ayyubid Sultan al-Malik al-Kamil Nasir al-Din Abul Ma'ali Muhammad (d. 1238) – better known as al-Malik al-Kamil – recruited Bitar into his service in 1224. Bitar was in his late twenties at the time. This enabled Bitar to extend his research into Egypt and Syria, thus adding to the list of new discoveries he was making on a daily basis. After the Sultan's death, he continued to serve other Ayyubid rulers.

He combined his role as a physician and herbalist to the Ayyubids with his study of medicine, botany and pharmacology for more than two decades, coupled with his extensive study of Dioscorides's Latin work, *De Materia Medica* (On Medical Materials), an encyclopaedia of medical drugs, and Book Two of Avicenna's *al-Qanun fi al-Tibb* (The Canon of Medicine), which dealt with the same subject. As a result, he attained sufficient mastery of medicine, botany and pharmacology to author a comprehensive compendium of plants, herbs, scrubs, foodstuffs, drugs and substances that could cure different types of ailments and illnesses.

The book Bitar compiled was *Kitab al-Jami li Mufradat al-Adwiyah wa'l-Aghdhiyah* (A Compendium on Simple Medication and Foodstuffs), although some scholars have confused this with his much smaller work, titled *Kitab al-Mughni fi Adwiyat al-Mufradat* (Independent Treatise on Simple Medicines).[4] However, both books were written during his time serving the Ayyubids and, unsurprisingly, he dedicated them to his patron and supporter, Al-Malik al-Salih Najm al-Din ibn Ayyub (d. 1249), who ruled Egypt from 1240 to 1249.

The other books he authored on medicine include *Mizan al-Tibb* (The Balance of Medicine) and *Tafsir Kitab al-Diyusquridis* (Commentary on the Book of Dioscorides). Bitar's reputation and fame as an outstanding physician and, arguably, the greatest botanist and pharmacist of the medieval period rests mainly on his *Kitab al-Jami li-Mufradat al-Adwiyah wa'l-Aghdhiyah*. This book is nothing short of an encyclopaedia of plants, medicines, herbs and foodstuffs, listing around 1400 items in alphabetical order, explaining their use and benefits in the treatment of various ailments and illnesses.

Being a very diligent and hard-working scholar and researcher, Bitar had made very good use of around 150 works of his predecessors and contemporaries, both Muslims and non-Muslims including Dioscorides, Galen, Abu Hanifah al-Dinawari, Ibn Sina (Avicenna), Ibn Bajjah (Avempace), al-Zahrawi (Abulcasis), Abul Abbas al-Nabati, al-Idrisi (Dreses) and al-Ghafiqi, among others. He also developed their ideas and thought substantially due to his copious notes, explanations and corrections of past misconceptions on different types of medical remedies and prescription, all of which were based on his own experiments, observation and experience as a physician and pharmacist.

Furthermore, he discovered and incorporated more than 300 new plants, herbs and scrubs into his work in a systematic way and did so in an easy-to-use format, thus enabling both specialists and ordinary people to read and understand it. It should also be pointed out here that Bitar did not neglect the issue of storage and preservation of medicine and drugs. He made an invaluable contribution to the development of an empirical scientific methodology by suggesting different ways to store medication, whether they were plants, herbs or foodstuffs based on his experiments and observations. Needless to say, modern science has benefited tremendously from the experimental approach of the early Muslim scientists such as Bitar, despite the fact that such wide-ranging contributions and achievements are not always acknowledged.

For instance, referring to a plant which was known as Brinjasif, otherwise called the Yarrow Plant, Bitar goes on to provide a detailed description of the plant, its place of origin, its benefits and possible side effects. He also highlights the views of previous physicians, botanists and pharmacists with regards to the plant. Here is a brief summary of his long explanation and assessment of the medicinal value of this plant:

It is called Artemisia in Greek and Shuwilah in Arabic. It is found to grow profusely by riverside, and comes out of the ground every year. It is counted to be among the vegetables that are similar to wormwood (afsantin). It produces a secretion that sticks to the hands...The wood pieces of the plant are small, the stem delicate and small with clusters of flowers...All of its varieties are attenuant and calorific. It acts as lithontriptic and diuretic (in the event of the blockage of urine). An excessive quantity of poultice of the bruised plant, if applied to the lower portion, will release menstrual flow...Also by sitting in a bath containing its decoction, the corrupt matter is expelled...The spraying of its decoction or application thereof is useful in headache arising out of colds, and it is a curative for colds and sinus.[5]

Unlike the writings of many of his predecessors, Bitar's encyclopaedia is fortunately still extant and its modern Arabic edition consists of nearly one thousand pages. It was first published in four volumes in Egypt in 1874. His work was rated so highly that it was later translated into Latin in 1758, French from 1877 to 1883 and German from 1840 to 1842, respectively. Accordingly, it was used as a standard work of reference on the subject of medicine, botany and pharmacology up until the modern times. Manuscripts of this historic work are preserved to this day in London, Vienna and Aleppo. According to George Sarton, the celebrated historian of science, Bitar became the greatest authority on these subjects in the Islamic East, as well as in the Western world, during the Middle Ages and beyond.[6]

As expected, Bitar's work influenced generations of prominent scientists and physicians, including Abd al-Razzaq al-Jaza'iri, Abul Abbas al-Hasani al-Tunisi, Amir al-Dawlah al-Amasi, Ibn Abi Usaybi'a and Carolus Linneaus.[7] On a personal level, he was a devout Muslim who was equally kind, courteous and loyal to his friends, family members and supporters. He never returned to his native Malaga, and died in Damascus at the age of around 51, while still busy researching and writing about science. This was, of course, an achievement for a young man born into an ordinary European Muslim family, in a remote Spanish port-city who, by the sheer dint of his character, imagination and hard work, went on to carve out a unique place for himself in the history of science and medicine.

1.  Seyyed Hossein Nasr, *Islamic Science: An Illustrated Study.*

2.  See Lisan al-Din ibn al-Khatib, *al-Ihata fi Akhbar Gharnata.*

3.  Michael Wolfe, *One Thousand Roads to Mecca.*

4.  See, for example, Seyyed Hossein Nasr, op. cit.

5.  Abdul Ali, *Eminent Arab-Muslim Medical Scientists.*

6.  George Sarton, *Introduction to the History of Science.*

7.  Syed Ashraf Ali, *Men of Letters, Men of Science.*

# 16

# ABU ISHAQ AL-SHATIBI

B. 1320 – D. 1388

GRANADA

Islamic thought and scholarship had been dominated by the Muslim jurists (*fuqaha*) from the early days of Islam. Renowned Companions (*sahabah*) of the Prophet (peace be on him), such as Abu Bakr al-Siddiq (d. 634), Umar ibn al-Khattab (d. 644), Ali ibn Abi Talib (d. 661), Abdullah ibn Mas'ud (d. 650), Abdullah ibn Umar (d. 693) and Aishah bint Abi Bakr (d. 678), among others, were some of the first jurists in the history of Islam.

They were succeeded by their prominent followers (*tabi'un*) who became the leading scholars of Islamic law and jurisprudence of their generation, including Alqama ibn Qays al-Nakha'i (d. 682), Sa'id ibn al-Musayyib (d. 715), Urwah ibn al-Zubair (d. 713), Qasim ibn Muhammad (d. cir. 730), al-Hasan al-Basri (d. 728), Ja'far al-Sadiq (d. 765) and Abu Hanifah (d. 772). These early jurists, in turn, paved the way for Malik ibn Anas (d. 795), Abu Yusuf Yaqub ibn Ibrahim (d. 798), Muhammad ibn Hasan al-Shaybani (d. 805), Muhammad ibn Idris al-Shafi'i (d. 820), Ahmad ibn Hanbal (d. 855) and Ibn Jarir al-Tabari (d. 923).

Needless to say, their collective contribution advanced Islamic law and legal thinking substantially. Indeed, al-Shafi'i's celebrated *Kitab al-Risalah fi Usul al-Fiqh* (Treatise on Islamic Jurisprudence) is considered to be the first extant systematic work on the theoretical foundation of Islamic jurisprudence. This, and other similar contributions, therefore inspired generations of Muslim jurists to emerge and engage with the science of Islamic jurisprudence (*usul al-fiqh*) in order to make it more relevant to their time and circumstances.

Some of those luminaries include Abu Bakr Muhammad al-Baqillani (d. 1013), Abul Ma'ali Abd al-Malik al-Juwayni (d. 1028), Ibn Hazm (see chapter 7), Abu Hamid al-Ghazali (d. 1111), Ibn Rushd (see chapter 13), Fakhr al-Din al-Razi (d. 1209), Sayf al-Din al-Amidi (d. 1233) and Badr al-Din Muhammad al-Zarkashi (d. 1392), among countless others. However, one of the most innovative and influential Muslim jurists and legal thinkers of all time was none other than Abu Ishaq al-Shatibi of Islamic Granada.

Abu Ishaq Ibrahim ibn Musa ibn Muhammad al-Lakhmi al-Shatibi, known as Imam al-Shatibi for short, was born into an ordinary Muslim family of Granada that traced their ancestry back to the Arabian tribe of Lakhm. Unfortunately, information about his early life and subsequent activities are shrouded in mystery and, as a result, his biographers have advanced conflicting explanations regarding his ancestry and formative years. His forefathers may have settled initially in the Andalusian town of Jativa or Shatiba (present-day Xativa, located towards the south of Valencia) which would explain why he subsequently became known as al-Shatibi (or 'from Shatiba'). However, most of his biographers agree that he was not born there, despite claims made by some writers to the contrary.[1] So therefore, the question is left unanswered: if not Shatiba, where was he born?

There are two plausible explanations: firstly, he may have actually been born in Shatiba, but it was his parents who moved to Granada soon after his birth. As Muslims were being expelled from different parts of Spain by the conquering Christians at the time, it would not have been unreasonable for a devout Muslim family to move to the relative safety and security of Granada which was under Muslim rule. Some of al-Shatibi's biographers, such as Muhammad Khalid Masud, have argued that the last Muslims to be driven out of Shatiba was in 1247, but that view is far from being definitive given the complex political, economic and cultural challenges of the time.[2] The other explanation would be that he was born in Granada, while his *nisba* (attribution) merely points to his family's place of origin, namely Shatiba. In the absence of any other conclusive evidence, the above explanations appear to be the most plausible.

Nevertheless, what is known is that young al-Shatibi grew up and received his early education in Granada during a chaotic and turbulent period in its history. The *Imarat Gharnatah*, or the Nasrid Kingdom of Granada, was established by Muhammad I ibn Nasr (1191–1273) in 1238. The city was ruled by the Nasrid dynasty for the following 250 years, up until 2 January, 1492, when Muhammad XII (Spanish Boabdil) was forced to surrender by Ferdinand and Isabella. During this long period of Nasrid rule, Granada experienced considerable political, economic, social and cultural difficulties and challenges, as well as intervals of development, prosperity and growth. As vassals of the Kingdom of Castile, the Nasrids were required to pay tributes to the Castilian

Kings. This meant that the city was not only politically vulnerable, but also economically beholden to the Christian rulers. To add to that, Granada was, at the time, locked in a fierce contest with the Kingdom of Fez over the city of Ceuta. Between 1305 and 1415, they repeatedly annexed the city only for it to be recaptured before finally losing control in 1415.

Despite the politico-economic uncertainty and upheaval of the time, the Nasrids transformed Granada into a thriving and prosperous centre of trade and commerce, in addition to being one of the most populous cities in Europe at the time. This was perhaps inevitable. As Muslims were being expelled from other parts of Spain or forced to convert to Christianity, the Nasrids offered them refuge in Granada, as a result, the city became a notable centre of Arabic culture, arts and scholarship with many writers, poets and Islamic scholars choosing to settle there rather than moving to North Africa or the Islamic East. In the words of the historian Stanley Lane-Poole (1854–1931),

> During this period of comparative tranquillity, Granada had taken the place of Cordova as the home of arts and sciences. Its architects were renowned throughout Europe; they had built the marvellous 'Red Palace', *Alhambra*, so called from the colour of the ferruginous soil on which it stands, and they had covered it with the splendid gold ornament and Arabesque mouldings which are still the wonder of artists of all countries. Granada itself, with its two castles, was a pearl of price. It stands on the border of a rich plain, the famous 'Vega', lying at the feet of the snowy 'mountains of the moon,' the Sierra Nevada. From the heights of the city, and still better from the Alhambra, which stands sentinel over the plain like the Acropolis of Athens, the eye ranges over this beautiful Vega, with its streams and vineyards, its orchards and orange groves. No city in Andalusia was more favoured in site or climate; the breezes from the snowy mountains made the hottest summer tolerable, and the land was fertile beyond compare.[2]

Growing up during the long reign of Sultan Muhammad V of Granada (r. 1354–1359 and 1362–1391), al-Shatibi swiftly memorised the whole Qur'an. He then went on to study the Arabic language, grammar, poetry, literature and traditional Islamic sciences under the tutelage of many prominent scholars of Granada, as well as those who had settled there during the political chaos and confusion that had spread across Muslim Spain in the wake of the *Reconquista*. Some of the leading native scholars who taught him include Abu Abdullah Muhammad ibn Ali al-Fakhkar al-Biri, Abu Sa'id ibn Lubb, Abu Ja'far al-Shaqquri and Abu Abdullah al-Balansi. Al-Biri was one of al-Shatibi's teachers who specialised in Arabic language and grammar and, on account of this, he became known as *Shaykh al-Nuhat* (master grammarian).

Young al-Shatibi not only learned the art of reciting the Qur'an under his guidance, but also became thoroughly familiar with Arabic grammar and literature.

He continued to study with al-Biri until the latter died in 1353, when al-Shatibi was in his early twenties. Thereafter, he attended the lectures of Ibn Lubb who was an expert in Islamic jurisprudence, while al-Shaqquri taught him advanced Arabic grammar and jurisprudence. He also benefited from al-Balansi's extensive knowledge of the Qur'an.

In addition to the above teachers, al-Shatibi received advanced training in aspects of Islamic jurisprudence (Maliki *fiqh* in particular) under several North African scholars who had either settled in, or frequently visited Granada at the time, including Abu Abdullah al-Maqqari, Abu Ali Mansur al-Zawawi and Abu Abdullah al-Sharif al-Tilmisani. Al-Maqqari was a gifted scholar of Islamic sciences of Sufi-inclination, and it was he who introduced al-Shatibi to the science of Islamic spirituality (*ilm al-tasawwuf*), while al-Zawawi, who also taught in Bijaya (in modern Algeria), guided him in aspects of philosophy (*falsafa*) and theology (*ilm al-kalam*). Likewise, al-Sharif al-Tilmisani was rated highly for his mastery of Islamic and rational sciences. After receiving a thorough education in Arabic, traditional Islamic sciences, aspects of philosophy, theology and spirituality, al-Shatibi became particularly interested in Islamic jurisprudence. In his own words,

> Ever since the unfolding of my intelligence for understanding (things) and ever since my anxiety was directed towards seeking knowledge, I always looked into its (the Shari'a's) reasons and legalities; its roots and its branches. As far as the time and my capacity permitted I did not fall short of any science among the sciences nor did I single one out of the others. I exploited my natural capacity or rather plunged myself into this tumultuous sea…so much so that I feared to destroy myself in its depths…until God showed His kindness to me and clarified for me the meaning of Shari'a which had been beyond my reckoning…From here I felt strong enough to walk on the path as long as God made it easier for me. I started with the principles of religion (*usul al-din*) in theory and in practice and the branches based on these problems. (It was) during this period (that) it became clear to me what were the *bida* and what was lawful and what was not. Comparing and collating this with the principles of religion and law (*fiqh*), I urged myself to accompany the group whom the Prophet had called *sawad al-azam* (the majority).[4]

Historically speaking, the Islamic West contributed more to philosophy, mysticism and scientific research and scholarship than Islamic jurisprudence. Other than Ibn Hazm and Averroes, that part of the Muslim world did not produce many great jurists and legal thinkers. That is why al-Shatibi's interest in Islamic jurisprudence and his single-minded devotion and dedication to this subject requires further clarification. Political upheaval and uncertainty of the time aside, he lived during a socially, culturally and intellectually confusing period in the history of the Islamic West. Intra-religious rivalry and sectarianism was widespread in Granada at the time, as different Muslim groups and factions engaged in endless debates and discussions on Islamic theological and legal issues, thus often leading to considerable misunderstanding and conflict. Such conflict, in turn, undermined Muslim unity and solidarity.

Al-Shatibi was also concerned by the huge diversity of opinion and contradictions that existed within the Maliki *madhhab* (school of Islamic law), which he found to be confusing and bewildering. Such a state of affairs may have contributed to his decision to specialise in Islamic jurisprudence, focusing especially on the higher aims and objectives (*maqasid*) of the Shari'ah rather than concentrating only on substantive law (*fiqh*). Pursuing a critical approach to Islamic jurisprudence convinced him that the norms and practices of his people held more similarities with local traditions than with the scriptural sources of Islam, namely the Qur'an and authentic Prophetic instructions and guidance. As soon as he began to point out such contradictions in public, he was immediately accused of heresy and misguidance. As he recalled,

> I had entered into certain public professions (*khutat*) such as *khataba* (preaching) and *imama* (leading the prayers). When I decided to straighten my path, I found myself a stranger among the majority of my contemporaries. The custom and practice had dominated their professions; their stains of the additional innovations had covered the original tradition (*sunna*)... I wavered between two choices; one to follow the *sunna* in opposition to what people had adopted in practice. In that case I would inevitably get what an opponent to the [social] practice would get, especially when the upholders of this practice claimed that theirs was exclusively the *sunna*... The other choice was to follow the practice in defiance of the *sunna* and the pious ancients. That would get me into deviation [from the true path]... I decided that I would rather perish while following the *sunna* to find salvation... I started acting in accordance with this decision gradually in certain matters. Soon the havoc fell upon me; blame was hurled upon me... I was accused of innovation and heresy.[5]

Despite the harassment, abuse and charges of heresy that were levelled against him by the other *ulama* (religious scholars), al-Shatibi was determined to question, scrutinise and evaluate the prevailing customs and practices of his society, which he did so in the light of Islamic scriptural sources. As a result of his research and examinations, he found many of the existing customs and practices to be innovations (*bida*) that were, in his opinion, not only unsubstantiated by Islamic law or theology, but also the main reasons for social conflict and religious disunity in Granada at the time. This, in turn, inspired al-Shatibi to explore the origins of the principles of Islamic law, their meaning, purpose and relevance to people, society and the institutions in general.

His deep and profound understanding of the philosophy of Islamic law enabled him to take a step further and explore the 'intentions' of the Legislator (Law-giver), in addition to identifying the purpose, relevance and outcome of the rules or regulations as such. He summarised his research findings in the form of two books titled *al-Muwafaqat* (The Reconciliation) and *Kitab al-I'tisam* (The Book of Devotion). The original title of the former was *'Unwan al-Ta'rif bi Asrar al-Taklif* (Exposition of the Mysteries of Accountability before the Divine Law), although it subsequently became popular as *al-Muwafaqat fi Usul al-Shari'ah* (The Reconciliation of the Fundamental Principles of Islamic Law). In this pioneering work, first published in five volumes in 1884, al-Shatibi set out to systematically delineate the *raison d'etre* of the Shari'ah, and its implication for law-making and possible impact on individuals and society as a whole. He explained,

> When the secret which had been so well concealed manifested itself, and when God in His bounty granted me access and guidance to that which He willed to reveal thereof, I proceeded to record its wonders and gather together its scattered pieces from the most specific to the most general, citing the evidence thereof from the sources of Islamic rulings with attention to every detail. In so doing, I relied upon all-inclusive inferences rather than limiting myself to isolated particulars, demonstrating the textual and rational foundations [of Islamic rulings] to the extent that I was enabled by grace to elucidate the objectives of the Qur'an and Sunnah. Then I sought guidance from God Almighty as to whether it was His will for me to string these precious pearls, assembling these treasure troves into explanations which would trace them back to their origins and be a source of assistance toward their comprehension and acquisition. As a consequence, they were brought together to explain the fundamentals of jurisprudence, and their splendid threads were woven together into a book in five parts.[6]

His desire and determination to explore the aims and objectives of the Divine law paid handsome dividends, as al-Shatibi delved deep into the science of Islamic jurisprudence. In the process, he formulated his theory of *maqasid al-Shari'ah*, revolving around the concept of *maslaha* or 'public interest'. Although he was not the first scholar to write on the importance and relevance of the concept of *maslaha* in Islamic law, he was certainly one of the first to liberate it from the grip of *Madhhab*-centric interpretation and understanding, by emphasising the flexibility and universality of this important source of the Shari'ah. In other words, al-Shatibi argued that, far from being relative, *maslaha* has a fundamental role in law-making in the Shari'ah.

Refuting theological determinism and the relativity of *maslaha*, he divided *maqasid al-Shari'ah* into two categories: namely, the aims of the Legislator and the aims of the subjects, or those accountable before the law. This prepared the ground for him to propose that, since the protection and promotion of 'public interest' was the first and foremost *maqasid* of the Legislator, it is the latter who decides what is *maslaha*, not the *mukallaf* (those subject to the law), who are required to abide by the aims and objectives of the Shari'ah. This is because the Legislator has already taken the public interests into consideration.

That means that *maslaha* is constant and flexible, being open to consideration, not least because individuals and societies are always open to change and flux. He found ample evidence for such an approach in the scriptural sources of Islam. The following Qur'anic verse is an example: 'God does not want to impose any hardship on you, but wants to make you pure, and to bestow upon you the full measure of His blessings, so that you might have cause to be grateful.' (Sura [chapter] 5: verse 6)

Needless to say, al-Shatibi's deep and penetrating analysis of the foundational principles of Islamic law and jurisprudence was nothing short of a remarkable contribution to the history of Islamic thought. This is not least because his theory of *maqasid al-Shari'ah* centred around the concept of *maslaha*, but without ignoring other equally important concepts like *Niyya* (intention), *Ada* (tradition or continuity), *Bida* (innovation and change), *Ijtihad* (independent juristic thinking), *Ikhtilaf* (diversity of interpretation), *Taklif* (legal obligation and accountability) and *Dalala* (language and law), it did provide an antidote to the philosophical and methodological inadequacy that was inherent in *fiqh* (substantive law) at the time – being completely oblivious of political exigencies, social change and cultural flux.

As expected, his innovative legal ideas and thought helped revitalise Islamic thinking and scholarship, inspiring not only his colleagues and disciples, but also generations of Muslim scholars and thinkers up to this present day. Some of the leading Muslim scholars who had engaged with his legal theory and philosophy included Abu Bakr Muhammad ibn Asim, al-Hafid ibn Marzuq, Ahmad Baba, Muhammad Makhluf, Muhammad Abduh, Muhammad Rashid Rida, Musa Jarullah (see chapter 34), Abdullah Draz, Muhammad Abu Zahra, Muhammad Mustafa Zarqa, Sayyid Abul A'la Mawdudi, Fazlur Rahman and Muhammad Khalid Mas'ud, among others.

By comparison, al-Shatibi's *al-I'tisam* is an important contribution to the subject of *bida* or religious innovation. In this work he examines some of the popular innovations that had crept into the lives and practices of the scholars and masses of Granada. He subjects them to careful analysis and scrutiny in the light of the Qur'an and Prophetic norms, and finds them to be baseless and unsubstantiated by scriptural evidence. Although he clarified that *bida* only related to the area of ritual obligations (*ibadat*), the local officials and *ulama* were far too incensed by his censure of their long and well-established practices to pay any attention to his explanations or clarifications. Such practices included his refusal to mention the names of local rulers or the rightly-guided Caliphs in Friday prayer sermons, or his repudiation of collective supplication (*du'a*) after obligatory congregational prayers.

Despite being a spiritually-inclined scholar himself, he vehemently criticised certain Sufi beliefs and practices which, no doubt, infuriated his opponents. As a result, they subjected him to considerable hardship and suffering, but al-Shatibi patiently endured the tests and trials. Eventually he responded to his critics in writing; this book was the outcome of his research on the topic of religious innovation. In addition to the above, al-Shatibi authored scores of manuscripts or articles on aspects of Arabic grammar, syntax, Prophetic traditions, Islamic jurisprudence and medicine.

On a personal level, al-Shatibi was an adherent of the Maliki *madhhab* and was known to have been a pious, frugal and upright individual. However, nothing is known about his family life or career, other than the fact that he trained and tutored scores of students in Islamic sciences and jurisprudence. His students and disciples continued to popularise his ideas and thought for the benefit of posterity. Although Abd al-Rahman ibn Khaldun (d. 1406), the celebrated historian and father of sociology, and Lisan al-Din ibn al-Khatib (see chapter 51), a renowned polymath and politician, were his contemporaries and they knew al-Shatibi, neither of them mentioned him in their writings. He seemed to have spent all his life in Granada as there is no mention of him having travelled to North Africa for any particular reason, or even to the Islamic East to perform the annual pilgrimage to Makkah. He died at the age of around 68 and was laid to rest in his native Granada during the reign of Sultan Muhammad V 'al-Ghani bi'llah', the eleventh ruler of the Nasrid dynasty.

Imam al-Shatibi's writings have now been published in many languages including Turkish, Urdu and English. Muhammad Khalid Mas'ud (b. 1939), a renowned Pakistani scholar and jurist, was one of the first to write a doctoral thesis on the life and works of al-Shatibi in English at McGill University in Canada in 1973. Subsequently published in the form of a book in 1977, he paid al-Shatibi the following tribute:

There are frequent references in modern Muslim writings to Shatibi's doctrines and their relevance to the problems of modern Islamic legal theories…The conservative Muslim as well as a number of non-Muslims…view Islamic law to be immutable. The modernist Muslim and a few non-Muslim scholars regard Islamic law adaptable to social changes. While the conservative oppose legal reforms as interference in Divine law, the non-Muslim scholars support them arguing that it was a religious law and that reform and change were modern concepts and cannot be justified by medieval or pre-modern Islamic legal history or theory. These scholars do not consider Islamic law a law in the proper sense. The modernists, including a few non-Muslim scholars, on the other hand, treat Islamic law as law and find it adaptable in theory as well as in practice… I found Shatibi engaged in a similar debate.[7]

Ⓝ

1. Muhammad Khalid Masud, *Shatibi's Philosophy of Islamic Law*.

2. Ibid.

3. Stanley Lane-Poole, *The Muslims in Spain*.

4. Al-Shatibi, *al-I'tisam*, quoted by M. K. Mas'ud, *Journal of Islamic Studies*, 1975. See also Ahmad al-Raysuni, *Imam al-Shatibi's Theory of the Higher Objectives and Intents of Islamic Law*.

5. Ibid.

6. Al-Shatibi, *al-Muwafaqat*, quoted by Ahmad al-Raysuni, op. cit.

7. M. K. Mas'ud, op. cit.

# 17

# KHAYR AL-DIN BARBAROSSA

B. 1478 – D. 1546

GREECE

The British historian, Simon Sebag Montefiore, published two volumes of short biographies under the titles of *Monsters: History's Most Evil Men and Women* and *Heroes: History's Greatest Men and Women* in 2008 and 2009, respectively. Though beautifully written and very attractive in presentation, both volumes are, however, more fun and entertaining than serious and thoughtful scholarly works of history and biography. The author concluded his short introduction to the first volume, confessing that his list of 'heroes' and 'monsters' was made randomly without much thought, reflection and certainly without a thorough study and evaluation of each individual and their life and works. As such, his whole approach to selection and coverage of the historical figures in both volumes was not only highly subjective, but also historically questionable and flawed.

Although, the author finalised his short introduction saying, 'the important thing is knowledge, remembrance and judgement. We should all know these characters, remember these crimes and make our own judgements.'[1] As I flicked through the contents of *Monsters*, I was rather surprised to find Khayr al-Din Barbarossa listed there among some of history's most evil men and women, whilst his patron and master, Sulaiman the Magnificent, was more fortunate to find a place in the volume titled *Heroes*. Was

Barbarossa a monster, as Montefiore would have us believe, or was he a great European Muslim, as the Ottomans and Muslims in general have always considered him to be?

'Khayr al-Din' Khizr Yaqub, better known in Europe as 'Barbarossa' and in Turkey as 'Hayreddin', was born into a lower middle-class Muslim family in the village of Palaiokipos, today located in the Greek island of Lesbos, situated towards the north of the Aegean Sea off the coast of Turkey. Though Yaqub Aga, the father of Khizr, was of Albanian origin, his family members served the Ottomans, thus over time they became thoroughly assimilated into the expanding culture and empire of the Ottomans. So much so that he actively participated in the Ottoman conquest of Lesbos in 1462.

In recognition of his loyalty and valiant efforts, his superiors granted him a generous fief of a local village called Bonova, where he settled with his wife, Katerina, who hailed from a Greek Christian family and was a widow of an Orthodox priest. Yaqub and his wife soon established a thriving pottery business whilst raising their growing family of four sons and two daughters. Though little is known about the daughters, the four boys grew up under the watchful gaze of their father and eventually joined the family business. As the business expanded, Yaqub responded by building several boats to transport his pottery products to neighbouring territories and, in so doing, hoped to increase his commercial stakes.

As expected, he was actively supported in his efforts by his four sons; with Ishaq and Ilyas initially choosing to support their father at home, Aruj and Khizr opted to venture beyond Lesbos to promote their pottery products. As the brothers travelled regularly to other coastal towns and cities, they soon became skilled and competent sailors. According to the historian Adrian John Tinniswood (b. 1954), at the time:

> The dominant power in the Mediterranean, and the largest market, was the Ottoman Empire, a vast conglomerate of conquered territories and vassal states... Christian Europe was frightened of the Empire. Ever since Sultan Mehmed II's armies conquered Constantinople in 1453, Spain and Venice, the major Catholic powers in the Mediterranean, had felt challenged by the threat that the Turks posed to Catholic Europe's cultural identity. Some of that same anxiety was also permeating the nations of northern Europe.[2]

The fear of Ottoman power and expansion not only gripped most of Europe at the time, it also led to the rise of demonisation of Muslims as 'cruel, aggressive and debauched, and it legitimised those who wished them harm. Ideologically motivated attacks on Moslem shipping in the eastern Mediterranean by the religious and military order of the Knights of St John were just one expression of a crusader mentality which taught that it was a Christian's duty to fight...'[3] As it turned out, the sons of Yaqub, namely Ishaq, Aruj, Khizer and Ilyas, became experts in marine affairs at a time when the coasts of the Mediterranean had become the main theatre of clash between the Ottoman navy and the Christian powers of Europe. Though Ishaq and Ilyas became notable seamen in their own right, it was Aruj and Khizer who were destined to fight for undisputed naval supremacy in the waters of the Mediterranean during the first half of the sixteenth century on behalf of the Ottomans, and they did so by repeatedly crushing their European rivals.

It is true that Aruj, better known as Oruc Reis, was the first to take to sailing and his brothers followed suit. He was, in many ways, an extraordinary individual who, having quickly established his reputation as a gifted sailor, then went on to assert his territorial authority at sea without any fear or favour. He was only two years older than Khizer and was fluent in more than half a dozen languages, including Turkish, Italian, Spanish, Greek and Arabic. His pursuit of business took him to distant places such as Anatolia, Syria and Egypt.

Indeed, it was on his way back from yet another business trip to Tripoli (in present-day Lebanon) that Aruj and his brother were attacked at sea by the Knights of St John who were, at the time, based on the island of Rhodes. In the ensuing battle, Ilyas, the younger brother of Aruj, was killed and the latter was taken and incarcerated in Bodrum Castle, located towards the south-west of Turkey, also known as the Castle of St Peter. As soon as news of the plight of his brothers reached Khizer, who was hitherto busy pursuing business in the Aegean Sea from his headquarters in the Greek port-city of Thessaloniki, he set out in the direction of Bodrum Castle and successfully rescued his brother from captivity.

Convinced that the Knights Hospitaller were a major threat to them and their business activities, Aruj wasted no time in joining hands with the Ottomans to take the fight to the fanatical Knights. It was Sehzade Korkut (b. cir. 1467 – d. cir. 1513), an Ottoman prince, who was in charge of Antalya, an Ottoman territory located on the Mediterranean coast, who offered to support him. This was perhaps because the Knights were also proving to be a thorn in the path of the Ottomans at the time. When the prince subsequently became the governor of the Manisa province, he granted Aruj a large fleet and permission to use the port of Izmir, thus enabling Aruj to show off the skills he held. He also participated in the Ottoman naval expedition to Apulia in the Kingdom of Naples. Thereafter, Aruj engaged in regular battles with Italian, Spanish and other European galleys in the waters of the Mediterranean, and his efforts were supported by the Sultan of the Banu Hafs dynasty in Tunisia.

However, his fame spread far and wide between 1504 and 1510, when he successfully managed to transport many Spanish Muslims to North Africa as they were being actively persecuted in Spain by the Catholics at the time. This earned him the honorific title of Baba Oruc (Father Aruj), which the Europeans mispronounced as Barbarossa, meaning 'red beard' in Italian, due to his red, bushy beard. Hereon, Aruj and Khizer became widely known in Europe as the Barbarossa brothers. Also, being half Albanian and half Greek in parentage, the brothers looked more European in their appearance than Ottoman. As it happened, the Ottoman Empire, which at the time established itself across the three continents of Europe, Africa and Asia, never hesitated to recruit people of different cultures, race and background into its service. That clearly added to its political, economic, military and cultural diversity, vigour and strength.[4]

However, from their secure base at La Goulette, the brothers now launched naval attacks on Sicily, southern Italy, coastal areas of Andalusia and captured Genoese galleys close to Genoa. This was in addition to repulsing Spanish efforts to take Bougie, Oran and Algiers too. In so doing, they asserted their territorial authority across the waters of the Mediterranean and beyond. Then, in 1516, the brothers went on to liberate Jijel and Algiers from the Spanish. Subsequently, Aruj lost no time in declaring himself the Sultan of Algiers, before expanding his kingdom by annexing Miliana, Medea, Tenes and the island of Capo Rizzuto, among others.

In due course, he joined hands with the Ottomans and the Sultan, in turn, appointed him a *Bey* (governor) of Algiers and the Western Mediterranean. Aruj eventually died in 1518 whilst fighting the Spanish in Tlemcen. However, it was his younger brother Khizer, better known as 'Khayr al-Din' (Goodness of the Religion of Islam) – a title that was conferred on him by his boss, Sulaiman the Magnificent (1494–1566) – who picked up the baton from his elder brother and went on to establish complete Ottoman mastery of the Mediterranean.

Once the Ottoman Sultan Salim I (1470–1520) confirmed Khayr al-Din as the *Beylerbey* (chief governor) of Algiers and the Western Mediterranean, the latter lost no time in launching a fresh assault on Tlemcen, successfully recapturing it from the Spanish in December 1518. He also continued his brother's policy of transporting Spanish Muslims to North Africa as they were being actively persecuted by the Catholics. This, in turn, won the new governor considerable support at home and abroad. Indeed, for the next quarter of a century, the waters of the Mediterranean were firmly under the control of Khayr al-Din. In fact, his contribution to the expansion and consolidation of the Ottoman Empire was such, that the whole of Europe at the time felt threatened by his extraordinary naval power and invincibility.[5] Perhaps this is not surprising given his outstanding record of military successes, both on sea and on land.

Soon after recapturing Tlemcen, Khayr al-Din annexed Bone and repulsed a combined Spanish-Italian attack on Algiers a year later. Then he went on to raid parts of southern France, before capturing Spanish ships returning from Cadiz. His forces participated in the Ottoman conquest of the island of Rhodes, leading to the departure of the fanatical Knights of St John in January 1523. For the next four to five years, Khayr al-Din repeatedly launched raids against ports, coastal towns and cities of Spain and Italy in order to keep them at bay. In August 1529, he again attacked the Mediterranean coasts of Spain and this enabled more than 70,000 Spanish Muslims to safely escape to North Africa. Two years later, he faced Admiral Andrea Doria (1466–1560) who was entrusted by Emperor Charles V to recapture their lost territory, but Khayr al-Din defeated the combined Spanish-Genoese fleet. Following Ottoman loss of several cities to the Spanish in 1532, Sultan Sulaiman summoned Khayr al-Din, his star admiral, to Istanbul, and entrusted the task of maintaining Ottoman naval supremacy to him.[6]

He responded by raiding Sardinia and several neighbouring islands. Thereafter, he encountered the forces of Andrea Doria once again at Preveza before the latter fled. His successes delighted the Sultan so much that he summoned Khayr al-Din again to his palace in Istanbul where he conferred the title of *Kapudan–i Derya* (Grand Admiral) of the Ottoman navy on him and also confirmed his position as chief governor of North Africa. This was no mean achievement for the son of Yaqub, who first learnt to sail in order to promote his father's pottery products off the coast of Lesbos, but through sheer hard work, loyalty and dedication, he now occupied the highest post in the most powerful navy in the world at the time! And, yes, there is more to come.

During 1533 and 1534, Khayr al-Din Pasha and Francis I, the King of France, exchanged messages. The latter requested the former's support against his Habsburg rivals. In the following years, the Pasha was forced to abandon Tunis due to tactical reasons, but soon led a successful naval attack on the Kingdom of Naples, as well as several islands belonging to the Republic of Venice.

However, one of the greatest achievements of the Grand Admiral's naval career took place in 1538, when his forces took on the combined might of Christian Europe and soundly crushed them at sea. Concerned by Khayr al-Din's growing territorial threat to mainland Europe, Pope Paul III called for a Holy League consisting of Spain, Venice, Genoa, Malta and other Papal States. This led to the formation of a massive fleet of more than 300 ships of different shapes and sizes, under the command of some of Europe's foremost admirals, with Andrea Doria, the great Genoese Condottiero and Admiral, being entrusted with the overall leadership of the entire Christian fleet. By contrast, the Ottoman navy, under the admiralship of Khayr al-Din Pasha, only consisted of just over 120 galleys. The two navies came face to face near Preveza (today located in north-western Greece) on 28 September and a fierce battle, the Battle of Preveza, ensued.

During the battle Andrea Doria, concerned about his fleet, ordered his ships to disengage, leaving the Venetians outnumbered and exposed. The Europeans lost thirteen ships and another thirty-six were captured. Doria's own fleet, although it escaped battle unscathed, was caught in a storm two days later. Up to seventy galleys were lost. The Turks, on the other hand, lost not a single ship, although a few were seriously damaged. Probably the greatest Ottoman naval victory over the Europeans, the battle established Ottoman naval supremacy in the eastern Mediterranean and compelled Venice to surrender fortresses along the Dalmatian coast and the Aegean islands.[7]

European defeat at Preveza not only established Ottoman dominance over the Mediterranean and North Africa, it also confirmed Khayr al-Din Pasha's reputation as one of the greatest European Muslim admirals and war strategists of all time. Clearly Emperor Charles V recognised his strategic value and military genius, hence why in

September 1540, he sent an agent to the Pasha offering him the whole of North Africa in exchange for his services, but the latter was far too loyal, honest and principled to be bribed. Unable to convince the Pasha to switch sides, in desperation the Emperor laid siege to Algiers in October 1541, but a combination of adverse weather and tactical errors eventually forced Charles to withdraw his forces.

Two years later, a combined Ottoman and French expedition captured Nice before Khayr al-Din reached the mouth of River Tiber. Rome would have been captured by the Ottomans, had it not been for the French, who requested the Pasha to spare the Pope's city. Khayr al-Din was now roaming around much of Europe without facing any serious resistance. Therefore, this forced the Republic of Genoa to finally agree to pay Khayr al-Din substantial sums of money to protect its territories from being annexed. In due course, Sultan Sulaiman and Emperor Charles V agreed a truce and this, no doubt, improved relations between the two rivals for a period. The Pasha's final expeditions were launched against the Spanish provinces of Majorca and Minorca in 1545, before he returned to Istanbul to retire. He died a year later in his palace, which was located close to the Bosphorus; he was around 68 at the time. But his son, Hasan Pasha, continued to serve the Ottomans as the ruler of Algiers.

Before his death, Khayr al-Din dictated his memoirs, entitled *Gazavat-i- Hayreddin Pasa* (The Conquests of Khayr al-Din Pasha), consisting of five volumes. It is now preserved in the Topkapi Palace in Istanbul. In 2003, this historic document was thoroughly edited and published in Turkey for the benefit of present and future generations.[8] A memorial was also erected next to his mausoleum in 1944, as a tribute to this great Muslim admiral, warrior, nation-builder and politician.

Finally, returning to the question: Was Khayr al-Din a monster or was he a great hero? I have no doubt that he was not a monster, for if he was, I would not have included him in my selection of fifty eminent Western Muslims. But of course, he was far from perfect too. He was in many ways a unique individual who lived during a very difficult, complex and turbulent time, and as such, he was very loyal, honest and dedicated to his Ottoman masters, and equally hard, uncompromising and even ruthless against his European opponents. In other words, he was a man of his own times and circumstances, and therefore the answer to the above question would very much depend on who is answering. Indeed, he clearly remained a persistent thorn in the path of Christian Europe for nearly half a century but, at the same time, he was a great blessing for the Muslims of Spain, North Africa and the vast Ottoman Empire.

Either way, however, no one can deny his remarkable and enduring impact on both European and global political, economic, military and cultural affairs. That is why the life and legacy of Khayr al-Din Barbarossa needs to be more widely recognised by the present and future generations. If he had been British, French, Spanish, German or Italian – instead of being called a pirate, privateer or corsair – he would have been hailed as one of history's great military figures.

(N)

1. Simon Seabag Montefiore, *Monsters: History's Most Evil Men and Women*.

2. Adrian Tinniswood, *Pirates of Barbary*.

3. Ibid.

4. Stanford J. Shaw, *History of the Ottoman Empire and Modern Turkey, 1280–1808*.

5. Ernle Bradford, *The Sultan's Admiral*.

6. Andre Clot, *Sulaiman the Magnificent*.

7. Alexander Mikaberidze (ed.), *Conflict and Conquest in the Islamic World: An Historical Encyclopaedia*, volume 1.

8. See Ahmet Simsirgil, *Gazavat-i Hayreddin Pasa*.

# 18

# GAZI HUSREV BEY

B. 1480 – D. 1541

BOSNIA HERZEGOVINA

The Ottoman Empire (*al-Khilafa al-Uthmaniyyah*) was established during the beginning of the fourteenth century. It subsequently expanded into three continents, thus becoming one of history's foremost political, economic and military powers. It continued to endure such power for more than six centuries before it was formally abolished during the early part of the twentieth century.

Indeed, it was during the reign of Sultan Muhammad II (r. 1451–1481) that Ottoman rule expanded rapidly: soon after the conquest of Constantinople in 1453, the Sultan instigated a series of campaigns that led to the conquest of parts of Serbia, Anatolia, Greece, in addition to attacking Hungary, Moldavia and the island of Rhodes, and he was even eyeing Italy when he died. Many parts of the Balkans, including Bosnia and Herzegovina, were also annexed by the Ottoman's during the remarkable reign of Sultan Muhammad II, although it was left to his successors (such as Bayazid II [r. 1481–1512], Salim I [r. 1512–1520] and Sulaiman the Magnificent [r. 1520–1566]) to expand and consolidate their presence in the newly conquered territories.

Whilst the Islamic history of Arabia, Persia, Central Asia, Andalusia, Ottoman Turkey and the Indo-Pak subcontinent are widely known and accepted, unfortunately the Muslim history and culture of the Balkans has remained peripheral and largely neglected. Most books on Islamic history barely mention the Balkans, and as such, the rich and remarkable contribution and achievements of the Muslims of this region are rarely acknowledged. One such outstanding Muslim personality was Gazi Husrev Bey, who was one of the main founders and benefactors of Islam in Bosnia and Herzegovina during the first half of the sixteenth century.[1]

Ghazi Khusraw Beg, better known as Gazi Husrev Bey in both Bosnia and modern Turkey, hailed from a family that traces its origins from, on his father's side, Bosnia and Herzegovina, and from his mother's side, the Ottoman royal family. He was born in Serres, today located in northern Greece. His father, Ferhat Bey, son of Abd al-Ghafur, became a prominent member of the Ottoman political and military service. Quick to recognise his merits, Sultan Bayazid married his daughter, Seljuka, to the talented young officer. Husrev Bey was therefore the grandson of Sultan Bayazid and the great-grandson of Sultan Muhammad II, the conqueror of Constantinople. He was barely six when his father died during the Battle of Aden, where the Ottomans were, at the time, locked in a battle against the Mamluks of Egypt, and to add to his misfortune, his mother also died thereafter.

Accordingly, young Husrev Bey was brought up by the royal family in Istanbul, and they ensured that he received a good education under the tutelage of private teachers, thus becoming thoroughly familiar with Arabic, Qur'an, Turkish and aspects of Islamic sciences, among other subjects. He must have been a talented student because he was appointed a diplomat while he was still in his early twenties, accompanying his uncle in the latter's role as governor of Crimea in 1503. As such, he began his political and military career under the guidance of his uncle on the one hand, and his grandfather, the Sultan himself, on the other, who was keen to consolidate and strengthen his expanding empire before launching any further military expeditions. In the words of the historian Stanford Jay Shaw (1930–2006):

> The reign of Mehmet's son Bayezit II marked a period of transition from the old heroic age of the fourteenth and fifteenth centuries to the new age of grandeur. Mehmet II had made substantial conquests in the East and the West, restoring the empire of Bayezit I and adding to it. But he had left severe economic and social problems that had to be resolved if the empire was to be retained and new conquests made. Bayezit II's reign was a period of consolidation before conquests were resumed.[2]

He barely served for a year in Crimea before he was transferred to the city of Shkodra, which is today located in the north-west of Albania, in his capacity as *Beylerbey* or chief governor. Again, he proved his worth here by swiftly establishing Ottoman rule and substantially improving the socio-economic condition of the local people. By all accounts, Husrev Bey, like his maternal grandfather, was a devout Muslim who preferred the company of religious scholars and Sufis than that of soldiers or politicians, but he was equally fearless and brave, and was not found wanting whenever he was called upon to fight for the Ottoman army.

On more than one occasion he fought directly on the battlefield, and did so especially during the reign of Sulaiman the Magnificent, when the Ottomans laid siege to the

Hungarian fortress of Belgrade in July 1521. This subsequently paved the way for the decisive Battle of Mohacs (*Mohac Muharesbes*), where the Hungarian forces of King Louis II were crushed by the Ottomans, led by Sultan Sulaiman himself. This victory not only led to the division of Hungary, but its consequences were to be felt across central Europe for many centuries to come. Husrev Bey's successful participation in the conquest of Belgrade won him the title of 'Ghazi' or 'war hero' from none other than the Sultan himself, and he was also rewarded with the governorship of Bosnia. He served his first term there from 1521 to 1525 before he was recalled to participate in the Battle of Mohacs in which, again, he enhanced his reputation as an able and gifted military commander and strategist.[3]

Soon after the battle, Husrev Bey was sent to Bosnia for the second time in 1526 as its governor. He served there for another eight years, distinguishing himself as an outstanding political administrator and benefactor of Sarajevo, formerly known as Vrhbosna, the capital city of the present-day Republic of Bosnia and Herzegovina. During his first tenure as governor, Husrev Bey focused his attention on establishing his authority and consolidating Ottoman rule in a region that was first conquered in 1463, although it is true that Bosnia's first contact with Islam pre-dates Ottoman conquest of that region. In the words of the British historian Noel Malcolm (b. 1956):

> The arrival of the Turks in the fifteenth century was probably not the first contact between Bosnia and Islam. The early Arab expansion in the Mediterranean, which by the ninth century had established Muslim rule in Crete, Sicily, southern Italy and Spain, must have brought Muslim merchants and raiders frequently to the coast of Dalmatia. The slave trade from that coast, which, as we have seen, spread Bosnian slaves round the western Mediterranean throughout the later middle ages, was certainly operating during this earlier period: enslaved Slavs from the Mediterranean region were present in early Muslim Spain, and the Saracen rulers of Andalusia are known to have had a Slav army of 13,750 men in the tenth century. But we can only speculate about whether any Bosnians converted to Islam, obtained their freedom and returned to their homeland.[4]

However, it is equally true that the arrival of the Ottomans in the mid-fifteenth century led to the gradual Islamisation of Bosnia and its neighbouring territories for the first time. Although Ottoman conquest of the region took place during the reign of Sultan Muhammad II, it was Husrev Bey, his great-grandson, who was destined to consolidate Ottoman rule in the region and accelerate the process of Islamisation like never before. So much so, that less than a decade after the death of Husrev Bey, almost forty per cent of the population of north-eastern Bosnia was Muslim, although it took much longer, in fact no less than 150 years, before the majority of the population of Bosnia became Muslim. The process of Islamisation pursued by governors like Husrev Bey were incremental and non-coercive, notwithstanding the mass propaganda that was disseminated by the Serbs and others during the Balkan conflicts of the 1990s, aiming to distort and falsify the history of Muslim presence in that region.

It should also be pointed out here that the Muslims of the Balkans are some of Europe's most indigenous population, more so than the Muslim population of Islamic Spain (Andalusia). Therefore, Serbian efforts to project them as being Ottoman settlers have been thoroughly discredited by some of Europe's leading historians. As it happens, Sarajevo is called the 'Jerusalem of Europe' with its Muslim, Orthodox, Catholic and Jewish populations having coexisted side-by-side for centuries, and that also provides a befitting answer to the peddlers of propaganda. So if the credit for Ottoman conquest of Bosnia goes to Sultan Muhammad II, then the credit for securing a permanent place for Islam in Bosnia and Herzegovina must go to none other than the visionary Husrev Bey.

It was, however, during his second tenure as governor of Bosnia (from 1526 to 1534) that Husrev Bey initiated a large programme of reorganisation and rebuilding, and did so with the backing and support of Sultan Sulaiman, whose reign marked the height of Ottoman power and glory during the mid-sixteenth century. During this period, Husrev Bey started constructing new settlements, roads, schools, hospitals, markets, dormitories, public baths and places of worship, thus building on the foundation laid by his predecessors like Ishakoglu Isa Bey, who was the first Ottoman governor of Bosnia in the mid-fifteenth century. Under Husrev Bey's stewardship, Sarajevo became the foremost centre of Bosnia, being renowned for its cultural and religious diversity, bustling marketplace and imposing mosques, and the city's population also grew rapidly. So much so, that Sarajevo soon became one of the most important and largest Ottoman cities in the region, even rivalling Istanbul for its diversity, tolerance and creativity.[5]

Thanks to his outstanding political and administrative abilities, coupled with his farsightedness and vision, Husrev Bey was nominated to serve his third term as governor of Bosnia from 1536 until his death in 1541. During this period, he expanded and further consolidated Ottoman rule and, being a devout and mystically-oriented individual, he went out of his way to establish several endowments as an act of perpetual charity (*sadaqat al-jariya*) for the benefit of his people and his own spiritual gain. According to Enes Karic (b. 1958), a prominent Bosnian scholar and historian,

> Gazi Husrev Bey made many endowments in the city of Sarajevo. Among these, as well as the *Madrasa* he built in 1537, one may single out the large and famous mosque (built 1530), known for centuries in Sarajevo and throughout Bosnia as the *Begova dzamija* or Bey's mosque, the *khanaqa* and *maktab* (1531), and the *Kutubkhana* or library, which he endowed in 1537. Of course, the basic institution founded by Gazi Husrev Bey was his *waqf*. This endowment has financed almost all his institutions, and in particular the *Madrasa*, for centuries.[6]

Unlike many other senior Ottoman politicians and military leaders, Husrev Bey was a very learned and cultured individual who never lost an opportunity to perform an act of charity. In his own words, 'Good deeds drive away evil, and one of the most worthy of good deeds is the act of charity, and the most worthy act of charity is one which lasts forever. Of all charitable deeds, the most beautiful is one that continually renews itself.'[7] Indeed, his *waqfnama,* or deed of endowment, is a living testament to his piety, selflessness and burning desire to use his wealth for the benefit of others. In fact, in those days, it was fairly common for Ottoman governors serving in different parts of Europe to write *waqfnama* for their spiritual gain: the endowments of Turahan Bey in Thessaly and that of Gazi Mihalogullari in northern Bulgaria are two other prominent examples.[8]

To achieve his objective, Husrev Bey went on to build one of Bosnia's first and foremost institutions for further and higher education, namely the Gazi Husrev Bey Madrasa on 8 January, 1537. As though that was not enough, he then went further by clearly stipulating that a suitably qualified superintendent or professor, assisted by a deputy, should be employed on a full-time basis to teach religious and related sciences to the younger generation in pursuance of public benefit and welfare. Since its inception, this historic Islamic seminary has continued to play an important role in the preservation and dissemination of Islam and Muslim culture in Bosnia for nearly five hundred years now. Some of the leading contemporary graduates of this seminary include Esad Durakovic, a notable philologist, Arabist and translator; Enes Karic, an academic, historian, politician and author; Mustafa Ceric, an Islamic scholar and former *Rais al-Ulama* of Bosnia and Herzegovina; Fikret Karcic, an academic and author, and Haris Silajdzic, a notable politician and academic, among hundreds, if not thousands of others.

One of Bosnia's most famous and largest mosques, *Begova Dzamija* or Bey's Mosque, built by Husrev Bey in 1530 in Sarajevo, stands to this day despite the ravages of time and history. It is an impressive example of classical Ottoman architecture, designed and executed by Acem Esir Ali of Persian descent, at the behest of the city's governor. Later, during the time of the Austro-Hungarian Empire, this became one of the first mosques in the world to have electricity installed, thus the mosque was illuminated in 1893. The mosque, along with the madrasa, a *maktab* (Islamic primary school), lodge for the Sufis (*khanqa*) and *hammam* (public bath), among other projects, consisted of Husrev Bey's three massive endowments written in November 1531, January 1537 and November 1537. They were intended to benefit the people of not only Bosnia and Herzegovina, but the people of the Balkans as a whole. For example, the purpose of the Sufi lodge, according to the founder of the endowment, was to provide residence for:

Believing *shaikhs* known for the sincerity which characterizes their mystics and for their virtue, who are clad in the garments of God-fearingness and piety, who are steadfast on the path of the glorious Shari'ah, who follow the deeds of *shaikhs* and pious people, who emulate the behaviour of the *awliya,* who always conduct themselves according to the provisions of the Shari'ah, who are obedient, who are among those who pray *namaz* in *jama'at*, who fast, who perform *dhikr*, who eradicate evil impulses from their souls, and who in addition to this maintain the customs of other believing people and the sayings of those who know and who are familiar with the right path.[9]

On a personal level, Husrev Bey was educated, upright, brave and unrelenting in the pursuit of his aims and objectives, but very little is known about his family life and children. According to one account, he died fighting in battle in Montenegro, which is now an independent Balkan country, at the age of around 61. His body was subsequently transferred to Sarajevo, where he was buried within the precinct of his mosque. As expected, his life and legacy has been – and continues to be – an enduring source of inspiration for the Muslims of Bosnia and Herzegovina to this day. According to Enes Karic, a leading Bosnian scholar and historian:

> It is important to recall that the Gazi Husrev Bey *madrasa* and the other institutions of the Gazi Husrev Bey *waqf* were the focus of national resistance to the invading Austro-Hungarian forces in 1878…the formation of the National government and the 'development of the first rebel banner' took place in the shadows of the Gazi Husrev Bay institutions: *madrasa*, mosque, *khanaqah*, *khan*, *imaret* and *waqf*…the majority of the resistant leaders, Muhamed *efendi* Hadijamakovic, *hafiz* Abdullah *efendi* Kukcija and others, were themselves linked through their work to the Gazi Husrev Bey institutions…the names of these people remain to this day important symbols of Sarajevo and major links in the chain of Muslim patriotic and religious and Bosniak national memory.[10]

1. Noel Malcolm, *Bosnia: A Short History*.

2. Stanford J. Shaw, *History of the Ottoman Empire and Modern Turkey, 1280–1808*.

3. Noel Malcom, op. cit.

4. Ibid.

5. Ilhan Sahin, 'The Story of the Emergence of a Balkan City: Sarayova' in *Proceedings of the International Symposium on Islamic Civilisation in the Balkans*.

6. Enes Karic, *Contributions to Twentieth Century Islamic Thought in Bosnia and Herzegovina*, volume 1.

7. See *Proceedings of the Second International Symposium on Islamic Civilisation in the Balkans*.

8. See website of Gazi Husrev Bey Mosque.

9. *Vakufname iz Bosne i Hercegovine*, quoted by Enes Karic, op. cit.

10. Enes Karic, op. cit.

19

# ROXELANA

B. 1502 – D. 1558

UKRAINE

Although the leadership of great Muslim empires – like the Umayyad (r. 661–750), Abbasid (r. 750–1258), Caliphate of Spain (r. 711–1031), Fatimid (r. 909–1171), Ottoman (r. 1300–1924) and Mughal (r. 1526–1857) – were almost entirely dominated by men, it is equally true that many Muslim women, often linked with the ruling families, went on to exercise considerable power and authority within their dominions, particularly at a time when it was not common for women to assume such influential positions. For example, during the time of the Abbasids, Caliph Harun al-Rashid's (r. 786–809) wife, Zubaida bint Ja'far (d. 831), became a prominent player in her husband's administration. She not only influenced policy-making, but also established her reputation as an outstanding philanthropist and canny political operator.

Likewise, during the Umayyad rule of Spain, Lubna of Cordova (d. 984), who was of Spanish origin, was recruited into the Caliphal palace in Cordova on account of her considerable learning and scholarship, and soon established her position there as an influential policy-maker, strategist and advisor to Caliph Abd al-Rahman III (d. 961) and his successor, al-Hakam II (d. 976). And, during the Mughal rule in India, Mehr al-Nisa (d. 1645), better known as Nur Jahan (Light of the World), completely dominated the Mughal administration of her husband, Nur al-Din Muhammad Salim, otherwise known as Jahangir (r. 1605–1627), so much so that she was widely considered to be the real mover and shaker behind the Mughal throne at the time.[1]

Like her illustrious predecessors and contemporaries, Roxelana, the wife of Sultan Sulaiman the Magnificent of the Ottoman Empire, became the most influential European Muslim woman of the sixteenth century.

According to an unconfirmed Polish story, Hurrem Haseki Sultan, better known as Roxelana or Roxolana, was born during the early years of the sixteenth century. She was supposedly born into a notable Orthodox family in the town of Rohatyn, in the Kingdom of Poland, today located in western Ukraine.[2] At the time, the Kingdom of Poland consisted of both present-day Poland and Lithuania, and was ruled by the Jagiellon dynasty that reigned there from 1385 to 1569. Unfortunately, very little is known about Roxelana's family background and early years, other than the fact that her father was an Orthodox priest of Ukrainian origin, who must have arranged for her to receive education in Polish, Russian and aspects of Orthodox Christianity during her early years.

She grew up at a time when different European ruling families, particularly those in Eastern Europe, were busy fighting each other to gain political supremacy whilst, at the same time, the Ottomans were directly or indirectly threatening to expand their hegemony across the region by ousting the warring Hungarians, Poles, Moldavians and Habsburgs. Disturbed by growing Ottoman threat, the Poles launched a major offensive to break the Ottoman, Crimean Tatar, Moldavian and Muscovite alliance in 1497, but the Ottomans inflicted a crushing defeat on the Poles, thus the latter were forced to make peace. This resulted in the Crimean Tatars having a major empire consisting of 'the entire steppe north of the Crimea from the Dniester to the Volga, under the suzerainty of the sultan. This, however, subsequently led to an inevitable break with Muscovy, which would soon become a rival instead of an ally.'[3]

Young Roxelana may have been captured by the Crimean Tatars during one of their many conflicts with the Kingdom of Poland, which led to her being sold into slavery. From Crimea, she eventually found herself in the bustling slave market of Constantinople (present-day Istanbul). Needless to say, slavery played an important role in the Ottoman system, although, according to the historian Paul Coles:

> Turkish slavery did not in the least resemble the slavery which Europeans imposed upon field workers in the plantations of the New World in the course of the sixteenth century; nor was it in most cases as onerous as the serfdom which was inflicted upon the peasant class of Eastern Europe during the same time. The comparatively mild character of Turkish slavery derived from the fact that slaves were not valued primarily for the economic utility of their labour. They were used instead to satisfy the ambition of Ottoman notables (often slaves themselves) to accumulate a large household of attendants as a public expression of their personal wealth and power...Slave women played the role of concubines

and mothered the heirs of the Ottoman ruling class. The sultan himself was almost always the son of a slave mother. Great dignitaries directed the affairs of the empire through the agency of their slave households. The royal slave-family administered the secular side of the sultan's government and furnished the corps d'elite of his army.[4]

Roxelana's journey – from her native Rohatyn in present-day Ukraine, to captivity in Crimea, and from there to the largest slave market in Kaffa or Theodosia, a city in Crimea, before being brought to the slave market in Constantinople – is nothing short of an extraordinary tale of test, trial and uncertainty. But that was far from being the end of her story, because the best was yet to come: for, at the slave market of Constantinople, she must have attracted the attention of the chief keeper of the Sultan's harem (private quarters), as she soon found herself there until Sulaiman I ascended the throne on 30 September 1520, following the death of Sultan Salim I on 21 September 1520.

In due course, the Sultan met her in his private quarters and she became his favourite (*haseki*) consort, thanks to her sheer beauty, sharp wit, intelligence and equally attractive character and personality. As the Sultan fell for her beauty and charm, not surprisingly, the other women in his private quarters became intensely jealous and envious of Roxelana. Being blonde, blue-eyed, slim but of medium height, no one could have possibly guessed that the daughter of an Eastern European Orthodox Christian priest would end up conquering not only the heart of the most powerful Muslim ruler of the sixteenth century, but also leave her indelible marks on Ottoman domestic and foreign affairs like no other woman of the time.

The Sultan, being a scholar, linguist and poet of considerable repute and standing himself, expressed his burning desire, love and longing for his beloved Roxelana in verse:

Throne of my lonely niche, my wealth, my love, my moonlight.
My most sincere friend, my confidant, my very existence, my Sultan, my one and only love.
The most beautiful among the beautiful…
My springtime, my merry faced love, my daytime, my sweetheart, laughing leaf…
My plants, my sweet, my rose, the one only who does not distress me in this world…
My Constantinople, my Caravan, the earth of my Anatolia
My Badakhshan, my Baghdad and Khurasan
My woman of the beautiful hair, my love of the slanted brow, my love of eyes full of mischief…
I'll sing your praises always
I, lover of the tormented heart, Muhibbi of the eyes full of tears, I am happy.

Although the modern Turks fondly refer to Roxelana as 'Haseki Sultan' (favourite wife) or 'Hurrem Sultan' (happy and joyous wife); thanks to her outgoing, bubbly and pleasant character and personality, she was barely 16 years of age when she first met the Sultan in his private quarters in Istanbul. He was around 26 years of age at the time. For the next four decades, she completely dominated the life and career of Sultan Sulaiman, who went on to become one of the most successful rulers of the Ottoman Empire, hailed as *il magnifico* or 'the Magnificent' in the West, as well as *qanuni* or 'the Lawgiver' in the East. Sulaiman was also the longest serving Ottoman Sultan, ruling over 30 million people spread across three continents of Europe, Asia and Africa, being one of the largest empires in history. According to the literary historian Galina Yermolenko,

> Roxolana's emergence in the Ottoman imperial harem has been compared to the projectory of a meteorite or a bright comet in the night sky...for after giving birth to her first son Mehmed in 1521, she bore the Sultan four more sons – Abdullah (b. 1522), Selim (b. 1524), Bayazid (b. 1525), and Jahangir (b. 1531, a hunchback) – and a daughter Mihrimah (b. 1522). That Roxolana was allowed to give birth to more than one son was a stark violation of the old royal harem principle, 'one concubine mother – one son,' which was designed to prevent both the mother's influence over the sultan and the feuds of the blood brothers for the throne. The violation of this principle signalled to the outside world the emergence of a powerful female in Suleiman's court.[5]

As Roxelana strengthened her hold on the Sultan, his other notable consorts like Gulfem Hatun (d. 1561), who hailed from Montenegro, and Mahidevran Hatun (d. 1580), who was of Albanian origin and the mother of Sehzade Mustafa (d. 1553), knew only too well that their power and position within the extended family of the Sultan was now on the wane. This was especially the case after Roxelana was allowed to give birth to Muhammad (Mehmed) in 1521, followed by four more sons, thus overriding Mahidevran's claim to be the mother of the Sultan's only son and his heir apparent. The only other woman who was still alive at the time, and could check Roxelana's growing power and standing, was Ayse Hafsa Sultan, the mother of Sulaiman.

However, her death in March 1534 removed yet another barrier from the path of the former. Nonetheless, another challenge for Roxelana was yet present: namely Mahidevran and her son Mustafa, who was Sulaiman's heir apparent. Soon, rivalry broke out between the two women and when matters became too intense and destabilising for the liking of the Sultan, he sent Mahidevran to go and live with their son, Sehzade Mustafa, who was serving as the governor of the province of Manisa (Magnesia) at the time. This cleared the way for Roxelana's instant rise to power and authority within the highest echelons of the Ottoman Empire.

Indeed, her unrivalled position as the Sultan's favourite consort was confirmed by Sulaiman's decision to break the long established family tradition by formally marrying Roxelana, thus she became his only legal wife and the first to be so for nearly 200 years. The public ceremony marking their wedding was an impressive affair, as one would expect, but the Sultan's offer of a daily allowance of 2000 aspers or silver coins to his favourite consort and only wife, which was an eye-watering amount at the time, confirmed Roxelana's position as the highest paid consort in Ottoman history. In return, she remained steadfastly loyal, loving and committed to her husband throughout her life. In the words of Galina Yermolenko:

> Her authority showed not only in her firm grip over Suleiman's heart but also in her ability to compete with the male rivals in Suleiman's court, and to be a skilful sovereign and ruler. She was a keen advisor to Suleiman in political matters, particularly when he was absent from Istanbul on his numerous military campaigns. She regularly sent him letters to the Sultan, in which, in addition to expressing her great love and longing for him, she also informed him of the situation in the capital and of any events that required his immediate attention or action. In being thus vigilant, she protected Suleiman's interests and contributed to the success of his reign. There is no doubt that Suleiman trusted her more than he did his male advisors.[6]

Given Roxelana's great love and unflinching devotion to her husband, it is not surprising that the Sultan, yet again, violated long established Ottoman imperial tradition of *Sanjak Beyligi,* which required the consort to move to a distant province where the son would serve as governor, and she would not be permitted to return until the son was recalled back to Istanbul to ascend the throne. But Sulaiman made an exception in the case of his beloved Roxelana and kept her with him permanently. Subsequently, when the Sultan was forced to leave the Old Palace (*Eski Saray*) for the New Palace (*Topkapi*) due to a devastating fire, she followed suit and moved into her husband's new residence without facing barriers or restrictions. Needless to say, as the Sultan grew older, he became more dependent on Roxelana for advice, guidance and support on both domestic policies and foreign affairs. So much so, that she eventually became Sulaiman's chief advisor and was widely considered to be the most powerful woman in the history of the Ottoman Empire.

As expected, she exercised huge influence on Ottoman politics and policy-making which, in turn, earned her considerable praise as well as criticism. This was especially because she went out of her way to actively promote her sons at the expense of Mustafa, who was Sulaiman's eldest son by Mahidevran and his heir apparent. Although Sehzade Mustafa was highly respected by the senior Ottoman officials – on account of his unusual intelligence, strategic abilities and considerable military experience – unfortunately, he was executed on the orders of his father and unsurprisingly, Roxelana was blamed for his untimely death.[7] Again, the reasons for the removal of several other senior officials, civilian and military from their posts, was laid squarely at the doors of Roxelana until Damat Rustem Pasha, her son-in-law, was appointed the grand vizier. Roxelana's undue influence on her husband, coupled with her involvement in the political affairs of the Ottoman Empire, rightly or wrongly, tarnished her image and standing.

It is unfortunate because Roxelana was an equally devout and generous Muslim lady who became renowned for her charitable contribution, and played an equally important role in forging good relations between the Ottomans and Poland at the time. Good relations subsequently paved the way for the establishment of a Polish-Ottoman alliance during the time of King Sigismund II Augustus, who reigned from 1548 to 1572. As a fabulously wealthy lady and generous philanthropist, Roxelana funded the construction of many mosques, *madrasas* (Islamic seminaries), public baths *(hamam)*, fountains and other similar building projects for the benefit of her people.

However, her most important contribution includes the construction of a large and exclusive hospital for women in Istanbul, which was designed and executed by Mimar Sinan (1489–1588), the great Ottoman architect who served Sultan Sulaiman as his chief designer and builder at the time. Her other important contribution was the establishment of a public kitchen, known as *Haseki Sultan Imaret*, which fed more than 500 poor and needy people twice a day, and this project was subsequently replicated in Makkah, the most sacred city of Islam, and Jerusalem, the third sacred city of Islam, and again it was funded entirely from her personal fortune. In that sense, Roxelana was very much like Zubaida bint Ja'far, the wife of Caliph Harun al-Rashid, who was hailed as a wise and very generous lady for her wide-ranging charitable and philanthropic activities during her life time.

After dominating Ottoman domestic politics, foreign policy, and social and cultural life for nearly four decades, Roxelana eventually died at the age of around 56. Although her death broke the Sultan's heart, he continued to serve his people for another eight years and died at the age of around 72. Needless to say, Roxelana's remarkable life and career captured the imagination of Europeans and Ottomans, Christians and Muslims alike. So much so that,

> Folk legends, historical and quasi-historical narratives, and fictional stories about Roxolana have circulated in Europe since the early modern times, and more stories emerged in the Turkish, French, German, Italian, English, Serbo-Croatian, Hungarian, Romanian, Polish, Ukrainian, and Russian languages in the later centuries…In the nineteenth and twentieth-century Western art and literature, the legend of Roxolana continued to expand and magnify in proportions, often acquiring romantic overtones – a practice inherited from the West's romantic fascination with Turkey and Near East.[8]

Ⓝ

1. Diana and Michael Preston, *Taj Mahal: Passion and Genius at the Heart of the Moghul Empire.*

2. Andre Clot, *Suleiman the Magnificent.*

3. Stanford J. Shaw, *History of the Ottoman Empire and Modern Turkey, 1280–1808.*

4. Paul Coles, *The Ottoman Impact on Europe.*

5. Galina Yermolenko, Roxolana: "The Greatest Empress of the East", in *The Muslim World*, vol. 95, number 2, 2005.

6. Ibid.

7. Andre Clot, op. cit.

8. Galina Yermolenko (ed.), *Roxolana in European Literature, History and Culture.*

# 20

# HASAN KAFI PRUSAC

B. 1544 – D. 1615

BOSNIA HERZEGOVINA

Most books on the Islamic history of the West focus on the origin, development and eventual decline and disintegration of more than seven hundred years of Muslim presence in Andalusia, while the Islamic history of the Balkans is largely neglected, if not ignored. Although historians of the Islamic West have identified the beginnings of a significant Muslim presence in the Balkans during the Ottoman expansion in the region during the fifteenth century, it is equally true that the Islamic history of the Balkans can be traced back to the early Muslim expansion into the West during the eighth and ninth centuries, when Crete, Sicily, parts of southern Italy and Spain came under Islamic rule for the first time. As a result, direct contact and interaction took place between the Muslims and the people of the Balkans – facilitated no doubt by traders and merchants -- even if, at the time, it did not lead to the spread of Islam in the region in a significant way.[1]

As such, the history of Muslims in the Balkans is not only important to the Muslims of the West, but equally important to the rest of the Muslims around the world, as it is crucial to be aware of this rich and remarkable history and heritage. Likewise, it is not widely known that the Islamisation of the Balkans was an incremental process that took place over many centuries, spearheaded by prominent local Muslim governors and officials, as well as scores of influential religious scholars and preachers. One such

prominent Muslim scholar, thinker and writer of the sixteenth century Balkans was
Hasan Kafi Prusac of Bosnia.

Hasan Kafi ibn Turhan ibn Dawud ibn Yaqub az-Zibi al-Aqhisari al-Bosnawi, better
known as Hasan Kafi Prusac, was born into a learned and highly regarded Muslim
family in the Ottoman village of Aqhisar, today located in the Bosnian town of Prusac.
Hasan Kafi's grandfather, Dawud ibn Yaqub, of Albanian origin, was recruited by
the Ottomans into their army, thus he took part in many military expeditions. He
eventually died at the age of 70 during the Ottoman siege on the Croatian fortress of
Buruna. Hasan Kafi's father, Turhan ibn Dawud, was a learned and devout Muslim who
lived and died in his native Aqhisar when he was in his mid-nineties.[2]

Brought up and educated in an Islamic ambience, young Hasan Kafi assimilated
Islamic principles and practices from an early age and inherited his father's unquenchable
thirst for learning. After completing his early education at home, he was enrolled at his
village school at the age of 12 where he studied Arabic, Qur'an and aspects of traditional
Islamic sciences. As a talented student, he swiftly completed his further education and,
being keen to pursue higher education, he left Bosnia and moved to Constantinople
(present-day Istanbul), which was the capital of the Ottoman Empire.

Here, he attended the classes of the city's leading Muslim scholars including Haji
Efendi, Mawla Ahmad al-Ansari and Shaykh Bali ibn Yusuf, among others. It was a
good time to pursue higher education in Istanbul because under the generous patronage
of Sulaiman the Magnificent (r. 1520–1566), the city became a prominent centre of
learning and scholarship, thus attracting scholars from many parts of the Muslim world
who specialised in the religious, philosophical and scientific subjects of the time.

Haji Efendi, also known as Kara Yilan, was a leading expert in religious sciences
at the time, thus Hasan Kafi benefited from his extensive knowledge and scholarship,
while Mawla Ahmad al-Ansari and Bali ibn Yusuf taught him Qur'anic exegesis (*tafsir*)
and Prophetic traditions (*ahadith al-nabawi*), respectively. He also attended the classes
of Jalal al-Din Akbar and Shaykh Anwar (Enver), who were both leading scholars of
the Qur'an and Islamic theology of the time. In other words, during his stay of nine
years in the Ottoman capital, Hasan Kafi attended the classes of dozens of prominent
scholars and received certification (*ijaza*) in aspects of Islamic sciences, thus acquiring
mastery of Arabic, Qur'anic exegesis, Prophetic traditions, Islamic theology (*ilm al-
kalam*) and philosophy (*falsafa*), among other subjects. An average seeker of knowledge
would have returned home to take up a teaching position after such a long period of
rigorous training.

However, Hasan Kafi was a true seeker of knowledge and, as such, he moved
to Madinat al-Nabi, the city of the Prophet, where he engaged in advanced Islamic
education under the city's leading scholars (such as Mir Ghadanfar ibn Ja'far a-Husayni).
Hasan Kafi's time in the city also enabled him to master the intricacies of the Arabic
language and literature, thus consolidating his reputation as one of the great Muslim

scholars and Arabists of the Balkans, if not the Ottoman Empire as a whole, during the sixteenth century.

After studying for more than a decade in Istanbul and Arabia, Hasan Kafi eventually returned home to Aqhisar in 1575 at the age of around 31, and started lecturing on aspects of Arabic language, grammar and Islamic sciences.[3] Due to his vast learning and oratory skills, he soon became a popular teacher and students would come from far and wide to listen to his lectures. This enhanced his reputation and standing with the public and, as expected, he soon attracted the attention of the local governor who appointed him to the post of *Qadi* (judge) of Aqhisar. He continued to serve in this capacity until he was promoted to the judgeship of the district of Srem or Syrmia, today located in the north of Belgrade, before setting out for the sacred pilgrimage to Makkah in 1591. On his return from the annual hajj, Hasan Kafi resumed his duties as a judge and served in various locations, until he opted to retire and return to teaching.

He also served in the army of several Ottoman governors and actively participated in military expeditions in and around Bosnia. During one such expedition, he proved his worth and the governor's army subsequently returned home victorious and, in appreciation, he was re-appointed as judge of Aqhisar in 1596. A year later, he resigned and went to Istanbul where he was granted a warm welcome by the ruling elite, thanks to his literary contribution and achievements. Indeed, he presented some of his writings to the senior Ottoman officials who were clearly impressed by his vast learning and scholarship. They also requested him to resume the post of judge on his return to Aqhisar, with the added responsibility of teaching Islamic sciences to the local students, which he agreed to do.

Despite working full-time as a judge for the Ottoman authorities, Hasan Kafi found time to research and write profusely on aspects of Islamic law, theology, philosophy, logic and linguistics, among other subjects. He was a senior or contemporary of many other prominent Muslim scholars and writers, including Muhammad ibn Musa Allamak al-Bosnawi (d. 1636), Sijahi Mustafa (d. cir. 1617), Abdullah al-Bosnawi (d. 1644), Ali Boshnaq (d. 1594), Ahmed Sudi Bosnawi (d. 1598) and Beyazizade Ahmed Efendi (d. 1687), among others. But despite this, he stood over and above all of them on account of his mastery of Islamic sciences and enduring contribution to the development of Balkan Muslim thought, culture and literature during the sixteenth century.

As a prolific writer, Hasan Kafi authored seventeen books and treatises, although the Gazi Husrev Bey Library based in Sarajevo has only fourteen titles. According to some scholars, he became known as 'Kafi' – not because it was a part of his name – but on account of his attachment to Abu Amr Uthman ibn Umar ibn al-Hajib's (d. 1248) *al-Kafiyah*, a famous work on Arabic grammar, which Hasan taught throughout his career as a scholar and teacher.[4] However, according to another view, he first used 'Kafi' as his artistic name upon completing his two treatises on logic, namely *Mukhtasar al-Kafi min al-Mantiq* (Kafi's Summary of Logic) and *Sharh Mukhtasar al-Kafi min al-Mantiq* (Commentary on Kafi's Summary of Logic).[5]

Being one of his first books, written when he was in his mid-thirties, the author explained why he composed *Mukhtasar al-Kafi min al-Mantiq* in these words:

> As I noticed that today's students who are immersing themselves in logic are not getting from it what they are looking for, due to an abundance of discrepancies in the texts on logic and as it is hard to give exact interpretations in sciences, I chose a clear compendium based on the books by old authorities and their followers, and thus analysed for those eager to know more, and simplified for those who research, elaborating on the basis of my modest understanding and aware of my limited capacities...[6]

In these two treatises, Hasan Kafi defines the basic terms and principles of logic in the format of textbooks for the benefit of students following in the footsteps of his predecessors, focusing especially on two fundamental aspects of logic, namely 'conceptions' and 'assertions'. He explains the origins of both in logical discourse and their relevance to the study of this subject. His *Mukhtasar* was an introduction to logic while the *Sharh*, composed three years later, was a detailed commentary on the former to help students develop a better knowledge and understanding of the science of logic. Some of his other well-known books and treatises include *Usul al-Hikam wa Nizam al-'Alam* (Principles of Wisdom about the Political System of the World), *Rawdat al-Jannah fi Usul al-I'tiqadat* (Gardens of Paradise in the Principles of Beliefs), *Nur al-Yaqin fi Usul al-Din* (Light of Certainty in the Principles of Religion) and *Nizam al-Ulama ila Khatm al-Anbiya* (Order of the Scholars leading to the Seal of Prophets).

Unlike his introductory texts on logic and aspects of Arabic grammar, Hasan Kafi's *Usul al-Hikam* was a treatise on political thought and administration. Originally written in Arabic around 1596 and subsequently translated by the author into Turkish for the benefit of his Ottoman patrons, this short treatise is divided into an introduction and three chapters As in the *Nasihat al-Muluk*, attributed to Abul Hasan Ali al-Mawardi (Latinised: Alboacen, d. 1058), in which the author offers sincere advice to the rulers of his time, Hasan Kafi went out of his way to highlight the reasons for the political, economic and military challenges that faced the Ottomans at the time. Concerned by the gradual decline of the Ottoman Empire, coupled with increasing internal strife, growing corruption and moral laxity, the author was keen to restore a semblance of 'order' (*nizam*) in the prevailing chaos and disorder that had gripped the Ottoman power and administration.

Not surprisingly, soon after completing his treatise, Hasan Kafi presented copies to the Ottoman hierarchy for them to read and reflect on his political advice and guidance. He hoped that in so doing, they would address the challenges facing them at the time without any hesitation or delay. Impressed by his insight and scholarly discourse, the Ottoman elite encouraged him to develop his thesis further and, in response, Hasan Kafi authored a detailed commentary on his treatise and subsequently presented it to his patrons during one of his journeys to Istanbul. As expected, he was praised for his scholarly contribution and efforts.

By comparison, Hasan Kafi's *Rawdat al-Jannah* and *Nur al-Yaqin* are theological works focusing on aspects of Islamic beliefs and practices. His books are based on the theological and legal works of early Islamic luminaries like Abu Hanifah (d. 767), Abul Hasan al-Ash'ari (d. 936), Abu Ja'far al-Tahawi (d. 933) and Abu Mansur al-Maturdi (d. 944) as well as Sa'd al-Din al-Taftazani (d. 1390), Mir Sayyid Sharif Jurjani (d. 1339), Fakhr al-Din al-Razi (d. 1209), Abu Hafs Umar al-Nasafi (d. 1142) and Jalal al-Din al-Suyuti (d. 1505), not to mention the prominent Ottoman scholars of the time. A quick browse through his treatises shows that Hasan Kafi was not only thoroughly familiar with *ilm al-kalam* (dialectic theology), *usul al-din* (fundamental beliefs and practices of Islam) and *usul al-fiqh* (science of Islamic jurisprudence), but his knowledge and understanding of the complexities and intricacies of these sciences are equally impressive.

Indeed, his profound scholarship is reflected in his multi-dimensional understanding of Islam: despite being an admirer of Imam al-Maturidi, he preferred Imam al-Tahawi's traditionalism over the former's rationalistic tendencies and, although he was a staunch Hanafi, he was closer to the Salafis in his literalist approach to the scriptural sources of Islam. In other words, 'one can say that Hasan Kafi Akhisari combined Hanafite Maturidism with some Salafi principles in order to present the essentials of Islamic faith in a clear way, and to avoid disputations in the matters of religion.'[7]

Growing up in sixteenth century Ottoman Bosnia, Hasan Kafi witnessed first-hand the dangers of theological disputation and wrangling, as different sects emerged to misguide the masses. For example, Hasan Kafi was highly critical of the Ibahi and Hamzawi Tariqas of the Balkans. Likewise, he refuted the Mu'tazilite, *falsafa*, *Ahl al-Kitab*, deviant Sufi groups and others. After studying and analysing each one of them, he repudiated their beliefs and practices, and in so doing, he became a champion of traditional Islam. He was one of the first Bosnian Muslim scholars to emphasise the importance of adhering to the Prophetic guidance and methodology (*minhaj al-sunnah al-nabawiyyah*) in public and private, individually and collectively. He made this very clear in his explanation of the meaning, purpose and relevance of a Prophetic tradition that is otherwise known as *Hadith* of Jibril (Gabriel).

In addition to the above, Hasan Kafi authored two other books, namely *Nizam al-Ulama* and *Risalah fi Tahqiq Lafz 'Calabi'* (Treatise on Exposition of the Word 'Chalabi'). The former is essentially a biographical work, which also includes his own autobiography, being the penultimate entry of the book. In total, the book consists of thirty biographies of prominent Muslim personalities. The entry on his own life and work has been translated into English but, unfortunately, the original Arabic version is yet to be thoroughly edited and published.[8]

However, according to some scholars, Hasan Kafi's *Risalah* was in fact his first book and, as the title suggests, it provides a detailed explanation of the meaning, origin and development of the word 'Chalabi' for the benefit of his readers. Needless to say, this book is also an important contribution to the study of aspects of language, literature, culture and history of the Balkans during Ottoman rule. In addition to the above, he wrote a commentary on *Mukhtasar al-Quduri* of Imam Abul Husayn Ahmad al-Quduri al-Baghdadi (d. 1036), which is a standard work on Hanafi *fiqh*, and published it in four volumes for the benefit of the Muslims of the Balkans and beyond.

Needless to say, Hasan Kafi combined his study of Arabic, Islamic sciences, theology, philosophy, logic and history with his passion for teaching, for which he was granted a pension for life by the Ottoman authorities. Although he was a pious and frugal individual, very little is known about his personal and family life. However, what we do know is that he spent most of his money on charitable and philanthropic work, such as establishing religious endowments (*awqaf,* sing. *waqf*), through which he himself funded the establishment and running of several mosques, *madrasas* (Islamic seminaries), *maktabs* (Islamic primary schools), public baths, kitchens, lodges for travellers, water supply systems and other similar projects.

After a very productive and fruitful life, Hasan Kafi died at the age of around 71 and was laid to rest in his native Aqhisar. The Muslims of the Balkans, especially Bosnia and Herzegovina, will no doubt, remain forever grateful to Hasan Kafi for his remarkable and enduring contributions. In the words of the historian Caterina Bori,

> Today, Hasan Kafi al-Aqhisari represents a major reference point in the revival of the Bosniac Islamic legacy, in the spirit of which some of his theological works are now being edited. In spite of this, his theological views remain to be studied, and many of his works are still in manuscript form.[9]

Ⓝ

1. Noel Malcolm, *Bosnia: A Short History*.
2. IRCICA, *Proceedings of the Second International Symposium on Islamic Civilisation in the Balkans*.
3. Amir Ljubovic, *The Works in Logic by Bosniac Authors in Arabic*.
4. IRCICA, op. cit.
5. Amir Ljubovic, op. cit.
6. Ibid.
7. IRCICA, op. cit.
8. Jan Just Witkam, *Manuscripts of the Middle East*.
9. Emad El-Din Shahin (ed.), *Encyclopedia of Islam and Politics*.

# 21

# SAFIYE SULTAN

B. 1550 – D. 1605

ALBANIA

The popular view that Muslim women, historically speaking, did not play a worthwhile role in the political, economic and cultural development of the Muslim world is not only misleading, but also factually inaccurate. During the heyday of the Ottoman Empire alone, several Muslim women who were of European origin became the real movers and shakers within the empire which, at the time, had spread over three continents, being one of the most powerful in history. We have already covered the life and works of Hurrem Sultan (Roxelana), who was of Polish/Ukrainian origin and was the wife of Sulaiman the Magnificent, the tenth ruler of the Ottoman Empire (see chapter 19 for more information).

Like Roxelana, Afife Nurbanu Sultan (d. 1583) was another powerful European Muslim woman who went on to exert huge influence on Ottoman political and economic affairs in the sixteenth century. Of Venetian origin, her original name was Cecilia Venier-Baffo and she may have been of Jewish background. In her role as the consort of Sultan Salim II (r. 1566–1574) and subsequently as the mother of Sehzade Murad (b. 1546), the heir to the Ottoman throne, she exerted huge influence on Ottoman administration and, in the process, played a key role in forging closer ties between the Ottomans and her native Kingdom of Venice.

Like Roxelana and Nurbanu, Safiye Sultan was also an immensely influential woman of European origin, who went on to dominate Ottoman politico-economic affairs for more than a quarter of a century. Along the way, she became the first Muslim lady to exchange correspondence with Queen Elizabeth I of England.

According to one account, Safiye Valide Sultan, better known as Safiye Sultan, hailed from Venice and was the daughter of the governor of Corfu. She was reportedly captured by the Ottomans during one of their raids and subsequently found herself recruited into the private quarters (*harem*) of the Sultan.[1] According to others, however, she was of Moldavian, Bosnian or Slavic origin. Although, if the Venetian Giovanni Francesco Morosini (1585) is to be believed, she actually hailed from the village of Rezi, most probably modern Kryezi, located in the mountains of north-western Albania, and the majority of historians now accept this as the most reliable account of her origins.[2]

Like so many of her predecessors, Safiye must have been brought to Istanbul, the capital of the empire, by the Ottoman army during one of their raids in the Balkans. At the time, Istanbul had one of the biggest and busiest slave markets where young girls often found themselves. Safiye (Arabic: *Safiya*, meaning the 'pure one') may have been recruited into the household of Mihrimah Sultan (1522–1578), the daughter of Sulaiman the Magnificent, before the former presented her to Murad, the eldest son of future Sultan Salim II. Safiye was still a teenager at the time but, due to her youthful beauty, charming personality and jovial character, the 17 year old Murad instantly fell in love with her.

Born in Manisa in 1546, Murad was adored by his parents, Salim and Afife Nurbanu, and a year later his circumcision ceremony was celebrated with much pomp and pageantry. His grandfather, Sulaiman the Magnificent, was the reigning Sultan at the time. Later he was appointed as a *Sanjakbey* (or senior governor), first in the Ottoman district of Aksehir and subsequently in Saruhan. After the death of Sultan Sulaiman, Salim II ascended the Ottoman throne on 7 September 1566. He posted Murad, his eldest son, to Manisa as governor of the province, thus he continued to serve in this capacity until his father died in December 1574.

During this period, Murad lived in Manisa with his beloved Safiye and, unlike other Ottoman princes, did not take any other partners at the time. In the meantime, Safiye had given birth to Sehzade Muhammad (Mehmed), Murad's only son. He was around 28 when his father died and, being the oldest son of Sultan Salim II, he occupied the Ottoman throne. However, he found himself facing a series of political and economic crises at home and abroad. If the Ottoman defeat at the hands of the Holy League on 7 October 1571, otherwise known as the Battle of Lepanto, represented a major political setback, then the economic condition within the empire was not much better either. Hitherto the Ottoman economic model was one of self-sufficiency. Unfortunately, such a closed economic system was now facing serious challenges from a 'centralised mercantilist economy' that was emerging across Europe, coupled with European expansion into the Americas and Africa, whilst the Ottomans were busy with their internal politics, in-fighting and rivalry.[3]

That is why the reign of Salim II is regarded by the historians of the Ottoman Empire as the beginning of the 'sedentary rule' because, unlike the early sultans, he confined himself to his palace and engaged in merry-making, whilst leaving the affairs of the empire to his senior officials who often fought each other to protect their personal gains, positions and power. In the process, the officials allowed corruption, bribery and disorder to spread. Like his father, Sultan Murad III was a 'sedentary' ruler who never took to the battlefield and instead, confined himself to his private quarters where he led a life of nothing but fun, pleasure and prayers. The Sultan's regimented lifestyle has been vividly described by his personal physician as follows:

> In the morning he rises at dawn to say his prayer for half an hour, then for another half hour he writes. Then he is given something pleasant as a collation, and afterwards sets himself to read for another hour. Then he begins to give audience to the members of the Divan on the four days of the week that occurs, as has been said above. Then he goes for a walk…then he goes back again to studying until he considers the time for lunch has arrived. He stays at the table only for half an hour…Then he goes to say his midday prayer. Then he stops to pass the time and amuse himself with the women…[until] the evening prayer…Then he dines and takes more time over dinner than over lunch, making conversation until two hours after dark, until it is time for prayer…He never fails to observe this schedule every day.[4]

Thanks to the Sultan's self-imposed seclusion and disinterest in politics, the affairs of the empire were once again left in the hands of the senior officials and particularly his ambitious and domineering mother, Nurbanu, who accordingly became the most powerful person in the Ottoman administration at the time. After 1581, when Sultan Murad was in his mid-thirties, his private life also became increasingly complicated, partly due to his mother who urged him to father more children for the sake of political stability and continuity. Prior to this, Safiye was his only partner and the mother of Sehzade Muhammad, his only son and heir apparent.

Though Safiye initially resented Murad's proclivities and excesses, she retained her dignity and fully co-operated with the Sultan and his mother until the latter died in December 1583. This cleared the way for Safiye to exercise more influence on the Sultan and, according to the Ottoman historian Gelibolulu Mustafa Ali Celebi (1541–1600), she also became Sultan Murad's legal wife. Indeed, as the only wife of the Sultan and the mother of his successor, Safiye was now more close to the ruler than anyone else within the Ottoman administration. Indeed, her presence was felt within the Inner and Outer services of the empire. According to the historian Stanford Jay Shaw (1930–2006),

> Proximity to the ruler has traditionally enhanced the importance of individuals throughout Middle Eastern history. Those in the palace had the special power and authority not only to provide, educate, and maintain rulers – and also to ensure that there would always be at least one prince who would be able to rule

when needed – but also to make the entire Ottoman system operate. The Palace itself was divided structurally and symbolically between the isolated rear areas, the harem, and the Inner Section (*Enderun*), on the one hand, and the more accessible Outer Section (*Birun*), on the other.[5]

As the *haseki sultan* (mother of the heir to the throne), Safiye now wielded considerable power and authority, especially as the Sultan also trusted her more than anyone else. Not surprisingly, she had a say in the appointment of senior Ottoman officials, including the post of grand vizier. Indeed, after the death of the influential Sokolovic Muhammad (Mehmed) Pasha (1506–1579) – a Serbian convert to Islam who had served as grand vizier to three successive Ottoman sultans, namely Sulaiman the Magnificent, Salim II and Murad III – Safiye made use of her influence.

With much credit to Sayife, Damat Ibrahim Pasha (1517–1601), who was of Bosnian origin and her son-in-law, became the grand vizier of the Ottoman Empire. Ibrahim was a clever and crafty political operator and was equally renowned for his military skills in the battlefield. After serving as governor of Egypt during the reign of Murad III, he returned to Istanbul following the latter's death in December 1595 and served Muhammad (Mehmed) III, who was his brother-in-law, as chief advisor and confidant. Hereon, the Ottoman administration was completely dominated by the trio, namely the Sultan himself, Safiye as the *valide sultan* (mother of the reigning sultan) and Ibrahim Pasha as the grand vizier, although in reality the real influence was driven by Safiye.

During Sultan Muhammad III's reign of nearly eight years, Safiye was in full control of both the internal and external affairs of the empire. In addition to consolidating her grip on power within the royal family, for which she was admired by some and equally criticised by others, she also went out of her way to establish Ottoman relations with the two leading European powers of the time: namely Venice and England. As it happened, the military encounters between the Ottoman's and their European rivals had overshadowed other aspects of their relations, particularly the thriving commercial and cultural contact that existed since the early days of the empire. As early as 1352, the Italian republic of Genoa was offered trading licences by the Ottomans, and the same was granted to Venice in 1403 and France in 1536.

Keen not to be left behind,

By the late 1570s England was ready to join its European neighbours in establishing diplomatic and commercial ties with the Ottoman Empire. The first formal contact between England and the Porte commenced with the arrival of William Harborne, who was a factor of Sir Richard Osborne, one of the well-established merchants in London, in Istanbul in 1579. Harbone's visit signals the launching of diplomatic and mercantile relations between Sultan Murad III and Queen Elizabeth.[6]

William Harborne (1542–1617), the son of William Harebrowne of Great Yarmouth, Norfolk, became the first ambassador sent by the Queen to Istanbul. This happened as a result of an exchange of correspondence between Sultan Murad III (r. 1574–1595) and Queen Elizabeth I (r. 1558–1603) in 1579. This heralded a new era in Anglo-Ottoman relations, paving the way for Safiye, in her capacity as a prominent figure in the Ottoman administration, as well as the wife of Sultan Murad III and subsequently as the mother of Sultan Muhammad III, to take further steps to strengthen Ottoman diplomatic and commercial relations with England.[7] Just as she had previously dissuaded her husband from launching an attack against Venice in the face of maritime provocation, this time she took the initiative and exchanged three letters with Elizabeth I: the first of which was sent in 1593, and the two following letters were sent in 1599, when her son was the sultan. A summary of the first letter reads as follows:

> After elaborate praises of God and eulogies of the Prophet [Muhammad], Safiye, mother of the heir-apparent Mehemmed, sends greetings to the Queen of England. Briefly alluding to the Queen's gifts, she acknowledges the letter which the Queen's ambassador delivered with them to the Qapuagha who, for his part, had handed them to her attendant. The letter has been read to her and its message understood; further correspondence is encouraged so that the Queen's requests to the Sultan may be transmitted to him by Safiye in person.[8]

Along with her letter, Queen Elizabeth had sent Safiye several gifts. For example, she gifted Safiye with a ceremonial carriage that was used by her as transport from time to time, which the ordinary Ottomans no doubt found rather strange and bemusing. In return, she sent the Queen of England a robe, two gold-embroidered bath towels, handkerchiefs and a ruby, among other things. Looking beyond the friendship struck by the two remarkable ladies, there is no doubt that Anglo-Ottoman relations were also strengthened by their mutual anti-Spanish and anti-Catholic policies. The issue of maritime trade and commerce was equally important to both parties. The fact that two influential women on both sides were the real catalysts in forging such an important and enduring diplomatic relationship is something that needs to be known and recognised more widely.

Safiye's efforts to improve Ottoman relations with its European counterparts aside; her continuous meddling in the administrative affairs of the empire, coupled with the financial mismanagement that was taking place at the time, soon made her unpopular at home. This was a time when the Ottoman coffers were shrinking fast, her personal daily allowance was 3000 aspers (silver coins), making her the highest paid woman in the history of the empire.

To make matters worse, some of her personal officials had amassed large quantities of wealth and properties which eventually prompted the imperial cavalry to instigate a rebellion, only for Sultan Muhammad III (r. 1595–1603) to intervene and reassure the soldiers that he would address their concerns. Safiye was also blamed for the execution of her grandson, Sehzade Mahmud, because she intercepted a message that suggested the latter was destined to become sultan upon the death of his father within a few months. Upon hearing this, the sultan had his son strangled to death, perhaps because his son was becoming more popular with the army and the masses, thus he may have felt threatened by him.

On a personal level, however, Safiye was a pious, educated and independent-minded lady who initiated many charitable and philanthropic activities. She funded several public projects, including the construction of Yeni Cami or the 'New Mosque' in Istanbul in 1597, but unfortunately it was not completed during her life time due to financial and other problems. It was eventually completed by Turhan Hatice Sultan (1627–1683), who was of Ukrainian origin and the mother of Sultan Muhammad (Mehmed) V, in 1665. Originally known as Valide Sultan Mosque because Safiye had initiated its construction when she became the mother of the reigning sultan, it is located on the Golden Horn and is today regarded as one of the most impressive works of architecture in Istanbul.

The Al-Malika Safiye Mosque or 'Queen Safiyya Mosque', located in Safiye Square in Cairo, is another important edifice that bears her name. This mosque was initiated in 1610 by Uthman Agha, who was one of Safiye's officials there, and the endowment created for its upkeep was very generous, stipulating that thirty-nine people should be employed to oversee all aspects of its daily operation and activities for the benefit of the local people and all its visitors.

However, after the death of Sultan Muhammad III in December 1603, he was succeeded by his devout son, Ahmad I (1590–1617), whose mother, Handan Sultan (Helena), was of Greek origin. He was around 13 years of age when he ascended the Ottoman throne. One of the first decisions he made after becoming sultan was to deprive Safiye, his grandmother, of all her powers. Thereafter, she moved to the Old Palace where she continued to live until her death at the age of around 68. One of her great legacies was that all the subsequent Ottoman sultans descended from her.

1. Lord Kinross, *The Ottoman Centuries: The Rise and Fall of the Turkish Empire*.

2. Leslie P. Peirce, *The Imperial Harem: Women and Sovereignty in the Ottoman Empire*.

3. Stanford J. Shaw, *History of the Ottoman Empire and Modern Turkey*.

4. Ozgen Felek, *Re-creating Image and Identity: Dreams and Visions as a Means of Murad III's Self-Fashioning*.

5. Stanford J. Shaw, op. cit.

6. Fatima Essadek, *Representations of Ottoman Sultans in Elizabethan Times*.

7. Christopher J. Walker, *Islam and the West: A Dissonant Harmony of Civilisations*.

8. S. A. Skilliter, 'Three Letters from the Ottoman "Sultana" Safiye to Queen Elizabeth I' in *Documents from Islamic Chanceries*.

# 22

# EVLIYA CELEBI

B. 1550 – D. 1605

TURKEY

Historians have agreed that the Ottoman Empire had the most profound impact on Europe from the mid-fourteenth to the late seventeenth century. It was again, their failure to take Vienna in 1683, coupled with the signing of the Treaty of Karlowitz on 26 January, 1699, that marked the beginning of their retreat from Europe. At the time, the Ottoman's were also locked in a military confrontation with another powerful foe in the East, namely the Safavids of Persia who reigned from 1502 to 1716. Facing such mounting political, economic and military challenges and difficulties in Europe and Asia, the Ottoman's tried to consolidate their presence in Africa, having successfully overthrown the Mamluk Sultanate during the second decade of the sixteenth century.[1]

By conquering vast sways of territories across three continents, the Ottoman's successfully established their suzerainty as far as central Europe, parts of Asia and North Africa, and in so doing, it became one of the most influential and enduring dynasties in history. Following in the footsteps of Ibn Jubayr, Marco Polo and Ibn Battutah; Evliya Celebi, an Ottoman nobleman and scholar, travelled extensively across Europe, Central Asia and Africa. He meticulously recorded his views and observations about the places he visited in the form of a multi-volume travel account that is today regarded as one of the great monuments of global history, culture and heritage. In the process, Evliya Celebi became one of the most outstanding and gifted travel writers of all time.

Evliya ibn Dervis Muhammad (Mehmed) Zilli, better known as Evliya Celebi, was born to an Ottoman father and Caucasian mother in the historic city of Constantinople (present-day Istanbul) during the early part of the seventeenth century. His father, Muhammad (Mehmed) Agha, also known as Mehmed Zilli, was a jeweller and goldsmith by trade who worked for the Ottoman elite. Through his mother's side, Evliya Celebi was related to Melek Ahmad Pasha (1604–1662), who was a renowned Ottoman statesman and served as the grand vizier to Sultan Muhammad (Mehmed) IV (r. 1648–1687).

Also, Evliya (Arabic *Awliya*, which is literally 'friends [of God]') traced his spiritual and paternal genealogy back to Khwajah Ahmad Yasawi (1093–1166), the founder of the Yasawiyya Sufi *tariqa* (Order). This was an off-shoot of the more famous Naqshbandi *tariqa* that originated in Central Asia in the twelfth century, which subsequently spread to Turkistan, Persia, Afghanistan and India.

Brought up in a relatively wealthy and devout Muslim family, Evliya assimilated Islamic principles and practices from the outset. He studied Arabic, Ottoman Turkish, the Qur'an and aspects of religious sciences from prominent local tutors who were hired by the Ottoman elite to impart a sound education on young boys from notable Turkish families, hoping to prepare them for political, economic, administrative, religious and military roles within the ever-expanding Ottoman Empire.

As a bright student, Evliya swiftly memorised the Qur'an when he was still a teenager and, impressed by his personal piety and retentive memory, he was selected to receive one-to-one tuition from Evliya Muhammad (Mehmed) Efendi, who served as the prayer leader (Imam) to Sultan Murad IV (r. 1623–1640) at the time. Under the tutelage of this scholar, he not only studied traditional Islamic sciences, but also acquired a thorough knowledge of the Qur'an. In his own words,

> From Evliya Efendi I mastered the science of reciting the Koran from memory, and I could recite the entire Koran in eight hours, without addition or subtraction, and without error whether open or hidden …And every Friday eve (Thursday night) I appointed to complete a Koran-recital. God be praised, from childhood until present, whether at home or during my travels, I have not abandoned this practice.[2]

Due to the rigorous training he received under Evliya Efendi's guidance, Evliya soon became an accomplished reciter of the Qur'an. This prompted the religious authorities in Istanbul to invite him to regularly recite the Qur'an in his beautiful and melodious voice at public events. When he was in his early twenties, he was invited to recite the Qur'an in the Aya Sophia, one of the city's most famous mosques. On this occasion, he attracted the attention of Sultan Murad IV (r. 1624–1640). Impressed by his skills and ability, the Sultan recruited him into his palace where Evliya continued to entertain his patron with his recitations of the Qur'an, poetry and story-telling until the latter set out in the direction of Baghdad in 1638. Evliya considered Sultan Murad IV to be a great warrior because he personally led the Ottoman forces into the battlefield against the Safavids, annexing Azerbaijan and other neighbouring territories, before spearheading the Ottoman conquest of Baghdad. In Evliya's own words,

> God be praised that my noble father served as chief goldsmith to all the Ottoman sultans from Suleyman to Ibrahim, and that I was honoured with the companionship of such a noble sovereign and jihad warrior as Murad Khan Gazi. Just before the Baghdad campaign I received his blessings and graduated from the harem into the cavalry corps with a daily allowance of forty *akce*.[3]

After graduating into the Ottoman cavalry corps, Evliya did not become a full-fledged member of the Ottoman military because if he had, he would have become an Agha or Pasha, but destiny had other plans for him. Instead of joining the army and fighting for the imperial forces who were, at the time, locked in fierce battles in Europe, Asia and Africa; Evliya claimed to have seen the Prophet Muhammad (peace be on him) in his dream who approved of his plans to travel extensively, not only to perform the pilgrimage to Makkah and explore the sacred sites of Islam, but also to propagate the faith and meticulously record his travels for the benefit of posterity.

That aside, as an individual, Evliya was far too restless and inquisitive to lead a routine, monotonous and sedentary existence and, not surprisingly, he never stayed in a job for long. Although throughout his career he had worked for many senior Ottoman officials in his capacity as secretary, advisor, religious instructor, courier, interlocutor and Qur'an reciter, he soon established his reputation as Celebi or 'gentleman' on account of his educational attainment, cultural refinement and scholarly disposition.

Indeed, despite hailing from a notable family with considerable wealth and properties in Istanbul, he remained materially detached with virtually no worldly ties, and did so throughout his life. In that sense, Evliya can be considered to have been a wandering Sufi who lived in, and travelled extensively, across three continents, but he did not become unduly attached to any one person or place. He remained a confirmed bachelor all his life and travelled for more than forty years across Europe, Asia and Africa.

Throughout this period, Evliya enjoyed the support, patronage and assistance of many prominent Ottoman governors, military leaders, religious scholars, administrators and other officials, although it was the patronage of Melek Ahmad Pasha that he later recalled with gratitude and much admiration. Melek Pasha was not only his maternal uncle, but he was also an influential Ottoman statesman and governor who actively encouraged his nephew in his travels, providing generous patronage as well as facilitating access to places he may not have otherwise seen. In the words of the historian Rhoads Murphey,

> If a travel account can be said to have a hero, that hero must be the traveller himself. While the *Book of Travels* is no exception to this, it can also be said to have another hero: Melek Ahmed Pasha. For it is not simply a travel account *(seyahatname)*; it is also a chronicle *(tarih)* of Evliya's life and times. The narrative thread, accounting for roughly 5 per cent of the huge ten-book

text, is an autobiographical memoir. And the 'hero' in Evliya's life, from his own perspective, is not himself but his patron. Of the various patrons who sponsored Evliya's career, Melek Ahmed was by far the most important. Their bond of kinship provided the basis for Evliya's attachment to Melek and his household. Evliya served Melek, not only in religious and official capacities, but above all as confidant – we might say, as friend, although their differences in age and in position clearly made Evliya a subordinate.[4]

After fully exploring his native Istanbul and its surroundings whilst in his early twenties, Evliya travelled across Anatolia, the Caucasus and the island of Crete, before proceeding to Azerbaijan in Central Asia. His account of his experience and observations in these places were recorded in volume one and two of the *Seyahatname*, respectively. The first volume is perhaps the most vivid and comprehensive description of Istanbul to have ever been written, and certainly the most important historical and geographical survey of the city to have been produced during the seventeenth century. It provides a detailed description of Istanbul's mosques, schools, buildings, roads, parks, markets, gardens, food, dress, crafts, jobs and its population. Not surprisingly, historians consider this volume as a rich and invaluable source for the study of Ottoman antiquity, as well as social history during the seventeenth century.

By comparison, volume two covers Evliya's account of his travels in the Ottoman city of Bursa, before he joined the company of Ketenci Umar Pasha, who was appointed the governor of Trabzon, located in north-eastern Turkey. However, he returned home having suffered a shipwreck on the Black Sea in October 1642. Thereafter, in August 1646, he set out in the company of Defterdarzade Muhammad (Mehmed) Pasha, who was appointed the governor of Erzurum, located in eastern Turkey. It was during this period that he visited Tabriz, the provincial capital of Safavid Persia, and Baku, the capital of Azerbaijan, before rushing back to Istanbul upon hearing the news of the death of his father in July 1648.

Here, he witnessed, to his surprise, considerable political uncertainty and turmoil which led to the ousting of Sultan Ibrahim I (r. 1640–1648) and the enthronement of Muhammad (Mehmed) IV at the age of only six. Replacing his erratic and unpredictable father, the new Sultan delegated much of his executive powers to his Albanian grand vizier, Koprulu Muhammad (Mehmed) Pasha (b. cir. 1575–1661), and subsequently to the latter's son, Koprulu Fazil Mustafa Pasha (1637–1691). Both individuals proved to be highly competent and accomplished statesmen as they helped transform Ottoman fortunes for the better.

However, being the restless traveller that he was, Evliya did not stay in Istanbul for long, thus he joined the company of Silihdar Murtaza Pasha who had been appointed governor of Damascus in September 1648. From there he moved to Sivas, today located in the Central Anatolian region of Turkey, before returning to Istanbul in July 1650. As he was approaching his fortieth birthday, Evliya decided to accompany Melek Ahmad Pasha to various locations in the latter's capacity as governor. Volume three of the *Seyahatname* records his visits to Thrace, today bordering Bulgaria, Greece, Turkey and the Balkans. He spent the next twelve years in the service of his maternal uncle and in volume four, he documents his time with Melek Pasha in Van, located in eastern Turkey, and his sojourns in Bitlis, Tabriz, Azerbaijan, Persia, Iraq and Kurdistan.

In May 1656, at the age of 45, Evliya returned to Van. However, on this occasion, his patron Melek Pasha sent him to Bitlis to collect tax before he participated in a series of Ottoman military campaigns against the Poles, Cossacks and Moldavians, among others, and re-joined his patron in Sarajevo in 1660. Volume five also covers his visit to Split, where he carefully observed Venetian customs and practices, in addition to polishing up his Italian. He then moved on to Sofia, the capital of present-day Bulgaria, with Melek Pasha who was appointed governor there a year later.

While volumes six and seven largely cover Evliya's travels and adventures in Europe especially in Albania, Austria, Hungary and southern Russia. During this period, Evliya accompanied an Ottoman mission to Vienna, the capital of King Leopold I, under the leadership of Kara Mustafa Pasha, who later served as Sultan Muhammad (Mehmed) IV's military leader and grand vizier from October 1676 to December 1683. Of Albanian origin, Kara Pasha was related to the powerful Koprulu family and he spearheaded Ottoman efforts to expand into Central and Eastern Europe at the time.

Volume eight records his visit to Crimea before returning to Istanbul in May 1667. Later that year, he joined Ottoman efforts to annex the island of Crete from the Kingdom of Venice, this being the longest siege in history from 1648 to 1669. Thereafter, Evliya moved to Adrianople, today known as Edirne, where he presented the reigning Sultan with some hawks that he obtained from Circassia. Sultan Muhammad (Mehmed) IV was a passionate hunter and became known as *Avci Mehmed* (Mehmed the Hunter), thus he appreciated the gift. From here, Evliya set out in the direction of Greece before participating in the last Ottoman campaign to conquer Crete in September 1669. This volume also covers his mission to Albania and other Balkan countries, before returning back to Istanbul in December 1670; he was in his late fifties at the time.

By comparison, volume nine of the *Seyahatname* provides a comprehensive account of Evliya's pilgrimage to Makkah. Prompted by a dream, at the age of 60 he set out for the annual hajj and carefully recorded his views and observations about Makkah and its population. He also visited Madinah, the city of the Prophet, Palestine and the sacred city of Jerusalem, as well as Damascus. His account of the annual hajj is vivid, detailed and one of the most interesting to have been penned by a Muslim during the seventeenth century. That is why Michael Wolfe's failure to include Evliya Celebi in his *One Thousand Roads to Mecca* (1997) is an unfortunate oversight and omission on his part.[5]

Last but not least, volume ten of *Seyahatname* covers the final decade of Evliya's life in Cairo where he decided to settle after completing the pilgrimage to Makkah. Despite also visiting Alexandria, Ethiopia and Sudan during this period, Evliya's account of Cairo, like that of his description of Istanbul, is one of the most vivid and detailed since Taqi al-Din al-Maqrizi's (1364–1442) account of Cairo more than 200 years earlier. After more than half a century of travelling across Europe, the Caucasus, Ottoman Turkey, Central Asia, the Middle East and Persia, Evliya eventually retired at the age of 72. It was here in Cairo that he completed his monumental *Seyahatname* for the benefit of posterity. What motivated him to write this book?

According to the historian Robert Dankoff (b. 1943), a leading authority on the life and works of Evliya Celebi:

> It is clear that Evliya kept systematic notes en route, and that during the periods he was home – first in Istanbul, then in Cairo – he organised the notes into a coherent narrative, the *Book of Travels*…An analysis of the ten volumes shows that throughout the work there is a clash between two organising principles: on the one hand, spatial or geographical; on the other hand, temporal or chronological. Evliya's first aim was to provide a complete description of the Ottoman Empire and its hinterlands. In pursuing this aim, the spatial or topographical survey is the favourite mode…His second aim was to provide a complete record of his travels. In pursuing this aim, the first-person account of his itineraries and adventures comes to the fore. The first mode is imperial in scope, having sources in the 'Roads and Kingdoms' (Arabic: *masalik wa mamalik*) tradition of Muslim geographers…The second mode is personal or autobiographical, with sources in the *rihla* tradition of Muslim travellers, the best known of whom is Ibn Battuta (fourteenth century), whose life and travels overlapped with those of Marco Polo.[6]

Two years after completing his book, Evliya died at the age of around 74 and was most likely buried in Cairo. However, his name and fame soon spread across Ottoman Turkey and beyond, thanks to the discovery of his remarkable ten-volume *Seyahatname*, which is today regarded as a unique travelogue, providing detailed and first-hand information, views, observations and descriptions of life during Ottoman rule in the seventeenth century. According to the historian Ilber Ortayli (b. 1947),

> Today it is not just Turks who find what he has to say interesting but also historians across the world, as well as ordinary Europeans. With his penchant for satire and his sharp wit, Celebi liked to turn to extraordinary contradictions. Because he had a good ear, he also proved to be an excellent documenter of languages. In his travel books it is possible to find traces of Caucasian languages

which are no longer spoken, and this is why people from the Caucasus regard him as an indispensable source.[7]

Little was known about this extraordinary travel account until Evliya's own signed copy was discovered in Cairo in 1742 and brought to Istanbul. Subsequently, it was translated into modern Turkish, while parts of the *Seyahatname* have since been translated into Arabic, Armenian, English, French, Greek, Hungarian, Romanian, Russian and Serbian. Also, a German translation of parts of the *Seyahatname* was undertaken by Joseph von Hammer-Purgstall (1774–1856) in 1814.

Recently, Robert Dankoff and Sooyong Kim have produced a condensed, but highly readable translation of the *Seyahatname* into English under the title of *An Ottoman Traveller: Selections from the Book of Travels of Evliya Celebi* (2010) for the benefit of the English-speaking world.

**(N)**

1. Paul Coles, *The Ottoman Impact on Europe*.
2. Evliya Celebi, *Seyahatname*, quoted by Robert Dankoff & Sooyong Kim, *An Ottoman Traveller*.
3. Ibid.
4. R. Dankoff and R. Murphey, *The Intimate Life of an Ottoman Statesman*.
5. See Michael Wolfe, *One Thousand Roads to Mecca; Ten Centuries of Travelers Writings about the Muslim Pilgrimage*.
6. R. Dankoff and S. Kim, *An Ottoman Traveller: Selections from the Book of Travels of Evliya Celebi*.
7. Ilber Ortayli, *Discovering the Ottomans*.

THE MODERN
PERIOD

# 23

# AYUBA SULAIMAN DIALLO

B. 1701 – D. 1773

UNITED KINGDOM

The history of the transatlantic slave trade is not as widely known today as it ought to be. It transformed the lives of millions of helpless African individuals, both men and women and young and old, who were forcibly taken away from their homes only to die at sea or find themselves working as slave labourers in the plantations of the Americas, West Indies and Europe. The fact that a significant number of the enslaved individuals were African Muslims is equally unknown and unacknowledged. Unsurprisingly, most European history books are silent on the subject.

Although this inhumane and barbaric trade was spearheaded by the British, other European nations were actively involved in it too. Such involvement was inevitable seeing as the profit from slave trade was a quick and easy method of building wealth and gaining the power of influence in society at the time. The fact that such gains were being made at the expense of colossal and unprecedented human suffering, pain and brutality was overlooked, if not deliberately ignored, for a long time.

However, this was until 1787 when a group of Quakers and Anglicans, led by Thomas Clarkson (1760–1846), Granville Sharp (1735–1813) and others, established *The Society for the Abolition of the Slave Trade* in London, the headquarters of the British Empire. Otherwise known as the Abolitionists, the members of the *Society* actively campaigned to end slave trade and thus, their efforts culminated in the passage of the Abolition of the Slave Trade Act in 1807, outlawing British involvement in the transatlantic slave trade. However, it was not until 1833 that the enslavement of African individuals in the British colonies was finally brought to an end, following the Great Reform Act a year earlier.

As the transatlantic slave trade lasted for almost four centuries, historians rightly consider it to be the single most horrific act of forced migration in human history.[1] Yet very little is known about those who perished during this period, other than a handful of individuals who were fortunate enough to not only survive the ordeal, but to also tell the tale of their lives and experiences. Umar ibn Sa'id was one of them. Born around 1770 in a region bordering present-day Senegal and Gambia, he hailed from a wealthy and educated Muslim family and went on to become a teacher of Arabic and Islamic studies. Thereafter, he engaged in trade and soon established a thriving business.

Whilst he was travelling in pursuit of trade, he was captured and sold into slavery by the Portuguese. After a gruelling journey across the Atlantic, he found himself in America at the age of around 38. There, he worked in the plantations and subsequently lived with a Christian family, creating a harmonious blend between his inner Islam and Christian surroundings until his death in 1859 in North Carolina. To his credit, Umar wrote a short account of his early life, his experiences as a slave and his time spent with the American family. Written in Arabic, his autobiography consisted of only twenty-five pages which was later translated into English.

Bilali Muhammad was another prominent Muslim to be enslaved in America. Born in the 1780s in Timbu (Timbo), the capital of the Muslim State in the Futa Djallon of Guinea in West Africa, he was brought up in a traditional Muslim family. He acquired sufficient education during his early years, hence his abilities to read, write and speak Arabic. Before his fifteenth birthday, he was captured and sold into slavery. He was first taken to the Bahamas before arriving in Georgia, America where he worked at the Spalding Plantation, which was owned by Thomas Spalding (1774–1851).

As a devout Muslim, Bilali prayed regularly, fasted during the month of Ramadan, engaged in other devotional activities and reportedly died with a copy of the Qur'an tied to his chest. He worked hard and was later appointed supervisor of around 500 other slaves by his master. During his lifetime, Bilali also wrote a short manual of Islamic jurisprudence (*fiqh*) in Arabic, drawing on the well-known *Risalah* (Treatise) of Ibn Abi Zayd of Qayrawan (922–996) for the guidance of his fellow Muslims.[2]

Like Bilali Muhammad, Abd al-Rahman Ibrahim ibn Sori was born in 1762 in Timbu and hailed from a princely family. He was highly educated, having studied Arabic and Islamic sciences in Timbuktu, Mali, but was captured by the slave traders during a military expedition; he was in his mid-twenties at the time. He was subsequently transferred to Mississippi, America and worked there on a cotton plantation before securing his release from captivity, due to the intervention of Sultan Abd al-Rahman of Morocco. He had a large family and died in Monrovia, Liberia at around the age of 67. Like Bilali, Abd al-Rahman also wrote in Arabic and composed two short autobiographies, documenting his life and career for the benefit of posterity.

Two other individuals worth mentioning here are Lamen Kebe and Abu Bakr Sadiq. The former was born into a notable African Muslim family and received a thorough education in Arabic and Islamic sciences during his early years. He excelled in his studies and went on to become a headmaster of a local school, of course, before he was captured and transferred to America in 1804. He was enslaved in Alabama, Georgia and South Carolina for nearly three decades. Eventually he was freed and, in 1835, he returned to Africa. Abu Bakr Sadiq, on the other hand, was born in 1790 in Timbuktu, the ancient seat of Islamic learning in Mali, Africa. He hailed from a distinguished Muslim family and learned the Qur'an as a child.

He was barely 15 when he was captured and sold into slavery, before being shipped to Jamaica to spend more than a decade working as a slave. Like all of these individuals, thousands of other noble and educated African Muslims were captured and sold into slavery during the sixteenth, seventeenth, eighteenth and nineteenth centuries by the Europeans. As a result, they found themselves working in locations across the Americas, West Indies and Europe, and their lives, stories and tales must never be forgotten nor neglected. However, only one individual was able to transcend the untold struggle, hardship and suffering that was endured by millions of enslaved Africans at the time. He was Ayuba Sulaiman Diallo, whose life and career is a shining example of an African who was equally at home in the West.

Ayuba Sulaiman Diallo, better known in Europe and America as Job ben Solomon, was born into a prominent Muslim family in the West African State of Bundu, located today in eastern Senegal. His father was a notable Muslim scholar who served the local Fulani (Fulbe) people in his capacity as a religious advisor and guide (Imam). The Fulanis were the majority at the time, unlike the Mandingos, who, however, dominated trade and commerce. According to the American historian Michael Gomez, the State of Bundu was a Muslim polity that had,

> Played a major role in the development of commerce in Senegambia in the eighteenth and nineteenth centuries. Strategically placed between the Senegal and Gambia rivers, Bundu served as a major staging area through which the gold of neighbouring Bambuk and slaves from Segu and kaarta flowed westward, in exchange for European goods. A focus for competition between French and British trading interests, Bundu was also a major source of cotton and sustenance for the entire Senegambia region.[3]

Despite growing up during a politically and economically turbulent period, Young Ayuba studied Arabic and traditional Islamic sciences under the guidance of his father,

Sulaiman, who was a prominent scholar in his own right, as was his grandfather, Ibrahim. The latter was an unusually learned Muslim scholar and the founder of Bundu town which, at the time, was the capital of Futa, an African Muslim dynasty ruled by King Abu Bakr. After completing his formal education at the age of around 15, Ayuba assisted his father in his duties as a religious guide. In due course, he married into a notable Muslim family and his young wife bore him three sons, namely Abdullah, Ibrahim and Sambu. In addition to being tall, slim, with long curly black hair, Ayuba had an equally likeable personality and character. A devout Muslim since his early years, he combined his role as an Assistant Imam to his father with trade, enabling him to take good care of his family.

He proved to be successful in both roles and, at the age of around 28, he married another lady who bore him a daughter called Fatimah, named after the younger daughter of Prophet Muhammad (peace be upon him). Growing up in a polygamous society, it is not surprising that Ayuba married two wives and fathered four children before he had attained his thirtieth birthday. It was also common for young men who hailed from learned and respectable families to engage in business and trade. During one of his business trips to a neighbouring territory, he was captured and sold to Captain Pike (Pyke), an Englishman who was involved in the slave trade.

Although Ayuba hailed from a prominent African Muslim family who had strong links to the rulers of the Futa dynasty, he happened to be in the wrong place at the wrong time. This resulted in many Africans of princely backgrounds being caught up in the thriving transatlantic slave trade of the time. Despite his frantic efforts to communicate with his family to inform them of his plight, unfortunately help did not arrive in time. The ship soon set off from Africa bound for the United States with Ayuba on-board.

Resigned to his fate, the long journey across the Atlantic was, no doubt, fraught with considerable hardship and danger for the 30 year old African nobleman, before the ship finally reached Annapolis, located in the present-day US State of Maryland. Along with the other slaves, he was handed over to Mr Vachell Denton, who was in the service of a more influential trader called Mr Hunt, perhaps Captain Henry Hunt of Liverpool. Thereafter, he was sold to another trader, named Mr Tolsey, who, according to Thomas Bluett (1690–1749), Ayuba's contemporary and first biographer, employed him in his tobacco plantation in Kent Island, Maryland only to find that,

JOB [Ayuba] had never been used to such Labour. He every Day shewed more and more Uneasiness under his Exercise, and at last grew sick, being no way able to bear it; so that his Master was obliged to find easier Work for him, and therefore put him to tend the Cattle. JOB would often leave the Cattle, and withdraw into the Woods to pray; but a white Boy frequently watched him, and whilst he was at his Devotion would mock him, and throw Dirt in his Face. This very much disturbed JOB, and added to his other Misfortunes; all which were increased by his Ignorance of the *English* Language, which prevented his complaining, or telling his Case to any Person about him.[4]

Unable to communicate in English and explain his plight to his master, Ayuba soon escaped from captivity in desperation. After travelling for many days through the local forests and jungles, he found himself in the County of Kent. Ayuba was subsequently captured and put behind bars as he could not account for himself. According to the prevailing local law, any slave who was unknown to the authorities, did not carry a valid pass or could not explain themselves to the law enforcement agencies would automatically be imprisoned until a valid claim was made for their release by their owner. Whilst Ayuba was struggling to explain himself to the authorities in the local courthouse, Thomas Bluett, who was a Christian priest and lawyer, encountered him for the first time. In Reverend Bluett's own words,

> This happened about the Beginning of *June*, 1731, when I, who was attending the Courts there, and had heard of JOB, went with several Gentlemen to the Gaoler's House, being a Tavern, and desired to see him. He was brought into the Tavern to us, but could not speak one Word of *English*. Upon our Talking and making Signs to him, he wrote a Line or two before us, and when he read it, pronounced the Words *Allah* and *Mahommed* [Muhammad] by which, and his refusing a Glass of Wine we offered him, we perceived he was a *Mahometan* [Muslim], but could not imagine of what Country he was, or how he got thither; for by his affable Carriage, and the easy Composure of his Countenance, we could perceive he was no common Slave.[5]

However, with the help of a local African interpreter, it became clear to Mr Tolsey, his master, that Ayuba was not an ordinary slave; rather, he was a learned individual who hailed from a noble African family. Accordingly, Mr Tolsey took pity on the young man and treated him well, encouraging him to write a letter to his father in Arabic. Subsequently, the letter found its way to James Oglethorpe (1696–1785), who was initially the Director and later became the Deputy Governor of the Royal African Company.

Unable to read Arabic, he sent the letter to John Gagnier (b. cir. 1670–1740), a Frenchman who was then serving as the Laudian Chair of Arabic at Oxford University, for it to be translated into English. As soon as the authenticity of the letter was confirmed, James Oglethrope took steps to free Ayuba from bondage, which was achieved on the payment of £40 and another £20 was raised to pay for his travel and related costs. Accordingly, Ayuba boarded a ship called *William*, which was under the command of Captain Wright, and sailed to England in April 1733 where he lived with Rev. Thomas Bluett in Cheshunt, Hertfordshire, as James Oglethorpe was on a business trip to

Georgia, America at the time. During his stay with Rev. Bluett, Ayuba made efforts to learn English and was soon able to speak and write reasonably well.

In the meantime, Ayuba's English patrons and supporters in London had collected sufficient funds to purchase an official document from the Royal African Company confirming his freedom from enslavement. Now officially freed from bondage, Ayuba was able to move around London without the fear of being enslaved or put away into captivity again. His new-found freedom enabled him to mingle and socialise with London's elite. In the process, he befriended many wealthy and prominent people including their Royal Highnesses, the Earl of Pembroke and members of the Royal African Company, receiving numerous gifts, awards and recognition in the process.

He also became a member of the Gentlemen's Society of Spalding. He was arguably the first Muslim to achieve such a notable position in the City of London back in the mid-eighteenth century, as he did so without diluting or undermining his faith and culture as an African Muslim. Indeed, according to Thaddeus Mason Harris,

> Job's knowledge of Arabic rendered him serviceable to Sir Hans Sloane, often employed him in translating Arabic manuscripts, and inscriptions upon medals. To bring him into due notice, Sir Hans had him dressed in the customs of his country, and presented to the king and royal family; by whom he was graciously received; and her majesty gave him a beautiful gold watch. The same day he dined with the Duke of Montague; who afterwards took him to his country seat, where he was shewn, and taught the use of, the tools employed in agriculture and gardening. The same nobleman procured for him a great number of these implements, which were put into cases, and carried aboard the vessel in which he was to return to his native country.[6]

With Ayuba's assistance, Sir Hans Sloane (1660–1753), who was a renowned physicist, naturalist and the curator of the Museum at the time, was able to rearrange the Arabic manuscripts at the British Museum and translate many Arabic coin inscriptions. After staying in London for almost a year and a half, in July 1734, Ayuba, accompanied by Thomas Moore, boarded a ship belonging to the Royal African Company and set off for Gambia and from there, to his native Bundu where he stayed until his death at the age of around 72. He left London with gifts and presents worth in excess of £500, which was a significant sum in those days.

However, before his departure, his friend Thomas Bluett wrote a short account of his life which was later published in English and French. The full title of his memoir was *Some Memoirs of the Life of Job, the Son of Solomon, the High Priest of Boonda in Africa; Who was a Slave about Two Years in Maryland; and Afterwards Being Brought to England, Was Set Free and Sent to his Native Land in the Year 1734.* This account of his life was published in London by R. Ford in 1734 and was sold for one shilling a copy. It is today considered to be one of the first biographies of a former slave to have been written in English, thus marking the beginning of the genre of slave literature.[7]

A portrait of Ayuba was also painted in 1733 by William Hoare of Bath (1707–1792), which is now based at the National Portrait Gallery in London, following the gallery's successful campaign to raise more than half a million pounds to keep the portrait in London.

Ⓝ

1. See Allan D. Austin, *African Muslims in Antebellum America*; Sylviane A. Diouf, *Servants of Allah: African Muslims Enslaved in the Americas*.

2. M. A. Al-Ahari (ed.), *Five Classic Muslim Slave Narratives*.

3. Michael Gomez, 'Bundu in the Eighteenth Century', *The International Journal of African Historical Studies*.

4. Thomas Bluett, *The Memoirs of the Life of Job, the Son of Solomon, the High Priest of Boonda in Africa*; also Al-Ahari, op. cit.

5. Ibid.

6. Thaddeus Mason Harris, *Biographical Memorials of James Oglethorpe: Founder of the Colony of Georgia in North America*.

7. Douglas Grant, *The Fortunate Slave: An Illustration of African Slavery in the Eighteenth Century*.

# 24

# LORD HENRY STANLEY OF ALDERLEY

B. 1827 – D. 1903

UNITED KINGDOM

What does it mean to be British? Who decides what it means to be British? Who is or is not a Muslim? Is there such a thing as 'British Muslim' and, if so, how is one to make sense of the complexity and diversity of Britishness on the one hand, and the equally complex and cosmopolitan nature of the Muslim communities in the United Kingdom on the other? At a time when British Muslims are, once again, in the spotlight and their faith, identity and loyalty are being openly questioned and contested by many politicians, policy-makers, journalists and the mass media, it is worth considering how the early converts to Islam made sense of their faith and identity as British Muslims.

According to the historian Humayun Ansari, for the early converts to Islam, '…it has not been a question of simply making Islam indigenous but, more urgently, of reconfiguring Islamic ideas to make meaningful connections between Islam and British norms. During the late Victorian, Edwardian and interwar eras, Muslims, whether converts or from outside Britain, looked for similarities between Islam and Christianity and tried to disturb cultural practices as little as possible by a deliberate building of bridges. Jesus was acknowledged as a prophet of God, and no distinction was made between him and the prophet Muhammad as deliverers of the divine message. Indeed being a Muslim was presented as being a better Christian.'[1]

One such individual was Lord Henry Stanley of Alderley, who reconciled his Islamic faith with his identity as a loyal member of the British Establishment during the nineteenth century, and did so with considerable tact, pragmatism and success.

Henry Edward John Stanley, better known as Lord Henry Stanley of Alderley, was born into an aristocratic English family that traced its ancestry back to Adam de Audithlegh. Adam de Audithlegh fought at the Battle of Hastings in October, 1066 on the side of Duke William I of Normandy, better known as William the Conquerer (b. cir. 1028–1087), who became the first Norman King of England due to his decisive victory over the incumbent Anglo-Saxon ruler, King Harold Godwinson (b. cir. 1022–1066). Adam de Audithlegh's bravery in the battlefield impressed William the Conquerer, thus the latter rewarded him handsomely for his services by offering him a number of large estates. His immediate descendants, particularly his three great-grandsons, Sir William de Stanley in particular, substantially increased the family fortunes through a combination of business and marriage.

Sir William's successors continued to play prominent roles as politicians, rulers and administrators of justice under Richard de Vere, the Duke of Ireland (1362–1392), King Richard II (1367–1400), King Henry IV (1367–1413) and King Henry VI (1421–1471) of England. It was Thomas Stanley, the son of Sir John Stanley and Elizabeth Harrington, who became the first Baron Stanley, and together they became the founders of the Stanley family of Alderley. After Sir Thomas's death in 1721, he was succeeded by his two sons, namely James and Edward. The latter's son, Sir John Thomas Stanley (1766–1850), in turn, was created Baron Stanley of Alderley by none other than Queen Victoria on 9 May, 1839.[2]

Unlike his brother Edward Stanley, who became the rector of St. Mary's Church in Alderley before being appointed the Bishop of Norwich in 1837, Sir John was a scholarly individual having published several books, including *A Voyage to the Orknies* (1789) and *Leonora* (1796). His eldest son was Edward John Stanley (1802–1869), who married Henrietta Maria (1807–1895) in 1826, as she hailed from an aristocratic Irish family. She not only bore him ten children; six daughters and four sons, namely Henry Edward John, John Constantine (1837–1878), Edward Lyulph (1839–1925) and Algernon Charles (1843–1928); but also became one of the first and foremost campaigners of women's rights at Cambridge University at the time.

As the eldest son of the second Baron Stanley of Alderley and first Baron of Eddisbury, Henry was brought up on his family's large estate of Alderley Park in Cheshire. Since Baron Edward Stanley was an influential and wealthy English politician, it is not surprising that young Henry received a thorough education during his early years, though it is equally true that his parents were not particularly attached to one religion as such. Likewise, they did not actively encourage their children to follow a particular religion or denomination, despite most members of the Stanley family being attached, one way or another, to Anglicanism.

Unsurprisingly, even before he had reached his teens, young Henry became interested in things Eastern, including a desire to learn the Arabic language and explore the Orient. By contrast, his youngest brother, Algernon Charles, later became a Roman Catholic Bishop of Emmaus, and his other brother Edward Lyulph, became an agnostic, whilst his parents were themselves freethinkers. Despite being religiously unconventional, the Stanleys were equally committed to their individual causes, whether it be as champions of constitutional monarchy and toleration of political non-conformity, or as advocates of female liberty and freedom (It is worth mentioning here that Henry's father served as a member of the House of Commons as a Whig MP for Hindon in 1831 and subsequently as a Member of Parliament for North Cheshire).

As the Stanleys' eldest son, Henry received a lot of attention from his parents and other members of the extended family. His grandmother, Lady Maria Josepha (d. 1863), who was the daughter of John Holroyd, the first Earl of Sheffield, was particularly fond of her grandson, whilst predicting that his innocence and open-mindedness may lead to his adoption of 'the colour of those he lives with'.[3] Clearly Henry found the idea of exploring Oriental countries more exciting and exhilarating than leading a quiet and undisturbed life of luxury in England, but before he could embark on his journeys, he needed to complete his formal studies.

Accordingly, at the age of nineteen he joined Trinity College, Cambridge to study Arabic and, a year later, he moved to the Foreign Office where he worked under Lord Palmerston (1784–1865), who was the Foreign Secretary, with a view to qualifying for the diplomatic service. At the time, Britain and other European countries were preoccupied with the 'Eastern Question', namely how to deal with the Ottoman Empire and the growing demand for autonomy by its subjects in parts of Europe, Africa and Asia. The British position vis-à-vis the Ottomans at the time was that the Turks were far more advanced and civilised than the Russians and, accordingly, adopted a more friendly and lenient foreign policy towards the Ottoman Empire than some other European powers, which young Henry would no doubt have approved and endorsed, being a Turkophile himself.

Despite being an able aide to Lord Palmerston and an admirer of his foreign policy, Henry's time in the Foreign Office was not a happy one. During this period, he experienced deep spiritual and philosophical crises and, as a result, he began to question aspects of Christian theology and its implications, leading to his eventual withdrawal from the church. This was not surprising considering the fact that Henry grew up during the Victorian age when Biblical literalism in general, Protestantism in particular, faced serious challenges from new scientific discoveries. Much of these discoveries directly contradicted Biblical accounts of the origin of creation and human life, coupled with growing philosophical scepticism and rationalistic tendencies that were ushered in by the European Enlightenment of the seventeenth and eighteenth centuries.

This led to a radical transformation of the British elite's attitude and behaviour towards religion, science, culture and literature in general. Although Henry was a product of his age, he – in many ways – also transcended the linguistic, cultural and geographical boundaries of that age due to his burning desire to explore the Orient and acquire first-hand knowledge and understanding of the 'Other'. His parents were acutely aware of his personal dissatisfaction and religious uncertainty and so, instead of encouraging him to pursue a career in politics, they persuaded him to take up a junior post at the British Embassy in Constantinople (Istanbul) in 1850.

At the age of 23, Henry found himself working in the heart of the Ottoman Empire and, for the first time, came into direct contact with Muslim culture and the Islamic way of life. He already had profound respect and regard for Oriental culture and so his time in Istanbul only served to reinforce this. At the same time, Henry observed international politics and policy-making being played out by the European imperial powers, including the British government, for their own ends and to the detriment of the Turks. This clearly was a rude awakening for the idealistic young man who soon decided that international politics and diplomacy was not to his liking after all.

As expected, in 1852, he wrote to his mother informing her of his desire to study further on whatever allowance his father was able to provide him. The Stanleys knew that their son was a fiercely independent-minded young man and coercing him to do what pleased them was not an option, thus they wisely decided to support him in his desire to travel and study in the East. By now, Henry had become an accomplished linguist, having learned several European languages, in addition to Arabic, Turkish, Persian and Chinese. This was no mean achievement considering the fact that the Victorians were not known for their linguistic skills, but the senior officials in the British diplomatic service appreciated his knack for Oriental languages.

Despite his doubts and reservations about aspects of British foreign policy vis-à-vis the Turks, Henry continued to serve his country loyally and, no doubt, his parents were very pleased that he did do so, not least because his father was wary of his son's increasing move towards Islam as his spiritual home. Although Henry had befriended several Muslims during his time in the Foreign Office in London, his exposure to a cosmopolitan Muslim city like Istanbul confirmed his desire to explore Islam further. He continued his study of Eastern languages and culture, and Islam in particular, during his diplomatic service in Bulgaria, Athens and the Danubian Provinces in the 1850s.

As a consequence of his personal study and deep reflection, he not only became very fond of Islam, but he also started wearing Ottoman attire, much to the dismay of his father. As British policy towards the Ottomans hardened, in 1859, Henry decided to travel around the Muslim world and, in so doing, he set off in the direction of Egypt.

From there, he went to Jeddah in the present day Kingdom of Saudi Arabia, although it is not clear whether he had actually visited Makkah, the sacred city of Islam.

Nonetheless, Henry was clearly impressed by Islam as a religion and way of life. Consequently, unbeknown to his family back in England, he embraced Islam and, thanks to his eastern attire, he was a Muslim both in spirit and form. Unlike many other Western converts to Islam, Henry did not leave behind any formal documentation to confirm the exact date, time, place or circumstances that led to his conversion to Islam, but like most other early converts, he became a Muslim after many years of personal study, reflection and extensive travels across the Islamic world, especially in the Middle East and Asia. When the news of his conversion eventually reached his family back in England, his father was furious; indeed, he could not understand why his son would want to embrace the religion of the Turks, whom he considered to be lowly, backward and uncivilised.

However, in a letter to his brother John Stanley, who was on diplomatic service in Calcutta at the time, Henry explained that he had 'always been a Mussulman at heart' and preferred to be known as 'Hafiz' (preserver), although, according to others, he was known as 'Abd al-Rahman' (servant of the Merciful). As expected, his parents were far from impressed, despite his efforts to reassure them before returning to England in 1860. They could not agree with his decision to 'become a Turk' and so he set out again; this time spending most of his time in Europe where he also met Serafina Fernandez Funes (b. cir. 1835–1905), better known as Fabia, who was a Catholic lady of Spanish heritage. They later married in Algeria according to Islamic law.

After spending almost a decade travelling in Europe and the Ottoman Empire, Henry made preparations to return to the East again, but destiny had planned otherwise. His father suddenly died in June 1869 and at the age of nearly 42, Henry automatically inherited the title of third Baron Stanley of Alderley and second Baron of Eddisbury, thus returned immediately to England to settle there permanently with Fabia, his wife.

In so doing, Henry Stanley became the first Muslim member of the House of Lords and spent the rest of his life managing the family estates in Cheshire and Anglesey whilst, at the same time, serving in his capacity as a peer of the realm. Prior to this, Henry had already joined the Council of the Hakluyt Society, which was founded in 1846 to print and promote rare and unpublished travel accounts. He also became a member of the Royal Asiatic Society in 1858 and remained so for the rest of his life. He earned both honours on account of his remarkable linguistic skills, profound knowledge and understanding of Oriental culture and society, and his life-long interest in Middle Eastern and Asian affairs.

Upon assuming the leadership of the Stanley family, Henry closed all the public houses on his estates due to the consumption of alcohol being forbidden in Islam, including The Wizard, The Edge, The Eagle and Child and The Iron Gates, but he was more than happy to fund the restoration of several churches including the St Mary's

Church in Anglesey. Despite being a devout Muslim who prayed five times a day, often waking up in the middle of the night to stand in prayers (*tahajjud*) before his Lord in imitation of the Prophet Muhammad (peace be upon him), he had a soft spot for all good causes and never hesitated to support them, especially through his membership of the East India Association and the Aborigines Protection Society.

He was particularly fond of the Prophet of Islam, whom he considered to be an ideal role model for humanity and a paragon of spirituality, ethics, morality and justice. He came to this conclusion after decades of studying Arabic language, literature, Islamic theology, history and religious practices, in addition to his first-hand knowledge and experience from travelling in the Muslim world. Unlike what Sir Bertrand Russell (1872–1970) would have us believe, who was his nephew and a renowned British philosopher, Lord Henry Stanley was an able diplomat, gifted linguist, seasoned traveller and equally capable politician, writer and editor. He translated and single-handedly edited six volumes of travelogues for the Hakluyt Society and regularly spoke at the meetings of the Royal Asiatic Society in London.

Whilst his religious views were clear and unambiguous, his politics were less so. Thus, on the one hand, he was keen to retain British rule in India, while on the other, he resented and opposed any form of injustice or oppressive measures that were taken by the British government at the time. He was particularly eager to see Indian laws being interpreted and applied by both Hindus and Muslims according to their religious laws and dictates, and favoured the establishment of an Indian version of the Privy Council and a Court of Appeal.

In other words, he was keen to see more natives taking up senior positions in the Indian Civil Service because he felt that would help redress the Indian sense of injustice and grievance. Likewise, despite being an English patriot, he never shied away from defending the rights of the Ottomans whenever he felt that Britain and other European powers acted against the interests of the Turks. In the words of the historian Jamie Gilham,

> He was particularly agitated by further fragmentation of the Ottoman Empire, and exasperated by Gladstone's championing of Russia and denunciation of the Turks. Indeed, at the height of the Bulgarian agitation in 1876, Stanley was a Committee member and largest financial donor to the Turkish Wounded Soldiers' Relief Fund, established to support the Ottoman troops…He protested through the Patriotic Association against Turkey in 1880, pleading that it abide by the treaties of Paris and Berlin (1878), which guaranteed the independence of the Ottoman Empire by Europe.[4]

In the same way, Henry never lost an opportunity to highlight and defend the rights of the African people, Muslims and non-Muslims alike. Much the same as India, the

Ottoman Empire and the Islamic East, he was very fond of the continent of Africa and championed African people's right to independence and self-determination, and to that end, he opposed any efforts to extend or prolong Western imperial ambitions in the continent. Ultimately, however, he knew that his lobbying on behalf of India, the Ottomans and the African people would only have limited impact on British foreign policy at the time, but to his credit, that did not deter him from trying to make a difference. What was even more surprising, perhaps, was his unwillingness to engage in public discussions and debates about Islam, even though his commitment to his faith was unwavering.

Unlike many of his contemporaries, both Muslims and non-Muslims; including Wilfrid S. Blunt (1840–1922), Sir Sayyid Ahmad Khan (1817–1898), Rt Hon. Syed Ameer Ali (1849–1928), Rt. Hon. Sir Rowland George Allanson-Winn (1855–1935), better known as Lord Headley or Shaykh Rahmatullah al-Farooq, and William Henry Quilliam (1856–1932), also known as Abdullah Quilliam; he steered completely away from public discussion on the subject, perhaps to avoid reigniting bad feelings within his extended family as a result of his rejection of Christianity in favour of Islam.

Indeed, being a man of unusual abilities, considerable political tact and wisdom, extensive learning as well as being spiritually at home in the East and the West, Henry was in many ways a model British Muslim. His dedication and commitment to his faith should be a source of inspiration to the present and future generations, thus enabling them to build on his remarkable legacy and, in so doing, foster a uniquely British Muslim identity for the benefit of everyone, Muslims and non-Muslims alike.

After a lifetime devoted to learning, travelling, politics and diplomacy, Lord Henry Stanley of Alderley passed away in the sacred month of Ramadan at the age of around 75. He was buried in his family estate in Cheshire, following a simple funeral prayer led by the Imam at the Turkish Embassy in London. Another funeral prayer was performed for the deceased in Liverpool by Abdullah Quilliam, and his obituaries were subsequently published in *The Review of Religions* and *The Crescent*. Referring to her brother, Henrietta Blanche (1830–1921), who was the Countess of Airlie and the grandmother of Clementine Churchill, stated that,

> I do not think […] that he has been a sad man, for he has had joys of his own, being at one with his God, from whom he takes all willingly without repining, and in his submission there is great content, and he loved nature and real sport, and Oriental learning, and order and obedience, and he had a fair estate to rule over, and he enjoyed improving it in his own way. No, I think he had been a happy man.[5]

As Lord Henry Stanley had no children of his own, his titles automatically passed on to his younger brother, Edward Lyulph, who accordingly became the fourth Baron Stanley and third Baron of Eddisbury. After attending Eton College and subsequently studying at Oxford University, Edward established his reputation as a leading politician and educationalist. He died in 1925 at the age of 84.[6]

1. Humayun Ansari, *The Infidel Within: Muslims in Britain since 1800*.

2. See *Oxford Dictionary of National Biography*, Oxford University Press.

3. Quoted by Jamie Gilham, *Loyal Enemies: British Converts to Islam, 1850–1950*.

4. Ibid.

5. Jamie Gilham, op. cit.

6. See his *Our National Education*, published in London in 1899.

25

# ALEXANDER RUSSELL WEBB

B. 1846 – D. 1916

UNITED STATES OF AMERICA

According to some historians, the presence of Muslims in the Americas can be traced back to the pre-Columbus period, while others have argued that the presence of Islam in that part of the world only became noticeable after the arrival of the African Muslims during the transatlantic slave trade.[1]

However, what is not so widely known is that most North American Muslims, like their European counterparts, are heirs to a triple heritage. First and foremost, they are Americans by virtue of their citizenship and domicile. America is a wealthy, powerful and equally cosmopolitan country, underpinned by its founding principles of freedom, democracy, pluralism and respect for human rights. These principles and values are not only American, but they are also universal and that is why American Muslims should never have any problems or difficulties in subscribing to them.

Secondly, they are heirs to the same great Abrahamic tradition and spirituality as their Jewish and Christian brethren. In other words, if the God of Abraham is the God of the Jews, Christians and Muslims, which I firmly believe to be the case, then their spiritual heritage is alike, too. Thirdly, most American Muslims are also heirs to a distinct ethnic and cultural heritage, namely Asian, African, Arab, European, Hispanic, Latino or Native American, among others. Such diversity and cosmopolitanism is surely nothing more than a reflection of our common human origin, history and heritage, thus transcending race, colour, creed, culture and background.

One of the earliest Americans to convert to Islam and travel around the Muslim world was Alexander Russell Webb, who hailed from an equally diverse culture and heritage, being white, American and Muslim, he was undoubtedly the quintessential triple-heritager!

Alexander Russell Webb was born in Hudson, located in present-day Columbia County in the US State of New York, into a middle class Anglo-American family. His parents, Alexander Nelson Webb and Caroline Elizabeth Lefferts, were New Yorkers who traced their ancestry back to England. They later moved to Hudson from Syracuse city, Onondaga County, a few years before Russell's birth. Nelson initially worked for a local newspaper, the *Columbia Washingtonian*, before purchasing it from its proprietor, Warren Rockwell, in 1847, a year after the birth of Russell. Thereafter, Nelson Webb founded the *Hudson Daily Star*, which was the first daily newspaper to be published in Columbia County at the time. He combined his work as a printer, publisher and editor, with that of a committed family man who took good care of his large, extended family of six children; four boys and two daughters; and many other relatives including his parents.

As religion played a prominent role in people's lives in mid-nineteenth century America, Hudson was a noteworthy centre of religious activities at the time. Although Quakerism was most dominant in that area, the followers of other denominations were also present there, including Methodists, Presbyterians, Baptists and Episcopalians, among others. The Webb family were devout Presbyterians and Nelson, Russell Webb's father, was the secretary of the Columbia Temperance Society, although it is not clear if the latter ever joined the Cadets of Temperance, the youth wing of that organisation. As a youngster, Russell Webb was more interested in playful activities than religious observance or education. In his own words,

> When I was young I went to Sunday school. In those days I was a pretty wild kind of a boy, and I used to go to church simply for the sake of seeing nice-looking girls and escorting them home. It was a most delightful task. When I was a little older, I changed from the Presbyterian church , to the Episcopal one, as there were equally nice young ladies to look at in the latter church...I gave religion no thought. About the age of 20 I met a family of Universalists, and they began to preach religion to me, and I began to think of religion. The more I thought of it, the more absurd it seemed to me.[2]

Despite his early playfulness, Russell Webb received a thorough education during his early years. His father enrolled him at local private schools, where he no doubt studied mathematics, history and literature, among other subjects, before joining Claverack

College in Columbia, which operated very much like a military academy at the time. It is not clear if he had completed his education or training at this college, although his interest in writing essays and short stories probably developed during this period. If his claim that he was not a devout Christian during his early years is open to question, the fact that he never ceased to think, ponder and reflect is beyond doubt. Again, in his own words,

> Fortunately I was of an enquiring turn of mind – I wanted a reasonable foundation for everything – and I found that neither laymen nor clergy could give me any rational explanation of this faith, but either told me that such things were mysterious or that they were beyond my comprehension.[3]

With his probing philosophical and theological questions aside, Russell Webb found aspects of Christianity to be irrational and illogical too, which added to his growing doubts and uncertainty about his ancestral religion. He especially found the doctrine of Trinity to be confusing and problematic and, in the absence of any satisfactory answers or explanations, he felt compelled to reject it altogether. He explained,

> I abandoned the system improperly called Christianity, soon after I attained my majority, because its teachers could not give me a convincing reason for the faith that was in them. When I was asked to believe that one was really three, and that a just and merciful Creator committed an act of unnatural cruelty simply to gratify a mere whim, I demanded corroborative testimony and was told that none had ever been filed. This very grave omission compelled me to throw the case out of court.[4]

Some of Russell's biographers have suggested that he may have completely lost faith in Christianity and became an agnostic in the mid-1860s. This state of affair persisted for nearly a decade during which he not only led a hedonistic and materialistic lifestyle, without showing any interest in religion, he went further and developed a measure of antipathy towards all things religious. However, the materialistic phase of his life ended following his encounter with Theosophy in the 1870s and Buddhism in particular, which took place during the early 1880s. Indeed, it was his interest in Theosophy that prompted him to study and explore eastern religions and philosophies in the first place, and as a consequence, he became deeply attracted to Buddhism due to its simplicity and rationality. At the time, he was working as an assistant editor for the *Missouri Republican* in St. Louis.

Prior to that, Russell had spent two years training as a watchmaker in New York and worked as a jewellery salesman in Chicago, where he met and married the daughter of Lucian. W. Conger, a local businessman, in 1869. In the following year, he returned to

New York and, thanks to his father's intervention, he secured a job at a local jewellery shop and worked there for three years before returning to Chicago with his wife who was unwell at the time. It was in Chicago that his father-in-law persuaded Russell to take up journalism and become the editor of the *Unionville Republican* in Missouri. So, Russell continued in this capacity until 1876, when he assumed editorship of the *St. Joseph Gazette*. Thereafter, he became an associate editor of the *Missouri Morning Journal* and this enabled him to polish his journalistic and editorial skills to the extent that he was subsequently able to secure the post of assistant editor of the *Missouri Republican* in 1883; he was around 37 at the time.

In total, he spent fourteen years in Missouri working mainly as a journalist but, at various times, he worked as a jewellery salesman, circus publicity manager, drama director and playwright, in addition to meeting and marrying Ella Hotchkiss, his second wife, in June, 1877. He spent the rest of his life with her and her daughter from a previous marriage, but, for some unknown reason, he never made any reference to his first marriage. Ella subsequently bore him a son and a daughter, namely Russell L. Webb (b. 1879) and Mary C. Webb (b. 1885), while his second daughter, Nala D. Webb, was born in Manila in 1888.

As Russell privately studied and looked into eastern religions and philosophies, he became well acquainted with Asian cultures, languages and customs, and regularly communicated with prominent personalities from that part of the world. He had access to a large collection of books, reportedly more than 10,000 volumes and, on average, he read for four to five hours daily on a wide range of subjects, focusing particularly on religion, philosophy, literature and history. Not surprisingly, according to a reference statement,

> His knowledge of Oriental peoples and customs is extensive…He uses neither wines, beer, nor tobacco nor stimulants nor narcotics of any sort and his physical health is as perfect as anyone could desire. He comes from a long-lived family and his regular habits, systematic course of diet, composed mainly of vegetables and fruits, coupled with a naturally vigorous constitution render him capable of enduring extremely severe physical strains. He has not been ill enough to go to bed nor to require the services of a physician for more than twenty-five years.[5]

It was perhaps on account of his extensive knowledge and understanding of Asian history and culture that prompted the US administration, under the presidency of Grover Cleveland (1837–1908), to appoint Russell as America's Consular Representative in Manila, Philippines. Although he wanted to be posted to India or Singapore, the government officials offered him Manila and, accordingly, he boarded a ship bound for Asia. From 1 January, 1888 to 5 September, 1892, he served his country loyally and diligently, despite the fact that the Democrats were replaced by a Republican administration during his time in Manila and, as a result, America's foreign policy in Asia also shifted considerably. During this time, Russell also began to study and explore Islam seriously for the first time. He had already been corresponding with several Indians, including Mirza Ghulam Ahmad, the so-called Messiah and founder of the Qadiani sect, and in so doing, he became deeply interested in Islam as a religion and way of life. After his initial fascination with Buddhism, he subjected it to scrutiny and, once the results of his investigation proved to be unsatisfactory, he shifted his attention towards Islam. He explained his intellectual and spiritual journey to Islam during a lecture he delivered at the Framji Cowasji Institute in November, 1892, as follows:

> About eleven years ago I became interested in the study of Oriental religions… I saw Mill and Locke, Kant, Hegel, Fichte, Huxley and many other more or less learned writers discoursing with a great show of wisdom concerning protoplasm and monads, and yet not one of them could tell me what the soul was or what became of it after death…I have spoken so much of myself in order to show you that my adoption of Islam was not the result of misguided sentiment, blind credulity, or sudden emotional impulse, but it was born of earnest, honest, persistent, unprejudiced study and investigation and an intense desire to know the truth… The essence of the true faith of Islam is resignation to the will of God and its corner stone is prayer. It teaches universal fraternity, universal love, and universal benevolence, and requires purity of mind, purity of action, purity of speech and perfect physical cleanliness. It is the simplest and most elevating form of religion known to man.[6]

Russell Webb stated on more than one occasion that he was in search of the truth, and if the trajectory of his life is anything to go by, then his claim is undisputable. He started off life as a Christian only to renounce it in favour of materialism. He then became a Theosophist and pursued Buddhism, only to be disillusioned with that, too. Thereafter, he studied Islam most fervently before formally becoming a Muslim in 1888; he was 42 at the time. Islam's focus on the concepts of Divine unity (*tawhid*), chain of prophecy (*risalah*) and life after death (*akhirah*) clearly attracted his attention, which he considered to be the simplest, most rational, practical and authentic religious truths ever to be revealed.

Needless to say, the path leading to that truth had been anything but straightforward: 'And let me assure you that in seeking for the truths I have found, I have had to overturn a vast deal of rubbish in the shape of false history, false opinions, and false reasoning, before I caught the faint gleam of that priceless jewel which has been preserved to man through all the ages, although the bigots and Pharisees of orthodoxy have striven most earnestly to destroy it.'[7]

In other words, Russell Webb embraced Islam after a long period of study and reflection. He read the writings of many prominent scholars, Muslims and non-Muslims, including Rt. Hon. Syed Ameer Ali (1849–1928), Thomas Patrick Hughes (1838–1911), Chiragh Ali (1844–1895) and Mawlana Muhammad Ali Lahori (1874–1951), among others. And, in so doing, he acquired an intimate knowledge and understanding of Islam and its teachings. During a lecture he delivered in Hyderabad, India in November, 1892 on the topic of 'philosophic Islam', he stated – and I quote him at some length – to show the depth of his knowledge and reverence for the Prophet of Islam,

Our Holy Prophet – peace be with him forever – knew all the mysteries of life and death, and so did Jesus of Nazareth, and so did every other truly inspired prophet the world has ever known. The one truth – the only real science – has been handed down from the beginning of human development, through the long line of prophets to Mohammed – *Hazrat Mohammed Sallal laho aliehi wasallam* – and this truth has been offered to mankind earnestly and eloquently, while the masses have turned their backs upon it and have wandered off in search of money and comfort and pleasure…There comes to my mind the picture of a grand and noble figure in history – one of the grandest and noblest that man has ever known; calm, majestic man, in whose personality there is something that commands respect, admiration and awe. His countenance beams with the glory of divine inspiration as he stands with his back against one of the rough pillars of the rude little mosque in Medina, in the erection of which his own hands assisted. Around him are seated a company of men who listen with eager attention to the words that fall from his lips, while they gaze upon him with rapt reverence and devotion. He has given up all that men of the world prize and toil for, has submitted to the cruellest, most inhuman insults and persecution that could be invented by wicked, selfish people who were formerly his admirers and friends; has endured pains and sorrows and disappointments that would have utterly broken an ordinary man. And yet in his heart there is no malice, no desire for revenge, no selfish ambition, no hatred; his soul is full of peace and joy and love, for the divine light pervades his whole being. Patiently and earnestly he points out to his humble followers the true way to eternal life, while they listen gratefully and attentively, letting his words sink deep into their hearts, and treasuring them there in all their daily lives. They do not question the truth of his teachings – they do not doubt – but say: 'Show us the way and we will walk in it truthfully and we will walk in it trustfully and loyally until we have found the priceless jewel of eternal truth.' And what is the way pointed out by this grandest of all prophets? Islam! Resignation to the will of God; the omniscient, omnipresent, omnipotent God, who stands ready to lead the aspiring soul out of the darkness of materialism into that light which shines for all as a guide to Paradise.[8]

Although Russell Webb became a Muslim in 1888, the American public did not know anything about it until the news of his conversion was picked up by the newspapers there in September, 1892. Prior to that, he had met up with several Indian Muslims and they collectively established the American Islamic Propaganda with a view to promoting Islam in their country. Hajji Abdullah Arab of Bombay, a wealthy merchant, agreed to fund Russell Webb's religious activities and the latter, in turn, went on a tour of the Muslim world including India, Egypt and Ottoman Turkey where he met many prominent Muslim figures and delivered lectures, before finally returning to America on 16 February, 1893.

Soon after his return, he began to organise the work of the American Islamic Propaganda, whose main objectives were to raise awareness of Islam through a series of educational activities, namely the publication of a weekly journal, establishment of a publishing house, setting up lecture rooms and establishing a library of Islamic literature, both classical and modern books in Arabic, Persian, Turkish, Urdu and English. As soon as the news of his plans became public, he was mocked, ridiculed and caricatured. Undeterred, he continued his religious and educational work, but the level of funding that was required to carry out his programme of activities was far greater than that forthcoming from Hajji Abdullah of India and, ultimately, that undermined the viability of his entire project.

Even so, in partnership with The Oriental Publishing Company in New York, Russell published his first book in 1893 under the title of *Islam in America*, which was largely based on his lectures that were delivered in India. In the same year, he went to Chicago to attend the First World Parliament of Religions as Islam's official representative and delivered two lectures there, titled 'The Spirit of Islam' and 'The Influence of Islam on Social Conditions', both of which were received well by the audience. Thereafter, he established the Moslem World Publishing Company which published several books and produced *The Moslem World* newspaper, the mouthpiece of the American Islamic Propaganda. This paper reprinted articles by prominent Muslims and Western scholars, as well as news from around the Muslim world.

Shortage of funding led to the closure of the paper after only seven issues. It was replaced by *The Voice of Islam*, a much smaller publication than *The Moslem World*, but it too became defunct in August 1894. The combined publication of both journals under the title of *The Moslem World and Voice of Islam* continued until it, too, ceased to exist in 1896. Russell Webb's financial situation became dire after he fell out with other members of the American Islamic Propaganda. The news of their break-up soon reached India, leading to more complications for Russell. Although he was determined to continue his activities, his failure to build links with other Muslims in New York did not help his cause. According to some of his biographers, he was an elitist who did not easily mingle with Muslims who hailed from lower class backgrounds, and his views and opinion about them were often negative, if not racialistic or dismissive.[9]

Eventually, he and his family moved to Rutherford, New Jersey, and very little is known about the last eighteen years of his life. He is said to have played an active part in local political and civic affairs, and continued to advocate Islam and speak in defence of Ottoman Turkey, for which Sultan Abd al-Hamid II of Turkey formally recognised him in 1901. Although Russell Webb remained a committed Muslim until his death on 1 October, 1916, his wife, who, having earlier embraced Islam, subsequently joined the Unitarian Church in Rutherford and died three-and-half-years after him. He was laid to rest in the Hillside Cemetery at the age of 69.

His life and legacy remained largely forgotten until quite recently, thanks to the growing American Muslim community's desire to rediscover and revive its past. Some have even hailed him as the 'First American Muslim' and books about his life, contribution and achievements are now proliferating, which will indeed help raise awareness and understanding of America's rich Islamic history and heritage for the benefit of the present and future generations.

1. See Allan D. Austin, *African Muslims in Antebellum America* and Sylviane A. Diouf, *Servants of Allah: African Muslims Enslaved in the Americas.*

2. Brent D. Singleton (ed.), *Yankee Muslim: Mohammed Alexander Russell Webb.*

3. S. A. Khulusi (ed.), *Islam Our Choice.*

4. Umar F. Abd-Allah, *A Muslim in Victorian America: The Life of Alexandra Russell Webb.*

5. Brent D. Singleton, op. cit.

6. S. A. Khulusi, op. cit.

7. Umar F. Abd-Allah, op. cit.

8. Brent D. Singleton, op. cit.

9. Ibid.

# 26

# ISMAIL BEY GASPIRALI

B. 1851 – D. 1914

CRIMEA

At a time when significant parts of the Islamic world were firmly under colonial rule, many prominent Muslim scholars and reformers emerged during the nineteenth and early twentieth centuries to liberate their lands from foreign occupation, and, in so doing, reinvigorate Muslim faith and culture. Whilst the lives and contributions of some of those scholars and reformers are widely known today, others have been largely forgotten, if not completely ignored.

For example, the contribution and achievements of Sir Sayyid Ahmad Khan (1817–1898), Jamal al-Din al-Afghani (1838–1897), Muhammad Abduh (1849–1905), Rt. Hon. Syed Ameer Ali (1849–1928) and Sir Muhammad Iqbal (1877–1938) are widely known in the Muslim world and the West. By comparison, the names of scholars and reformists like Nawab Bahadur Abd al-Latif (1828–1893), Abd al-Rahman al-Kawakibi (1855–1902), Abd al-Hamid ibn Badis (1889–1940) and Malik Bennabi (1905–1973), among others, are only familiar to the academics and educated Muslims.

At the same time, the lives and works of other equally important nineteenth and early twentieth century Muslim scholars and reformers have been blanked out entirely both in the Muslim world and the West. For that reason, in this volume, an attempt has been made to briefly introduce their lives and works, focusing particularly on their contribution to Islamic thought and culture for the benefit of Muslims and non-Muslims alike. One such inspiring, but equally neglected Muslim scholar, educator and reformer of the nineteenth and early twentieth centuries, was Ismail Bey Gaspirali of Crimea.

Ismail Bey Gaspirali, also known as Ismail Bay Gasprinski, was born into a notable Crimean Tatar Muslim family in the village of Uchukoy, not far from the present-day Crimean city of Bakhchisaray, which is considered by the majority of the countries to be an integral part of the Eastern European State of Ukraine. Following Russian annexation of Crimea in 2014, it now forms a part of the Russian Federation. His father, Mustafa Agha, was a secretary and translator to a Russian prince and hailed from a distinguished Muslim family from the village of Gaspira, located on the coast of the Black Sea, which explains why Ismail later became known as Gaspirali. Likewise, his mother, Fatma Hanim, came from a prominent Crimean Muslim family. According to Rizaeddin bin Fakhreddin (see chapter 51), who was himself a distinguished Tatar Islamic scholar and writer, Ismail's parent's initially settled in Sevastopol (or Sebastopol), which is today a coastal city in the south-western region of Crimea located on the Black Sea, but they moved to Bakhchisaray when their son was only four years old.[1]

Young Ismail received his early education at home under the tutelage of his learned father before enrolling at the local Qur'an school (*maktab*) where he studied Arabic and aspects of Islamic beliefs and practices. Thereafter, he joined a Russian gymnasium (state-sponsored secular school) where he studied the Russian language, history, geography, mathematics and science. At the age of around 15, he moved to Moscow and enrolled at the Military Academy for further education, but two years later, in 1867, he abandoned his formal education and set out in the direction of Istanbul to support the Ottomans against their Greek foes. However, the Russian authorities stopped him at Odessa and sent him back to Bakhchisaray, much to his dismay and disappointment.

Ismail grew up at a time of considerable change and upheaval in Crimea, so much so that the very survival of the Crimean Tatars was at stake at the time, not least because relations between the Russian government and Muslims had been a source of tension for some time. However, after the Crimean War and Polish Rebellion, the forces of Pan-Slavism and anti-Turkish sentiments grew louder and popular in Russia, leading to the gradual marginalisation and disenfranchisement of its Muslim population. Although, 'Catherine II had adopted a tolerant stance toward Islam after she had annexed the Crimea in 1783, her "Greek project" and the following colonization had stripped the Crimean Tatars of their means of subsistence. The result was the continuous emigration of Crimea's Muslim population to the Ottoman lands…The exact number of emigrants is still unknown, but it is possible to say that the total number of people who migrated from Russia to the Ottoman Empire between 1855 and 1866, including the immigrants from the Caucasus, is over one million.'[2]

This, of course, was compounded by the political failures and economic impoverishment of the Russian Muslim elite, in addition to the challenges they faced from the Christian missionaries who were determined to Christianise and, by extension, Russify the Muslim population. This, in turn, forced the Muslim community to gradually withdraw from the mainstream political, social, cultural, economic and educational spheres of their society, leading to increasing resentment and alienation.

As Ismail grew up and pursued his education, the challenges facing his people clearly had an impact on his thinking, which perhaps prompted him to move to Istanbul where he stayed for a year, thus becoming familiar with Ottoman policies and practices. He then went to Paris, where he lived for two years and became proficient in French. Ismail's travels across the Ottoman Empire and France convinced him that the road to advancement and progress for the Russian Muslims was dependent on proactive engagement with the status quo rather than self-imposed withdrawal and isolation from mainstream society. Accordingly, he returned to Russia in 1874 and became a teacher of Russian language and literature in Yalta. Then, in 1876, he moved to his native Bakhchisaray where he taught Russian at the Zinjirli Madrasah, in addition to aspects of Muslim thought, history and culture.

During this period, he established his reputation as a gifted teacher and proactively encouraged the Muslim community to play their full part in their society. He was not only respected by the local Muslims, but the senior government officials also found him to be loyal, committed and trustworthy. His ability to break down barriers, unify the Muslim community and promote co-operation between the authorities and the masses subsequently prompted him to stand for the post of mayor (*golova*) of Bakhchisaray. He was successfully elected in 1879 and served in this capacity for the following four years.[3]

During this period, he worked hard to improve the social, educational and economic conditions of his people, which he considered to be the fruits of his proactive engagement and constructive collaboration with the Russian authorities, locally and nationally. After successfully serving his term as mayor, in 1884, he focused his attention on more pressing and pertinent issues facing not only the Crimean Tatars, but also the Muslims of Russia as a whole. He felt that the Russian Muslims were not only cut off from the rest of the Muslim world, but that they were also on the verge of religious and cultural extinction. Needless to say, the Muslims of the region needed someone to awaken them from their slumber through inspirational leadership and intellectual regeneration – was there anyone more qualified and experienced than Ismail to carry out the task?

Indeed, as early as 1881, Ismail had published a series of articles on the subject of 'Russkoe musul'mantsvo' (or 'Russian Islam'), in which he argued that the Muslims of Russia were united by their common faith, language and culture despite their political, economic and educational backwardness. However, unfavourable government policies towards the Muslim community, he contended, only served to make matters worse by insisting that the members of the community pay their taxes without the government providing adequate help and support to them in return. He therefore called for an overhaul of Russia's policy and attitude towards its Muslim population, that is to say, he advocated the need for the unification and empowerment of his people on the basis of freedom and equality of opportunity on the one hand, and sound education and economic development on the other. He wanted the Muslims of Russia to remain true to their Islamic faith and culture, but also become loyal and productive members of their society.

In other words, Ismail wanted them to be Russian Muslims, being proud of their Russian identity and their Islamic faith which, ultimately, he felt was in the best interests of Russia as well as its Muslim population.[4] For that reason, he did not get involved in domestic Russian politics but instead, became an advocate of the Tatar language as a medium of learning, as a champion of religious educational reform, as well as the need for intellectual renewal in the Muslim community. Unlike his other contemporaries (such as Ahmad Mahdum Donish [1826–1897] of Central Asia and Ziya Gokalp [1876–1924] of Ottoman Turkey), he was not only a critic of his community, but an active participant in its development and regeneration. As a result, he became the chief architect of Islamic modernism among the Muslims of Russia during the nineteenth and early twentieth centuries.

Although he encouraged the Russian Muslims to engage in educational and literary activities to achieve cultural renewal and progress, the question remains: how were they supposed to go about achieving that? Firstly, he was not only in favour of translating modern Western literature on medicine, science, philosophy, mathematics, history and geography into the Tatar language, but also advocated their introduction into the *maktab* and *madrasah* curriculum to enable the Muslim students to become familiar with Western thought, history and culture.

Secondly, being a respected teacher, journalist and scholar himself, Ismail argued that Islam was a simple and equally modern faith at its core. That is why it only made two fundamental demands on Muslims, namely the need to pursue education and observe regular prayers. But, the Russian Muslim community of the time were very backward in both areas. Therefore, it inspired Ismail to engage in his reformist activities to improve his people's dire and pitiful existential condition. As expected, his thoughtful and balanced approach to Islam, cultural identity and citizenship soon won him recognition within the government circles. As a result, the Russian authorities were happy to grant him permission to publish a bilingual newspaper called *Tercuman* (in Tatar) and *Perevodchik* (in Russian), meaning 'translator' or 'interpreter' in both languages.[5]

As it happened, Ismail founded the *Tercuman* in 1883 and pursued his reformist activities through publication for the next 31 years without any government censorship or intervention. This in itself was a major achievement, considering the fact that the Muslims of Russia had always struggled to publish their own journals, newspapers and periodicals due to interference or censorship from the authorities. That was because, unlike the other publications, Ismail's newspaper adopted a non-confrontational and conciliatory tone from the outset.

His aim was to 'elucidate the nature of Islamic and Russian/Western cultures for wide-spread public consumption across cultural lines so as to encourage both the revitalization of Islamic society and its *sblizhenie* (rapprochement) with the Russian. The anticipated consequences were, on the one hand, an end to the mental complacency of Muslims that stifled economic development, encouraged social indifference, and engendered political weakness; on the other, a beginning to an equal partnership between Muslim and Russian in shaping a more just, harmonious, and strengthened empire.'[6] Although he had set himself a monumental task, Ismail was a confident, optimistic and visionary reformer who was determined to transform the social, educational, cultural and economic condition of his people, not only in Crimea but across the Russian Empire. In his own words,

> At the present time, despite the fact that the Muslim subjects of Russia lag far behind [other peoples], and that they share in so little of modern life, this great [Muslim] society is not all that incognizant [of what is happening around it]; and one cannot deny that within Islam a revival is taking place. Granted that this revival is not imposing; and so long as you do not pay close attention you will not even notice it. Yet it is enough for us that with some attention it can be observed, because it undoubtedly represented the beginning of progress and civilization.[7]

During the next three decades, the *Tercuman* (*Tarjuman* in Arabic) established itself as the most influential publication not only within the Tatar Muslim community, but also across Central Asia and beyond. Its confident and refreshing tone, coupled with its vision and foresight, not to mention its innovative approach to problem-solving, soon captured the imagination of its readers, Muslim and non-Muslim alike. As its readership and popularity continued to increase, Ismail was forced to print more copies to meet the growing demand. Three years after the launch of the *Tercuman*, he referred to its *raison d'etre* and growing popularity in the following words:

> Let us inform our readers what we see as the use and purpose of *Terjuman* that it has aimed at that improving the health and happiness of our homeland [*vatan*], of the Turks as well as other Muslims who live in Russia. We have aimed at providing the essentials for the education of our nation, of the Turks and all Muslims in Russia. When the first issue of *Terjuman* was printed, we produced only 320 copies, and we perhaps thought that we would find it difficult to have a readership warranting that many. In December 1883, though, we needed to print 406 copies. For 1884 we had to increase our operating budget, and by December we had 1000 subscribers. Let us describe briefly whose those 1000

subscribers were. 300 were in Crimea; 300 were in Astrakhan, Samara, Orenburg, Ufa, Kazan, and Perm; 150 in Dagestan; 50 were Siberian Muslims; 200 were in Central Asia and Turkistan. 150 appeared to be from the upper and wealthy classes; 300 were ordinary working people; 500 were urban merchants, teachers, [and] artisans. Our readership comes from all over the Russian Muslim world, and includes all sorts of people.[8]

Convinced that his message had struck a chord with Muslims at home and abroad, Ismail then travelled extensively in Russia, Central Asia, the Islamic East and South Asia to disseminate his reformist message, which, in turn, won him respect and recognition in many parts of the Muslim world. For example, he visited Baku (the capital of present-day Azerbaijan) in 1885 and 1893, respectively, before proceeding to Bukhara (in Uzbekistan) in 1907. Thereafter, he went to Cairo in 1908 and eventually made his way to India in 1911.

During his stay in Egypt, he not only attended the General Islamic Congress there, but was also invited by his peers to deliver a lecture to an audience of 300 prominent Islamic scholars, jurists, government officials, writers and journalists. He spoke eloquently, highlighting the challenges and difficulties faced by the Muslims at the time. When he proceeded to Bombay a few years later, he delivered several lectures there under the auspices of the *Anjuman-i-Islam* (The Islamic Society) on the condition of the Muslim *ummah* (global community). As expected, he found that the Indian Muslims were suffering from the same problems and difficulties that confronted the Muslims in Russia, Central Asia and the Islamic East. In his own words – and it is worth quoting him at some length:

In the Muslim world, madrasas continue for the most part to be institutions of the past and continue to play the part of obstacle to progress and renewal. Muslims appear to be under the domination of traders and commercial interests. They appear unable to take charge of these affairs on their own…We have no successful commercial companies, no successful banking establishments, no leaders in international trade and commerce. We have inherited from our ancestors, fertile lands and rich forests and great commercial traditions. But we cannot discover how to make use of them, to profit from them. We are dependent on others, from non-Muslim lands and traditions, to exploit our own riches…It is my belief that if the present situation continues for long, not only the traditions and values of the Muslims but their very existence is in question. It is ignorance that is primarily to blame. Greeks, Bulgarians, Jews, Hindus, all have in less than half a century made such strides in progress that they have left us far behind…Are Muslims, who today appear to be without knowledge, without talents, slaves of outmoded ideas and systems, to remain in this condition indefinitely? Islam is a religion that should be able to offer us a solution to the current state of affairs. Islam is a religion that fosters science, knowledge, education, progress. Islam is not a religion opposed to any of the above. Why does it seem to be so today?[9]

He eventually returned home from his journeys across the Islamic world, convinced that the Muslims were in such a pitiful condition due to their outmoded educational systems, coupled with the absence of intellectual creativity, social enterprise, scientific innovation and cultural progress, rather than any form of weakness that can be attributed to Islam as such. He was an advocate of change and reform in Muslim societies, so long as they did not entail a complete break with the Islamic past, for the past must always inform the present, just as the present determines the future.[10]

Not surprisingly, he argued in favour of female education at a time when Muslim girls were discouraged by their families from attending schools due to fear of being influenced by foreign ideas and thought. Likewise, he wanted Muslim jurists to revisit aspects of *fiqh* (Islamic jurisprudence) to ensure that they were fully in tune with the spirit of the Shari'ah (Islamic law) and its fundamental principles to enable Muslims to respond to the challenges of modernity and Westernisation.

Despite being a modernist thinker and reformer, however, he was convinced that the spirit of Islam was forward-looking and progressive, unlike many other religions and ideologies, and therefore he expected it not only to survive the challenges it faced at the time but also, in the future, to play its rightful role in the progress and development of the Muslim world as well as humanity as a whole. In that sense, Ismail had a lot in common with several other nineteenth century Muslim scholars and reformers, including Nawab Bahadur Abd al-Latif of Calcutta, Sir Sayyid Ahmad Khan of Aligarh and Muhammad Abduh of al-Azhar. However, unlike the other Muslim reformers, his activities were focused on Muslims who were living in predominantly non-Muslim societies as minorities at the time.

Likewise, as a writer and editor, Ismail was prolific and truly indefatigable. He not only edited the *Turcuman* for more than thirty years, but also contributed regular editorials and articles in the newspaper, in addition to writing many other books and essays on religious, educational and cultural topics that were of relevance to the Russian Muslims in general and the Crimean Tatars in particular, including *Tonguch* (First-born, 1881), *Shefak* (Daybreak, 1881) and *Salname-i Turki* (Turki Yearbook, 1882), among others. Indeed, two decades after the launch of the *Turcuman* and his single-handed struggle to revive Russian Islam, Ismail was of course delighted to see his efforts eventually bore fruit. He acknowledged this himself in an editorial published on the twentieth anniversary of the newspaper:

Schools for Muslims in Russia are changing, are improving, and we believe some of the credit for this development belongs with what has been published in

*Terjuman*. Foundations for more than one thousand primary schools have been laid, and in many of them, our 'phonetic method' of instruction is employed. Our young writers and scholars have produced in these twenty years as many as three hundred scientific and literary treatises. In eight of our cities, societies have been established to work for the social and cultural benefit of our people. The spiritual and intellectual health of our world of Islam is greatly improved. We hope that God is pleased with what has been achieved. But much more still remains to be accomplished.[11]

Likewise, his reformist efforts and activities later influenced generations of Russian, Crimean, Turkish and Central Asian Muslim scholars, thinkers and reformers. So much so that a new school of thought, known as Jadidism (or *usul-i Jadid* [New School] as opposed to *usul-i Qadim* [Old School]), subsequently emerged in that part of the world, inspired by the ideas, thoughts and activities of Ismail Bey Gaspirali.

On a personal level, he was a devout and frugal Muslim who also smoked tobacco as a treat. He used to walk to his office every morning and stay there until all his tasks for the day were complete. He was a busy individual who disliked idleness. He admired things that were attractive and beautiful. He was also hopeful and optimistic, and equally determined and hard-working. He was fond of classical Turkish music and always wore traditional dress and clothing. He married three times and had six children, three sons and three daughters.

However, as a workaholic, his heavy workload eventually took its toll on his health and he died of a heart attack at the age of 63. His funeral prayer took place on Friday after the congregational prayer, and he was laid to rest next to the Mengli Giray Khan *turbe*. His final words were:

God is great! I have lived more than sixty-three years. I have devoted more than thirty-five of them to Muslim movements and Islamic renewal. I hope my efforts have provided long-lasting benefit to my nation and that my work has helped everyone else's work too. I have one more hope. But I do not know whether this hope will be granted. It is that God will be pleased with what I have done and that God will approve of what all of you do after me.[12]

Ⓝ

1. Gaspirali's obituary in Edward Allworth (ed.), *Tatars of the Crimea: Their Struggle for Survival.*

2. Mustafa Ozgur Tuna, 'Gaspirali v. Il'minskii: Two Identity Projects for the Muslims of the Russian Empire' in *Nationalities Papers*, vol. 30, No. 2.

3. Charles Kurzman, *Modernist Islam, 1840–1940.*

4. Alan W. Fisher, 'Ismail Gaspirali, Model Leader for Asia' in Edward Allworth (ed.), op. cit.

5. Helene Carrere d'Encausse, *Islam and the Russian Empire: Reform and Revolution in Central Asia.*

6. Edward J. Lazzerini, 'Ismail Bey Gasprinskii's *Perevodchik/Tercuman*: A Clarion of Modernism' in Hasan B. Paksoy (ed.), *Central Asian Monuments.*

7. Ismail Bey Gasprinkskii, 'First Steps toward Civilizing the Russian Muslims' in Charles Kurzman, op. cit.

8. Edward Allworth (ed.), op. cit.

9. Ibid.

10. Pinar Batur-Vander Lippe and John M. Vander-Lippe, *Young Ottomans and Jadidists: The Continuity of Debates in Turkey, the Caucasus and Central Asia.*

11. Edward Allworth, op. cit.

12. Ibid.

# 27

# WILLIAM HENRY QUILLIAM

B. 1856 – D. 1932

UNITED KINGDOM

During the eighteenth and nineteenth centuries, Britain became, according to David Samuel Margoliouth (1858–1940), a prominent British Orientalist, 'the greatest Moslem power in the world'. His words simultaneously echo those of Maulvi Chiragh Ali (1844–1895), a modernist Indian Muslim scholar, who wrote in 1883 that, 'the British Empire is the greatest Mohamedan power in the world', having established its rule in many parts of the Muslim world including the Middle East, Africa and Asia.[1]

So much so, that more than half of the world's Muslim population lived under British governance at the time. Britain's involvement and interaction with the Islamic world prompted many Britons to take a closer look at, and explore the faith, culture and history of the Muslims for themselves and, in the process, they became fascinated by Islam. They were particularly attracted and impressed by the simplicity and rationality of the Islamic faith.

Defying well-established Victorian stereotypes and caricature of the Muslim faith as a religion of the backward and uncivilised people of the Middle East, Africa and Asia, many prominent English men and women openly embraced Islam. In addition to Lord Henry Stanley of Alderley (see chapter 24), Lord Hedley Churchward (d. 1929), Lady Evelyn Cobbold (see chapter 29), Sir Charles Edward A. W. Hamilton

(d. 1939), Yahya (John) Parkinson (see chapter 32), Rt. Hon. Sir Rowland George Allanson-Winn (d. 1935), better known as Lord Headley (see chapter 51), and Marmaduke William Pickthall (see chapter 33) among others, converted to Islam. However, unlike the aforementioned British converts, William Henry Quilliam became the first English Muslim in the nineteenth century to establish a mosque and Islamic centre in England, and, as a result, he became a catalyst for the formation of a thriving community of hundreds of English converts to Islam in the north-western port-city of Liverpool.

William Henry Quilliam, better known as Abdullah Quilliam, was born into a relatively wealthy middle class English family in Liverpool who traced their ancestry back to the Isle of Man. His parents were devout Methodists who belonged to the Temperance movement and actively campaigned to outlaw alcohol. Robert Quilliam (d. 1889), his father, was a successful watchmaker by trade and Harriet Burrows (d. 1901), his mother, was the daughter of a prominent local physician. Being their only child, young Quilliam grew up under the watchful gaze of his parents and regularly attended his local Methodist church where, at the age of seven, he took the pledge of total abstinence under the guidance of Mary Quilliam, his grandmother. Like the other members of his family, William thus became an active nonconformist and often spoke in public in favour of banning liquor while he was still in his teens.

He combined his religious activism with his education at Liverpool Institute. Prior to that, he had also attended the King William's College on the Isle of Man, where his family owned a house. In addition to English, he studied arithmetic, history, science and aspects of religion at school before choosing to specialise in law. During his student days, he also dabbled in journalism and, for a short period, served as the editor of the Good Templar newspaper. He also contributed regular articles to local newspapers and magazines including the Liverpool Albion.

At the same time, Quilliam was an able student who excelled in his studies and, in the process, won several prizes and awards at the Liverpool Institute. Eventually, he passed his final law examination in 1878 and pursued a career in law, which was not an unusual choice for young Quilliam to make because it was considered to be both prestigious, as well as financially very lucrative in those days. In the words of the historian and biographer Ron Geaves,

> As commerce expanded and trade with the world brought untold wealth to Liverpool...William Quilliam chose a new career in law, one that would flourish as commercial activity increased. Quilliam became renowned for his legal work. As a solicitor, he built one of the most successful practices of law in the northwest of England, but he was also known as an advocate, taking on thirty or forty cases per week from the courts.[2]

Whilst Quilliam was busy working as a lawyer, representing both petty criminals as well as high profile individuals (such as Henry Burton and James Gilbert, who were at the time accused of plotting to detonate bombs in the City of London), he – like Alexander Russell Webb (see chapter 25), his American contemporary – may have developed doubts about Christianity and its conflicting theological claims. This was nothing unusual as scientific discoveries, coupled with growing interests in philosophy and literary criticism had called into question some of the fundamental tenets of Christianity, leading to widespread agnosticism and loss of faith, not only in Victorian England but across Western Europe and America.[3] To make matters worse, religious rivalry and in-fighting between the different Christian denominations and sects, especially that between the Protestants and Catholics, became widespread, much to the annoyance and dismay of Quilliam.

In other words, a combination of heavy workload, ill-health, as well as theological doubts about his ancestral faith, coupled with Christian disunity and schism in Liverpool, may have prompted Quilliam to take a break from his legal practice and go abroad to recuperate. It is worth pointing out here that Quilliam was a widely read and scholarly individual who was well-versed in philosophy, theology, history and aspects of science, with a well-stocked personal library of more than two thousand books. His spiritual crisis, if it can be called a crisis at all, was not due to cultural alienation, dislike of things Western or lack of personal success; it was perhaps precipitated by his personal study and inquiry into the ultimate meaning of life and its purpose in the wider scheme of things.

He was around 26 when he went to France and from there, proceeded to Algeria and Tunisia where, for the first time, he came in direct contact with Islam and Muslim culture. He was profoundly impressed by what he witnessed in North Africa, a traditional culture and way of life that revolved around faith, morality and ethics, unlike in late Victorian England where religion had become a major source of disunity, conflict and confusion. This may have inspired him to make another journey in 1883; this time he went to Gibraltar, Spain and Morocco.

Yet again, he was struck by Islam's ability to foster a culture of spirituality, solace, security and contentment without undermining human reason and rationality. On his return from the Maghreb in 1884, he began to study Islam seriously for the first time and the more he explored its scriptures, theology, history and culture, the more he admired it. A year later, he published an article under the title of 'The Mysteries of Muslim Theology' before visiting North Africa yet again in 1887. He may have embraced Islam during his stay in Morocco, although he did not publicly announce his conversion until 1888; he was 32 at the time. What was the main reason for his conversion to Islam? In his own words,

One of the glories of Islam is that it is founded upon reason, and that it never demands from its followers an abnegation of that important mental faculty. Unlike certain other faiths, which insist upon their votaries implicitly accepting certain dogmas without independent inquiry, but simply on the authority of 'The Church', Islam courts inquiry and counsels its disciples to study, search and investigate prior to acceptation. The Holy Prophet, of ever blessed memory, said: 'Allah hath not created anything better than reason, or anything more perfect or more beautiful than reason, the benefits which Allah giveth are on its account, and understanding is begotten on it.' On another occasion, he said: 'Verily, I tell you, a man may have performed prayers, fasts, charity, pilgrimage and all the other good works; but he will not be rewarded but by the manner in which he hath used and applied his reason.'[4]

On another occasion, Quilliam explained,

Those who cannot understand how, 'Islam can be accepted by a European', have no proper comprehension of Western peoples. In the British Isles we are taught to be logical, and to think and reason for ourselves. Islam as a reasonable and logical faith appeals to men's reason, and therefore is likely to be adopted by those who reflect and think and have the courage of their conscience.[5]

In other words, unlike Christianity, he considered Islam to be a reasonable and logical faith that did not require its adherents to accept or believe in doctrines that did not make sense –logically, philosophically or theologically. In addition to this, Quilliam felt that there was no confusion or ambiguity about Islamic morality because it was inclusive and practical, unlike the highly idealistic moral code that was advocated by his former faith, which appeared to him to be out of touch with reality and the challenges of modern life. His first-hand experiences of daily life in Muslim North Africa only served to confirm his doubts and misgivings about Christianity and his eventual conversion to Islam. Not surprisingly, soon after returning home from North Africa, he began to deliver lectures on a range of topics including religion, history, and social justice, often going out of his way to warn the masses of the dangers of alcohol, gambling and other social vices that were prevalent in Liverpool at the time.

Keen not to generate any fuss or hostility amongst the public, he deliberately pursued a subtle and gradualist approach to explaining Islam to the locals. As a popular, learned and eloquent public speaker, he was frequently invited to deliver lectures at churches, public halls and educational institutions across Liverpool. As a result, Quilliam took advantage of these opportunities to point out to his audiences that Islam provided an alternative and more vibrant vision of life, culture and society than the status quo. Despite his subtlety and careful articulation of Islamic principles and values, his views were often greeted with dismay and hostility by local Christian groups who soon considered him to be a renegade and traitor. That was certainly the case following the public announcement of his conversion to Islam in 1888.

Indeed, his task was compounded by a combination of historical hostility towards Muslims as well as the public's negative perception of Islam, due to General Charles Gordon's crushing military defeat at the hands of the Mahdi of Sudan (1844–1885), which created a huge storm in Britain at the time. Undeterred, Quilliam soon gathered around him a handful of followers, all being recent converts to Islam, and they rented a property in Mount Vernon Street, which effectively became their first mosque and meeting place until the landlord discovered, to his utter shock and horror, that his tenants were far from being faithful Christians.

During this period, Quilliam developed his future plans and strategy, which were fourfold, namely 1) to establish an institution for his followers, 2) the need to expand Islamic work in order to gain more converts and supporters from the wider community, 3) to initiate the publication of Islamic journals, books and magazines to disseminate their message nationally and internationally, and 4) to develop and strengthen their links with the Muslim world. In 1891 Quilliam and his followers moved into Brougham Terraces in West Derby Road, which became known as the Liverpool Mosque and Institute (LMI), thus marking the beginning of his mission to institutionalise Islam in Britain for the first time.

According to the historian Humayun Ansari, these premises were subsequently expanded and housed several different projects including:

> A mosque, a *madrassa*, a library and reading-room, a printing-press, a museum, a boys' boarding- and day-school, a girls' day-school, a hostel for Muslims and an office for a literary society. Quilliam and his adherents also established a home for unwanted children. The LMI conducted Friday congregational prayers and celebrated the many annual Muslim festivals. The first funeral prayer according to Muslim custom was said at the Institute in 1891, and many weddings thereafter were solemnised in the Islamic tradition. At the core of LMI's ethos was a sense of belonging to a global Muslim community; Quilliam believed in the 'complete union of Islam and of Muslim peoples', and worked hard towards the accomplishment of this goal. 'Here within the walls of this institution', he declared, 'who knows but that the scattered cords may not be able to be gathered together and woven into a strong rope?'[6]

While the Mosque served as a centre of religious, cultural and ceremonial activities, the Institute played an important role in disseminating Islam in Liverpool and other parts of the country. Quilliam's Islamic activities proved to be such a success that within just over twenty years, he managed to establish the first indigenous Muslim community in Britain consisting of hundreds of British converts. He achieved this by proactively preaching Islam in a language and style that the natives could readily understand and appreciate. This was undertaken through a combination of one-to-one preaching, classroom-based tuition, public lectures and the publication of many books, journals and magazines which were disseminated locally and nationally for the benefit of Muslims and non-Muslims alike. Though he received moral and financial support from some of his adherents, however, the majority of the work was funded by Quilliam out of his own pocket. As an editor, prolific writer and poet, Quilliam published widely and some of his most notable publications include *The Crescent*, *The Islamic World*, *Fanatics and Fanaticism* and *The Faith of Islam*, in addition to more than fifty poems on different subjects.

*The Crescent* was a pioneering weekly newspaper, founded in 1893 by Quilliam, which he continued to edit until 1908. Most of the articles published in this newspaper were written by Quilliam himself, focusing mostly on foreign policy, social justice, Islam, Sufism, freemasonry and critique of Christianity. As a supporter of the Ottoman Empire and an admirer of Sultan Abd al-Hamid II (r. 1876–1909) in particular, Quilliam resented European, particularly British, involvement and meddling in Ottoman internal affairs, and he regularly wrote articles in defence of the sultan and his empire. Although Abd al-Hamid was widely perceived to be a totalitarian and repressive monarch in Europe at the time, Quilliam vehemently disagreed with this view and instead he considered the sultan to be an enlightened Muslim ruler who was fighting valiantly to preserve the unity and integrity of the Ottoman Empire in the face of Western encroachment and hegemony.

If Quilliam's conversion to Islam and subsequent proselytisation in Liverpool did not raise too many eyebrows within the British Establishment at the time, his clear and unequivocal support for, and endorsement of Sultan Abd al-Hamid and his policies, must have alerted, if not alarmed the British security services of his activities. According to Ron Geaves, Quilliam's first biographer, the latter was an 'Ottomanist' through-and-through, although it is fair to say that he was more a Pan-Islamic activist (like Alexander Russell Webb [see chapter 25], Jamal al-Din al-Afghani [838–1897], Muhammad Abduh [1849–1905] and Shakib Arslan [1869–1946]) than a nationalist.[7] Writing in *The Crescent* on 22 April 1896, Quilliam stated,

> All praise be to God Who, in His unlimited goodness, has favoured us with the gift of the True religion of Islam, and Who has ordered the brethren to be united…Among Muslims none should be known as Turks, Arabs, Kurds, Ajem, Afghan, Indians or English. They are all Muslims, and verily the True-Believers are brethren. Islam is erected on the Unity of God, the unity of His religion, and the unity of the Muslims. History demonstrates that the True-Believers were never defeated while they remained united, but only when disunion crept

into their ranks. At the present time, union is more than ever necessary among Muslims.[8]

Along with *The Crescent*, Quilliam published a monthly journal entitled *The Islamic World*. As expected, the articles published in the latter were more in-depth and critical than those in the former, but both publications enabled Quilliam to present his interpretation and understanding of Islam to Muslims and non-Muslims alike – locally, nationally and internationally. *The Islamic World*, first published in 1894, was widely circulated with more than 5000 subscribers but, unlike *The Crescent*, it failed to generate enough income to sustain itself in the long-term.

However, Quilliam's other publication, entitled *The Faith of Islam*, which consisted of a collection of his lectures on aspects of Islam, became an instant hit soon after its appearance in 1889. Reprinted many times and translated into several languages, *The Faith of Islam* was read widely in England and many parts of the Muslim world, including Turkey, Egypt and India. This was his most widely read publication with more than 22,000 copies being printed and disseminated in English alone.

In recognition of his contribution and achievements, Quilliam was hailed as an *alim* or 'Islamic scholar' by the University of al-Qarawiyyin in Fez, Morocco, and Sultan Abd al-Halim II, in turn, conferred the title of 'Shaykh al-Islam of the British Isles' on him, thus officially recognising him as a religious authority in his own right. The rulers of Afghanistan, Egypt, Morocco and Persia also confirmed his position as a champion of Islam and they often provided financial support to Quilliam's Liverpool Mosque and Institute. His other notable publications include *Fanatics and Fanaticism* (1890), *Religion of the Sword* (1889), *Studies in Islam* (1898), *Manx Antiquities* (1898) and *The Balkan Question from a Turkish Standpoint* (1903), among others.

Moreover, Quilliam was an accomplished novelist and poet who published two novels, namely *Polly* (1891) and *The Wages of Sin* (1894), in addition to a large collection of verses on a range of topics including Islam, spirituality, love and family history. Like his other writings, Quilliam's poems have yet to be collected, critically edited and published for the benefit of posterity. Titled 'Hymn for the Prophet's Birthday', here is an example of his beautiful and inspiring Islamic poetry, which was originally published in *The Crescent* on 12 August, 1896:

The people that in darkness sat
A glorious light have seen;
God's prophet now to them hath come –
Muhamed, Al Emin.

We hail thee, Allah's prophet true,
Of prophecy the seal!

We read with reverence the book
Thou wast sent to reveal.

For thou the burden did'st remove,
Idolatry's fell rod;
And in thy day the idols fell
Before the sword of God.

To bless Arabia and the world
Most surely thou wast raised:
We'll sing thy praises evermore,
Our Mustapha, the praised.

We watch with gentle, fostering care
The seed that thou hast sown;
And trust to hear the world declare
God's prophet as its own.

We laugh with scorn at those who say
That God has had a son;
With confidence we do declare
"La Allah," God is One.[9]

Needless to say, Quilliam was a gifted scholar, successful lawyer, charismatic preacher and dedicated Islamic activist who tried to raise awareness and understanding of Islam in England at a time when it was not fashionable to do so. His efforts led to the conversion of a large number of people to the fold of Islam in the nineteenth century, thus laying the foundation of the first indigenous British Muslim community consisting of around 500 people, if not more. Many of those individuals subsequently went on to become prominent early British or European Muslim personalities in their own right, including William Obeidullah Cunliffe (b. cir. 1831-1894), Elias Johan Valfrid Hedman (1872–1939), John Yahya Parkinson (see chapter 32), Amherst Daniel Tyssen (see chapter 51), William Richard Williamson (see chapter 51) and Bertram William Sheldrake (see chapter 51), among many others.

Although Quilliam did not have any formal education in Arabic or traditional Islamic sciences, it is equally true that he read widely enough to thoroughly assimilate Islamic principles and practices. Indeed, his knowledge and understanding of Islamic theology, philosophy, history and culture was more informed and sophisticated than that of any other nineteenth and early twentieth century English convert to Islam, other than Marmaduke Pickthall. As a voracious reader of Islamic literature in

English, Quilliam had access to an English translation of the Qur'an, in addition to the biographies of the Prophet by Thomas Carlyle (1795–1881), Sir William Muir (1819–1905) and Rt. Hon. Syed Ameer Ali (1849–1928), among others.

Due to the success of Quilliam's Islamic activities in Liverpool, he attracted considerable attention from both Muslims and non-Muslims in England and from abroad. Most Muslims were very happy to see Islam grow and expand in Britain while others – especially the Christian missionaries – were utterly dismayed and disgusted by his success. As a result, Quilliam and his adherents 'experienced sustained threats and discrimination. This was hardly surprising for a marginal and provocative group in a city which had been persistently disorderly throughout the nineteenth century and, in its final decades, was strained as a result of growing poverty, rising immigration and appalling public health.'[10] This, coupled with serious financial problems, family issues and other difficulties he faced at the time, eventually forced Quilliam to move to Istanbul in 1908 before returning to London in 1914.

He continued to live there under the new name of Henri de Leon or Harun Mustapha Leon, perhaps in order to avoid attracting unnecessary attention and scrutiny. During this period, Quilliam also became involved with the Woking Muslim Mission* and often delivered lectures on Islam under his new identity. Accordingly, in 1920 he presided over an Indian Muslim delegation led by Mawlana Muhammad Ali Jauhar (1878–1931) at the Woking Mosque. The purpose of this meeting was to promote the

---

* The Woking Muslim Mission was founded in 1912 by Khwaja Kamaluddin, an Indian barrister from Lahore, and based at the site of the Woking Mosque (now called the Shah Jahan Mosque). The Mosque had been established in 1889, the first purpose-built mosque in Britain, after the initiative of an Orientalist named G. W. Leitnar and with the substantial funding of Begum Shah Jahan, the female ruler of the state of Bhopal in India. Kamaluddin belonged to the Ahmadiyya or Qadiani sect, albeit to the Lahori branch which historically has been closer to the orthodox community, despite also falling under the anathematising edict (*takfir*) of the Pakistani government in 1974 that declared them to be non-Muslims. The Woking Muslim Mission, according to the words of Kamaluddin's 'disciple and collaborator' Ya'qub Khan, operated a 'no-sect-in-Islam' policy, whereby 'the Sunni, the Shi'a, the Wahhabi, the Ahmadi – all met as fellow brethren in Islam' (as quoted in Arslan Bohdanowicz, 'To the Memory of al-Hajj Khwaja Kamal-ud-Din (1870–1932): A Pioneer of the Re-birth of Islam', *The Islamic Review*, December 1949 – available at http://www.wokingmuslim.org/pers/kk/life-dec49.pdf). As such, we see notable and outright Sunnis, like Abdullah Quilliam and Marmaduke Pickthall, working with the Woking Muslim Mission; See Ron Geaves, *The Life and Times of Abdullah Quilliam*. According to the current Shah Jahan Mosque website, it remained under 'Ahmediya administration' until the 1970s, when it transferred to Sunni control that continues until today (see http://www.shahjahanmosque.org.uk/history-mosque-part-3).

cause of the Khilafat movement which was being spearheaded by the Indian Muslims at the time. Likewise, in August 1928, he visited Cairo, Egypt where he delivered a lecture on 'Half a Century of Islam in England', which was very well received by his hosts. Unlike many of his friends and family members, Quilliam (or Henri de Leon) remained a dedicated and committed Muslim until his death.

Shaykh Abdullah William Henry Quilliam died in Bloomsbury, London at the age of 76 and was buried in Brookwood Cemetery near Woking, following a simple funeral prayer which was led by the Imam of the Woking Mosque. To raise awareness and understanding of his life, work and contribution, the Abdullah Quilliam Society was established in Liverpool in the 1990s. The founders of this project hope to renovate and reopen the historic Liverpool Mosque and Institute as a tribute to his memory, and for the benefit of the present and future generations.

1. John Slight, *The British Empire and the Hajj, 1865–1956*.

2. See Ron Geaves, *Islam in Victorian Britain: The Life and Times of Abdullah Quilliam*.

3. Simon Heffer, *High Minds: The Victorians and the Birth of Modern Britain*.

4. S. A. Khulusi (ed.), *Islam Our Choice*.

5. Quoted by Jamie Gilman, *Loyal Enemies: British Converts to Islam 1850–1950*.

6. Humayun Ansari, *The Infidel Within: Muslims in Britain since 1800*.

7. Ron Geaves, op. cit.

8. Ibid.

9. Brent D. Singleton (ed.), *The Convert's Passion: An Anthology of Islamic Poetry from Late Victorian and Edwardian Britain*.

10. Jamie Gilman, op. cit.

# 28

# PHILIPPE GRENIER

B. 1865 – D. 1944

FRANCE

The nineteenth century was a fascinating period in the history of modern Islam. At no other time in the history of modern Europe did so many scholars, writers and politicians of Christian heritage choose to convert to Islam, notwithstanding centuries of Western myth-making, demonisation and hostility against Islam, its Prophet and the Qur'an.

Indeed, according to the British historian Norman Daniel, the Western view of Islam across the centuries was so negative that, 'nonsense was accepted, and sound sense was distorted…A communal mode of thought developed. Establishing a great internal coherence, it represented the doctrinal unity of Christendom in its political opposition to Islamic society, a clear social function that correlated military and intellectual aggression.'[1] During this period, the Prophet of Islam was particularly attacked and vilified across Europe. That of course prompted Thomas Carlyle (1795–1881), the celebrated nineteenth century British philosopher and writer, to rush to the defence of the venerable Prophet. Why?

The popular European image of the Prophet bore, in the words of Minou Reeves, 'no resemblance to the Muhammad familiar to Muslims, seen by them as the noblest of men, kindest of husbands and fathers, most faithful and forgiving of friends…who in victory was magnanimous towards his enemies.'[2] Although Carlyle defended the Prophet and hailed him as a 'hero', other prominent Westerners at the time went further and converted to Islam.

Such converts included Ivan Agueli (see chapter 51), a celebrated Swedish painter and author; Alexander Russell Webb, an American diplomat and social reformer (see chapter 25); Lord Henry Stanley of Alderley, an English aristocrat and member of The House of Lords (see chapter 24); Rene Guenon, an influential French metaphysician and author (see chapter 38); Sir Charles Archibald Hamilton (see chapter 51), an English aristocrat; and Lord Headley (see chapter 51), a British peer of the realm. Dr Philippe Grenier, the first Muslim member of the French parliament, also belonged to the generation of Westerners who had left their indelible marks on the history of modern Islam, and Western Islam in particular.

Philippe Grenier was born in the city of Pontarlier (ancient Ariolica), which is today located in the eastern province of Doubs, a department in the Bourgogne-Franche-Comte region of France. He was born into a middle-class, Christian family belonging to the Catholic denomination. His father, Hippolyte Grenier, was an army officer who served Louis-Napoleon Bonaparte (1808–1873), better known as Napoleon III. The latter was the nephew of Napoleon I (1769–1821) and served as the Emperor of the Second French Empire from 1852 to 1870. Hippolyte served Napoleon III in his capacity as a Cavalry Captain in the French military outpost based in Mostaganem, Algeria.[3]

Marie Thiebaud, the mother of Philippe Grenier, was the daughter of Charles Thiebaud, who was a prominent lawyer and a public notary in Pontarlier. Unfortunately, Grenier was only six when his father passed away, thus Marie took on a more prominent role of taking care of her young son and ensuring he received a thorough education. During his early years, Grenier was a playful and active individual. Though on one occasion whilst playing, Grenier leapfrogged only to land awkwardly and, in the process, dislocated his hip. He made a good recovery, although a slight limp was noticeable and for that reason, he often walked with a cane. Being a devout Catholic, his mother was a regular church-goer and she always took her three children with her. Therefore, young Grenier assimilated Catholic principles and practices from the outset.

In other words, young Grenier combined religious training with a thorough education in French literature, history and science. He grew up at a time when philosophical positivism had become one of the most dominant ideologies in French educational and intellectual circles. This was thanks to Auguste Comte's (1798–1857) critique of European Enlightenment thought and humanism on the one hand, and his formulation of a historical sequence on the other, that charted the progress of the human mind through the law of three stages; namely theology, metaphysics and positivism, which proved to be immensely influential. He argued that in the first two stages, attempts were made to interpret and understand the nature of things largely through religious and metaphysical explanations, often relying on revelation or supernatural sources that were beyond human reason, rationality and individual scrutiny.

By contrast, the positivist approach, he contended, was fundamentally based on individual or collective observation and experimentation, and therefore positivist theory and methodology in science was the key to the intellectual development and progress of humanity.[4] As positivism was highly fashionable in those days, Grenier was exposed to this new school of thought at high school and became deeply interested in the physical sciences, particularly human physiology. He was a bright student and, as expected, excelled in his studies which, in turn, enabled him to pursue intermediate and undergraduate studies. He successfully completed his diploma in 1883 at the age of 18.

Keen to pursue further education and training, Grenier applied to the University of Paris to study medicine. He was offered a place at the Faculty of Medicine where he spent the next five years studying all aspects of medicine, with specialisation in human physiology, health and hygiene. Exposure to positivist philosophy, coupled with increasing doctrinal disputes and uncertainty within the Catholic Church in late nineteenth century France, forced many educators, scholars, writers and intellectuals to ask serious questions about their faith and practices. Indeed, as the age of religious certainty and security paved the way to philosophical scepticism and religious uncertainty, Grenier and his contemporaries also subjected their faith to philosophical and scientific scrutiny during this period.

In the process, many of them found Catholicism to be wanting – some even drifted into other forms of spirituality (such as mysticism, theosophy or Vedantic philosophy). This state of affair persisted until Grenier successfully completed his medical education in 1889 and returned to his native Pontarlier, where he soon established a thriving medical practice. It was not long before he decided to go to North Africa and see his brother who, at the time, was based in Algeria.

Algeria was very close to Dr Grenier's heart because his father had previously served in the army of Emperor Napoleon III in Mostaganem. At the age of around 26, Dr Grenier set off for Blida (a city that is located towards the south-west of Algiers), where he encountered Islam and traditional Muslim culture for the first time. He liked what he saw and, as a result, his interest in Islamic teachings and the Muslim way of life intensified. Accordingly, he began to study Islam very closely, focusing particularly on the Qur'an, in addition to first-hand observation of local Islamic culture and practices.

By the same token, Dr Grenier's visit to Algeria was a real eye-opener for him insofar as French colonial policy and administration in North Africa was concerned. He was shocked and appalled by the widespread poverty, social injustice and the oppressive manner in which the French colonial machinery operated and its negative impact on the Algerian people. Historically speaking, France had developed contact with North Africa, particularly Algeria, during the time of Charles Philippe (1757–1836), better known as King Charles X, who reigned from 1824 to 1830. Keen to divert attention away from his domestic challenges and difficulties, the King initiated a military expedition against Algiers.

Subsequently, during the reign of his successor, King Louis-Philippe (r. 1830–1848), much of Algeria was annexed and a colonial administration exercised power over two million Muslims. Although France benefited substantially from its colonisation of

North Africa, Algeria in particular, its behaviour and conduct towards the Muslims of the region was nothing short of ghastly and reprehensible. Nearly half a century before Dr Grenier's visit to Blida, Alexis de Tocqueville (1805–1859), the well-known French political thinker and historian, had observed:

> As far as I am concerned, I came back from Africa with the pathetic notion that at present in our way of waging war we are far more barbaric than the Arabs themselves. These days, they represent civilization, we do not. This way of waging war seems to me as stupid as it is cruel. It can only be found in the head of a coarse and brutal soldier.[5]

Needless to say, the political, economic, social and security situation in Algeria did gradually improve. However, improvements were not quick enough to impress Grenier who, upon his arrival in Blida in 1889, was appalled by the injustice, partiality and oppressive nature of the French colonial administration on the one hand, and the abject poverty, helplessness and growing resentment of its Muslim population on the other. Not surprisingly, on his return to France, Dr Grenier continued to study Islam and, in the process, he became thoroughly familiar with the Qur'an and its teachings. The Qur'anic concept of Divine Oneness (*tawhid*) particularly appealed to him, as did its rationalistic approach to, and understanding of, the meaning and purpose of humanity and the natural world as a whole. In addition to this, Dr Grenier found Islam to be a simple, logical and attractive way of life because it was, in his opinion, based on fairness, justice, charity and spirituality.

Being a medical doctor by profession, he was also impressed by Islam's repeated emphasis on personal hygiene and cleanliness. During this period, he spoke to his mother, Marie Grenier, about Islam and explained his growing interest and inclination towards the religion. Being a devout Catholic, she may have discouraged him but he was not to be deterred. Accordingly, during his second visit to Blida in 1894, he formally embraced Islam; he was 29 at the time.

Thereafter, he went to Makkah to perform the annual pilgrimage (hajj) and eventually returned to France donning the traditional Muslim headgear and robe which, as expected, raised many eyebrows in the Catholic neighbourhoods of Pontarlier. This, however, did not bother the young Muslim doctor in the least because Islam had, at last, offered him what he had been earnestly longing for: namely peace, solace, serenity and contentment. Back home, Dr Grenier resumed his work as a medical doctor and often went out of his way to help the poor and needy by providing them with free treatment and medication. Such efforts impressed the locals, despite their reservations about Dr Grenier's new faith and traditional Arab dress.

A few years later, the local member of the French Parliament died and many people, especially the poor and the downtrodden, urged Dr Grenier to stand as a candidate.

He was understandably apprehensive and considered his chances of winning to be very slim as the other two candidates were prominent individuals in their own right: one being the son of the deceased member of the Legislature, while the other candidate was a leading lawyer from Vesoul, a city located in eastern France. However, Dr Grenier was keen to make a real difference in Pontarlier because he saw how the place suffered from considerable political, economic, social and health problems at the time. Being a doctor by profession, he had no previous experience of politics nor was he an active member of any political party.

However, thanks to the support and encouragement of the local people, he eventually put himself forward as a candidate. Real change and transformation could only take place from a position of power and strength, thus for that reason, being a spectator or bystander was not an option for Dr Grenier. He was equally aware that standing for public office would inevitably lead to closer scrutiny and examination of his private life, religious beliefs and cultural practices. He was fully prepared for a media frenzy and free-for-all. Indeed, as soon as he had announced his intention to stand as a candidate for parliament, journalists rushed to his house to interview him. They wanted to know why he had become a Muslim and what his chances were of winning an election in a staunchly Catholic area. He responded:

> You want to know why I became a Muslim. Due to taste, inclination and faith rather than whim, as some have insinuated. From a young age, Islam and its beliefs became very attractive … but only after a careful reading of the Qur'an, followed by extensive studies and long meditations, did I embrace Islam. I adopted this faith, this dogma, because it seemed to me to be just as rational and more in line with science than Catholic dogma. I would add that the requirements of Islamic law are very suitable since, socially Arab society revolves around the organisation of the family and the principles of fairness, justice and charity towards the poor. From a hygiene point of view, which has some importance for a doctor, it prohibits the use of alcoholic beverages and enjoins the frequent washing of the body and clothing.[6]

After clarifying his position, Dr Grenier fought a determined political campaign, as did the other five candidates, before the results of the first round of the by-election were announced: Emile Grillon, the lawyer, had received 4853 votes; Maurice Ordinary, the son of the deceased MP, had secured 3497 votes; and Dr Philippe Grenier stood in third place, with only 1659 votes. Although the chances of him being able to turn things around from such an unfavourable position were very slim, Dr Grenier decided to stay in the contest and hope for better results in the second round. As a result, Dr Grenier successfully secured 5138 votes, enough for him to win the election outright as his closest rival had only received 4855 votes. By virtue of winning this by-election, he became the first and only Muslim member of the French Parliament in 1896.

This was no mean achievement for the 31 year old doctor who, despite being a devout Muslim, won the hearts and minds of the Catholic population of Doubs and, in so doing, left his indelible mark on modern French parliamentary history. If Dr Grenier had attracted only limited publicity in the mainstream national French press during his election campaign, the situation changed overnight following his by-election victory. Suddenly, the prominent national newspapers, including the *Li Figaro*, *La Croix*, *The National* and *The Sun*, among others, focused their attention on Dr Grenier, his religious views, cultural practices and charitable activities.

Needless to say, Dr Grenier received a mixed reaction from the press. Some papers, such as *The National* and *The Sun*, cautiously welcomed his election to the French National Assembly, while others, such as *Li Figaro* and *La Croix*, were very critical and disparaging, if not downright offensive. As expected, he did not pay much attention to the press and continued to serve his constituents very conscientiously and loyally. Being a man of uncompromising principles, values and morals, Dr Grenier often spoke in the National Assembly and highlighted the on-going crimes, injustice and oppression that was being perpetrated by the imperial powers in many parts of the world, including Algeria, Tunisia, Mali and Senegal. This, of course, did not please the French government officials, but he was not to be frightened or deterred.

In addition, he spoke on poverty alleviation, the need for better transportation, the importance of hygiene and cleanliness, as well as the need for financial support for education, agriculture and medical care in his constituency. Being a practising Muslim, a room was set aside for him in the French National Assembly, allowing him to perform his ablutions and daily prayers. Despite his dedication as an MP and the achievements he made, Dr Grenier unfortunately lost his seat in the 1898 general election. Four years later, Dr Grenier put himself forward in the election but did not regain his seat, perhaps because he repeatedly condemned the consumption of alcohol in a constituency where distilleries became the backbone of the local economy. This effectively marked the end of his short political career.

After leaving politics, Dr Grenier resumed his work as a medical doctor and became heavily involved in charitable activities, especially helping the poor and needy in his locality through the provision of free healthcare and medication. On a personal level, he was pious and ascetic. He not only prayed regularly and observed fasting, he was also a devout and dedicated scholar of the Qur'an. One of Dr Grenier's favourite mottos was: 'Man can always improve or worsen his condition in the hereafter by his good or bad actions.' After becoming a Muslim, he lived the rest of his life according to this fundamental principle, that is to say, always with one-eye fixed to the hereafter. This inspirational and outstanding European Muslim politician, medical doctor and Islamic scholar died at the age of around 79; he was laid to rest in his native Pontarlier.

A decade after his death, Robert Fernier (1895–1977), a notable painter and writer, produced the first biographical sketch of Dr Grenier in French consisting of eighty-six pages; it was published in Pontarlier by Faivre-Vernay Publishing in 1955. Based on Fernier's earlier work, Robert Bichet (1903–2000), a Gaullist MP himself, subsequently authored a biography of Dr Grenier under the title of *Un Comtois Musulman, Le Docteur Philippe Grenier* (The Muslim Comtois, Dr Philippe Grenier). Consisting of 197 pages, this book was published in Besancon (Doubs) by Jacques and Demontrond in 1976.[7] As a tribute to his memory, the main mosque in Pontarlier has been named after him, as well as a local street and college.

1.  Norman Daniel, *Islam and the West: The Making of an Image.*

2.  Minou Reeves, *Muhammad in Europe: A Thousand Years of Western Myth-Making.*

3.  *The Dictionary of French Parliamentarians (1889–1940).*

4.  Auguste Comte and Fredrick Ferre, *Introduction to Positive Philosophy.*

5.  Alexis de Tocqueville, *Travail sur l'Algerie.*

6.  Robert Bichet, *Un Comtois Musulman, Le Docteur Philippe Grenier.*

7.  Sadek Sellam, *Islam and Muslims in France.*

# 29

# LADY EVELYN COBBOLD

B. 1867 – D. 1963

UNITED KINGDOM

The hajj or pilgrimage to Makkah is the fifth pillar of Islam, although it is only obligatory on those who are physically and financially in a position to make the journey. According to the Qur'an, it was Abraham (Prophet Ibrahim) and Ishmael (Prophet Ismail) who constructed the Ka'bah, the cube-shaped structure in the Arabian citadel of Makkah, and called humanity to the worship of God (Allah in Arabic)[1]. Thus the Ka'bah not only came to symbolise the Oneness of Divinity, but also as a reminder to humanity of its oneness and commonality. Ever since then, the sacred mosque became the focus of pilgrimage and, following the advent of Prophet Muhammad (peace be on him) in seventh century Arabia, the Ka'bah was re-dedicated to the worship of One God. In other words, Islam's unusual and extraordinary ability to attract people from all walks of life and unify them into one human family is best showcased by the annual pilgrimage to Makkah.

Indeed, stripped of racial, social, political, economic and other worldly trappings, the pilgrims respond to their burning desire and urge to return back to the centre – the spiritual axis; the primordial origin of all that exists. That is why over the last fifteen centuries of Islam, millions of Muslims – and even some non-Muslims – went out of their way to undertake the life transforming journey and experience the hajj for themselves.

Some even recorded their experiences of the journey, often providing moving accounts of their spiritual transformation and renewal which, in turn, continue to impress and inspire Muslims and non-Muslims, Westerners and Easterners alike to this day.

From Ibn Jubayr, the medieval Spanish traveller (see chapter 14), to Malcolm X (1925–1965), a prominent American civil rights leader, and from Jean Louis Burckhardt (1784–1817), a renowned Swiss explorer, to Michael Wolfe (b. 1945), a contemporary American poet and author, Westerners have been fascinated by the hajj, as have those from the Islamic East. Lady Evelyn Cobbold was another trail-blazer who, by virtue of being able to perform the pilgrimage to Makkah in the early part of the twentieth century, became the first British Muslim woman to successfully accomplish the momentous journey.

Evelyn Murray, better known as Lady Evelyn Cobbold or Sayyida Zainab, was born into a wealthy and aristocratic Scottish family that traced its ancestry back to William I (1028–1087), the first Norman King of England – otherwise known as William the Conqueror. Her father, Charles Adolphus Murray (1841–1907), was not only the 7th Earl of Dunmore, but also a notable Scottish peer and a Conservative politician. Her mother on the other hand, Lady Gertrude Coke (1847–1943), was the third daughter of the Rt. Hon. Thomas William Coke (1822–1909), the 2nd Earl of Leicester. The Earl and Countess of Dunmore married on 5 April, 1866 and they had six children, of whom Evelyn was the eldest. Though she was fond of her parents, young Evelyn had more in common with her father than her mother.

A traveller and explorer of indefatigable energy and dedication, Lord Dunmore was, according to the historian Sydney Ernest Fryer, a powerful man who, 'travelled in many parts of the world, including Africa and the Arctic regions; but his chief fame as an explorer rests on a year's journey made in 1892 …through Kashmir, Western Tibet, Chinese Tartary and Russian Central Asia…He had ridden and walked 2500 miles, traversing forty-one mountain passes and sixty-nine river passes…'.[2]

Along with Sir Francis Younghusband (1863-1942), Lord Dunmore was a founding member of the Central Asian Society (now Royal Society for Asian Affairs). His interest in geography and regular trips to North Africa and Asia fascinated his daughter, Evelyn, who completed her formal education under the supervision of a private tutor or governess at their family villas in Cairo and on the outskirts of Algiers. It was during these sojourns in North Africa that Evelyn first came in contact with Muslim faith and culture. In her own words,

> As a child I spent the winter months in a Moorish villa on a hill outside Algiers, where my parents went in search of sunshine. There I learnt to speak Arabic and my delight was to escape my governess and visit the Mosques with my Algerian friends, and unconsciously I was a little Moslem at heart. After three years' wintering at Mustapha Superieure we left the villa for good, much to my despair,

but in time I forgot my Arab friends, my prayers in the Mosque and even Arabic language.[3]

Whilst in Cairo, she also witnessed the Mahmal, an annual ceremony that marked the completion and departure of the *kiswa* (or the embroidered cover of the Ka'bah) from Cairo to Makkah. Evelyn found the occasion to be interesting and very colourful. As it happened, aspects of the Muslim faith and culture always appealed to her, thus her fascination with Islam was destined to become a permanent part of her life. Like her French contemporary, Isabelle Eberhardt (see chapter 51), Evelyn found Islam and Muslim culture to be authentic and attractive, but unlike the former, she never settled permanently in the Muslim world. Being very fond of her native Scottish Highlands, that part of the world was to remain her original home. Despite being a seasoned traveller and adventurer, having travelled extensively through many parts of the Muslim world and also having lived in Suffolk, East Anglia during her married life, it was her beloved Scotland that was to be her permanent home and final resting place.

Although Evelyn had more in common with her father, she did share her mother's spiritual tendencies and inclinations. Despite initially leaning towards Islam, Gertrude never became a Muslim, unlike her daughter, and around 1900, she and her husband eventually embraced Christian Science as their religious denomination. Prior to that, in 1891, whilst Evelyn was in her mid-twenties, her parents blessed her marriage to John Dupuis Cobbold, which took place on 23 April at the All Saints Church in Cairo. John hailed from the wealthy Cobbold family of Suffolk, East Anglia, who made their fortune from their brewery business. Whilst the Cobbold family were not aristocratic in their origins, they were, however, more wealthy and prosperous than the Murray's and that, no doubt, encouraged Charles and Gertrude to approve their daughter's marriage.

Born in 1861, John was an educated, handsome and wealthy young man, who had fallen in love with the slim, attractive, intelligent and elegant Evelyn as soon as he saw her. After their marriage, the couple left Cairo and moved to Holywells, the Cobbold's family estate in Ipswich, which was located in a 67-acre park. Their three children, namely Winfried Evelyn Cobbold (b. 1892), John Murray (Ivan) Cobbold (b. 1897) and Pamela Cobbold (b. 1900) were born during this period. Although Suffolk was very different from the Scottish Highlands or North Africa for that matter – places that Evelyn was most familiar with and had shaped and influenced her during her formative years – she played an active part in her children's upbringing, even if her husband was not always at hand to provide necessary help and support. Although, to be fair to John, he did provide her with everything she needed materially. According to Evelyn's biographers,

> Married life provided every material comfort available and imaginable at the time. We see Evelyn as a handsome, if somewhat austere-looking, woman with a

penchant for large hats and long intricate dresses, cinched at her wasp-like waist. She is shown spending much time reading alone in the garden, sometimes on her horse, and frequently entertaining large family parties. To alleviate the *longueurs* of this gilded cage, there were family visits to the seaside to stay with 'Uncle Felix' at another Cobbold house, The Lodge at Felixstowe, which the children adored, as well as annual jaunts to Ascot and Cornwall, fishing and stalking in Scotland, holidays in Monte Carlo, visits to Cairo, and regular social and shopping trips to London.[4]

Despite having all the material comforts that money could buy at the time, Evelyn never really felt at home in Suffolk and, accompanied by her husband, she often travelled abroad, such as to Norway, Ireland and Scotland. Both husband and wife combined their passion for travel with their duties as parents but, over time, as John spent more and more time away from his family, it was rather inevitable that he and his wife would drift away from one another. Evelyn's longing for the Islamic East was evident from the fact that she, accompanied by a female companion, soon visited North Africa and an account of her adventures in that part of the world was subsequently published in 1912 under the title of *Wayfarers in the Libyan Desert* (London: Arthur L. Humphreys).

In this travelogue, Evelyn provided a detailed and sympathetic description of Muslim life and culture. An impartial reader of this book cannot help but feel that she was describing a culture that she herself belonged to, rather than a culture she was an alien or an outsider to. Although it is not possible to say categorically whether she had embraced Islam by that time, the fact that the first chapter of her book begins with the Islamic invocation of *Bismillah al-Rahman al-Rahim* (In the name of God, the Most Beneficent, the Most Merciful), inscribed most probably in her own hand-writing, indicates that she considered herself to be a Muslim. Her description of the prayer performed by the Bedouins in the desert is also moving and inspirational, thus confirming her growing commitment to Islam. In her own words,

> When the desert assumes the blue veil of approaching night, the Bedouins halt for the evening prayer. They stand, their hands outstretched, their eyes turned to Mecca, while they recite the opening chapter of the Koran, occasionally prostrating themselves, their foreheads touching the ground. In the silence of these vast unlived-on tracts the nomads pray to the God of Islam with perfect faith that knows no doubts. There is something very impressive in the desert prayer. To believe in Allah and his Prophet, to await without fear or impatience the inevitable hour of death, this is the simple faith of Islam.[5]

Again, towards the end of her book, Evelyn gently reminded her Western, non-Muslim readers of Islam's positive impact on world history and its remarkable contributions to human civilisation:

> Nearly 1300 years ago, when Christian Europe was in a state of semi-barbarism, its literature dispersed or lost, the finer arts extinct, Islam arose, binding the wild hordes of Arabia together in the brotherhood of a powerful faith; and in a short time these Arabs established brilliant centres of advanced civilisation in the chief cities of Asia, Africa, and southern Europe. Bagdad became the home of philosophers, poets, and men of letters, and in Cairo, Cordova, and many another city, libraries were collected, schools of medicine, mathematics, and natural history flourished, while Europe is indebted to Islam for the preservation of much of the classical literature of the ancient world…To the Arab his religion is a living thing, ever present in his daily life; a power to console in sorrow, a faith enabling him to face trouble with resignation, death without flinching. Truly is Islam a powerful and great force.[6]

Being an intelligent, outward-looking and fiercely independent-minded woman, Evelyn was determined to carve out her own moral and spiritual path in life. Clearly her attachment to Islam was genuine and profound, and that of course became gradually clear to her husband during their two decades together. Since his wife's love and longing for the 'religion of common sense' was far from being a moment of madness, coupled with his own pre-occupation with travelling and other business interests, eventually prompted John to agree to an amicable separation.

Although some writers have stated that Evelyn was divorced, according to her great-grandson, Angus Sladen, Evelyn supposedly died as a widow of John Dupuis Cobbold.[7] As per the terms of the settlement, John purchased her a house in Mayfair, London; agreed to an annual allowance of £10,000; and offered Evelyn Glencarron in Wester Ross, which was a 15,000 acre estate in Scotland. By all accounts, this was a generous settlement, thus it enabled Evelyn to live in considerable luxury and comfort for the rest of her life; pursuing her own interests in stalking deer, shooting grouse, fishing salmon and trout, and of course, her life-long fascination with Islam. But a question still remains unanswered: when did Evelyn actually become a Muslim? In the introduction to her book, *Pilgrimage to Mecca*, she explained – and it is worth quoting her at some length:

> *'If this be Islam,' asks Goethe, 'do we not all live in Islam?"Yes,' answers Carlyle, 'all of us that have any moral life, we all live so.'*

I am often asked when and why I became a Moslem. I can only reply that I do not know the precise moment when the truth of Islam dawned on me. It seems that I have always been a Moslem. This is not so strange when one remembers that Islam is the natural religion that a child left to itself would develop. Indeed, as a Western critic once described it, 'Islam is the religion of common sense'... Some years went by and I happened to be in Rome staying with some Italian friends, when my host asked me if I would like to visit the Pope. Of course I was thrilled, and, clad all in black with a long veil, I was admitted into the august presence in company with my host and his sister. When His Holiness suddenly addressed me, asking if I was a Catholic, I was taken aback for a moment and then replied that I was a Moslem... A match was lit and I then and there determined to read and the more I studied, the more convinced I became that Islam was the most practical religion, and the one most calculated to solve the world's many perplexing problems, and to bring to humanity peace and happiness. Since then I have never wavered in my belief that there is but one God; that Moses, Jesus, and Muhammed and others were Prophets, divinely inspired, that to every nation God sent an apostle, that we are not born in sin, and that we do not need any redemption, that we do not need anyone to intercede between us and God, Whom we can approach at all times...and that our salvation depends entirely on ourselves and our actions. The word 'Islam' means surrender to God. It also means peace. A Moslem is one who is 'in harmony with the Decrees of the Author of This World', one who has made his peace with God and His creatures.[8]

This passage shows that Evelyn's understanding of Islam was broad and inclusive, being less ritualistic and more universal, focusing as she did on its principles, values and ethos. Her knowledge of Islam was considerable, thanks to her first-hand knowledge and understanding of Muslim culture which she acquired during her travels and extensive reading of Islamic literature. In addition to prominent pro-Islamic Western scholars and thinkers like Johann Wolfgang von Goethe (1749–1832), Thomas Carlyle (1795–1881) and Wilfrid Scawen Blunt (1840–1922), she was familiar with the writings of leading Muslim scholars of the time, including Rt. Hon. Syed Ameer Ali (1849–1928), William Henry Quilliam (see chapter 27), Marmaduke Pickthall (see chapter 33) and Mawlana Muhammad Ali Lahori (1874–1951), among others.

Evelyn had access to several English translations of the Qur'an and she considered the five pillars of Islam (*Arkan al-Islam*) to be its heart and soul. She repeatedly emphasised the importance of the first and fifth pillars of Islam, namely Divine Oneness (*Tawhid*) and the Prophethood of Muhammad (peace be on him), along with the pilgrimage to Makkah. However, it is not known whether she regularly performed the five daily prayers (*Salah*), observed fasting during the month of Ramadan (*Siyam-i-Ramadan*) and paid the annual obligatory levy on excess wealth (*Zakat*), although she was generous in her support of various Islamic causes, including funding the publication of Islamic literature.

After her separation from her husband in 1922, Evelyn did not remarry and divided her time between London and Glencarron. But after the death of her husband in 1929, she moved around more freely. Now in her mid-sixties, she decided to perform the pilgrimage to Makkah, but it was never going to be an easy undertaking considering the political, economic and cultural uncertainty and upheaval of the time. Oil had not been discovered yet and Saudi Arabia was on the verge of financial bankruptcy at the time, mostly due to widespread poverty, financial mismanagement and reduction in the number of pilgrims, who otherwise brought in much-needed revenue to boost the local economy.

Being a wise lady, however, Evelyn contacted the Saudi Arabian Ministry in London for guidance and support. In Shaykh Hafiz Wahba (1889–1969) – who served as the first Saudi ambassador to London from 1930 to 1956 and was an Islamic scholar in his own right – she found a great supporter who later contributed a glowing foreword to her book on the pilgrimage. The Shaykh agreed to help her and immediately dispatched a letter to King Abd al-Aziz ibn Saud (1875–1953) seeking permission from the Saudi monarch.

As she was not willing to simply idly wait for a response from Riyadh, Evelyn made her own arrangements and set out for Jeddah where she stayed with Harry (Abdullah) St John Bridger Philby (see chapter 37) and his wife. After being vetted by the Saudi authorities, she was granted permission to perform the annual hajj in 1933, which she completed successfully and then proceeded to Madinah, the city of the Prophet, on 15 March, which was, of course, facilitated by Philby. As expected, she found Madinah to be calm, peaceful and spiritually exhilarating, but her description of the city, its people and the Prophet's mosque is most vivid and unusually informative.

During her journey to and from Makkah, Evelyn maintained a detailed diary which enabled her to write a meticulous account of her extraordinary pilgrimage on her return to London. First published in 1934 under the title of *Pilgrimage to Mecca* (London: John Murray) and recently reprinted in London and Riyadh (2008), the book was positively reviewed in the leading British newspapers of the time including the *Sunday Times*, the *Manchester Guardian*, the *Morning Post*, the *Scotsman* and the *News Chronicle*, among others. The only exception was the *Geographical Journal* which was unduly negative. Reviewing the book in the *Sunday Times*, Sir John Collings Squire (1884–1958), who was himself a renowned scholar and literary figure, wrote:

Lady Evelyn will deserve a place of her own in the records of Arabian travel; she is the first European woman convert to Islam to have visited and described its Holy Places...and, had she been the hundred and first visitor, her book would still have been interesting, charming and even amusing...the author, though the digressions in her personal narrative are never very long, puts eloquently the case for Islam, particularly with regard to bellicosity and the position of women.[9]

Sir John was right to point out that Evelyn's book was much more than a story of her journey to the sacred cities of Islam, not least because she robustly defended traditional Islamic teachings and practices throughout the book, but also as she highlighted the similarities between Islam and Christianity. However, his designation of her as the 'first European woman convert to Islam' to have performed the pilgrimage is far from being accurate.

As it happened, several other European Muslim women had accomplished that feat before her, although she was certainly the first British Muslim woman to perform the sacred hajj. She was also the first British Muslim to publish an account of her journey to Makkah. As expected, her book received a glowing review in the *Islamic Review* (January 1935), the monthly journal of the Woking Muslim Mission, but undoubtedly the most positive review was published by her contemporary and fellow convert, Marmaduke Pickthall (see chapter 33), in the *Islamic Culture*, which he edited and published from India at the time under the patronage of the Nizam of Hyderabad. According to Pickthall,

> There are certain false ideas about Islam which still prevail in Europe: that Muslims believe that women have no souls, [and] that Islam, as a religion, may appeal to men (because it allows polygamy) but cannot possibly appeal to any civilized enlightened woman, and so forth. These misapprehensions the delighted account which Lady Evelyn Cobbold has given of her pilgrimage to Al-Madinah and Mecca and her performance of the hajj ought completely to dispel: for there can be no doubt either of Lady Evelyn's sincerity as a Muslimah or of the freedom of her choice of Al-Islam as her religion; and the story of her pilgrimage is sufficient refutation of the ancient calumny concerning souls.[10]

Almost two years after her pilgrimage, Evelyn set off on another journey. This time she visited Kenya, accompanied by Toby Sladen, her grandson, and on her return she published her diary under the title of *Kenya: The Land of Illusion* (London: John Murray, 1935). However, unlike the *Pilgrimage to Mecca*, it did not receive widespread acclaim or recognition. According to Evelyn, 'this little book, which is but an elaborated diary, was originally written for my [Evelyn's] own amusement and to fill in the idle hours when flying over the African deserts', rather than being a scholarly account of her African sojourn.[11]

Although she was now approaching her seventieth birthday, she subsequently found the time and energy to visit North Africa again, spending time in Algeria and Morocco. During the Second World War (1939 to 1945), her movements were restricted to London, being unable to even visit Glencarron. She later moved to her large estate in Scotland

and eventually died in a nursing home in Inverness on Friday 25 January, 1963 at the ripe old age of 95. As per her instruction, Lady Evelyn (Sayyida Zainab) Cobbold was laid to rest on a Scottish mountain facing towards the *Qibla*, the direction of Makkah, much to the amusement of the locals. Her funeral prayer was conducted by the Imam of Woking Mosque, Shaykh Muhammad Tufail, whose detailed description of the funeral was published in Urdu in Lahore a month later. She requested the following Qur'anic verse, known as the 'Verse of Light' (*Ayat al-Nur*) to be inscribed on her tombstone:

Allah is the light of the heavens and the earth;
A likeness of His light is as a niche in which is a lamp,
The lamp is in a glass,
(And) the glass is as it were a brightly shining star,
Lit from a blessed olive-tree,
Neither eastern nor western,
The oil whereof almost gives light though fire touch it not –
Light upon light –
Allah guides to His light whom He pleases,
And Allah sets forth parables for men,
And Allah is Aware of all things.[12]

N

1. See Qur'an, *Surah Baqara* [chapter] 2: verse 127.

2. Sydney Ernest Fryer, *Dictionary of National Biography* (1912 Supplement).

3. Lady Evelyn Cobbold, *Pilgrimage to Mecca.*

4. William Facey and Miranda Taylor, Introduction, *Pilgrimage to Mecca*, op. cit.

5. Evelyn Cobbold, *Wayfarers in the Libyan Desert.*

6. Ibid.

7. Anthony Cobbold, a descendant of the Cobbold family, also confirmed this to be true to this writer.

8. Lady Evelyn Cobbold, *Pilgrimage to Mecca.*

9. *Sunday Times*, 17 June 1934.

10. *Islamic Culture*, vol. 8, 1934.

11. Lady Evelyn Cobbold, *Kenya: The Land of Illusion.*

12. See Qur'an, *Surah Nur* [chapter] 24: verse 35.

# 30

# MEHMED DZEMALUDIN CAUSEVIC

B. 1870 – D. 1938

BOSNIA HERZEGOVINA

In his acclaimed book, *Bosnia: A Short History* (1994), Noel Malcolm (b. 1956), a leading British historian of the Balkans, wrote:

> While the term 'Muslim' was acquiring political significance in this way, the strictly religious basis of the term was being gradually eroded by the secularizing influences of the twentieth century. Islamic observance in Bosnia had never been generally 'fanatical', though casual visitors had sometimes described it as such; there had indeed been some fiercely orthodox Muslim clergy, but the population at large was more relaxed in its practices…Since 1878 a slow process of secularization had been under way; increasing numbers of Muslims had acquired a Western education at state schools, and some had gone on to study subjects such as medicine or engineering at Vienna or Budapest. As the old advantages of economic power from land-owning declined, the upper stratum of Muslim society naturally began to move into the professions, for which a Western education was required. One observer in 1920 was struck by the number

of young Muslims studying at universities and technical colleges. Meanwhile ordinary Muslim women had been encouraged to go to work in factories in Sarajevo – something unthinkable in strict Muslim societies at the time.[1]

During this momentous time in the history of the Balkans and Bosnia in particular, a remarkable Muslim scholar, reformer and thinker was born, who was in fact destined to leave his imperishable mark on the history of Islamic thought and culture across the region. He was none other than the indomitable Dzemaludin Causevic of Bosnia and Herzegovina.

Muhammad Jamal al-Din Causevic, better known as Mehmed Dzemaludin Efendi Causevic or Dzemaludin Causevic for short, was born into a well-respected Muslim family in the Bosnian village of Arapusa in the municipality of Bosanska Krupa, located towards the north-west of the present-day Republic of Bosnia and Herzegovina.[2] His father, Ali-hodza Causevic, was an Islamic teacher who was known locally for his religious and social activities. As expected, he ensured his son received a thorough Islamic education during his early years.

In addition to learning Arabic, the Qur'an and aspects of Islamic jurisprudence from his father, young Causevic attended the classes of several local teachers to prepare himself for further and higher Islamic education. Being a bright and ambitious student, he soon impressed his family members and teachers by swiftly learning and memorising the Arabic Qur'an. His eagerness to learn more prompted his father to enrol him at the Islamic seminary (*madrasah*) in Bihac, a city located in north-western Bosnia on the River Una, when he was only seven. Here, he soon attracted the attention of Ahmad Sabit Efendi Ribic, who was the principal tutor at the seminary and also the city's *Mufti* (jurisconsult). Under the guidance of the scholar and jurist, Causevic improved his knowledge and understanding of Arabic, Qur'anic exegesis, Prophetic traditions and Islamic jurisprudence, in addition to learning aspects of the Turkish language and literature.

Whilst Causevic was busy pursuing his further education at the seminary in Bihac, the political condition in Bosnia had undergone a radical transformation. Centuries of Ottoman rule gave way to the Austro-Hungarian Empire (fl.1878–1918), soon establishing its sovereignty over Bosnia, leading to a combination of political, economic, cultural and educational transformations across the region.

Although the imperial rulers neither condoned nor opposed Islamic customs and practices, the Muslim population of Bosnia, which at the time consisted of more than thirty-five per cent, were treated unfairly and often harassed by the authorities, thus forcing many Muslims to move to Ottoman Turkey. In addition to this, the imperial government went out of its way to undermine Bosnia's political and cultural links with the Ottoman State. In the words of Enes Karic, a notable Bosnian scholar and historian,

With the coming of the Austro-Hungarian Empire to Bosnia in 1878, the Austro-Hungarian authorities attempted to establish a certain distinct religious Islamic hierarchy, unknown until then in Bosnia and Herzegovina. The Austro-Hungarian authorities sought in this way not only physically but spiritually to separate the Bosnian Muslims from the Ottoman Empire. For example, when the Austro-Hungarian troops entered Bosnia in 1878, they found that Husein Nur ef. Hafizovic as the supreme Shari'ah judge in Sarajevo that year, and the Austro-Hungarian occupation authorities considered him as the supreme representative of the Islamic community in Bosnia and Herzegovina. However, since the Austro-Hungarian Empire had undertaken, at the Berlin Congress of 1878, respect to religious freedom when 'bringing order to Bosnia and Herzegovina', and not to disrupt the connections of the Istanbul *Shaykh al-Islam* with the Bosnian Muslims, the Bosnian Muslims expected that their principal religious representative would be appointed from Istanbul. The Austro-Hungarian authorities, however, did not wholly honour this international commitment.[3]

It was during this period of political, economic and cultural upheaval that Causevic completed his further education at the Islamic seminary in Bihac under the tutelage of Ahmad Ribic and his colleagues. He was barely 17 years old at the time and, being eager to pursue higher education in Arabic and Islamic sciences, his erstwhile mentor recommended that he should proceed to Istanbul. After bidding farewell to his family and relatives, Causevic moved to the capital of the Ottoman State and joined the class of Salih Efendi Tokatli.

During his time in Istanbul, young Causevic not only received advanced training in Arabic, Turkish and Islamic sciences, he was also exposed to the political, social, economic and cultural challenges that Muslims faced at the time, both in the Balkans as well as in the heart of the Ottoman State. His hard work and dedication to his studies bore fruit as he was granted *ijaza* (certification of proficiency) by none other than Hasan Husni Efendi, one of Istanbul's leading Islamic scholars at the time.

He combined his traditional Islamic education with specialisation in law at *Madrasah al-Huquq* (Faculty of Law) in Istanbul, enabling him to acquire an in-depth knowledge and understanding of Islamic jurisprudence as well as secular Ottoman State law. During this period, he visited his native Bosnia at regular intervals and, due to his extensive knowledge of Arabic and Islamic sciences, he was invited to deliver lectures at different venues in his locality. Here, he urged the masses to remain faithful to Islam and its teachings, which of course won him many plaudits and admirers.

Causevic completed his higher education at a time when the Muslim world was firmly under the grip of the European colonialists, especially the French and British. The former had established themselves in North Africa and parts of the Middle East, while the latter had secured their rule in Mughal India and Egypt, among other places. European subjugation and exploitation of Muslim lands during the eighteenth, nineteenth and early twentieth centuries eventually prompted many Muslim scholars and reformers to emerge to rally the masses in order to liberate Muslim countries from foreign occupation and hegemony.

Two of the leading Muslim scholars and reformers of the time included Jamal al-Din al-Afghani (1838–1897) and his prominent disciple, Muhammad Abduh (1849–1905). Both men became the standard-bearers of Islamic modernism at a time when most of the Muslim world was firmly under Western political, economic and military control. They advocated the need for religious renewal, political liberation, economic development and cultural advancement across the Islamic world, and did so through their intellectual efforts, political activism and journalistic endeavours.[4]

During his time in Istanbul, Causevic became so interested in the modernist message of the Muslim reformers that, in the year 1900, he even went to Cairo where he met and attended Muhammad Abduh's lectures for several months. Like Abd al-Rahman al-Kawakibi (1849–1903), Muhammad Rashid Rida (1865–1935), Qasim Amin (1865–1908), Ahmad Lutfi al-Sayyid (1872–1963) and others, Causevic was inspired by Abduh's bold and farsighted vision for the Muslim world. However, he never became a blind or uncritical follower of any religious scholar or school of thought, unlike some of Abduh and al-Afghani's other disciples.

After completing his formal education, Causevic was offered a teaching role in *Madrasah al-Huquq,* but he turned down the offer and returned home to Bosnia to take up the post of an Arabic teacher at the main Gymnasium in Sarajevo, a prominent high school at the time. Causevic's impressive command of Arabic and Turkish, coupled with extensive knowledge of Islamic and modern sciences, prompted his appointment to the *Majlis al-Ulama* (The Council of Religious Scholars) of Bosnia and Herzegovina. That was no mean achievement for someone in his mid-thirties at the time. His role within the Council was to promote and improve Islamic education across Bosnia, and for that purpose, he travelled extensively up and down the country between 1905 and 1909 in order to acquire first-hand knowledge and understanding of Islamic schools and colleges.[5]

After completing his survey of Islamic educational institutions and their conditions, he realised that most of them were not fit for purpose. The governing authorities, teachers, students, as well as the textbooks that were being taught at those institutions were, he felt, completely out of touch with reality and as such, the graduates of those religious institutions would be incapable of dealing with the complex and ever-changing challenges and difficulties facing the Bosnian Muslims and their societies.

Indeed, the prevalence of rote learning and uncritical thinking within the Islamic educational establishments had, in his opinion, led to blind imitation of religious customs and practices which were undermining Islamic education, culture and institutions across the country. Causevic therefore recommended the provision of additional training for the teachers and the production of religious textbooks in the

Bosnian languages, replacing the existing Arabic and Turkish ones, in order to promote and popularise sound Islamic knowledge and practices within the Bosnian societies. In his own words,

> Each of you, brothers, sees clearly and lucidly the state of our Islamic world. The *maktabs* and *madrasas*, and all our educational institutions, need a major overhaul. To find the remedy and assistance for this, we must instruct our people. I know that we cannot do everything overnight, but reading to them or speaking to them of what is written will gradually bring them to awareness, and then everything will go better. I ask you, and draw your attention to the fact that this task must be seriously addressed. All of us together must move things forward, must not lag behind, but must accept the culture that is inseparable from Islam and that teaches us the wisdom of our forgotten things, that we must once again accept and embrace wherever we find.[6]

Causevic's impressive and in-depth knowledge of Arabic and Islamic sciences, especially Islamic jurisprudence and Ottoman *Qanuni* (Kanuni) law as promulgated by the sultans, soon prompted the authorities to appoint him to the post of professor of Islamic jurisprudence at the Faculty of Shari'ah in Sarajevo in 1909. This school was established and financed by the imperial rulers to train up a new generation of specialists in Islamic law, focusing particularly on the needs and requirements of the Muslim population of Bosnia. He soon established his reputation as an outstanding and erudite scholar, being equally at home in the religious and secular sciences, which no doubt endeared him to the ruling elite as well as the Muslims of Sarajevo and Bosnia as a whole.

Being confident, learned and a reformist, he promulgated and espoused a comprehensive and integrated approach to the Islamic worldview and the Shari'ah, which was at once inclusive, outward-looking and of course islamically well-informed and authentic. This clearly impressed those around him, so much so that four years later, while he was still in his mid-forties, Causevic was nominated to replace Hafiz Sulaiman Efendi Sarac (1850–1927) as the *Rais al-Ulama* (Grand Mufti) of Bosnia and Herzegovina. However, his unwillingness to dilute or compromise fundamental Islamic principles and practices did not impress or please the ruling Yugoslav authorities, until the subject of administration of religious endowments (*awqaf*) flared up during the late 1920s.

This happened following the collapse of the Austro-Hungarian rule after the First World War (1914–1918) and the creation of the Kingdom of Yugoslavia in 1918, which continued to endure until the outbreak of the Second World War in 1941. This was, again, a momentous period in the history of Bosnia and Herzegovina, when the forces of secularisation were unleashed, coupled with the political, social and economic uncertainty and upheaval of the time, leading to considerable religious and cultural conflicts and confusion across the region. According to Noel Malcolm, 'the main threat to tolerance came, as so often in Bosnia's history, from outside Bosnia's borders. The unresolved political tensions between the centralists and their opponents grew more and more severe during the 1920s…King Alexandra tried at first to defuse the crisis and to set up a new government under Korosec. But then, in January 1929, the King took more drastic action, suspending the constitution, and imposing a far more unitary political system than anything the Serbian politicians had hitherto attempted.'[7]

Causevic served as *Rais al-Ulama* during a testing and turbulent time and, coupled with the fact that he was a reformist scholar and jurist, he often found himself out of tune with the conservative *ulama* as well as the incumbent government, which was often unpredictable and unwilling to accommodate religious needs and requirements. Combining his role as a religious leader of his people with that of a senior government official was, therefore, far from being easy or straight-forward at the time, but he persisted and continued to urge the Muslims of Bosnia to unite and work together for their collective benefit.

However, he often found himself alone in his quest for concessions from the government and, needless to say, this was often compounded by the conservative *ulama*, who were never in a mood to understand and appreciate, much less accept and accommodate alternative views and opinions on a range of religious and legal issues affecting the Bosnian Muslims at the time. Unsurprisingly, Causevic felt that he was fighting a lonely battle on behalf of his people. In his own words,

> I carried out and continue to carry out my duties as has no other Ra'is. I have been interpreting the religious truth in the Bey's mosque for almost eight years, and state and recommend what is beneficial to the Islamic community. Pointing the finger at our deficiencies in religious upbringing, I proposed certain remedies…I said then that it is not right to expect of the Ra'is that he alone will take everything like this into account. I have said that if we were all together, I would be there too.[8]

Causevic served as *Rais al-Ulama* for nearly two decades during which he not only championed the cause of the Bosnian Muslims, but also instigated much-needed reforms in the religious, legal and cultural practices that prevailed in Bosnia. Inspired by the modernist message of Muhammad Abduh and other nineteenth century Muslim reformers, Causevic attempted to harmonise Divine revelation with human reason; thus seeking to overcome the conflict between fundamental Islamic principles and values with the growing demand for modernisation and progress that was sweeping Western societies, as well as parts of the Muslim world at the time. The reform measures he instigated during his time as *Rais al-Ulama*, therefore, need to be analysed and understood in the existential condition in which he operated. He stated,

It would be madness to think that others will wait for us and have regard for us, and that with time they will pay attention to our wishes. Everything has changed now. Schools and education have changed, and those who cannot cope with novelty will be lost. The world is moving ahead, and if we cannot keep up with the spirit of the times, we shall be overrun. In the past we were asleep, but we have to wake up now.[9]

In keeping with the spirit of the age, he argued that *waqf* land, located in prime locations in parts of Bosnia, should be utilised more effectively by building schools and other educational institutions for the benefit of local people, rather than left as graveyards which, as expected, incensed the conservative *ulama*. However, he did not budge an inch. On another occasion, he argued that the *niqab* (full veil worn by some Muslim women) was not a requirement of the faith, although modesty in dress and behaviour was, in his opinion, an integral part of Islamic ethics and morality. In his own words, 'I had rather see a Muslim girl unveiled and honourably earning her living, than a girl who walks round the streets veiled in the daytime and spends the evening in a café.'[10]

His intention was to encourage more Bosnian Muslim girls to attend school and pursue higher education as the conservative Muslims were, at the time, reluctant to allow their daughters to attend secular schools due to un-Islamic practices and influences at those institutions. Likewise, he authorised Bosnian Muslim youth to enlist for service in the Austro-Hungarian military despite stiff opposition from other Muslim scholars, but he took no notice of such criticism. Rather, he accused the Bosnian Muslim intelligentsia of having distanced themselves from their people, as well as ignoring their collective benefits and national interests.

In 1930, at the age of 60, Causevic resigned as Grand *Mufti* in protest against a royal decree that stipulated the creation of a single post of *Rais al-Ulama*, consisting of a single Council, serving the whole of Yugoslavia with its headquarters being located in Belgrade. During this period, he worked closely with Hafiz Muhammad Pandza and, after nearly a decade of collaboration, they produced one of the first complete translations of the Qur'an into Bosnian under the title of *Kur'an casni, prevod i tumac* (The Holy Qur'an, Translated and Interpreted). Published in 1937 in Sarajevo by Causevic himself and, consisting of more than one thousand pages, the main purpose of this translation and commentary was to introduce the message of the Qur'an to the people of the Balkans in general, and that of Bosnia in particular.

Another reason for this translation and commentary was, as explained by Causevic in his introduction, to inform

Our brothers in the world at large to see and discover that we Muslims in this part of Europe, too, although few in number, are able and willing to translate and interpret the sublime source of our fate as is being done in the major centres of the Islamic community. I wanted to demonstrate that our generosity of spirit should not be measured in terms of our small numbers in this corner of Europe.[11]

For their commentary, Causevic and Pandza relied heavily on the following scholars: Omer Riza Dogrul, Muhammad Abduh, Sir Sayyid Ahmad Khan, Muhammad Rashid Rida, Mawlana Muhammad Ali Lahori and Tantawi Jawhar, among others. Needless to say, their efforts inspired other Bosnian scholars to subsequently produce their own Qur'anic translations, revisions and commentaries, but the credit for initiating this trend must go to none other than Causevic and Pandza for their seminal contribution to Qur'anic studies in the Bosnian language. Needless to say, 1937 was an important year in the history of Qur'anic studies in Bosnia because another Qur'anic scholar, Ali Riza Karabeg of Mostar, also produced his own translation into Bosnian in the same year.

Likewise, Adem Bise, a notable Bosnian scholar of the time, published a short, but invaluable book on the Qur'an in the same year in Tuzla, entitled *Da li moze Musliman zivjeti evropskim kulturnim zivotom i ostati dobar Musliman (Kur'an teoriji i praksi)* [Can a Muslim live a European Cultural Life and Remain a Good Muslim: The Qur'an in Theory and Practice]. However, according to Enes Karic, who is himself a contemporary Bosnian Qur'anic scholar, Causevic's contribution and achievement was nothing short of remarkable. He explained,

> The magnitude of Causevic's work of commentary should be viewed in the context of the Bosnia of his day and position of Bosnian Muslims between the two world wars of the twentieth century. Causevic was a 'son of his times', and did not write his commentary for the purpose only of resolving those eternal theological, metaphysical and other-worldly issues. With his translation of the Qur'an Causevic sought above all to provide the Bosnian Muslims with a redemptive reformist theory of Islam that would prompt them to reflect on their existence in this world…Causevic was not an unreserved admirer of either scientism or modernism, or indeed of any other western isms then making inroads…These isms served him as the decorative wrapping for the message of his translation of the Qur'an.[11]

Causevic passed away at the age of around 67. He became rather frail and lonely towards the end of his life, perhaps on account of his hard work and dedication to his literary and administrative tasks. However, as soon as the news of his death was relayed across Bosnia and Herzegovina, tens of thousands of people from across the country flocked to his funeral prayer, proving the fact that he was more popular with the masses than the conservative *ulama*. He was laid to rest in the precinct of the famous Gazi Husrev Bey Mosque in Sarajevo, following a simple funeral prayer led by Hafiz Asad Efendi Sabrihafizovic.

His life and work has, however, continued to inspire generations of Balkan scholars and thinkers to this day, including Adem Bise, Sukrija Alagic, Salih Hadzialic, Alija Nametak, Mehmed Handzic, Husein Efendi Dozo, Smail Balic, Alija Izetbegovic, Hasan Kalesi, Nerkez Smailagic and Muhamed Filipovic, among others. To his credit, Enes Karic (b. 1958) devoted no less than four chapters to the life and works of Causevic in his *Contributions to Twentieth Century Islamic Thought in Bosnia and Herzegovina* (2011), while Hafiz Mahmud Traljic (1918–2002), a notable scholar and writer, published an anthology of biographies of influential Bosnian personalities under the title of *Istaknuti Bosnjaci* in Sarajevo in 1998, wherein he provided a detailed survey of the life and works of Mehmed Dzemaludin Causevic.

1. Noel Malcolm, *Bosnia: A Short History*.

2. See Mahmud Traljic, *Istaknuti Bosnjaci*.

3. Enes Karic, *Contributions to Twentieth Century Islamic Thought in Bosnia and Herzegovina*, volume 1.

4. Albert Hourani, *Arabic Thought in the Liberal Age, 1798–1939*.

5. Enes Karic, op. cit.

6. Quoted by Enes Karic, op. cit.

7. Noel Malcolm, op. cit.

8. Quoted by Enes Karic, op. cit.

9. Ibid.

10. Quoted by Noel Malcolm, op. cit. Also see Charles Kurzman (ed.), *Modernist Islam 1840–1940: A Source Book*.

11. Quoted by Enes Karic, op. cit. Also see E. Karic, *Essays (on behalf) of Bosnia*.

# 31

# HAFIZ ALI KORCA

B. 1873 – D. 1956

ALBANIA

Before the creation of the republics of Bosnia-Herzegovina and Kosova in 1992 and 2008, respectively, Albania was the only European country with a Muslim majority population. Although the history of Albania can be traced back to the pre-historic period, during the Middle Ages it remained firmly under Roman (Byzantine) control until it succumbed to Bulgarian encroachment during the late thirteenth century. After the Serbian interlude, the Ottoman Empire expanded its rule into southern Europe and, in the process, Albania and other parts of the Balkans were secured during the first half of the fourteenth century.

Following the establishment of Ottoman rule, the people of Albania, who had hitherto been predominantly Catholics, gradually began to embrace Islam and that, in turn, enabled them to swiftly make progress and become influential players in the political, economic, military and cultural sphere of the vast Ottoman Empire. This continued to be the case until the early part of the twentieth century, when Albania – like many other parts of the Ottoman Empire – formally declared its independence in 1912. However, according to Noel Malcolm (b. 1956), a leading historian of the Balkans, the popular view of nineteenth and early twentieth century Balkan history is far too simplistic, whereas the reality was more complex and complicated.

Far from being simply a case of autocratic and oppressive rule versus popular desire to reclaim freedom and independence; during 'the reign of Sultan Mahmut II (1808–39), the Ottomans introduced an ambitious sequence of reforms, designed to turn the Empire into a modern (which meant, in many respects, Westernized) state. However, in order to implement any of the reforms, it was necessary for the central administration in Istanbul to win back real power from the local lords who had usurped it in most provinces of the Empire. The move to centralise power, while it may have been the strategic ally of a liberalization programme, was sometimes indistinguishable at the tactical level from sheer brutal oppression.'[1]

Born during this period of political, economic and cultural uncertainty and upheaval in Ottoman Albania, Hafiz Ali Korca not only went on to become one of the most influential Muslim scholars and reformers of nineteenth and early twentieth century Albania, but also the Balkan region as a whole.

Ali Korca, better known as Hafiz Ali Korca, was born into a notable Muslim family in Korce, a municipality that is today located in south-eastern Albania, being the sixth largest city in the country with a population of more than fifty thousand people. However, during the 1870s, it was a much smaller settlement with barely a few thousand people, a place where Ottoman officials reigned supreme politically, economically and culturally at the time. Ali's father, Iljaz Efendi, was a well-known local Muslim scholar and preacher, and his mother, Naime, was a pious lady who ensured their son received a thorough religious education during his early years.

Young Ali was a bright student who was blessed with a powerful memory, thus successfully committing the entire Qur'an to memory before his twelfth birthday, which clearly impressed his parents. It was very common for traditional Albanian Muslim families to encourage their children to memorise the Qur'an prior to joining local *ibtidaije* or *rushdije*, primary and secondary Islamic schools, for their early and further education. According to the historian Ramiz Zekaj, these educational institutions,

> Mainly functioned near the mosques and were directed by the imams. In many cases an appointed cleric acted as a teacher. The number of pupils of these Mejteps was composed by both genders (male and female). The age of admittance was not fixed but generally the mejteps accepted pupils from the age of 6–7 till the age 14–16. The subjects taught in the Mejteps had religious characteristics (Islamic) and a considerable Arabic terminology was used while the explanations were in the Albanian language. Quranic teachings and commentary filled the greatest part of the time. In the same time pupils used to learn even the principles of arithmetic. On the occasions in some Mejteps other subjects were taught as well. This educational cycle that was also called 'Rushdije' normally lasted three years, while the primary education Mejteps were called 'Ibtidaije'.[2]

Ali pursued the same curriculum and successfully completed his elementary and high school education in Arabic language, Qur'anic studies, aspects of Islamic jurisprudence and Prophetic traditions, coupled with a thorough grounding in Albanian, his mother-tongue. This, of course, earned him the respect of his family as well as the local population. Being a dedicated student and keen to serve his people, Ali eventually left Korce when he was just a teenager and decided to proceed to Istanbul for higher education in languages, Islamic studies, jurisprudence, philosophy and sciences.

It was very common for aspiring Muslim students from the Balkans to travel to Istanbul for higher education as it was the capital of the Ottoman State and one of the foremost centres of education and scholarship in the Muslim world at the time. With a population of nearly a million people, it was also one of the most populous and cosmopolitan cities in the Western world. Thus, in addition to hundreds of beautifully decorated mosques and mausoleums, Istanbul was known for its numerous schools, colleges and Islamic seminaries (*madrasas* or *medreses*), which were often attached to the city's prominent mosques.

Teachers and students flocked from other parts of the Ottoman Empire – and especially from the Balkans – to study and pursue research there. A thorough and successful education in such institutions were often seen as the quickest route to securing jobs as religious scholars, preachers, teachers, political and civil administrators, lawyers, military officers and physicians, among other career options that were available at the time. Driven by his own ambition to become an Islamic scholar and jurist, Ali arrived in Istanbul as a youngster and joined a local Islamic seminary to pursue higher education.

It was during this period that he polished his knowledge of the Arabic language and grammar, in addition to becoming thoroughly familiar with Ottoman Turkish and Persian. He then received advanced training in Qur'anic exegesis, Prophetic tradition, Islamic jurisprudence and aspects of modern philosophy and science, which enabled him to become proficient in both traditional Islamic sciences and familiar with modern ideas and thought.

For a student of Albanian background who had never visited or studied in Persia, Ali became renowned for his knowledge and understanding of Persian literature and poetry. Through his own efforts, he also learned French and English, thus becoming a prominent linguist in his own right. It was during one of his journeys from Korce to Istanbul via Sofia (in present-day Bulgaria) that he was stopped and detained by the authorities in Sinop, a northern coastal Turkish city, for apparently carrying religious books in the Albanian language. This took place in 1893 when Ali was only 20 and was well on his way to completing his higher education in Istanbul.

Needless to say, it was a time of considerable uncertainty and turmoil within the Ottoman State itself, which was further compounded by rising nationalistic fervour across Ottoman territories in the Balkans and elsewhere. The Albanians had initiated their political campaign and struggle for independence from Ottoman hegemony at the time, leading to mutual suspicion and misunderstandings on both sides, and of course Ali became a victim of the on-going political tussle and rivalry. Contrary to what some Albanian scholars have suggested; being a student, Ali was neither interested nor actively involved in any nationalistic activities at the time.

After nearly six centuries of Ottoman rule, Albania became independent in 1912. This was the result of a long and protracted political campaign pursued by the Albanian people against Ottoman rule. Indeed, the origin of Albanian national consciousness is often traced by the historians back to the formation of the League of Prizren, which was established in June 1878. Although the League's founding principle was to defend the integrity of the Ottoman Empire, it eventually lost the support of Ottoman officials and instead, focused its attention towards the establishment of Albanian autonomy. The League became directly involved in military operations to prevent the annexation of parts of Albanian territory, thanks to the decisions made by the Congress of Berlin on 13 July 1878, which consisted of the Great Powers (namely Great Britain, Russia, Germany, Ottoman Empire, Italy and Austria-Hungary). The League was, however, forced to retreat and withdraw as a result of pressure from the Great Powers before the Ottoman military defeated them in the battlefield.

Also during this time, considerable political and economic changes were underway in Istanbul, the heart of the Ottoman State, where the Young Turks movement was launched during the early part of the twentieth century. The Young Turks wanted to replace absolute monarchy by forming a constitutional monarchy in order to address the growing political, economic, military and cultural challenges and difficulties facing them at the time. This culminated in the Young Turk Revolution in 1908 against the absolute rule of Sultan Abd al-Hamid II, leading to the establishment of the Second Constitutional Era which, in turn, paved the way for multi-party democracy in the Ottoman State for the first time in its history.[3]

Whilst political and economic changes were sweeping across the fledgling Ottoman State, the Albanian revolt against the Young Turks taxation, conscription and military policies broke out in January 1912, coupled with the Ottoman defeat in the Balkan Wars (8 October 1912–18 July 1913), culminated with the proclamation of Albania's independence on 28 November, 1912. During this period of unprecedented political transformation and realignment, Ali became actively involved in pro-independence political campaigns of the time. Being a devout Muslim and an equally proud Albanian, who was very fond of this mother-tongue, he resented direct government interference in the economic, cultural and religious affairs of his people. The authorities were uncompromising in their response and, as a result, he was repeatedly harassed, exiled and interned.

During this period, Ali served as a teacher in an Islamic school in Korce, being one of the first to combine the teaching of traditional Islamic sciences with aspects of modern ideas and thought. If the Albanian people were to advance and make progress in an increasingly secular and modern age, he felt, there was an urgent need to pursue traditional Islamic learning with modern sciences in order to address the challenges and difficulties facing the people.

As an influential advocate for the promotion of mass education, Ali implemented his new reformist educational model in various institutions in Albania, including the Islamic seminary in Tirana, the capital of Albania, where he served as a teacher for a long period. He also served in his capacities as teacher, jurist, advisor and director of education in Durres, Elbasan, Dibra, Mat and Shkodra, among other locations across Albania. As a religious and cultural pragmatist, Ali was a champion of the pursuit of Islamic learning and education in the Albanian language because, he felt, that was the most suitable language in which to convey the message of Islam to his fellow Albanians.

According to the Albanian nationalists, Ali was also a nationalist but, to be fair to the latter, he was more a religious activist and scholar, unlike the former, who were largely secular nationalists. Indeed, the emergence of 'Albanianism' during the 1920s must have worried Ali as it was a form of civic nationalism that advocated the need for secularisation, leading to the de-Ottomanisation of the political system on the one hand, and the de-Islamisation of the society on the other hand. In the words of the historian Ina Merdjanova,

> Islam was not a central nation-building component for the Albanians in the Albanian nation-state. Divisions along religious lines, going far back in history, made language rather than religion a dominant factor in the Albanians' efforts to define their national identity…Public space was de-Islamized, especially in the administrative and educational sphere, even though the state provided funds for the building of some mosques. This limited further the role of Islam as a marker of Albanian national self-definition, given that the majority of Albanians followed the Islamic faith.[4]

Like the proponents of 'Albanianism', Ali was a linguistic nationalist and an advocate of the de-Ottomanisation of the political system but, unlike the former, he was undoubtedly opposed to the secularisation of the public space in a Muslim country where the masses remained largely committed to a traditional interpretation and understanding of Islam, which were of course based on a combination of Arabic, Ottoman Turkish and Persian sources. Ali wanted the Albanian language to play a more prominent role in the dissemination of Islam in Albania, along with the other classical languages especially Arabic, the language of the Prophet of Islam and the Qur'an.

His wise, nuanced and pragmatic approach to the question of Albanian self-identity and nation-state building prompted the ruling elite to promote him to the office of the Chairman of the Supreme Shari'ah Council (*Keshilli i Larte i Sheriatit*), which was at the time, one of the most influential religious posts in the land. Ali served in this capacity from 1918 to 1924. Now, as the leader and one of the most powerful spokesmen of the Albanian *ulama* (religious scholars) of the time, he argued, in the words of the historian Nathalie Clayer, that:

Islam itself did not need to be reformed. It was a modern and healthy religion, adapted to science, progress and civilisation. If Muslims were not in a good position, it was because they were not good Muslims, because they were not involved, because they had not kept alive the earlier knowledge. Therefore, the solution for Hafiz Ali Korca and the leading group of Albanian Islamic institutions of that time was to establish a good *madrasa*, with modern methods of teaching and a program including contemporary sciences. With this madrasa, they hoped to prevent the young Albanian Muslims from going to [other parts of] Europe to study, so that they would not be cut off from their religion and the nation... Hafiz Ali Korca and his reformist colleagues also attempted to improve the cultural level by other means: the publication of social, moral, economic, technical and historical papers in the journal published by the Islamic religious Community, as well as the translation and publication of books.[5]

In addition to working full-time as a teacher, advisor, religious scholar and jurisconsult, Ali worked and collaborated with many leading Albanian scholars, politicians, writers and journalists of the time, including Dervish Hima, also known as Ibrahim Mehmet Naxhi (1872–1928); Akif Pasha Elbasani (1861–1926); Pandeli Sotiri (1843–1892); Kristo Luarasi (1876–1934); Mati Logoreci (1867–1941); and Sali Navica (1890–1920). He was also a contemporary of prominent Albanian Islamic scholars like Hoxha Vehbi Dibra (b. 1867), who was the *Mufti* of Diber and one of the best commentators of the Qur'an in Albanian; Vejsel Naili (b. 1860), a leading jurist and judge (*Qadi*) from Libohova in southern Albania; Sa'id Najdeni (b. 1864), a prominent scholar and political activist; and Mulla Jusuf Kraja (b. 1849), an outstanding Islamic thinker, religious leader and theologian from Kraja, among others.

These scholars and religious leaders formed 'the nucleus of the Albanian Islamic institutions, supposed to administer and control the diffusion and the practice of Islam in the country; yet, for various reasons, these representatives of official Islam had difficulty imposing themselves on the whole Islamic sphere.'[6] That was because the political leaders, unlike the *ulama*, not only wanted to nationalise Islam, but also reduce its role in Albanian society at the time. Although the *ulama* supported the government's efforts to indigenise Islam, however, they opposed the wholesale secularisation of Islamic institutions and the public sphere as a whole. During this period, Ali was forced to resign from his position as the Chairman of Supreme Shari'ah Council due to his disagreement and differences of opinion with the country's political elite.

Though he resigned from government service in 1924, Ali certainly did not retire from teaching, pursuing research and writing. Indeed, despite being an influential Islamic scholar, jurist, educationalist and public figure, he found the time to write prolifically on a wide range of subjects, including Qur'anic studies, Islamic theology, history, poetry and literature. He authored and translated more than thirteen books and manuscripts; some of them were published during his own lifetime, while others had remained unpublished.

His most notable literary contributions included *Muvludi* (1900), *300 Fjale te Imam Ali* (1910), *Historia e Shenjte dhe te Kater Halifete* (1913), *Gjylistani* (1918), *Jusufi me Zelihane* (1923), *Tefsiri i Kur'anit* (1924) and *Rubijjati Khajjam* (1930), among others. The *Muvludi* was a work of celebration of the birth and life of the Prophet Muhammad (peace be on him), being very similar to those written by other Muslim scholars and writers in many parts of the Muslim world, whilst the *Historia* consisted of an account of early Muslim history.

He also translated 300 sayings and exhortations of Ali ibn Abi Talib (599–661), the fourth Caliph and son-in-law of the Prophet, from the original Arabic into Albanian for the benefit of his people. Likewise, he translated Shaykh Sa'di's *Gulistan* (The Rose Garden), Abd al-Rahman Jami's *Yusuf-i-Zulaikhah* (Joseph and the Wife of Potiphar) and Umar Khayyam's *Ruba'iyyat* (Collection of Quatrains) from Persian into Albanian and, in so doing, he successfully introduced the works of these three famous Persian poets to the masses in Albania. However, his most extensive work was the translation and commentary of the Qur'an into Albanian, which he undertook from 1920 to 1924. This monumental work consists of 2000 pages and has remained unpublished to this day.

Perhaps Ali's most popular work was *Bolshevizma e Ckaterrimi i Njerezimit* (Bolshevism is a Destruction for Mankind), which he wrote and published in March 1925. He wrote this booklet to remind his people of the looming dangers of the 'black cloud' of Communism following the Bolshevist Revolution in Russia in March 1917. His warning was very timely and pertinent as Communism soon made in-roads into much of Eastern and Southern Europe.

As expected, Albania subsequently found itself firmly under Communist sway, thus confirming Ali's worst fear and trepidation. Unsurprisingly, his anti-Communist and anti-Marxist writings and activism soon earned him the wrath of the ruling authorities. Ali narrowly escaped assassination attempts on several occasions, although he remained firmly opposed to the atheistic and totalitarian political ideology. He made his brave and uncompromising stance against Communism very clear at the outset of this work. In his own words:

> With the religion of Muhammad
> The Bolshevism is never reconciled
> In an open war they will be
> Until the Day of Judgement.[7]

However, a close reading of this short work shows that Ali's knowledge and understanding of Communism was based on secondary sources, namely Turkish newspapers and journals of the time. As a journalist and writer, he not only read, but also regularly contributed to several Arabic and Turkish publications. He was equally proficient in Persian, French and English, but did not seem to have access to primary literature on Communism and Marxism, and much less on Judaism as a religion and culture. Consequently, he not only conflated Judaism with the Jews, but also confused Karl Marx with Marxism and Communism with Leninism, and Bolshevism with Stalinism and, in the process, failed to explain their full meaning and implication.

However, his critique of the economic policy pursued by the Bolshevists in Russia at the time was more informed and largely accurate. He was also thoroughly familiar with the writings of the Muslim modernists like Jamal al-Din al-Afghani (1838–1897), Muhammad Abduh (1849–1905) and Musa Jarullah (see chapter 34 for more details), among others, and referred to their views and opinions in his work before concluding that 'Islam has no need of Bolshevism because in Islam rules the democracy and the overall brotherhood [of humanity]'.[8]

Despite Ali's best efforts, Albania formally became a Communist State after the Second World War and, accordingly, religion in general, Islam in particular, was actively suppressed in the country at the time. The Communist rulers of Albania referred to it as the 'world's first atheist state' in 1967, barely a decade after Ali's death at the age of around 83. This must have figuratively made him turn in his grave.

However, as he had already prophesied, Communism as a political and economic force was bound to fail due to its theoretical inconsistencies and impractical methodology. So, this was proved with the break-up of the Eastern Bloc in the late 1980s, followed by the dissolution of the People's Republic of Albania during 1991–1992. Defying all odds, he died of natural causes and was buried in the old cemetery in the city of Kavaja, today located within a municipality in Tirana County in the Western Lowlands of Albania. He left behind six children, four sons (Iljas, Selaudin, Alaydin and Mexhdedin) and two daughters (Fiqiret and Mediha).[9]

Needless to say, Hafiz Ali Korca's indefatigable energy, personal bravery, prolific pen and wide-ranging educational reforms, coupled with unshakeable faith and conviction in the message of Islam, contributed to the preservation and promotion of Islamic culture in Albania and the Balkans, not only during the first half of the twentieth century, but also up to this day. Unfortunately, his life and legacy remains largely unknown in Europe and the Muslim world as a whole. If this entry on his life and contribution inspires others to pursue further study and research on this topic, then I will feel my effort had not been in vain. The Albanian historian Ramiz Zekaj paid Hafiz Ali Korca this fitting tribute,

> He was 'one of many scholars who were prosecuted – for their ideas, worldviews and activities...His life is an excellent model of a devoted patriot, who doesn't separate words from actions, and invites all to collaborate for the sake of [their] mother country and not to forsake it.'[10]

Ⓝ

1. Noel Malcolm, *Kosovo: A Short History*.

2. Ramiz Zekaj, *The Development of the Islamic Culture among Albanians during the 20ᵗʰ Century*.

3. Caroline Finkel, *Osman's Dream: The Story of the Ottoman Empire 1300–1923*.

4. Ina Merdjanova, *Rediscovering the Umma: Muslims in the Balkans between Nationalism and Transnationalism*.

5. Nathalie Clayer, 'Adapting Islam to Europe: The Albanian Example' in Christian Voss and Jordanka Telbizova-Sack (eds.), *Islam and Muslime in (Sudost) Europa im Kontext von Transformation and EU-Erweiterung*.

6. Nathalie, Clayer, 'The Building of an Albanian and European Islam in Interwar Albania' in Edward E. Curtis IV, *The Bloomsbury Reader on Islam in the West*.

7. Hafiz Ali Korca, *Bolshevism is a Destruction for Mankind*.

8. Hafiz Ali Korca, op. cit.

9. Information provided to this writer b Aled Korca, Hafiz Ali Korca's great-grandson.

10. Ramiz Zekaj, op. cit.

# 32

# JOHN YAHYA PARKINSON

B. 1874 – D. 1918

UNITED KINGDOM

Historians often trace the origin of the growing presence of Islam in Scotland back to the period of the British Empire when many Scots travelled to different parts of the Muslim world, including the Middle East and India. They served there with great success and distinction and, in so doing, many of them developed close relations and affinity with local Muslims. Some even brought their Indian aides and relatives back with them to Scotland which, in turn, encouraged the Indian seamen, most of whom were Muslims, to follow suit and eventually settle in this part of the world. From such humble beginnings, Scotland's growing Muslim community now consists of around 100,000 people, being the second largest religious group after the Christians.

However, it is not widely known that Scotland's links to the Muslim world, especially with Andalusia or Muslim Spain (711–1492) and the Abbasid Empire (750–1258), were very cordial and extensive from very early on. The discovery of silver coins in 1912 at Talnotrie, Glen of the Bar, Kirkcudbrightshire, bearing – in Arabic – the name of al-Mutawakkil ala Allah (r. 847–862), the Abbasid Caliph, shows that Scotland had developed strong trading and cultural ties with the Muslim world as early as the ninth century, if not earlier. Similar contacts were also established with Andalusia, where the

Muslim rulers played an active role in forging close relations with friendly northern European countries.

Indeed, Caliph Abd al-Rahman II (r. 822–852) sent Yahya ibn Hakam al-Ghazal, one of his senior officials, as an emissary to a 'northern country' during the mid-ninth century, which may have been Scotland. Given Scotland's long history of active engagement with the Muslim world, it should not surprise anyone if some Scots did develop an interest in Islam, maybe even to the extent of converting. One such prominent and pioneering Scottish convert to Islam was John (Yahya) Parkinson of Kilwinning.

John Parkinson, also known as Yahya an-Nasr (Yehya-en-Nasr) Parkinson, was born into a lower middle-class Scottish family in the town of Kilwinning, located in North Ayrshire; about 20 miles south of Glasgow. His family traced their ancestry back to both Ireland and the clan of the Featherstonehaugh's in the northern English city of Durham. However, his father, Samuel Parkinson (b. 1843), and mother, Mary Jane Clockie (b. 1856), married in Kilwinning in January, 1874. Their only son, John, was born in February, 1874, although some writers have suggested that he was born in 1876. However, that would not have been possible because his mother had died on 17 September 1874, only seven months after his birth. Indeed, John had lost his parents as a child and therefore, his maternal grandparents, John and Jane Clockie – who were born in Ireland but subsequently moved to Scotland and settled in Kilwinning – took on the role of caring for their grandson.[1]

Therefore, John grew up under the watchful gaze of his loving grandparents, both of whom were in their fifties at the time, and attended a local boarding school. He was, by all accounts, a gifted child who became very fond of geography, literature, mathematics, science and poetry during his early years. After completing his primary and secondary schooling up to the sixth grade, he could not continue his further and higher education due to his grandparent's limited financial circumstances, thus forcing young John to seek employment to support himself and his aging grandparents.[2]

According to one account, in 1890, at the age of sixteen, John left formal education and secured employment as a wool spinner at the local Busby Spinning Company while, according to others, he was forced to abandon his studies at the age of 13 and seek work to make ends meet. Either way, he grew up at a time when the Industrial Revolution had transformed the textile industry like never before, thanks to the availability of large and good quality machinery for the development and expansion of the manufacturing industries, especially the textile sector.[3] And that, in turn, led to the rapid growth of the population as more manpower was needed to meet the growing demand for textile products across Scotland and beyond. Thus, people travelled from as far as Ireland and the Scottish Highlands seeking employment in the cotton mills of Ayrshire where they soon settled.

By all accounts, the Busby Spinning Company was a large cotton mill and it employed hundreds of people, but life was far from being easy for the workers. They were required to work up to fourteen hours a day, six days a week, with only two days paid holiday per year. Working conditions were often dangerous and accidents and injuries were common. The temperature inside the mills was hot and cleanliness and hygiene was well-below acceptable standards, which explains why the mill workers frequently suffered from, and often died of, diseases like tuberculosis, bronchitis and pneumonia. However, as the demand for textile dipped towards the end of the nineteenth century, the cotton industry began to decline irreversibly. That, in turn, had a negative socio-economic impact on the local population, thus many people were forced to move out of the area in search of employment opportunities elsewhere.

However, John was fortunate enough to secure full-time employment at the Busby Spinning Company and worked in such capacity for most of his working life. As an intelligent and hard-working young man, he also remained committed to completing his education in his spare time. Being very fond of books, he read extensively during this period and became thoroughly familiar with science, biology, geography, romantic literature, philosophy, poetry and history. He became an accomplished astronomer and biologist, and contributed articles on both subjects in local newspapers, while still only in his teens. Not surprisingly, he was later elected a member of the West Scotland Branch of the British Astronomical Association.

Thereafter, he embarked on an in-depth study and exploration of philosophy and world religions, focusing particularly on the history and theology of Christianity, the Indic religions and Islam. His command of Latin was good and some of his writings also demonstrate familiarisation with basic Arabic, which he acquired after his conversion to Islam. This clearly was a remarkable achievement considering that he lived in a small, remote Scottish town, being far away from prominent cities like London, Cardiff or Liverpool; locations that were, of course, more cosmopolitan in their cultural make-up at the time than rural Kilwinning. Needless to say, not having access to a good and well-stocked library made John's task much harder, not to mention the fact that John was forced to combine his studies with full-time work that required him to exercise considerable physical exertion for no less than twelve hours a day, six days a week. Writing in January 1915, he explained his personal difficulties and challenges as follows:

> Every working day except Saturday I have to attend to business not less than twelve hours. All my writing, studying, and recreation has to be got through in the few hours left in the evening. I am sorry to say I also find it necessary to sleep some. It is, therefore, impossible for me to reply to the letters coming from various parts of the globe requesting me to deal with various questions. I have not the time to do so, even though I possess the knowledge and ability. I propose going on in the future as I have done in the past, writing just as I feel impelled to do so, and on whatever subject the inspiration leads me.[4]

Although born and raised in a conservative Christian family, John subsequently joined the United Presbyterian Church, which was a denomination of the Scottish Presbyterian Church. As a reformed tradition within Protestantism, Presbyterianism originated in the British Isles during the sixteenth century but, over time, several reformist movements emerged and they broke away from the established Church of Scotland. The United Presbyterian Church was one such denomination that was formed in 1847. This strand of Presbyterianism was characterised by its liberal approach to Protestant principles and practices, which may have attracted John's attention, hence why he became a member of the Church as a young man.

However, his thirst for knowledge, coupled with his burning desire to discover the truth, eventually compelled him to abandon Christianity altogether as it failed to stand up to his critical analysis and evaluation. Indeed, he rejected Christianity on both historical and theological grounds. He later wrote – and it is worth quoting him at some length:

> In the early ages of Christianity the so-called 'Epistles of Paul' were accepted as the genuine writings of an Apostle Paul by Christians in general. There were a few exceptions; in the second century the heretical Sevesians looked upon them as spurious. From that time onward to the sixteenth century criticism was practically stagnant and barren of result. No mental life of any consequence was possible under the iron sway of Rome, or within range of the creatures of the Inquisition, when that refined method of religious appeal came into operation. After the outbreak of the Reformation...criticism moved slowly, but surely, onward. The Old Testament was the first to be taken in hand. But it was a long time before Christians gathered courage to make an attack on the bedrock of their faith and beliefs, the New Testament. Even today it appears to the majority of them sacrilege to attempt to shatter the ideal romances woven round the history and life of the central figure in the Gospels. The illusion is going, the whole superstructure is crumbling into atoms, and soon not a wrack nor cloud will be left behind...It is to be understood that the above remarks apply to criticism by Christian scholars; Rationalistic criticism goes still further.[5]

John not only examined the history of the New Testament and found it wanting, he was equally unimpressed by Christian theology, which contributed to his detachment from his ancestral faith. Indeed, his rejection of Christianity prompted him to explore the Indic religions, especially Buddhism and Hinduism, but none of them impressed him either. He then turned his attention to Islam and carried out a thorough study of its history, theology and culture. The more he studied, the more he was impressed by Islam's encouragement of learning, education and scholarship. He found the philosophical and rationalistic trends in medieval Islamic thought to be most appealing, not least because he was already thoroughly familiar with aspects of ancient Greek, Continental and British philosophical traditions. During this period, he studied the writings of prominent Muslim and non-Muslim scholars of Islam, including George Sale (1697–1736), Sir William Muir (1819–1905), Stanley Lane-Poole (1854–1931), Rt. Hon. Syed Ameer Ali (1849–1928), Dr T. J. De Boer (b. 1866), Duncan Black MacDonald (1863–1943) and of course William Henry Quilliam, better known as Abdullah Quilliam (see chapter 27), among others.

His thorough and detailed study of Islam, its Prophet and the Qur'an convinced him of their clarity, soundness and authenticity. He found the Islamic concept of Oneness of Divinity to be particularly attractive and appealing, unlike Christology, which he considered to be both illogical and irrational, and therefore confusing and contradictory. In his essay titled 'An Outline of Christian Theology before Muhammed' (1914), he later argued that it was the Prophet of Islam who had restored pure monotheism, as the original message of Jesus was not only changed but completely distorted following Christianity's encounter with Roman Paganism on the one hand, and the Gnostic movements of the second century on the other. If Paganism had heavily influenced Christian rituals during its formative period, then Gnostic ideas and doctrines, he argued, played a pivotal role in re-moulding Christian theology and philosophy during the second century before the Council of Nicaea, in 325 C.E., attempted to finally settle the question of Christian beliefs and dogmas.

However, that did not work out as numerous sects emerged, one after another, to make claims and counter-claims and, in the process, they contradicted one another, which led to more confusion and strife. Needless to say, these disputes and disagreements revolved around the question of 'the Divine and human nature in Jesus, another over the position and personality of the Holy Ghost. It was a complete muddle. The Pagans looked upon their opponents as insane…The whole population was rent into factions. Fighting took place in the very churches. Massacres and persecutions of the most savage and brutal nature occurred. The Church was completely powerless for good. No voice was raised against the social conditions, against the moral degradation…There was no intellect behind it. A few generations of Christianity had banished intelligence. No lofty thought, no high ideals, were possible in such an environment. Such social chaos and moral disorder was unable to breed minds of a calibre high enough to carry a religious or even purely moral revival.'[6]

By contrast, the mission of Prophet Muhammad (peace be on him) represented the restoration of the original message of not only Jesus, but all the other previous Divinely-inspired Prophets and Messengers, argued John. According to him, the Prophet of Islam was an outstanding religious teacher, spiritual guide and practical moralist whose exemplary life and high ethical standards was nothing short of a beacon of light for humanity as a whole.

In a detailed, but equally interesting essay he later wrote on the life and career of the Prophet titled 'The Messenger', which was serialised in the *Islamic Review*; he concluded, 'Beloved by all, of the noblest generosity and of becoming humility, a smile was ever on his lips, kindness shone from his dark, beaming eyes, and gentleness revealed itself in every aspect of his manner. Enthusiastic when enthusiasm was required, and heroic in the face of persecution and injustice. Adamant in the face of evil and error, merciful when mercy could be given. By steadfastness, courage and devotion he changed the whole current of Arabian thought and custom, and remoulded the history of the world.'[7]

Around 1900, when he was in his mid-twenties, John formally embraced Islam, although exact details about his conversion are not known. Far from being a moment of madness, his conversion was the result of a detailed and systematic exploration and engagement with Islamic thought and history over many years. Not surprisingly, he devoted the remaining eighteen years of his life to the study and exposition of his new faith and its teachings. In so doing, he became one of the most important and influential figures within the British Muslim community at the time. He not only became involved with the religious activities of his mentor and spiritual guide, Shaykh Abdullah Quilliam of the Liverpool Muslim Institute, but also established his reputation as a prolific writer and poet.

Indeed, soon after embracing Islam, he contacted Quilliam, who was based at his Muslim Institute in Liverpool at the time, and began to contribute regular articles and poems to the latter's journals, namely *The Crescent*, and *The Islamic World*. Both of them were established in 1893 and they became a vehicle for John to disseminate his views on a wide range of subjects including Islam, social, political, inter-religious and literary topics.

Thus, from 1901 to 1907, John contributed numerous articles and poems to both journals, initially under his pen-name, Igomar, and thereafter under his real name, John, as well as his adopted Muslim name, Yahya. Unlike most of Quilliam's followers and disciples, John never moved to Liverpool and remained a resident in Scotland. Only occasionally did he visit the Muslim Institute, where he delivered lectures on aspects of Islam and recited his inspiring poetry. Most of the poetry he published at the time eulogised heroic Muslim figures of the past, including Musa ibn Nusayr (640–716); Almanzor (see chapter 6); Salah al-Din ibn Ayyub, better known as Saladin (1138–1193); Nur al-Din Zangi (1118–1174); Musa ibn Abu'l-Gazan, a brave Muslim warrior of Granada; Amir Abd al-Qadir of Algeria (1808–1883); Sultan Abd al-Hamid II of Ottoman Turkey (r. 1876–1909); and of course the Prophet of Islam, among others.[8]

His 'The Sword of Islam' was also serialised in *The Crescent* in 1901. As Quilliam's journals were read in many parts of the Muslim world, in addition to Britain and America, it is not surprising that Yahya's poetry soon attracted the attention of the Ottoman officials who were very impressed by his Islamic fervour and patriotism.

Indeed, his poems in praise of the Ottomans and especially Sultan Abd al-Hamid II, earned him the Mecidiye Medal from none other than the Sultan himself in 1905. Some of his verses, as a result, were translated into Turkish. In the same year, he was elected Vice-President of the British Muslim Association, which was based in London.

Three years later, John received an invitation from Abd al-Karim Jamal, a notable Muslim leader and businessman of Rangoon, Burma (present-day Myanmar) and, accordingly, he moved there in 1908. The invitation to move to Rangoon was timely as he was living with his aunts in Belfast at the time, having resigned from the Busby Spinning Company on 1 April 1908. During his two-year stay there, he worked as a deputy editor of a Rangoon-based newspaper and reportedly engaged in Pan-Islamic activities, including participating in a campaign to restore the burial site of the exiled Mughal emperor, Bahadur Shah Zafar II (1775–1862).[9] In addition, he authored several works during his stay in Burma, including *Essays on Islamic Philosophy* and *Muslim Chivalry*, both of which were published in 1909.

The former consisted of six short essays of fifty-four pages in total. In his preface to this short volume, John wrote, 'Sketchy and all as it is I can only hope that in Islam it may create a renewed interest in the subject. If it should, I trust present day Muslims will not rest satisfied with the conclusions arrived at by their fathers, but remember that philosophy has been enriched since their time by generation after generation of further experiences, and been developed by a long line of earnest workers, and that it has been illuminated by the valuable and epoch-making discoveries and more reliable methods of modern science.'[10]

By contrast, his *Muslim Chivalry* (1909) and *Lays of Love and War* (1904, reprinted 1927) are works of prose and poetry reflecting Islamic principles and values of honesty, courage, bravery, brotherhood, unity and solidarity. Here is an example of his unique and inspiring Islamic poetry:

Lift I say the flag of Islam
Place it on the hills again,
Every beauteous fold revealing
To the world-wide sons of men;
You remember how your fathers
On the hill-tops of the world
Careless of all opposition
Every spotless fold unfurled.
Let us follow their example,
Staunch of heart and strong of hand,
Till the sacred light of learning
Brightens every Muslim land;
In the thunder of the conflict

Raise the voice and wield the pen,
We shall plant the flag of Islam
In the fields of thought again;
Even as the Lord Muhammed
In the "Times of Ignorance,"
Touched the heart and broke the idols
Of Arabi's pagan lance.
Then, all worthy sons of Islam,
Gird your armour on I say,
For the morning light is dawning
Heralding the coming day.[11]

Ill-health eventually forced John to leave Rangoon and return home to Scotland in 1910 but, being a devout Muslim and scholar of tireless energy, he continued to research and write prolifically. During this period, he published many essays and poems in several other journals and magazines, including the *Journal of Moslem Institute* (Calcutta), *Crescent* (Lahore), *The Review of Religions* (Punjab) and *The Islamic Review and Muslim India* (London). Indeed, he became a regular contributor to the latter and soon established his reputation as one of the most gifted Western writers and expositors of Islam during the first half of the twentieth century.

Indeed, from 1913 until his death in 1918, John published some of his most important essays and articles in the *Islamic Review*, including 'Al-Ghazali', 'The Messenger', 'The Ethics of War', 'The War and the Muslims', 'The Days of Ignorance', 'Some of the Sayings of Muhammed', 'A Story of Islam', 'The Age of the New Testament', 'Monism', 'Type of the Red Heifer', 'Byeways and Highways', 'Meditations', and 'Muhammed – Personality'[12], among many others.

A careful reading and analysis of his writings shows that he was a gifted scholar and thinker, who was equally steeped in Western intellectual thought, in addition to being an assiduous critic of Christian theology and history. In other words, he pursued a more systematic and scholarly approach to aspects of Islamic thought, Western philosophy and Christology than any of his contemporaries, including Abdullah Quilliam, Lord Headley, Khalid Sheldrake, Ameen Neville J. Whymant, Noor-ud-Din Stephen and Dudley M. S. Wright. Only Marmaduke Pickthall was more systematic and accomplished as an Islamic scholar, thanks to his excellent command of Arabic and thorough knowledge of Islamic thought and culture, being the first English Muslim to have translated the entire Qur'an into English (see next chapter for more information).

However, John's knowledge and understanding of Western philosophy, thought and history was far superior to that of Pickthall. According to *The Islamic Review*, 'The supreme literary gift of Mr. Parkinson has gained him a well-deserved fame and popularity. His contributions to these pages, well known for their versatile character, display deep philosophy, sound logic, and vast information. He has got a facile pen, which he wields with clearness of expression and vigour.'[13]

Despite his valuable literary contributions, John was not an intellectual hermit; he was aware of the challenges and difficulties that confronted the British Muslim community – and indeed the Islamic world as a whole – at the time. Accordingly, he became involved in the affairs of the *Ummah* – locally, regionally and internationally. In addition to being elected a Vice-President of the British Muslim Association, he published several articles in defence of Muslim India and the Ottoman Empire.

He also served as a Vice-President of The Islamic Society in London and, despite being of modest means, he was generous when it came to supporting Muslim causes. He donated five shillings to the Society's 'Indian Muslim Soldiers' Widows and Orphans War Fund' in 1915, when the Woking Mosque congregation as a whole contributed only fifteen shillings. However, he was unable to attend the Society's large gathering, which was held at the Woking Mosque on Sunday 20 December, 1915. Instead, he sent a letter, dated 17 December, 1915 which was read out to the whole assembly and subsequently published in *The Islamic Review*. He wrote – to quote him at some length:

> The tree of Islam is flourishing in Britain; it has borne fruit, and the British Muslim Society is the first offerings of its activities…Such a society was badly wanted – urgently needed to fulfil in reality the command of the Prophet on the hill without Mecca after the fall of the city; the command that all Muslims should be brothers…It will, I hope, also serve to keep us in touch with the other parts of our world-wide brotherhood. Union is strength. May it be a uniting link not only between every British Muslim but between us and the Muslims everywhere, consolidating and binding the whole into one unbroken and unbreakable chain, stretching through the Orient and Occident, Africa, and the South and North American States! We have now planted the banner of Islam in the heart of the British Empire…Let us keep it flying on the winds unstained, untarnished, as spotless as when it was first unfurled on Arabia's burning sands over fourteen hundred years ago…Our heritage is a glorious one; be it ours to maintain it unsullied, and to hand it on undimmed to those who may follow after us, leaving to the generations yet to be an example of which they may be proud, and which will enable them to tread more securely the paths of justice and truth, and help them to climb to higher heights than we shall ever climb limn ideals we never saw or dreamt of. 'Fear not, the future shall be better for thee than the past.' Be earnest, be honest in your endeavours in the cause you have pledged yourselves thereto…Strong of heart and steady of hand, and faithful in all your dealings, even as he was, whom the Arabs of the desert call Al-Amin, and victory will crown your efforts…May Allah be with you all![14]

Being very fond of the Prophet, it was fitting that John's last article should have been entitled 'Muhammad – Personality' which was published in the *Islamic Review* in December 1918, the same month in which he died of pneumonia at the relatively young age of 44. He was laid to rest in an unmarked grave in his native Kilwinning. He was a devout Muslim, notable scholar, prolific writer and a gifted poet, but also one of the foremost British – indeed Western – admirers and followers of the Prophet of Islam.

Unfortunately, his life and legacy is not widely known today, perhaps because he had no family or friends to remember him after his death, unlike the other prominent British Muslims of the early twentieth century. I hope this short entry will inspire others to pursue further study and research on his life and work for the benefit of the present and future generations.

Ⓝ

1. See www.boards.ancestry.co.uk (Ayrshire, Scotland).

2. See Yehya en-Nasr Parkinson, *Muslim Chivalry*.

3. See Christopher A. Whately, *The Industrial Revolution in Scotland*; Barrie Trinder, *Britain's Industrial Revolution: The Making of a Manufacturing People, 1700–1870*.

4. John Parkinson, 'The Pauline Literature and Christ' in *Islamic Review and Muslim India*, vol. 3, no. 1.

5. Ibid.

6. John Parkinson, 'An Outline of Christian Theology before Muhammed' in *Islamic Review and Muslim India*, vol. 2, no. 9.

7. John Parkinson, 'The Messenger' in *Islamic Review and Muslim India*, vol. 2, no. 7.

8. Brent D. Singleton (ed.), *The Convert's Passion: An Anthology of Islamic Poetry from Late Victorian and Edwardian Britain*.

9. John Parkinson, 'Inversion of Times: An Appeal for the Erection of a Memorial at Rangoon to Abu-Zafar Bahadur Shah'.

10. John Yehya-en-Nasr Parkinson, *Essays on Islamic Philosophy*.

11. Ibid.

12. *Islamic Review and Muslim India*, volumes 1 to 8 (1913 to 1918).

13. *Islamic Review and Muslim India*, vol. 2, no. 2.

14. *Islamic Review and Muslim India*, vol. 3, no. 1.

# 33

# MARMADUKE WILLIAM PICKTHALL

B. 1875 – D. 1936

UNITED KINGDOM

Islamic civilisation is first and foremost a civilisation of books. Throughout its history, books dominated Muslim thought, history and culture, and did so at an un-precedented level, the like of which was unknown and unheard of in human history. It is true that books played an equally important role in the formation and evolution of many other world cultures and civilisations. However, it is only the Islamic civilisation that can proudly claim to be based on a single book, namely the Qur'an.

Indeed, the influence and impact of the Qur'anic revelation on not only Muslims, but humanity as a whole, spanning no less than fifteen centuries, remains prodigious and unprecedented in world history. It all began back in seventh century Arabia with the revelation of the Arabic word *iqra* ('to read' or 'to recite') to an unlettered merchant from Banu Hashim, a noble tribe from the Arabian citadel of Makkah. During the following twenty-three years, the Qur'anic revelation was vouchsafed to the Prophet Muhammad (peace be on him) piecemeal.

Today, like the earliest Muslims, more than one billion believers consider the Qur'an to be literally the 'Word of God' (*kalam Allah*). Consisting of over 6000 verses, divided into

114 chapters of variable length, the Qur'anic revelation thus became the foundation of a civilisation that was destined to dominate human thought and culture unlike any other before or since. Though revealed in pure, classical Arabic; later the Qur'an was translated into other prominent languages to convey its meaning and message to non-Arabs. In the process, the Divine revelation became more widely accessible, thanks to translations into Persian, Latin, Urdu, Turkish, Bengali and English, which is today the most widely spoken language in the world.

However, the credit for producing the most popular and authentic translation of the Qur'an into English must go to none other than Marmaduke Pickthall, being the first English Muslim to achieve the remarkable feat during the first half of the twentieth century.

Marmaduke William Pickthall, better known as Muhammad Marmaduke Pickthall, was born into a notable English family that traced its ancestry back to Sir Roger de Poictu, who served as a senior army officer to William I, the famous Norman King of England, otherwise known as William the Conqueror (r. 1066–1087). The family name, Pickthall, was therefore a corruption of de Poictu. His father, Charles Grayson Pickthall (1822–1881), was an Anglican priest, and his mother, Mary O'Brien (1836–1904), was of Irish descent and traced her family roots back to Admiral Donat Henchy O'Brien, who was actively involved in the Napoleonic Wars from 1803 to 1815. They both met and married after the untimely death of Ellen Louis Christie, Charles's first wife who bore him no less than 10 children.

At the time, Charles worked in his capacity as the rector of the village of Chillesford, today located in the Suffolk Coastal District in the English county of Suffolk, which has a unique distinction of being the home of two English translators of the Qur'an (the other being J. M. Rodwell, who was born in 1808 in Barnham Hall, Suffolk, and was also an Anglican clergyman).[1]

As expected, Mary lived at the rectory with her husband, young stepsons and daughters, and successively bore him two sons, Marmaduke and Rudolph George, the former being the eldest. Despite the rectory being a ten-bedroomed house, it was barely big enough for their large family of twelve children and several adults. This explains why Mary subsequently moved to Cambridge Terrace in west London, where she gave birth to Marmaduke before returning back to Chillesford with her son. The youngster spent his early years in rural Suffolk with his parents, until his father was taken seriously ill when he was only five. In the absence of his father, who was not only a prominent figure in the village, but also the main bread-winner in the family, his mother had no choice but to move to London permanently where Marmaduke grew up under the care of his mother and the family nursemaid. He was, by all accounts, a bright, well-behaved and contemplative boy who was, according to his earliest biographer, 'born with an Eastern mind'.[2]

Unsurprisingly, Marmaduke had a natural and precocious talent for arithmetic and languages. He was very shy, reserved and disliked unruly behaviour, unlike the other children of his age. Marmaduke was also fond of geography and cricket, in which he excelled. However, his health was always fragile. He was barely nine when he was taken seriously ill suffering from brain-fever, thus as a result, he was sent back to Chillesford to recover. There, his father's successor, Reverend B. J. St Patrick, granted him all the freedom in the world to do as he wished. He not only made a speedy recovery, but also thoroughly enjoyed his stay in rural Suffolk.

However, the illness was to have a lasting impact on his ability to perform even basic mental arithmetic, although he made up for this by reading English literature extensively. In such a process, Marmaduke eventually became thoroughly familiar with the works of prominent literary figures like Lord Byron (1788–1824), Sir Walter Scott (1771–1832), Algernon C. Swinburne (1837–1909), Charles J. H. Dickens (1812–1870), William M. Thackeray (1811–1863) and Benjamin Disraeli (1804–1881), among others. He also learnt swimming, horse-riding and walking, which was to become a lifelong hobby.

Subsequently, Marmaduke's mother enrolled him at Harrow School, one of the leading public schools in London at the time, where Sir Winston Churchill (1874–1965) and Leopold. S. Amery (1873–1955) were some of his contemporaries. However, he stayed there for only six terms and left at the age of 16, before focusing his attention on learning languages, thanks to his mother's encouragement and support. A year later, he met Muriel Smith, who was a daughter of a leading educationalist, and they soon became engaged. He then prepared for examination to qualify for the Consular Service under the supervision of Reverend H. P. Waller, who was the headmaster of St Catherine's School where he was a boarder at the time. Although he performed well in the languages, overall he came seventh on the list with only three vacancies to fill in the Eastern Department. He was, of course, devastated, as he later recalled:

> Early in the year 1894 I was a candidate for one of two vacancies in the Consular Service for Turkey, Persia, and the Levan, but failed to gain the necessary place in the competitive examination. I was in despair. All my hopes for months had been turned towards sunny countries and old civilisations, away from the drab monotone of London fog, which seemed a nightmare when the prospect of escape eluded me. I was eighteen years old, and, having failed in one or two adventures, I thought myself an all-round failure, and was much depressed. I dreamed of Eastern sunshine, palm trees, camels, desert sand, as of a Paradise which I had lost by my shortcomings. What was my rapture when my mother one fine day suggested that it might be good for me to travel East, because my longing for it seemed to indicate a natural instinct, with which she herself, possessing Eastern memories, was in full sympathy![3]

Thereafter, his mother, a quiet but fiercely independent-minded lady, offered him a choice between re-joining his younger brother at Harrow before proceeding to Oxford, or, travelling to Palestine. As expected, he chose 'Eastern sunshine, palm trees, camels, desert sand, as of a Paradise which I had lost by my shortcomings' over 'the drab monotone of London fog'. His mother raised sufficient funds to pay for his sojourn so that he may learn eastern languages to enable him to secure a position within the Foreign Service. Accordingly, he set off in the direction of Naples where he boarded a ship destined for Port Said in Egypt. Soon after his arrival in the Islamic East, he went native in his dress, language and mannerism, much to the disapproval of the other Europeans who lived there at the time. During this period, he travelled extensively across Egypt before heading to Palestine where, accompanied by a local guide, he swiftly acquired proficiency in Arabic and explored the length and breadth of the country, including Jerusalem.

During his long eighteen month sojourn, Marmaduke also visited Lebanon and Syria, and indeed, was very impressed by what he saw. He found daily life in Lebanon and Syria to be similar to the famous stories that he had once read in *Alf Layla wa Layla* (One Thousand and One Nights), otherwise known as *The Arabian Nights*. As he later wrote, 'What struck me, even in its decay and poverty, was the joyousness of that life compared with anything that I had seen in Europe. The people seemed quite independent of our cares of life, our anxious clutching after wealth, our fear of death. And then their charity! No man in the cities of the Muslim empire ever died of exposure at his neighbour's gate. They undoubtedly had something which was lacking in the life of Western Europe...It was only afterwards that I learnt they had once possessed the material prosperity which Europe now can boast, in addition to that inward happiness which I so envied.'⁴

He later recorded in his travelogue, *Oriental Encounters* (1918) that he found life in the Islamic East to be not only physically liberating, but also emotionally soothing and spiritually uplifting. That was because the Muslim countries he had visited at the time were still traditional in their culture and outlook, being largely undisturbed by the forces of modernism and westernisation that were so prevalent in Western Europe, and were rapidly spreading across the Ottoman Empire and heading in the direction of the Islamic East.

During this period, Marmaduke even considered converting to Islam, which no doubt would have horrified his mother, herself a devout, church-going Christian, but the grand Mufti and Imam of the Umayyad Mosque in Damascus dissuaded him by reminding him of his duties to his mother. 'No, my son,' exhorted the venerable Shaykh, 'wait until you are older, and have seen again your native land. You are alone among us as our boys are alone among the Christians. God knows how I should feel if any Christian teacher dealt with a son of mine otherwise than as I now deal with you.'⁵

His encounter with the wise Shaykh was timely because his conversion at the time would have been motivated more by the romance and pageantry of Eastern life, than as a result of in-depth study of, and reflection on, Islamic teachings, ethos and values. Even so, his travels in the Islamic East opened his mind and intellect to a new and fascinating world, indeed, a great culture and civilisation that, unlike Western Christendom, was very traditional in its outlook. Although, despite such traditionalism, the Islamic East was remarkably progressive in its principles and values, revolving as it did around the universal teachings of the great Arabian Prophet.

Upon completing his sojourn, Marmaduke returned home to resume normal life. He was 20 at the time and still remained a committed Christian who attended Church regularly, but his enchantment with the Islamic East persisted. As he prepared to return to the Islamic East, his mother was taken seriously ill, forcing Marmaduke to postpone his plans. Encouraged by his mother, he married Muriel, his childhood sweetheart and, to his credit, he remained faithful to her for the rest of his forty years. Keen to earn a living, he then published several stories in various journals. Marmaduke had eventually earned enough to rent a cottage in Holton, Suffolk where he lived for the next five years.

During this period, Marmaduke published several novels including *All Fools* (1900), *Sa'id the Fisherman* (1903), *Enid* (1904) and *Brendle* (1905). Of these, *Sa'id the Fisherman* proved to be very popular, so much so that it was hailed as an important contribution by prominent writers like A. J. Dawson (1872–1951), Sir James M. Barrie (1860–1937) and H. G. Wells (1866–1946). His literary admirers also included D. H. Lawrence (1885–1930) and E. M. Foster (1879–1970). Thereafter, he moved to a flat in Maida Vale, London and, in 1906, his *House of Islam* was published, though it was far from being a bestseller.

Perhaps it was his failure to make a literary impression in England which prompted him a year later to go to Cairo as the guest of a British official. Here, Marmaduke met several notable publicists and administrators, including Sir Mark Sykes (1879–1919), George Lloyd (1879–1941) and Lord Cromer (1841–1917), who was the British Consul-General at the time.[6] From Egypt, he moved to Damascus before finally returning home via Marseille. His fifth novel, *The Myopes* was published in 1907, followed by *The Children of the Nile*, although the latter received more positive reviews than the former. He spent a good part of 1908 in Egypt, Syria and Lebanon where he perfected his knowledge of classical Arabic under the guidance of a local headmaster.

On his return back to England, he rented a house in Buxted, Sussex where he lived with his wife for the following six years. Soon after, he published another novel, *The Valley of the Kings* (1909), followed by a collection of short stories titled *Pot au Feu* (1911), and two other novels, *Larkmeadow* (1912) and *Veiled Women* (1913), in addition to many articles in various journals on Middle Eastern themes. During this period, he visited many European countries including France, Switzerland, Italy, Belgium and Holland. From 1912 to 1920, Marmaduke published articles in the weekly *New Age*, which was, at the time, edited by A. R. Orage (1873–1934), a leading

British intellectual and journalist of the time. He focused on Middle Eastern cultural and political topics, expressing his independent and well-informed views and opinions on the burning issues of the day without any fear or favour.

Privately, however, he continued to study, explore and reflect on Islam and its teachings more than ever before. In addition to books that were readily available in European languages on Islam at the time, he read the Qur'an and classical Islamic literature, thanks to his proficiency in Arabic. The more he studied and reflected, the more he moved closer to Islam – spiritually, emotionally and politically. Unsurprisingly, his writings in the *New Age* and *The Nineteenth Century and After* reflected such a personal transformation as he wielded his pen in defence of Ottoman rights and deplored European Christian designs against the burgeoning Muslim empire.

Marmaduke lived during a politically, economically and culturally turbulent and testing period in modern history. Although significant parts of the Islamic world were still firmly under the grip of colonial powers, a number of Muslim revivalist movements had already emerged in Egypt, India and Ottoman Turkey to call the masses back to Islam on the one hand, and pro-actively engage in socio-political activism on the other, to regain their freedom from foreign subjugation. The Young Turk Revolution of 1908 was one such movement that ushered in much-needed internal socio-political reforms within the Ottoman State and, needless to say, Marmaduke was a supporter of the Turkish reformists who established the Committee of Union and Progress (*Ittihat ve Terakki Cemiyeti*) to bring about democratisation and reformation in the Ottoman Empire.

However, his knowledge and understanding of the internal dynamics within the empire was far from being well-informed and in-depth. This prompted him to travel to Istanbul in 1913 where he stayed for four months and, in addition to learning Turkish, he met many prominent officials including Ali Haidar Bey, the son of a former vizier, and Prince Sa'id Halim Pasha (1865–1921), who served as the Foreign Minister at the time. His observation of Ottoman life, culture and ethos reinforced his belief that Islam, as represented by the reformist Turks, was very progressive and that they needed help and support from the British Government. When the Anglo-Ottoman Society was founded in London in 1914, Marmaduke became an active member. Even when Britain declared war against Turkey on 5 November, 1914 though heart-broken, he continued to argue for Turkish freedom and independence.

In other words, Marmaduke's writings during this period focused on two important themes: firstly, the emergence of a reforming Islam within the Ottoman State in the form of Young Turks, and why it was important to support their reform initiatives, and secondly, highlighting the universal message of Islam which transcended race, colour and geographical boundaries. As the Ottoman Caliphate transcended such categories, he opined, it had to be protected and preserved due to its high political and religious standing in the Muslim world as a whole, not just Turkey.

In his own words, 'The question of the Khilafat is no concern of Christians any more than it is the concern of Muslims to decide who shall be Pope of Rome...The Muslim world as a whole accepts the Ottoman Sultan as its Khalifah with enthusiasm and impassioned sympathy.'[7] His subsequent encounter with the Indian Muslims, who were actively engaged in a campaign to preserve the Caliphate at the time, only served to confirm his thinking on the issue.

Indeed, as the tone of his writings during this period indicated, Marmaduke was now moving closer to Islam spirituality, in addition to his political and emotional affinity with the Muslim world. Thus, unsurprisingly, in January 1917, Marmaduke not only delivered a speech marking the Birthday of the Prophet, he also contributed an article titled 'The Prophet's Gratitude' in *The Islamic Review and Muslim India*, the monthly journal of the Woking Mosque.

He summarised the character and personality of the Prophet in the following words: 'To the last he was a pious Muslim, simple in his habits, regular in prayer, vigorous and far-seeing in affairs of state, gentle and forgiving in his private inter-course with men, a loyal friend, a noble enemy, faithful in all things that he undertook. His followers were bound to him by the ties of love, not fear.'[8] By now, he was a Muslim in all but name and it was only a matter of time before his conversion would be publicly announced. It took place on 19 November, 1917 when he was invited by the Muslim Literary Society in Notting Hill, West London to deliver a lecture on 'Islam and modernism'. According to *The Islamic Review*, he was:

> Listened to in rapt silence. His intonation of suitable verses from Holy Qur'an in the original text to illustrate the beauties of Islam, with which he frequently punctuated his most learned discourse, threw those who were not used to listening to such recitations from a Westerner's lips into ecstasies. From start to finish Mr. Pickthall held his audience as if in a spell by his erudition, by his deep thinking, and lastly by the most genuine and rock-like faith which every word of his breathed into the splendour and beneficence of Islam...When he sat down, every one of his hearers felt that they had lived through, during that one short hour, the most remarkable period of his or her life.[9]

After his conversion, he became known as Muhammad Marmaduke Pickthall and, as a leading figure of the British Muslim community, he was regularly invited to deliver lectures, Friday sermons and lead prayers at the Mosque in Notting Hill, in addition to publishing articles in *The Islamic Review* on Islam and related topics. He also led Eid al-Fitr prayers at the Woking Mosque in 1919 and helped to edit *The Islamic Review* for a short period. Unlike other prominent British converts to Islam (such as Abdullah Quilliam, Khalid Sheldrake, Dudley M. S. Wright, Noor-ud-Din Stephen, Ameen Neville J. Whymant, Lady Evelyn Cobbold and John Yahya Parkinson), Marmaduke was fluent in both classical and colloquial Arabic. Unsurprisingly, his knowledge and understanding of Muslim thought, history and culture was intimate as it was authentic, which was not always the case with the other converts.

Likewise, his approach to Islam was theologically sophisticated and orthodox, but socially and culturally progressive. He repeatedly emphasized the importance of material and cultural advancement, but never at the expense of spiritual growth and development. A balanced approach to their faith required Muslims to combine the two aspects, just as it was exemplified in the life and career of the Prophet of Islam. Success, he argued, did not 'refer to the success of a business man or a politician, or a social magnate, or any of those vulgar triumphs which are acclaimed in the daily papers, with a portrait of the successful one. "Success" in El-Islam is something very different. The Qur'an defines it in a later Surah: "He is indeed successful who improves it (the soul) and gives it growth; and he is indeed a failure who stunts and starves the soul".'[10]

On a more personal level, however, Marmaduke struggled to make ends meet, having been without a regular job for some time. So, when the editorship of the *Bombay Chronicle* was offered to him with a salary of 1400 rupees a month, he accepted it without any hesitation. He soon completed the *Early Hours*, his last novel, and sent the manuscript to the publisher before setting off to India, where he stayed for the next fifteen years. He stayed in Bombay for four years and then moved to Hyderabad, where he worked for the Nizam for over a decade.

This was, by all accounts, the most peaceful and happiest period of Marmaduke's life. Being a gifted linguist, he soon learned Urdu and became a leading editor, teacher and headmaster of a boy's high school. His patron, Sir Uthman Ali Khan Bahadur, the Nizam of Hyderabad (r. 1911–1948), was himself a noted literary figure, and also contributed to transforming the princely State into a prominent cultural centre in India. It was during this period that Marmaduke was invited by The Committee of 'Madras Lectures on Islam' to deliver their second series of public talks on 'The Cultural Side of Islam' in English. He obliged by delivering eight lectures on different aspects of Islamic culture. Towards the end of his first lecture, he explained his approach to the subject as follows:

> You may think that in this lecture I have wandered off from my appointed subject, which is culture, into the religious field. Islamic culture is so intricately bound up with religion, so imbued with the idea of Allah's universal sovereignty that I could not treat the subject properly without first giving you the indications I have given in this first address. In its grandeur and its decadence, Islamic culture – whether we survey it in the field of science, or of art, or of literature, or of social welfare – has everywhere and always this religious inference, this all-pervading ideal of universal and complete theocracy. In all its various productions – some of them far from being what is usually called religious – this is evident. It is this

which makes Islamic nationalism one with internationalism. For, acceptance of the fact of Allah's universal sovereignty entails acceptance of the complementary fact of universal human brotherhood.[11]

In his lectures, Marmaduke provided a clear and unambiguous exposition of Islamic teachings on a range of subjects, including the importance of combining modern education with a traditional understanding of the faith; the need for progress and advancement along with spiritual growth and development; he advocated the rights and duties of individuals, especially that of Muslim women in a grossly unfair, and often oppressive society; and, of course, he highlighted the importance of good character and conduct in the formation of a healthy Islamic culture and society. His lectures were not only received positively at the time, they were also published in 1927 and subsequently translated into several languages, such as Urdu and Bengali, and reprinted many times. Thanks to these lectures, Marmaduke became widely known as a prominent Islamic scholar and thinker. As a result, he was offered the editorship of the *Islamic Culture*, a new quarterly journal that was published under the patronage of the Nizam.

He edited this scholarly publication for about 10 years and some of its notable contributors included David S. Margoliouth (1858–1940), Fritz J. H. Krenkow (1872–1953), W. E. Gladstone Solomon (1880–1965), Freya Stark (1893–1993), Julius Abd al-Karim Germanus (see chapter 36), Leopold Weiss (better known as Muhammad Asad – see chapter 39) and Muhammad Hamidullah (see chapter 51). Alongside his editorial job, he continued his regular review of books on different subjects published in Arabic, Persian, Turkish, German, French, Spanish and Urdu. For example, he translated Josef Horovitz's (d. 1931) monograph titled 'The Earliest Biographies of the Prophet and Their Authors' from German into English and serialised it in the early issues of the *Islamic Culture*. Through this journal, Marmaduke became well-known in the scholarly and academic circles, both in the Muslim world and the West.

However, the crowning achievement of his life was the translation of the whole Qur'an from the original Arabic into English and, in the process, he became the first English convert to Islam to achieve this remarkable feat. His patron, the Nizam, granted him two years fully paid leave from work so that he could complete his task for the benefit of the English-speaking world. Being unhappy with the existing translations, most of which had been undertaken by non-Muslims, Marmaduke was motivated to produce an accurate, but equally readable rendering of the meaning of the Qur'an into English. After completing the task, he went to Egypt to seek approval for his translation from the senior scholars at al-Azhar University in Cairo. The authorities hesitated to approve his work, despite considering it to be 'the best of all translations'.

Soon after his return from Egypt in March 1930, it was published under the title of *The Meaning of the Glorious Koran* by A. A. Knopf in New York in December 1930; he was in his mid-fifties at the time. Subsequently, it was published in England by Allen and Unwin in 1939. As expected, the work established his reputation as an outstanding Islamic scholar and translator, thus his work has continued to be reprinted and read widely to this day. Although the language and tone of his translation do appear to be somewhat archaic today, it does remain one of the most literal and authentic translations to have been produced by a Muslim whose mother-tongue was English. Dedicated to his patron, the Nizam, in the foreword to the translation, he wrote:

> The Koran cannot be translated. That is the belief of old-fashioned Sheykhs and the view of the present writer. The Book is here rendered almost literally and every effort has been made to choose befitting language. But the result is not the Glorious Koran, that inimitable symphony, the very sounds of which move men to tears and ecstasy. It is only an attempt to present the meaning of the Koran – and peradventure something of the charm – in English. It can never take the place of the Koran in Arabic, nor is it meant to do so.[12]

Soon after its publication, Marmaduke's translation was hailed as a major achievement. According to the *Times Literary Supplement*, 'it is not only a translation. It is provided with historical, explanatory, chronological, and critical notes: some of these are most illuminating, as they make clear to readers imperfectly acquainted with Arabian customs, the events of contemporary Arabian history…The whole is a fine literary achievement, a labour of love on behalf of the creed of the author's choice and adoption.'

After ten years of dedicated service to the Nizam, Marmaduke finally retired in 1935, just before his sixtieth birthday. He returned to England via Europe and settled in St. Ives in Cornwall. As he was making preparations to revise his *The Cultural Side of Islam* and go to Makkah to perform the annual pilgrimage, he died of a heart attack at the age of 61. He was laid to rest at the Brookwood Cemetery in Surrey following a simple funeral prayer led by the Imam of Woking Mosque. Soon after his death, the *Islamic Culture* paid him this glowing tribute:

> Soldier of Islam! True servant of Islam!
> To thee 'twas given to quit the shades of night
> And onward move, aye onward into Light
> With strengthen undaunted, heart assured and calm![13]

Ⓝ

1. See J. M. Rodwell, *The Koran*.

2. Anne Fremantle, *Loyal Enemy: Life of Marmaduke Pickthall*.

3. Marmaduke Pickthall, *Oriental Encounters: Palestine and Syria (1894–6)*.

4. Quoted by Anne Fremantle, op. cit.

5. Ibid.

6. Peter Clark, *Marmaduke Pickthall: British Muslim*.

7. *Islamic Review and Muslim India*, vol. 7, no. 11.

8. *Islamic Review and Muslim India*, vol. 5, No. 1.

9. *Islamic Review and Muslim India*, vol. 7, No. 1.

10. *Islamic Review and Muslim India*, vol. 7, No. 6.

11. Marmaduke Pickthall, *The Cultural Side of Islam*.

12. Marmaduke Pickthall, *The Meaning of the Glorious Koran: An Explanatory Translation*.

13. Quoted by Peter Clark, op. cit.

# 34

# MUSA JARULLAH

B. 1875 – D. 1949

RUSSIA

The history of Tatarstan (or 'the land of the Tatars') can be traced back to the Palaeolithic period, thanks to the discovered remains from the Stone and Bronze Ages, although its territorial boundaries were first established during the time of the Volga Bulgars, from the eighth to the mid-thirteenth century. Today located in the centre of the east European plain, less than 500 miles from Moscow, Islam first made in-roads into this region during the early part of the tenth century.

It was the Muslim preachers and traders from Abbasid Baghdad who moved into this area and played a pivotal role in the Islamisation of that part of the world. The Mongols subsequently invaded Volga Bulgaria and that, in turn, led to the formation of a Volga Tatar ethnicity during the fourteenth century. The Khanate of Kazan (Qazan), a medieval Volga-Tatar and Turkic kingdom, was then formed around the mid-fifteenth century. It continued to rule for over a century until Ivan the Terrible (r. 1547–1584), a fearsome Russian Tsar, conquered the Khanate kingdom in 1552.

The Russian troops killed those Tatars who opposed them and also forced many to embrace Christianity. They went out of their way to achieve the complete Russification of Tatar culture and heritage. For example, all the mosques in Kazan, the capital of Tatarstan, were destroyed during this period and replaced by churches and cathedrals. Prohibition on the building of mosques was strictly enforced until Catherine the Great (r. 1762–1796) eventually lifted the ban and the first mosque was, therefore, constructed during the eighteenth century under her patronage.

The nineteenth and early twentieth centuries witnessed a revival of Islam across the region and beyond, thanks largely to the efforts of many outstanding and influential Muslim reformers from within the Russian Empire. Musa Jarullah was one such gifted scholar and intellectual whose life, contribution and achievements are, strangely enough, not as widely known today as they should be, both in the Muslim world and the West.

Musa Bigiyev, better known as Musa Jarullah, was born in Novocherkassk, a Russian city in present-day Rostov Oblast, into a notable Muslim family that traced its ancestry to Tatarstan, which is today a federal subject of the Russian Federation. According to another account, he was born in the village of Kikine in the Kamenskiy region which, at the time, was a part of the Penza Governorate, an administrative division of the Russian Empire. As it happens, his biographers have provided conflicting information about his family history and early years due to the fact that he did not write anything on the subject himself.

However, most of his biographers have agreed that his father, Mullah Yarullah Delikam, was a devout and learned Muslim who served as an Islamic scholar and preacher (Persian *Akhoond* and Arabic *Imam*), and, unfortunately, died when his two sons, Zahir and Musa, were still young. Fatima, his wife, was the daughter of a local Muslim preacher and a devout Muslim herself, who then took full responsibility for raising her sons, providing them both with a good education and upbringing.[1] As the majority of the population in their locality were ethnic Russians who were Greek Orthodox Christians, there were very few opportunities available there for Fatima to provide a good Islamic education to her sons. As a result, Fatima decided to send Musa to Kazan in 1888, when he was only 13 years old.

Being the capital of Tatarstan, Kazan was a thriving multicultural centre of commerce, trade and education at the time. Consisting of Kipchaks, Bulgars and Tatars of the Golden Horde, the city not only developed strong cultural links with other great Muslim capitals like Baghdad, Bukhara and Samarqand, but also many Islamic scholars, traders and travellers came to Kazan from different parts of the Muslim world to pursue trade, education and learning, thanks to the generosity of its rulers. Indeed, Kazan was renowned at the time for its prominent Islamic schools (*maktabs*) and seminaries (*madrasahs*), where students came from across the Russian Empire to pursue further and higher education in Arabic language and literature, Persian poetry, traditional Islamic sciences, and aspects of history, logic and traditional philosophy, among other subjects. Successful completion of madrasah education enabled graduates to seek relatively well-paid employment and, at the same time, gain considerable respect and standing in their communities.

Young Musa, like most other students, would have needed some knowledge of Arabic and Persian before acquiring thorough proficiency in the Qur'an. This would have enabled the students to study a range of texts including *Adab-i-Muta'allimin* (dealing with ethics and etiquette of being a student), followed by *Sharh-i-Mulla* (a commentary on Ibn Hajib's *Kafiya*) by Abd al-Rahman Jami (1414–1492), and basic texts on logic and theology (such as *Shamsiya* of Najm al-Din Qazwini [1203–1276] and *Aqa'id* of Abu Hafs Umar al-Nasafi [1067–1142]), in addition to aspects of Islamic jurisprudence (*fiqh*), Prophetic traditions (*ahadith an-nabawi*) and early Islamic history (*ta'rikh*) – often based on commentaries of works produced by earlier scholars. Such readings would have provided the students with a good grounding in traditional Islamic sciences to enable them to pursue further and higher education, and, thereby, qualify as Islamic scholars and preachers. Referring to the method of teaching that was prevalent at the time, one historian wrote:

> A student entered a madrasa when a mudarris allowed him to listen to his lectures; there was no formal matriculation…As in the maktab, progress through the madrasa was marked by successful completion of books; each student proceeded along the curriculum at his own pace. Attendance at lectures coincided with more informal peer learning in study circles organized by students. Members of a circle studied the same book, and those with a better command of the material helped others in return for food or clothing, since it was considered 'a kind of vileness' to receive money in return for knowledge. Some texts were studied only in groups, and others were prepared thus before students listened to lectures on them from the mudarris. When the student had satisfied the professor of his command of a book (which often involved memorization), he could pass on to the next book by joining another study circle, possibly with another teacher.[2]

Young Musa spent just over two years studying at Kazan's two leading seminaries, namely Apanay and Kulbue Madrasahs. This enabled him to learn Arabic and Persian, in addition to acquiring familiarisation with Ottoman Turkish and aspects of traditional Islamic sciences and literature. Being a gifted student who was equally ambitious, he returned home to enrol at the local technical school where he studied Russian language, literature, mathematics and sciences.

After graduating from school at the age of 20, Musa moved to Central Asia and studied in Bukhara and Samarqand under the tutelage of prominent teachers and scholars. He studied there for several years, although the rote, monotonous and uncritical method of their teaching did not impress him, and, therefore, he moved to Istanbul to pursue advanced Islamic education. During his stay in Istanbul, Musa studied Islamic jurisprudence and philosophy, and discovered that senior Turkish students went to Cairo to complete their higher education.

Musa lived and pursued his education at a time when the forces of modernity and Westernisation had begun to transform Tatar culture and society, mainly due to Russian interference and influence. This prompted the *ulama* (religious scholars) to revisit and review their own history and Islamic culture, and devise ways to protect their people from foreign influence on the one hand, but also make efforts to reinvigorate their stagnant communities on the other. The enlightened Tatar *ulama* were, of course, aware that preservation of their religious belief and national culture was critical for their survival.

And that, in turn, could not be achieved without a thorough study and dissemination of Islamic principles and values across all sections of their society. Indeed, the young Tartars, 'sensing the problematic political and geographical environment surrounding them, were aware of the carefulness that was required for them, unlike other Muslim communities. After a short span of time, educated Tatars found themselves at the fork of a road. Were they to stay as easterners, or to move towards the West, or was there a third way composed of a mixture of these two?'[3]

Prominent Kazan and Crimean Tatar reformers, educators and *ulama* (like Abdunnasr Qursavi [1771–1812], Shihabuddin Merjani [1818–1889], Rizaeddin bin Fakhreddin [see chapter 51], Alimajan Barudi [1857–1921], Sheikh Zeynullah Rasuli [1833–1917] and Ismail Bey Gaspirali [see chapter 26]) wrestled with the above questions and formulated responses that could be categorised as modernist, reformist or traditionalist. The modernists were of the opinion that the degeneration of Muslim society was not due to Islam, but instead, as a result of Muslim failure to respond to the challenges of modernity and Westernisation. The reformists, on the other hand, argued that social and material progress was, undoubtedly, dependent upon reformation of existing educational policies and practices, which was entirely religious at the time through the introduction of secular subjects.

By contrast, the traditionalists considered religion to be complete and permanent, and, therefore, there was no need for Islamic modernism or reformation.[4] In other words, at a time when discussion and debate about the role of Islam in Tatar society was at its most intense, reflecting a diversity of views on social, cultural and educational conditions that were prevalent at the time, Musa left Istanbul and moved to Egypt to pursue advanced education under the leading Muslim scholars of Cairo.

Needless to say, the capital of Egypt was one of the foremost centres of Islamic learning and scholarship, mainly because it was the home of the historic al-Azhar University, which was (and still is) one of the most famous institutions of further and higher Islamic education in the world. Here, Musa attended the lectures of several prominent Islamic scholars, including Muhammad Abduh (1849–1905), Muhammad Rashid Rida (1865–1935) and Muhammad Bakhit al-Muti'i (d. 1935). During his four year stay at al-Azhar, he became thoroughly proficient in Islamic theology (*ilm al-kalam*), philosophy (*falsafa*) and jurisprudence (*fiqh*), in addition to Arabic grammar, syntax, poetry and literature. He conducted extensive research on the history and codification of the Qur'an during this period, before heading to Makkah to perform the annual pilgrimage. He spent nearly two years in Makkah and Madinah studying in the local seminaries, but he was far from impressed by the quality of education that was offered in Islamic seminaries across the Muslim world at the time. In his own words,

Seeds of love for religious sciences were planted into my heart by the hands of the Almighty; after wasting ten years in religious schools of Qazan and Mawaraennahr, I departed to the Muslim countries full of hopes. I used to travel in the Islamic lands of Turkey, Egypt, Hijaz, India and Sham for nearly five years; and was staying at religious *madrasahs* of those countries for either short or long periods. I have seen every famous religious school of those lands. But, unfortunately, the thing that I was able to find least in these 'great religious madrasahs' was religious education.[5]

Unlike the *ulama* in Tatarstan, Central Asia and many other parts of the Muslim world, Musa found Abduh and his disciples to be both informed and inspiring. Influenced by Jamal al-Din al-Afghani (1838–1897), they became champions of a new trend in Islamic thought which was known as 'Islamic Modernism'. These reformers rejected uncritical traditionalism, as well as blind imitation of Western ideas, thoughts and values. Instead, they advocated the need to reinterpret Islam in the light of modern challenges and difficulties which confronted the Muslim world at the time, and they especially emphasized the free use of rational faculty in understanding Divine revelation and its application to human life and society.[6] As expected, Musa found this new message of reform (*tajdid*) and renewal (*islah*) to be refreshing and timely. Inspired by the Islamic modernists, he returned home with a mission to reform Tatar culture and society for the benefit of his people.

Back home, one would have expected Musa to get married, which he did, and settle down to teaching at a local Islamic seminary. Instead, however, he moved to St Petersburg in 1905 to pursue legal training at the local university. This enabled him to acquire knowledge of modern legal systems and undertake a comparative study of Islamic and Western legal thought and practice. Musa also became familiar with Russian politics, culture and society, but was far from impressed by his experience in St Petersburg. During his twelve year stay there, he became actively involved in the affairs of the Russian Muslim community and attended the All-Russian Muslim Congresses from 1905 to 1917.

Working in partnership with other Pan-Islamic leaders like Abd al-Rashid Ibrahimov (1857–1944), Musa combined political activism with research and writing. He published numerous articles in pro-Islamic publications like *Tilmiz* and *Ulfat*, and served as an Imam (preacher and prayer-leader) at St Petersburg mosque. For about a year, he also taught Arabic and traditional Islamic sciences at Khosaeniya Madrasah in Orenburg, located on the Ural River towards the south-east of Moscow. His writings and political activism reflected the modernist approach of Abduh and his disciples, coupled with the reality of life in Muslim communities in Russia, Tatarstan and Central Asia, along with the diversity of Islamic thought that was prevalent across the region.

However, when the Russian Revolution of 1917 erupted, dismantling the Tsarist autocracy and paving the way for the emergence of the Soviet Union, Musa initially welcomed the revolution. However, he was soon disappointed. Indeed, the establishment of a Communist regime and its encroachment into the Volga-Urals region, the Caucasus and Muslim Central Asia began to raise alarm bells. His fears were not misplaced as the new regime instigated reforms that attempted to undermine, if not completely eradicate, Islam and Muslim culture. In response to Nikolai Bukharin's *The Alphabet of Communism* (1919), Musa wrote his *Alphabet of Islam* (*Islam Alifbasi*, 1920).

His stinging criticism of Communist-Marxist ideology and robust defence of Islam angered the regime and its leaders, leading to his arrest and incarceration at the age of 45. Three months later, he was released, thanks to pressure from Turkey and Finland. A year later, he went to Makkah to participate in an International Conference as a Russian delegate, but the authorities considered him to be a foreign spy, thus forcing him to flee, leaving his wife and six children behind.[7]

During this period, he travelled extensively and visited Chinese Turkistan, Afghanistan, India, Finland, Turkey, Germany, Japan, Sumatra and Singapore, in addition to the Middle East. He planned to settle in Afghanistan or India but the British authorities arrested and imprisoned him in Peshawar, thinking that he was a foreign spy, only to release him eighteen months later following the intervention of Muhammad Hamidullah Khan (1894–1960), who was the ruler of Bhopal at the time. He stayed in India until 1947 and became proficient in Urdu and Sanskrit before finally moving to Egypt in October 1949, when he was in his mid-seventies. Writing to a friend in Finland, he explained why he travelled extensively across the Muslim world and beyond:

> My journeys were the journeys of education. In order to awaken the thinking *fuqaha*, I always use small and short ideas in each of my works. My main aim was to initiate revolutionary movements in the thoughts of Muslims. My hope, will, and wishes for this have increased today. My dream might become a reality as the establishment of small or huge revolutionary trends in the Islamic scholarship and religious thought in one of the Islamic States of the Muslim World seems to be possible today.[8]

During his journeys, Musa found time to write prolifically and authored more than sixty books and manuscripts of varying sizes on a wide range of subjects, including Arabic grammar, Qur'anic studies, Prophetic traditions, Islamic theology, philosophy, jurisprudence and the social, political and cultural conditions of the Muslims of Russia and Tatarstan. Though he was proficient in more than half a dozen languages, he preferred to write in Arabic, perhaps because the majority of the *ulama* were conversant in the language. Musa's *Alphabet of Islam* aside, some of his other prominent works include *Tarihu'l Qur'an ve'l Mesahif, Sheru'l Luzumiyat, Rahmet-i Ilahiyye Burhanlari, Hukuku'n-nisa fi'l Islam, Uzun Gunlerde Ruze* and *Buyuk Mevzularda Ufak Fikirler*.

In the *Tarihu'l Qur'an*, the author provides a critical account of the history and codification of the Qur'an, arguing in favour of translating the Divine revelation into the Tatar language, thus making the Qur'an more accessible to the masses. Musa was reported to have produced a Tartar translation but it is no longer extant. By contrast, *Sheru'l Luzumiyat* is a commentary on the work of Abul Ala al-Ma'arri (973–1057), who was a blind poet, philosopher and writer. Like al-Ma'arri, in his commentary, Musa questions received wisdom and formulates a rationalistic and sceptical approach to religion. In the same way, in his *Rahmet-i Ilahiyye*, he argues that God's mercy and forgiveness is limitless, thus encompassing not only believers, but also non-believers. As expected, his views infuriated the traditional *ulama,* as well as the modernist scholars who published a refutation under the title of *Din va Magishat* (Religion and Life).[9]

As a religious scholar and reformer, Musa was appalled by the behaviour and attitude of Muslims towards women, particularly because Islam grants women more rights and recognition than any other religion. Yet, the disconnection between the Islamic ideals and reality of life in Muslim societies prompted Musa to become an advocate of women's rights, which he espoused in *Hukuku'n-nisa* (Rights of Women).

Likewise, his *Uzun* is a highly innovative, but equally controversial, work on Islamic law of fasting in the northern hemisphere where there is often an overlap between the length of daylight and darkness, unlike in the Islamic East. For a modernist Muslim thinker who advocated the need for reform in Islamic education and renewal of Muslim culture and societies in tune with the march of time, Musa had a soft spot for Sufism (or Islamic spirituality). Unsurprisingly, in his *Buyuk*, he criticised those who opposed Sufism because the Sufis, in his opinion, contributed to the preservation and dissemination of Islam throughout its history. In addition to the above, Musa authored many textbooks on Arabic grammar, commentaries on certain Qur'anic chapters, Prophetic traditions, the life of the Prophet, early Islamic history and Persian poetry.

By all accounts, he was a gifted scholar and prolific writer, although he was far from being a rigorous and systematic thinker, perhaps because he was always on the move and often wrote during his journeys from one country to another. And, despite being an heir to the Jadidist strand of Islamic thought that was prevalent in Russia, Crimea and Tatarstan at the time, he did not consider himself to be an exponent of Jadidism (Islamic modernism), nor was he associated with their Qadimist (Islamic traditionalist) opponents. He respected both strands of Islamic thinking but, ultimately, he carved out his own distinctive path that combined elements of traditionalism and modernism.

Nonetheless, he was one of the first Tatar scholars to explore the reasons for the decline of the Muslim world and the progress and advancement of Europe. He tried to answer this question in an essay titled *Khalq Nazarina Bir Nich Mas'ala*, which he wrote in 1912. He argued that there were many reasons for the decline of the Muslim world, but one of the main factors was educational backwardness and absence of intellectual creativity.[10] Having no obvious successors, unlike Ismail Bey Gaspirali, his ideas and thought remained largely scattered. Thus, Musa did not enjoy the same level of popularity or influence in the Muslim world, unlike many of his other prominent contemporaries.

After a lifetime devoted to Islamic learning, writing, political activism and travels across the Muslim world, Musa eventually passed away in Egypt at the age of 74; in fact, he died in a hospice for the poor and needy with no immediate family members or relatives to claim his body. However, thanks to the efforts of a number of contemporary scholars like Ahmet Kanlidere, Mehmet Gormez and Elmira Akhmetova, the life, contribution and achievements of this important Tatar Muslim reformer are being revived again for the benefit of everyone, Muslim and non-Muslim, alike.

1. See Ahmet Kanlidere, 'Musa Carullah (1875–1949): Tatar Alimi ve Dusunuru', *Turkiye Diyanet Vakfi Islam Ansiklopedisi*.

2. Adeeb Khalid, *The Politics of Muslim Cultural Reform: Jadidism in Central Asia*.

3. Ahmet Kanlidere, 'The Kazan Tatars in the 19th and 20th Centuries' in *The Turks*.

4. Ahmet Kanlidere, *Reform within Islam: The Tajdid and Jadid Movement among the Kazan Tatars (1809–1917)*.

5. Elmira Akhmetova, *Ideas of Muslim Unity at the Age of Nationalism: A Comparative Study of the Concept of the Ummah in the Writings of Musa Jarullah and Sa'id Nursi*.

6. Nikki R. Keddie, *An Islamic Response to Imperialism: Political and Religious Writings of Sayyid Jamal al-Din 'al-Afghani'*.

7. Azade-Ayse Rorlich, 'Bigi, Musa Yarullah', *The Oxford Encyclopedia of the Modern Islamic World*.

8. Elmira Akhmetova, op. cit.

9. Azade-Ayse Rorlich, op. cit.

10. Musa Jarullah Bigi, 'Why Did the Muslim World Decline While the Civilized World Advanced?', Charles Kurzman (ed.) *The Modernist Islam, 1840–1940*.

# 35

# YUSUF ZIYAEDDIN EZHERI

B. 1879 – D. 1961

BULGARIA

The history of Islam in Bulgaria is often traced back to the mid-ninth century when the first Muslim traders and preachers went there to pursue commerce and disseminate their faith. It was this which prompted Pope Nicholas I (820–867), otherwise known as St Nicholas the Great, to write to the ruler of Bulgaria to request him to expel the Muslims. Further contacts took place between Bulgaria and Islam during the eleventh and twelfth centuries with the arrival of the nomadic Turks (or Turkomans). This was followed by the migration of Seljuk Turks during the thirteenth century which, of course, paved the way for Ottoman expansion into the region during the mid-fourteenth century.

In 1364, the Ottomans captured Plovdiv and, two decades later, Sofia, the capital of present-day Bulgaria, was annexed. During the next 500 years, the Ottomans maintained their tight grip on Thrace, Macedonia, Kosova and parts of Albania, whilst Romania and Hungary remained a part of the Ottoman Empire for around 300 and 150 years, respectively. It was during Ottoman rule in Bulgaria that Islam became firmly established in the country, although the majority of its Muslim population consisted of a combination of Turks, Pomaks, Romas and Tatar, who lived (and continue to live) in north-eastern parts of the country.[1]

Consisting of just under one million people, the Bulgarian Muslims today constitute around fifteen per cent of the country's population and, along with their counterparts in Western Europe, they are now proud members of the European Muslim family. In other words, far from being an alien and unwelcome intrusion into continental Europe, Islam as a religion and way of life has been an integral part of Europe – and, by extension, the Western world – since the seventh century.

Although most Europeans, both Muslims and non-Muslims, now recognise and accept this historical fact, very few people know that the first European Muslim scholar and reformer to have fully understood and accepted this reality was none other than Yusuf Ziyaeddin Ezheri of Bulgaria who, during the first half of the twentieth century, went on to formulate a new, integrated and constructive interpretation of Islam to enable Western Muslims to become active members of their societies. In so doing, he contributed significantly to the creation of tolerant, inclusive and vibrant multicultural communities across Europe and the Western world as a whole.

According to most of his biographers, Abul Khayr Yusuf Diya al-Din al-Azhari, better known as Ebu'l Hayr Yusuf Ziyaeddin Ezheri, was born in the village of Khan Hacimusa in the north-western Turkish province of Duzce, located on the coastline of the Black Sea. His father, Hasan Efendi, and grandfather, Sahin, traced their family ancestry to the Caucasus before their preceptors came to Ottoman Turkey where they became known for their piety and learning. During his early years, Yusuf's father ensured his son attended the village Qur'an school (*maktab*) where he swiftly memorised the entire book, much to the delight of his family and relatives. Thereafter, he was enrolled at the local Junior High school before joining the Islamic seminary (*madrasah*) in Kastamonu, located in the Black Sea region to the north of Turkey.

By all accounts, he was a gifted student who was blessed with a highly retentive memory. From Kastamonu, the brightest and most ambitious students often proceeded to Istanbul to pursue further education in Arabic language and literature, traditional Islamic sciences, and aspects of Sufism, philosophy and logic, in addition to acquiring familiarisation with Ottoman history, geography and Persian literature.[2] Accordingly, Yusuf moved to Istanbul where he pursued higher Islamic education for several years under the tutelage of some of the city's prominent Islamic scholars and spiritual guides, including Ahmad Ziyaeddin Gumushanevi (1813–1893) and Omer Ziyaeddin Dagistani (1850–1920).[3]

Indeed, during his stay in Istanbul, he not only became proficient in traditional Islamic sciences, but his teachers also initiated him into the Naqshbandi Order of Sufism (or Islamic spirituality) that was widely followed throughout the Ottoman Empire; this Order was especially popular in Istanbul. This was because specialisation in the formal sciences of Islam was not considered to be enough, unless it was combined with a period of spiritual training under the guidance of a respected and accomplished Sufi. Only after completion of such an all-round training would the certificate (*ijaza*) of proficiency in the religious sciences be formally issued to the students. Being products of such a system of education themselves, most of Yusuf's teachers (like Ahmad Gumushanevi and Omer Dagistani) were well-known experts in traditional Islamic learning, as well as being prominent Sufi leaders in their own right.

Despite their thorough education in the exoteric and esoteric dimensions of Islam, the majority of the Ottoman *ulama* were, however, completely out of touch with the social, political, economic and cultural changes and transformations that were taking place, not only within the Ottoman State, but also across Europe and the Muslim world as a whole. Indeed, Yusuf completed his higher Islamic education in the heart of the Ottoman State during an unprecedented time in modern history when the balance of power had radically shifted in favour of European countries, while the Muslim world remained idle and static. Though interaction between the Islamic world and the Western countries increased during this period, Muslims had now fallen way behind – politically, economically and culturally. According to one scholar,

> In the post-Enlightenment era the relationship between Europe and the Islamic world grew immensely. This was manifest not only in scientific and technological but also in intellectual and religious spheres. Gradually the West began to exercise an increasing influence on various aspects of the Muslims' lives…It is also significant that Western cultural influence was quite pronounced even in the major centres of Muslim intellectual life.[4]

During this period of political flux and intellectual realignment, Yusuf moved from Istanbul to Cairo in order to acquire mastery of Arabic and become an expert in the traditional Islamic sciences under the guidance of prominent Egyptian Islamic scholars. He was only 22 at the time, yet his knowledge of Arabic and Islamic sciences was so impressive that Muhammad Abduh (1849–1905), the Grand Mufti (chief jurisconsult) and rector of al-Azhar University, (the most famous centre of learning in the Muslim world), took him under his care and taught him Islamic theology (*ilm al-kalam*), philosophy (*falsafa*) and Qur'anic exegesis (*tafsir*), among other subjects. Yusuf stayed in Cairo for the next four years and eventually graduated from al-Azhar in 1905, which explains why he subsequently became known as Ezheri.

Needless to say, his time in Cairo proved to be both an eye-opener, and immensely productive for a number of reasons. Firstly, his stay in Egypt enabled him to attain mastery of Arabic and traditional Islamic sciences which, of course, earned him considerable respect and standing within the circle of *ulama* in Istanbul upon his return. Secondly, his study with many influential scholars at al-Azhar opened his mind to the existential problems facing Muslims. His teachers were not only experts in the traditional Islamic sciences, but they were also aware of the challenges and difficulties confronting the Muslim world due to the spread of Western culture in that part of the world.

The French occupation of Egypt from 1798 to 1801, followed by the establishment of British hegemony in 1882, exposed Egyptian society and intelligentsia to the forces of modernity and Westernisation, and, of course, some of the leading *ulama* (like Muhammad Abduh, Muhammad Rashid Rida, Muhammad Farid Wajdi [1875–1954] and Muhammad Bakhit al-Muti'i [d. 1935], among others) endeavoured to respond to such challenges to the best of their abilities.

Thus, in addition to becoming thoroughly familiar with the prevailing discussion and debate on how to reconcile traditional Islam with Western modernity, at the time, Yusuf also witnessed the emergence of three different intellectual trends among Muslims; namely reformist, conservative and secularist strands. Influenced by Jamal al-Din al-Afghani (1839–1897), the reformists/modernists were led by Abduh and his disciples who emphasised the role of human reason and rationality in the interpretation of the Qur'an, to make its meaning and message directly relevant to their existential condition. However, on his return to Istanbul in 1906, he continued his education under the guidance of prominent local *muderris* (teachers) like Mustafa Asim Efendi and Ismail Hakki Efendi (d. 1912) who, at the time, were based at the city's Fatih Mosque Complex.

It was during this period that Yusuf encountered other Ottoman scholars like Mustafa Sabri Efendi (1869–1954) and Zahid ibn Hasan al-Kawthari (1879–1951) who were staunch traditionalists and conservatives in their scholarship and outlook. Islam was, in their opinion, complete as a religion and way of life, and therefore, there was no need for Islamic modernism or reformation. Given their anti-modernist stance, it is not surprising that both men were eventually forced to move to Egypt following the emergence of the Young Turks in 1908. By contrast, prominent writers and activists like Ziya Gokalp (d. 1924) and Abdullah Jawdat (d. 1932) espoused a line of thinking that not only repudiated both Islamic traditionalism and modernism, but also openly advocated secularisation and westernisation of Muslim societies.[5]

Needless to say, Yusuf wrestled with the differing approaches adopted by Muslim scholars and writers at the time, but he was far from impressed by some of them. Indeed, their conflicting and contradictory positions were, in his opinion, unlikely to resolve the challenges and difficulties confronting the Muslim world. He felt the traditionalists were out of touch with reality, while the secularists were suffering from an inferiority-complex and cultural alienation. However, the reformist approach appeared to him to be more appropriate for the regeneration of the Muslim world as it did not entail a complete break with the Islamic past, unlike what the secularists and westernisers advocated.

Likewise, the reformists were open to change and adjustments, contrary to the rigid and uncompromising stance adopted by the traditionalists and conservatives. Following in the footsteps of Abduh, his mentor and guide, Yusuf therefore became an advocate of change and reform in Islamic thought and culture whilst, at the same time, remaining faithful to the Islamic past. For example, Yusuf was a great champion of freedom of thought and expression, but not at the expense of other people's rights and liberties. In other words, he argued that freedom of thought and expression was a gift from God, a basic human right, but certainly not a free licence to curse and abuse as one wished, and, therefore, it needed to be exercised with due care, understanding and responsibility. In his own words,

> Freedom of thought and action is [a] human's required condition, and his natural right. Taking away this right is [an] encroachment and the greatest injustice to human being[s]. But yet the meaning of freedom should not be misunderstood, and should not be abused. Absolute liberty and freedom belongs to Allah [*sic*]. Only He may do whatever He wills. Human freedom is not absolute, but limited. The person's use of freedom in his actions, taking it as absolute, would eventually damage the self and the society.[6]

Informed by his experiences in Egypt and Istanbul, coupled with his expertise in Hanafi *fiqh*, Islamic theology and Qur'anic exegesis, in addition to being an adherent of the Naqshbandi Sufi Order, Yusuf emphasised the importance of following the fundamental principles and practices of Islam at an unprecedented period of socio-political uncertainty and upheaval within the Ottoman Empire. Although he initially worked as a Mufti (jurisconsult) in his native Duzce, he was later transferred to the Orphan's Office and, in the process, he established his reputation as a competent scholar and official.

Not surprisingly, in 1920, when he was around 45, he was promoted to the prestigious post of Mufti of Duzce. He worked in this capacity for a few years before he received an invitation to move to the Bulgarian city of Shumen, located in the north-east of the country. Though the city was ethnically very diverse (consisting of Pomaks, Turks, Romas and Tatars), the Turks formed a significant proportion of its population, and, at the time, they were actively searching for a prominent Islamic scholar to come and serve their community. Needless to say, the socio-political situation in Bulgaria at the time was considerably different from that in mainland Ottoman Turkey. According to one historian,

> Among Muslims of the Ottoman Empire, many intellectual and political currents developed concurrently and combined: Ottomanism, Islamism (sometimes in a version of pan-Islamism), and Turkism (also in a pan-Turkist version). But in the European part of the Empire, including in the capital, Albanianism was also spreading, in close connection with the question of the fate of Ottoman Balkan territories. Among Muslims in Bulgaria and Romania, who maintained close relations with the Empire, the politicization of identities was also stimulated by resentment of mistreatment and by failure to respect rights of Muslims, but also by the ongoing process of nation building.[7]

Politically speaking, this process of nation building was initiated after the Russo-Turkish War of 1877–1878, when Bulgaria was liberated from Ottoman rule and then, in September 1908, Prince Ferdinand of Bulgaria (r. 1908–1918) finally declared their independence after the Young Turk Revolution which took place in July that year. As a result, the social, political and cultural condition of the Muslims in Bulgaria began to rapidly deteriorate until the Treaty of Istanbul was signed in 1913 by Turkey and Bulgaria. Thereafter, the Treaty of Neuilly was signed in 1919 and, as a result, the Bulgarian government made some efforts to implement policies that promoted tolerance and co-existence in the country. In response, the Bulgarian Muslims established many Turkish and Islamic schools in different parts of the country to meet their cultural and spiritual needs.[8]

It was during this period that Yusuf moved to Shumen where he became a prominent teacher, reformer, spiritual guide and one of the most influential scholars at the Madrasat al-Nuwwab (Mederesetu'n Nuvvab), which was established in August 1920, but later became known as 'the Azhar of the Balkans'. He worked closely with other scholars and intellectuals of the time (such as Hocazade Sadeddin, Huseyin Husni, Mehmed Celil, Osman Nuri and Abdullah Fehmi). In so doing, he transformed this seminary into one of the foremost centres of Islamic learning and scholarship in Europe during the first half of the twentieth century.

Indeed, referring to this renowned Islamic seminary, a Bulgarian government official stated in 1935 that, 'Madrasat al-Nuwwab is gradually becoming a religious and civilized centre for numerous Muslim inhabitants living in the Balkan Peninsula...[it] is the most vivid and brilliant monument to freedom of religion in Bulgaria.' During the next thirty years of his stay in Shumen, Yusuf not only trained up a new generation of European Muslim scholars, but he also developed an innovative approach to Islamic thought and culture in the light of his experience of living with the Bulgarian Muslims.

As it happened, soon after his arrival in Shumen, Yusuf was struck by the diversity and multicultural nature of Bulgarian society where, unlike in Cairo, Istanbul or Duzce, the Muslims were a minority in a predominantly secular Orthodox Christian country. If the challenge for the Muslims in Egypt was one of how to reconcile traditional Islam with the influx of Western culture and values, and for the Ottomans, how to respond to the socio-political transformation that was sweeping across the empire, then the situation of the Muslim minorities in an increasingly secular Bulgaria could not be more different.

At the time, the Muslims in Bulgaria consisted of Pomak, Turkish, Roma and Tatar ethnicities, with the Turks being the largest community, although the Bulgarian policy-makers did not always make a clear distinction between the different groups within the Muslim community. Once Yusuf became aware of the internal diversity of the community, along with the awareness of the minority status of Muslims within the country as a whole, he began to explore how to create a new identity for Bulgarian

Muslims that would enable them to remain faithful to Islam whilst, at the same time, become active and loyal citizens of their country. Inspired by the reformist ideas and thought of Muhammad Abduh, his erstwhile mentor and guide, coupled with his own mastery of Arabic and traditional Islamic sciences, he responded by formulating an integrated and constructive (*inshai*) approach to Islamic sources. This enabled him to reconcile the stark choice between total assimilation into secular Bulgarian culture on the one hand, and inevitable alienation from the mainstream society on the other.

The first option, he felt, would lead to the total de-Islamisation of Bulgarian Muslims through their superficial adoption of secular Western culture and values, while the latter approach would certainly contribute to their marginalisation and ghettoisation, which would be highly detrimental not only for the Muslim community, but also for the country as a whole. He therefore became an advocate of an inter-disciplinary approach to the Islamic sciences, as well as Western thought and history, which became known as *inshai* or constructive way forward. Such an approach, he argued, would lead to the harmonisation of knowledge of the sciences, cultures and societies which, in turn, would contribute to the formation of a multifaith and multicultural society.

Of course, his critics argued that he was playing with fire and his experiment would lead to a dilution, if not complete distortion of Islam, but he was convinced that a new, and equally authentic, approach to Islamic thought, Western culture, citizenship and inter-community engagement was required in an increasingly secular and multicultural Europe. His critics could not, of course, question his Islamic credentials, being a graduate of al-Azhar who initially served as an Imam of Solak Sinan Camii (mosque) in Istanbul, before preaching for no less than three decades at the Sherif Halil Pasha Mosque (also known as Tombul Mosque) in Shumen, which was Bulgaria's largest mosque.

In other words, his impeccable Islamic scholarship and high standing within the Muslim community in Bulgaria enabled him to advocate an integrated approach to learning and education in Europe for the benefit of Western Muslims, and Bulgarian Muslims in particular. In so doing, he hoped that Bulgarian Muslims would forge a new European Islamic identity for themselves. Unlike the majority of *ulama* at the time, he espoused positive views of Western culture and society, and encouraged European Muslims to benefit from their rich intellectual history and heritage, which was both Islamic and Western in its origins. In his own words,

Western people do not put the scientific books they got from the Islamic world into museums, contrary to what we do. They establish enormous libraries open to the public for their scientific and educational benefit. Beside their own scientific books, they study and examine our books as well. Recently, we have started learning many Islamic topics from European orientalists due to our ignorance of Arabic language, the main language of Islamic culture and civilization. It is widely known by learned people that many thinkers and authors who write about any branch of Islamic sciences, even Islamic history, hadith or *tafsir* quote passages from European scholars' books. They interpret and rely on their reasoning and methodology.[9]

During this period, Yusuf not only trained up hundreds of students who later became notable Muslim scholars, who of course were equally proud of their Bulgarian heritage, (including Osman Seyfullah [d. 1989] and Mehmed Fikri [d. 1941]), but he also wrote prolifically. He authored and translated more than twenty books and manuscripts, some being small and others much larger in size, on different aspects of Islam including Arabic grammar, Qur'anic studies, Prophetic traditions, Islamic history, and ethics and morality.

Some of his prominent books included *Tarih-i Islam* (2 volumes, 1932), *Telhisu'l Fusul fi Ehadisi'r Rasul* (1941), *Tabiiyyun Dava ve Gayeleri* (1923), *Vahdaniyet-i Ilahiyyenin Burhanlari* (1930), *Dini Terbiye ve Adab-i Muaseret* (1936) and *Ilm-i Ahlak* (1940).[10] He was particularly known for his expertise in *tafsir* and wrote commentaries on several chapters of the Qur'an, in addition to a manuscript on his appreciation of aspects of European thought and history. Some of these works were used as textbooks at Madrasat al-Nuwwab and were also distributed widely within the Muslim community in Bulgaria in order to promote knowledge and understanding of Islam among the masses.

After three decades of dedicated service to the Muslims of Bulgaria, in 1950, Yusuf returned to Turkey where he initially served as a Mufti (jurisconsult) in Ankara, before being promoted to the Directorate of Religious Affairs as an advisor. He delivered his last lecture at the Nasrullah Mosque in Kastamonu and died of a heart attack on his way back to Duzce. He was around 80 years of age at the time and was laid to rest in the local cemetery. Ibrahim Hatiboglu, a contemporary Turkish scholar and leading authority on the life and works of Yusuf Ziyaeddin Ezheri, paid him this fitting tribute:

> Ezheri's books offer a variety among discipline... His works on *tafsir* and hadith which brings out his academic and methodical upbringing, his philosophic works on philosophers who nurtured French revolution, his works where he aimed to discuss and criticize naturalistic tendencies of his time, his pedagogical studies which intended to provide Islamic education and training for children, his books on social ethics aiming to protect Islamic morality in society and books about Islamic history are all the reflection of his *inshai* and inter-disciplinary systematic approach...I think, the example of Ezheri model which combines all these elements can reduce conflicts in the minority-majority relations as well as among minorities, and also form a spirit of togetherness in harmony with members of other religions.[11]

1. Nathalie Clayer, 'The Muslims in Southeastern Europe: From Ottoman subjects to European citizens', *Routledge Handbook of Islam in the West*.

2. Ahmed Hasanov, 'Seyh Yusuf Ziyaeddin Ezheri'nin Hayati, Kilsiligi ve Hizmetleri', *Journal of Islamic Institute of Bulgaria* and *Yusuf Ziyaeddin Ezeri'nin Hayati, Eserli ve Tariih-i Kur'an Adli Calismasi*.

3. Ibrahim Hatiboglu, 'The Interpretation of Islamic Sciences by the Muslim Minority in Bulgaria during the First Half of the 20th Century' in *The Muslim World*, January 2008.

4. Ibrahim Hatiboglu, 'Religio-Intellectual Relations between Bulgarian and non-Bulgarian Muslims in the First Half of the 20th Century', *Journal of Islamic Studies*, Spring 2007.

5. T. Parla, *Social and Political Thought of Ziya Gokalp, 1876–1924*.

6. Ibrahim Hatiboglu, 'Inshai Interpretation of Islamic Sciences…' *Proceedings of the Second International Symposium on Islamic Civilisation in the Balkans*.

7. Nathalie Clayer, op. cit.

8. Ina Merdjanova, *Rediscovering the Umma: Muslims in the Balkans between Nationalism and Transnationalism*.

9. Quoted by Ibrahim Hatiboglu, op. cit.

10. Ibid.

11. Ibid.

# 36

# JULIUS GERMANUS

B. 1884 – D. 1979

HUNGARY

The Republic of Hungary is a small, central European country, surrounded by seven neighbours including Slovakia in the north, Romania to the east, Serbia to the south and Slovenia to the west. For a country of just under 10 million people, it has an unusually rich history and culture that can be traced back to ancient times. From the earliest Roman settlements of ninth century BC, to the establishment of the Huns Empire around 370 CE, the territory that is today known as Hungary witnessed considerable socio-political changes.

However, it was the legacy of the Eurasian nomadic Huns who hailed from Central Asia, China, the Caucasus and, of course, eastern Europe, that had the most powerful and enduring impact on the subsequent history and culture of Hungary, so much so that the name Hungary itself, is said to have originated from the word 'Hun'.

Given its ethno-historical diversity, it is not surprising that the presence of Islam in Hungary dates back to as early as the ninth and tenth centuries, as Yaqut ibn Abdullah al-Hamawi (1179–1229), a renowned medieval Muslim geographer, pointed out in his celebrated *Mu'jam al-Buldan* (Dictionary of Countries). He noted how a Hungarian Muslim youth arrived in Aleppo to study Islam, and he had mentioned that there were many well-established Muslim villages in Hungary at the time.

Then, following the expansion of Ottoman rule during the early part of the sixteenth century, Islam became more entrenched in that part of the world and many Hungarian Muslims went on to become influential figures within the Ottoman administration, including Kanijeli Siyavus Pasha (d. 1602), who not only married the daughter of Sultan Selim II, but also served as his Grand vizier. Ottoman rule of Hungary continued for more than 150 years before they were eventually forced to cede the territory to the Habsburg dynasty in 1699.

Thanks to Hungary's rich cultural history and heritage, an impressive tradition of Oriental studies emerged in the country during the nineteenth and early twentieth centuries. Unsurprisingly, Hungarian Orientalists like Arminius Vambery (1832–1913) and Ignac Goldziher (1850–1921), dominated the study of eastern history, culture and languages in Europe at the time. A renowned Turkologist and traveller, Vambery, learned more than half a dozen languages and published extensively on Oriental subjects, including a book on Islam in the nineteenth century.[1]

Likewise, Goldziher became one of the founders of modern Islamic studies in Europe along with Theodor Noldeke (1836–1930), who was a German Orientalist and author of a history of the Qur'an, and Christiaan Snouck Hurgronje (1857–1936), a renowned Dutch Orientalist, who wrote a dissertation on the festivities of Makkah and taught Arabic at the University of Leiden.[2] Needless to say, Vambery and Goldziher's contributions and legacy profoundly influenced another Hungarian Orientalist who, by all accounts, became one of the foremost scholars of Oriental languages, history and culture in Europe during the twentieth century. He was none other than Julius Germanus.

Julius Germanus, also known as Gyula Germanus or Abd al-Karim Germanus, was born in Budapest into a lower middle-class Jewish family. His father, Alexandra Germanus (b. 1852), was a shoe-maker by trade, while his mother, Rosalia Zobel (b. cir. 1858), was of German origin. Being assimilated Jews, Alexandra and Rosalia raised their children in a secular environment as religious activities did not appeal to them. Unsurprisingly, they did not provide their children with a traditional Hebrew education, which was common among European Jewry, but instead, enrolled their children in local secular schools.

Thus young Julius, like his brother, Franz Germanus, and sister, Johanna Germanus, attended State-funded primary and secondary schools where Hungarian was the medium of education, with additional focus on mathematics, science, history and geography. Since his mother spoke German at home, he grew up learning both Hungarian and German, although his academic performance at school was rather poor, especially in the technical subjects. Perhaps his love of languages, history and geography during his early years indicated that a career in Oriental studies was a real possibility for the youngster. During this period, he also studied Greek, Latin and French, enabling Julius to read history and literature extensively, in addition to learning to play the violin and the piano with considerable skill.

After successfully completing high school in 1902, Julius decided to visit Bosnia and Herzegovina during the summer vacation, having already acquired a familiarisation with Ottoman Turkish. On his arrival there, he instantly fell in love with Muslim culture. His encounter with the Bosnian Muslims inspired him to pursue a career in Oriental studies, although his parents wanted him to become an engineer. He later recalled his first experience of travelling in a Muslim country as follows:

> During a summer vacation I was lucky to travel to Bosnia, the nearest Oriental country adjacent to ours…As soon as I settled in a hotel I dashed forth to see living Muslims, whose Turkish language had only beckoned to me through its intricate Arabic script from the pages of grammar books. It was night, and in the dimly-lit streets I soon discovered a humble café in which on low straw stools a couple of Bosnians enjoyed their *kayf.* They wore traditional bulging trousers kept straight at the waist by a broad belt bristling with daggers. Their headgear and the unfamiliar costume lent them an air of truculence. It was with a throbbing heart that I entered the *kahwekhane* and timidly sat down in a distant corner. The Bosnians looked with curious eyes upon me and I suddenly remembered all the bloodcurdling stories read in fanatical books about Muslim intolerance… One of them offered me a cigarette and at its flickering light I noticed that their martial attire hid a hospitable soul. I gathered strength and addressed them in my primitive Turkish. It acted like a magic wand. Their faces lit up in friendliness akin to affection…Instead of hostility they invited me to their homes; instead of the falsely anticipated daggers they showered benevolence upon me. This was my first personal meeting with Muslims.[3]

He returned home from Bosnia with an even greater desire and passion for eastern languages, culture and history than before, much to the disappointment of his father, who wanted his son to pursue a technical or scientific subject to enable him to secure a stable, well-paid job. Instead, Julius enrolled at the local university to read Latin and history with specialisation in Ottoman history. Prominent Orientalists and linguists like Arminius Vambery, Ignac Goldziher, Ignac Kunos (1860–1945), Balint Kuzsinszky (1864–1938) and Henrik Marczali (1856–1940) taught him during this period. Four years at university provided several opportunities for foreign travel in order to learn Oriental languages and, as a result, Julius visited Turkey on more than one occasion to improve his knowledge of Turkish. This included a period studying law and Turkish at the *Dar ul-Funun* (The Academy of Arts) in Istanbul and travelling in Anatolia, which enabled him to become thoroughly familiar with Turkish language, culture and history.

In addition to this, in 1906, he travelled to Austria and joined the University of Vienna where he pursued Arabic, history and literature for a period, before returning to Budapest to receive his doctorate with *summa cum laude* in Turkish, Arabic and ancient history at the age of 23.[4] This was, by all accounts, a remarkable achievement considering that he became proficient in no less than half a dozen languages at the time.

Although Julius studied under the supervision of both Goldziher and Vambery, he was very fond of the latter who considered him to be a promising young scholar. He was more close to Vambery than Goldziher due to the fact that the former was one of the leading European scholars of eastern languages and culture, unlike Goldziher, who was more interested in Arabic language, Islamic thought and sciences, which were of less interest to Julius at the time. During this period, he authored several publications including *Evliya Celebi on 17th-Century Turkish Guilds* (1907), and an essay in German titled *Geschichte der Osmanischen Dichthunst* (History of Ottoman Poetry), in addition to a detailed review of Elias J. W. Gibb's *A History of Ottoman Poetry* (1901).

Indeed, his scholarly demeanour and commitment to his tasks impressed Vambery, so much so that the latter secured sufficient funding to enable Julius to travel to London in 1908 with the intention of undertaking a detailed study of Oriental books and manuscripts at the British Museum and other institutions. This clearly enriched Julius's knowledge and understanding of Turkish, Arabic and Persian, as well as historical sources related to Islamic history and culture.

On his return to Budapest, Julius converted to Calvinism, which was a branch of Protestantism that was founded by John Calvin (1509–1564), a reformist theologian who lived during the Reformation. His motivation for conversion was not clear as he did not become an active member of the Hungarian Reformed Church and, instead, began to teach Ottoman Turkish and Arabic at the Oriental Academy and the Theological Academy of the Reformed Church in 1909 and 1910, respectively. He continued to teach at the Oriental Academy until in 1915, he proposed the establishment of a Department of Islamic Studies to teach the history of Islam, and Muslim law and culture, which he felt was the most appropriate step to take for the students after learning Turkish and Arabic languages. Although the Academy did not implement his proposal, the need to directly engage with Islam as a religion and way of life now attracted his attention. A year later, he delivered a lecture on Islam, a topic which he also taught during the following academic year.

Then, in 1918, he met and married Rozsa G. Hajnoczy (1892–1944), who hailed from a Hungarian Christian family. Both husband and wife lived in their flat in Budapest, until Julius was promoted to the post of ordinary professor at the Royal Pazmany Peter University at the age of 38.[5] Subsequently, he published his *Turkish Grammar* in 1925 and worked as a translator at the Justice Court of Budapest. In due course, he met Rabindranath Tagore (1861–1941), an acclaimed Bengali poet and Nobel laureate, who was visiting Budapest during his European tour, and the latter invited him to Santiniketan (in the present-day Indian State of West Bengal) to help establish a Department of Islamic Studies at Visva-Bharati University that Tagore had founded in December 1921. Accordingly, he applied for the post of Chair of Islamic Studies, which was funded by the Nizam of Hyderabad, on a monthly salary of 400 rupees. Once his application for a three-year paid sabbatical leave was granted, he moved to West Bengal with his wife in 1929.[6]

Upon his arrival in India, Julius settled into his new teaching role at Visva-Bharati and freely mingled with local Muslims. At the time, he was going through a period of intellectual and spiritual turmoil as Christianity did not satisfy his personal quest for meaning and purpose in the modern world. By contrast, the Islamic concept of Divine Oneness, coupled with his interaction with Indian Muslims, prompted him to become a Muslim. Another explanation he provided for his conversion to Islam was his encounter with the Prophet Muhammad (peace be on him) in the form of a dream. In his own words,

> My brain was satiated but my soul remained thirsty. I had to divert myself of much of that learning I had gathered, in order to regain it through an inner experience ennobled in the fire of suffering, as the crude iron which the pain of sudden cold tempers into elastic steel. One night the Prophet Muhammad appeared before me. His long beard was reddened with *henna*, his robes were simple but very exquisite, and an agreeable scent emanated from them. His eyes glittered with a noble fire and he addressed me with a manly voice, 'Why do you worry? The straight path is before you, safely spread out like the face of the earth; walk on it with trusty treads, with the strength of Faith'... 'I cannot sleep,' I groaned with pain. 'I cannot solve the mysteries which are covered by impenetrable veils. Help me, Muhammad, O Prophet of God! Help me!' A fierce, interrupted cry broke forth from my throat. I tossed chokingly under the burden of a nightmare – I feared the wrath of the Prophet. Then I felt as if I had dropped into the deep – and suddenly I awoke. The blood knocked in my temples, my body was bathed in sweat; my every limb ached. A deadly silence enveloped me, and I felt very sad and lonely.[7]

Rozsa was aware of her husband's intellectual and spiritual crises which she recorded in her personal diary during their three-year stay in India, later published in Hungarian as *Bengali Tuz: Harom ev Tortenete* (Fire of Bengal: The Story of Three Years, first published in 1943). She wrote, 'My husband's spiritual turmoil is of an intellectual nature. He longs to know Islam as a Muslim understands it. He knows every sentence of the Koran, and can break down each word to its constituents; but the word and the sentence do not constitute the whole. If I set out to analyse a temple, I shall end up with a great pile of stones: but the stones are not the temple...Sooner or later, his sincere approach and hard work are bound to bring success. I tried to calm his inner conflict'.[8]

His encounter with the Prophet of Islam, coupled with much-needed reassurance and support from his wife, eventually convinced Julius of the authenticity of Islam and, on the following Friday (19 December 1930), at the age of 46, he publicly announced his conversion to Islam at the *Jami Masjid* (Central Mosque) in Delhi after *Salat al-Jumu'ah* (Friday Congregational Prayer) in-front of around 5000 people. He did not lead the prayers, unlike what Imre Bangha has suggested, but was only requested by his hosts to address the congregation.[9] He did so in an inspirational and eloquent way, as he later recalled:

> '*Ayyuh al-Saadaat al-Kiram*,' I started in Arabic – 'I came from a distant land to acquire knowledge which I could not gain at home. I came to you for inspiration and you responded to the call.' I then proceeded and spoke of the task Islam has played in the world's history, of the miracle God has wrought with His Prophet. I expatiated on the decline of present-day Muslims and of the means whereby they could gain ascendancy anew. It is a Muslim saying that all depends on God's will, but the Holy Qur'an says that, 'God betters not the condition of a people unless they improve themselves'. I built my speech on this Qur'anic sentence and wound up with the praise of pious life, and the fight against wickedness... Men stood before me and embraced me. Many a poor suffering fellow looked with imploring eyes on me. They asked for my blessing and wanted to kiss my hand. 'O God!'I exclaimed, 'don't allow innocent souls to lift me above them! I am a worm from among the worms of the earth, a wanderer towards Light, just as powerless as the other miserable creatures.'[10]

After his conversion, Julius became known as Abd al-Karim Germanus and always introduced himself using his new name when meeting other Muslims, both at home and abroad. Although some of his non-Muslim biographers have questioned his motivation for conversion, if Rozsa Hajnoczy, his wife, is to be believed, then his conversion to Islam was nothing other than a natural progression of his spiritual growth and development, a perfect solution for his 'spiritual turmoil'.[11]

After his three-year contract with Visva-Bharati came to an end, he decided to return to Budapest in March 1931, turning down an offer of professorship at Calcutta with a handsome salary of 1800 rupees a month from none other than Sir Hasan Suhrawardy (1884–1946) himself, who was the Rector of the University of Calcutta at the time. It is worth pointing out here that during his time in India, Julius had met and befriended many prominent Muslim scholars and intellectuals like Sir Muhammad Iqbal, Sir Abd al-Karim Ghaznavi, Dr Zakir Husayn and Marmaduke Pickthall. He was also invited to deliver lectures at the universities of Delhi, Dhaka, Aligarh, Lucknow, Agra, Calcutta, Hyderabad and Punjab.

However, upon his return home, he became a curator of the Library of the Oriental Institute and started work on a Hungarian translation of the Qur'an, which unfortunately he never completed. He also became active in the Muslim community in Hungary, before applying for a government scholarship to pursue research in Egypt. As soon as the grant was approved, he set off in the direction of Egypt in 1934. On his arrival in Cairo, he studied at al-Azhar University for a short period and met prominent Egyptian scholars and writers, including Muhammad al-Zawahiri (the Grand Shaykh of al-Azhar), Muhammad Abdullah Inan, Mahmud Abbas al-Aqqad, Mahmud Taimur and Muhammad Husayn Haykal, among others.

From Cairo, he went to Jeddah, before being allowed to proceed to Makkah for the annual pilgrimage, thanks to the timely intervention of Harry St John Philby, better known as Abdullah Philby (see next chapter), who was a close friend and advisor to King Abd al-Aziz ibn Saud (1875–1953) at the time.

A year later, he published his account of his pilgrimage and travels in the Middle East under the title of *Allah Akbar!* This book instantly became a hit and established his reputation as one of Hungary's foremost orientalists, and certainly the first Hungarian to perform the hajj. It was subsequently translated into German and Italian. During this period, he also became a familiar voice on radio, delivering regular lectures in both Hungarian and English, attracting listeners from as far as Cairo.[12]

Then, in 1939, he set off again for Egypt before completing his second pilgrimage. Two years later, he became the Director of the Eastern Institute in Budapest, but the Second World War soon broke out which forced him to help the poor, injured and the displaced. His beloved wife, Rozsa, also committed suicide during this period. To make matters worse, the Eastern Institute soon closed down, forcing Julius to resume teaching Turkish philology at the Pazmany Peter University where, in due course, he produced a book on Arabic poetry which was subsequently published under the title of *Ibn al-Rumi's Dichtkunst* (1956). This book confirmed his credentials as an outstanding scholar of Arabic language and literature. In the meantime, he married for the second time and his wife, Kajari Kato (Aishah), also converted to Islam.

He devoted the rest of his academic career to teaching Arabic, Turkish and aspects of Islamic thought and history, until finally retiring in 1964, at the age of 80. As expected, he combined teaching with research and writing, and authored more than twenty books and manuscripts in several languages, including Hungarian, Turkish, Arabic and English. Likewise, he wrote on a wide range of subjects such as Ottoman history, Arabic poetry, Turkish literature, and Islamic thought, history and culture. Some of his noteworthy books and essays include *Modern Movements in Islam* (1932), *The Role of Turks in Islam* (1934), *Allah Akbar!* (1936), *The History of Arabic Literature* (1962), *The Lights of the East* (1966), *Ibn Khaldun, the Philosopher* (1967) and *The Mystical East* (1975).

In addition to being a devout Muslim, Julius was a Pan-Islamist in his thinking and scholarship. For example, he was of the opinion that it was not the Turks who had made Islam great but, on the contrary, it was Islam that unified and transformed the Turks into a powerful force for good, thanks to its uncompromising message of Divine Unity, socio-political solidarity and brotherhood of humanity.

In other words, the message of Islam, he argued, unequivocally repudiated all forms of racial discrimination, cultural segregation, tribal affiliation and nationalistic jingoism which, in turn, enabled the Turks to establish an empire that expanded into three continents and become one of the most powerful in modern history. In his own words, 'Islam and its martial spirit was one of the greatest motives in the uninterrupted success of the Turks. They had fought, as idolaters before, for the sake of rapine and glory, but the propagation of the faith gave a moral aim to their valor and enhanced their fighting quality.'[13]

Likewise, despite his reverence and regard for prominent European Orientalists (such as Josef Horovitz, Ignac Goldziher and Arminius Vambery), in the end, he felt they failed to project Islam as a Divinely-inspired religion and way of life and, at times, even misrepresented Muslim contributions to world civilization. Accordingly, he was critical of some Orientalists for being far too political – as supporters of colonialism and subjugation – rather than being true seekers of knowledge and wisdom for the benefit of humanity.

After dedicating more than fifty years of his life to research and writing on Arabic, Turkish and Persian literature, as well as Islamic thought and history, in 1965, Julius was invited to Saudi Arabia by King Faisal ibn Abd al-Aziz (1906–1975) to participate in the meeting of the Organisation of Islamic Conference (OIC), and it was on this occasion that he performed his third pilgrimage; he was accompanied by his wife. Thanks to his impeccable scholarship in Arabic, he was appointed a Correspondent Member of the Academy of the Arabic Language in Cairo; the Academy of Baghdad; the Academy of Damascus; and, he was also offered an honorary membership of the Arab Writers' Association in Cairo. Al-Hajj Julius Abd al-Karim Germanus had no children of his own and died at the age of 95. He was laid to rest in the Farkasreti Cemetery, one of Budapest's well-known cemeteries, with the following Qur'anic verses inscribed on his tombstone:

> O (you) the one in (complete) rest and satisfaction!
> Come back to your Lord,
> Well-pleased (yourself) and well-pleasing unto Him![14]

The renowned Egyptian writer and scholar, Mahmud Taimur (1894–1973), paid Julius Germanus the following tribute:

> During his long journeys Professor Germanus has penetrated deeper into Islamic culture than any of his predecessors. Besides his thorough scientific background he never lost sight of the practical requirements of life...We, the Arabic speaking peoples can return with respect, admiration, and affection – only to some extent – all the great services he has done for our culture and nation...Every Arabic reader, writer, and scholar greets and congratulates the scholar and the true man in him.[15]

1. Arminius Vambery, *Arminius Vambery, His Life and Adventures*; Gy. Kaldy-Nagy (ed.), *The Muslim East: Studies in Honour of Julius Germanus*.

2. Robert Irwin, *For Lust of Knowing: The Orientalists and Their Enemies*.

3. *The Islamic Review*, June 1950.

4. Adam Mestyan, 'Materials for a History of Hungarian Academic Orientalism' in *Die Welt Des Islams*, 2014.

5. Ismail Durmus, 'Julius Germanus' in *Diyanet Islam Ansiklopedisi*.

6. Imre Bangha, *The Hungry Tiger*.

7. *The Islamic Review*, June 1950.

8. Rozsa Hajnoczy, *Fire of Bengal* (translated by Eva Wimmer and David Grant).

9. Imre Bangha, op. cit.

10. *The Islamic Review*, June 1950.

11. Rozsa Hajnoczy, *Fire of Bengal* (translated by Eva Wimmer and David Grant).

12. Adam Mestyan, op. cit.

13. Julius Germanus, *The Role of the Turks in Islam*.

14. Surah (chapter) al-Fajr (The Dawn), verses 27–28.

15. Quoted in Gy. Kaldy-Nagy, op. cit.

37

# HARRY ST JOHN PHILBY

B. 1885 – D. 1960

UNITED KINGDOM

During the nineteenth and twentieth centuries, many British individuals went to Arabia to explore its history, geography, demography and climate, and, in the process, they became some of modern history's most renowned explorers and adventurers. Sir Richard Francis Burton (1821–1890) was born in Torquay, Devonshire and became a pioneering explorer who travelled extensively across Africa, Asia and the Middle East during the mid-nineteenth century. He earned his fame as one of the first Westerners to be able to enter the sacred city of Makkah, disguised as a Pathan (Pashtun) pilgrim, Hajji Abdullah, and observed the annual pilgrimage (hajj) in 1854, in addition to exploring Midian (now north-west Saudi Arabia) in search of gold and silver. He left behind a detailed account of his observation of the hajj, entitled *Personal Narractive of a Pilgrimage to Al Madinah and Meccah* (1855).

Charles Montagu Doughty (1843–1926), born in Saxmundham, Suffolk, was another important British writer, poet and explorer of the time. He travelled through Arabia and lived with the Bedouins from 1876 to 1878. He then recorded his experiences of life in the deserts of Arabia in a two-volume book titled *Travels in Arabia Deserta* (1888). Born in Bombay but educated in Portsmouth and the Isle of Man, William Henry Shakespeare (1878–1915) also became a linguist and explorer of considerable distinction, having led no less than seven expeditions to Arabia and, in the process, becoming the first European to map the Nafud desert. He was shot dead during the Battle of Jarrab at the age of 36.

Gertrude Bell (1868–1926) was another trail-blazer. Born in Durham and educated at Queen's College, London and Lady Margaret Hall, Oxford, she became a distinguished political operator, linguist, archaeologist and explorer, having travelled across Arabia no less than six times over a period of twelve years, and being only the second foreign woman to visit the Arabian oasis of Ha'il in 1913. Considered to be one of the greatest female British mountaineers, she has been hailed as the 'Queen of the Desert'.

Likewise, Bertram Sidney Thomas (1892–1950) was a notable Arabist. Born in Bristol and educated at Trinity College, Cambridge, he became famous as the first Westerner to cross the Rub al-Khali (The Empty Quarter) in the Arabian Peninsula from 1930 to 1931, covering around 250,000 square miles, a significant part of southern Arabia, including present-day Saudi Arabia, Oman, the United Arab Emirates and Yemen.[1] He recounted his journey in minute detail in a book titled *Arabia Felix* (1932). However, according to others, the greatest British Arabist, traveller and explorer of all time was none other than Harry St John Philby.

Harry Saint John Bridger Philby, better known as Jack Philby or Shaykh Abdullah Philby, was born into a respectable Christian family of traders at Badulla in British Ceylon (today known as Badula, the capital city of Uva Province in Sri Lanka). His father, Harry Montagu Philby (also known as Montie, d. 1913), moved to Ceylon in the 1870s, seeking his fortune in coffee trade, where he met and married Queenie (otherwise known as May) in 1884, who was the eldest daughter of Colonel John Duncan, a senior British army officer.

She bore Montie Philby four sons, of whom Harry was the second, although her husband's erratic behaviour and lack of success in trade eventually forced Queenie to return to England and settle in Queen's Gate, London with her sons. Harry and his brothers attended a local preparatory school, paid for by their maternal grandfather. Thus, they received a thorough grounding in English, grammar and arithmetic. By all accounts, he was a bright and hard-working student who soon outshone his brothers by winning a coveted scholarship to Westminster College when he was only 13. According to Elizabeth Monroe (1905–1986), Harry's earliest and most notable biographer:

> Westminster, more than any other English public school, is woven into the national fabric of Church and State. It has existed since its foundation in the shadow of Westminster Abbey, where its school prayers are said daily; it commemorates its foundress, Queen Elizabeth I, by singing a Latin service in the light of candles, round her tomb. Its pupils participate in national and royal ceremonies that include the Coronation. Across the road lies Parliament; of its ceremonial opening they have a privileged view from the green opposite, and

they have a right to attend its debates. Big Ben is comfortably within earshot. Little Dean's Yard, where most of the school's buildings are, has something of air of a college quadrangle with its alternating quiet and bustle. Its boys are free to roam the Abbey and its precincts, and, if they like, to imbibe tradition and history in that way.[2]

At Westminster, Harry studied under the tutelage of several scholars (such as W. G. Rutherford and James Gow) who admired his academic and sporting abilities. So much so, that he was appointed captain of the school and was a prominent member of its cricket team. In March 1904, he secured a place at Trinity College, Cambridge to read Classics. Unlike urban and loud Westminster, rural and leafy Cambridge was more appealing to him. There, some of his contemporaries included Donald Robertson (later Regius Professor of Greek at Cambridge), J. R. M. Butler (who later became a prominent historian and fellow of Trinity), Jawaharlal Nehru (who became the first prime minister of independent India) and Muhammad Iqbal (later Allama Iqbal and knighted for his literary output). After initially studying classics, he switched over to modern languages, a subject in which he thrived under the guidance of Edward Granville Browne (1862–1926), who was a renowned Orientalist and scholar of Persian, acquiring proficiency in Persian and Urdu (Hindustani), in addition to French and German, which he knew very well.

His time at Cambridge also had a profound impact on his faith and beliefs. That, of course, was expected as Trinity became the centre of theoretical and philosophical sciences at Cambridge under J. M. E. McTaggart (1866–1925), Alfred N. Whitehead (1861–1947), Bertrand Russell (1872–1970) and George E. Moore (1873–1958). These philosophers subjected religion, Christianity in particular, to critical scrutiny and that, in turn, led to considerable philosophical and religious scepticism which had a profound impact on students' religious beliefs and convictions. Harry's Christian faith was seriously tested and undermined at the time, although he did not completely abandon it.

Academically, however, he thrived at Trinity. In 1907, when he was 22, he obtained a First in modern languages and that, in turn, enabled him to secure a posting in the Indian Civil Service.[3] Upon his arrival in Bombay in December 1908, he was instructed to proceed to Lahore. He worked in Jhelum district as a judicial officer and it was during this period that he improved his knowledge of Urdu, in addition to learning about the Muslim faith and culture under the guidance of a local *Maulvi* (religious instructor). Being a junior officer, his salary was barely 400 rupees a month. However, the cost of living was low which enabled him to save money to help his mother make ends meet in London. After passing an examination in Urdu, Harry was promoted to sub-district officer, and it was during this period that he met and married Dora Johnston, who was the daughter of Adrian Hope Johnston, a senior railway engineer, at the age of 25. His son Harold 'Kim' Philby (d. 1988) – the notorious British spy who defected to the Soviet Union, and was part of the 'Cambridge spy ring' – was born a year later.

During the following years, Harry became proficient in several other languages and dialects including Arabic and Baluch, which not only earned him 10,000 rupees in prize money, but also made his entry into the prestigious Political Department easier. In the meantime, thanks to his remarkable linguistic abilities, Harry was promoted to the post of head of the language board in Calcutta, having already served as a District Commissioner. He worked in this capacity at a time when the Great War (also known as the First World War) was raging in Europe. His brothers were already actively involved in the war efforts and he was itching to do the same, but he preferred to serve in the Middle East. This opportunity finally came in 1915 when Sir Percy Cox (1864–1937), then, a British Political Resident in the Persian Gulf (1904–1919), needed more Arabic linguists in Mesopotamia (present-day Iraq), thus Harry was selected for service. Accordingly, he moved to Basra in November that year.

Needless to say, Cox was a shrewd and experienced political operator who was intimately familiar with Arab politics and personalities whilst, at the same time, keeping a close eye on the Turks. In addition to protecting the oilfields, he encouraged Abd al-Aziz ibn Saud (1875–1953), the Amir of Najd, to attack Ibn Rashid of Ha'il, located in central Arabia. He did not trust Sayyid Talib ibn al-Naqib of Basra (1862–1929), but co-operated with Shaykh Mubarak ibn Sabah of Kuwait (1837–1915); Khaz'al ibn Jabir al-Ka'bi (1863–1936); the Shaykh of Muhammara (in present-day Khuzistan province, Iran); and, Husayn ibn Ali (1854–1931), the Sharif of Makkah, who had of course allied himself with the British.

This was the political context in which Harry arrived in Basra, where Cox had assigned him the task of establishing a viable system of financial record-keeping, which he accomplished to Cox's satisfaction and was subsequently promoted to the post of Revenue Commissioner. Harry was also made a Commander of the Indian Empire (CIE), being one of the youngest to have received the honour at the age of 31. During this period, Harry travelled extensively across Iraq (Arabic name for Mesopotamia) and became familiar with the language, culture and customs of the local tribes, in addition to serving Cox as his personal assistant in Baghdad. Handling Cox's papers enabled Harry to acquire first-hand knowledge of British policy and politics in the Middle East, Turkey and India.

In other words, Harry soon became aware of the complexity of local and regional politics; for the British and the Turks were bitter foes, whilst Ibn Saud regarded the Sharif of Makkah as a sell-out and Ibn Rashid of Ha'il as his enemy, and, needless to say, Baghdad was firmly under British occupation at the time. It was under a tense and complex political time that

Harry was assigned a task that became the most defining moment of his life, namely to undertake a mission to Ibn Saud on behalf of Sir Percy Cox. He set out in November

1917, accompanied by two companions, and travelled by caravan through the harsh and burning sand of the desert from al-Uqayr to Jeddah, destined for Riyadh. They stopped at al-Hasa to recuperate, before continuing their journey to the headquarters of the future king of Saudi Arabia. He took meticulous notes of people he met, places he visited and challenges he faced during his sojourn, in addition to photographs of important sites. This was later recorded in the form of an extensive travelogue, entitled *The Heart of Arabia* (2 volumes), and was published by Constable of London in 1922.

Upon his arrival in Riyadh, he met Ibn Saud and his ailing father, Abd al-Rahman ibn al-Faisal al-Saud, and discussed ways to strengthen relations between the British and the House of Saud. During his 10-day stay in Riyadh, Harry was granted a private audience with Ibn Saud which enabled him to discuss a wide range of political, cultural and religious issues with the latter. He found him sharp and accommodating, but also very determined to achieve his political and religious objectives, namely the ousting of the Sharif of Makkah and the dissemination of a pure and unadulterated interpretation of Islam as championed by Muhammad ibn Abd al-Wahhab (1703–1792), the spiritual founder of the modern Kingdom of Saudi Arabia.[4]

From Riyadh, Harry moved to Jeddah for a meeting with the Sharif of Makkah, whilst political manoeuvring in London and Washington was happening at pace. The Balfour Declaration, made public in London in 1917, promised a national homeland for the Jewish people in Palestine at a time when Lloyd George promised self-determination to Arabia, Palestine, Syria and Mesopotamia, among others. By contrast, in Washington, President Woodrow Wilson advocated the autonomy of different nationalities that lived under Turkish rule. Being unaware of radical policy shifts in London and Washington, Harry returned to Cairo in January 1918, only to be sent back to Ibn Saud to encourage the latter to attack Ha'il. Whilst the former prepared to launch an expedition, Harry went to Riyadh with the intention of travelling and surveying other parts of Arabia.

Indeed, he spent most of 1918 in Arabia working with Ibn Saud to oust the Rashidis from Ha'il, when, suddenly, he received an order from Baghdad to end his mission in Arabia which, of course, baffled him, being completely unaware of the political changes that had taken place elsewhere in the Middle East. General Allenby had captured Palestine, Faisal I ibn Husayn (1885–1933) had taken Damascus and the Turks were in full retreat in northern Iraq. However, Harry's long stay with Ibn Saud enabled him to observe him, his character and personality more closely than any other Westerner, and, of course, he was profoundly impressed by what he saw: a friend who was 'beyond all price'.[5]

After a whole year away from his family, Harry was granted an extended leave, thus he returned to England. But in October 1919, he was requested by the Government to entertain the royal family led by Amir al-Faisal, the 14 year-old son of Ibn Saud. As he toured the country with the young Amir, his longing for the wild and emptiness of the desert grew. He wanted to explore other parts of Arabia but he could not pay for such an adventure himself. He soon needed to secure a job as his paid leave was fast coming to an end. As luck would have it, Sir Percy Cox, who rated Philby highly for his intelligence, linguistic abilities and industry, included him on a list of people he wanted to take with him to Iraq. Harry thus decided to move to Baghdad with his family in 1920 and, thanks to his handsome annual salary of £2,500, he lived comfortably.

Nonetheless, this comfort did not last long as Cox opted to install Faisal I as king of Iraq, rather than offering a democratic choice to the Iraqi people; this inevitably infuriated Harry because that, in his opinion, amounted to betrayal. As an advocate of Arab independence, he could not accept the status quo and, accordingly, found himself at odds with Sir Percy Cox. The latter, in turn, was fully aware of Harry's dissent and displeasure, and recommended him for a post in the Middle East Department of the Colonial Office in Transjordan in 1921. He was vetted for the position of Chief British Representative by many senior officials including T. E Lawrence (1888–1935), better known as Lawrence of Arabia, Sir Herbert L. Samuel (1870–1963), a notable Zionist Jew and British Commissioner in Palestine, and, of course, Winston Churchill (1874–1965). He passed his vetting and went to Amman to take up the new post.

However, he was not impressed by British policy vis-à-vis the Arabs in general and the Palestinians in particular. He expressed his views clearly during a visit to London in 1922, when he stated that Arabs should be granted genuine independence as stipulated in the Anglo-French Declaration of November, 1918, rather than a truncated version of the agreement. Furthermore, Samuel's meddling and intervention in the discharge of his duties in Transjordan, coupled with his growing resentment and disapproval of the British betrayal of the Arabs, prompted Harry to eventually hand-in his resignation and return home in 1924.

Thereafter, he wrote and published numerous articles on Middle Eastern policy and politics in leading British newspapers and journals, in addition to delivering rousing speeches at meetings held in prominent venues across London, much to the annoyance and irritation of the government. To earn a living during this period, Harry became a partner in a trading company based in Jeddah and authored two books titled *Arabia of the Wahhabis* (1928) and *Arabia* (1930), both published by Constable which, of course, established his reputation as a writer, traveller and explorer. He was elected member of the Royal Geographical Society in 1925 and awarded Sir Richard Burton Memorial Medal in the same year for his travels and expertise in Arabian culture and geography.

In May 1930, Ibn Saud visited Jeddah where Harry was resident at the time, and it was on this occasion that he became the King's chief advisor on foreign affairs. Previously he had informed Dora, his wife, of his desire to embrace Islam, but his personal circumstances prevented him from taking the step. Now was the time, he felt, to enter the fold of a religion and way of life that he admired so much. Although he was not an Islamic scholar, unlike Marmaduke Pickthall and Abdullah Quilliam, he was a distinguished Arabist whose conversion was based on a sound knowledge and understanding of Islam. Elizabeth Monroe has hinted that his conversion may have been politically motivated, which, of course, reflects her own prejudice rather than Harry's lack of sincerity and commitment to his new faith.

Indeed, his view of Islam was clear, well-informed and positive. In his own words, 'Islam at any rate uncompromisingly demands adherence to its moral code in spite of any inconvenience it may entail. At the same time its code is based on recognition of the frailty of human nature and none of its demands are excessive. That is probably due to the fact that, although divinely inspired, the Prophet Muhammad himself never claimed to be anything but a human being like the rest of mankind. "Ana bashrun mithlukum" he declared. "I am a human being like yourselves".'[6] On another occasion, he stated,

> The word [Islam] is generally understood as signifying 'peace' or 'resignation to the will of God'. In my opinion, however, if I may venture to express it in the presence of many better qualified to express an opinion than I am, those meanings are secondary or derivative meanings of the word. After all the word is, as you all know, an Arabic word derived from the root SLM, the basic idea of which seems to me to be safety or salvation…in the strictest ecclesiastical sense salvation from hell-fire but in general salvation from danger or misfortune. And you must remember that in the strictest Muslim sense such salvation depends entirely on the will of God.[7]

Elsewhere, he wrote:

> The logic of Islam is unassailable, and it is the only way of life yet propounded which has attempted – with no mean measure of success – to apply the basic principles of democracy to human society. Islam has largely succeeded where Britain, America and France have failed, despite all their great charters of liberty, equality and fraternity. Let us beware of all efforts to extinguish the shining light of its independence or cover it with the bushel of a mechanised civilisation.[8]

After his conversion at the age of 45, Harry took the name of Abdullah, and 'for the first time [in] many years I [Harry] felt strangely at peace with the world', he later wrote in his book titled *Arabian Days*. However, back home in London, he was severely criticised for 'going native', but his wife robustly defended her husband's decision to convert to Islam, referring to herself as 'Mrs Abdullah'. Thereafter, Ibn Saud offered him a house in Makkah where he settled and began to advise the king on foreign affairs, particularly in his negotiations with the British, American and other Western powers.

During the following two decades, he not only became the king's trusted advisor, but also pursued personal business interests and, in his spare time, he travelled extensively across Arabia. He made contacts with, and negotiated, oil exploration contracts with several Western companies on behalf of Ibn Saud, including a 60-year agreement with Standard Oil of California (Socal) which, in 1936, joined forces with Texaco and formed the Arabian-American Oil Company (ARAMCO) in 1944, thus becoming one of the richest companies in the world. Needless to say, the discovery of oil beneath the barren deserts of Arabia during 1930s and 1940s was destined to transform the poor kingdom into one of the richest countries in the world. Harry played an active part in this transformation by faithfully and ably representing Saudi interests which, of course, impressed Ibn Saud, his friend and benefactor.[9]

Politically speaking, however, he was aware that the implementation of the Balfour Declaration would lead to the establishment of a Jewish State in historic Palestine, and this would inevitably lead to considerable political tension and upheaval in the Arab world. As a political realist, he knew that the Arabs were too disorganised to resist such an imposition whilst, at the same time, he felt that the indigenous population of Palestine had to be protected from being completely overwhelmed by the Zionists. Although his proposal came to nothing, he continued to champion the Arab cause and never failed to remind the British of their betrayal and treachery against the Arabs in general, and the Palestinians in particular. This irritated and annoyed the British, so much so that he was detained in Karachi in August 1940. He was forced to return to London while the Second World War was raging across Europe and beyond. He eventually returned to Arabia in 1945 and continued to serve Ibn Saud, pursue business as a director of Mitchell Cotts (Sharqieh) Ltd, and explore the country in his spare time.

In the meantime, a number of his books were published in London, including *The Empty Quarter* (1933), *Harun al Rashid* (1934) and *Sheba's Daughters* (1939). The *Empty Quarter* was an account of his remarkable journey across Rub al-Khali, one of the largest deserts in the world, which he undertook in 1932, while *Harun al Rashid* was a short biography of the famous Abbasid Caliph who reigned from 786 to 809. By contrast, *Sheba's Daughters* covered his journeys to Shabwa and the Aden Protectorates in 1936. As a prolific writer, over the next fifteen years or so, he authored the following books: *A Pilgrim in Arabia* (1943), which provides an account of his pilgrimage, while the *Arabian Days* (1948) is essentially autobiographical, covering his life up to his fiftieth birthday.

However, in *The Background of Islam* (1947), he provides an overview of the pre-Islamic history of Arabia, which he in fact self-published. The *Arabian Highlands* (1952) is another travelogue, covering his journey to Asir on the Saudi-Yemeni borders. And despite its title, the *Arabian Jubilee* (1952) is a biography of Ibn Saud, while *Saudi Arabia* (1955) is an updated version of his earlier work titled *Arabia* (1930). Like the *Arabian Highlands*, *The Land of Midian* (1957) is a travelogue covering his first journey to Midian from Madinah to Tabuk. His *Forty Years in the Wilderness* (1957) consists of eleven essays on his life and career, while the *Arabian Oil Ventures* was posthumously published in 1964.

As a writer, Harry was more descriptive and vivid than analytical or evaluative; his prose was fluent and readable, but equally dry and unexciting. However, as an individual, he was a proud Muslim and equally passionate libertarian. He was a man of principles and integrity, but equally down-to-earth and pragmatic. His life, career, politics and writings provide an extraordinarily complex picture of an Arabist who explored Arabia more extensively than any other Westerner before him. He summed up his ideas and thought in the following words, 'My ideals have been all-embracing, excluding no people and no part of the earth from its birth right of freedom. But my individual effort has inevitably been limited by circumstances, and I shall be content indeed if the light of freedom, real freedom, dawns upon India and these countries of the Arab world before I pass on from the scene of my endeavours to serve the cause of humanity.'[10]

Harry continued to live in Saudi Arabia and made sure he never missed an opportunity to perform the annual pilgrimage during this period. After the death of Ibn Saud in 1953, however, he fell out with King Saud (1902–1969), his son and successor, which forced him to move to Beirut where he eventually died at the age of 75, three years after the death of his beloved wife. He was laid to rest in a Muslim cemetery in Basta, one of the oldest districts in Beirut, following a simple funeral prayer.

Needless to say, Harry was a remarkable explorer and one of the foremost British Arabists of his generation. He was also a man of principles and never allowed his personal interests to cloud his judgement on the political, economic and cultural issues of his time. F. A. Davis, a former Chairman of the Board of Directors of the Arabian-American Oil Company, paid Harry (Abdullah) St John Philby this glowing tribute:

> I first had the pleasure of meeting Philby in 1937 on his home grounds in Jidda. He was a raconteur of great wit and charm, but it was for more substantive reasons that I came away from our first meeting, and our many subsequent ones, with a greater respect for the man and his accomplishments. His integrity and wholehearted devotion to the purposes he had set himself in life made a deep impression. Saudi Arabia is better for his having been a part of it.[11]

(N)

1. See Eid al-Yahya, *Travellers in Arabia: British Explorers in Saudi Arabia*.

2. Elizabeth Monroe, *Philby of Arabia*.

3. Umar bin Salih al-Umuri, 'Abdullah Philby: Hayatuhu wa Asaruhu' in *Addarah*, No. 3, 1999.

4. Michael Crawford, *Ibn 'Abd al-Wahhab* (Makers of the Muslim World).

5. Quoted by Monroe, op. cit.

6. Quoted by M. A. Sherif, *Brave Hearts: Pickthall and Philby*.

7. Ibid.

8. Harry St John Philby, *The Evening Standard*, October 1, 1943.

9. Harry St John Philby, *Arabian Oil Ventures*.

10. Harry St John Philby, *Forty Years in the Wilderness*.

11. Quoted in Harry St John Philby, *Arabian Oil Ventures*.

# 38

# RENE GUENON

B. 1886 – D. 1951

FRANCE

In 1784, the famous German philosopher, Immanuel Kant (1724–1804), wrote an essay entitled *Beantwortung der Frage: Was ist Aufklarung?* (Answering the Question: What is Enlightenment?). As one of the most influential thinkers and philosophers of modern Europe, he argued in his essay that Enlightenment represented nothing short of man's release from his self-imposed ignorance, error and superstition. For Kant, the Enlightenment period (also known as the 'Age of Reason') was the beginning of humanity's emergence from the darkness of the past to the brightness of a future that was to be designed and determined solely by human reason and rationality. And that, he felt, could only be achieved by overcoming the intellectual incoherence and mental immaturity of our closed and captivated minds.[1]

However, in his *Candide*, a philosophical novel, the French thinker Francois-Marie Arouet (1694–1778), better known as Voltaire, clearly demonstrated how reason divorced from experience and sensitivity can lead to error and absurdity. Indeed, other exponents of Enlightenment went even further and argued that feeling, faith, intuition and authority were equally essential for understanding human nature and analysing our existential condition if we were to create a better world for everyone. Those who attempted to take the middle-road between unfettered rationalism on the one hand, and blind imitation of tradition on the other became known as 'philosophers' (French *philosophes* and German *Aufklarer*). They included prominent thinkers and reformers like Charles-Louis de Montesquieu (1689–1755), Voltaire, David Hume (1711–1776), Edward Gibbon (1737–1794), Jean-Jacques Rousseau (1712–1778) and Benjamin

Franklin (1706–1790).[2] The contributions of Julien de La Mettrie (1709–1751), Jeremy Bentham (1748–1832), Adam Smith (1723–1790) and Thomas Jefferson (1743–1826), among others, also fall within this category.

Such thinkers and philosophers not only argued for a more nuanced approach to understanding nature and man's role in the modern world, unlike most contemporary philosophers, they also wanted to change and transform our existential condition. In other words, they wanted to move away from a traditional view of human life and the natural world in order to develop a new and modern perspective, one that was to be informed and inspired by innovative thinking and a forward-looking outlook. This was to enable human progress and development to take place in the face of widespread prejudice, backwardness, injustice and enslavement. The development and dissemination of this new vision of human life and nature was meant to herald the 'Age of Progress', leading to much-needed peace, security, prosperity and advancement, not only in the West, but also across the world. Have we managed to achieve that goal?

According to Rene Guenon – one of the twentieth century's foremost Muslim thinker, metaphysician and critic of modernity – humanity has certainly made progress but, unfortunately, in the wrong direction.

Rene Jean-Marie Joseph Guenon, better known in the Muslim world as Shaykh Abd al-Wahid Yahya al-Shadhili, was born in the ancient French city of Blois, located about 100 miles from Paris, into a middle-class Catholic family. His father, Jean-Baptise Guenon, was of French stock and hailed from a small landholding family who managed vineyards. But keen to pursue an alternative career, Jean-Baptise went on to study architecture and eventually qualified as an architect. He subsequently married and settled in a small house in the suburbs of Vienne, today located in the Nouvelle-Aquitaine region of south-western France, where he worked as an architectural designer.

The family were devout Catholics who attended their local church regularly. When their son was born, Jean-Baptise and his wife were 56 and 36 years old, respectively.[3] His birth was a real boon for the family, mainly because they had previously lost a daughter who died in her infancy, and, therefore, the birth of their son was a great blessing. Though tall and slender, young Guenon was of weak and fragile health, so much so that the family baptised him at the earliest opportunity. In the meantime, Jean-Baptise had secured employment as an auditor and adjuster for a local assurance company which, in turn, enabled the family to move into a more spacious property with a garden facing the river.

Guenon grew up here under the watchful gaze of his parents and was initially home-tutored by them on account of his fragile health. But then his aunt, Madame Veuve Duru, who lived next-door and was a teacher, became one of his first instructors. He was barely 11 when he joined St. Nicholas, his local church, and became a regular attendee along with his aunt, who was an influential role model for him during his formative years. During this period, he enrolled at the Notre Dame des Aydes, a religious school led by priests who were equally secular in their views and outlook. Young Guenon was a bright student who soon assimilated French language, literature, arithmetic, aspects of history and Catholic teachings, but did not like poetry. Although poor health frequently interrupted his education, his devotion to his studies and unusual abilities were admired by his teachers. In 1902, at the age of 16, he enrolled at the College Augustin-Thierry, which was a renowned educational institution in Blois at the time, extending over fourteen hectares of land today. Here, he studied Latin, philosophy and science, but struggled in poetry, history and geography.

However, during his time at Augustin-Thierry, Guenon won prizes in physics, philosophy and religion, in addition to excelling in mathematics. Guenon not only completed his Baccalaureate, but he also fell under the influence of Albert Leclere, who was a leading philosophy teacher and author of *Essai Critique sur le Droit D'affirmer*. Keen to pursue an academic career, in 1904, he moved to Paris to study mathematics at the College Rollin. However, soon he left his studies, perhaps due to a combination of ill-health and home-sickness which forced him to abandon formal education.[4]

For the next twenty-five years, Guenon lived in a small apartment in the centre of Paris and became actively involved in various occultist groups, esoteric cults and masonic movements, which were mushrooming in the capital of France at the time. The unfettered rationalistic tendencies of the Enlightenment era had created a spiritual vacuum which, as expected, was being filled by 'spiritualists' of all shades and colours. In the words of one scholar, 'Since the Catholic Church identified itself with the old order, and since the reason of the *philosophes* by itself was impotent, they sought a way out in "the new religion," or more precisely in the religion of a new period, which was to be the heir of the persecuted ancient traditions that were preserved in occult sanctuaries. The secrecy and the style of secret societies accompanied the rise of the democratic age, particularly in Italy and France.'[5]

Operating in such a cultural, intellectual and spiritual ambience in Paris, Guenon soon joined many occultist groups and, in the process, became a leading member of theosophical, masonic and spiritualist secret societies. So much so that, in 1909, while he was still in his mid-twenties, he founded and edited *La Gnose*, which was an occultist journal, and published numerous articles on aspects of 'gnostic' teachings. Unfortunately, the publication folded two years later. His interaction with the occultist groups enabled him to undertake a comparative study of prevailing spiritualist thought and practices. As a result, he was able to critique their artificial character and theories, which he argued, were actually underpinned by the materialistic philosophies of modernity, as opposed to being inspired by genuine metaphysical traditions. The outcome of his study was later published in two separate volumes entitled *Le Theosophisme: Histoire d'une pseudo-religion* (Theosophy: History of a Pseudo-Religion, 1921) and *L'Erreur Spirite* (Spiritist Fallacy, 1923).

Far from being impressed by the secretive and obscure origins of the occultist teachings and practices, Guenon soon abandoned the counterfeit spiritualities and, instead, focused his attention on eastern esoteric traditions, which he considered to be repositories of genuine metaphysics and spirituality. The traditional Catholic culture of France, he felt, was being systematically undermined by the onset of Western modernity, being as it were a product of post-Enlightenment rationalistic and scientific hedonism, leading to the loss of genuine faith, tradition and spirituality. During this period, he became actively involved in social and intellectual circles in Paris, befriending prominent scholars like Jacques Maritain (1882–1973), Leon Champrenaud (1870–1925) and Albert Puyou (1862–1939), among others. He also attended lectures on philosophy at the Sorbonne and became a family man, having married a teaching assistant, although he struggled to make ends meet.

Around this time, he met several Hindu visitors who arrived in Paris, and was initiated into the Advaita Vedanta strand of spirituality.[6] In due course, he also encountered Ivan Gustaf Agueli (1869–1917), a Swedish painter and convert to Islam, who introduced him into the Sufi *tariqa* of Shaykh Abd al-Rahman Ilaysh al-Kabir (1840–1921) of Egypt, thus adopting the Muslim name of Abd al-Wahid Yahya. Agueli had not only embraced Islam in Cairo under the guidance of Shaykh al-Kabir, but also went on to study Arabic and Islamic philosophy at al-Azhar University, being one of the first Westerners to do so. Subsequently, he was initiated into the al-Arabiyya Shadhiliyya Order of Islamic spirituality (*tasawwuf*) by his teacher and guide. He took the Muslim name of Abd al-Hadi and returned to Paris to disseminate Islam there (see chapter 51 for more information).[7] Guenon's encounter with the Vedantists, as well as Sufism, completely transformed his worldview, thus enabling him to distinguish genuine faith, tradition and spirituality from pseudo-religion and spirituality that was widespread in Paris at the time.

When the First World War broke out in July 1914, he was exempted from military service due to ill-health, but his income was drastically reduced and he was forced to earn a living. A year later, he obtained a first degree in philosophy from the Sorbonne which enabled him to teach at various educational institutions from 1915 to 1929, including spending a year in Setif in Algeria where he taught French, Latin and philosophy, in addition to improving his knowledge of Arabic.

During this period, Guenon combined his work as a teacher with extensive research and writing, authoring numerous books such as *Introduction Generale a l'etude des Doctrines Hindoues* (An Introduction to the Study of Hindu Doctrines, 1921); *Orient et Occident* (East and West, 1924); *L'Homme et son Devenir selon le Vedanta* (Man and his Becoming according to the Vedanta, 1925); *L'esoterisme de Dante* (Esoterism of Dante, 1925); *Le Roi du Monde* (The Lord of the World, 1927); *La Crise du Monde Moderne* (The Crisis of the Modern World, 1927); and *Autorite Spirituelle et Pouvoir Temporel* (Spiritual Authority and Temporal Power, 1929), in addition to *Le Theosophisme: Histoire d'une pseudo-religion* (Theosophy: History of a Pseudo-Religion, 1921) and *L'Erreur Spirite* (Spiritist Fallacy, 1923), among others.

It is true that his *Introduction to the Study of Hindu Doctrines* was intended to be an academic dissertation, but the university authorities did not rate it highly, perhaps because he was not a trained Orientalist or a recognised academic. Furthermore, he did not follow a standard system of academic documentation or referencing, and his arguments were dismissed by the university authorities as being far too esoteric and unverifiable, and, therefore, did not carry academic weight or recognition.

Although he was trained at the Sorbonne, he did not belong to the mainstream French academia and, as such, his writings only attracted minimal attention in France and elsewhere during his lifetime. Even so, his writings and thought defy classification, as one admirer rightly pointed out.[8] Perhaps it would not be unfair to say that his works were aimed at a select audience rather than intended for mass dissemination.

Not surprisingly, his influence within the Western academic circles has remained minimal, despite his seminal contribution to the revival of traditional thought and philosophy during the twentieth century, along with Ananda Coomaraswamy and Frithjof Schuon.

* In other words, Guenon's *Man and his Becoming according to the Vedanta* and *Esoterism of Dante* are important works on traditional metaphysics, whilst his *Theosophy, Spiritist Fallacy, Lord of the World, Crisis of the Modern World* and *Spiritual Authority and Temporal Power* directly address contemporary issues and worldly concerns. However, the key to understanding Guenon's thought and writing lies in his idea of Primordial Tradition, which is both universal and revealed, he argued. Therefore, it is pure and changeless metaphysical knowledge, unlike modern Western thought, which focused its

---

* The movement inspired by Guenon and Schuon is often referred to as the 'Perennialist' or 'Traditionalist' school. Schuon explains one of the central tenets of this school – namely, 'the transcendent unity of religions' – in the following terms: 'In reality, it means that all [true religions] are right, not in their dogmatic exclusivism, but in their unanimous inner signification, which coincides with pure metaphysics, or in other terms, with the *philosophia perennis*' (quoted in Michael Oren Fitzgerald, *Frithjof Schuon: Messenger of Perennial Philosophy*). The addition of 'true religions' in the aforementioned quotation is necessary because the perennialists do not see *all* religions as valid before God at the present time, but only *true* religions as valid in this sense; and for them, the latter consists of prime examples like Hinduism, Buddhism, Judaism, Christianity, Islam and Native American religion. This 'metaphysical' understanding is one that is categorically rejected as anti-Islamic (*kufr*) in orthodox Islamic theology, whereby God's sending of the Prophet Muhammad (peace be upon him) is understood as signifying the finality of prophethood and God's final religious form for all humankind who have the ability to receive the message. [Rev.]

attention on 'intellectual progress' and, in the process, dragged truth down to our level rather than seeking to transcend the material plane through the incessant pursuit of the 'knowledge of the Universal'.

Likewise, in his *Crisis of the Modern World,* he severely criticised modernity and the idea of 'progress', which he argued, explained modern man's obsession with, and longing for, material power. This reflected 'the illusion of ordinary life' as opposed to seeking authentic knowledge and acquiring insight into the nature of Ultimate Reality as such, leading to nothing but shallowness and spiritual destitution of the Western world, compared with the richness of traditional Eastern cultures and civilisations. To Guenon, the East was undoubtedly the repository of Tradition and Metaphysics, while the modern West was in total denial of both, thus precipitating the spiritual crisis that has engulfed the Western world today. The only way to save the West from ruin, he felt, was to recover the traditional and sacred roots of Western civilisation that had been systematically undermined and eroded due to the desacralising forces of 'modernity' and 'progress'. In his own words,

> To be resolutely 'anti-modern' is not to be 'anti-Western' in any sense of the word; it means, on the contrary, making the only effort that can be of any value to save the West from its confusion…There are those who speak today of a 'defence of the West', which is really remarkable when, as we shall see further on, it is the West that is threatening to submerge and drag down the whole of mankind in the whirlpool of its own confused activity; remarkable, as we say, and completely unjustified, if they mean, as despite certain reservations they really seem to do, that this defence is to be against the East, for the true East has no thought of attacking or dominating anybody and asks no more than to be left in independence and tranquillity – a not unreasonable demand, one must admit. Actually, the truth is that the West really is in great need of defence, but only against itself and its own tendencies, which, if they are pushed to their conclusion, will lead inevitably to its ruin and destruction; it is therefore 'reform of the West' that should be demanded, and if this reform were what it should be, that is to say a real restoration of tradition, it would entail as a natural consequence an understanding with the East.[9]

By all accounts, Guenon was a prolific writer who published extensively during the 1920s, authoring at least one book a year except in 1928, when his beloved wife, Berthe, suddenly died of meningitis. This was followed by the death of his mentor and guide, Madame Duru, which of course represented a double-blow for him. Although his friends and relatives provided much-needed support and comfort, by 1930, Guenon had made-up his mind to leave Paris and settle in the East, longing to move to and settle in, what he considered to be, a traditional culture and society. His friends and relatives tried to dissuade him but he was not to be deterred and, accordingly, he left the 'profane' West for the 'sacred' Islamic East, never to return.

He settled in Cairo, which was a bustling cosmopolitan city at the time, and quickly improved his command of Arabic, both spoken and written. Being an accomplished linguist, he was well-versed in more than half a dozen languages including Latin, Greek, German, French and Arabic. His knowledge of Arabic was so impressive that, from 1931, he became a regular contributor to *al-Ma'rifah*, a leading Cairo-based literary journal of the time. He also experienced financial hardship during this period and published articles and reviews in *Etudes Traditionnelles*, a French periodical, which was edited by Paul Chacornac, his friend and biographer, to make ends meet.[10]

In Cairo, Guenon led a traditional Islamic lifestyle and renewed his contact with the Shadhili Sufi order through a notable Shaykh, Sayyid Salamah ibn Hasan al-Radi (1867–1939), and became increasingly known in Cairo's literary and Sufi circles. He then married Fatimah, the daughter of another Sufi Shaykh, Muhammad Ibrahim, in 1934, and she bore him four children, two daughters (Khadijah and Layla) and two sons (Ahmad and Muhammad); the latter was born just after the death of his father.

It was during this period that he authored and published a number of important books on metaphysics, symbolism, esoterism and criticism of the modern world, including *Le Symbolisme de la Croix* (The Symbolism of the Cross, 1931); *Les etats Multiples de l'Etre* (The Multiple States of Being, 1932); *La Metaphysique Orientale* (Oriental Metaphysics, 1939); *Regne de la Quantite et les Signes des Temps* (The Reign of Quantity and the Signs of the Times, 1945); and, *La Grande Triade* (The Great Triad, 1946). The *Symbolism of the Cross* was completed before he moved to Cairo, but it was dedicated to Shaykh al-Kabir, his Sufi master. The *Multiple States of Being* further expanded this metaphysical doctrine of multiple states of Being from an esoteric perspective. By comparison, his *Oriental Metaphysics* was first delivered as a lecture at the Sorbonne in 1925 and published more than a decade later.

Perhaps Guenon's most powerful, pertinent and popular work is *The Reign of Quantity and the Signs of the Times*. In this book, he provides a detailed and systematic exposition of the 'precise nature of the modern deviation, and devotes special attention to the development of modern philosophy and science, and to the part played by them, with their accompanying notions of progress and evolution, in the formation of the industrial and democratic society which we now regard as "normal". Guenon sees history as a descent from Form (or Quality) toward Matter (or Quantity); but after the Reign of Quantity – modern materialism and the "rise of the masses" – Guenon predicts a reign of "inverted quality" just before the end of the age: the triumph of the "counter-initiation", the kingdom of Anti-christ.'[11]

Guenon published seventeen books and treatises during his lifetime, and hundreds of articles. According to some of his biographers, he authored more than 600 books, essays and articles in total. However, a large collection of his writings remained unpublished at the time of his death, but they were later collected and published in France. Most of his books have since been translated into more than twenty languages, including Italian, English, German, Spanish, Portuguese, Hindi and Tibetan.

As expected, his ideas, thoughts and writings have inspired generations of Western and Eastern scholars, thinkers and writers, Muslim and non-Muslim alike: including, Ananda K. Coomaraswamy (1877–1947); Frithjof Schuon (1907–1998); Titus Burckhardt (1908–1984); Martin Lings (see chapter 43); Marco Pallis (1895–1989); Michel Valsan, otherwise known as Shaykh Mustafa Abd al-Aziz (1907–1974); Leo Schaya (1916–1986); Jean-Louis Michon, also known as Ali Abd al-Khaliq (1924–2013); Charles Le Gai Eaton (1921–2010); Huston Smith (b. 1919); and Seyyed Hossein Nasr (b. 1933), among others.

On a more personal level, Guenon was a polite, humble and generous man, who was an equally devout and dedicated Muslim. He meticulously observed fundamental Islamic practices (for example, the five daily prayers and fasting during the month of Ramadan) during the last two decades of his life in Cairo.[12] Although he was granted Egyptian citizenship in 1949, he rarely ventured outside and, instead, preferred to lead a quiet and secluded life. In the words of Martin Lings, who knew Guenon very well, he 'never went out practically, and I would send a car to fetch him, and he would come with his family to our house about twice a year. We lived at that time just near the pyramids outside Cairo. But I did go with him once to visit the mosque of Sayyidina Husayn in the centre of Cairo, near the Azhar. He had a remarkable presence, and it was very striking to see the respect with which he was treated.'[13]

Needless to say, Guenon was profoundly influenced by Sufism (namely the esoteric dimension of Islam) as interpreted by Ibn al-Arabi (see chapter 51), the famous Andalusian metaphysician and Sufi scholar, despite being an adherent of the Shadhili order of North Africa, which was one of the most orthodox branches of Islamic spirituality. After a lifetime devoted to research, writing and spiritual quest, Shaykh Abd al-Wahid Yahya eventually passed away at the age of 64. He was busy repeating 'Allah' when he departed this world for the hereafter. Martin Lings, who was one of Guenon's close friends and admirers in Cairo, paid him the following tribute:

Guenon…was the pioneer, and already as a young man he saw clearly that in the West human intelligence, generally speaking, had come to be left out of religion. It no longer participated in the things of the spirit, and he was acutely conscious of the need to express spiritual truths in such a way as to win back the intelligences of virtually intelligent men and women for the only object that could truly satisfy them, namely Divine Reality, the Object for which intelligence exists. To do this, in a world increasingly rife with heresy and pseudo-religion, he had to remind twentieth century man of the need for orthodoxy, which presupposes firstly a Divine Revelation and secondly a Tradition that has been handed down with fidelity what Heaven has revealed…Guenon's function as pioneer went, no doubt providentially, with a style of writing wherein he could be likened to an archer. His teachings came forth like arrow after arrow, shot from a basis of unwavering certitude and hitting, in the vast majority of cases, the very centre of the target. The undeniable attraction that lies in such spontaneity explains the immense attraction that Guenon's writings continue to have for his readers.[14]

Ⓝ

1.  Immanuel Kant, *An Answer to the Question: 'What is Enlightenment?'*

2.  Roy Porter, *The Enlightenment.*

3.  Robin Waterfield, *Rene Guenon and the Future of the West.*

4.  Paul Chacornac, *The Simple Life of Rene Guenon*; John Herlihy (ed.), *The Essential Rene Guenon: Metaphysics, Tradition, and the Crisis of Modernity.*

5.  Jean-Pierre Laurant, 'The Primitive Characteristics of Nineteenth-Century Esoterism', Antoine Faivre and Jacob Needleman (ed.), *Modern Esoteric Spirituality.*

6.  Martin Lings, *Enduring Utterances: Collected Lectures (1993–2001).*

7.  Jean Borella, 'Rene Guenon and the Traditional School,' in Antoine Faivre and Jacob Needleman (ed.), *Modern Esoteric Spirituality.*

8.  Charles Le Gai Eaton, *The Richest Vein: Eastern Tradition and Modern Thought.*

9.  Rene Guenon, *The Crisis of the Modern World.*

10. Robin Waterfield, op. cit.

11. See 'editorial note' to Rene Guenon, *The Reign of Quantity and the Signs of the Times.*

12. Jean-Louis Michon, 'In the Intimacy of Shaykh Abdul Wahid – Rene Guenon – in Cairo 1947–1949', *Sophia: A Journal of Traditional Studies* vol. 3, no. 2.

13. Martin Lings, op. cit.

14. Martin Lings, 'Frithjof Schuon and Rene Guenon', *Sophia: A Journal of Traditional Studies* vol. 5, no. 2.

39

# LEOPOLD WEISS

B. 1900 – D. 1992

AUSTRIA

Just as medieval Europe had produced some of the Muslim world's foremost scholars and thinkers (including Abulcasis [see chapter 5], Ibn Hazm [see chapter 7], Avenzoar [see chapter 9], Avempace [see chapter 10], Abubacer [see chapter 12], Averroes [see chapter 13], Bitar [see chapter 15] and al-Shatibi [see chapter 16]), modern Europe also gave birth to some of the leading Muslim scholars, thinkers and writers of contemporary times, even if it is not widely recognised in the West and the Muslim world today. For that reason, the lives, thoughts and achievements of the medieval European Muslim scholars and thinkers has been highlighted in the first part of this book, whilst the contribution of the leading contemporary Western Muslim scholars is the focus of attention in the second part.

In other words, the lives and contributions of John Yahya Parkinson (see chapter 32), Marmaduke Pickthall (see chapter 33), Musa Jarullah (see chapter 34), Yusuf Ziyaeddin Ezheri (see chapter 35), Julius Germanus (see chapter 36) and Rene Guenon (see chapter 38) have been largely neglected by both Muslims and non-Muslims, just as much as the achievements of scholars like Mehmed Handzic (see chapter 42), Martin Lings (chapter 43) and Husein Dozo (see chapter 44) are equally unknown in the Muslim world today – despite being some of the most gifted European Muslim scholars and thinkers of modern times.

In the same way, the life, contribution and achievements of Leopold Weiss deserve special attention, not least because he was arguably the single-most influential Muslim scholar and thinker of the modern West. Unfortunately, as yet, there are no full-length and critical biographies of these great scholars available in English or any other languages, which is an unfortunate, but equally true reflection on contemporary Muslim intellectual failure and poverty.

Leopold Weiss, better known as Muhammad Asad, was born in the city of Lemberg in the Austrian Kingdom of Galicia, which was once a part of the Habsburg Empire. Although, from 1867 to 1918, it became known as Austro-Hungarian Empire, and today it is known as the city of Lviv in western Ukraine, located around fifty miles from the border of Poland. He hailed from a notable Jewish family of Rabbis (teachers of Jewish law and preachers in the synagogues). His grandfather, Benjamin Weiss, continued the family tradition by becoming an Orthodox Rabbi and soon established his reputation as a Jewish scholar and preacher in Czernowitz, the capital of the Austrian province of Bukovina, and was especially known for his mastery of rabbinic learning.

Rabbi Weiss wanted his son, Akiva, the father of Leopold, to continue the family tradition by qualifying as a Rabbi, but his son had other ideas: he had set his mind on studying secular law, as opposed to Jewish law, with the intention of becoming a barrister. He combined his study of the Talmud with secular law and eventually qualified as a lawyer, practising his profession in Lviv before moving to Vienna, the capital of Austria, where his family settled just before the Great War (also known as the First World War).[1]

Despite their religious family background, Akiva and his wife, Malka, who was the daughter of a wealthy banker, led a secular lifestyle and only paid lip service to Jewish teachings and practices. Even so, they ensured that during his early years, their son, the second of their three children, learned Hebrew and became familiar with the Jewish scriptures including the Talmud, Mishna and the Hebrew Bible. Referring to his early years, Leopold later recalled:

> It was a happy childhood, satisfying even in retrospect. My parents lived in comfortable circumstances; and they lived mostly for their children. My mother's placidity and unruffled quiet may have had something to do with the ease which in later years I was able to adapt myself to unfamiliar and, on occasion, most adverse conditions; while my father's inner restlessness is probably mirrored in my own... In accordance with our family's tradition, I received, through private tutors at home, a thorough grounding in Hebrew religious lore. This was not due to any pronounced religiosity in my parents. They belonged to a generation which, while paying lip service to one or another of the religious faiths that had shaped the lives of its ancestors, never made the slightest endeavour to conform its practical life or even its ethical thought to those teachings...Thus, by the age of thirteen, I not only could read Hebrew with great fluency...I studied the Old Testament in the original; the *Mishna* and *Gemara* – that is, the text and the commentaries of the Talmud – became familiar to me; I could discuss with a good deal of self-assurance the differences between the Babylonian and

Jerusalem Talmuds; and I immersed myself in the intricates of Biblical exegesis, called *Targum*, just as if I had been destined for a rabbinical career.[2]

As destiny would have it, Leopold did not pursue a rabbinical career and, instead, his father wanted him to become a scientist. However, by his own admission, he was 'a very indifferent student' at school and found mathematics and science to be dull and boring, preferring to read literature and history, which no doubt would have disappointed his father. His love of Polish and German literature, along with history, may have been a bit of a consolation for his learned, ambitious and successful father who wanted his talented son to shine and become equally successful. But at the age of 14, unbeknown to his father, he escaped from school and joined the Austrian army, only for his father to track him down and take him home.

However, the youngster was still restless, being intellectually detached from his Jewish faith and equally disinterested in formal education. Accordingly, he officially joined the Austrian army at the age of 18, although he was far from impressed by his experience in the military service. A few years after the Great War, he joined the University of Vienna to study philosophy and history of art, but again, he was not happy. In his own words, 'My heart was not in those studies. A quiet academic career did not attract me. I felt a yearning to come into more intimate grips with life, to enter it without any of those carefully contrived, artificial defences which security-minded people love to build up around themselves; and I wanted to find by myself an approach to the spiritual order of things which, I knew, must exist but which I could not yet discern.'[3]

Leopold grew up during an unpredictable and unprecedented time in the history of modern Europe. The Great War had devastated the politico-economic landscape of the whole continent, creating widespread fear and insecurity. This was coupled with the necessary loss of faith and trust, mainly due to modern philosophy and science's over-reliance on human reason and cognition to solve humanity's social and intellectual problems, with no clear and reliable standards of morality and ethics – this eventually led to growing spiritual restlessness and confusion across the continent. During this period, at the age of 20, Leopold abandoned his formal education for good, despite his father's protestation, and left Vienna for Prague in pursuit of a career in journalism.

He spent the next year travelling across Central Europe, surviving on little income from odd part-time jobs, before becoming a reporter for United Telegraph, which was an American news agency based in Berlin, where he soon became a sub-editor, thanks to his knowledge of European languages. According to Leopold, at the time, he was 'not unhappy: but my inability to share the diverse social, economic and political hopes of those around me – of any group among them – grew in time into a vague sense of not quite belonging to them, accompanied, vaguely again, by a desire to belong – to whom? – to be part of something – of what?'[4]

He was barely 22 when he received a letter from a maternal uncle who lived and practised psychiatry in Jerusalem, inviting him to spend some time in the Islamic East, which, of course, provided him with a golden opportunity to escape from his intellectual restlessness and quest for meaning in an increasingly competitive, dull and spiritually dissolute European capital. He resigned from United Telegraph and left Berlin for Constanza, before setting off for Alexandria destined for British Mandate Palestine.

As a young European, he went to the Muslim world with no prior knowledge of Islam or experience of Muslim culture, other than a Eurocentric and romanticised view that considered Islam to be an Abrahamic heresy and aberration, whilst only Christianity and Judaism deserved to be taken seriously as viable spiritual and ethical worldviews. During his stay in the Middle East, he worked as a foreign correspondent for the *Frankfurter Zeitung*, a leading German newspaper, on a freelance basis. Then, in 1924, he published his first book, *Unromantisches Morgenland* (The Unromantic Orient), being a descriptive account of his experience in the Middle East, for the benefit of his German readers.[5] His bosses at the *Frankfurter* were so impressed that they sponsored him to travel more extensively to collect information for a more comprehensive travelogue.

Needless to say, his journeys to Palestine, Jordan, Arabia, Egypt and Syria, among other places, not only improved his knowledge of Arabic and understanding of Islam, but also led him to become an admirer of the authenticity and spiritual depth of Islamic faith and culture. In addition to meeting prominent Muslim scholars and reformists (such as Shaykh Mustafa al-Maraghi [1881–1945], the rector of al-Azhar University in Cairo), he lived, travelled and broke bread with ordinary Muslims on a daily basis, and what he witnessed profoundly impressed him – a people at peace with God, with themselves and their environment – unlike the fear, insecurity and restlessness that was so prevalent in Europe at the time.

As it happened, observing an elderly gentleman perform his five daily prayers in Jerusalem, he later recalled, opened the door to Islam for him because 'I began to feel an unwonted humility whenever I saw, as I often did, a man standing barefooted on his prayer rug, or on a straw mat, or on the bare earth, with his arms folded over his chest and his head lowered, entirely submerged within himself, oblivious of what was going on around him, whether it was in a mosque or on the sidewalk of a busy street: a man at peace with himself.'[6]

At the same time, he became aware of the political games that were being played by the Western powers in the Middle East, often at the expense of the Arabs and especially the Palestinian people. Unsurprisingly, he became a vociferous critic of Zionism. In his own words, 'Although of Jewish origin myself, I conceived from the outset a strong objection to Zionism...I considered it immoral that immigrants, assisted by a foreign Great Power, should come from abroad with the avowed intention of attaining to majority in the country and thus to dispossess the people whose country it had been since time immemorial.'[7]

His outspoken criticism of Zionism, coupled with his pro-Palestinian political stance, did not of course, impress the prominent Zionist leaders of the time, including Chaim Weizmann, but he did not relent: 'How was it possible', he asked, 'for people endowed with so much creative intelligence as the Jews to think of the Zionist-Arab conflict in Jewish terms alone? Did they not realize that the problems of the Jews in Palestine could, in the long run, be solved only through friendly co-operation with the Arabs? Were they so hopelessly blind to the painful future which their policy must bring? – to the struggles, bitterness and the hatred to which the Jewish island, even if temporarily successful, would forever remain exposed in the midst of a hostile Arab sea?'[8]

After almost two years of travelling in the Middle East, he eventually returned to Frankfurt to put pen to paper, but unfortunately failed to complete the travelogue, leading to the termination of his contract. He also married Elsa, a widow 15 years his senior, and moved to Berlin where he worked as a reporter for local newspapers. Also during this time, he read Islamic literature extensively, including the Qur'an – in French and German translation – as his command of classical Arabic was still weak. It was during this period, whilst still in his mid-twenties, he opened the Qur'an and was moved by the power and majesty of the following verses: 'You are obsessed by greed for more and more until you go down to your graves. Nay, in time you will come to understand! And once again: Nay, in time you will come to understand!'[9]

This, coupled with his considerable knowledge and experience of the Islamic East, not to mention his on-going personal quest for meaning and purpose in the modern world, eventually convinced Leopold of the truth of Islam. He went straight to the head of the Islamic Society in Berlin and formally became a Muslim, taking the name of Muhammad Asad (Asad is an Arabic word for Leopold, meaning 'lion'). Elsewhere he stated, 'Islam appears to me like a perfect work of architecture. All its parts are harmoniously conceived to complement and support each other; nothing is superfluous and nothing lacking, with the result of an absolute balance and solid composure. Probably this feeling that everything in the teachings and postulates of Islam is "in its proper place," has created the strongest impression on me.'[10]

After his conversion, his wife followed suit and embraced Islam, and so together they moved to Arabia where Leopold lived for the next six years. During this period, he perfected his command of Arabic and performed the annual pilgrimage no less than five times, whilst contributing articles to a Swiss newspaper as a freelancer. Unfortunately, his wife died soon afterwards, so Leopold married twice during his stay in Arabia. Munira, his second wife, bore him a son, Talal Asad (b. 1933), who went on to become a respected anthropologist and academic. Like Harry (Abdullah) St John Philby (see chapter 37), during his stay in Arabia, Leopold became a close associate of King Abd al-Aziz ibn Saud (1880–1953), the founder of the Kingdom of Saudi Arabia, and served the Saudi monarch in various capacities. Although he initially rated Ibn Saud highly as a political leader – hoping that he could unify the Muslim world under his able leadership

– in due course, however, he was to be disappointed by the Saudi ruler who, in his opinion, proved to be anything but a political visionary. His criticism of Wahhabism, the official creed of the Saudi kingdom, was equally incisive and devastating, as he later wrote:

> The spiritual meaning of Wahhabism – the striving after an inner renewal of Muslim society – was corrupted almost at the same moment when its outer goal – the attainment of social and political power – was realized with the establishment of the Saudi Kingdom at the end of the eighteenth century and its expansion over the larger part of Arabia early in the nineteenth. As soon as the followers of Muhammad ibn Abd al-Wahhab achieved power, his idea became a mummy: for the spirit cannot be a servant of the power – and power does not want to be a servant of the spirit. The history of Wahhabi Najd is the history of a religious idea which first rose on the wings of enthusiasm and longing and then sank down into the lowlands of pharisaic self-righteousness. For all virtue destroys itself as soon as it ceases to be longing and humility: Harut! Marut!'[11]

Disappointed by Ibn Saud's lack of political ambition and vision, Leopold left Arabia in 1932 in favour of British India. He initially stayed in Kashmir, before moving to Lahore where he befriended Sir Muhammad Iqbal (1877–1938), who was one of the foremost Muslim poets and philosophers of his generation. Iqbal encouraged him to formulate an intellectual response to the political, social, educational and cultural problems confronting the Muslim world at the time. Less than two years later, his *Islam at the Crossroads* was published and it instantly became a bestseller. Consisting of seven essays and a short foreword and conclusion, in this book, Leopold argued for the regeneration of Islam for the benefit and welfare of humanity. In order to achieve that objective, he felt, Muslims had to stop blindly imitating the West and, instead, rediscover their own inner strength and energy. In his own words,

> What appears to be the decay of Islam is in reality nothing but the death and the emptiness of our hearts which are too idle and too lazy to hear the eternal voice. No sign is visible that mankind, in its present stature, has outgrown Islam. It has not been able to produce a better system of ethics than that expressed in Islam; it has not been able to put the idea of human brotherhood on a practical footing, as Islam did in its supra-national concept of *ummah*; it has not been able to create a social structure in which the conflicts and frictions between its members are as efficiently reduced to a minimum as in the social plan of Islam; it has not been able to enhance the dignity of man; his feeling of security; his spiritual hope; and last, but surely not least, his happiness.[12]

In other words, in this book, he not only pitted Islam against the West, but he also established the superiority of the former over the latter, which of course impressed the Indian Muslim scholars and politicians. 'This work', stated Iqbal, 'is extremely interesting. I have no doubt that coming as it does from a highly cultured European convert to Islam it will prove an eye-opener to our younger generation.'[13] Iqbal was right; Leopold's stinging criticism of the materialistic West subsequently inspired generations of Muslim revivalists and reformers across Asia, Europe, the Middle East and Africa, including Sayyid Abul A'la Mawdudi (1903–1979), Sayyid Qutb (1906–1966), Alija Izetbegovic (see chapter 48) and Hasan al-Turabi (1932–2016), among others.

Two years after the publication of his *Islam at the Crossroads*, Leopold was appointed editor of *Islamic Culture* by the Nizam of Hyderabad. This monthly journal was first edited by Marmaduke Pickthall (see chapter 33), but after his retirement and subsequent demise in 1936, Leopold took charge of the publication and soon established his reputation as a gifted Muslim scholar, thinker and editor. However, when the Second World War broke out in Europe in September 1939, he was interned in India as a foreign national and spent the next six years in captivity until he was eventually released in August 1945.

He then founded and – for a short period – edited a journal called *Arafat*, wherein he surveyed and critiqued Muslim thought and culture in order to awaken his fellow Muslims from their intellectual slumber. And, after the establishment of Pakistan in 1947, he became a champion of the new Muslim country, serving as the director of the Department of Islamic Reconstruction with a view to formulating its constitution and future political direction. Like Iqbal and Muhammad Ali Jinnah (1876–1948), he wanted Pakistan to be a liberal, democratic and pluralistic Muslim country, underpinned by Islamic principles and values.

However, he soon found himself in conflict with prominent Pakistani Islamic ideologues (like Sayyid Abul A'la Mawdudi), for they were determined to establish a rigid political framework in Pakistan. This forced him to move away from domestic politics in favour of international diplomacy through Pakistan's Foreign Ministry, before being transferred to New York as its representative to the United Nations in 1952.

In addition to *Islam at the Crossroads*, during his time in Pakistan, Leopold authored several other works, including *Sahih al-Bukhari: The Early Years of Islam*; *The Principles of State and Government in Islam*; and, *This Law of Ours and Other Essays*. The *Sahih al-Bukhari* was intended to be the first complete translation of one of Islam's earliest and most important anthologies of Prophetic traditions (*ahadith an-nabawi*) – accompanied by insightful and critical notes – but he was unable to complete the work due to the outbreak of the Second World War and the political chaos and confusion that ensued during the partition of India.

As a result, only the first instalment of this work saw the light of day in 1935. *The Principles of State and Government in Islam,* on the other hand, was first published in 1961 by the University of California Press and, *This Law of Ours and Other Essays* appeared much later in 1987. In these works, Leopold formulated a liberal and pluralistic interpretation of Islamic law, jurisprudence and morality, as well as political principles and rules of governance, characterised by maturity of thought and reflection, unlike the simplistic and one-dimensional approach adopted in *Islam at the Crossroads*.

For example, in his 'Author's Note' to *The Principles of State and Government in Islam*, he wrote: 'the past thousand years or so of Muslim history can offer us no guidance in our desire to achieve a polity which would really deserve the epithet "Islam". Nor is the confusion lessened by the influences of which the Muslim world has been subjected in recent times…And so, the Muslims' longing for a truly Islamic polity stands today, despite – or perhaps because of it – its intensity, under the sign of utter confusion.'[14]

His solution to this problem was simple: Muslims have no other option other than to return to the fundamental sources of Islam for spiritual, as well as political guidance, namely the Qur'an and authentic Prophetic teachings. By comparison, his *Road to Mecca* became an instant bestseller soon after its publication in 1954. HailHailed as a work of 'great power and beauty' by the *Times Literary Supplement* and a 'rare and powerful book' by the *New York Post*, in this work, the author provides an insightful and vivid account of his life and travels in Arabia, covering the period from 1900 to 1932. This book is undoubtedly Leopold's most widely read work, thus it has also been translated into many prominent languages.

Soon after his arrival in New York, Leopold met and married Pola Hamida, an American Polish convert to Islam, having already divorced Munira, his Arab wife of twenty years. He subsequently spent the next forty years of his life with his new wife, Pola Hamida – first in Geneva, and then in Gibraltar. It was during this period that he worked on his *magnum opus*, *The Message of the Qur'an: Translated and Explained* under the patronage of King Faisal of Saudi Arabia (r. 1964–1975) and Shaykh Ahmad Zaki Yamani (b. 1930), who served as Saudi Arabia's Minister of Oil and Mineral Resources from 1962 to 1986. He expressed his gratitude to the latter by dedicating *This Law of Ours and Other Essays* to him. Leopold began surveying the existing English translations of the Qur'an and being unimpressed by them, he decided to work on a fresh translation and commentary of the Divine revelation. He spent the next twenty years of his life on this project and eventually completed the task in 1980.

Consisting of 1000 pages, this monumental work is nothing short of an encyclopaedia on Qur'anic sciences and exegesis, as well as reflection on Islamic thought, history, culture and civilisation. Dedicated to 'people who think', this translation is based on an intimate awareness and understanding of classical Arabic, although the same cannot be said about its commentary, which – being heavily influenced by Ibn Hazm (see chapter 7), Fakhr al-Din al-Razi (1149–1209), Muhammad Abduh (1849–1905), Muhammad Rashid Rida (1865–1935) and Muhammad Iqbal (1877–1938) – is far too allegorical and modernist in its tone and content. Unsurprisingly, the conservative *ulama* (Islamic scholars) categorically rejected his rationalistic views and tendencies, prompting the

Saudi authorities to impose a ban on his translation and commentary even before its full publication, which of course annoyed and angered Leopold.

He considered the Saudi reaction to be yet another example of contemporary Muslim deviation from fundamental Islamic principles and values of intellectual freedom, respect for scholarship and toleration of diversity of views and interpretation. In his foreword to *The Message of the Qur'an*, he wrote:

> In order to bring out, to the best of my ability, the many facets of the Qur'anic message, I have found it necessary to add to my translation a considerable number of explanatory notes ... [and] to this end, drawn amply on the works of the great Arab philologists and of the classical commentators. If, on occasion, I have found myself constrained to differ from the interpretations offered by the latter, let the reader remember that the very uniqueness of the Qur'an consists in the fact that the more our worldly knowledge and historical experience increase, the more meanings, hitherto unsuspected, reveal themselves in its pages. The great thinkers of our past understood this problem fully well. In their commentaries, they approached the Qur'an with their *reason*: that is to say, they tried to explain the purport of each Qur'anic statement in the light of their superb knowledge of the Arabic language and of the Prophet's teachings...Hence, it was only natural that the way in which one commentator understood a particular Qur'anic statement or expression differed occasionally – and sometimes very incisively – from the meaning attributed to it by this or that of his predecessors. In other words, they often contradicted one another in their interpretations: but they did this without any animosity, being fully aware of the element of relativity inherent in all human reasoning, and of each other's integrity [because] ... such differences of opinion are the basis of all progress in human thinking and, therefore, a most potent factor in man's acquisition of knowledge.[15]

In 1982, Leopold moved to Sintra, located on the outskirts of Lisbon, before finally settling in Mijas in southern Spain. During his final years, he was busy working on a sequel to *The Road to Mecca* under the title of *Homecoming of the Heart,* covering his life from 1933 to 1992, but death intervened before he could complete this work. His wife, Pola Hamida Asad (d. 2007), subsequently completed the manuscript and it was eventually published in Lahore in 2012.

Leopold Weiss, or Muhammad Asad, died at the age of 91 and was buried in a Muslim cemetery in Granada. In recognition of his contribution to inter-religious dialogue and cultural understanding, an open space in-front of the UNO City in Vienna, known as 'Muhammad Asad Square', was officially named after him in 2008. Pakistan Post also issued a stamp in honour of 'Allama Muhammad Asad' in March 2013 as a tribute to his memory.

(N)

1. Martin Kramer, 'The Road from Mecca: Muhammad Asad' in *The Jewish Discovery of Islam*: *Studies in Honor of Bernard Lewis*.

2. Muhammad Asad, *The Road to Mecca*.

3. Ibid.

4. Ibid.

5. Translated into English by Elma Ruth Harder in 2004.

6. Muhammad Asad, *The Road to Mecca*.

7. Ibid.

8. Ibid.

9. Muhammad Asad, *The Message of the Qur'an: Translated and Explained*.

10. Muhammad Asad, *Islam at the Crossroads*.

11. Muhammad Asad, *The Road to Mecca*.

12. Muhammad Asad, *Islam at the Crossroads*.

13. See M. Ikram Chughtai (ed.) *Muhammad Asad: Europe's Gift to Islam*, 2 volumes.

14. Muhammad Asad, *The Principles of State and Government in Islam*.

15. Muhammad Asad, *The Message of the Qur'an*, op. cit.

# ABDULLAH ALI AL-HAKIMI

B. 1900 – D. 1954

UNITED KINGDOM

Elizabeth I was the Queen of England and Ireland from 17 November, 1558 until her death in 1603. Upon her accession, Pope Pius V wanted Elizabeth to enter the Catholic fold; however, she refused and was swiftly ex-communicated in 1570. She was unruffled by papal censure and went on to become one of the greatest monarchs in the history of England. It was during her successful reign that England became truly outward-looking and internationalist in its policy and politics, forging ties with prominent Muslim powers that were locked in battle against Catholic Spain at the time, leading to considerable cultural, economic and political exchanges between England and the Muslim world.

This laid the foundation for further interaction during the subsequent centuries with the expansion of British trade and commercial interests in many parts of the Islamic world, which, of course, eventually led to the establishment of British political, as well as military hegemony, in Mughal India, Africa and the Middle East during the eighteenth and nineteenth centuries.[1]

It was during this period that Muslims first began to arrive in England and other European countries; the lives and careers of notable individuals like Ayuba Sulaiman Diallo (see chapter 23), Mirza Abu Talib Khan (1752–1806), Sake Dean Mahomed

(Shaykh Din Muhammad, 1759–1851), Mirza Abul Hasan Shirazi (1776–1845) and Rifa'a al-Tahtawi (1801–1873), highlights the formative period of Muslim presence in England. These pioneers paved the way for the arrival of more Muslims during the late nineteenth and early twentieth centuries. And, although the history of migration of the Sub-continental Muslims to Britain is widely known, the story of the arrival and settlement of Yemeni Muslims in the British port cities of Cardiff, Liverpool, South Shields and Hull has received very little attention.

This explains why the life and career of Abdullah Ali al-Hakimi, a prominent Yemeni scholar and spiritual leader, and one of the pioneers of the British Muslim community, is hardly known today.

Shaykh Abdullah Ali al-Hakimi al-Alawi al-Shadhili, known as Abdullah Ali al-Hakimi for short, was born into a conservative Muslim family belonging to the tribe of al-Hakim in Dhubhan, located in the province of al-Hujariya, not far from the present-day Yemeni city of Ta'izz, which is the headquarters of Ta'izz Governorate and was once the cultural capital of Yemen.[2] In the absence of a full and well-documented biography based on primary data, it is not surprising that historians have struggled to reconstruct his life and career, using largely secondary sources instead.

As such, very little is known about his early years and education, other than the fact that he grew up in a pious Muslim family and attended local religious schools, and, in the process, became thoroughly proficient in Arabic (which was his mother-tongue), the Qur'an and aspects of Islamic teachings. Members of his family may have been involved in trade as he later became a merchant himself, thus successfully combining learning and scholarship with business and trade. He grew up at a time when Yemen as a country emerged, in the words of the historian Paul Dresch, 'in a context shaped by outside powers. Much of Yemen's history through the twentieth century connects with efforts to form that state, which was finally established in 1990. Before that there were two states, North and South, with their capitals at Sanaa and at Aden, each with its view of the country's past and future, and in the years around 1900 there were myriad little centres of power – hence myriad different histories, were there space to give them – and a few great claimants, two of which were foreign empires.'[3]

The strategic geo-political positioning of Yemen, bordering Saudi Arabia to the north, the Red Sea to the west, and, crucially, the Gulf of Aden and Arabian Sea to the south, and of course Oman to the east and north-east, explains why the colonial powers (especially the Ottomans and the British) were so eager to establish and retain their hegemony in that part of the world during the eighteenth, nineteenth and early twentieth centuries. But international politics and colonial rivalry aside, Yemen also occupies an important place in early Islamic history, culture and literature, being mentioned in the Qur'an and numerous Prophetic traditions. For example, the collapse of the great dam of Ma'rib, the capital of ancient Kingdom of Saba, which was caused by the great flood of Arim, is alluded to in Surah Saba (chapter 34 of the Qur'an).

Likewise, referring to the people of Yemen, the Prophet of Islam once remarked, 'They are tender hearted and more delicate of soul. The capacity to understand is of the Yemenis and wisdom is that of the Yemenis.'⁴ In other words, the Islamic values and virtues of the people of Yemen were not only recognised and acknowledged during the early days of Islam, but their contribution to the preservation and dissemination of Islamic learning, education and spirituality has been equally invaluable and noteworthy. Perhaps inspired by the contribution and achievements of his countrymen, young Abdullah completed his early and further Islamic education in his homeland before pursuing trade to earn a living.

Needless to say, in those days, young and ambitious merchants and traders travelled far and wide in order to expand their businesses and increase profit margins. No doubt, Abdullah was one such trader who travelled extensively in pursuit of business but, thanks to his love for Islamic learning and education, he combined the two by attending the lectures of prominent Muslim scholars of the time. It was during one such visit to North Africa that he encountered Shaykh Abul Abbas Ahmad ibn Mustafa al-Alawi al-Shadhili, a renowned Algerian Islamic scholar and Sufi master. According to some scholars (such as Fred Halliday and Mohammad Siddique Seddon), he may have met al-Alawi in Morocco during the 1920s, perhaps when he was in his late twenties. Born in the Algerian port city of Mostaganem in 1869, Ahmad al-Alawi received his early education at home under the tutelage of his father, before moving to Morocco in 1894 ,where he studied under the guidance of Shaykh Muhammad al-Habib Hamu al-Buzaydi (or Buzidi, 1824–1909), who was a leading Islamic scholar and Sufi master of the time. He spent more than a decade in the company of the spiritual master before he was initiated into the al-Darqawi Order of Sufism.⁵

Then, in 1914, he established his own Alawi Sufi Order. Thus, he and his prominent disciples became the leading disseminators of Islamic spirituality (*tasawwuf*) across North Africa and Europe during the twentieth century. The disciples were often accepted as *faqir* (initiate) and, after an intensive period of learning and spiritual development, they were appointed *muqaddam* (representative) of the Shaykh, before being dispatched to the other cities and countries in order to establish a *zawiya* (Sufi lodge) and popularise the Alawiyya Order of Sufism in that location. Like Isa Nur al-Din Ahmad al-Alawi al-Shadhili (1907–1998), better known as Frithjof Schuon, Abdullah also became a prominent disciple of al-Alawi who, upon obtaining permission from his Shaykh, left North Africa and moved to Europe in order to disseminate the message of Islam and spirituality.

Whilst Isa Nur al-Din Ahmad had established a Sufi lodge in Switzerland and disseminated Sufism there for four decades, he eventually moved to America where he subsequently attracted many disciples, Muslims and non-Muslims alike. Abdullah, on the other hand, initially settled in France and established a *zawiya* in Marseilles; he was in his early thirties at the time. In due course, he moved to the Netherlands and engaged in religious proselytising in Rotterdam where there was a sizable Muslim community consisting mainly of Yemeni sailors (lascars). In addition to establishing an Alawi Sufi lodge, he served as an Imam (prayer leader) and spiritual guide in the small Muslim community.

After staying in France and the Netherlands for a few years, Abdullah was granted permission by his Shaykh to proceed to England to disseminate the Alawi order of Sufism in the British Muslim community. As expected, the Muslim population in Britain, at the time, consisted of no more than 10,000 people, and they had settled in prominent cities like London, Cardiff, Manchester and Birmingham. For such a small community, however, it was unusually diverse and consisted of those of Indian, Yemeni and Somali origin, as well as some English converts to Islam, most of them being women who often embraced the faith through marriage to Muslim settlers. For those early Muslims, life in Britain was far from being easy; they faced considerable social, cultural, economic and racial barriers and challenges.

Accordingly, some became 'more like their white counterparts and less like members of their communities of origin. But the more Muslims attempted to maintain their distinct community identities during this period, the less they seemed to be accepted by the society as a whole. Being a Muslim in Britain during these years was not easy: it involved trying, in an atmosphere of racial hostility, to claim the rights that went with being British while still hanging on to what distinguished these communities from those around them. To some extent Muslim communities succeeded in both endeavours, but their successes were won in the face of resentment from sections of the wider society, which resisted their presence for economic as well as social reasons.'[6]

This is the social, political and economic context in which Abdullah arrived in Britain in November 1936 while he was in his mid-thirties. He initially settled in South Shields, which was a coastal English town located less than five miles from the city of Newcastle upon Tyne, and he was surprised to find that it had a thriving Muslim community consisting of several thousand Yemeni sailors. They not only stayed in local Arab boarding houses, but many of them had also taken English wives who, in turn, had converted to Islam.

As expected, the women and children had very little knowledge and understanding of their faith and its teachings. He was equally disappointed to see that there were no religious facilities or educational institutions available to meet the local community's spiritual and educational needs and requirements. This prompted him to establish the Zawiya Islamia Alawia Religious Society of the United Kingdom (Zaouia Islamia Allawouia Religious Society) in order to inform and educate the local Muslims in their faith and its teachings, establish religious and educational institutions to cater for the community's needs, and promote inter-religious understanding and dialogue with the wider society in order to remove barriers and misconceptions, thereby fostering social harmony and cultural integration. During this period, Abdullah travelled extensively between South Shields and Cardiff, which also had a substantial population of Yemeni sailors, and endeavoured to organise and institutionalise the Muslim communities in both locations, but financial problems hampered his efforts.

Although the Yemeni sailors had been visiting the British port cities like Cardiff, Liverpool and South Shields since the mid-nineteenth century, most of them came to Britain after the Great War (also known as the First World War). The majority of the early Yemeni settlers were poor and illiterate, but equally loyal and hard-working. They primarily worked on British merchant ships that travelled via Aden, a strategically important port city that came under British control in 1839, and earned just about enough to make ends meet. This explains why Abdullah initially struggled to raise sufficient funds in South Shields and Cardiff to purchase suitable properties to convert them into religious and community centres for the benefit of his congregations.

Unsurprisingly, in November 1938, he sent a letter to Sir Bernard R. Reilly (1882–1966), the British Governor of Aden at the time, in his capacity as the president of the Zawiya based at Bute Street in Cardiff, requesting him to help raise £4000 to build a mosque and Islamic school on a piece of land they had already purchased for £500 because 'there are a large number of Moslems resident in Cardiff, and many of us have become citizens, married, and have families, and we are very anxious that our children shall be given the opportunity of being educated, and in this connection we hope to have your able assistance…'.[7]

Although it is not clear if any financial contribution was made by the British authorities at the time, by 1938, Abdullah had not only established a thriving Zawiya on Peel Street, Cardiff – thus laying the foundation for what later became known as the Nur al-Islam Mosque and South Wales Islamic Centre – he also purchased *The Hilda Arms*, a former public house, which was located on Cuthbert Street, South Shields. He soon converted it into a mosque and Islamic school where daily prayers and regular Islamic classes were organised for the benefit of local Muslims, in addition to serving as a venue for weddings, religious ceremonies and cultural events and activities.

He eventually moved from South Shields to Cardiff, which may have been precipitated by his desire to establish a thriving mosque there for the city's Muslim community which, at the time, had no less than 4000 Muslims of Yemeni origin alone. After the Second World War, the Colonial Office provided generous funding to the Muslim community to help rebuild the mosque as a token of gratitude for their loyalty and support during the war efforts. Robert B. Serjeant, a Cambridge-based academic and prominent Arabist, happened to be there in 1943 and witnessed the opening ceremony of the new mosque where the Mayor of Cardiff was the chief guest.[8] Needless to say, Abdullah's efforts and activities were not only confined to South Shields and Cardiff, he was also instrumental in establishing mosques and Islamic schools in several other British cities including Liverpool, Manchester, Birmingham and Sheffield.

Thanks to Abdullah's vision, leadership and dedication, the Zawiyas he founded were open, inclusive, outward-looking and vibrant institutions that welcomed both men and women, young and old, rich and poor, and Muslims and non-Muslims alike. As a wise scholar and visionary leader, Abdullah was fully aware that he was operating in a non-Muslim country and therefore, it was in the long-term interest of the Muslim community to establish contacts and strengthen relationships with the local authorities and institutions, as well as the wider society in general. In other words, just catering for the spiritual needs of the community was not enough; this had to be combined with the educational, health, social welfare, employment and other individual and collective needs of the whole community. To achieve that, he felt,

> Collective action would be needed to persuade the institutions of the wider society to allow some space for Muslim living, such as access to *halal* food and approved burial grounds, and Al-Hakimi became a key figure in the attempts of the South Shields and Cardiff Muslim communities to negotiate on those matters with the local authorities. In his efforts to achieve a firm basis for Muslim community life, al-Hakimi painstakingly cultivated connections with local officials such as the mayor, town councillors and the Chief Constable. For their part, the local authorities seemed to welcome the establishment of the order in these towns, since by strengthening the religious organisations of the community it provided a useful means of controlling the behaviour of its members and exerting social discipline.[9]

During this period, Abdullah trained up several young scholars (such as Shaykh Hasan Ismail and Shaykh Sa'id Ismail of Cardiff, and Shaykh Muhammad Qasim al-Alawi of Birmingham) who went on to become some of the leading British Muslim scholars and community leaders of their generation. Shaykh Hasan Ismail served as a deputy to Abdullah, until the two men clashed and eventually parted company due to their differing stance on Yemeni domestic policy and politics which, of course, had a considerable impact on the British Yemeni community at the time.

Being an advocate of Yemeni political unification, Abdullah supported the Free Yemen Movement, and was a fierce critic and opponent of the Zaydi Imams who were ruling Yemen at the time. He wanted the division between the North and South of Yemen to be consigned to history, thus paving the way for the country's unification. Hasan Ismail, on the other hand, being pro-Zaydi Imamate, profoundly disagreed with his teacher and mentor, and campaigned to maintain the status quo in Yemen. In the ensuing tussle, Hasan Ismail prevailed because the majority of Yemeni people in Cardiff supported his political stance.[10]

This forced Abdullah to resign from his position as chief Imam, only to be succeeded by his one-time disciple and deputy. By comparison, Sa'id Ismail was raised and educated in Britain and Yemen where he studied at prominent Islamic seminaries before qualifying as a scholar. After completing his formal Islamic education, he returned to Cardiff and succeeded Hasan Ismail as Imam of the Nur al-Islam Mosque. He continued to serve in this capacity until his death in 2011. By comparison, Muhammad Qasim al-Alawi moved to Birmingham during the early 1940s and, soon after his arrival, he established a new Zawiya in the city. He continued to serve in his capacity as a notable religious scholar, community leader and spiritual guide to the local Muslims until his death in 1990.

In addition to being a prominent Islamic scholar, social reformer and institution-builder, Abdullah was also a notable spiritual leader and writer. He not only became a pioneering British Muslim scholar and Sufi who remained faithful to Shaykh Ahmad al-Alawi, his spiritual master and guide, he also went on to establish a firm place for Islam and traditional Sufism in Britain for the first time in its history, having recruited and trained thousands of Muslims across Britain.

To this end, he authored a number of Arabic books on Islamic teachings and practices, as well as interfaith relations for the benefit of his flock, including *Din Allah Wahid* (The Unity of Divine Religion) and *al-As'ilah wa'l-Ajwibah bayn al-Masihiyyah wa'l-Islam* (Questions and Answers about Christianity and Islam). He was motivated to write the former because he wanted to 'bring closer together the religious Moslems and Christians, and others, but as regards Religion, God's religion is one. For those of the past age and those of this present age, and on the tongues of all the Prophets, was one religion and no other.'[11] In the latter, however, he endeavoured to explain the similarities and differences between Islam and Christianity, and once again, Abdullah emphasized the importance and value of inter-religious understanding and co-operation in a world ravaged by suspicion, hostility and hatred.

His views and opinions on this issue were no different from that of his own spiritual master whose message he faithfully championed and promoted throughout his life, despite the fact that he lived for a quarter of a century in Western Europe, unlike al-Alawi, and faced considerable challenges and difficulties, and always endeavoured to tackle those issues with wisdom, tact and diplomacy. The only area where he never budged an inch was his strong political views and opinions vis-à-vis the Zaydi Imamate, which he considered to be not only corrupt, but equally unprincipled and unpatriotic. He felt that the Yemeni people deserved much better and actively campaigned in favour of the Free Yemen Movement.

Although his strong political views landed him in trouble in Cardiff, where, he served as president of the Yemen Union for several years. He also authored a book titled *Da'wat al-Ahrar* (Call to Freedom), in addition to launching the first Arabic periodical in Britain, which was known as *Al-Salam* (The Peace), to raise awareness and understanding of the challenges facing the Yemen and the Muslim world as a whole at the time. However, upon his arrival in Aden in January 1953, he was immediately arrested and imprisoned for apparently attempting to smuggle arms into the country. He was, of course, framed by the authorities and, after a court hearing, he was eventually released from prison in October 1953.

A year later, he was hospitalised due to a kidney infection. Whilst he was recovering in hospital, he was reportedly poisoned by his political opponents, of whom the Zaydi ruler, Ahmad, was the most active and powerful. Shaykh Abdullah Ali al-Hakimi died at the age of around 54. Mohammad Siddique Seddon, a British historian and author of *The Last of the Lascars* (2014) paid him this glowing tribute:

> His extraordinary efforts not only transformed the British Yemeni community from a disparate and invisible group of transient docklands settlers into a fully-fledged religious community that was both organized and dynamic, locally and nationally, but they also resulted in the formation of a nascent and authentic manifestation of 'British Islam' that stretched from South Wales to north-east England. The introduction of the 'Alawi *tariqah* to British Yemenis also precipitated a significant identity shift from race and ethnicity in a distinctly discriminate and excluding minority context to a religious identity that was both, geographically transcontinental, linking Arabia, Africa and Europe, and spiritually universal, developing a distinctly *ummatic* sense of British Yemeni 'Muslimness'.[12]

1. Sarah E. Stockwell, *The British Empire: Themes and Perspectives*.

2. Fred Halliday, *Britain's First Muslims: Portrait of an Arab Community*.

3. Paul Dresch, *A History of Modern Yemen*.

4. *Sahih al-Bukhari*, Hadith no. 4129.

5. Martin Lings, *A Sufi Saint of the Twentieth Century: Shaikh Ahmad al-Alawi, his spiritual heritage and legacy*.

6. Humayun Ansari, *The Infidel Within: Muslims in Britain since 1800*.

7. Full letter printed in Fred Halliday, op. cit.

8. Robert B. Serjeant, 'Yemeni Arabs in Britain', *The Geographical Magazine*, 1944.

9. Humayun Ansar, op. cit.

10. M. S. Seddon, 'Shaykh Abdullah Ali al-Hakimi, the 'Alawi Tariqa and British-Yemenis', Ron Geaves and Theodore Gabriel (eds.), *Sufism in Britain*.

11. Quoted by M. S. Seddon, *The Last of the Lascars: Yemeni Muslims in Britain, 1836–2012*.

12. Ibid.

41

# KNUD HOLMBOE

B. 1902 – D. 1931

DENMARK

Denmark is a small Scandinavian country with a population of just under six million people. Bordering Sweden, Norway and Germany, its history and culture can be traced back to ancient times. Archaeological evidence of human habitation dates back to around 12,000 BC, although it was not until the pre-Roman Iron Age that the first tribal Danes came to this part of the world and established trade links with the Roman provinces. Historians have also found evidence of Celtic cultural influence in ancient Denmark prior to the arrival of the Angles and Saxons (Anglo-Saxons), which led to further racial and cultural assimilation.

Thus, modern Danes trace their ancestry back to those early settlers, including the Vikings who established their presence in the Scandinavian region between the eighth and tenth centuries. To avoid being overwhelmed by the Holy Roman Empire (*Sacrum Imperium Romanum*), Danes converted to Christianity during the mid-tenth century, only for Canute the Great to emerge in the eleventh century and politically unify Denmark, England and Norway. Being Danish by origin, Canute the Great reigned from 1016 to 1035 and left his indelible marks on the history of the country. However, following the Protestant Reformation of the sixteenth century (led by seminal figures like Martin Luther [1483–1546], John Calvin [1509–1564] and John Knox [1513–1572], among others), the Danes embraced Lutheranism in 1536.[1]

Nonetheless, during its early modern history, Denmark experienced considerable politico-economic upheaval and uncertainty until, eventually, it became a constitutional monarchy in June 1849. Industrialisation of the country then helped transform its infrastructure and economy in the second half of the nineteenth century. Despite maintaining neutrality during the Great War, Denmark was quickly invaded by Nazi Germany during the Second World War regardless of having a 10-year non-aggression pact with the Germans. After the war, however, Denmark became a founding member of NATO and, in 1973, it formally joined what is today known as the European Union. In terms of population, around eighty-five per cent consists of ethnic Danes, while the remaining fifteen per cent are of other backgrounds.

Likewise, more than seventy per cent of Danes belong to the Church of Denmark, which is an offshoot of Protestantism rooted in the Lutheran tradition, with Islam being the second largest religion in the country and, as such, Muslims now make-up around five per cent of the population. Historically speaking, it was after the Second World War that Muslims first moved to Denmark, although the majority of them immigrated there after the 1970s.[2] Furthermore, since the 1950s, an increasing number of Danes have been converting to Islam and, needless to say, they now make-up a significant minority within the Danish Muslim community. One of the first Danes to convert to Islam and travel around the Islamic East during the early part of the twentieth century was none other than the brave and indomitable Knud Holmboe, whose short, but remarkable life and career is hardly known in the Muslim world and the West today.

Knud Valdemar Gylding Holmboe, also known as Ali Ahmad el-Gheseiri, was born into a middle-class Danish family of traders and merchants in the city of Horsens, which is located in east Jutland and well-known today for its cultural vibrancy. His father, Jens Christian Gylding Holmboe, was a merchant by trade, and his mother, Signe Adolfine Marie Dryer, ensured her six children received a good upbringing and education during their early years. Though the family nominally belonged to the Church of Denmark, in truth, their life revolved more around their thriving family business, leaving very little time for other activities. Being a manufacturer and supplier of colours and lacquers, Knud's father was a successful businessman who, like his wife, was an amateur musician, and both of them loved to play the piano during their spare time.

Brought up and educated in a family where music was not only practised, but also loved, young Knud may have learnt to play the piano and violin during his early years like Vagn Holmboe (1909–1996), his younger brother. Vagn Holmboe became a violinist at the age of only 14, before enrolling at Copenhagen's Royal Danish Music Conservatory in 1926, and he later went on to become a renowned composer and teacher.[3] However, unlike his younger siblings, Knud became interested in religion, philosophy and journalism during his school days and, soon after completing his primary and secondary education, he began to explore religion and philosophy more closely, whilst actively looking for opportunities to pursue a journalistic career.

He was around 16 when he started contributing short pieces and stories to his local papers. This was his first journalistic experience which enabled him to not only polish his writing skills, but also to become familiar with the fiercely competitive world of journalism. It was also a politically and economically challenging time as the Great War was still raging across Europe. Fought between the Allies (consisting of the British Empire, France and the Russian Empire) on the one hand, and the Central Powers of Germany and Austria-Hungary on the other, this global war lasted more than four years, and close to 40 million people lost their lives, both military and civilian, thus it was one of the most horrific conflicts in human history. As Great Britain and Germany were also two main trading partners of Denmark prior to the outbreak of the war, there is no doubt that the social, political and economic impact of the conflict on Danish society was massive and far-reaching despite its political neutrality.[4]

As a result, fear, insecurity and uncertainty about the future spread across Denmark and indeed, Europe as a whole, leading to widespread disenchantment, loss of faith and hopelessness. It may have been this which prompted Knud to explore religion and philosophy in his personal quest for meaning and purpose in the modern world in the face of unspeakable bloodshed, hatred and destruction. Accordingly, at the age of 20 he converted to Catholicism and moved to France where he joined a monastery of religious monks and nuns in Clairvaux.

Being adventurous, contemplative and inquisitive, Knud may have found life in the monastery to be too repetitive, timid and unexciting for his liking and soon left this religious order. However, his unfavourable experiences at the monastery did not deter him from his personal quest for the truth as he continued his religious and philosophical studies. Thereafter, he read widely and became familiar with different religious beliefs and philosophical schools of thought, both Western and Eastern, and it was perhaps during this period that he first became aware of Islam.

That, in turn, may have prompted him to go to Morocco in 1924 to observe and study the Muslim faith and culture for the first time. His stay in the North African country opened a new window in his religious and cultural horizon; indeed, meeting an elderly Shaykh (Islamic scholar and sage) in his rather old, but spiritually peaceful mosque and Sufi lodge, may have convinced him that the truth he was seeking was nothing other than Islam. In his own words, 'The difference between Islam and all other religions is that other religions say that through faith you may act; Islam says, rather, that through action faith must be born.'[5]

According to another account, Knud first went to Morocco in his capacity as a reporter for *Dagens Nyheder*, which was a Copenhagen-based newspaper, and contributed many articles about the French military campaign against the inhabitants of Rif (Berber *Arif*), a mountainous region located in the north of Morocco. However, upon his return to Denmark, he collected and published the articles in the form of a book titled *Between the Devil and the Deep Sea – a dash by plane to seething Morocco*, in addition to a short anthology of poems. Having observed foreign aggression and brutality against the Muslims of Rif at first-hand 'bore heavily on Holmboe's conscience. Overtaken by a painful crisis of identity and faith, he gave up his writing and sought refuge in a French monastery, with the intention of reading and reflecting on the large questions of history and religion which troubled him. We do not know what he read…But something must have struck a chord, for a year on, we find him emerging from his retreat with his early interest in Islam confirmed.'6

Either way, in 1925, Knud finally embraced Islam at the age of 25. We do not know the exact details of his conversion, but later he explained the reasons for his conversion in the following words: 'First of all, I saw how Islam preached that you must live according to your religion. Other religions only demand faith in fossilized dogmas. Secondly, I consider Islam to be the only religion which will be able to survive our modern times. It is clear and concise, tolerant towards everybody as long as they do not deny God, and it grips you because you soon find out that following it leads you onward.' Again, he explained that he joined Islam because he believed that 'you can be happy if you live according to the teaching of the Prophet Mohammed and the Prophet Isa [Jesus].'7

In other words, Knud embraced Islam because he considered it to be the true religion of Jesus, unlike Christianity, which, in his opinion, was a corrupted version of the original teachings of the Messiah. Likewise, he considered the Prophet of Islam to be the natural successor of Jesus, who not only acknowledged and praised the Messiah but, like the latter, he also proclaimed the absolute Unity and Oneness of God without compromising or diluting the original message of all the previous prophets and messengers, namely Islam.

Soon after embracing Islam, Knud decided to travel to the Islamic East to learn more about Arab and Islamic culture, and, in the process, he toured prominent Muslim countries including Turkey, Syria, Palestine, Iraq and parts of Persia. He visited these countries at a time when much of the Muslim world was still under colonial occupation. Witnessing at first-hand Western meddling and interference in the affairs of the Muslim world must have had a profound impact on Knud, being both European and Muslim.

Upon his return home, he met and married Leonora Borup, who was in her early twenties, and she later bore him a daughter by the name of Aisha (b. 1927), otherwise known as Nette Holmboe. Two years after his Middle Eastern sojourn, he set out again, but this time he decided to tour the Balkans with his wife. His decision to tour the Balkans was mainly because that part of Europe had a large Muslim population since the early Ottoman times, especially in Albania and Bosnia and Herzegovina (formerly known as Yugoslavia).

During his Balkan trip, he witnessed, to his shock and horror, Italian brutality and oppression in Albania. Historically speaking, although Italy and Austria-Hungary played a pivotal role in the creation of Albania as an independent state before the Great War; in 1915, however, Italy invaded the southern parts of Albania, perhaps to prevent an Austro-Hungarian military intervention. And, whilst Italy was forced to withdraw from the Albanian territories in 1920, after Benito Mussolini (1883–1945) of the National

Fascist Party assumed power in Italy in 1922, he renewed their political, economic and military interests in Albania, which contributed to the Italian colonisation of Albania. During his tour of the Balkans, Knud contributed a series of articles on Italian excesses and mistreatment of the Albanian population, thus raising awareness of their plight across Europe but, as expected, this infuriated the Italian Fascists.

After his Balkan tour, Knud returned to Denmark and continued to work as a freelance reporter and editor for local papers. However, not having a permanent job meant that he struggled to make ends meet, not least because he now had a family to maintain, namely his wife and a newly-born daughter. Accordingly, in 1928, while he was in his late twenties, Knud left Denmark and settled in Morocco with his family for nearly two years and became known by his Muslim name of Ali Ahmad el-Gheseiri.

Two years later, his wife decided to return to Denmark with her daughter, whilst Knud prepared to go to Egypt by crossing the Sahara desert. This long, unpredictable and harrowing journey was destined to make him famous in Europe, America and parts of the Muslim world. He set out from Morocco in his battered Chevrolet Model 1929 and, as he travelled across the burning, merciless and sand-dusted Sahara, he discovered new tribes who welcomed him into their communities. He was not only a fluent Arabic speaker and a devout Muslim, but his ability to recite the Glorious Qur'an at the drop of a hat and don traditional Arab gear with relative ease enabled him to win over the locals throughout his journey.

Likewise, Knud was a perceptive observer of people's customs, habits and behaviours. For example, seeing Tarbox, his American co-traveller, pouring salt into a cup of coffee instead of sugar, prompted him to make the following observation:

> This was the reason for our first and, I am happy to say, last quarrel and it shows how deeply rooted the human being is in habits and prejudices, even when mere trifles are concerned. When as Arab eats with his fingers instead of using knife and fork it is barbaric; when a Spaniard eats octopus or a Frenchman snails it is disgusting – though most of us derive great pleasure from swallowing live oysters![8]

After a long journey, fraught with danger and difficulties, Knud eventually reached Libya, and from there he was able to proceed to Egypt. However, during his time in Libya, Knud saw first-hand how the Italian Fascists, led by Mussolini, Pietro Badoglio (1871–1956) and Rodolfo Graziani (1882–1955), among others, perpetrated unspeakable brutality and oppression against the local people. They not only hanged their opponents, mutilated corpses and burnt crops and livestock, but also raped and pillaged whole tribes and villages in their quest for total political subjugation and military victory in Libya. So much so that Graziani was subsequently nicknamed 'the Butcher of Fezzan' by the locals.

By contrast, the brave, but ill-equipped Muslims resisted the might and power of the Fascist military machine under the heroic leadership of Umar al-Mukhtar Muhammad ibn Farhat Bredan (1858–1931), who was a prominent Islamic scholar and teacher in Cyrenaica.[9] He and his followers bravely resisted the Fascists for nearly two decades until Shaykh Umar al-Mukhtar was eventually captured and hanged in 1931 at the age of 73. Needless to say, seeing the horrors that were being perpetrated by the Fascists in Libya at the time prompted Knud to support the Libyan resistance movement, but the Italians soon arrested and deported him. Why? Simply because he was a first-hand witness to their monstrous crimes and genocide. Knud was of course aware of this, as he later wrote, 'In Europe one is only told that the peaceful Italians in Cyrenaica have been attacked by the blood-thirsty Arabs. Only I, who have seen it, know who the barbarians are.'[10]

In Egypt, Knud tried to mobilise public support for the Libyan resistance. However, the British officials responded by arresting him, then they eventually sent him back to Denmark at the behest of the Italian authorities. Being the first – and probably the only European Muslim – to have witnessed such horrific and ghastly crimes and atrocities being committed by the Western colonial powers against the innocent and helpless people of North Africa and the Middle East as a whole, inspired Knud to write a book based on his first-hand knowledge and experience of the Islamic East. He completed and published this travelogue in 1931 under the title of *Orkenen braender* (The Desert on Fire) and, five years later, it was translated into English and published as *Desert Encounter* by Helga Holbek.

Soon after its publication, the book became a bestseller in Europe and America. However, unsurprisingly, the book was immediately banned in Italy by the Fascists who, of course, wanted to suppress any accounts of them committing mass murder and genocide against the Muslims of North Africa, and Libya in particular. It was eventually translated into Italian in 2004 and published there amidst controversy generated by the right-wing opponents of the book.

However, Knud was a gifted writer and traveller who was equally wise, discerning and impartial in his observation and assessment of facts and figures. He robustly defended the Arabs, the Muslims in particular, against the European accusation of being somehow uncivilised and backward, thus providing the justification for Western colonisation and subjugation of the Muslim world.

As expected, he profoundly disagreed with such an ignorant and misguided view of Islam and the Muslim world, arguing that, 'The Oriental differs widely from the European, especially in the way in which the latter has developed during the last generation. The Oriental does seek development and progress, but he seeks it in very different spheres from the European. The Oriental holds that spirit and the development of the spirit is the most important thing. And how does he arrive at the most perfect development of his spirit? By following his religion and its ethical demands, by continually trying to make himself better, more able to grasp beauty in all its ethical and aesthetic forms; by trying to approach that ethical and artistic perfection which is God.'[11]

Likewise, he did not consider all the Italian officials in Libya to be cold, calculated and trigger-happy, although the majority were certainly guilty of committing crimes against humanity. In his own words, 'the Italian colonization of Cyrenaica is such that any European who obtains a glimpse of it must feel ashamed to belong to the white race – for here it is waging a modern war barbarically and ruthlessly – Commandant Diodiece was a rare and redeeming feature, for he possessed that culture which so many think can be replaced by civilization.'[12] Ultimately, however, Knud was keen to promote co-operation, understanding and dialogue between the Muslim world and the West for the benefit of humanity as a whole. He stated, 'I think we ought to try to come to some understanding with the Arabs. Only by friendly co-operation between European civilization and Oriental culture can any good results be obtained.'[13]

Soon after the publication of his travelogue, in May 1931, Knud set out again in the direction of the Islamic East with the intention of performing the annual pilgrimage to Makkah. He travelled via Turkey, Jordan and Syria but, upon his arrival in the Middle East, the Italian secret agents were on his trail, closely monitoring his movements and activities. He was reported to have escaped many attempts on his life during his stay in Amman, Jordan but, undeterred, he set out in the direction of Aqaba, which is today a Jordanian port on the Red Sea, with a view to entering Arabia for the sacred pilgrimage. On his arrival in Haql (a town today located in the north-west of Saudi Arabia near the Gulf of Aqaba), he was brutally attacked and martyred by a group of Bedouins who were reportedly in the pay of the Italian intelligence services; he was only 29 at the time.

In short, Knud was a champion of knowledge, understanding, truth, justice and fair-play in a world that was being ravaged by ignorance, hatred, conflict and warfare. Therefore, his short but inspirational life should serve as a shining example for those who are keen to promote understanding and dialogue between different faiths and cultures – Western and Eastern, Muslim and non-Muslim alike.

Tim Winter, an academic at the University of Cambridge and himself a British convert to Islam, paid Knud Holmboe the following tribute:

Perhaps the most striking of Holmboe's many achievements was his ability to rise above...stereotypes, more powerful in his day even than in ours. He gives us a soberly factual and unadorned account which is always innocent of all prejudice. Considering his loyalties, and the cruelties to which he is a witness, this is an impressive accomplishment...At a time when the barriers are being thrown up everywhere; when the mutual blindness of the two Mediterranean shores seems to threaten us more than ever, voices such as Holmboe's deserve to be heard widely.[14]

Ⓝ

1. Knud J. V. Jespersen, *A History of Denmark*.

2. Jorgen Nielsen (ed.), *Islam in Denmark: The Challenge of Diversity*.

3. Stanley Sadie and John Tyrrell (eds.), *The New Grove Dictionary of Music and Musicians*.

4. Nils Arne Sorensen, 'Denmark' in *International Encyclopedia of the First World War*.

5. Quoted by S. A. Khulusi, *Islam Our Choice*.

6. Tim Winter, 'Introduction' to Knud Holmboe's *Desert Encounter*.

7. Knud Holmboe, *Desert Encounter*.

8. Ibid.

9. Ali Muhammad as-Salabi, *Omar al-Mokhtar: Lion of the Desert*.

10. Knud Holmboe, op. cit.

11. Ibid.

12. Ibid.

13. Ibid.

14. Tim Winter, op. cit.

42

# MEHMED HANDZIC

B. 1906 – D. 1944

BOSNIA HERZEGOVINA

Muslim historians, scholars and thinkers agree that Islamic thought and scholarship has been dominated by the *ulama* (religious scholars) since the early days of Islam. Unsurprisingly, some of the first and foremost scholars of Islam included prominent Companions of the Prophet, such as Abdullah ibn Mas'ud (d. 650), Ali ibn Abi Talib (d. 661), Aishah bint Abi Bakr (d. 678), Abdullah ibn Abbas (d. 687) and Abdullah ibn Umar (d. 693), among others. The early pioneers were then succeeded by generations of classical scholars like Hasan al-Basri (d. 728), Ibn Shihab al-Zuhri (d. 741), Ja'far al-Sadiq (d. 765), Abu Hanifah (d. 767), Malik ibn Anas (d. 795), al-Shafi'i (d. 820) and Muhammad ibn Ismail al-Bukhari (d. 870) – to name but a few – who not only dominated Islamic thought and scholarship, but they also profoundly influenced those who came after them.

Their collective contribution and achievements in the field of Qur'anic exegesis (*tafsir*), Prophetic traditions (*ahadith al-nabawi*), Islamic jurisprudence (*fiqh*) and Prophetic biography (*sirah al-nabawi*), in addition to their unrivalled expertise in classical Arabic, helped to lay the foundation of traditional Islamic sciences that was destined to influence Islamic thought, history, culture and civilisation like never before.

Thereafter, influential medieval Islamic scholars like al-Tabari (838–923), al-Ash'ari (874–936), Ibn Hazm (see chapter 7), Abu Hamid al-Ghazali (1058–1111), Averroes (see chapter 13), al-Shatibi (see chapter 16) and Ibn Taymiyyah (1263–1328), among others, contributed substantially to the development of Islamic thought and scholarship

– and did so, knowing full well that they were standing on the shoulders of giants.[1] The input and accomplishments of prominent modern Islamic scholars and reformers like Shah Waliullah of Delhi (1703–1762), Ibn Abd al-Wahhab (1703–1792), Uthman Dan Fodio (1754–1817), Muhammad Abduh (1849–1905), Muhammad Rashid Rida (1865–1935) and Badiuzzaman Sa'id Nursi (1877–1960) are widely known today.

Unfortunately, the same cannot be said about the lives and legacies of many modern Islamic scholars and thinkers from the Balkans, whose contributions to Islamic thought and scholarship were, in fact, no less valuable and impressive. Hailed as one of Bosnia and Herzegovina's most outstanding Islamic scholars and writers of the modern period, the life and works of Mehmed Handzic has yet to receive the recognition it deserves, both in the Muslim world, as well as the West.

Hajji Mehmed efendi Handzic, also known as Shaykh Muhammad Handzic al-Bosnawi, was born into a wealthy and prominent Muslim family in Sarajevo (the capital of present-day Bosnia and Herzegovina), whose members traced their ancestry back to the first Muslims who settled there during the Ottoman period. His parents were devout Muslims who ensured their son received a traditional education and upbringing, thus the youngster was enrolled at a local *maktab* (Qur'an school) where he studied Arabic and learnt to recite the Qur'an with considerable fluency.

He was a bright student who was equally dedicated to his studies. As a result, he was able to successfully complete his primary education before joining an elite high school (Shari'ah gymnasium) in Sarajevo. Here, he studied Arabic grammar, syntax and literature, as well as aspects of Islamic theology, Qur'anic exegesis, Prophetic traditions and Islamic jurisprudence, in addition to history, geography, logic, religious poetry and related subjects. Funded by the government and attended mainly by children from prominent and wealthy Bosnian Muslim families, the Shari'ah gymnasiums – like the Shari'ah judges' schools – were highly respected institutions of further education which, at the time, provided a varied, but also rigorous education in both the traditional and modern subjects over a period of eight years.[2]

Young Mehmed studied at the Shari'ah gymnasium in Sarajevo and, being a talented student, he excelled in his studies much to the delight of his family and teachers alike. He grew up and pursued his education at a time when Bosnia was passing through considerable social, political and economic change and transformation.

According to the historian Xavier Bougarel, although the Austro-Hungarian authorities (1878–1918) pursued the same socio-economic policies in Bosnia as they had originally inherited from the Ottomans, this state of affairs changed during the time of the Kingdom of Yugoslavia (1918–1939) with the introduction of agrarian reforms in 1920, thus 'hastening the economic decline of Muslim *agas* and *begs* (landowners), and transforming the relationship between peasants, local political elite and the state bureaucracy. Party politics, which had started to develop in the last years of the Austro-Hungarian period, resumed in the 1920s…Finally, educational and cultural institutions continued to develop, and ethno-religious identities also continued to evolve, as illustrated by the activities of Muslim cultural societies such as *Gajret* ("Effort", founded in 1903 and showing an increasingly "pro-Serbian" orientation) and *Narodna uzdanica* ("Popular Hope", founded in 1924 with a "pro-Croatian" orientation).[3]

During this period of considerable social, political and economic change across Bosnia, Mehmed pursued his higher secondary education in Sarajevo's Shari'ah gymnasium and, after almost eight years of dedication and hard work, he passed his final examination with flying colours; he was only 20 at the time. Although his mother-tongue was Bosnian and his overall academic performance was above average, his knowledge and understanding of Arabic was particularly impressive for a high school graduate who could not only read, but could also analyse Arabic works with relative ease. It may have been this which prompted Mehmed to move to Cairo in 1926 and enrol at the prestigious al-Azhar University to master Arabic and pursue higher Islamic education, as he hoped to secure a senior teaching or administrative post on his return home to Bosnia.

Another reason for wishing to pursue higher education may have been government legislation which, at the time, stipulated that all teachers and lecturers at elite Islamic high schools and seminaries must be graduates of recognised educational institutions (such as elite high schools) in Yugoslavia, in addition to having obtained an undergraduate or postgraduate qualification from a reputable university. According to the Bosnian scholar and historian Enes Karic,

> During this period both Istanbul and Vienna became less important for the Bosniaks as university centres. From now on a relatively large number of Bosnian Muslims would go to Cairo to study at the famous al Azhar Islamic university to acquire their university degree. Many graduates of the Gazi Husrev Bey *madrasa*, the Shari'ah judges' school and the Shari'ah gymnasium went to Cairo and gained their degrees from al Azhar. With their return to Bosnia, Islamic thought in our country gained greatly from the modernist influence of the reformist al Manar school founded by Muhammad Abduh.[4]

Mehmed stayed in Cairo for four years and, during this period, he became proficient in not only Arabic language and literature, but also in traditional Islamic sciences. Again, he proved to be a diligent and dedicated student at al-Azhar, whose love of learning endeared him to his fellow students and teachers alike. He was particularly attracted to Prophetic traditions (*hadith*), and Islamic ethics (*adab*) and morality (*akhlaq*), so much so that he contributed extensive and insightful notes and commentaries to two classical Islamic books during his time at al-Azhar, namely *Hayat al-Anbiya* (The Lives of the Prophets) by Abu Bakr Ahmad ibn Husayn al-Bayhaqi (994–1066) and *al-Kalim al-Tayyib min Adhkar al-Nabiyy* (The Goodly Word from the Supplications of the Prophet) by Abd al-Halim ibn Taymiyyah. This not only earned him plaudits from his teachers, but one of his professors even went out of his way to publish them in Cairo in 1930. Widely respected for his considerable learning and personal piety, Mehmed was now addressed by his peers and teachers as *al-Alim al-Fadil* (honourable scholar) and *al-Ustad al-Shaykh* (teacher and professor), which, of course, was no mean achievement for someone in his mid-twenties.

In addition to pursuing his advanced Islamic education at al-Azhar during his four-year stay in Cairo, Mehmed also came in contact with three powerful movements for change and reformation in the Islamic world. The first group consisted of secularists who wanted the Muslim world to make progress and development, just like the Western world, and the only way this could be achieved, they felt, was by marginalising the role of religion in society through the gradual secularisation of the public sphere. This, in turn, was to be achieved by promoting philosophical rationalism and scientific enlightenment across the Muslim world.

The second group, on the other hand, consisted of Muslim modernists who were inspired by the message of Muhammad Abduh and his prominent disciples. Unlike the secularists, the modernists were committed Muslims who not only wanted to improve and increase the role of Islam in the modern world by harmonising reason (*aql*) with revelation (*wahy*), they also wanted to transform Muslim culture and society through the adoption of democracy, freedom, modern science and technology, not to mention educational and intellectual progress based on Islamic values and principles. In other words, the modernists considered the tension between Islamic and modern Western values to be a historical accident rather than a civilisational conflict – one that could be repaired through political liberalisation, economic reorganisation and educational reformation.[5]

By contrast, the Islamic revivalists were led by Hasan al-Banna (1906–1949) and his Muslim Brotherhood (*Jami'yat al-Ikhwan al-Muslimun*), which he founded in 1928. Being religiously conservative, but equally keen to improve their societies, the revivalists advocated the need for social, political and economic transformation of Muslim countries, but they wanted to achieve this without undermining the existing religious, ethical, moral and spiritual fabric of Muslim cultures and societies. Needless to say, Mehmed observed and closely studied the conflicting views and arguments that were, at the time, being advanced by the protagonists of these intellectual trends with considerable interest and eagerness. As expected, after completing his higher education in Cairo, he returned home to Bosnia in 1930 and embarked on his short, but remarkably productive career as a teacher, scholar, reformer and writer.

Although he was only 24 at the time, Mehmed started his teaching career at the famous Gazi Husrev Bey Madrasah in Sarajevo where he taught Arabic, aspects of Qur'anic exegesis and Prophetic traditions, in addition to Islamic jurisprudence, theology and early Islamic history. Needless to say, his extensive knowledge of Arabic literature and

Islamic sciences (especially Hadith literature) not only impressed his students, but the other teachers at the seminary considered him to be a gifted scholar of Islam.

Regarded as a prominent member of the circle of traditional *ulama* (religious scholars), during this period, Mehmed found himself drawn into the main religious debates and discussions that were taking place in Bosnian society. The religious, cultural and intellectual activities of Edhem Mulabdic (1862–1954), Osman Nuri Hadzic (1869–1937), Safvet-Beg Basagic (1870–1934) and Musa Cazim Catic (1878–1915), among others, were – one way or another –influenced by the modernist discourse of nineteenth century Muslim scholars and reformers like Muhammad Abduh, Ismail Bey Gaspirali (see chapter 26), Sa'id Halim Pasha (1865–1921) and Mehmed Akif Ersoy (1873–1936). However, during the inter-war period, the debates about the role of Islam in Bosnia had shifted from generic issues (such as the 'backwardness' of the Muslim community) to the specifics, namely the role of Muslim women in society and the adoption of Western-style attire.[6] As expected, Mehmed soon became embroiled in these debates and discussions.

As a conservative *alim*, he not only bitterly opposed the secularists (such as Edhem Bulbulovic and Dzevad-Beg Sulejmanpasic) who wanted to privatise religion by gradually removing it from the public sphere, he also profoundly disagreed with the modernists (like Mehmed Dzemaludin Causevic and Fehim Spaho) who advocated the need for fresh interpretation of Islamic law to address burning issues, such as dress-code for Muslim women and the administration of *awqaf* (religious endowments). By the same token, he was critical of the religious literalism of a section of Bosnian *ulama* who, he felt, were completely out of touch with reality.

In other words, he pursued a traditional approach to the interpretation of the fundamental scriptures of Islam whilst, at the same time, being a realist in the application of Islamic laws and procedures. He therefore condemned both religious fatalism and negation of faith, and, instead, became an influential advocate of moderate traditionalism in his beloved Bosnia. In his own words, 'We condemn both stupidity and obscurity. We call on Muslims to be truly *ulu'l-albab*, people of reason. In this year's assembly there were references to the fact that some unenlightened types had published some stupid pamphlets and flyers, based on some kind of dream of some sort of graveyard keepers – in short, on lies, acceptable neither to Islam nor to common sense. Every Muslim and every reasonable man condemn such idiocies.'[7]

During his time as a teacher at Gazi Husrev Bey Madrasah, Mehmed not only trained hundreds of young scholars, but he also co-founded an influential periodical titled *El-Hidaje*, which he edited from August 1937 to July 1944. The purpose of this journal was to revive Islamic teachings, values and morality in Bosnia on the one hand, and also improve the social, economic and educational condition of the Muslim community on the other. According to Enes Karic, this periodical – like its versatile and gifted editor – 'made a powerful appearance, shinning like a bright meteorite in the

Bosnian skies' before it folded in February 1945, after dozens of issues were published and disseminated in Bosnia and other parts of the Balkans.[8]

However, after teaching for more than seven years at the Gazi Husrev Bey, Mehmed eventually moved to the *Visa Islamska Serijatsko-Teoloska Skola* (Higher Islamic Shari'ah Theological Faculty) in Sarajevo, where he taught advanced classes in Arabic literature and philology, Qur'anic exegesis, Prophetic traditions and Islamic ethics. He was thoroughly familiar with the writings and thought of prominent classical scholars and writers like Abu Muhammad al-Qasim ibn Ali al-Hariri (1054–1122), Abu Hafs Umar ibn Muhammad al-Nasafi (1067–1142), Abu Abdullah Muhammad ibn Sa'id al-Busiri al-Shadhili (1211–1294), Abd al-Haqq ibn Ghalib, better known as Ibn Atiyyah (1088–1150), and Taqi al-Din Muhammad ibn Ali, also known as Imam Birgivi (1522–1573), in addition to many influential modern Islamic scholars and reformers including Sayyid Mahmud ibn Abdullah al-Alusi (1802–1854), Muhammad Abduh and Muhammad Rashid Rida.

Although Mehmed was well-versed in the different branches of traditional Islamic sciences, he particularly excelled as a *Muhaddith* (master of Hadith literature), *Mufassir* (commentator of the Qur'an) and *Faqih* (Islamic jurist). He was not only thoroughly familiar with the *sahih sittah* (six canonical anthologies of Prophetic traditions compiled by al-Bukhari, Muslim, Abu Dawud, al-Tirmidhi, al-Nasa'i and Ibn Majah), but was equally learned in the Hadith writings and scholarship of Abu Hanifah (699–767), Malik ibn Anas (711–795), al-Shafi'i (767–820), Ahmad ibn Hanbal (780–855), Abd al-Razzaq al-San'ani (744–802), al-Hakim al-Nisaburi (933–1012), Ibn al-Salah (1181–1245), al-Nawawi (1233–1277) and Ibn Hajar al-Asqalani (1372–1449), not to mention al-Bayhaqi, al-Daraqutni (918–995), al-Tabarani (873–918) and Ibn Hibban (883–965), among others.

Likewise, in the field of *tafsir*, he made extensive use of the commentaries of al-Jassas (d. 942), al-Zamakhshari (1070–1143), Abu Bakr ibn al-Arabi (1076–1148), al-Qurtubi (1214–1273) and al-Baydawi (d. 1286). Furthermore, his knowledge and understanding of *fiqh* was impressive, and despite being an adherent of the *madhhab* of Imam Abu Hanifah, he was thoroughly familiar with the views of Imams Malik, Shafi'i and Ahmad ibn Hanbal.

In short, he became intimately acquainted with classical and modern Islamic literature which, in turn, enabled him to write scores of books and hundreds of articles on all aspects of Islam, numbering more than 350 items in total. Although he was fluent in several languages, he wrote most of his works in Arabic and Bosnian. Most of his writings have since been collected and published in six hefty volumes covering a wide range of subjects, including Arabic language and literature, history and biographies of Muslim luminaries of Bosnia, Qur'anic topics and aspects of Hadith literature, Islamic law and jurisprudence, and socio-cultural issues facing the Muslims of Bosnia at the time.

However, some of his notable literary contributions include *Obnavljanje Islama* (The Renewal of Islam), *Rad Bosanskohercegovackih Muslimana na Knjizevnom Polju* (Literature of the Muslims of Bosnia-Herzegovina), *Uvod u Tefsirsku i Hadisku Nauku* (Introduction to Tafsir and Hadith Sciences), *Predavanje iz Usuli-Fikha* (Lectures on Islamic Jurisprudence), *Ilmul-Kelam* (Islamic Theology) and *Opci Pogled na Razvoj Islamskih Sekta* (Short History of the Development of Muslim Sects), in addition to translations of several treatises from Arabic and Turkish into Bosnian.

What were the aims and objectives of his social and literary activities? Actually, he was not interested in reconciling Islam and modernity, nor did he intend to remove misunderstanding and misconceptions between the Islamic world and the West; on the contrary, his real mission in life was to call the Bosnian Muslims back to pristine, unadulterated Islam. In his own words, 'Unlike other faiths, in the opinion of all sincere friends of Islam, revival in Islam cannot mean additions and changes, since Islam is perfect and complete. The way to revival is only to return to the pure faith and its pristine forms, setting aside all accretions and false understanding.'[9]

Evidently, his rigid traditionalism was tempered by a big dose of religious pragmatism which, for example, enabled him to praise and openly acknowledge the contribution of the Sufis of Bosnia and Herzegovina. To this end, he also actively campaigned to preserve and protect the interests and welfare of the Bosnian Muslims from a highly volatile and unpredictable geo-political situation in the Balkans at the time, working under the banner of the Committee of National Salvation – established on 26 August 1942 – of which he was an influential member.[10]

On a more personal level, Mehmed was a pious and frugal individual who was deeply spiritually-inclined, but certainly not an adherent of a traditional Sufi Order. Likewise, he proudly donned religious dress – befitting as it did a traditional Islamic scholar – and, at the same time, maintained an open, welcoming and tolerant attitude towards people of other faiths and cultures. He devoted all his time, efforts and energy to Islamic research, writing and revivalist activities, and died at the young age of only 38; he was buried in his native Sarajevo where a street was later named after him as a tribute to his memory. As it happened, he had accomplished more during his short career than most people achieve in a whole lifetime.

Enes Karic, who is himself a leading contemporary Bosnian Islamic scholar, paid him this glowing tribute:

The writings of Mehmed Handzic, if considered from a broad perspective without subjugation to the ephemeral details contained in them, confront the Muslims of this part of the world with their faith, and even confronts the faith of Islam with the Muslims of his time. Handzic was an *ulama* and intellectual personality who was neither an Islamic radical, nor a revolutionary, nor a reactionary. With fine words and wise advice, edifying texts and *wa'z*, he appealed to faith…In saying that Handzic was a moderate traditionalist that is not to say that he displayed his traditionalism in a geometrically precise and mathematically determined way. This is not the case at all. To say that he was a moderate traditionalist is to say that with him the moderate approach to Islamic tradition prevailed.[11]

1. William M. Watt, *The Formative Period of Islamic Thought*.

2. Enes Karic, *Contributions to Twentieth Century Islamic Thought in Bosnia and Herzegovina*, vol. 1.

3. Xavier Bougarel, 'Farewell to the Ottoman Legacy? Islamic Reformism and Revivalism in Inter-War Bosnia-Herzegovina', Nathalie Clayer and Eric Germain (eds.), *Islam in Inter-War Europe*.

4. Enes Karic, op. cit.

5. Charles Kurzman, *Modernist Islam, 1840–1940*.

6. Xavier Bougarel, op. cit.

7. Quoted by Enes Karic, op. cit.

8. Enes Karic, op. cit.

9. Mehmed Handzic quoted by Enes Karic, op. cit.

10. Hazim Fazli, 'Modern Muslim Thought in the Balkans: The Writings of Mehmed ef. Handzic in the El-Hidaje Periodical in the Context of Discrimination and Genocide', *Journal of Muslim Minority Affairs*, vol. 35, no. 3.

11. Enes Karic, op. cit.

# 43

# MARTIN LINGS

B. 1909 – D. 2005

UNITED KINGDOM

The period between the seventeenth and eighteenth century is generally considered to be the 'Age of Reason' or 'Enlightenment' in Europe, when a group of influential philosophers, scientists and thinkers formulated a new worldview based on the primacy of human reason. That worldview represented the revolt of reason against revelation, matter against the spirit and empiricism against intuition. Culturally speaking, it signified the triumph of man against the forces of nature, man being the ultimate arbiter of right and wrong, whilst nature being the object to be mastered and subjugated for his sole benefit and utility.

Such a materialistic conception of man and nature became popular in Europe at a time when absolute monarchies were in decline, coupled with the marginalisation of the Church, and modern secular political ideologies gradually became influential in the Western World, especially in Europe and America. The transition from 'tradition' to 'modernity', and from 'religion' to 'secularism' was expected, according to the proponents of Enlightenment, to be the beginning of a new chapter in human history when the forces of 'progress' and 'development' would finally consign poverty, squalor and ignorance to history.

As it happened, modernity's promise of progress soon banished into thin air as the Great War broke out in Europe during the early part of the twentieth century, wherein nearly 40 million people perished within a period of just four years. Written and published during the war, in his *Der Untergang des Abendiandes* (The Decline of the West), Oswald Spengler (1880–1936), the renowned German historian and philosopher, predicted the inevitable decline of the West in the face of growing pessimism across Europe at the time.[1] He depicted modern man to be a proud but tragic figure who, in his attempts to master and subdue, turned out to be the biggest of losers. As expected, modernity's false promise of progress drove many young but thoughtful Europeans to look to the East for answers to humanity's quest for meaning and purpose in the modern world. Martin Lings was one such prominent Muslim scholar, metaphysician and writer.

Martin Lings, later known also as Abu Bakr Siraj al-Din, was born in Burnage, located on the outskirts of the northern English city of Manchester, into a Protestant family. As his father worked in America at the time, he spent his early years there and received a thorough elementary education, not only in literature, mathematics, science and history, but also in aspects of Christianity. After completing his early education in America, he returned home to England where his family soon enrolled him at Clifton College, which was a private boarding school based in the city of Bristol, located in the south-west of England. He thrived at Clifton College and was subsequently appointed as head boy.

Although Clifton was renowned at the time for its strength in science and mathematics, with a large number of its students going on to pursue engineering, Lings preferred English literature and poetry over other subjects. He participated in the formal religious activities at the school but, at the same time, he became increasingly detached from Christianity because it did not satisfy his personal quest for meaning and purpose in life. If modernity led to confusion and uncertainty, he felt that true faith must always engender stability and spiritual certainty. His longing for the spiritual past, as opposed to the secular present, was noticeable from an early age. In his own words, 'From my childhood I had seen that something was very wrong with the world and I was conscious of a nostalgia for past times. What struck me above all was the extreme ugliness of the modern civilization. Why had I not been born into an earlier age?'[2]

Perhaps it was his disillusionment with the spiritual crisis of the modern world that prompted Lings to pursue language and literature rather than science and engineering. Another explanation could be that he liked humanities more than physical sciences because the former still retained a sense of the sacred, unlike modern science and technology, which were the products of the 'Age of Reason'. Either way, after completing his secondary education at Clifton, he was offered a place at Magdalen College, Oxford to study English literature; he was in his early twenties at the time. At Oxford, he thrived under the tutelage of C. S. Lewis (1898–1963), who was a notable British academic, novelist and literary figure at the time. During this period, Lings experienced considerable spiritual challenges and difficulties.

As a result, he not only abandoned Christianity, much to the dismay of C. S. Lewis, his teacher and associate, but also 'had altogether given up any form of worship except individual prayer. But man is essentially, by his very nature, religious, and if he ceases to follow the religion he was brought up in, he will be likely to make a creed of something else. Looking back, I see now that I made for myself a "religion" of beauty, centred on nature and art.'³ At the same time, he successfully completed his Bachelors and Masters degrees in English literature in 1932 and 1937, respectively, specialising in the life and works of William Shakespeare (1564–1616).

Whilst at Oxford, Lings had discovered the writings of Rene Jean-Marie Joseph Guenon (see chapter 38), a French metaphysician and prolific writer, who had converted to Islam in 1912 and took the Muslim name of Abd al-Wahid Yahya al-Shadhili. Finding Guenon's writings represented a major turning point in his life, not least because he had already rejected Christianity's claim to be the only true path to God, but Guenon's writings confirmed to him that 'the great religions of the world, all of them equally Heaven-sent in accordance with the various needs of different sectors of humanity, can be graphically represented by the points on the circumference of a circle, each point being connected with the centre, that is, with God, by the radius.'⁴

The idea that all revealed religions were true at an esoteric level, notwithstanding their exoteric differences, instantly made sense to Lings. He must have read Guenon's books and articles in original French as his works were not translated into English until after 1945. In fact, Lings may have first read Guenon's articles in the *Etudes Traditionnelles*, a journal that was devoted to the study of metaphysics, of which he was the editor and principal contributor.⁵

During this period, Lings embraced Catholicism with a view to leading a life of prayer, solitude and meditation. He not only attended the Mass every morning and Vespers in the evening, Guenon's *L'Homme et son Devenir selon le Vedanta* (1925) also inspired him to learn Sanskrit with the intention of converting to Hinduism. In due course, he learned that a spiritual circle had recently been formed in Basle, Switzerland by a group of European Sufis who were inspired by the message of Shaykh Ahmad al-Alawi al-Shadhili of Algeria (1869–1934).

At a time when he was poised to make Christianity or Hinduism his spiritual home, Lings found himself drawn into Islam instead, thanks to al-Alawi's Swiss disciple, Isa Nur al-Din Ahmad (Frithjof Schuon), and the latter's group of around sixteen followers. Accordingly, he went to Basle and formally became a Muslim. However, according to another account, Lings actually came into contact with a group of French Muslims of North African origin in around 1937–1938, and he was very impressed by them. In his own words,

> In all my life I had never been so deeply impressed as I was by these men. They patiently answered all my questions but made not the slightest attempt to convert me to Islam; and it was always with the very greatest reverence that they spoke of Jesus Christ and of his mother, the Blessed Virgin Mary. I soon made up my mind, and they received me into Islam, gave me the name which is now mine,

and taught me the ablutions and the prayers and the other basic elements of the religion.[6]

Lings became a Muslim at the age of 29 and took the Muslim name of Abu Bakr Siraj al-Din. During this period, he stayed in Poland for a year and taught English there before being appointed a lecturer in Anglo-Saxon and Middle English at the University of Kaunas, located in south-central Lithuania, and continued to teach in this capacity until 1939. A year later, he went to Egypt to see a friend and it was in fact, on this occasion, that he met Guenon for the first time.[7] The latter had not only embraced Islam and moved to Cairo in 1930, he also led an entirely Islamic life for the rest of his living years and became known as Shaykh Abd al-Wahid Yahya.

During his stay in Cairo, Lings became closely associated with Guenon, and, at the same time, he taught English literature at the city's Fuad I University, which subsequently became known as the University of Cairo. As a Shakespearean scholar, the university authorities requested him to lecture on the life and works of the famous English bard, which he undertook much to the delight of his students and fellow teachers, in addition to studying and acquiring considerable fluency in Arabic himself.

Four years later, he married his childhood sweetheart, Lesley Smalley, who converted to Islam and took the Muslim name of Sayyida Rabi'a, and the couple soon settled in a traditional village on the outskirts of Cairo. In 1948, both husband and wife went on to perform the annual pilgrimage to Makkah, which was financed by his parents. However, in 1951, Guenon died at the age of 64 and, a year later, the Egyptian Revolution (also known as the 23 July Revolution) broke out. This marked the end of constitutional monarchy in Egypt and the creation of a secular republic under the leadership of the Free Officers Movement led by Muhammad Naguib (1901–1984) and Jamal Abd al-Nasir (1918–1970), thus formally ending British occupation of Egypt. During the ensuing chaos and confusion, many British residents were forced to leave the country and return home due to growing anti-British feelings and sentiments. Likewise, Lings and his wife were forced to return to London penniless where, as expected, he experienced considerable personal and financial difficulties.

Lings decided to resume his studies and, as a result, he successfully completed a degree in Arabic at the School of Oriental and African Studies, University of London. That, in turn, enabled him to secure the post of Keeper of Arabic Manuscripts and Printed Books at the British Museum in 1955. He combined his day job with doctoral research at the University of London on the life and works of Shaykh Ahmad al-Alawi, whose Sufi teachings had not only inspired Guenon and Schuon, but through the latter, Lings himself.

After extensive studying and research, Lings eventually completed his thesis in 1959, for which the University of London awarded him a doctorate in Islamic Studies. Two years later, it was published as a book under the title of *A Moslem Saint of the Twentieth Century* by George Allen and Unwin in 1961 (it was later reprinted as *A Sufi Saint of the Twentieth Century: Shaikh Ahmad al-Alawi, his spiritual heritage and legacy* by Islamic Text Society in 1993). Soon after its publication, this work earned Lings considerable academic acclaim. It was hailed as being 'masterly' and an 'original' contribution by Arthur J. Arberry (b. 1905 – d. 1969), who was a renowned British Arabist and translator of the Qur'an into English. It was not only a biographical study of an influential North African Sufi but, arguably, one of the most readable and equally insightful introductions to *ilm al-tasawwuf* (Islamic spirituality) to have been written in English at the time. This prompted the editors of the celebrated *Encyclopaedia of Islam* to request Lings to write an entry on the life and works of al-Alawi for inclusion in the prestigious publication, under the title of 'Ibn Aliwah', which he completed in due course.

Lings continued to work at the British Library as Keeper of Oriental Books and Manuscripts until his retirement in 1973; he was 64 at the time. During his decades of service, Lings had the opportunity to read some rare Arabic manuscripts and books, enabling him to acquire an in-depth knowledge and understanding of Islamic thought, culture and history. Among the European converts to Islam during the twentieth century, he was arguably the most knowledgeable and accomplished scholar of Islam, having authored more than twenty books on the Qur'an, the Prophet of Islam, Sufism, Islamic poetry and traditional thought. Some of his notable works include *The Book of Certainty: The Sufi Doctrine of Faith, Vision and Gnosis* (1952), *Shakespeare in the Light of Sacred Art* (1966), *What is Sufism?* (1975), *The Qur'anic Art of Calligraphy and Illumination* (1976), *Muhammad: His Life Based on the Earliest Sources* (1983), *A Return to the Spirit* (2005), and, *Enduring Utterance: Collected Lectures (1993–2001)*, in addition to a biography of Shaykh Ahmad al-Alawi.

As is evident from his writings, Lings' greatest intellectual debt was to Schuon. Moreover, throughout the latter's life, Lings remained a spiritual disciple, or *murid*, of Schuon, and fulfilled the role of Schuon's deputy, or *muqaddam*, for the Sufi order in London (which operated in secrecy). Lings maintained a significant connection throughout the controversies which beset Schuon (including his late-life involvement in primordialism), although Lings was arguably still a more Islamically-inclined perennialist.[*]

His first book, *The Book of Certainty*, was originally written in Arabic and was subsequently translated by the author himself into English and thereafter published in 1952. This is a small, but insightful treatise on the fundamentals of Islamic spirituality based on his first-hand knowledge and understanding of the original Arabic sources

---

[*]  See Mark Sedgwick, *Against the Modern World: Traditionalism and the Secret Intellectual History of the Twentieth Century*, (New York: Oxford University Press, 2004).

including the Qur'an. By comparison, his book on the secrets of Shakespeare was a unique contribution. In his foreword to this book, His Royal Highness The Prince of Wales, a long-time admirer of Lings, wrote, 'It is a book which I found hard to put down as it is clearly written from an intimate, personal awareness of the meaning of the symbols which Shakespeare uses to describe the inner drama of the journey of the soul contained, as it is, within the outer earthly drama of the plays.'[8] This book has since been reprinted several times under different titles, both in the United Kingdom and America.

However, it was his life of Prophet Muhammad (peace be on him) which earned Lings international recognition and awards from several Muslim countries, including from the presidents of Egypt and Pakistan. It was also declared to be the best biography of the Prophet written in English at a national *Sirah* conference held in Islamabad in 1983. Although based on Ibn Hisham's recension of Ibn Ishaq's *Sirat Rasul Allah*, Lings made extensive use of other original Arabic sources (such as Ibn Sa'd's [784–845] *Kitab al-Tabaqat al-Kubra* and Waqidi's [745–822] *Kitab al-Maghazi*, in addition to al-Bukhari, Muslim, Abu Dawud and other anthologies of Prophetic traditions). He also had access to reputable classical historical works of al-Azraqi, al-Tabari and as-Suhayli, among others. Despite its linguistic beauty and eloquence, his biography of the Prophet was not free from factual errors but, to his credit, he continued to improve and enhance it in the face of stinging criticism from a small number of conservative Muslim scholars and activists.[9]

Like his earlier work, *The Book of Certainty*, Lings' *What is Sufism?* was a short but incisive introduction to *tasawwuf,* aimed primarily at his Western audience. Based on his interpretation of Qur'anic verses, Prophetic traditions and classical Sufi sources, in this treatise, Lings attempted to introduce his readers to the spiritual dimension of Islam, which he felt had been largely misunderstood, if not, misrepresented by the Orientalists. In his own words, 'The title of this book is a question; and that question, as far as the Western world is concerned, has been given some dubious and suspect answers in recent years. Moreover the rapidly expanding interest in Sufism increases still further the need for a reliable introductory book – introductory in the sense that it requires no special knowledge, and reliable in that it is not written any more simply than truth will allow.'[10] This work was reviewed widely and has since been reprinted many times.

Lings was actively involved in the World of Islam Festival which took place in London in 1976, and it was on this occasion that his *The Qur'anic Art of Calligraphy and Illumination* was published as part of the Festival's illustrated series of books, covering aspects of Muslim history, culture and heritage. Whilst Muslim contribution to architecture has received considerable attention from scholars, Muslim and non-Muslim alike; in this invaluable book, the author highlights Islamic contributions to calligraphic art which, he argues, has remained unknown and inaccessible for too long. Consisting of more than 100 coloured plates of stunning Qur'anic calligraphy, the author chose the samples from libraries and museums in the Muslim world and the West, including from Cairo, Istanbul, Tehran and the British Library.

By comparison, Lings' *A Return to the Spirit* (2005) and *Enduring Utterance: Collected Lectures (1993–2001)* were published posthumously. The former consists of some of his last essays and articles, in addition to scores of tributes written by many of his friends and admirers from around the world, while the latter is a collection of lectures on metaphysics, Perennialism, Islam, Sufism, Qur'an and English literature. In his *Enduring Utterances* – edited and introduced by Trevor Banyard – Lings attempted to answer a number of pertinent and equally challenging questions, namely: Is Islam a tolerant faith? What is the meaning and purpose of Divine guidance? What is our ultimate fate and destiny? How do we explain the presence of evil and injustice? What is the value of beauty and art? And, what is spirituality and gnosis, and are they relevant in an increasingly materialistic age?

For example, in answering the question: 'what is Islam?', Lings stated that it was nothing but 'submission to God' based on the teachings of the Qur'an and the Prophet, adding that 'One of the basic themes of Islam is that one must not take anything for granted; one's hearing, one's sight, one's speech are things for which one must be profoundly thankful, whereas these things man has come to take for granted. And this is one aspect of the primordiality of Islam. As the last religion, Islam claims to be the primordial religion, and this wonderment recalls the wonderment of the first men who were created on Earth and who took nothing for granted, and who saw the marvels of creation and marvelled at them spontaneously.'[11]

Again, according to Lings, 'it is a characteristic of Islam that you will find a tremendous veneration for all the Prophets, and above all, for the Messengers. In Christianity one does not find that, and one does not find that in Judaism, because there is not so much mention of the Prophets; but in Islam one finds a very great veneration and love for Prophets such as Aaron, for example – who means practically nothing to the average Christian – Joseph, David, Solomon. David and Solomon are counted as Prophets in Islam; in Judaism they are kings of Israel, they are not counted as Prophets. And of course Zachariah, John the Baptist – they are among the Prophets who are venerated in Islam.'[12]

Likewise, Lings considered modern notions of 'progress' and 'advancement' to be anything but progression because 'the passage of time always produces the contrary of progress. The Prophet said, for example, No time cometh upon you but is followed by a worse…There is a verse in the Qur'an referring to certain people, of which the meaning is: A long time passed over them, so that their hearts were hardened, meaning that the inevitable result of the passage of time is the hardening of hearts.'[13] The cure for such hearts, according to Lings, is the enduring message of peace, wisdom and spirituality in Islam, which provides nourishment for the body (material) and the heart (spiritual) alike. Like Rene Guenon (see chapter 38), Frithjof Schuon and Titus

(Ibrahim Izz al-Din) Burckhardt, Lings was an astute and uncompromising critic of secularism and modern Western civilisation. He wrote and published a number of books on the topic, including *Ancient Beliefs and Modern Superstitions* (1964) and *The Eleventh Hour: The Spiritual Crisis of the Modern World in the Light of Tradition and Prophecy* (1989).

In addition to the above, Lings was a notable poet who published several volumes of poetry, such as *The Elements and Other Poems* (1967), *The Heralds and Other Poems* (1970), both of which were subsequently published as *Collected Poems: Revised and Augmented* (2002) and *Sufi Poems: A Medieval Anthology* (2004), which he collected and translated from Arabic. His poetry reflected his love of nature, spirituality and the beauty of God's creation, among other things. He contributed scores of articles on Sufism and Sufi poetry to a number of prestigious publications, including *Encyclopaedia Britannica* and *New Cambridge History of Arabic Literature*. He was also a regular contributor to several journals including *Studies in Comparative Religion* and *The Islamic Quarterly*.

He was not only intimately acquainted with the Qur'an, Prophetic traditions and Islamic jurisprudence, but he also lived by the legal dictates of his faith and its teachings until his death. Although his works betrayed his firm perennialist tendencies, Lings' profound understanding and awareness of the spiritual challenges and difficulties which face humanity deserves more attention in an increasingly materialistic and nihilistic age. He travelled extensively and delivered numerous lectures on Islamic and spiritual topics. On a personal level, Lings was a pious, frugal and studious individual who deliberately avoided publicity and only rarely did he attend public events. He was very fond of his garden which he cultivated with great love and affection.[14]

He died at the age of 96 and was laid to rest in his beloved garden in Westerham, Kent. His wife, Sayyida Rabi'a, survived her husband by another 13 years before she passed away in 2013. Though the Lings had no children of their own, they had many friends and admirers in the Muslim world and the West.

Ⓝ

1.  Oswald Spengler, *The Decline of the West*, vol. 1.

2.  Martin Lings, *A Return to the Spirit: Questions and Answers*.

3.  Ibid.

4.  Ibid.

5. John Herlihy (ed.), *The Essential Rene Guenon: Metaphysics, Tradition, and the Crisis of Modernity*.

6. See 'Profile: Alhaj Dr Abu Bakr Siraj ad-Din', *Muslim News International*, vol. 1, no. 8.

7. Martin Lings, *Enduring Utterance: Collected Lectures (1993–2001)*.

8. 'Foreword' to Martin Lings, *The Secret of Shakespeare*.

9. See 'Letters against Martin Lings' Biography of the Prophet', published by Jam'iat Ihya Minhaj al-Sunnah, 1990; and G. F. Haddad, 'A Critical Reading of Lings' *Muhammad:His Life Based on the Earliest Sources*'.

10. Martin Lings, *What is Sufism?*

11. Martin Lings, op. cit.

12. Ibid.

13. Ibid.

14. Michael Fitzgerald, 'In Memoriam: Dr. Martin Lings', *Sacred Web*, vol. 15, 2005.

44

# HUSEIN DOZO

B. 1912 – D. 1982

BOSNIA HERZEGOVINA

The political history of Bosnia and Herzegovina – often divided by the historians into four periods, namely the Ottoman (1463–1878), the Austro-Hungarian (1878–1918), the Kingdom of Yugoslavia (1918–1945) and the Socialist periods (1945–1992) – has been thoroughly and systematically studied and documented.[1] However, the same cannot be said about the origin and development of Islamic thought and scholarship in Bosnia and Herzegovina, not to mention the Balkans as a whole. Unsurprisingly, there is a lack of quality work around the subject both in English and the Balkan languages. In his *Contributions to Twentieth Century Islamic Thought in Bosnia and Herzegovina*, Enes Karic attempted to fill that gap. However, the main focus of his work, as the title indicates, was the twentieth century, although, to his credit, he also briefly highlighted the pivotal role played by the Gazi Husrev Bey Madrasah in Bosnia during the Ottoman times and subsequently.

Yet, the need for a systematic and comprehensive history of the origin and development of Islamic thought in Bosnia remains, not least because Karic's work provides no more than a brief overview of the contribution and achievements of only a handful of modern Bosnian Muslim scholars, reformers and activists, such as Mehmed Dzemaludin Causevic (see chapter 30), Mehmed Handzic (see chapter 42), Adil Bey Zulfikarpasic (see chapter 51) and Nerkez Smailagic (1927–1985), among others.

By all accounts, one of the most outstanding Bosnian Muslim scholars of his generation was Husein Dozo. He not only dominated the field of Islamic studies in

Bosnia during the second half of the twentieth century (particularly Qur'anic sciences and Islamic jurisprudence), he was an equally influential reformer and writer. For that reason, his contributions and achievements deserve to be known more widely, not only in the Balkans, but also across the Muslim world and the West.

Husein Dozo, also known as 'Abu Jim' Husein efendi Dozo, was born into a traditional Muslim family in the village of Bare, today located in the city of Gorazde (Gorajde) in eastern Bosnia and Herzegovina on the Drina River.[2] Being devout Muslims, his parents enrolled him at the local *maktab* (Qur'an school) where he learnt basic Arabic and Islamic rituals, before enrolling at the Islamic seminary in Foca, which is also a municipality located in eastern Bosnia. After studying there for a period, he joined Mehmet Pasha Madrasah at the age of 11. At this seminary, he improved his knowledge of Arabic and aspects of Islamic sciences sufficiently enough to be able to move to Merhemic Madrasah in 1925. Being a devout and talented student, he pursued his studies with considerable dedication which, of course, won him the respect and admiration of his teachers and fellow students alike.

After completing his primary education at this seminary, he moved to the Atmejdan Madrasah in Sarajevo for further studies in Arabic and aspects of Islam. As Sarajevo was the main centre of both secular and religious education in Bosnia and Herzegovina at the time, ambitious and talented students from across the country often moved to the capital to pursue further and higher education there, not least because Sarajevo had more educational institutions than any other part of Bosnia during the early part of the twentieth century. Another reason for students moving to Sarajevo for further and higher education at the time was the high quality of education that was provided in the city compared to institutions in other parts of the country.[3]

Furthermore, like Dozo, a large number of madrasah students in Sarajevo were from rural backgrounds. This was because the majority of Sarajevans abandoned religious education after the *maktab* and opted, instead, to pursue secular education at further and higher levels in order to secure well-paid government jobs compared to insecure, financially less rewarding teaching roles at mosques, *maktabs* and madrasahs. However, Dozo was a committed young man who was determined to become an Islamic scholar and, as such, he pursued his further education at the Atmejdan Madrasah until he passed his final exams with flying colours at the age of 16.

Dozo grew up and pursued his education at a time of considerable uncertainty and upheaval in the history of Bosnia and Herzegovina. After the Great War, Bosnia became a part of the South Slav Kingdom of Serbs, Croats and Slovenes. Supported mainly by the nationalist forces, the new kingdom attempted to forge a new common identity for all its subjects including the Bosnian Muslims, but the latter were justifiably apprehensive of the new order given the past conflicts. Although the ruling authorities initially promised a new beginning in inter-community relations, one where the political and religious rights of the Muslims would be protected, subsequently, they implemented policies that were highly detrimental to the political, economic and cultural benefits and welfare of the Muslim community.

In response, the Muslims of Bosnia attempted to form a political party of their own, namely *Jugoslovenska Muslimanska Organizacija* (Muslim Organisation of Yugoslavia) to protect their rights and interests. Unfortunately, the party had very limited impact until King Alexander, who was himself a Serb, effectively became the ruler and enacted new measures that strengthened his power, forcing *Rais al-Ulama* Mehmed Dzemaludin Causevic (see chapter 30) to resign in April 1930 in protest. A year later, the political structure of the country changed from a parliamentary system to a monarchy which took the form of the Kingdom of Yugoslavia. Thereafter, the Muslims of Bosnia had no choice but to unite and work together to preserve and protect their political, economic and religious rights under the leadership of the *Rais al-Ulama* (Religious Head) and the *Majlis al-Ulama* (Council of Islamic Scholars).

Dozo not only graduated from Atmejdan Madrasah during this unpredictable period, but, being equally unhappy with the quality of Arabic and Islamic education that he had received so far, he joined the Shari'ah Judges School in Sarajevo where he specialised in Arabic, Qur'anic sciences and Islamic jurisprudence. During this period, he may have attended lectures at various other Islamic institutions in Sarajevo, including the famous Gazi Husrev Bey Madrasah. After studying at the Shari'ah Judges School and other local institutions for more than four years, Dozo eventually passed his final exams at the age of 22, having 'conducted himself excellently'.[4]

Some of his teachers at the institution included prominent Islamic scholars like Sacir Sikiric (1893–1966), Besim Korkut (1904–1975) and Salih Safet efendi Basic (1873–1948), while his certificate of graduation was jointly signed by Dragoslav Jovanovic from the Ministry of Education; Dr Sacir Sikiric, who was the director of the School at the time; and, Semiz Muhamed, the then president of *Majlis al-Ulama*. Young Dozo must have been delighted that they considered him to be learned and competent enough to serve as a judge (*Qadi*) in the local Shari'ah courts, despite the fact that he was only in his early twenties at the time.

Tall, slim, handsome-looking and beardless in his appearance, Dozo did not always look like an Islamic scholar, although, behind his modern image, there resided a restless soul that was essentially Islamic. Impressed by his scholarly abilities and moral rectitude, his preceptors recruited him to a religious seminary in Sarajevo, where he soon proved to be an inspirational teacher and mentor to all his students. It was during this period that he decided to pursue further Arabic and Islamic education in Egypt to improve his career prospects, as well as to acquire proficiency in the traditional Islamic sciences, in addition to mastering Arabic language and literature. With that in mind, he left Bosnia and moved to Cairo where he enrolled at the historic al-Azhar University for advanced Islamic education.

Whilst Dozo was busy studying at al-Azhar's Faculty of Islamic Jurisprudence, he came in contact with the modernist ideas and thought of prominent Islamic scholars and reformers like Muhammad Abduh (1849–1905), Muhammad Rashid Rida (1865–1935), Mustafa al-Maraghi (1881–1945) and Mahmud Shaltut (1893–1963), among others. In addition to this, he became thoroughly familiar with the religious ideas and thought of classical Islamic scholars, including Abu Hanifah (699–767), Malik ibn Anas (711–795), al-Shafi'i (767–820), Muhammad ibn Hasan al-Shaybani (749–805), Abul Ma'ali al-Juwayni (1028–1085) al-Ghazali (1058–1111), Ibn Taymiyyah (1263–1328) and al-Nawawi (1233–1277).

Like Mehmed Dzemaludin Causevic and Yusuf Ziyaeddin Ezheri (see chapter 35), Dozo found the modernist's approach to Islam refreshing and appealing because, unlike the religious conservatives, they argued that reason and revelation were not only theologically compatible, but that the religious texts (namely the Qur'an and authentic Prophetic traditions) must also be reinterpreted by reputable Islamic scholars and jurists in the light of changing times and circumstances. Since culture and society are fluid, interpretation of religious texts must also be a continuous process to remain relevant in people's daily lives and affairs. For that reason, the modernists advocated the need for on-going *ijtihad* (independent legal discourse and interpretation), as opposed to wholesale blind imitation (*taqlid*) of the medieval jurists.

Dozo was, indeed, impressed by Islamic modernism. Thus, soon after completing his formal education in Arabic and Islamic jurisprudence at al-Azhar in 1939, as expected, he became an advocate of religious reform and revival. Indeed, his approach to Islam was 'characterized by two important features: the absolute affirmation of the compatibility between the Qur'anic revelation and reason and thus between Islam and Science, and his distinction between the eternal "concepts" contained in the Qur'anic message and the historicity of the interpretation of these very concepts.'[5] Unsurprisingly, he rejected wholesale imitation of medieval jurists in favour of independent reasoning to enable flexibility in the interpretation of Islamic scriptures to meet the growing challenges facing Muslims at the time.

If Islamic modernism provided Dozo with an intellectual methodology for questioning and reforming Muslim thought, culture and society, then as a teacher and writer, he was equally engaging and forward-looking. Upon his return to Bosnia in 1940, he became a teacher of Arabic and traditional Islamic sciences at Okruzna Madrasah in Sarajevo. By all accounts, he was an interesting and inspirational teacher who actively encouraged his students to think, reflect and ask questions. He argued that the Qur'an had enjoined on its readers to ponder and reflect on its message but, unfortunately, modern Muslims have completely deviated away from that contemplative and inquisitive Qur'anic approach and methodology.

As a result, wholesale blind imitation of religious concepts and practices became the norm, creating a culture of unquestioning respect and reverence for not only the fundamental beliefs, rites and rituals of Islam, but also for many out-dated and retrogressive practices which, in reality, had nothing to do with the Qur'an or authentic

Prophetic norms. Whether he taught at a junior madrasah or senior students at college or university, Dozo never failed to be engaging, questioning and even provocative. In the words of Enes Karic – and it is worth quoting him at some length:

> Dozo's classes at the Islamic Theological Faculty (later to be known as the Faculty of Islamic Studies) were like his articles. They consisted of a main strand, of 'principles and principle concepts', as he liked to say, and the 'development and elaboration of those principles in historical circumstances'. They were always dynamic classes, full of discussion and provocative remarks, sometimes made by him. I recall, as do all other colleagues of my generation, that Dozo would begin his classes with some improbable assertion, so as to get our attention, as pedagogues say. Once (indeed, not only once) he said that he did not consider *Iblis*, or *Shaytan*, as some personal, personalized entity. '*Shaytan* is in fact the human tendency to evil, the power of the nafs that we must tame', he liked to say. And then a lively discussion would begin, some students did not defend the 'existence of *Shaytan*' and agreed with Professor Dozo, while others would quote ayats and *hadiths* which show that *Iblis* really exists and that he is present at every step. I would say that practically all his classes were agreeable debates. Of course, during those classes he expounded his great knowledge, walking about the room constantly citing Arabic classic terms, works, names, years, but he was never a slave to detail. 'You know, if you don't link the details to the concept, if the details have no connection with the principles, then what are they the details of?'[6]

While he was busy teaching at madrasah, he was swiftly promoted to the post of director of religious education in the Department of Religious Affairs by the government officials. During this period, the Second World War broke out and the Kingdom of Yugoslavia was invaded by the Axis powers led by Nazi Germany. It was during this politically tumultuous time that Dozo was enlisted to serve as a chaplain (Imam) in the notorious 28th SS regiment. Political confusion, coupled with on-going Serbian (especially Cetnik) aggression and propaganda against the Muslims of the Balkans as a whole, eastern Bosnia in particular, clearly motivated many Muslims at the time to support the German army as a bulwark against Serb aggression and brutality.[7]

However, after the war, the Federation of People's Republic of Yugoslavia was formed in 1945 and Dozo was immediately arrested and convicted for 'raising morale in enemy units through his [religious] activities'. His critics have wrongly accused him of perpetrating numerous crimes, although he only served as a chaplain to the regiment and, therefore, did not directly participate in any military activities. Even so, he was put on trial by a partisan government and sentenced to five years incarceration; the verdict was subsequently confirmed in June 1945 by the Military Court in Sarajevo. This was a very difficult period for him, but he served his sentence and was eventually released in 1950. Having been charged and imprisoned for treason, he was banned from all political and religious activities, and that, in turn, forced him to earn his living working at a leather factory before securing the post of a bookkeeper for another local company.[8]

Although he resumed his religious and literary activities towards the end of the 1950s, he was formally granted permission to join the Department of Religious Affairs in 1960 as an advisor to the Grand Mufti of the then Yugoslavia. He also served as Head of Religious and Educational Affairs, in addition to teaching at the famous Gazi Husrev Bey Madrasah. For the next two decades, Dozo combined his work as a government official with Islamic reformist and literary activities. He contributed regular articles to the *Glasnik Vrhovnog Islamskog Starjesinstva* (Herald of the Senior Islamic Scholars) for more than twenty years and, from 1964 to 1979, he served as the head of the Association of *Ulama* (*Udruzenje Ilmijje*), in addition to editing its annual journal called *Takvim* (Calendar).

Furthermore, from September 1970, he was the founding editor of a new biweekly newspaper titled *Preporod* (Renaissance), whereby he proved to be an influential and effective champion of the Muslims of Bosnia. Although there were several other Muslim publications available at the time, the '*Preporod*, from its very first issue, began to address a number of topics which were out of the narrowly defined "profession" of *ulama* in a socialist country: observance of Islamic regulations in a secular state, social engagement of Muslims, religion and education, Islam and ethnicity, contemporary trends in the Muslim world, development of Islamic institutions in the then Bosnia and Yugoslavia and the like. Husin Djozo, as the founding editor of *Preporod*, was assisted by a group of young Bosniak students coming mainly from state universities but conscious that something should be done for the preservation of the Bosniaks' Islamic identity'.[9]

Dozo not only became actively involved in literary activities, but he also pursued a critical and engaging approach to Islamic thought and reform. Thanks to his mastery of Arabic and traditional Islamic sciences (especially the Qur'an and Islamic jurisprudence), he was able to ask and answer questions that were both challenging and pertinent to his people, which the majority of Bosnian *ulama* had singularly failed to address at the time. Although he authored nearly 250 treatises, articles and reviews on a wide range of topics during a career spanning almost half a century, he was in fact very fond of *tafsir* and *fiqh*. Having specialised in these subjects at al-Azhar, he was considered to be an expert in Qur'anic interpretation and Islamic jurisprudence. So much so that when the Islamic Theological Faculty was established at the University of Sarajevo in 1977, he became a professor of Arabic and Qur'anic sciences there.

According to Enes Karic, it was Dozo's habit to come to the 'faculty not only for classes during the day, and he would sit in his office writing in the early evening, staying until late. The following day, when as his assistant I would type up the manuscript, I would see that he had written between eight to twelve pages. He had a fine style, logical and clear. Dozo liked to use reason and logic to defend what he wrote, and that is how he wrote…He liked to dress in bohemian style, too; we recall him usually in a light jacket with a large beret, but he would most often walk bare-headed, showing his characteristic mane of white hair that sometimes fell over the collar of his shirt.'[10]

Despite being an eminent Islamic scholar and writer, Dozo's reformist approach to Islam proved to be controversial with certain Muslim groups in Bosnia, especially the members of the *Mladi Muslimani* (Young Muslims) organisation, who considered him to be too close to the Socialist government. Conversely, Josip Tito's repressive regime considered Dozo to be too Islamic for their liking and, as a result, he often found himself caught between a rock and a hard place. Needless to say, walking on such a tight rope was never going to be an easy and straight-forward task but, to his credit, he persisted until the pressure from the Communists proved to be unbearable, thus forcing him to resign from most of his government posts in 1979.

To make matters worse, the traditional *ulama* were not happy with his creative and engaging interpretation of Islamic scriptures either, leading to heated debates and discussions over some of his *fatawa* (Islamic legal edicts). Many of his legal edicts and commentaries on Qur'anic chapters were subsequently published in the form of books, including *Fetve-Pitanja i Odgovori* (1996), *Fetve II* (2006), *Islam u Vremenu* (1976) and *Prijevod Kur'ana sa Komentarom* (2006).

In fact, as a leading Islamic jurist, Dozo issued more than 800 fatwas on a wide range of subjects, including issues affecting the Bosnian youth, their role in a secular society, and the position of Muslim women in their families and communities. As a European Muslim scholar and reformer, his ideas and thought on spiritual, theological, legal and social matters were informed and underpinned by the need to address and reconcile their dual identity, namely of being Muslims and Bosnians living in an increasingly secular Europe. It was not only possible to forge such an identity, he felt, such a task needed to be undertaken if Islam is to survive and prosper in Europe and the West as a whole. The precedent for that already existed in Islamic thought, history and culture, he argued. In his own words,

> The great [Islamic] scholars of the past spoke and acted in accordance with their own times. Likewise, we must speak and act according to our own times. The views of the past scholars do not necessarily have to be the same as ours… By this, we are not neglecting the tradition *per se* but rather putting more emphasis on critical thinking and the need for revival instead of blind following.[11]

As an individual, Dozo was very pious, generous and studious. He devoted his entire life to the pursuit of Islamic knowledge and scholarship, and served the Muslims of Bosnia and Herzegovina with such a distinction that today he is rightly regarded as one of the most influential Muslim scholars, thinkers and reformers to have emerged in the Balkans during the second half of the twentieth century. He died in Sarajevo at the age of 70.

In recognition of his services to Islam, a school in his native Gorazde was named after him, and in 1990, the Supreme Council of the Islamic Community in Bosnia and Herzegovina hailed him as a benefactor of his people. Several scholars and writers have since published books and articles on his life and works, including Fikret Karcic, Enes Karic, Adnan Aslan and Sejad Mekic.

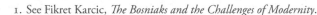

1. See Fikret Karcic, *The Bosniaks and the Challenges of Modernity*.

2. Sejad Mekic, *A Muslim Reformist in Communist Yugoslavia*.

3. Cornelia K. Sorabji, *Muslim Identity and Islamic Faith in Sarajevo*, unpublished PhD thesis, Kings College, Cambridge, 1989.

4. Enes Karic, *Contributions to Twentieth Century Islamic Thought in Bosnia and Herzegovina*, vol. 1.

5. Armina Omerika, 'The Role of Islam in the Academic Discourses on the National Identity of Muslims in Bosnia and Herzegovina, 1950–1980', *Islam and Muslim Societies: A Social Science Journal*, vol. 2, No. 2.

6. Enes Karic, op. cit.

7. Fikret Karcic, 'The Eastern Question – A Paradigm for Understanding the Balkan Muslims' History in the 20th Century', *Islamic Studies*, vol. 41, No. 4.

8. Marko A. Hoare, *The Bosnian Muslims in the Second World War: A History*; Adnan Aslan, 'Huseyin Efendi Djozo' in Oliver Leaman (ed.), *The Biographical Encyclopedia of Islamic Philosophy*.

9. Fikret Karcic, 'PREPOROD Newspaper: An Agent of and a Witness to Islamic Revival in Bosnia', *Intellectual Discourse*, vol. 7, No. 1.

10. Enes Karic, op. cit.

11. Quoted by Sejad Mekic, op. cit.

45

# NOOR INAYAT KHAN

B. 1914 – D. 1944

UNITED KINGDOM

The First and Second World Wars were, by all accounts, two of the most devastating and destructive conflicts in human history. During the former, it is estimated that there were around 40 million casualties, both military and civilian, whilst in the latter, the total number of human losses rose above 60 million, which was equivalent to three per cent of the world's population in the year 1940. As both wars originated in Europe and were fought between imperialistic, nationalistic and fascist powers – who were, at the time, bent on wreaking havoc not only in Europe, but also around the world – the global powers of the time had no choice but to fight back and defend liberty, freedom and democracy in the face of unspeakable hatred, aggression and injustice.

In the battle between right and wrong, justice and injustice, and freedom and oppression, the champions of liberty and freedom prevailed over the nationalistic forces of darkness and destruction. As the fight against the Serb nationalists (who instigated the First World War) and the Nazis of Germany (who were responsible for the Second World War) were truly decisive battles, people from around the world – regardless of their race, faith and background – actively participated in both wars in order to preserve human dignity and freedom.[1]

Whilst the contribution of the prominent Western nations (such as France, Britain, Russia and America) are widely known today, and rightly so; the important role played by other countries (like Canada, Australia, New Zealand, India and South Africa), however, are not as widely recognised. In the same way, the contribution of more than half a million Muslim soldiers during the First World War, and more than a million during the Second World War, is still yet to be recognised. Although the majority of Muslim soldiers who fought for the Allies (especially Britain and France) had hailed from British India and the French colonies of North Africa, others were, in fact, of European or Western origin too. One such extraordinary freedom-fighter was Noor Inayat Khan, who became the first Muslim woman to fight and make the ultimate sacrifice for Britain and France during the Second World War.

For that reason, her life and contribution deserves to be known more widely today, especially at a time when the faith, identity and loyalty of Western Muslims are not only being openly questioned, but also publicly mocked, ridiculed and demonised across Europe and America, due to the same dark forces of nationalism and xenophobia that instigated the First and Second World Wars.

Noor-un-Nisa Inayat Khan, better known as Noor Inayat Khan, was born into a notable Muslim family of Indian origin. Her father, Hazrat Inayat Khan (1882–1927), was from Baroda (today known as Vadodara in the Indian State of Gujarat) and traced his ancestry back to Pashtun Sufis of Afghanistan on the one hand, and the royal family of Tipu Sultan (1750–1799) on the other. Trained in classical Indian music and initiated into a branch of the Chishti Sufi Order of India by Abul Hashim Madani, who was a Shaykh of this branch of Sufism, Inayat Khan soon earned the respect and affection of his spiritual mentor and guide. While he was still in his late twenties, Madani encouraged him to travel to the West to disseminate the message of Islamic spirituality or Sufism.

Being an accomplished musician who specialised in classical Indian music, he travelled across Europe and America and soon established Sufi centres in several Western countries, attracting many followers. It was during this period that he met and married Ora Ray Baker (Ameena Begum). Ora was born in 1892 in New Mexico of half-English and half-Irish parentage, and was an attractive young lady who she first met Inayat Khan in San Francisco. They later married in London in 1913, despite facing opposition from Ora's immediate family.[2] A year later, Noor Inayat Khan, the eldest of their four children (two daughters and two sons) was born while her father was working as a musician in Moscow. Although Inayat Khan was very fond of Moscow for its cultural richness and vibrancy, the prevailing political tension and uncertainty soon forced him to move to France.

In the meantime, the First World War broke out in Europe. As soon as German weapons were pointed towards France, the Inayat family were forced to return to London, where, unfortunately, the family initially struggled to make ends meet because

Inayat Khan could not find regular work while the war was raging across the continent. During this period, young Noor experienced much poverty and hardship, so much so that there were days when the family had no food other than just bread. However, her parents made up for the hardship by showering her with generous amounts of warmth, affection and love, not least because she was their first-born.

In 1915, her father formally established his Sufi Order in the West – which was defined by a novel understanding of religion, rather than being strictly-speaking Islamic – and, a year later, her brother, Vilayat Inayat Khan (1916–2004) was born. Noor was very fond of her brother – she grew up with him and became his best friend. However, as the war continued to rage across Europe, her father responded by actively disseminating his Sufi message of peace, happiness and spirituality at a time of considerable turmoil, hardship and uncertainty. Needless to say, his message of oneness of Divinity and Truth (*tawhid*); oneness of religion and morality; oneness of brotherhood and humanity; and, peace with one self and nature soon resonated, as new branches of the Sufi Order were soon opened in London, Brighton, Harrogate and elsewhere.[3]

When Noor was only 3 years old, her family moved from their modest residence on Ladbroke Road to a more spacious property in Gordon Square, thanks to the financial support provided by her father's growing number of *murid*s (spiritual followers or disciples). Here, the Inayat family lived in more comfortable circumstances, although financially, they still continued to struggle to make ends meet. By all accounts, Noor was a bright, caring, but equally sensitive child who enjoyed listening to music and fairy tales. Indeed, on one occasion 'when she heard that children in Russia had nothing to eat she took it to heart, although she was only four. She began demanding chocolates from the adults, and as soon as she got one she would leave the room. Later her parents found she had a big box full of chocolates in her room, which she was collecting for the Russian children.'[4] After six years in London, Noor's family were forced to move again, as the British authorities became increasingly suspicious of her father's religious activities, as well as his growing links to prominent Indian nationalists (such as Mahatma Gandhi and Sarojini Naidu), who were, at the time, actively campaigning for India's freedom and independence from British rule.

Thankfully, the First World War had formally ended in November 1918 and that, in turn, prompted the Inayat family to make preparations to leave London in favour of France. In 1920, when Noor was only six, they moved to an old house in the French village of Tremblaye, located towards the north of Paris, which belonged to one of her father's English disciples. Being cold and damp, the family struggled to settle in this property and soon moved to Wissous, a small town located towards the south of Paris. They stayed there until 1922, when one of Inayat Khan's Dutch disciples offered to buy him and his family a property at Suresnes, which is today a commune in the western suburbs of Paris. He named it Fazal Manzil (or the 'House of Grace') and it lived up to its name. The family found it to be an open, spacious and peaceful residence, not only for themselves, but also for Inayat's growing stream of visitors who came from far and wide seeking spiritual guidance.

It was at Fazal Manzil that Inayat formally initiated the practice of Universal Worship, which combined aspects of Sufi teachings (such as the communal performance of *Dhikr*) with Christian devotion, and was influenced by other eastern traditions and faiths. Noor grew up observing and learning from her father's eclectic approach to religion, and as such, she was encouraged by her parents to read Buddhist, Hindu and Christian literature, in addition to the Qur'an. At the age of eight, she enrolled at the local College Moderne de Fille and soon became fluent in French. She wrote short stories and poems in French and English during this period, and became proficient in both Sufi and Western music with the help of her father.

As Inayat Khan was busy promoting his Sufi movement – with new branches being established in England, America, Germany, Belgium, the Netherlands, Switzerland and Scandinavia – he was hardly at home to spend time with his family. Noor was barely 12 when her father was taken seriously ill, perhaps due to over-work and exhaustion. He therefore decided to go to India for recuperation, nominating his 10-year old son, Vilayat, as his spiritual successor. In September 1926, he left his family behind and set out for India where he visited several cities, including New Delhi, and visited the *Dargah* (mausoleum) of Sultan al-Mashaykh Hazrat Shaykh Nizam al-Din Awliya (1238–1325), the famous Muslim saint of India, to pay homage to the great spiritual preceptor of Muslim India. A few months later, he was taken seriously ill and died at the age of only 44.[5]

The news of Inayat's death came down like thunder from the heavens for his young family; Ameena Begum was too distraught to face reality, while Noor was forced to shoulder family responsibilities, despite only being 13 at the time. Thankfully, a few months later, the family were able to go to India to visit the tomb of Inayat Khan, as well as the *Dargah* of Khwajah Mu'in al-Din Chishti (1141–1236) in Ajmer, the founder of the Chishtiyyah Sufi Order in India, with financial support from Inayat's European disciples. This was the first time that Noor had visited her ancestral home and, needless to say, she was impressed by the religious and cultural diversity of India, but saddened by the widespread poverty and squalor that she had witnessed there.

On her return to Suresnes, Noor combined family responsibilities with high school education at the Lycee de Jeunes in St Cloud, where she studied European languages, including English, French and German, in addition to participating in sports. Noor dearly missed her father, but always kept her feelings to herself as her mother was struggling to come to terms with her husband's death. During this period, Noor read extensively and wrote poetry expressing her love, affection and support for her parents. In one poem, which was addressed to her mother, she wrote:

Beloved! Ah! Beloved Amma,
A treasure stored deep in our hearts,
'Tis flowers of our gratitude,
A treasure that n'er will depart.
Behold! For their petals are carved
With Allah's own heavenly art,
Their beauty on this longed for day,
To you and Abba we impart.
Through life's struggle and through life's strife,
May we treasure as our life's gem
The seed in our heart, you have sown,
Ah! Quote in the sacred Nirtan,
And always remember this:
The path of the heart is thorny,
Which leads in the end to bliss.[6]

By all accounts, this was a profoundly moving, deeply thoughtful and equally impressive poem for a 15-year old to compose, but Noor was an exceptionally gifted and insightful teenager. Two years later, she successfully completed her Baccalaureate (equivalent to a certificate of secondary education). Thereafter, she studied music at the Ecole Normale de Musique de Paris, along with child psychology at the Sorbonne, University of Paris. She soon became an accomplished musician, combining classical Sufi Indian music with the Western musical tradition, before graduating from the Sorbonne in 1938 at the age of 24.

By now, Noor had also become a gifted linguist, being fluent in German, Spanish and Hindi, in addition to English, French and Urdu. She also learnt to read the Qur'an in Arabic. Despite her education and language skills, Noor chose to become a writer rather than a teacher. Encouraged by Baroness van Tuyll, who was a family friend and a member of the Sufi fraternity, she translated twenty stories from the Jataka Tales for publication. Accompanied by illustrations produced by Henriette Willebeek le Mair, her collection of traditional Buddhist stories, shortened and simplified for young individuals, was subsequently published in London by George G. Harrap in 1939.[7] In addition to this, Noor became a notable journalist, contributing as she did, articles and stories to prominent French newspapers and magazines, including the *Le Figaro*, *Sunday Figaro* and *Paris Soir*, among other publications.

At a time when the young journalist was well on her way to becoming a professional writer, the Second World War broke out in Europe. On 1 September 1939, when Noor was only 25, the Nazis, led by Adolf Hitler (1889–1945), who became the Chancellor of Germany back in 1933, invaded Poland. Prior to this, the Nazis had annexed Austria without provoking a backlash from the other European powers. Emboldened by his gain, Hitler then laid claim to Czechoslovakia. Britain and France swiftly responded by declaring war against Nazi Germany. Needless to say, Noor and her family were gripped by fear and panic even though there were no visible signs of war in Paris at the time.

In the meantime, Germany had invaded Denmark and Norway, and Winston Churchill (1874–1965) succeeded Neville Chamberlain (1869–1940) as the British Prime Minister on 10 May 1940. Germany then launched an offensive against France while Belgium, the Netherlands and Luxembourg succumbed to the Nazis. As the war raged across Europe, the Sufi fraternity, established by Inayat Khan, found themselves facing a serious dilemma. The Sufi message was, of course, one of peace and harmony, but in the face of imminent danger of Nazi invasion, what were they supposed to do? Continue preaching the message of peace or take a principled stand against Nazi aggression and brutality? Noor and her brother, Vilayat, felt they could not stand by and watch the Nazis run riot across Europe, for that would certainly have been against spirituality, morality and common sense.

Determined to join the fight against the Nazis, Noor and her family decided to move to England in June 1940 and join the war effort. In the meantime, Paris had fallen into German hands and the Nazis now turned their attention to Britain. Noor and her family soon reached Bordeaux and, from there, the family reached Falmouth in Cornwall before moving to Southampton to stay with a family friend. They then travelled to Oxford, except Vilayat, who moved to London to enlist for service in the Royal Air Force (RAF), although, unfortunately, ill-health forced him to return to his family in Oxford.

However, London soon came under sustained attack from the Nazis after the declaration of the Battle of Britain in August 1940. As the situation in London became desperate, Noor volunteered at the Fulmer Chase Maternity Home for Officers' Wives, located near Slough. She then joined the Women's Auxiliary Air Force (WAAF), which was established in June 1939, to support the RAF by freeing the men to go and fight in the battlefield. Noor joined the WAAF in November 1940 as 424598 ACW2. Despite being a Muslim, the authorities registered her as Nora Inayat Khan who belonged to the Church of England (CoE); according to Noor's biographers, this was probably done to avoid unnecessary complications.[8]

After being recruited into the WAAF, along with forty other women, Noor received training to become a wireless radio operator at RAF Balloon Command in Edinburgh. During her six months of training there, her mother also moved to be close to her daughter. She passed all her exams and was promoted to the post of Aircraftswoman (First Class) to serve at RAF Bomber Command in Abingdon. She was, according to her colleagues, a helpful, efficient and effective transmitter of messages. The fact that none of her colleagues knew anything about her family, background or faith, must have been rather liberating for her as, prior to this, she had always been known as the daughter of Hazrat Inayat Khan of the Sufi Order in the West.

During this period, she worked long shifts and continued to receive training in Advance Signals and Wireless communication. To add to the confusion, the Indian independence movement became very active at the time, but Noor remained committed to the fight against the Nazis, for she felt, the campaign for Indian liberation from British rule must not be allowed to undermine the battle against Hitler's Germany. Soon, her brother, Vilayat, had passed his Royal Navy examination and joined HMS Collingwood and Noor, in turn, was promoted to the post of Leading Aircraftswoman on 1 December 1942. Needless to say, her skills, loyalty and hard work did not go unnoticed as the military intelligence now became interested in recruiting her for special operations, thanks to her linguistic and technical skills.

In due course she was invited to an interview, which she attended in November 1942 at the War Office in London, to join the Special Operations Executive (SOE), which was created by Prime Minister Winston Churchill in the summer of 1940 to 'set Europe ablaze' by conducting a covert war against the German Fascists, in addition to the overt military campaign that was already raging across Europe. Considering that Noor was only 28 at the time, it could be argued that she did not fully understand what her new role would be in the SOE. That is to say, she may not have realised that her new role involved carrying out espionage, infiltration, sabotage and counter-insurgency against the Nazi war machine and its intelligence services.

However, according to the British official who interviewed her for the job, Noor was not only fully aware of the task ahead and the serious risks associated with such work, but she was also raring to take the battle to the Fascists.[9] As expected, after being discharged from WAAF, she joined the First Aid and Nursing Yeomanry (otherwise known as the Women's Transport Service), which, in reality, was a cover for female secret agents to undertake their training without being detected. Her salary was fixed at £350 a year which was paid quarterly into her Lloyds Bank account, and she signed the Official Secrets Act on 15 February 1943 at the age of 29. Thereafter, she undertook all necessary training at SOE schools where she became known as 'Nora Baker', some of her superiors expressed their reservations regarding her suitability for undercover warfare, but her fluency in French and competence in wireless communication, along with the dire shortage of agents, worked in her favour.

Once her training was completed, Noor assumed her code name of 'Madeleine' and 'Jeanne-Marie Renie', before being flown into northern France. She became the first female radio operator to go to France to work as an agent, and made her way to Paris. She joined the 'Physician' network along with two other female agents, namely Diana Rowden (code named Paulette/Chaplain) and Cecily Lefort (code named Alice/Teacher), with Francis Suttill (code named Prosper) being in charge. The network consisted of several circuits and sub-circuits, often consisting of three agents, namely the organiser, the courier and the radio operator. The role of the latter was particularly important because all communication between the agents and the SOE headquarters in

London took place through the radio operator, and the notorious Gestapo (Nazi secret police) were only too aware of this.

Unsurprisingly, they deliberately targeted the radio operators in order to disrupt and undermine British counter-insurgency activities in occupied France. As a result, in just over a month, the Nazis had captured all the radio operators connected with the Physician network, except for Noor, who soon became a real thorn in their side. She not only eluded the Gestapo, but also continued to transmit messages to London despite numerous mishaps, miscommunication and incompetence in London, as well as in Paris, coupled with counter-infiltration by Nazi double agents.

In the face of such mounting challenges and difficulties, according to Colonel Maurice Buckmaster (1902–1992), who was the leader of the French section of SOE in London, Noor even turned down an offer to return to England and, instead, continued to communicate with London at a time when the rest of her circuit almost ceased to exist. That was, by all accounts, a truly brave and extraordinary achievement on her part. Frustrated by their failure to capture Noor, the Gestapo now considered her to be the most wanted British secret agent in Paris and pursued her actively. She, in turn, kept on moving from one place to another and transmitted messages to London intermittently to avoid being detected by wireless vans operated by the enemy. At a time when radio operators did not survive more than a few weeks, Noor continued her work for no less than four months before being captured on or around 13 October 1943; she was reportedly betrayed by a double agent, or a fellow SOE officer, who may have revealed her identity to the Nazis.[10]

After being captured, she made several attempts to escape but was unsuccessful. Eventually, she was taken to Germany on 27 November 1943 and spent the next ten months in solitary confinement at a high security prison, being classified as 'highly dangerous' due to her refusal to co-operate and disclose information to the Nazis. Then, in September 1944, Noor and three other SOE agents were moved to the Dachau Concentration Camp and, two days later, they were all executed; Noor was only 30 at the time of her death. Her last word was 'Liberte'.

Lest we should forget, it is worth remembering that Noor was a young Muslim woman of Indian-American origin, who made the highest sacrifice for our freedom, liberty and democracy, which we rightly cherish and enjoy today, both in Britain and the West as a whole. In recognition of her remarkable courage, bravery, loyalty and sacrifices for Britain and France, on 16 January 1946, Noor was posthumously awarded the Croix de Guerre with Gold Star by the French government, the country's highest civilian award.

Likewise, the British government awarded her the George Cross on 5 April 1949, which is also Britain's highest civilian honour. The award citation summed up her achievements in these words: 'Assistant Section Officer [Noor] Inayat Khan displayed the most conspicuous courage, both moral and physical, over a period of more than twelve months.'[11] On 8 November 2012, a statue of Noor Inayat Khan was unveiled in Gordon Square, London by The Princess Royal, and the Royal Mail also issued a stamp in memory of her life and contribution to Britain on 25 March 2014 under the caption 'Remarkable Lives'.

1. Donald Sommerville and Ian Westwell, *The Complete Illustrated History of the First and Second World Wars: An Authoritative Account of the Two of the Deadliest Conflicts in Human History.*

2. Elisabeth Keesing, *Hazrat Inayat Khan: A Biography.*

3. Pir Vilayat Inayat Khan, *The Message in Our Time: The Life and Teachings of the Sufi Master, Pir-O-Murshid Inayat Khan.*

4. Shrabani Basu, *Spy Princess: The Life of Noor Inayat Khan.*

5. Elisabeth Kessing, op. cit.

6. Quoted by Shrabani Basu, op. cit.

7. See Noor Inayat Khan, *Twenty Jataka Tales*, recently reissued by Inner Traditions India.

8. Shrabani Basu, op. cit.

9. Elisabeth Kessing, op. cit., and Shrabani Basu, op. cit.

10. Gaby Halberstam, *Noor Inayat Khan: Muslim Pacifist, British Spy, National Hero.*

11. Quoted by Shrabani Basu, op. cit.

46

# THOMAS BALLANTINE IRVING

B. 1914 – D. 2002

CANADA

The compelling need facing Islam today is for Muslims to regain their self-confidence, and to learn to deal effectively and constructively with the world around them. The world has long worried about Islam because as a religion, it possesses absolute values, and such a starting point was dangerous in a colonial society if these were taken seriously. France found it difficult to bribe or coerce someone who knew the difference between right and wrong. Now frustrated states like France and Japan still do not understand Islam much better, and they must learn to study it differently in order to be able to function satisfactorily in the Middle East. France especially must free herself and turn from the futile colonialist studies which lost her Algeria and Syria; while Japan has had no studies at all of its own up to now. The United States is in even worse shape because it has been misled by pressure groups who are hostile to the Islamic world; this is ironic, for it never needed hostility to further its interests there, but now it is enmeshed in miscalculations and attendant violence. The crisis has been only postponed, not solved; and the solution must be ethical if it is to become durable. We thus need to work intelligently towards peace and understanding.[1]

After devoting a whole lifetime to the study, research and teaching of history, languages, culture and religion (especially Islam), Thomas Ballantine Irving, one of the leading Muslim scholars of the twentieth century, succinctly but accurately summed up the uneasy and tense relationship that exists between the West and the Muslim world at the moment, except that his aforementioned words were first published in 1979 and not in 2017.

Observers of diplomacy and international affairs would be forgiven for thinking that not much has changed during this period; others might even argue that things have substantially deteriorated since then. Being a proud Westerner, who was also a devout Muslim, Irving became an important and proactive bridge-builder who was determined to breakdown cultural barriers, as well as promote knowledge and understanding between the Islamic world and the West, but, unfortunately, the life, thoughts and achievements of such a remarkable Muslim historian, scholar and translator are not widely known today.

Thomas Ballantine Irving, better known as T. B. Irving or al-Hajj Ta'lim Ali Abu Nasr, was born in Preston (now Cambridge), which is located in the east-central Canadian province of Ontario. His parents, William John Irving and Jessica (Jessie) Christina MacIntyre, were of Scottish ancestry and possibly Presbyterians by faith. His forefathers migrated to Canada and eventually settled there. However, according to Irving, 'My mother used to tell me, that the First World War broke out when she got out of bed after giving birth to me on 20 July 1914... My next remembrance, or rather my first one actually related to that conflict, was riding down on the local druggist, Mr Donald Fairbairn's shoulder, to watch a biplane that had flown over from the Royal Canadian Air Force base at Camp Borden, a few miles east of Orangeville, where my maternal grandmother, Annabelle MacIntyre, lived, and where mother used to take us to spend the summer holidays. I remember it clearly as a biplane, which became my image for aircraft for many years thereafter, through most of my early childhood.'[2]

Although young Irving grew up in a happy family, the Western world was being torn apart at the time by unspeakable violence and bloodshed as a result of the Great War which endured until November 1918. A war that was expected to last only a few months, dragged on for more than four years with nearly 40 million casualties, being one of the deadliest conflicts in human history. As expected, it had a deep and profound impact on Irving, as he later recalled that on the first Armistice Day, 11 November 1918, when he was only four years of age, all the church bells in Preston suddenly started ringing. In his own words,

> It was 11 o'clock in the morning of that memorable day, and the little girl from next door, Norma Eby, who was a year younger than I was, exclaimed that it was the 'Armistice'! It was a big word for a four year-old boy and a three year-old girl,

but when I went back into our house to tell my mother, she sat down suddenly at our kitchen table, and began to cry. Such was her emotion after four years of war on another continent... Other stories relating to the War were Irish rebellion when friends from Waterfront in southern Ireland...came to live in Preston. And then how the Greeks fled from the cities they had occupied in Asia Minor. This campaign confused me, for I hadn't heard those names before, although it was a tailend to the Gallipoli campaign that my father talked about. Both he and several aunts encouraged me, even at that early age, to read newspapers...[3]

Irving read several newspapers at the time, including the *Toronto Star*, the *Globe*, and the *Galt Reporter*. As a result, he not only became familiar with aspects of domestic policy, but also international affairs, much due to his parents and relatives' heated discussions and debates. Irving was a bright student who preferred languages and humanities at school over mathematics and science. In addition to English, he learned French and Spanish during his early years, and, after successfully completing primary education, he moved to high school (which was known as 'collegiate' in Ontario at the time). He also became familiar with German as Ontario was, to a large extent, founded by German-speaking settlers. Although the younger generation did not show much interest in the language, the elders in the community continued to converse in German.

Needless to say, Irving was fascinated by Ontario's cultural and linguistic diversity. It was also during this period that he first heard about the Muslim world and the Near East in particular (after the Second World War, the Near East became more popular as the Middle East). It was, in fact, a cousin of his father who gave him a copy of T. E. Lawrence's (1888–1935) *Revolt in the Desert*, which he read avidly and, as a result, his interest in Arabs and their language and culture was ignited. He must have been around 14 at the time, as the *Revolt in the Desert* was first published for mass circulation in 1927 by Jonathan Cape of London.

After completing his secondary education, Irving joined the University of Toronto (then known as University College) to study modern languages focusing on French, German and Spanish. Whilst he was busy studying European languages, he was informed that an academic based at the same institution, by the name of W. C. Taylor, taught a course on Middle Eastern language and literature. He attended his class and was impressed by Islamic history and culture, thanks to Taylor's critical, but also accurate presentation of the subject. Thereafter, he discovered that Arabic was taught at Toronto by Frederick V. Winnet, who specialised in Middle Eastern language and history, and he soon completed a course in Arabic language and literature.

In 1937, at the age of 23, he graduated with honours in modern languages before enrolling at the University of Montreal, where he obtained a *Maitrise es Lettres* (Master of Arts) degree a year later. He was keen to go to Paris for doctoral studies, but that offer soon fell through, and, instead, he applied to join the University of Chicago where

Martin Sprengling (1877–1959) was teaching at the time. As Sprengling did not have a spare place on the course, he advised Irving to enrol at the University of Princeton in New Jersey, where Philip Khuri Hitti (1886-1978) taught Arabic and Islamic Studies. Accordingly, he pursued research in Spanish and Arabic studies under Hitti's supervision, and wrote a thesis on the history of Islamic Spain, specialising on the life and works of Alfonso X, el-Sabio, who was the king of Castille from 1252 to 1284, for which he was awarded a doctorate in history in 1940; he was only 26 at the time.[4]

Hereon, teaching modern languages along with Arabic and the history of Islamic Spain became the main focus of Irving's academic career, while his devotion and commitment to Islam was nothing short of exemplary and inspirational. When Irving was asked to explain the reasons for his conversion (or reversion) to Islam, he stated:

> I can remember thrilling as a very small child to the Christian interpretation of Jesus's life, but yet I cannot say that I was ever truly Christian of my own conviction. Instead of absorbing the pretty Biblical tales, I began wondering why so many in the world were 'heathen', why Jew and Christian differed on the same Bible, why the unbelievers were damned when the fault was not theirs, and also why they could practice goodness as well as the self-called 'higher' nations... I remember especially a missionary returned from India stating how the 'Mahometans' were so obdurate in adhering to their religion; that was my first encounter with Islam, and it roused an unconscious admiration in me for their steadfastness to their faith and a desire to know more about these wicked people...[5]

On another occasion, he remarked 'I am an old-timer because I became a Muslim (never changed, never was anything else, just as the Prophet says) in the 1930s at Toronto. Please don't call me a convert because that implies change and what did I change from? I became a Muslim only in the sense that at a point in time I realized that I was what I was. I personally feel that I am not a convert and not an indigenous as opposed to an immigrant Muslim.'[6] Though he became a Muslim during the 1930s, his knowledge and understanding of Islam was rather poor and scanty at the time.

As it happened, it was only after many more years of studying and exploring Islam and its teachings that he eventually accepted 'Muhammad as a messenger of God: firstly, he was needed; secondly, my own conclusions had been independent and still coincided; and thirdly, apart from both the former, realization of the divine quality of the Holy Qur'an and the Prophet's teachings flooded upon me clearly.'[7]

He had access to Mawlana Muhammad Ali Lahori's (1874–1951) English translation and commentary of the Qur'an, in addition to Islamic literature in both French and English. He found Islam to be simple, logical and rational, unlike the other creeds and philosophies that he had studied and explored at the time.

After successfully completing his higher education, Irving began his teaching career at the University of California, Berkeley as an instructor in Spanish in 1940. Although he was keen to teach Arabic, very few opportunities were available to teach the subject at the American universities and colleges at the time. Soon afterwards, Canada became involved in the Second World War which had broken out in Europe on 1 September 1939 and, accordingly, he left his post at Berkeley and joined the Royal Canadian Naval Volunteer Force (Reserve) as a Lieutenant (SB). Prior to the war, the Royal Canadian Navy was very small in size, but during the war it rapidly expanded, consisting of just under 100,000 men and women who manned 471 fighting vessels of various types. After bravely contributing to the Canadian war effort, Irving resumed his teaching career at the Carleton University in Ottawa, before moving to South America where he became the director of Colegio Nueva Granada in Bogota, Colombia.

After teaching there for a short period, he moved to New York in 1945 and took up the post of Assistant Professor of Romance Languages at Wells College, Aurora. In the following year, he went to the Central American country of Guatemala and taught at the Catedratico University de San Carlos for two years, before returning to the United States in 1948 to establish the Department of Near Eastern Studies at the University of Minnesota, Minneapolis, where he began to teach Arabic for the first time. In his own words,

> My chance at Arabic came after the Second World War... when a former classmate from Princeton, Donald Swanson, asked my chairman (in Romance Languages, Professor Francis Barton) for permission for me to teach Arabic in his new Department of Linguistics. Don had been asked to set up a linguistic program at Minnesota. He was a pure linguist who specialised in Greek and Sanskrit, and did not want the languages of his new department to be exclusively European as happened in most academic programs in that day. From our acquaintance and friendship at Princeton, he offered me this golden opportunity.[8]

It was during his time at Minnesota that Irving published several books on Latin American culture and literature, including *Adventuras en Centro-America* (1951) and *Paisajer del Sur* (1954). However, it was his *Falcon of Spain: A Study of Eight-Century Spain, with special emphasis upon the life of the Umayyad Ruler Abdur Rahman I (756–788)* (1954) that earned Irving considerable recognition as a historian and linguist. Being fluent in Spanish, French, German, as well as Arabic, enabled him to read extensively about the formative period of Muslim Spain, and thus, allowed him to reconstruct the life and career of one of medieval Europe's most brilliant rulers and statesmen.

In his preface to this book, Irving wrote, 'Ever since the beginning of my studies of Arabic, I have been interested in the life story of Abdurrahman ibn Mu'awiyah, the first Umayyad ruler of Spain... No one has made a proper biography of this European ruler who controlled the destinies of Spain throughout thirty-two critical years. Dozy is moreover inclined to interpret Abdurrahman as an oriental despot and to consider any non-Christian as a renegade. I feel he should rather have compared Abdurrahman's reign with that of Charlemagne, and Spanish Islam with contemporary European Christianity.'[9]

Although Irving's biography of Abd al-Rahman I was not free from error, soon after its publication, it was widely reviewed and became a standard work of reference on the subject, and it was simultaneously published in Guatemala as *Halcon de Espana* (1954).

Irving's interest in Arabic and Islamic history subsequently earned him a Fulbright research fellowship at the College of Arts, University of Baghdad where he stayed from 1956 to 1957, and this enabled him to enhance his knowledge of Arabic literature. During this period, he met and befriended Shaykh Taqi al-Din al-Hilali (1893–1987), a leading Moroccan Islamic scholar and traditionist (*Muhaddith*), who urged him to translate the Qur'an into English. He also performed the first of his two pilgrimages to Makkah in July 1957 under the patronage of Dr al-Hilali. On his return from the Middle East, Irving resumed teaching and research at Minnesota. He soon earned recognition within academia and became a member of many distinguished learned societies, including the American Oriental Society, Medieval Academy of America, Middle East Institute, Middle East Studies Association and Latin American Studies Association.

From Minnesota, he moved to North Central College, Naperville, Illinois, where he became the Professor of Foreign Languages in 1965. Thereafter, he served at the University of Guelph, Ontario, as a Professor of Spanish, before assuming the post of Professor of Romance Languages at the University of Tennessee, Knoxville, where he was subsequently promoted as Professor Emeritus. He eventually retired in 1980.

Irving also served as a Visiting Professor at several universities in America, Africa, Asia and the Middle East, including the University of Texas at Austin, Bayero University in Nigeria and the University of Libya in Tripoli. After his retirement, he became a trustee and served as the Dean of Faculty of Arts and Sciences at the American Islamic College in Chicago from 1981 to 1986. He also travelled extensively around the world and delivered lectures on aspects of Islam, Muslim history of Spain, and the challenges facing the Muslim world at the time. By all accounts, Irving was a prolific writer and translator. Based on his travels around the Muslim world, he published a detailed and critical survey of the Muslim world under the title of *Islam Resurgent: The Islamic World Today*. Although this book was first published in Nigeria in 1979, it was later reprinted in America as *The Tide of Islam* (1982). In his preface to this volume, the author wrote:

This description of the contribution of the Muslim countries to world culture reaches from the beginnings of Islam to the present day... Continuing events in the Middle East have shown the need for knowledge about this area by the general public... This work is not a hastily compiled volume. The author has investigated these areas of the world for decades, and taught related courses in well-known universities in the United States and Canada. His lecture notes were constantly updated through reading, contacts with natives of the area, as well as travel, research and lecturing in many of the countries discussed... The Islamic world is at present a powerful force and one which can be understood only as its nature and history become better known.[10]

However, Irving is today better known for his English translation of the Qur'an. He became fascinated by the sacred book of Islam during his student days, which prompted him to study Arabic in the first place, and after decades of researching and mastering the subtleties and intricacies of the language, he translated and published a slim volume entitled, *Selections from the Noble Reading* in 1968, which was later reprinted in Nigeria in the 1970s. It represented the first attempt to present parts of the Qur'an into American English by a Western Muslim. This volume was later expanded by Irving in collaboration with the Islamic Foundation in the United Kingdom and reissued as *The Qur'an: Basic Teachings* (1979). That became the foundation for his full translation and commentary of the Qur'an into American English, a project which he worked on for nearly quarter of a century, before it was finally completed during the early 1980s. Lack of funding delayed its publication until Amana Books, based in Vermont, agreed to publish only the translation without the commentary due to financial constraints.

Titled *The Qur'an: An American Version*, this new translation was fluent, accurate and in contemporary American English, unlike Abdullah Yusuf Ali and Marmaduke Pickthall's (see chapter 33) translations, but it proved to be less popular due to its peculiar title, which many Muslims found off-putting. Unlike the Bible, there is only one version of the Arabic Qur'an, and by giving his translation the title of 'An American Version', Irving unwittingly gave the impression that there could be different 'versions' of the Qur'an. That also explained why some reviewers were not very appreciative of his translation. However, in the introduction to his translation, he wrote:

In this new translation, I have attempted to accomplish what the West has generally failed to do with Islam: to study it from within and in the light of its own texts. The Qur'an is obviously the best preparation for such an attempt. Moreover this book gives the young Muslim something to hold on to in this day when most authority on moral matters is being abdicated... This present volume has been prepared in order to spread greater understanding of the Islamic religion and to present the English-speaking world with a clear rendition of the original Arabic into intelligible modern English... Our aim is to give pride to young English-speaking Muslims in North America especially, and also in Britain, the West Indies like Trinidad and Guyana, and the English-speaking parts of Africa. It can also be used by college students and interested non-Muslims who want a contemporary translation of this great world classic.[11]

As it was rendered into simple and easy-to-understand contemporary American English, and being free from linguistic and conceptual jargon, meant that Irving's work was praised by several prominent Muslim scholars. For example, referring to Irving's translation, Ismail Raji al-Faruqi (1921–1986), a notable American academic and Islamic scholar, observed that 'No interpretation can express the whole range of meanings contained in any given verse. But it can bring to light many a connotation which has escaped our attention in the past. In this respect the present translation breaks new ground, making refreshing reading even after all other translations have been read.' Likewise, Shaykh Dr A. H. Abdel Kader, a former Dean of the Faculty of Law at al-Azhar University, fully endorsed Irving's translation.

Unsurprisingly, his translation of the Qur'an was subsequently reprinted many times in America, Iran and India, both with and without the original Arabic text. In addition to the above, he wrote and published hundreds of essays, articles and reviews on Islamic thought, culture and history in books, journals, magazines and newspapers across the world, including *Impact International* (London), *Islamic Literature* (Lahore), *Muslim News* (Cape Town), *Message* (New Delhi), *Islamic Review* (London), *Muslim Education Quarterly* (Cambridge) and *Muslim World League Journal* (Makkah), among others. It is hoped that one day someone will collect, edit and publish his articles and reviews in the form of a book for the benefit of posterity.

Thankfully, many of his other contributions, written in both English and Spanish, were published and disseminated in the form of booklets such as *Religion and Social Responsibility: The Muslim's View* (Lahore, 1979); *El Poema de Jose* (Casida de Yusuf) [Cedar Rapids, 1988]; *El Cautiverio Babilonica de Andalucia* (Cedar Rapids, 1989); *Ten Days in Tehran* (Kuala Lumpur, 1980); *Had You Been Born a Muslim* (Chicago, 1976); *God Alone: The Concept of Allah in Islam* (Chicago, 1978); *Polished Jade Pulido* (San Gil Buenavista, 1981); and, *The Shorter Chapters of the Qur'an* (Kuala Lumpur, 1986).

In a series of articles he wrote for *Impact International* from the 1970s until his death, Irving drew the Muslim world's attention to the power, vitality and relevance of Islam as a spiritual, moral, ethical and intellectual standard-bearer in an increasingly secular and polarised world that was being dominated by disbelief, ignorance, xenophobia and hatred. In one such article, he stated that 'the Islamic world never lived in the same middle ages as Western Europe, and it is an injustice to call Islam 'medieval' or backward as some orientalists have done. For 14 centuries the Islamic world has formed a vast cultural enterprise which gathered up and prolonged the legacy of antiquity, and transmitted this into the European Middle Ages and renaissance for use in modern times. Without this, much of our classical heritage would have been lost, while the agriculture, learning and mechanics of India and China were likewise passed on to Europe and America through the incredibly active Islamic world.'[12]

Needless to say, Irving was fully abreast of the social, political, economic and intellectual condition of the Muslim world. He felt that the Islamic world had the potential to become a truly powerful force for good in global affairs, but the absence of political unity, economic co-operation, educational progress and Islamic solidarity had undermined the Muslim *ummah*. That, in turn, had enabled external forces to enter the House of Islam like wolves in sheep's clothing to preserve and protect their own political, economic and cultural interests rather than that of Islam and Muslims.

Likewise, he was a vociferous champion of Palestinian rights and repeatedly warned the Muslims of America that certain political groups were actively seeking to exacerbate and undermine their relations with mainstream America, as well as the Western world as a whole, and that they must always remain alert and vigilant. In his own words, 'They do not know how to handle Islam as an intellectual concept that holds sway over one-fifth of the world's population, but treat us for sensationalism, as if Islam were still an alien phenomenon subject to visions of the medieval crusade, and not the religion of one-fifth of the world's population...United States needs to accommodate itself to the Islamic and Arab world, as well as to the mass of citizens who profess Islam in this country, and pray to God Alone.'[13]

Irving and his wife, Dr Evelyn U. Irving, eventually moved to Cedar Rapids in Iowa to be close to its 'Mother Mosque' (*Ummul Masajid*), being the oldest mosque in the United States. Here, he collaborated with several prominent local Muslims to establish the Unity Publishing Company in March 1975 to produce high quality, authentic and relevant Islamic literature for the benefit of American Muslims, but lack of financial support from the Muslim community hampered this much-needed publishing project.[14]

However, on Irving's eightieth birthday, his contribution to Islam and the Muslim community of Iowa in particular was officially recognised by Larry J. Serbousek, the then Mayor of Iowa, who proclaimed 20 July 1994 as 'Dr Thomas B. Irving Day', although the Muslim community sadly continue to neglect one of its foremost historians, scholars and linguists.

Just before his eightieth birthday, Irving also underwent heart surgery as well as a cataract operation, but he continued to read and write incessantly. However, after the death of his wife on 28 February 1999, he moved to Mississippi where he stayed with his son, Dr Nicholas Irving, a polymer scientist. Two years later, he fell into a coma but never failed to respond to the recitation of *Kalimat al-Shahadah* (Islamic credo). He eventually died at the age of 88, leaving behind a son, two daughters and seven grandchildren.

In conclusion, Thomas Ballantine Irving was a devout, committed and gifted Muslim historian, scholar and translator who not only devoted his entire life to the service of Islam, the Qur'an and the Muslim *ummah*, but continued to remind fellow Muslims to 'remain faithful to Islam.'

(N)

1. Thomas Ballantine Irving, *The Tide of Islam*.

2. T. B. Irving, 'Interesting life, friends all around the world', *Impact International*, September 1994.

3. Ibid.

4. Muhammad Abdul Jabbar Beg, 'T. B. Irving: An American Writer' unpublished obituary, October 2002.

5. S. A. Khulusi (ed.), *Islam Our Choice*.

6. Sheila Musaji, 'Interview with Prof. T. B. Irving', see www.theamericanmuslim.org

7. S. A. Khulusi (ed.), op. cit.

8. T. B. Irving, op. cit.

9. T. B. Irving, *The Falcon of Spain*.

10. T. B. Irving, *Islam Resurgent: The Islamic World Today*.

11. T. B. Irving, *The Noble Qur'an: Arabic Text and English Translation*.

12. T. B. Irving, 'Islamic Contribution to Culture', *Impact International*, 1978 (reprinted in 2004).

13. T. B. Irving, op. cit.

14. Yahya Aossey, Jr., *Fifty Years of Islam in Iowa 1925–1975*.

# 47

# ALIJA IZETBEGOVIC

B. 1925 – D. 2003

BOSNIA HERZEGOVINA

As a Muslim country, Bosnia and Herzegovina has more in common with Bangladesh than probably any other Muslim country. Born out of war, both are relatively new countries with rich and varied history and culture. Both countries have experienced numerous conflicts and partitions, and have survived the vicissitudes of time and change. Despite being proud Muslims, the people of both Bosnia and Bangladesh are, generally speaking, open, tolerant and respectful of people of other racial, religious, cultural and linguistic backgrounds.

Likewise, their contribution to Islamic thought and culture is nothing short of remarkable yet, within the context of the Muslim *ummah* as a whole, both countries have been relegated to the periphery. Historians and scholars, both Muslim and non-Muslim, have wittingly or unwittingly contributed to their marginalisation by overlooking, if not completely ignoring their contribution to the development and progress of Islamic thought, culture and heritage.

And although Islam made in-roads into both countries incrementally over many centuries, the majority of their population have remained committed to their faith, notwithstanding concerted efforts by various powerful ideological, nationalistic, religious and cultural forces to undermine them and their faith and culture. However, whilst Bangladesh seceded from Pakistan only to find itself at the mercy of a powerful and encroaching neighbour, Bosnia was forced to fight against an aggressor that was bent on its destruction.

Indeed, when war broke out in the Balkans during the 1990s, the people of Bosnia and Herzegovina were faced with two stark choices: to fight for their survival or be wiped away from the global map. Under the inspirational leadership of Alija Izetbegovic, the first philosopher-president of Bosnia, the brave and indomitable people of that country successfully fought against the forces of darkness and hatred and, in so doing, secured their future.

Alija Ali Izetbegovic was born into a respectable Muslim family in the village of Bosanki Samac, which is today a municipality in northern Bosnia. His father, Mustafa Izetbegovic, was a merchant by profession and his mother, Hiba, was a devout Muslim and homemaker who ensured that her five children, as well as the large extended family, received good care and attention. They lived in a modest but spacious house overlooking two of Bosnia's largest rivers, namely Bosna and the Sava. The family had been very wealthy and influential during the Ottoman times but, during the Austro-Hungarian period, their political and economic fortunes declined rapidly. This forced Izetbegovic's grandfather to leave Belgrade and settle in Bosanki Samac with his Turkish wife and five children in the mid-nineteenth century. He later served as the mayor of this town and became well-known for his political, social and cultural activities.

His son, Mustafa, grew up in Bosanki Samac and became a successful merchant but, by the time Izetbegovic was born, his father's business had suffered serious losses. Accordingly, the family moved to Sarajevo where they were forced to endure considerable social and economic predicaments, which was compounded by Mustafa's ill-health. According to Izetbegovic, 'My childhood was affected by my father's illness. He had been seriously wounded in the First World War, at the Italian front in Piava. This later turned into a kind of paralysis, so that, for the last ten years of his life, he was more or less bedridden. My late mother took great care of him, and we children helped as best we could, growing up with a good deal of freedom.'[1]

Young Izetbegovic grew up in a devout and educated Muslim family. He was particularly influenced by his mother whose devotion and commitment to her faith profoundly influenced him not only during his formative years, but throughout his adult life too. He later recalled how his mother would wake up regularly at dawn to perform her morning prayers and she encouraged him to do the same. In his own words,

I was reluctant to get up, naturally, being then only 12 or 14 years old, but I was always glad when returning home, especially on spring mornings. The sun would already have risen, and the old Imam Mujezinovic would be in the Mosque. He always recited the wonderful *Surah al-Rahman* from the Qur'an with the second *ruku* (bowing) of the *Sabah* prayer. The Mosque amid the spring blossom, the *Sabah* morning prayer that *Surah al-Rahman* and that *alim* – respected by everyone in the neighbourhood, form one of the beautiful images that I can still see clearly through the mists of the years that have long since passed.[2]

During his early years, Izetbegovic attended his local *maktab* (Qur'an school) for basic Arabic and Islamic education before enrolling at Sarajevo's First Boy's Gymnasium (*Prva muska gimnazija*), an elite school for children from prominent Bosnian families, where he studied for the next eight years. Whilst he was pursuing his primary and secondary education in mathematics, science, languages, history, geography and religious education, he became heavily influenced by secular ideologies (especially Communist propaganda) that were so strong and pervasive at his high school. As a result, he became sceptical about religious beliefs and practices during his teens.

However, a few years later, he regained his faith; never to waver again. And, although he was not academically very gifted, he was certainly a voracious reader of books. Indeed, during his final years at high school, he claimed to have not only read, but also became thoroughly familiar with the writings of many prominent European philosophers and thinkers like Francis Bacon (1561–1626), David Hume (1711–1776), Immanuel Kant (1724–1804), Georg Wilhelm Friedrich Hegel (1770–1831), Auguste Comte (1798–1857), Friedrich Engels (1820–1895), Henri Bergson (1859–1941) and Oswald Spengler (1880–1936), in addition to aspects of Indian philosophy and spirituality.

He graduated in 1943 at the age of 18. This was an unprecedented period in the history of modern Europe as the Second World War was raging across the continent at the time. But following the invasion of the Kingdom of Yugoslavia (fl. 1918–1945) by the Axis powers (led by Germany, Italy and Japan), Bosnia became a part of the fascist Independent State of Croatia (fl. 1941–1945). During this period, Serbian nationalists instigated atrocities and reprisal attacks against the Muslims of Bosnia and, as a result, more than 100 *ulama* or Islamic scholars (linked to the *El-Hidaje* organisation) convened and duly issued the 'Resolution of Sarajevo Muslims', which was authored jointly by Mehmed efendi Handzic (see chapter 42) and Kasim efendi Dobraca (1910–1979), in order to protect the Bosnian Muslims from ongoing persecution and brutality at the hands of the fascists.

Unfortunately, the Muslims did not help their cause by dividing into two opposing camps, namely those affiliated with 'Gajret' (Muslim Serbs) and those linked to 'Narodna Uzdanica' (Muslim Croats). At the same time, a severe shortage of food and other essentials led to widespread famine and suffering, thus adding to the people's misery and hardship.[3]

It was during this critical period in the history of Bosnia and Herzegovina that a group of Muslim students formed the *Mladi Muslimani* (The Young Muslims Association). Initially, members of this group consisted of Esad Karadozovic (b. 1918), a medical student; Tarik Muftic (b. 1920), a forestry student; Emin Granov, an engineering student, and Husref Basagic, who was a civil engineering student at the time. In due course, they were joined by several other students from the First Gymnasium in Sarajevo including Alija Izetbegovic, Nedzib Sacirbegovic and Esref Campara.

As it happened, Izetbegovic became an active member of the Association after hearing its members discussing and debating about Islam and its role in modern society. In his own words, 'They outlined some new ideas that were more in line with what I wanted to hear about my religion. It was all very different from what we had learned in the *maktabs*, the religious instruction we had had at school, the lectures we had attended, or the articles we read in the journals of the day. I see it as a matter of the relationship between essence and form – the *hojjas* (Islamic religious teachers or priests) were, in our view, more inclined to interpret the rituals or external forms of Islam, while neglecting the essence.'[4]

Thereafter, the members of the Association met regularly at 'Trezvenost' (The Sobriety), which was a cultural and literary society based in Sarajevo, and engaged in heated discussions and debates about Islam, its meaning and purpose in the modern world, as well as its role in Bosnian society. They also read Islamic revivalist literature like *Islam u Svijetlosti Istine* (Islam in the Light of Truth) by Mehmed Alija Metiljevic (d.1934), *Muhamed i Kur'an* (Prophet Muhammad and Qur'an) by Osman Nuri Hadzic (1869–1937) and other books by Halil Halid Bey (1869–1931), who was an Ottoman writer and reformer.[5] Although the members of the Association considered the traditional *ulama* to be out of touch with reality – thus being a barrier to Islamic revivalism in the Balkans – yet they agreed to work with *El-Hidaje* in order to revive the message of Islam in Bosnia.

However, unlike the *ulama*, the Association pursued an ideological interpretation of Islam because they not only wanted to transform the social, educational and intellectual condition of their people in the image of Islam, but they also advocated the need for unity and solidarity within the Muslim *ummah* as a whole. At the same time, the other members of the Association were fully aware that their Islamic activism could lead to direct confrontation with two of the most powerful ideological forces that dominated Europe's socio-political order at the time, namely Hitler's Fascism and Stalin's Communism.

Undeterred by such threats, Izetbegovic and his colleagues continued their Islamic activism and, in the process, they recruited hundreds of members across Bosnia, although the main centres of their activity were Sarajevo, Mostar and Zagreb. In fact, the Association became so successful that it soon established its presence in no less than thirty towns and villages across Bosnia, in addition to listing another 1000 members in Herzegovina alone. Needless to say, this must have shocked and horrified the ruling junta, although according to Izetbegovic,

During the 1941–45 War there was a kind of unspoken non-confrontation agreement between ourselves and the authorities of the day: we avoided direct confrontation, although we were clearly the opposition. During 1944, I became less and less active, unhappy that the organisation had made a pact with El-Hidaje… I never wholly agreed with the *hojjas*, although there were many among them whom I respected. I was of the opinion that there should not be a special social class or order either of *hojjas* or of sheikhs, and that they were the proponents of a view of Islam that impeded both internal and external development. I said as much publicly, and was to some extent denounced as a result. After the war ended, we continued our activities, to the horror of the communist authorities. They tried to dissuade us and, when they failed, began arresting us in early 1946 or thereabouts.[6]

As the Communist regime of Josip Tito (1892–1980) felt threatened by the Association's growing popularity, they not only began to closely monitor the activities of its senior leadership, but they also put considerable pressure on its general members to deter them from their religious activities. When such measures failed to undermine the Association and its expansion, they arrested around fourteen of its leading activists including Izetbegovic, who was only 20 at the time. Charged with subversive activities, the group were sentenced to three years imprisonment. Although this was the first time that the Communist regime had charged and imprisoned members of the Association, it was not the last time that they took such harsh measures against its senior leadership.

After serving thirty-six months in prison, Izetbegovic was released and soon afterwards, he enrolled at the University of Sarajevo to study Agronomy. He also married during this period but, a few years later, lost interest in his studies before transferring over to the Faculty of Law in 1954. He eventually graduated with a law degree in November 1956 at the age of 31. He combined his studies with Islamic activism, albeit in a covert form, and contributed scores of articles to the Association's journal *Mudzahid* (*Mujahid*) or 'warrior'. It was during this time that the regime tried to bludgeon the Islamic movement through mass arrest of its leading members. Some (such as Izetbegovic) survived the ordeal but most of his colleagues (including Hasan Biber, Halid Kajtaz, Omer Stupac and Nusret Fazlibegovic) were brutally tortured before being executed by a firing squad of the State Security Service.

As for Izetbegovic, after graduating from university, he was forced to seek employment to make ends meet. He began working for a construction company and continued to combine his work with Islamic activism in a covert form. During this period he wrote many articles on aspects of Islam and the challenges facing Muslims at the time. Some of those articles were later published under the title of *Problemi Islamskog Preporoda* (The Problems of Islamic Regeneration). After working for a decade as the head of the company's hydro-electricity generating plant site in Niksic, which is today located in

Montenegro, he wrote his *Islamska Deklaracija* (Islamic Declaration) in 1969; it was revised and published a year later. Although it consisted of only forty pages, this manifesto was later destined to become one of his most contested works. According to Izetbegovic,

> The dominant idea of the *Declaration* is that only Islam can reawaken the imagination of the Muslim masses and render them capable of being once again active participants in their own history. Western ideas are incapable of this. This message was attacked as fundamentalist, which it was, in one particular sense: it appealed to a return to the sources. It condemned authoritarian regimes, called for increased expenditure on education, and advocated a new position for women, non-violence and rights of minorities. The *Declaration* was received in the West with considerable reservation. In my view, they could not forgive the fact that it placed Islam at the heart of the solution.[7]

Although the document did not cause much of a stir or alarm at the time of its publication, however, during the early 1980s it became the main focus of contention due to Izetbegovic's determination to promote Islam in Bosnia and Herzegovina; at the time he worked as a legal advisor. Incensed by his Islamic activities, Yugoslavia's Secret Police arrested many Bosnian Muslim activists in 1983. In addition to Izetbegovic, other prominent Muslim intellectuals and activists (such as Edhem Bicakcic, Omer Behmen, Mustafa Spahic, Hasan Cengic and Melika Salihbegovic) were accused of conspiring against the State.

Dubbed the 'Sarajevo Trial', each one of them were separately interrogated and forced to sign false testimonies before being charged with offences that included hostility towards the State, fomenting Muslim nationalism and disseminating fundamentalist propaganda in Yugoslavia. Passages were plucked out of Izetbegovic's *Islamic Declaration* to prove that he was an Islamic fundamentalist who was determined to establish an Islamic State in Bosnia, despite the fact that the *Declaration* was more about the Muslim world as a whole and did not mention Bosnia by name even once.

Furthermore, evidence provided by the State prosecutors suggested that Izetbegovic was the leader of a dissident Muslim group when, in fact, such a group did not exist and, therefore, his being their leader was out of the question.[8] However, the prosecutors were not interested in facts or evidence; rather, they were determined to find them all guilty and, of course, the partiality of the presiding judge helped the prosecutors to make their case. Found guilty of subversive activities, they were all sentenced to fourteen years incarceration with hard labour, although prominent human rights organisations like Amnesty International and Helsinki Watch, among others, considered this to be no more than Communist propaganda and a travesty of justice.

Prior to this, Izetbegovic had completed his famous book, *Islam izmedu Istoka i Zapada* (Islam between East and West), which was translated into English and first published in the United States by American Trust Publications. Although the author claimed to have written this book as early as 1946 while he was still in his early twenties, however, according to Enes Karic, a leading Bosnian scholar and historian, textual evidence suggests that he continued to revise and improve the book over the next thirty years or so before it was finally published in 1984.[9]

In this work, the author attempted to provide a critical evaluation of modern Western thought and philosophy in the light of the Islamic worldview. He pursued a dualistic approach; just as man consists of matter and spirit, the world is also divided into the East and the West. Likewise, science and technology provide a conception of life that is different from the perspective offered by religion, art and ethics. Between the Old and New Testament, there is the Final Testament (Qur'an) and if Moses was a leader, then Jesus was no more than a preacher, whilst the Prophet Muhammad (peace be upon them all) combined both roles. That is why Izetbegovic considered Islam to be a synthesis. In his own words,

> Islam's middle position can be recognized by the fact that Islam has always been attacked from the two opposite directions: from the side of religion that it is too natural, actual, and tuned to the world; and from the side of science that it contains religious and mystical elements. There is only one Islam, but like man, it has both soul and body. Its contrary aspects dependent on a different point of view: materialists only see Islam…as a 'right wing' tendency, while Christians see it only as a socio-political movement, as a left-wing tendency. The same dualistic impression repeats itself when looking from inside as well…The mystics have always stressed the religious aspect of Islam, the rationalists the other one. All the same, both of them have always had difficulties with Islam, simply because it cannot be put into any of their classifications.[10]

In a bipolar world, argued Izetbegovic, Islam has to be an intermediary between 'ancient cultures and the West, it must again today, in a time of dramatic dilemmas and alternatives, shoulder its role of intermediary nation in the divided world. This is the meaning of the third way, the Islamic way.' However, as the author was not trained in Arabic and the classical Islamic sciences, some Muslim scholars (such as Enes Karic) have accused him of essentialising Islam, while others (such as Muhammad al-Ghazali, not to be confused with the Egyptian scholar) have hailed him as an outstanding European Muslim philosopher and thinker who provided one of the most penetrating and cogent critiques of modern Western thought and philosophy.[11] Either way, Izetbegovic's work soon became very popular and it was swiftly translated into many languages including Arabic, Albanian, Turkish, German, Urdu and Indonesian, thus establishing his reputation as one of the leading European Muslim scholars and thinkers of the second half of the twentieth century.

However, after the collapse of Communism in 1989–1990, perhaps triggered by the fall of the Berlin Wall, Izetbegovic was released by the new authorities, having already served six years in prison. During his time in prison, he kept a detailed diary which was subsequently published as *Moj bijeg u Slobdu: Biljeske iz Zatvora 1983–1988* (Notes from Prison, 1983–1988). Upon his release, he founded *Stranka Demokratske Akcije* (SDA) or the 'Party of Democratic Action' for the purpose of establishing an open, tolerant, democratic and inclusive society in Yugoslavia, not least because the Muslims had suffered terribly during forty years of Communist rule. In a multi-party system of governance, he felt democratic parties could foster a culture of openness and transparency in a country that had witnessed so much repression over such a long period of time. After elections were held on 18 November 1990, the SDA won 86 of 240 seats in the Bosnian parliament and, being the head of the largest single party, Izetbegovic became the chairman of the power-sharing Presidency. Unfortunately, ethnic conflict eventually broke out between the Serbs and Croats, followed by armed contest between Slovenia and Croatia in the summer of 1991.

As expected, Bosnia soon became embroiled in the conflict which, in turn, forced Izetbegovic to declare their independence in March 1992. The European Union and United States immediately recognised the Republic of Bosnia and Herzegovina but the Bosnian Serbs, encouraged by Belgrade as well as Bosnian Croats, instigated a separatist war that lasted for three and a half years. During this period, tens of thousands of people (especially Bosnian Muslims) were systematically slaughtered by both Serb and Croat nationalists. NATO eventually intervened, thus forcing the warring parties to cease hostilities by formally signing the Dayton Accord in Paris on 14 December 1995.[12] However, Izetbegovic continued to serve as a member of the Presidency of Bosnia and Herzegovina until October 2000.

Thanks to his outstanding contribution and achievements, the people of Bosnia fondly referred to him as *Dedo* (meaning 'grandfather') and the Kingdom of Saudi Arabia duly awarded him the King Faisal International Prize for his services to Islam in 1993. Towards the end of his life, Izetbegovic wrote his autobiography under the title of *Sjecanja: Autobiografski zapisi*, which was subsequently translated into English and published as *Inescapable Questions: Autobiographical Notes* in 2003 by the Islamic Foundation, United Kingdom.

He died of a heart attack at the age of 78 and was buried in his beloved Sarajevo. In 2007 a museum was established at Kovaci in Sarajevo as a lasting tribute to his memory. By all accounts, Izetbegovic was a devout, learned and committed Muslim who was equally proud of his European culture and heritage. Above all, he was an independent-minded scholar and thinker who never ceased to wrestle with the challenges and difficulties of his time because the quest for meaning and purpose in the modern world demanded nothing less. In his own words,

What we call happiness is sometimes the accordance between our life and circumstance, our biography and history, our personal aspirations and historical currents. If I look at things that way, I can say: I was born too early to be happy. But birth is one of the many things we do not get to choose. It is part of our destiny. If I were offered life again, I would refuse it. But, if I had to be born again, I would choose my life.[13]

1. Alija Izetbegovic, *Inescapable Questions: Autobiographical Notes*.

2. Ibid.

3. Noel Malcolm, *Bosnia: A Short History*.

4. Alija Izetbegovic, op. cit.

5. Fikret Karcic, 'Bosnian Young Muslims: A Review Essay', *Islamic Quarterly*, vol. 45, no. 1.

6. Alija Izetbegovic, op. cit.

7. Ibid.

8. Amina Selimovic, 'Dualism of the World: An Analysis of Islam between East and West', unpublished MA thesis, University of Oslo, 2009.

9. Enes Karic, 'Islam in "Islam between East and West" ', *Journal of Intercultural and Religious Studies*, vol. 4.

10. Alija Ali Izetbegovic, *Islam between East and West*.

11. Muhammad al-Ghazali, 'Islam between East and West: The Magnum Opus of Alija Izetbegovic', *Islamic Studies*, vol. 36, no. 2.

12. Noel Malcolm, op. cit.

13. Alija Izetbegovic, *Inescapable Questions: Autobiographical Notes*.

# 48

# LOIS IBSEN AL-FARUQI

B. 1927 – D. 1986

UNITED STATES OF AMERICA

Although Muslim women have played a hugely influential role in the development and progress of Islamic thought, culture and civilisation, however their contribution and achievements have not received sufficient recognition and acknowledgement, both in the Muslim world and the West. For example, al-Shafi'i's (767–820) pioneering contribution to Islamic jurisprudence is universally recognised – and rightly so – but the life and work of Sayyida Nafisa (762–824), who was the teacher of al-Shafi'i, is not widely known.

Likewise, historians consider the reign of the Abbasid Caliph Abu Ja'far al-Mansur (r. 754–775) as an important period in the history of the Abbasid Empire, yet very little is known about his influential wife, Umm Musa Arwa bint Mansur al-Himyari (735–764), who not only guided her husband from behind the scenes, but also forced him to sign a written agreement preventing him from taking a second wife whilst she was still alive. As for Caliph Harun al-Rashid (763–809), he is equally famous in the East and the West but the life and contribution of his influential and generous wife, Zubayda (d. 831), has been largely forgotten. Similarly during a chaotic period in the history of Islamic Spain, Subh or 'Aurora', the beautiful mother of Caliph Hisham ibn al-Hakam (r. 788–796), who was of Basque origin, became the real mover and shaker from behind the scenes.[1]

In the same way, many prominent Muslim female scholars and jurists actively assisted their equally learned fathers and husbands to resolve complex legal and theological problems, but once again, their contribution is not widely known or recognised. For instance, Lubna of Cordova was one of the leading mathematicians and intellectuals of the second half of the tenth century, who also served as a private secretary to her father, Caliph al-Hakam II (see chapter 51 for more information), but very little is known about her today. Likewise, Fatimah bint Muhammad ibn Ahmad al-Samarqandi was a prominent Islamic theologian and jurist who served as a personal advisor to the famous Sultan Nur al-Din Zangi (1118–1174), but her life and contribution has also been forgotten.

Many modern Muslim female scholars have suffered the same fate due to their personal humility and humbleness, and their desire to contribute from behind the scenes without seeking any self-promotion or publicity. One such gifted academic, Islamic scholar and prolific writer was Lois al-Faruqi of the United States of America.

Lois Ibsen al-Faruqi, better known as Lamya al-Faruqi, was born in the Western American State of Montana into a traditional Christian family. Her exact date of birth is contested; some writers have suggested that she was born in 1927, although the majority are agreed that Lois was born on 25 July 1926. Either way, she grew up in an ambience where arts and music were not only enjoyed but also actively encouraged and pursued by her family members. Thus unsurprisingly, she became interested in music and arts from an early age. She was very fond of the piano and became proficient at playing the large musical instrument, initially at home and subsequently at school. After completing her early and secondary education, she chose to pursue higher education in Western music with a view to becoming a pianist and musical performer.

Accordingly, she joined the University of Montana to study for a first degree in music and graduated in 1948 before moving to the University of Indiana for a master's degree in the same subject. In so doing, she successfully completed her higher education in 1949; she was around 21 at the time.[2] It was during her time at Indiana that she met and subsequently married Ismail Raji al-Faruqi (1921–1986). Born and raised in British Mandate Palestine, Ismail received his early education in Arabic, Islamic studies and French before obtaining a degree in philosophy from the American University of Beirut in 1941. After the establishment of the State of Israel, he was forced to move to the United States where he resumed his studies in the Graduate School of Arts and Sciences at the University of Indiana in 1948 and received his master's degree in philosophy. Thereafter, he obtained another Master of Arts degree in philosophy from Harvard University in 1951 before returning to Indiana University in Bloomington to complete another Master of Arts degree in philosophy.

It was during this time that Lois embraced Islam, although the reasons for her conversion are not known. Having married a Palestinian Muslim, perhaps she felt that the next appropriate step to take was to become a Muslim, although she was far too intelligent, educated and culturally sophisticated to embrace Islam only for worldly reasons. There is no doubt that she found Islam to be a simple, rational and authentic manifestation of the Divine Will as expressed in the form of the Arabic Qur'an and the teachings of the Prophet of Islam. Unlike the message of the Biblical prophets (such as Abraham, Moses and Jesus), she felt that the teachings of Prophet Muhammad (peace be upon them all) had remained unaltered and intact to the present day. In her own words,

> Both the Prophethood of Muhammad and the Qur'an he conveyed as the message dictated to him by the angel on behalf of God represent the highest and ultimate development of the phenomenon of prophecy. Unlike any prophet before him, were Muhammad to return today, he would doubtless acknowledge the Qur'an to be the same text he received from God and conveyed to his companions. The text has been preserved absolutely intact. Not one jot or tittle has changed. Diacritical marks have been added and the calligraphy has been improved to facilitate its correct reading and recitation. Its parts stand today in exactly the same order in which the Prophet was instructed by the Angel to arrange them. Moreover, the language the Prophet and his contemporaries spoke is still alive. It is read, written, and spoken by millions. Its grammar, syntax, idioms, literary forms – the media of expression and the constituents of literary beauty – all are still the same as they were in the Prophet's time. All this makes of the Qur'an as phenomenon of human culture without parallel.[3]

In other words, Lois embraced Islam because she found it to be intellectually sound, scripturally authentic and culturally tolerant and inclusive. However, on a personal level, both Lois and Ismail faced considerable financial difficulties and hardship after their marriage. Although her husband had successfully completed two master's degrees, he was unable to secure a regular job, thus he turned to working as a translator of Arabic books. During this period, Ismail translated several titles by prominent scholars and writers like Khalid Muhammad Khalid (1920–1996) and Muhammad al-Ghazali (1917–1996), for which the American Council of Learned Societies paid him one thousand dollars. With this money he set up a construction company that specialised in building and refurbishing properties. His eye for appealing décor and quality furnishings made his homes attractive to buyers which, in turn, transformed his economic fortunes as he sold enough homes to make his family financially independent.

Like Lois, her husband was a scholarly person who was convinced that 'the way to nonmaterial pursuits goes through the materiality of one's financial situation. It was a dangerous and vicious course, for means can become ends if pursued over a certain period of time; and so is the allure of money, which outstrips women as well as power.'[4] Unsurprisingly, as soon as he had made sufficient money, Ismail left the construction industry and returned to the real love and passion of his life, namely the pursuit of knowledge and wisdom. Thereafter he enrolled at the University of Indiana and submitted his doctoral thesis on 'Justifying the Good: Metaphysics and Epistemology of Value', for which he was awarded a doctorate in September 1952. After successfully completing their higher education, both Lois and Ismail travelled to the Middle East in 1953 in order to acquire mastery of Arabic as well as undertake an in-depth study of the traditional Islamic sciences.

During their four-year stay in Cairo, Lois became thoroughly familiar with Arabic language and literature whilst her husband pursued post-doctoral research in Islamic sciences at the University of al-Azhar. Although prior to her conversion to Islam, Lois had pursued extensive training in Western music and arts but, during her four-year stay in Cairo, she became interested in Arabic language, Islamic thought, history and culture. Her first exposure to traditional Muslim society had a profound impact on her ideas, thoughts and outlook on life. She not only visited local Muslim families, but she also found them to be open, welcoming and hospitable, unlike in modern Western societies where modernity and secularisation, she felt, had undermined respect and regard for traditional family values.

During this period, Lois also became familiar with aspects of Islamic music and arts which enabled her to combine the study of Western arts and music with the rich Islamic artistic tradition. After completing their Islamic education in Cairo, Lois and her husband eventually returned to the United States in September 1958. Soon afterwards, Ismail was invited to join the Institute of Islamic Studies at McGill University in Montreal, Canada, by none other than Wilfred Cantwell Smith (1916–2000), who was a renowned Orientalist and the director of the institute at the time.

At McGill, Ismail pursued extensive research in Arabism (*Urubah*) and religion, Jewish history and Christian theology, thanks to the offer of a Rockefeller Foundation Fellowship, and actively participated in seminars, conferences and debates. He wrote a number of monographs during this period including *Urubah and Religion: An Analysis of the Dominant Ideas of Arabism and of Islam as Its Highest Moment of Consciousness* (1962), *Usul al-Sahuniyyah fi Din al-Yahudi* (An Analytical Study of the Growth of Particularism in Hebrew Scripture, 1964) and *Christian Ethics: A Systematic and Historical Analysis of Its Dominant Ideas* (1968). Lois was not only a great supporter of her husband's academic and literary activities, she also continued her own study and research on aspects of Islamic thought and culture at McGill University.

A few years later, Lois and her husband moved to Karachi, Pakistan on the invitation of Ishtiaq Husain Qureshi (1903–1981), who was a leading historian and director of the Central Institute of Islamic Research, which was established by President Muhammad Ayub Khan. They came to Pakistan in October 1961 with the hope of establishing a research institute for undertaking serious academic study of Islam and Muslim culture, but their hopes were subsequently dashed by internal politics and wrangling, which eventually forced them to return to the United States in September 1963. However, Ismail's stay in Karachi did force him to reconsider his views on Arabism because he had discovered, much to his surprise, that the non-Arab Muslims were more interested in Islamic unity and solidarity than any nationalistic causes, Arab or otherwise.

After teaching at the University of Chicago's Faculty of Divinity for a year, Ismail was offered the post of associate professor of Islamic Studies and History of Religion at Syracuse University in New York. In the meantime, Lois became busy raising their young family but, as a true seeker of knowledge, in her spare time she continued her research in Islamic thought and culture. By that time she had become more interested in the Islamic artistic tradition than in Western music because her exposure to the Islamic world completely transformed her views and outlook on life. In other words, like her husband, she came to realise that the fountainhead of Islamic thought, culture and civilisation was the concept of *tawhid* (or Divine Oneness and Unity). In her own words,

> There can be no doubt that the essence of Islamic civilization is Islam; or that the essence of Islam is *tawhid*, the act of affirming Allah to be the One, absolute, transcendent Creator, Lord and Master of all that is. These two fundamental premises are self-evident. They have never been doubted by those who belonged to this civilization or participated in it. And only very recently have missionaries, Orientalists, and other interpreters of Islam subjected them to doubt. Whatever their level of education, Muslims are apodictically certain that Islamic civilization does have an essence, that this essence is knowledge and capable of analysis or description, that it is *tawhid*. Traditionally and simply expressed, *tawhid* is the conviction and witnessing that 'there is no God but God.' This negative statement, brief to the utmost limits of brevity, carries the greatest and richest meanings in the whole of Islam. Sometimes, a whole culture, a whole civilization, or a whole history lies compressed in one sentence. This certainly is the case of the *kalimah* (pronouncement) or *shahadah* (witnessing) of Islam. All the diversity, wealth and history, culture and learning, wisdom and civilization of Islam is compressed in this shortest of sentences '*La ilaha illa Allah*'.[5]

After teaching at Syracuse for four years, in September 1968, Ismail was appointed as a full professor in the Department of Religion at Temple University, whilst Lois enrolled for a doctorate in Islamic Studies in the Department of Humanities at Syracuse University. After many years of dedicated research and writing, she finally submitted her thesis on 'The Nature of the Musical Art of Islamic Culture: A Theoretical and Empirical

Study of Arabian Music'.[6] Although she was awarded a doctorate in 1974, for reasons unknown, her thesis was never published in its entirety.

However, parts of the thesis were subsequently published as chapters in a number of books and journals. For example, the following essays were partly based on her doctoral thesis: 'The Shariʿah on Music and Musicians' (published in *Islamic Thought and Culture* edited by Ismail al-Faruqi, 1982); '*Muwashshah:* A Vocal Form in Islamic Culture' (published in *Ethnomusicology*, vol. 19, no. 1); 'Ornamentation in Arabian Improvisational Music: A Study of Interrelatedness in the Arts' (published in *The World of Music*, vol. 22, no.1); 'The Status of Music in Muslim Nations: Evidence from the Arab World' (published in *Asian Music*, vol. 12, no. 1); and, 'Tartil al-Qurʾan al-Karim' (published in *Islamic Perspectives* edited by K. Ahmad and Z. I. Ansari, 1979), among others.

Needless to say, Lois's in-depth knowledge and understanding of Islamic arts and music established her reputation as a leading scholar and authority on those subjects. That, of course, enabled her to secure teaching posts at some of the leading institutions in the United States and abroad, including Temple University, Butler University in Indianapolis, Villanova University in Philadelphia, the University of Pennsylvania and Mindanao State University in the Philippines, among others. She was appointed an Adjunct Professor at Temple and Villanova Universities in 1977 and continued to serve in this capacity until her death. She combined her academic career with a busy family life and pursued research and writing during her spare time. Being able to achieve such a balancing act without compromising her academic career or family life is a testament to her vision, commitment and character.

Indeed, during the next decade and a half, she became a distinguished Islamic scholar and writer in her own right, so much so that she was not only regularly consulted by her husband, who was himself an internationally recognised Arabist, Islamic scholar, philosopher and author, but many prominent American learned societies offered her membership including the American Academy of Religion, the American Oriental Society, the American Musicology Society, the Islamic Arts Foundation, the Society for the Scientific Study of Religion and the Society for Asian Music, among others. She was regularly invited to seminars and conferences in the United States, Turkey, Malaysia, Europe, North Africa and the Middle East. During this period, she was awarded many fellowships by the Ford Foundation, the Danford Foundation, the National Education Association and the National Association of University Women.

In addition to this, she was a dedicated member of the Society for Ethnomusicology and served on its Council from 1982 to 1985, and was chair of the Mid-Atlantic Chapter from 1983 to 1984. Her expertise was also recognised at an international level because she was a member of the United Nations Educational, Social and Cultural Organisation (UNESCO)'s Working Group that prepared a Universal Scientific and Cultural History of Mankind. Since 1975, she also served as chairperson of the Arts and Literature Group of the Association of Muslim Social Scientists.[7]

Lois was not only a widely recognised authority on Islamic arts, according to one of her students, this subject was her real love and passion because it 'drew its form from the religious philosophy of Islam and never deviated from exalting the beauty of the oneness of Allah. To her, Islamic art was a means of contemplating the spiritual without confusing or fusing the Creator with His creation. Her influence can be seen in her husband's graduate level courses in Islamic art, despite his interest in the subject since the early days of his career in construction. In fact, their ideas are so similar that it is hard to tell who influenced whom.'[8] Unsurprisingly, in the preface to her *Islam and Art* (Islamabad, 1985), Lois wrote that it was her husband who actively encouraged her to explore the beauty and wonders of Islamic art and music. Conversely, in the first edition to his *Tawhid: Its Implications for Thought and Life* (1982), Ismail openly acknowledged his profound debt to his wife.

Indeed, their co-operation and collaboration eventually led to the publication of their *magnum opus*, *The Cultural Atlas of Islam* in 1986 by Macmillan of New York, published posthumously. Consisting of 23 detailed chapters, divided into four parts and accompanied by more than 300 photos, images and illustrations, in this monumental work, the Faruqis provided a comprehensive but equally authentic overview of Islam as a faith, culture and civilisation stretching from Spain to China and from Yemen to Indonesia. Prior to this, Lois also published *An Annotated Glossary of Arabic Music Terms* (Connecticut, 1981), which is today considered to be a standard work of reference on the subject in English.

In addition to the above, she published more than fifty articles and reviews in books, journals and magazines in many parts of the world including the United States, Europe, Asia and the Middle East. Being a loyal American and an equally proud Muslim, Lois found herself in a unique position to be a mediator and interpreter of both cultures. According to one of her colleagues,

> Armed with both the convictions of an insider to Islam and a native's ease of access to North American ways, she added to the ongoing discourse of our discipline a voice of a different ideological-cultural premise of music and music-making. She had the courage and the ability to challenge us to come to terms with the reality of such differences – something that is easily evaded as long as we only talk about it within the comfortable premises of the Western intellectual tradition. Indeed, Lois al-Faruqi's deliberately favourable approach constituted an often uncomfortable reminder that there are groups of people 'out there' who want to discuss music and music-making on their own terms, as a part of their quest for asserting their cultural identity vis-à-vis the West. It is this challenge that constitutes, I believe, the most valuable legacy Lois has left our Society.[9]

Like her husband, Lois was well aware of the social, political and cultural challenges and difficulties facing the American Muslims, as well as the *ummah* as a whole at the time. Referring to the former, she wrote:

> There is a rapidly growing community of Muslims in the United States of which most Americans – both non-Muslims and Muslims – have had little knowledge. It is true that scattered Muslim individuals have existed in the United States from very early times, but it was not until the turn of the last century that other than isolated cases of Muslim citizens can be documented. It is only in the past two decades that their numbers have become large enough to make a Muslim presence tangible to most Americans… If the United States is to gain from the presence of the Muslim community in this continent, whether artistically or in any way, that benefit will come only from an alive and productive community, not from a dead or dying tradition. The latter can only take from, rather than contribute to, the future aesthetic heritage and well-being of the New World.[10]

As for the Muslim *ummah*, Lois and her husband called for a return to the Qur'an and Prophetic norms and practices (*sunnah*) to solve the social, political, economic and cultural problems facing the Islamic world. Muslims, they argued, needed to be conscious of their role as 'witnesses unto humanity' (*shuhada' 'ala al-nas*) and thus face the challenges of the present and future with wisdom, tact and openness by establishing political unity, advocating economic parity, promoting social justice and actively encouraging learning and scholarship in order to regenerate Muslim cultures and societies.

Likewise, Lois was an uncompromising champion of women's rights and responsibilities from an Islamic perspective. She felt that Muslim women were lagging behind men in every sphere of life despite Islam's enlightened and progressive approach to gender relationship. In her own words, '[Women's] position in early Islam was really an exemplary one, one that should be studied and known by every woman as well as every liberationist in the twentieth century – in America as well as in the Muslim world. The Muslim woman, if she is true to the principles of her religion, has lessons in equality to teach the Westerner, and her descendants in the East have to learn anew the role demanded of them by their religion. Orientalists and Orientals zealous for modernization should cease to put the blame on Islam, a blame which instead deserves to fall on their own ignorance of the faith and on the political and social decline which their nations suffered in the past.'[11]

On a personal level, Lois was a devout Muslim who was known for her kindness, generosity and hospitality. Indeed, the Faruqis regularly invited their relatives, friends, colleagues and students to dinner at their family home on Bent Road in Wyncote, Pennsylvania and showered them with presents and gifts. Although her husband had a habit of coming home with guests at short notice, she was an unfailingly kind and caring hostess who always entertained her guests with a smile and cheer, especially during the month of Ramadan and the Muslim festivals of Eid. Despite leading busy lives, the Faruqis were a happy couple who not only supported, but also inspired each other to achieve their personal and collective goals in life.

Tragically, both of them were brutally murdered in their home by an assassin on 27 May 1986. According to investigators, they were killed in an act of premeditated murder, perhaps carried out by a hired assassin because Ismail al-Faruqi, who was of Palestinian origin, was an outspoken critic of the State of Israel and defender of his people's rights and freedom. However, according to others, they were killed during a burglary that went horribly wrong, although nothing was stolen from their house. Either way, the murder of Lois and her husband was a great loss to the world of Islamic thought and scholarship, at least in the United States. Both were laid to rest at Forest Hills Cemetery in Lower Moreland in Philadelphia following a simple funeral prayer that was attended by their family, friends, students and admirers alike.

Needless to say, the Faruqis trained and mentored hundreds of students during their academic career, both Muslim and non-Muslim, and some of them subsequently went on to become prominent scholars and academics in their own right including John L. Esposito, Anis Ahmad, Muhammad Shafiq, Ghulam Nabi Fai, Charles Fletcher, Imtiyaz Yusuf and Gisela Webb. Only a day before her tragic death at the age of 59, Lois Lamya al-Faruqi wrote to a friend expressing her hopes and concerns for the future in the following words:

> There is so much there of goodness, of warmth, of brotherly-sisterly feelings, that one wonders how it is possible that the Muslims are denigrated and despised and 'put down'. At the same time, one finds from among the people those who have no awareness of their identity, of what their culture and religion stands for, nor of what can benefit their community and themselves. Instead, they seem bent on their own destruction, whether that means self-destruction of their own person or of their community and nations. Sometimes I ask myself if this can be just happening willy-nilly, or if there is some evil mastermind directing their self-destructive decisions and actions. We shall continue to pray for their enlightenment and try to train the next generation to be better than its forerunners.[12]

(N)

1. Wiebke Walther, *Women in Islam: From Medieval to Modern Times*.

2. Muhammad Shafiq, *Growth of Islamic Thought in North America: Focus on Ismail Raji al-Faruqi*.

3. Ismail and Lois Lamya al-Faruqi, *The Qur'an and the Sunnah*; Lois Ibsen al-Faruqi, 'Unity and Variety in the Music of Islamic Culture', *The Islamic Impact* (ed. Y. Y. Haddad et al.).

4. M. Tariq Quraishi, *Ismail al-Faruqi: An Enduring Legacy*.

5. Lamya (Lois) al-Faruqi, *Women, Muslim Society and Islam*.

6. Regula Buckhardt Qureshi, 'In Memoriam: Lois Lamya al-Faruqi', *Ethnomusicology*, vol. 32, no. 2; Ismail R. al-Faruqi (ed.), *Islamic Thought and Culture*.

7. See Muhammad Shafiq, op. cit. and R. B. Qureshi, op. cit.

8. Muhammad Shafiq, op. cit.

9. R. B. Qureshi, op. cit.

10. Lois Lamya al-Faruqi, 'Artistic Acculturation and Diffusion among Muslims of the United States', *Essays in Islamic and Comparative Studies* (ed.) Ismail Raji al-Faruqi.

11. Lamya (Lois) al-Faruqi, op. cit.

12. Quoted by Muhammad Shafiq, op. cit.

# 49

# W. D. MUHAMMAD

B. 1933 – D. 2008

UNITED STATES OF AMERICA

The United States of America is a powerful, wealthy and ethnically diverse country, but it is also a deeply politically polarised and racially segregated nation. Although its founding fathers are idealistically presented as having a vision of an open, tolerant and prosperous America –politically pluralistic, socially inclusive and economically equitable – today more than 230 years later, this great vision remains largely unfulfilled. Walking on the streets of Washington DC, the capital of the United States, and Brooklyn, one of New York City's five boroughs, I witnessed first-hand the political, economic and racial problems confronting contemporary America. The divide between the south and north, the whites and blacks and the haves and the have-nots could not have been more noticeable. Such a state of affairs persists due to the collective failure of American politics and policy-making.

For instance, the leader of the free world can afford to spend up to 711 billion dollars per annum on defence – close to what the rest of the world spends combined – but it cannot afford to provide basic necessities of life for millions of its own hard-working and loyal citizens. Likewise, from 1968 to 2011, more people died on the streets of America as a result of gunfire than they did in all the wars it had fought from the War of Independence to Iraq. With more than 300 million such weapons in the country, owned by more than a third of its population, it is not surprising that the real threat to America's security and stability lies at home, and not abroad. Having buried their heads in the sand, American politicians and policy-makers have been unwilling to address the real challenges and difficulties facing their citizens, especially the large African-American population.[1]

Being the descendants of African slaves who were brought to the Americas by force to work on the plantations during the early seventeenth century, it is estimated that six to seven million slaves were brought to the New World during the eighteenth century alone, until a campaign to abolish slavery was eventually initiated during the mid-nineteenth century in the northern United States by prominent abolitionists like Frederick Douglass (1818–1895), William Lloyd Garrison (1805–1879) and Harriet Beecher Stowe (1811–1896), among others. This led to the Emancipation Proclamation in 1862 and, a year later, the adoption of the 13th Amendment finally abolished slavery.[2]

Even so, the political, economic, social and cultural progress of the African-American population in the United States was repeatedly frustrated, firstly by the rebirth of white supremacy in the form of racist organisations (such as the Ku Klux Klan). The continued resistance to on-going racism and discrimination inspired many prominent African Americans to launch Black nationalistic or religious movements during the late nineteenth and early twentieth centuries in order to press for their political empowerment and economic upliftment, which, in turn, paved the way for the civil rights movement of the 1960s.

Some of the leading African-American nationalist and religious movements of the time included Martin R. Delaney's (1812–1885) National Emigration Conference; Henry Highland Garnet's (1815–1882) African Civilization Society; Marcus Aurelius Garvey's (1887–1940) Universal Negro Improvement Association and African Communities League, and Noble (Timothy) Drew Ali's (1886–1929) Moorish Science Temple of North America. However, one of the most influential and enduring African-American separatist movements of all time was the Nation of Islam, which was originally founded by Wallace Fard Muhammad back in the early 1930s.[3]

Born around 1877, Fard Muhammad claimed to have hailed from Makkah (in the present-day Kingdom of Saudi Arabia) and worked as a street peddler during his early years before moving to Detroit, Michigan during the early 1930s where he attracted a sizable following. He preached a concocted version of Islam and black supremacy, and argued that Allah was the real God of the black people; the white man was a devil and black people were an Asiatic race, being the cream of God's creation. As the movement grew in size, Fard Muhammad appointed many ministers to administer the social, economic and religious activities of the Nation of Islam before he suddenly disappeared without a trace in the mid-1930s.

One of the first ministers Fard Muhammad appointed was Elijah Poole, who was an unemployed auto worker. Born in 1898 in Sandersville, Georgia, his father, Wali Poole, was a Baptist minister who struggled to provide for his large family of thirteen children. After receiving a basic education, Elijah was forced to work as a labourer to earn a living. Subsequently, he worked as a foreman for the Cherokee Brick Company and soon married Clara Evans who bore him six sons and two daughters. He was then employed by the Chevrolet Auto Plant in Detroit from 1923 to 1929 but he struggled to make ends meet during the early years of the Great Depression (1929–1939). It was during this period that he met Fard Muhammad and began to study Islam before changing his name to Elijah Muhammad.[4]

Being a devout follower of Fard Muhammad, he was appointed the chief minister of the Nation of Islam and, after Fard's sudden disappearance, he became the pre-eminent leader of the movement and moved its headquarters to Chicago. Under Elijah's tutelage, the Nation of Islam not only expanded rapidly, but its theological and political beliefs were formulated at the time. The members of the movement considered Fard Muhammad to be God in person; that black people were an Asiatic race from Africa, and that 'white man is the devil', in addition to advocating black separatism from mainstream American society. Accordingly, Elijah encouraged a programme of economic self-help through the establishment of independent businesses and the sharing of profits for the benefit of black people as well as the propagation of his teachings.

Soon after taking over the leadership of the Nation of Islam, Elijah established an educational institution called the University of Islam, which, in reality, was no more than a school where children studied basic maths, science, African-American history and religious studies. This initiative was later extended to include a series of educational institutions including schools, colleges and seminaries to cater for the needs of the members of the Nation of Islam.

However, during the Second World War, Elijah was arrested and sent to prison for four years for evading military duties. In his absence, Clara Muhammad guided the movement until her husband was paroled and returned to Chicago where he received a hero's welcome from his followers. Furthermore, during the 1950s, the Nation of Islam expanded rapidly under the inspirational leadership of Malcolm Little, who became known as Malcolm X (1925–1965) after joining the movement in 1952. Having helped establish the majority of Nation of Islam's 100 Temples across the United States, Malcolm was appointed the National Spokesman of the movement in 1959 by Elijah himself until, however, a rift developed between the two men which forced the former to leave the Nation of Islam on 8 March 1964. A month later, he went to Makkah for the annual pilgrimage (hajj) where he embraced mainstream Islam and returned to the United States as an orthodox Muslim, having renounced Elijah's concocted version of Islam.[5]

However, after Malcolm's assassination in February 1965, the Nation of Islam continued to prosper under Elijah's leadership until he died on 25 February 1975. Elijah's death paved the way for Wallace Muhammad to assume leadership of the movement and completely reorganise the Nation of Islam in the light of authentic Islamic teachings and practices. In other words, the credit for guiding millions of African Americans to mainstream Islam must go to none other than Wallace Muhammad, who was undoubtedly one of the most influential Western Muslim leaders and reformers of the twentieth century.

Wallace Delaney Muhammad, better known as Imam Warith Din Muhammad, was born in Detroit, Michigan a few years after his father had joined the Nation of Islam under the guidance of Fard Muhammad. Being one of the youngest of Elijah and Clara Muhammad's eight children, Warith's birth was apparently predicted by Fard Muhammad himself. In his own words, 'I was the only child born during his stay with us. I was chosen because a new baby, a new birth – they wanted a Christ figure, someone with a mystery about [him]. Here was this newborn baby predicted by Fard Muhammad to be a male and it so happened the guess was right.'[6]

Needless to say, young Warith grew up in a family that was the heartbeat of the black separatist movement in America at the time. During his early years, he attended the University of Islam which consisted of a primary and secondary school that was founded by his father in Chicago to provide basic secular and religious education to the children of his close disciples. After completing his early and high school education, Warith joined Chicago's Wilson and Loop Junior College where he studied English, history, social sciences and microbiology, in addition to studying Arabic under the tutelage of a Palestinian academic.

After completing his formal education, Warith was appointed a minister of the Nation of Islam during the late 1950s when he was in his mid-twenties. He proved to be an eloquent speaker, charismatic leader and very knowledgeable in Islamic teachings which, in turn, prompted his father to send him to Philadelphia to take charge of its Temple during the late 1950s and early 1960s. At the time, the Nation of Islam was expanding across the United States under the inspirational leadership of Malcolm X like wildfire. As more and more African Americans (especially young people) flocked to the fold of the Nation of Islam, new Temples mushroomed throughout the country to cater for their social, cultural, educational and spiritual needs. In Warith's own words,

> When I was a young man…Malcolm X was an influence in my life. The thing that distinguished Malcolm X among the ministers was his individuality. Malcolm X was converted in prison. He came right out of prison and became a minister for the Honorable Elijah Muhammad. He didn't take on the thinking and behavior of the old conservative ministerial body. When the Honorable Elijah Muhammad saw this new blood he was excited. He just gave Malcolm free reign to preach his doctrine. The Honorable Elijah Muhammad welcomed this new blood. He told the old ministerial body, 'I will never get anywhere with people like you.' He said, 'All you do is teach the same thing we taught in the thirties.' He would say, 'Look at this young man'; he would brag on Malcolm. He said, 'He's in modern times, he knows how to help me.' Malcolm's new thinking, courage and youth attracted most of the young people into following the Honorable Elijah

Muhammad and I was one of them. I used to admire the way he would uncover our own ignorance.[7]

If Malcolm X had inspired Warith to become a political activist and disseminator of the message of the Nation of Islam during his formative years, then the latter also encouraged the former to ask questions and re-examine his knowledge and understanding of Islam which eventually led to Malcolm's conversion to orthodox Islam. Unlike Elijah Muhammad and Malcolm X, Warith had studied Arabic and therefore he had access to authentic Islamic literature including the Arabic Qur'an and Prophetic traditions (*ahadith an-nabawi*). In other words, his study of the original Islamic sources enabled him – like his younger brother, Akbar Muhammad (1939–2016) – to acquire an informed but authentic understanding of Islam as a faith, culture and civilisation, unlike the other members of the Nation of Islam.

Indeed, Akbar Muhammad subsequently went on to study at the prestigious al-Azhar University in Cairo and the University of Edinburgh in Scotland and became an expert in Islamic thought, history and jurisprudence. Like Malcolm X and Akbar, Warith rejected the God-image of Fard Muhammad, Elijah's claim to be a prophet and the Nation of Islam's racialist and separatist interpretation of Islam. According to one prominent historian of the Nation of Islam,

> There is no question that during the lifetime of Elijah, the Nation of Islam did not have many doctrines that the world of Islam could have recognized as Islamic. The Arab and Islamic torn-away elements and practices were present in NOI religion rather as emblems: these psychologically triggered a radical dislocation and shift in the American elements, and some disengagement from them that gave a sense of being freed and empowered. Arabic's role in opening up and pluralizing the conceptualization of the world by African-Americans would finally lead most of the adherents out altogether of the American thought-world still pervasive in the 1930–1975 NOI religion, and onto the plane of standard Islamic tenets.[8]

Needless to say, Warith was destined to play an influential role in the Nation of Islam's transition from a heterodox religious sect to mainstream Islam, but the task ahead was, of course, far from being easy or straight-forward. Unsurprisingly, on more than one occasion he fell out with the senior members of the movement including his father, who was the supreme leader, due to his refusal to accept some of the key tenets of the Nation of Islam. Such refusal led to his first excommunication from the movement in 1964 when he was in his early thirties. He was subsequently reinstated only to be excommunicated again a few years later.

Indeed, his membership of the Nation of Islam was cancelled by his father at least three to four times and always for the same reason, namely his refusal to believe that

Fard Muhammad was a God reincarnated in the form of a man. In his own words, 'The longest period of my suspension was between the years 1964 and 1969. During that time I was stripped of all minister's privileges. In 1966, early 1967 all support – even family relations were denied to me. I couldn't even socialize with family members.'[9]

During this period, he was forced to work as a labourer to make ends meet before setting up his own carpet and furniture cleaning business. However, lack of funds prevented him from advertising his business widely and, as a result, he had to travel from one customer to another to earn enough money to make a living. After several years of hard work and dedication, he eventually secured a relatively well-paid job as a welder and his circumstances soon began to improve. As it happened, he suffered considerable personal and financial hardship at the time but, to his credit, Warith never compromised his beliefs and principles. He was convinced that it was the Nation of Islam that needed to change and reform because its core beliefs and practices contradicted traditional Islamic teachings. Despite his refusal to budge an inch on this issue, his father reinvited him back into the movement in 1970 only to be expelled again. Elijah eventually relented and readmitted his son into the Nation of Islam during the mid-1970s. In Warith's own words,

> It was in 1974 that the Honorable Elijah Muhammad accepted me back into the ministry. I started teaching here in Chicago. The Honorable Elijah Muhammad gave me complete freedom to teach here in Chicago with Imam Shaw. At one point he told me to assume authority of the Mosque here in Chicago. From that point I was free to propagate and preach as my own wisdom dictated. I say that because I would actually test the support for me from the Honorable Elijah Muhammad. Nobody else was restricting my movement; I answered only to the Honorable Elijah Muhammad. I would say things I know were different from some of the things people had been taught under the leadership of Elijah Muhammad. I would use my discretion. I would test what the Honorable Elijah Muhammad would accept. He never ever called me in and said what I was teaching was causing problems [or to] slow up or go in another direction. He was satisfied with it.[10]

Towards the end of his life, Elijah appeared to have accepted what his sons, Warith and Akbar, had been openly but very respectfully advocating, namely the need to reform the Nation of Islam in the light of traditional Islamic teachings and practices rather than continuing to peddle a concocted version of the faith that was first developed in the 1930s in Michigan and subsequently transported across America from its headquarters in Chicago. More importantly, they argued that the racialist and separatist message of the Nation of Islam was completely out of tune with orthodox Islam as it was followed and practised in Africa as well as the rest of the Muslim world.

This realisation, coupled with his own health problems, forced Elijah Muhammad to be more tolerant and accommodating towards his sons. For example, on one occasion, when several officers of the Fruit of Islam, who effectively operated as the police for the Nation of Islam, obtained a tape recording of Warith's talks and sermons, Elijah summoned his son and played the recording. Thereupon, he applauded Warith for having acquired a sound and solid understanding of Islamic principles and practices, much to the shock and surprise of the officers of the Fruit of Islam. This undoubtedly marked the beginning of the transfer of power from the father to the son and the concomitant transformation of the Nation of Islam from being a black, separatist religious sect to its realignment with mainstream Islam.

On 25 February 1975, Elijah Muhammad died in Chicago's Mercy Hospital and, as expected, a few weeks later, Warith was unanimously elected as the new national leader (Supreme Minister) of the Nation of Islam. Although hitherto he had kept a relatively low profile, Warith was a charismatic individual who had not only acquired an in-depth knowledge of Islam, but also worked as a carpet cleaner, painter, welder, bookshop owner, restaurant manager as well as a self-employed businessman, in addition to serving as a lieutenant of the Fruit of Islam and minister of the Philadelphia Temple. Furthermore, he had performed the annual pilgrimage to Makkah (*hajj*) in 1967 and two other non-mandatory lesser pilgrimages (*umrah*), and even served three years in prison (1958–1961) for flatly refusing to report to the US authorities as a conscientious objector.

Thanks to his all-round knowledge of Islam, extensive experience of life and work as well as awareness of the challenges and difficulties facing his people, Warith was able to gently steer his followers away from a racialist, separatist and pessimistic picture of the past to a new, tolerant, inclusive and optimistic vision of the future. That is to say, he 'moved the members of the movement towards embracing orthodox Islam. He explained that the teachings of Wallace D. Fard and Elijah Muhammad were to be understood allegorically, not literally. He opened the doors of the Nation to white people and encouraged his followers to join in the civil and political life in US… [He] had accomplished a series of changes and reforms in administrative structure and in their official policy towards race relations, and political involvement. He eradicated racist and separatist teachings and reinterpreted other doctrines to enhance their consistency with Sunni Islam… [He] completed the Islamization process of the Nation of Islam, by organisational overhauling so that ministers became "imams"; temples became "mosques" and later "masjids". He also changed his name from Wallace Delaney Muhammad to Imam Warith Deen Muhammad.'[11]

The transition took place in three stages, namely the religious, organisational and political which, in turn, can be classified as being the 'Bilalian', 'The World Community of Al-Islam in the West' and 'The American Muslim Mission' phases. The title of his journal also reflected the gradual change: it began as *Bilalian News* before it became the *American Muslim Journal* until it assumed the title of the *Muslim Journal*. Although

Warith received significant moral and financial support from Saudi Arabia, Qatar, the United Arab Emirates and other Muslim countries in his Islamisation efforts, he also faced considerable internal challenges and difficulties. For example, Minister Louis Farrakhan (b. 1933), who became the Nation of Islam's National Spokesman after the assassination of Malcolm X, defected in 1978 and revived the original teachings and ideals of Elijah Muhammad.

Others who defected and established their own splinter groups included notable figures like John Muhammad, Silis Muhammad and Caliph E. Muhammad. Despite facing such internal schism, Warith persisted with his religious and organisational reforms and, in the process, he single-handedly brought millions of African Americans back into the fold of mainstream Islam. By all accounts, that was a remarkable achievement on his part.

At an international level, Warith not only developed good relations with prominent Muslim countries in Africa, Asia and the Middle East but he also forged ties with the growing Muslim communities in Guyana, Trinidad and Tobago, Jamaica and even parts of Europe where branches of his Islamic movement were subsequently established. During this period, he became actively involved in interfaith dialogue and debate, and developed close working relationships with prominent Christian and Jewish leaders in America and Europe. In the course of his interfaith work, he met both Pope John Paul II and the Dalai Lama, and was invited to deliver an address at the Washington Hebrew Congregation in Washington D.C. He also went against American Muslim public opinion by opposing Reverend Jesse Jackson's candidature for the Democratic nomination for President of the United States. As a prominent public speaker and leader of millions of African-American Muslims, he became the first Muslim to read an invocation in the United Nations Senate in 1992. Three years later, he was selected to serve as a President of the World Conference of Religions for Peace (WCRP) in Copenhagen, Denmark.

In short, he was an advocate of an open, tolerant and inclusive interpretation of Islam based on the Qur'an and authentic Prophetic traditions, one that was scripturally authentic and equally applicable in the Western social, political, economic, legal and cultural context, without in any way undermining the full meaning and import of Islam as a faith and way of life. He expounded his views and opinions on Islamic teachings, race relations, interfaith dialogue, socio-political coexistence and the challenges facing American Muslims in his hundreds of public talks, lectures and numerous books. Some of his notable publications include *The Teachings of W. D. Muhammad* (1975), *An African American Genesis* (1986), *Al-Islam: Unity and Leadership* (1991), *Growth for a Model Community in America* (1995), *Return to Innocence: Transitioning of the Nation of Islam* (2007) and *Life: The Final Battlefield* (2008).

On a more personal level, Warith was a devout Muslim who married four times and fathered eight children. He earned his living from his real estate, and import and export businesses. He died of a suspected heart attack at the age of 74. His funeral prayer which was held at the Islamic Foundation Masjid in Villa Park, Illinois, attracted more than 8000 people. As a highly respected Muslim scholar, writer, lecturer, reformer, educationalist, community regenerator and promoter of interfaith understanding and dialogue, he had no equal in the American Muslim community.

Indeed, according to some observers, he was the most influential 'Imam' in the United States during his lifetime, while others consider him to be the 'most significant, recognized, and respected leader of American Islam, one whose vision highly influences American blacks, both Muslim and non-Muslim. He has been called the contemporary *mujaddid*, the renewer of the religion of Islam for his age.'[12] Characteristic of the man, he himself was more humble and modest in his assessment of his life, contribution and achievements. In his own words,

> I hope what I leave behind is enough evidence of my sincerity as a Muslim for people to say, well, maybe he had ups and downs, maybe he didn't do a lot of things we thought he should do, but one thing we have no doubts about: he was a sincere believer in his religion.[13]

Ⓝ

1. Robert J. Gordon, *The Rise and Fall of American Growth*.

2. John Stewart, *American History: The People and Events that Changed American History*.

3. Clifton E. Marsh, *From Black Muslims to Muslims: The Transition from Separatism to Islam, 1930–1980*.

4. Elijah Muhammad, *Message to the Blackman in America*.

5. Malcolm X and Alex Haley, *The Autobiography of Malcolm X*.

6. Clifton E. Marsh, op. cit.

7. Ibid.

8. Dennis Walker, *Islam and the Search for African-American Nationhood: Elijah Muhammad, Louis Farrakhan and the Nation of Islam*.

9. Clifton E. Marsh, op. cit.

10. Ibid.

11. Nuri Tinaz, 'The Nation of Islam: Historical Evolution and Transformation of the Movement', *Journal of Muslim Minority Affairs*, vol. 16, no. 2.

12. Jane I. Smith, *Islam in America*.

13. Steven Barboza, *American Jihad: Islam after Malcolm X*.

# 50

# MUHAMMAD ALI

B. 1942 – D. 2016

UNITED STATES OF AMERICA

Muslim contributions to theology, philosophy, science and mathematics are more widely known in the Islamic world and the West today than Muslim contributions to arts, architecture, music and global sports. Unsurprisingly, considerable amounts of literature have already been published on the lives and works of prominent Muslim theologians, philosophers, scientists and mathematicians who, I hasten to add, made a significant addition to the development and progress of human thought and civilisation.

Indeed, pioneering Muslim scholars, thinkers and writers like Jabir ibn Hayyan (721–815), al-Khwarizmi (780–850), al-Farabi (872–950), al-Ash'ari (874–936), Abu Bakr al-Razi (854–925), Abulcasis (see chapter 5), Ibn al-Haytham (965–1040), Ibn Sina (980–1037), al-Ghazali (1058–1111), Averroes (see chapter 13) and Ibn Khaldun (1332–1406), among many others, blazed a trail that have few parallels in human history.

Whilst their extraordinary contributions and achievements have been rightly recognised and acknowledged, both in the Islamic East and the Western world, Muslim contributions in the field of arts, architecture, music and global sports have, unfortunately, been largely neglected, if not completely ignored. However, one remarkable Western Muslim sportsman and philanthropist contributed more to global sports, philanthropy and intercultural understanding than probably anyone else during the twentieth century. His life and legacy represents nothing short of a beacon of light for both Muslims and non-Muslims, Westerners and Easterners. He was none other than the great Muhammad Ali.

Born Cassius Marcellus Clay Jr., in Louisville, located in the south-eastern American State of Kentucky, into a working African-American family, Muhammad Ali was no ordinary child. His father, Cassius, Sr., and mother, Odessa, were a hard-working couple who, like any other parents, tried to provide the best for their children. Young Ali inherited both the sweet, bubbly and steadfast qualities of his mother and the fast-talking, creative qualities and attributes of his artistic father.[1] Ali and his brother Rudy grew up in the happy but conservative environment of Western Louisville, which at the time was a mainly black area. Since the white areas of the city were strictly 'no-go' areas for its black population, the Clay family's movements were restricted to the city's black areas.

Like many other parts of America, the racial segregation of Louisville was symptomatic of the wider racial and cultural segregation which plagued American culture and society at the time. As a youngster, Ali was known to have been both shy and reserved but thanks to Rudy, his younger brother, and Joe Elsby Martin, a local police officer, he soon became interested in sports. According to Ali, when he was about 12, his father bought him a new bike for Christmas, but it was stolen from him by thieves. This prompted a disconsolate Ali to go to Joe Martin to make a complaint. Joe compiled a police report and asked Ali to join him at his Columbia Boxing Gym.[2]

A tall, slim and shy Ali went to the gym and put on his boxing gloves for the first time. His agility, athleticism and frightening speed impressed Joe Martin, who asked him to attend his gym on a regular basis. Keen to improve his boxing skills, he began to take additional lessons with his brother Rudy, who trained him by hurling stones at him, to improve his reflexes, and which he learnt to evade with ease. If Joe Martin introduced Ali to boxing, then Fred Stoner became his first serious boxing instructor. As a respected black boxer himself, Stoner taught Ali the art of boxing in a rigorous and systematic way. Indeed, he considered Ali to be highly-gifted and encouraged him to develop his stamina, technique and speed, something all aspiring professional boxers had to master at the outset.

Young Ali's ability to move with ease, dance around the ring and deliver crushing blows to his opponents with frightening speed soon convinced Stoner that he was a great boxing talent who could reach the heights of sporting stardom. Ali confirmed Stoner's prediction when he was barely 16 by winning the Louisville Golden Gloves lightweight tournament. Whilst still at high school, he progressed to the quarter-finals of the regional boxing championship in Chicago. Then, after graduating from Louisville's Central High school at the age of 18, he won the National Golden Gloves tournament and also the Amateur Athletic Union competition. His achievements at both the local and national level included a further six title fights, which established his reputation as an emerging star.

Thanks to his success, Ali was chosen to represent his country at the Olympics in Rome in 1960, where he won a Gold Medal and of course this made him instantly famous. Aware of his achievements, good looks and electrifying personality, he was also in the habit of bragging about his boxing ability and greatness even when he was a youngster. And no one (including his parents, trainers and fans) ever doubted his physical ability, boxing talent and way with words. Those who knew the 18 year old Ali described him as inspiring, energetic and sophisticated.[3]

After returning home from Rome with an Olympic Gold Medal, a group of white millionaire businessmen came together and formed the Louisville Sponsoring Group, a business consortium which sponsored and promoted his fights. He signed a lucrative contract with this consortium and began his professional boxing career at the age of 18. Sponsored by the company, he fought his first professional bout in 1960 and scored a sixth round victory. His emergence as a professional boxer created considerable interest in the sport; also, his flamboyant style, self-confidence, ingenuity and arrogance turned him into an overnight celebrity. Keen to show the world that he was not a one-time wonder, he then approached Angelo Dundee, a renowned boxing trainer, to join his team and supervise his training needs and requirements. The two men soon became good friends and Ali flourished under Dundee's tutelage.

During this period he trained hard, mastered his footwork and became a polished boxer. His physical power, coupled with his lightning speed, agile movement and quick-thinking made him a formidable boxer who, in 1962, thoroughly mesmerised and out-fought the former world light-heavyweight champion Archie Moore. The press and the American public were bowled over by the quick-witted, boastful and ferocious Ali, who was increasingly considered to be one of the most entertaining boxing sensations of his generation. In reality, however, Ali had barely started his professional boxing career.

Nevertheless, his convincing victory over Moore paved the way for him to challenge Sonny Liston, the then reigning heavyweight champion of the world. Ali, the challenger, entered the ring with Liston in 1964. Chanting 'Float like a butterfly, sting like a bee', he mesmerised the feared and revered Liston. By combining his unconventional boxing skills with his exceptional speed, Ali stunned the American public by becoming the heavyweight champion of the world. Prior to the bout Liston predicted, 'I might hurt that boy bad', and every American believed him (including the press, the public and the pundits), but a confident and arrogant Ali, then only 22, proved them all wrong. After soundly beating the world heavyweight boxing champion, he emerged to proclaim, 'I am the greatest!'[4]

The year 1964 represented an important period in American history. It marked the beginning of a decade of student protests under the banner of the Free Speech Movement. In the same year, the American army was given the green light to attack Vietnam, while the white supremacists affiliated with the Ku Klux Klan began to terrorise prominent civil rights activists in Mississippi (which led to the ratification of the Civil Rights Act) and, of course, the Beatles took America by storm. But it was Ali's historic victory over Liston in 1964 which represented a milestone in the history of global sporting achievements.

Even before the dust of his victory over Liston could settle, he announced his conversion to the Nation of Islam. This represented another bombshell as far as the mainstream American press and public were concerned. No one expected Ali to out-smart Liston, but he proved his critics wrong and then, to add insult to injury, he announced his conversion to an organisation which was widely considered to be a racist, black-separatist movement. As expected, soon after his conversion to the Nation of Islam, Ali's career and public image took a battering from the American press, both visual and print. He felt mainstream America had failed to understand him, not least because his conversion to Elijah Muhammad's Nation of Islam was far from being a moment of madness or a publicity stunt. Taught and mentored by none other than Malcolm X (al-Hajj Malik al-Shabazz), he closely studied the Nation's religious thought and methodology for more than a year before formally becoming a member.

In fact, his change of religion was a real change of heart and conviction, rather than a publicity stunt. Encouraged by Malcolm X (see chapter 51) and Elijah Muhammad (1897–1975), he then changed his name to Muhammad Ali, for he no longer wished to be known by his 'slave name'. Like him, tens of thousands of other African Americans found true freedom, liberation and self-respect in the fold of the Nation of Islam. Later, according to Ali, it was Warith Din Muhammad (see chapter 49) who was instrumental in his subsequent conversion to mainstream Islam after the death of his father in 1975[5]. In the meantime, Ali married for the first time and continued to box, allowing his fists to do all the talking inside the ring. He not only retained his heavyweight championship title by defeating Liston for the second time in 1965, but also successfully defended the title another six times in 1966, with five knockouts.

A year later, another public outcry broke out when Ali refused to sign up for military duties in Vietnam. As a conscientious objector, he responded to his critics in rhyme, 'Keep asking me, no matter how long. On the war in Vietnam, I sing this song. I ain't got no quarrel with the Viet Cong.' Found guilty of draft evasion by an all-white jury, he was fined ten thousand dollars and sentenced to five years in prison. Although freed on appeal, his boxing licence was suspended, and he was also stripped of his World Boxing Association (WBA) title. At a time when his promising boxing career appeared to be in ruins, an indomitable Ali remained as firm as ever. During this period he married for the second time, and three years later the Supreme Court quashed his conviction for draft evasion. He responded by returning to the boxing ring with a bang, winning two successive bouts before losing against Joe Frazier, his successor as the undisputed world heavyweight champion. But he regained his title in 1974 and successfully defended it against Frazier a year later in the 'Thrilla in Manilla'. Ali's autobiography entitled *The Greatest – My Own Story*, which he co-authored with Richard Durham, appeared in 1975.

Two years later, Ali married for the third time and in the following year fought one of his most memorable bouts against George Foreman in the famous 'Rumble in the Jungle' in Zaire, which earned him five million dollars. He then lost against Leon Spinks, but regained his title for the third time and, in so doing, he became the only man to have won the world heavyweight championship three times. After two more fights – one against Larry Holmes in 1980 and the other against Trevor Berbick in 1981 – Ali finally retired from boxing in 1981 at the age of 41, having fought a total of 61 bouts, with only five defeats.[6]

A few years later, he told the New York Times Magazine that he was suffering from Parkinson's syndrome, probably as a result of repeated blows to the head. As a result, he developed speech problems even though his mental faculties were not affected. Ali made more than 50 million dollars from boxing, and gave away a substantial amount to fund charitable activities. In other words, after his retirement from boxing, he became one of America's most prolific philanthropists and charity workers.

Moreover, as a sporting legend and a distinguished statesman, he went to Lebanon in 1985 and Iraq in 1990 to secure the release of hostages from those countries, in addition to being an active supporter of the rights and freedom of the Palestinian people. Likewise, in 2002, Ali went to Afghanistan as the United Nation's 'Ambassador of Peace'. He worked closely with Michael J. Fox, a prominent American actor, to raise awareness of Parkinson's disease and secured funding for medical research. In 1991, Thomas Hauser published his popular biography of Ali under the title of *Muhammad Ali: His Life and Times* and eight years later Robert Cassidy's definitive study *Muhammad Ali: The Greatest of All Time* was published. However, one of the most memorable sporting images of recent times was that of an ailing Ali carrying the Olympic torch in Atlanta in 1996. He also took part in the opening ceremony of 2012 Summer Olympics in London where he carried the Olympic Flag with the assistance of his wife.

The public story of this great sportsman and humanitarian activist culminated in the release of Michael Mann's Hollywood film-blockbuster *Ali* in 2001, starring Hollywood superstar Will Smith. Furthermore, Ali was honoured by the Kings of Saudi Arabia and Morocco for his services to Islam. The Muhammad Ali Centre for the Advancement of Humanity, which consists of a museum and resource centre, was unveiled in Ali's hometown of Louisville, Kentucky in recognition of his outstanding sporting achievements and charitable activities. The Ali Centre intends to 'preserve and share the legacy and ideals of Muhammad Ali' for the benefit of posterity.[7] Ali was hailed as one of the '100 Most Important People of the 20th Century' by *Time* magazine in 1999, while the *Sports Illustrated* crowned him the 'Sportsman of the Century' in the same year. Ali also won the BBC's 'Sports Personality of the Century' award in 1999. Ali lived with Lonnie Williams, his fourth wife, in Michigan and Kentucky before moving to Scottsdale, Arizona where he was admitted to hospital in June, 2016 suffering from respiratory illness. A day later, he passed away at the age of 74.

As expected, the news of his death soon spread like wildfire and glowing tributes poured in from around the world. His admirers included influential politicians, prominent sportsmen and religious leaders such as President Barack Obama, Bill Clinton, David Cameron, Michael Johnson, Tiger Woods and Greg Fischer, the Mayor of Louisville, who said that, 'Muhammad Ali belongs to the world. But he only has one hometown'. As a devout Muslim, his funeral prayer, held on a Friday at the Freedom Hall, Kentucky Exposition Center, was conducted according to Islamic guidelines before he was laid to rest at the Cave Hill Cemetery.[8] This was followed by a public multifaith memorial service, held at Louisville's KFC YUM! Center, where people of different faiths, races, colours and backgrounds gathered to remember the life and legacy of one of the twentieth century's most famous Muslims. The British newspaper, *The Guardian*, paid him this fitting tribute:

Muhammad Ali…was acclaimed by many as the greatest world heavyweight boxing champion the world has ever seen. He was certainly the most charismatic boxer. His courage inside and outside the ring and his verbal taunting of opponents were legendary, as were his commitment to justice and his efforts for the poor and underprivileged.[9]

Likewise, the well-known American poet Maya Angelou (1928–2014) wrote that,

Muhammad Ali was not just Muhammad Ali the greatest, the African-American pugilist; he belonged to everyone. That means that his impact recognizes no continent, no language, no color, no ocean.[10]

Ⓝ

1. Muhammad Ali, *The Greatest: My Own Story*.

2. Thomas Hauser, *Muhammad Ali: His Life and Times*.

3. Ibid.

4. Alan Goldstein, *Muhammad Ali: The Story of a Boxing Legend*.

5. Clifton E. Marsh, *From Black Muslims to Muslims: The Transition from Separatism to Islam, 1930–1980*.

6. David Remnick, *King of the World: Muhammad Ali and the Rise of an American Hero*.

7. See www.alicenter.org

8. See 'Thousands Celebrate Muhammad Ali's Life', www.abcnews.com

9. See 'Muhammad Ali obituary', www.theguradian.com

10. Maya Angelou, *Muhammad Ali: Through the Eyes of the World*.

HONOURABLE
MENTIONS

# AL-HAKAM II

B. 1914 – D. 2002

SPAIN

Al-Hakam II ibn Abd al-Rahman III was born in Cordova and received his early education in Arabic, aspects of Islamic sciences, poetry and literature under the tutelage of several private tutors in his father's caliphal palace. After completing his formal education, he became actively involved in political administration and served as an assistant to Caliph Abd al-Rahman III. He succeeded his father when he was in his mid-forties and assumed the title of al-Mustansir bi-'llah in the year 961. Unlike his father, he was not a brilliant political strategist and military commander but, like his illustrious father, he was a great patron of learning and education. Accordingly, he transformed Cordova, the capital of Andalusia, into a pre-eminent centre of research and scholarship in medieval Europe.[1]

Under his generous patronage, the Academy in Cordova became an unrivalled institution of higher education, thus attracting scholars from across the Muslim world and Europe. As an insatiable seeker and disseminator of knowledge, his personal library alone housed around half a million books and manuscripts, being the largest library in the world at the time. According to the historian Ibn Khaldun (1332–1406), the unfinished catalogue of al-Hakam's library consisted of more than forty volumes, each comprising of twenty to fifty pages, listing the names of all the books and their authors.[2] This was no mean achievement as printing was unknown at the time and every copy of the book had to be carefully inscribed by hand.

He was not only a collector of books but also a gifted scholar in his own right. Indeed, according to Philip K Hitti (1886–1978), he was one of the best scholars among Muslim rulers and wrote extensive notes on the margins of many scientific, philosophical and religious books and manuscripts which were rated very highly by other scholars and researchers alike. After ruling for about sixteen years, al-Hakam died at the age of 61 and was succeeded by al-Hisham II al-Mu'ayyad, his only surviving son, who was only 12 at the time. That paved the way for the emergence of the great Almanzor (see chapter 6 for more information).

# IBN HAYYAN

B. 987 – D. 1075

SPAIN

Abu Marwan ibn Khalaf ibn Husayn ibn Hayyan al-Qurtubi, known as Ibn Hayyan for short, was born in Cordova and also pursued his early, further and higher education in his native city. He went on to become a prominent scholar of Arabic, traditional Islamic sciences and history. He combined his research and scholarly activities with his day job working as an official in the administration of *al-Hajib* al-Mansur (Almanzor) who effectively ruled Andalusia after the death of Caliph al-Hakam II in September 976.

However, after Almanzor's successful reign came to an abrupt end during the early years of the eleventh century, Ibn Hayyan experienced considerable personal and financial problems. As a supporter of the Umayyad dynasty of Spain, he was dismayed by the social, political and economic chaos that ensued the demise of the Caliphate in 1031, which was followed by the turbulent period of *muluk al-ta'ifa* (reign of the petty rulers).[3] Although this proved to be a difficult time for Ibn Hayyan, he continued to pursue his scholarly activities and, in the process, he became one of the most prolific medieval writers on the political, intellectual and cultural history of Islamic Spain.

Some of the works that are attributed to him include *Ta'rikh al-Fuqaha Cordova* (History of the Jurists of Cordova), *Kitab Akhbar fi'l Dawla al-Amiriya* (History of the Amirid Rule in Spain) and *Kitab al-Muqtabis fi Ta'rikh al-Andalus* (A History of Andalusia) which focused particularly on the lives and works of its leading personalities. Most of his works are no longer extant. Ibn Hayyan died in his late eighties and was buried in his native Cordova.

# IBN AL-ARABI

B. 1165 – D. 1240

SPAIN

Abu Abdullah Muhammad ibn Ali ibn Muhammad ibn al-Arabi al-Hatimi at-Ta'i, better known as Ibn al-Arabi or Ibn Arabi (without the definite article *al*), was born in al-Mursiya, which is today located in the Region of Murcia on the Mediterranean coast of Spain. Of both Arabian and Berber origin, he pursued his education in Seville before moving to Fez, Morocco for further and higher education. After completing his education, he went to Makkah to perform the annual pilgrimage in around 1202 where he stayed for three years.[4]

From Makkah, he then proceeded to Syria, Palestine, Egypt, Iraq and parts of Anatolia. During his extensive travels across the Islamic East, he met and befriended many scholars and Sufi sages before eventually returning to Makkah where he continued to study Islamic sciences and spirituality. He was a prolific writer who authored many books and manuscripts on the mystical dimensions of Islamic teachings including *Tarjuman al-Ashwaq* (The Interpreter of Desires), *Fusus al-Hikam* (The Ringstones of Wisdom), *Diwan* (Collection of Poetry) and *al-Futuhat al-Makkiyyah* (The Makkan Illuminations), among others. Although some of his biographers have attributed as many as 800 works to Ibn al-Arabi, most of his works are no longer extant and the majority of those that are available have not been properly edited and authenticated to this day. Nonetheless, a number of works attributed to him have been translated into English, including a number of the aforementioned, as he has been the subject of much discussion.

There is no doubt that Ibn al-Arab was a gifted scholar and writer, but he is also one of the most controversial authors and spiritual figures in the history of Islam.[5]

His bold, innovative and equally provocative interpretation of aspects of *tasawwuf* (Islamic spirituality) has won him widespread acclaim as *Shaykh al-Akbar* (the Grand Shaykh) from his admirers as well as stinging censure from his detractors who often refer to him as *Shaykh al-Akfar* (The Unbelieving Shaykh). The fact that he continues to polarise Muslim scholars and Sufi sages to this day proves that he was one of the most original Sufi thinkers and writers of all time. He died at the age of 75 and was buried in Damascus, Syria.

# AL-QURTUBI

B. 1214 – D. 1273

SPAIN

Abu Abdullah Muhammad ibn Ahmad ibn Abu Bakr al-Ansari al-Qurtubi, better known as Imam al-Qurtubi, was born into a learned Muslim family in Cordova and received his early education in Arabic and Islamic sciences in his native city. He was in his early twenties when Cordova was annexed by the forces of Ferdinand III, the Catholic King of Castile and Leon (r. 1217–1252), and this forced young al-Qurtubi to leave Andalusia and move to Egypt. He settled in Cairo and pursued advanced training in Qur'anic sciences, Prophetic traditions and Islamic jurisprudence. Despite being an adherent of Maliki *fiqh*, he soon became well-known for his expertise in Qur'anic exegesis (*tafsir*) and comparative jurisprudence, so much so that his peers considered him to be one of the most outstanding Islamic scholars of his generation.

As a devout Muslim, he not only defended the traditional Islamic approach to law and theology but also repudiated the rationalistic views of the Mu'tazilah. He was a prolific writer on a range of Islamic subjects including Qur'anic exegesis, Prophetic traditions, Islamic jurisprudence and theology. However, al-Qurtubi is today best known for his *al-Jami li-Ahkam al-Qur'an*, otherwise known as *Tafsir al-Qurtubi*, which is a monumental commentary on the Qur'an in Arabic consisting of twenty volumes. He focused mainly but not entirely on the legal teachings of the Qur'an and provided a comprehensive and illuminating interpretation of the Qur'an from a largely Maliki perspective.[6] Widely regarded as a standard work of reference on the Qur'an, it has been translated into many languages including Bengali, English, Urdu and Spanish. He led a simple and pious lifestyle; he died in his late fifties and was buried in Munya Abi'l-Khusayb in Upper Egypt.

# AL-GHARNATI

B. 1256 – D. 1344

GRANADA

Abu Hayyan Muhammad ibn Yusuf ibn Ali ibn Yusuf ibn Hayyan al-Andalusi, better known as Abu Hayyan al-Gharnati, was born in Islamic Granada into a Berber family. He pursued his early Islamic education in Spain before travelling extensively in the Islamic East where he received advanced training in Arabic and Islamic sciences under the tutelage of prominent Muslim scholars. After completing his formal education, he was appointed as a teacher of Arabic and Qur'anic exegesis in both Alexandria and Cairo, and thereby established his reputation as a distinguished scholar in his own right.

Indeed, his mastery of Arabic and Qur'anic sciences was such that he could read standard works on both subjects directly from memory. Being an adherent of Zahiri *fiqh*, he was also very critical of many prominent Sufis whom he considered to be heretical including Ibn al-Arabi, Husayn ibn Mansur al-Hallaj (858–922) and Abu Muhammad Abd al-Haqq ibn Sab'in (1217–1271), among others. As a prolific writer, more than sixty works have been attributed to him on aspects of Arabic grammar, Qur'anic sciences and Islamic theology but only a handful of his writings have survived. Hailed as one of the foremost grammarians of his generation, he wrote one of the best commentaries on Abu Abdullah Jamal al-Din Muhammad ibn Malik's (1204–1274) *al-Khulasa al-Alfiya*, which is a famous work on Arabic grammar. He was also well-versed in several other languages and dialects including Berber, Turkic and Amharic.[7]

He was not only respected by the Mamluk rulers of Egypt for his scholarship, but the masses also revered him for his extensive knowledge of Islam. After the news of his death was relayed across Cairo, the masses flocked to his funeral in their droves. He died at the age of 87 and was buried in the Cemetery of Bab al-Nasir in Old Cairo.

# IBN AL-KHATIB

B. 1313 – D. 1374

SPAIN

Muhammad Abdullah ibn Sa'id ibn Ali ibn Ahmad, known as Lisan al-Din ibn al-Khatib, was born into a notable Muslim family in present-day Loja in southern Spain. He grew up during a turbulent time in the history of Muslim Spain and completed his formal education locally before entering the service of Nasrid Sultan Yusuf I. He was a skilful official who also became renowned for his love of literature and scholarship. He subsequently married Iqbal, who was the daughter of a low-ranking government officer and she bore him three sons. However, after the death of Ibn Ali ibn al-Jayyab in 1349, who was the chief vizier, he was promoted as a secretary to the Council of Viziers and continued to serve in this capacity until Sultan Yusuf was brutally murdered in October 1354. He then served the young Sultan Muhammad, the son and successor of Yusuf I, who was only 16 at the time, and the former valued the advice and guidance he received from Ibn al-Khatib.

Soon afterwards, Ibn al-Khatib's life was turned upside down by the political upheaval of the time and he was forced to flee to Fez in Morocco where he and his family were offered asylum by Abu Salim, the reigning Marinid Sultan. It was during this period that Ibn al-Khatib first met Abd al-Rahman ibn Khaldun (1332–1406), who was a young jurist and scholar, and they soon became good friends.[8] However, on his return to Granada, Ibn al-Khatib was appointed chief vizier during Sultan Muhammad's second reign, but he soon fell out of favour and was forced to flee to Morocco once again where he was reportedly murdered in prison by the agents of the Sultan; he was around 61 at the time.

In addition to being an influential politician and statesman, Ibn al-Khatib was also a prominent physician, historian and literary figure who soon became the focus of controversy due to his political intrigues rather than his theological views. Even so, some of his notable literary contributions include *Ta'rikh Isbaniya al-Islamiya* (A History of Islamic Spain), *Kitab Awsaf al-Nas* (Description of People) and *Kitab al-Ihata fi Akhbar Gharnata* (Comprehensive Source on the History of Granada).

# KOPRULU MEHMED PASHA

B. 1575 – D. 1661

ALBANIA

Koprulu Mehmed Pasha was born in Roshnik, located in present-day Berat County in central Albania, and he was inducted into the Ottoman administrative service during his early years. He was an able and diligent young man who soon graduated from the sultan's elite palace school. He initially worked in the imperial kitchen before being recruited into the Ottoman treasury. He soon proved his worth and was promoted to the office of the vizier where he established his reputation as a skilful political and administrative officer. In due course, he worked under the tutelage of the influential Gazi Husrev Pasha who served as the Grand Vizier to Sultan Murad IV from 1628 to 1631.

However, after the assassination of Husrev Pasha in March 1632, he was promoted to various important roles in and around Istanbul, including serving for a period as the head of the Sipahi (cavalry) corps. His loyalty and dedication earned him the respect of Ottoman elites, who not only appointed him to the rank of Pasha, but they also promoted him to the post of provincial governor (*beylerbey*) of Trabzon in 1644. Thereafter, he became the governor of the province of Egri (located in present-day northern Hungary) before moving to Karaman in 1648 and Anatolia in 1650.

His achievements as a governor prompted the senior officials to appoint him to the influential post of vizier to the Council of State (*divan*), but political intrigues within the sultan's palace soon led to his dismissal.

At a time when the Ottoman Empire faced mounting military challenges from its external enemies, as well as internal political plots and intrigues at home, the mother of the reigning Sultan Mehmed IV was forced to intervene to avert a political crisis by appointing Mehmed Pasha as the Grand Vizier in September 1656. As a result, he became one of the most powerful men in the Ottoman Empire at the time. This was no mean achievement for someone who had hailed from a humble Albanian family.

Although he was very old at the time, he served the sultan with unflinching dedication and loyalty for another five years before he died at the age of around 85. His son, Koprulu Fazil Ahmad Pasha (1635–1676), succeeded him as the Grand Vizier, and, in so doing, he became the founder of one of the most powerful families of politicians, viziers and statesmen in the history of the Ottoman Empire; so much so that the Koprulu family subsequently went on to produce no less than six grand viziers of the Ottoman Empire.[9]

# JOZEF Z. BEM

B. 1794 – D. 1850

POLAND

Jozef Zachariasz Bem, also known as Murad Pasha, was born in Tarnow, a city which is today located in south-eastern Poland, into a local Christian family. The political instability and confusion of the time forced his family to move to Krakow (Cracow) when he was in his early teens, and so he joined the local military school. Despite being rather short for his age, he was an able student who excelled in his studies before joining the Polish artillery regiment as a junior officer. His commitment and dedication was soon recognised by his superiors who swiftly promoted him to the post of Sub-Lieutenant and then Lieutenant. He played an active part in French military action against Russia in 1812; he was only 18 at the time. A year later, his heroic defence of the Free City of Danzig, which was established by Napoleon Bonaparte (1769–1821) in September 1807, won him widespread acclaim. So much so that the Knights Cross of the Legion of Honour, which is one of France's highest military awards, was bestowed on him.

A few years later, when the Duchy of Warsaw became the Kingdom of Poland, Jozef left the army and became a teacher and researcher at a military college, but his political activities in favour of Polish independence soon landed him in trouble with the Russian authorities. This forced him to move from one place to another until the Polish-Russian War broke out in 1830 and Jozef joined the Polish freedom-fighters. He not only served as a Major in the Polish army but also fought bravely against the Russian forces, and, in so doing, he saved the lives of thousands of soldiers.

Although he was promoted to the rank of Brigadier General on account of his bravery, the Polish army was forced to surrender by the superior Russian forces. As expected, this forced Jozef to move to Paris where he earned his living as a teacher of mathematics before settling in Portugal. Being a military officer *par excellence*, he soon became actively involved in the Hungarian Revolution of 1848. Thanks to his heroism in the battlefield, he is today known in Hungary as *Bem apo* or 'Grandfather Bem', and Sandor Petofi (1823-1849), the national poet of Hungary, also immortalised him in his poetry.

Though Jozef was well-versed in many European languages, he authored several books on aspects of Polish history, military campaigns and technology in German, French and Polish.

Needless to say, the failure of the revolution forced Jozef to flee to Istanbul where he converted to Islam and adopted the Muslim name of Murad Pasha. Impressed by his personal courage, upright character and poised military skills, the Ottomans recruited him into their military and administrative service. He subsequently served as a governor of Aleppo and died at the age of 56. He is not only revered in both Poland and Hungary as one of their national heroes, but the Bem Statute in Budapest also became the focus of attention during the Hungarian Revolution of October 1956.[10]

# AMHERST D. TYSSEN

B. 1843 – D. 1930

UNITED KINGDOM

Amherst Daniel Tyssen, better known as Amherst D. Tyssen, was born into a distinguished English family in Upper Clapton, which today is a district in the London Borough of Hackney. After successfully completing his early education, he joined Merton College, Oxford where he studied law, and he soon obtained two undergraduate degrees before completing his masters and doctorate in Common Law in 1877. During his time at the University of Oxford, he joined the city's Rifle Volunteer Corp and worked as a postmaster. His interest in religion and philosophy may have developed during the same period as he leaned more towards Theism, that is, belief in one God as the Creator and Sustainer of the entire universe, and Divine revelation as a medium of communication between God and man. Accordingly, he may have converted to Unitarianism which also explains why he chose to marry in a Unitarian Church in 1883.

However, being a successful lawyer and a scholar of comparative religion and philosophy, he continued his quest for meaning and purpose in the modern world, and, as a result, his interest in Islam began to grow. Indeed, the simplicity and clarity of the Islamic concept of Divine Unity may have inspired him to embrace Islam at a time when it was not very fashionable to become a Muslim in England. In due course, he linked up with William Henry Quilliam's Muslim Institute in Liverpool and contributed scores of articles and poems on aspects of Islam in several publications including *The Crescent, The Islamic World, Transactions of the Unitarian Historical Society* and the *Islamic Review*. He also authored several books such as *The Birth of Islam* (1895), *Law of Charitable Bequests* (1888), *Occasional Hymns* (1902) and *The Life and Teachings of Muhammad* (1907).[11]

Towards the end of his life, Amherst became a trustee of the Unitarian Church in Banbury, Oxfordshire and published a series of interesting articles in the *Islamic Review* including 'Some Thoughts from the Qur'an', 'The Prophet's Resolution' and 'The Result of Ignorance'. Dr Amherst D. Tyssen eventually passed away at the age of 87. Soon after his death, the *Transactions of the Unitarian Historical Society* published a short but informative obituary (see volume 4, no. 4, 1930).

# SAMI FRASHERI

B. 1850 – D. 1904

ALBANIA

Shams al-Din Sami efendi Frasheri, better known as Sami Frasheri, was born into a Muslim family in the village of Frasher (ash tree) in the Albanian district of Permet. His father, Halit Bey (1797–1859) and mother, Emine Hanim (1814–1861), took good care of their eight children before enrolling them in their local school. Young Sami attended Zozymee gymnasium in Loannina, Epirus, which was one of the best Greek-medium schools in the Balkans at the time, and soon became proficient in French, Italian and Greek, in addition to his native Albanian. His encounter with modern Western thought and philosophy proved to be life-transforming, although he subsequently learned Arabic, Persian and Turkish which, in turn, enabled him to combine his study of modern philosophy with traditional Islamic thought.

Like his brothers Abdul (1839–1894) and Naim (1848–1900), after completing his formal education, Sami was forced to seek employment to make ends meet. However, his real passion in life was the revival of Albania's social, political and cultural fortunes. Despite working in Istanbul for the Ottoman press bureau, he played a pivotal role in the establishment of the Society for the Publication of Albanian Writings. The purpose of this cultural organisation was the production of textbooks, curriculum, periodicals and related information in the Albanian language for the benefit of their people. Like Naim, Sami became a prolific writer whose mastery of Oriental languages enabled him to write a historical account on the Middle Eastern people, commentaries on Arabic grammar textbooks as well as an anthology of poetry attributed to Ali ibn Abi Talib (599–661), the cousin and son-in-law of the Prophet of Islam.[12]

In total, Sami authored around fifty books and treatises on a wide-range of subjects including religious topics, history, linguistics, education, science and non-fiction. However, the Ottoman authorities were concerned by his nationalistic overtures which led to the closure of the Society for the Publication of Albanian Writings. In other words, the Frasheri brothers played an influential role in the development of the Albanian people's national feelings and aspirations, both through their political and literary activities. Sami died at his home in Istanbul at the age of 54, leaving behind his wife, Emine, and son, Ali Sami Yen. In recognition of his wide-ranging contribution and achievements, many schools have been named after him in Albania including the Sami Frasheri High School in Tirana and Prishtina, among others.

# LORD HEADLEY

B. 1855 – D. 1935

UNITED KINGDOM

Rowland George Allanson-Winn, better known as Lord Headley or Shaykh Rahmatullah al-Farooq, was the only son of the Honourable Rowland Allanson of Glenbegh, County Kerry, Ireland, and Margaretta Stephana Walker, the second daughter of George Walker of Overhall, Essex. He was born in London and educated at Westminster School before joining Trinity College, Cambridge and Kings College London. He obtained his Bachelor's degree in 1878 and, a year later, joined Middle Temple to study law. He initially worked in education and journalism before qualifying as a civil engineer. Thereafter, he worked in Kashmir, British India and in Ireland. In 1913, at the age of 57, he succeeded his cousin, Charles Mark, as the fifth Lord Headley.

It was during his time in India that Lord Headley first came in contact with Islam, and, as a result, it had a lasting impact on him. Despite being brought up as a Protestant and being familiar with Catholicism, it was the Islamic concept of Divine Unity that really appealed to him. His conversion to Islam took place after many years of studying and reflection, as well as extensive discussion with several prominent Muslim scholars and activists including Khwaja Kamaluddin of the Woking Muslim Mission. Convinced of the truth of Islam, he became a Muslim in November 1913 and took the name of Shaykh Rahmatullah Farooq. Soon after his conversion, he became a leading light for the British Muslim community. He was keen to perform the annual pilgrimage to Makkah but the outbreak of the First World War prevented him from accomplishing his task. It was not until a decade later that he finally performed the pilgrimage in 1923, accompanied by Khwaja Kamaluddin (1870–1932), his friend and well-wisher.

As an active member of the Muslim community, he helped establish the British Muslim Society in 1914 and served as its first president. Under his leadership, several prominent British Muslims became actively involved with the Woking Muslim Mission including Henry William Quilliam (see chapter 27), John Yahya Parkinson (see chapter 32) and Khalid Sheldrake (see the entry on him below), among others. He was a regular contributor to the *Islamic Review*, which was the mouthpiece of the Woking Muslim Mission, and also published several booklets on aspects of Islam and comparative religion.

In his *A Western Awakening to Islam* (1914), he argued that 'Islam is the religion of grand simplicity; it satisfies the noblest longings of the souls, and in no way contravenes the teachings of Moses or Christ.'[13] He subsequently published two other booklets, entitled *The Three Great Prophets of the World: Moses, Jesus, and Muhammad* (1923) and *The Affinity between the Original Church of Jesus Christ and Islam* (1926). Lord Headley died at his home, Ashton Gifford House, near the village of Codford, Wiltshire at the age of 80.

# RIZAEDDIN BIN FAKHREDDIN

B. 1858 – D. 1936

TATAR REPUBLIC

Rizaeddin bin Fakhreddin, also known as Rizaeddin Fahreddin, was born into a notable Tatar Muslim family in Samara, today located in the Tatar Republic of the Russian Federation. His father was a local Muslim preacher who initially taught his son before enrolling him at the local Islamic seminary. He was a gifted student who successfully completed his Islamic education in 1889 at the age of 30. Although it was very common in those days to move from Tatarstan to Bukhara to receive advance Islamic training in Arabic and the traditional Islamic sciences, Rizaeddin did not pursue that path and, instead, continued his advanced Islamic studies locally.

Thereafter, he joined the Islamic seminary in Ilbek as a teacher and soon established his reputation as a learned scholar whose knowledge of Islamic jurisprudence and history was nothing short of impressive. A few years later, he was promoted to the post of judge (*Qadi*) and thus became known as Riza Qadi. He was also known for his expertise in Oriental languages including Arabic, Persian and Turkish, in addition to Russian and Tatar dialects. His linguistic skills enabled him to read widely and develop an intimate knowledge and understanding of Islamic thought, history and culture – focusing particularly on the Islamic culture and heritage of the Tatar people.[14]

It was during his late forties, however, that he turned his attention to journalism as the founding editor of *Shura* (Consultation), through which he was able to disseminate his considerable knowledge of Islamic thought, history and culture for the benefit of his people. He was a prolific writer who contributed scores of articles in his journal and authored many books and monographs on aspects of Islamic sciences, Tatar history, biographies of prominent Muslim personalities and religious textbooks for students. As a Muslim modernist, he not only wrote biographies of Ibn Taymiyyah (1263–1328) and Jamal al-Din al-Afghani (1838–1897), he was also profoundly influenced by their reformist ideas and thought.

However, he is best known today for his two-volume history of Tatar Muslim scholars. He combined his literary and scholarly activities with his work as *Mufti* (jurisconsult) of the European region of Russia. Although he was employed by the Russian government, he did not support their political and military activities, which he considered to be misguided and counter-productive. Thanks to his vast learning and scholarship, he was respected by the Russian authorities as well as the Tatar people. He died at the age of 74.

# J. W. LOVEGROVE

B. 1867 – D. 1940

UNITED KINGDOM

James William Lovegrove, otherwise known as 'Jimmie' or Habibullah Lovegrove, was born into a lower middle-class English family in Grove, Berkshire. His family traced their ancestry from the Lovegroves of Wantage, Berkshire and both his father, William James Lovegrove (d. 1913), and grandfather, David Lovegrove (d. 1943) were tailors by profession. His mother, Emma Clifton (d. 1927) was a homemaker and also assisted her husband in his role as a publican. After completing his basic education, young James followed in the footsteps of his father and became a tailor by profession.

Tall, handsome and spiritually-inclined, he began training as a cutter in Worksop, Nottinghamshire and moved to Battersea, today located in the London Borough of Wandsworth, after marrying Elizabeth Foster in 1892 at the age of 25.

He became a skilful and popular tailor who was especially known for designing and making coats, jackets, overcoats, hats, handkerchiefs and gloves. His stylish designs and attractive outfits won considerable acclaim, and were even featured in *Motoring Illustrated*. Founded in 1899, this motor car journal promoted his products widely especially in its 1902–1903 issues. Thanks to the success of his business, he was subsequently elected president of the Tailors and Cutters Guild, which was an influential and high-profile position at the time. He was also the chief petitioner of the Small Holdings and Allotment Act of 1908, which placed a duty upon local authorities to provide sufficient allotments, according to demand. However, it was only after the enactment of the Allotment Act of 1922 that the rights of allotment holders were strengthened.

On a more personal level, James was a true seeker of knowledge, wisdom and truth. Although Christianity was his ancestral faith, he found its teachings over-complicated and contrary to reason and rationality, and continued his quest for meaning and purpose in the modern world. Eventually, he came in contact with members of the Woking Muslim Mission and obtained copies of Islamic literature. After studying the Qur'an and the life of the Prophet of Islam, he reportedly saw the famous Sufi poet, Jalal al-Din Rumi (1207–1273) in the form of a vision, and the latter encouraged him to embrace Islam, thus adopting the Muslim name of Habibullah Lovegrove.[15]

However, in the foreword to his *What is Islam?* James wrote that, 'I wanted a simple, practical religion, free from dogma and tenets, which I could not accept without killing my reason. To do my duty to God, and my neighbour, undoubtedly is and ought to be the main object of every religious system, but Islam came to give the maximum as practical shape. We want precepts as well as example to meet all the contingencies and exigencies of life and directions to guide us in our difficult callings. This I found in Islam.'[16]

After confessing Islam, he became an active member of the Woking Muslim Mission and served as a vice-president and secretary of the British Muslim Society for a period. There is a beautiful photograph of James demonstrating how to perform the *Salah* (five daily prayers) in Khwaja Kamaluddin's booklet titled *Islam and the Muslim Prayer* (1914, revised edition 1960). He died in Sidcup, south-east London, at the age of 73 and was buried in Wantage Cemetery, Berkshire, according to Islamic rites.

# IVAN AGUELI

B. 1869 – D. 1917

SWEDEN

Ivan Agueli, also known as John Gustaf Agelii or Shaykh Abd al-Hadi Aqili, was born into a middle-class Swedish family in the town of Sala, which is today located in Vastmanland County in the north-west of the country. His father was a vet by profession and young Ivan became fascinated by arts, music and mysticism from an early age. After completing his early education in Gotland and Stockholm, he moved to Paris in 1889 and became a student of Emile Bernard (1868–1941) who was a notable French Post-Impressionist painter and writer. He continued his studies at an art school in Stockholm under the tutelage of Anders Zorn (1860–1920) and Richard Berg (1858–1919), both of whom were renowned Swedish artists of their generation. However, towards the end of 1892, he returned to Paris where he became involved with the French anarchists and was soon imprisoned for his activism.

Upon his release in 1895, he moved to Egypt where he encountered Islam for the first time. The simplicity of the faith and its spirituality, otherwise known as *tasawwuf* or Sufism, fascinated him, so much so that, a year later on his return to Paris, he converted to Islam and adopted the Muslim name of Abd al-Hadi. After a short sojourn to Colombo (capital of present-day Sri Lanka), he went to Egypt in 1902 where he became one of the first Western Muslims to study at the University of al-Azhar in Cairo. While he was busy studying Arabic and Islamic philosophy, he met the renowned Egyptian Islamic scholar and Sufi Shaykh, Abd al-Rahman Ilaysh al-Kabir (1840–1921), who initiated him into the al-Arabiyya Shadhiliyya Sufi Order.[17]

After completing his education, Ivan returned to Paris and established a Sufi society under the name of *al-Akbariyya*, revolving around the teachings of Ibn al-Arabi (see the entry on him above). The renowned French metaphysician and Sufi writer, Rene Guenon (see chapter 37), was one of its first members. However, during the First World War, Ivan was thrown out of France, having been suspected of being an Ottoman spy, which forced him to move to Spain where he apparently died in an accident in a location not far from Barcelona.

As a gifted artist, however, he is today widely recognised as one of Sweden's foremost painters. Most of his paintings are currently on display at the National Museum of Fine Arts (Stockholm), the Museum of Modern Art (Stockholm) and the Agueli Museum (Sala). In recognition of his contribution to the arts, the Swedish Postal Service printed six of his paintings as stamps in 1969. Just over a decade later, his remains were finally brought back to Sweden and re-buried in his native Sala as per Islamic guidelines.

# WILLIAM RICHARD WILLIAMSON

B. 1872 – D. 1958

UNITED KINGDOM

William Richard Williamson, also known as Hajji Abdullah Fadhil al-Zubayr, was born into a relatively well-to-do English family in the city of Bristol, located towards the west of England. He was inclined to being a daredevil and never hesitated to push the boundaries of acceptability, both at home and school. His father and teachers at Clifton College struggled to keep up with him until his uncle sent him off to the United States and Australia to learn the hard lessons of life, presumably with a view to returning home to continue his education, but the 13 year-old had other ideas. In San Diego, he abandoned ship and found work in a farm not far from Los Angeles, before he set off for France, only to return to the US again. He subsequently boarded a ship bound for the Caroline Islands, located towards the east of the present-day Philippines, where he engaged in trade but was imprisoned in Manila for selling illegal weapons to local tribesmen.

With the assistance of Alexander Russell Webb (see chapter 25), the then US consul in Manila, he set off for Hong Kong before heading for Bombay. He soon found employment in India and became fascinated by the diversity of its religious customs and practices. He also encountered Islam for the first time in the country and became interested in its teachings. However, it was during his voyage to Aden in Yemen that he discovered the writings of Henry William Quilliam (see chapter 27), the famous founder of the Liverpool Muslim Institute, which he read avidly and through which he was convinced of the soundness and simplicity of Islam.[18] Upon his arrival in Aden, he studied the faith more closely under the tutelage of local Islamic scholars and formally became a Muslim. Like most other Western converts to Islam, he found the Islamic concept of Divine Oneness very appealing, unlike the Christian doctrine of Trinity, which he considered to be both confusing and contradictory.

As expected, his decision to go native did not go down too well with the authorities in Aden and he was forced to return to India. However, while he was still in his early twenties, he joined a caravan destined for Makkah and successfully completed the annual pilgrimage, being one of the first English Muslims to accomplish that feat in 1894. During this period, he earned his living by trading in camels and horses from Arabia, Iraq, Kuwait and India. His relations with the British officials improved overtime and profits from his import and export business enabled him to undertake numerous adventures both on land and sea. Although he subsequently worked for several Anglo-Persian oil companies, he was always fair and equitable in his dealings with the Arabs which, of course, did not always go down well with his British superiors who wanted to secure the best deals as possible.

Fluent in Arabic and equally versed in Islam, he became a real thorn in the side of the Christian missionaries who were very active in and around Basra at the time. He engaged in fierce debates and discussion with them, and robustly defended Islam and its Prophet against their vitriolic attacks, much to the delight of the local Muslims. He eventually retired in 1937 and lived in the city of Zubair with his family. He was a devout Muslim who performed his daily prayers in his local mosque and died in his mid-80s.

# SIR CHARLES ARCHIBALD HAMILTON

B. 1876 – D. 1939

UNITED KINGDOM

Charles Edward Archibald Watkin Hamilton, also known as Sir Abdullah Archibald Hamilton, was born in London into an aristocratic British family of Scottish ancestry. His father, Sir Edward Archibald Hamilton, the fourth Baronet of Trebishun, Breconshire and his mother, Lady Mary Elizabeth Gill, were very wealthy and distinguished individuals who provided a privileged upbringing for their son. After completing his formal education, he became a naval officer and, in December 1897, he married Olga Mary Adelaide FitzGeorge, who was the granddaughter of the Duke of Cambridge and great-great-granddaughter of King George III. Although she bore him a son and daughter, the marriage ended in divorce after five years. To add insult to injury, he lost his son during the horrors of the First World War; he died in action while serving in France with the Grenadier Guards. He himself became a Lieutenant in the 4th Battalion, Royal Sussex Regiment, and played an active part during the First World War.

   He spent most of his life in southern England and served as a president of the Conservative Association in Selsey, County of Sussex. He married for the second time in 1906 but he was forced to separate after only two years due to his wife's erratic behaviour. In the meantime, his quest for meaning and purpose in life led to his conversion to Islam in December 1923. He wrote an article published in *The People* (13 January, 1924) which was reprinted in *The Islamic Review* (February 1924), wherein he explained his reasons for converting to Islam: 'Since arriving at an age of discretion, the beauty and the simple purity of Islam have always appealed to me. I could never, though born and brought up as a Christian, believe in the dogmatic aspect of the Church; and have always placed reason and common sense before blind faith. As time progressed, I wished to be at peace with my Creator, and I found that both the Church of Rome and the Church of England were of no real use to me. In becoming a Muslim I have merely obeyed the dictates of my conscience, and have since felt a better and a truer man.'[19]

Sir Charles remarried for the third time in 1927. His marriage to Lilian Austen, otherwise known as Lady Hamilton, was conducted according to Islamic guidelines, and she also became a Muslim. According to his fellow Muslims, he was an 'ardent preacher of the faith' and played an active part in the affairs of the Woking Muslim Mission. He died at the age of 62 and was laid to rest next to his friend and fellow convert, Lord Headley (see entry on him above), at the Brookwood Cemetery, Surrey. His funeral prayer was led by the Imam of the Woking Mosque. According to Edward Heron-Allen (1861–1943), the renowned English polymath and scientist, Sir Abdullah Archibald Hamilton was 'one of the most highly cultivated and most deeply read men that I have ever known.'[20]

# ISABELLE EBERHARDT

B. 1877 – D. 1904

SWITZERLAND

Isabelle Eberhardt was born in Geneva, Switzerland into a middle-class Christian family. Her father, Alexandre Trophimowsky, was a former Orthodox priest and her mother, Nathalie Moerder, hailed from both a Lutheran and Jewish background. She was initially educated at home by her father whose remarkable linguistic abilities rubbed-off on his daughter. In addition to French, Russian, German and Italian, she learned Latin, Greek and classical Arabic which enabled her to read the Qur'an for the first time. Like her father, Isabelle grew up to be a non-conformist who actively engaged in literary activities during her spare time and regularly published short stories in local journals, often under a pseudonym.

In due course, she became interested in learning more about North Africa, thanks partly to her knowledge of Arabic and partly due to the inspiration of her brother, Augustin, who was serving in Algeria at the time under the French Foreign Legion. Based on her regular correspondence with Augustin and Eugene Letord, a French officer, she subsequently authored and published an essay titled *Vision du Moghreb* (Vision of the Maghreb) in the *Nouvelle Revue Moderne* in 1895.

Although she was barely 18 at the time, her writing was well received and thus, this prompted Louis David, a prominent French-Algerian photographer, to invite her to visit him in Bone, Algeria. She and her mother followed suit and, in May 1897, for the first time, she came directly in contact with traditional North African Muslim culture. She and her mother were so impressed that both of them embraced Islam, much to the disapproval of the French expatriates whose colonial mentality and attitude was profoundly resented by the locals. She later wrote, '...I feel myself saturated by ancient, unshaken Islam, which here seems to be the very breathing of the earth; to the extent that my days go by calmly, the necessity for labour and strife is less and less real to me.'[21]

After the death of her parents in 1897 and 1899, respectively, Isabelle moved to Paris where she struggled to make ends meet before returning to Algeria in July 1900 and settled in El Oued. Subsequently, she was initiated into the North African branch of the Qadiriyya Sufi Order and hereon led an entirely Muslim lifestyle, although the French colonial authorities wrongly considered her to be a spy or political agitator. Being a committed anti-colonialist, however, Isabelle wrote scores of articles in support of Arab emancipation and criticised French foreign policy in North Africa. For that reason, she struggled to publish her writings in France at the time. In due course, she secured employment as a reporter for the *al-Akhbar* newspaper (based in Algiers), in addition to publishing short stories in the *Trimardeur*.

Having been struck by a flash flood, she died at the age of only 27. She left behind several unpublished manuscripts including *Dans l'Ombre Chaude de l'Islam* (In the Shadow of Islam) which received widespread acclaim soon after its publication in 1906, although it was not translated into English until 1993.

# KHALID SHELDRAKE

B. 1888 – D. 1947

UNITED KINGDOM

Bertram William Sheldrake, better known as Khalid Sheldrake, was born into a wealthy English family of pickle manufacturers. After completing his early education, he studied medicine and qualified as a physician. He was barely 16 when he had converted to Islam, which was as a result of his personal quest for meaning and truth. He subsequently enlisted for service during the First World War and attained the rank of sergeant in the British army, having fought on the side of the Allies against the Central Powers of Germany and Austria-Hungary. The unprecedented destruction and mayhem that ensued, coupled with the colossal loss of human life, prompted many Europeans to ask questions and engage in soul-searching both during and after the war; this prompted many to convert to Islam including Abd al-Aziz Peach, Charles Salman Schleich, Walter H. Williams and Joseph Abdullah Davidson, among others.

Although he had participated in the war efforts, Khalid struggled to make sense of the madness that had originated in Europe and soon spread to other parts of the world. Writing during the war, he observed that, 'Protestantism is too much occupied with its own internal dissensions to preach a united doctrine of peace to the world' and, although 'Christianity has had the power to enforce obedience, to make men good and pure and true; she has had churches and paid priests for centuries, and what is the result to-day? Appalling! Heart-breaking! Is Europe happy, united and peaceful?'[22]

He initially became a member of the Pan-Islamic Society in London which was founded by Sir Abdullah al-Ma'mun Suhrawardy in 1903, before establishing his own Young England Islamic Society a few years later (with the support of Ahmad Browning and Omar Flight), in addition to serving as the London correspondent of the *Crescent*, which was founded and edited by Henry William Quilliam in Liverpool (see chapter 27). However, after the founding of the Woking Muslim Mission and its mouthpiece, *Muslim India and Islamic Review* (which subsequently became known as *Islamic Review*), he became an active member and contributed scores of articles under the editorship of Khwaja Kamaluddin.

He later fell out with the senior leadership of the Woking Muslim Mission and, as a result, co-founded the Western Islamic Association with the help of several other English converts including Omar Richardson and Osman Watkins. The association not only had a prayer room (also known as Peckham Mosque) where he acted as an Imam, but it also published its own journal titled the *Minaret*. Most of the activities of the association were funded by Khalid and his supporters.

Being a Pan-Islamist, he was later invited to become the 'King of Islamistan' which was a territory in Xinjiang province, located in northwest of China. However, he never took up this role, but instead, spent the rest of his life travelling and pursuing business activities. He eventually died in London at the age of 59.

# MUHAMMAD HAMIDULLAH

B. 1908 – D. 2002

FRANCE

Muhammad Hamidullah was born in Mohalla Feelkhana, old town of Hyderabad, State of Hyderabad (in the present-day Indian State of Telangana) into a notable Muslim family of scholars and writers. His father, Abu Muhammad Khalilullah, worked as an Assistant Revenue Secretary and was a prominent Islamic scholar who initially taught his son at home before enrolling him at their local Islamic seminary. He graduated at the age of 20 and then joined the Osmania University to complete his postgraduate education, obtaining both MA and LLB degrees in 1930. Thereafter, he went to Germany and enrolled at the University of Bonn for doctoral studies and obtained his first PhD in 1933, whilst also serving as a European correspondent for the *Islamic Culture*, a quarterly journal published from Hyderabad.

Two years later, he obtained another doctorate from the Sorbonne. He returned to Hyderabad in 1936 only to find out that his beloved father had passed away. In due course, he joined the Osmania University and taught Islamic and international law for a decade, and soon after, he was promoted to the rank of a professor. He was barely 40 when the Nizam of Hyderabad sent him to Paris as his Constitutional Adviser, but following India's invasion of the princely Muslim State, he chose to settle in Paris rather than live under occupation. After a short stay in Pakistan, he returned to Paris where he served as a Research Fellow at the Centre National de la Recherche Scientifique for nearly a quarter of a century, in addition to being appointed Visiting Professor at universities in Malaysia and Turkey.

During this period, Hamidullah carried out original research on aspects of early Islamic history, the life of the Prophet of Islam (*sirah*) and Islamic International Law. Some of his leading publications include *Die Neutralitat im islamischen Volkerrecht* (Neutrality in Islamic International Law), which was published in Bonn and Leipzig in 1935; *La diplomatie musulmane a l'epoque du Prophete et des Khalifes Orthodoxe* (Muslim Diplomacy during the time of the Prophet and the Rightly-Guided Successors), which was published in Paris in 1935 in two volumes; and, *The Muslim Conduct of State*, originally a master's dissertation submitted to Osmania University, which was first published in 1941 from Lahore, Pakistan and this being one of his most popular books.

His other notable publications were *The First Written Constitution in the World* (1941), *Introduction to Islam* (1957), *Muhammad Rasulullah* (1979), *The Battlefields of the Prophet Muhammad* (1992) and the *Emergence of Islam* (1993). Steeped in classical Islamic sciences and Western academic methods and languages, Hamidullah was a gifted linguist and translator. He was fluent in more than a dozen languages including English, French, German, Arabic, Persian, Turkish, Italian and Urdu, which was his mother tongue. His linguistic abilities enabled him to read extensively and publish more than 150 books and around 1000 research papers and articles.[23] However, two of his most popular works include *Le Prophete de l'Islam* (1959), a seminal biography of the Prophet published in two volumes in French (translated into English as *The Life and Work of the Prophet of Islam* in 1998), and *Le Saint Coran*, a monumental French translation and commentary of the Qur'an (1959 onwards).

A Muslim by faith, Easterner in his principles and values, and a Westerner by academic training and citizenship, Hamidullah was a towering Muslim scholar, researcher and writer who led a pious and scrupulous lifestyle, being totally detached from material benefits and consideration. He never married and, instead, devoted his entire life to Islamic learning and scholarship. In recognition of his services to Islam, the Government of Pakistan awarded him the International Hijrah Award in 1985 but, typical of the man, he donated the cheque for one million rupees to the Islamic Research Institute in Islamabad. Although he suffered from ill-health from 1988 onwards, he found time to learn the Thai language at the age of 84. He was admitted to hospital in Paris for hypothermia in January 1996 and subsequently moved to the United States of America for medical treatment in October. He died and was buried in Jacksonville, Florida at the age of 94.

# KNUT BERNSTROM

B. 1919 – D. 2009

SWEDEN

Muhammad Knut Johan Richard Bernstrom, better known as Knut Bernstrom, was born into a middle-class Protestant family in Saltsjobaden, today located in Stockholm County, Sweden. His father, Seth Bernstrom, was an engineer by profession, and his mother, Erna von Hillern-Flinsch, was a homemaker. As a dedicated student, he successfully completed his primary, secondary and advanced education, before joining the Swedish diplomatic service as a subordinate. He soon won the support and confidence of his seniors and served in his capacity as a diplomat for forty years, including as Swedish ambassador to Venezuela from 1963 to 1966. He then moved to Spain and served there from 1973 to 1976 before transferring to Morocco as Swedish ambassador, and thus remained there until 1983. In addition to this, he worked in France, United States of America, Brazil and Senegal before finally retiring due to ill health.

Knut was a seeker of knowledge and wisdom from the outset and continued his personal quest for meaning until he became a Muslim when he was in his mid-sixties. Although raised as a Protestant, he abandoned his ancestral faith during the 1950s in favour of Catholicism because he was hungry for moral and spiritual certainty in an age of flux and uncertainty, but his new faith did not quench his spiritual thirst. Indeed, when Pope Paul VI decreed in December 1963 that Latin should no longer be the sole language of liturgy, he immediately renounced Catholicism because he considered this to be a corruption of faith and worship. However, after he was posted to Rabat as Swedish ambassador, he encountered traditional Islam for the first time and was impressed by its spiritual depth and moral certainty.

During his seven years of service in Morocco, he became actively involved in Moroccan society and culture, and that enabled him to learn Arabic. As an accomplished linguist who was already familiar with a dozen languages including English, French, Spanish, and German, it did not take him long to master Arabic which enabled him to read the Qur'an and classical Islamic literature for the first time. He was so impressed by the Qur'anic revelation that he continued to study it for nearly a decade before he finally embraced Islam in 1986. He then committed the entire sacred text to memory, much to the surprise and admiration of his friends and family.

Thereafter, he devoted the next 10 years of his life to meticulously translating and annotating the entire Qur'an into his native language, being the first Swedish translation to be officially approved by the University of al-Azhar in Cairo. Accompanied by the original Arabic text and valuable introductory notes, his contemporary Swedish translation, entitled *Koranen Budskap*, was printed in 1998 by Proprius Publishing, a Stockholm-based publishing house, to widespread acclaim. The success of his translation then prompted Knut to start work on preparing an anthology of Prophetic traditions into Swedish, although it was probably never completed. This remarkable Muslim scholar, linguist and translator eventually passed away at the age of 89.

# SMAIL BALIC

B. 1920 – D. 2002

BOSNIA HERZEGOVINA

Smail Balic, also known as Dr Smail Balic, was born in Mostar, which is today located in southern Bosnia and Herzegovina, into a notable Muslim family. His pious family ensured that he received a thorough religious education during his early years, and then moved to Sarajevo where he studied Arabic, Islamic theology and philosophy. As a talented student, he successfully completed his early and further education in his native Bosnia before moving to the universities of Vienna (Austria), Leipzig (Germany) and Wroclaw (Poland) where he pursued higher education in Turkish, Arabic and Slavic languages. In the process, he became a prominent linguist who also specialised in the intellectual and cultural history of Bosnia and Herzegovina. Indeed, he wrote his doctoral thesis on the development of Islamic thought and culture in his native Bosnia, for which the University of Vienna awarded him a Doctor of Philosophy Degree in 1945, when he was only 25.

Thereafter, he taught at several educational institutions in Europe and the Middle East including in Vienna, Kuwait and Jordan. Although he started his academic career as a lecturer at the Public School of World Trade in Vienna, he subsequently worked as a research librarian at the Austrian National Library where he was the head of Oriental languages and Keeper of its Arabic books and manuscripts; he served in this capacity from 1963 to 1984. As a devout but liberal Muslim scholar and author, during this period he pursued research on aspects of European Muslim history, culture and heritage focusing particularly on his native Bosnia and Herzegovina. He authored many books, monographs and research articles including *Islam in Medieval Hungary* (1965),

*The Culture of Bosniaks* (1973), *The Unknown Bosnia* (1992), *The Forgotten Islam or Euro-Islam* (2000), *Islam for Europe: New Perspectives of an Ancient Religion* (2001) and *Catalogue of Turkish Manuscripts in the Austrian National Library* (2006).

In his writings, Smail presented Islam as a democratic and pluralistic faith that was not only an integral part of Europe, both historically and culturally, but it was also in harmony with traditional Western thought and philosophy. Unsurprisingly, he espoused a liberal interpretation of Islamic scriptures, namely the Qur'an and Prophetic teachings, which emphasised the ethical and moral dimension of Islam, but he severely criticised the politicisation of the faith. Just as conflict and violence was alien to the Islamic worldview, he argued that the protection and preservation of human life was the *raison d'etre* of Islamic law.

However, his ideas and thought have been criticised by several European Muslim scholars (such as Murad Wilfried Hoffman) who considered his attempts to develop a 'European Islam' forced him to dilute traditional Islamic beliefs and teachings.[24] In other words, Smail rightly deplored the situation of Muslims in the East which, of course, contributed to the negative perception of Islam in the West but, at the same time, he failed to criticise the Western powers for contributing to the social, political and economic problems in the Muslim world. Having said that, there is no doubt that Smail Balic was one of the foremost European Muslim historians, thinkers and writers of his generation.

Furthermore, he was an active member of Austria's growing Muslim community and was awarded the country's Cross of Honour for Science and Art (First Class) in recognition of his contribution to research, scholarship and literature. He eventually died at the age of 82.

# ADIL BEY ZULFIKARPASIC

B. 1921 – D. 2008

BOSNIA HERZEGOVINA

Adil Bey Zulfikarpasic, better known as Adil Zulfikarpasic, was born in the town of Foca in Yugoslavia (in present-day Bosnia and Herzegovina) into a traditional Muslim family. His father, Husayn Bey, was a very wealthy individual who served as the mayor of Foca for twenty-five years, and his mother, Zahida, hailed from the noble Cengic family. He attended the local Qur'an school during his early years before enrolling at his local primary school. Thereafter, he moved to Sarajevo for his secondary education and subsequently graduated in political science and law. He then joined the Communist Party of Yugoslavia and, thanks to his dedication and commitment, he was promoted to the organiser of the party.

He participated in the Second World War and attained the rank of Lieutenant Colonel but was captured by the Croatian pro-Nazi forces, otherwise known as the Ustasha. With the assistance of the Yugoslav Partisans, he escaped from captivity but, after the war, he joined the Communist regime of Josip Broz Tito (1892–1980) and served as Deputy Minister of Trade for a period. Being unhappy with Tito's authoritarian tendencies and unpopular policies, he eventually left Yugoslavia and settled in Zurich, Switzerland where he became a highly successful businessman and philanthropist.

In 1987, he established the Bosniac Institute, a private non-profit foundation in Zurich, in order to preserve and promote the history and heritage of Bosnia and Herzegovina for the benefit of the present and future generations. Funded entirely by himself, the institute specialised in collecting, documenting, archiving and preserving social, cultural, historical, linguistic and religious data and artefacts about Bosnia and its people. The institute today houses an extensive library, large arts collection and initiates cultural projects in order to promote intercultural understanding and religious dialogue, both in Bosnia and abroad. Upon his return to Bosnia in 1990, Adil became actively involved in the political and cultural affairs of the country. Along with Alija Izetbegovic (see chapter 48), he founded the Party of Democratic Action (SDA) and served as its Vice-President for only one year.

Subsequently, both of them disagreed on the future political, economic and cultural direction for Bosnia and that, in turn, forced Adil to leave the SDA and establish his own party, the Muslim Bosniac Organisation, with the help of Muhamed Filipovic (b. 1929) and others. He eventually retired from politics and became more involved in cultural and philanthropic activities. Indeed, in 2001, he and his wife, Tanja, opened the Sarajevo branch of the Bosniac Institute and, a year later, he was elected an honorary member of the country's Academy of Sciences and Arts on account of his remarkable efforts to preserve and promote Bosnia's cultural heritage. He was also a notable writer and editor who founded a prominent journal, the *Bosanski pogledi*, in collaboration with Smail Balic, and published many essays, articles and interviews including *The Bosniak* (1998).

After a lifetime devoted to the service of the people of Bosnia and Herzegovina, Adil Zulfikarpasic died at the age of 86. Four years after his death, a detailed biography of this remarkable Bosnian Muslim politician, reformer and philanthropist was published by Sacir Filandra and Enes Karic. It was subsequently translated into English as *The Bosniac Idea* by Saba Risaluddin (Zagreb, 2004).

# ZAKI BADAWI

B. 1922 – D. 2006

UNITED KINGDOM

Muhammad Abul-Khayr Zaki Badawi, better known as Shaykh Dr Zaki Badawi, was born in Sharkia, a town on the outskirts of Cairo, into a devout Muslim family. After his early education at home, he joined al-Azhar Primary School before moving to the Secondary School where he proved to be a talented student. Encouraged by his tutors and family members, he then enrolled at al-Azhar University's Faculty of Theology and passed his first degree with flying colours; so much so that he was awarded the King Fuad First Prize for being the best student of 1945; he was only 23 at the time.

Two years later, he obtained his master's degree from the Faculty of Arabic Studies and, again, received a prize for being the best postgraduate student of 1947. Keen to pursue higher education in England, he enrolled at the University of London in 1951 and was awarded a degree in Psychology from University College London in 1954. As an insatiable seeker of knowledge and wisdom, he then pursued doctoral studies at London University and received his PhD degree with a thesis on the subject of modern Islamic thought and reform in Egypt. After completing his higher education, he returned to Cairo to teach at al-Azhar.

Zaki was not only steeped in traditional Islamic sciences but also thoroughly familiar with modern Western thought, research and scholarship. His unique ability to combine Islamic thought with Western scholarship, in addition to mastery of Arabic and English, encouraged the officials of al-Azhar University to send him to Malaysia to help establish a Muslim college there and teach Arabic and Islamic sciences at the universities of Singapore and Malaya in Kuala Lumpur. Thereafter, he moved to Nigeria and became a professor of Islamic Education at the Ahmadu Bello University and Bayero College, Kano (now known as Bayero University). After teaching in Nigeria for a decade, he moved to London as a researcher before being appointed director of Islamic Cultural Centre and the chief Imam of the Regent's Park Mosque in 1978.

During this period, he became an important institution-builder who played an instrumental role in setting up the UK Shari'ah Council, Imams and Mosques Council, and he was the founder-principal of Muslim College London in 1986. The college became one of the first institutions of postgraduate studies in Arabic and Islamic Studies in the Western world, providing courses that combined the study of classical Islamic sciences with modern thought and philosophy to enable its graduates to confidently engage with issues of faith, morality, ethics, citizenship and interfaith dialogue.

Although Zaki was a gifted scholar and writer, his involvement in the affairs of British Muslims did not leave much time for him to pursue research and scholarship, which was his real love and passion. Even so, he contributed regular articles in a number of journals and magazines including the London-based *Al-Arab*, the *Islamic Quarterly* (of which he was the editor for four years) and the *Islamic Banker*. He also authored or edited several books on Islamic thought, history and interfaith dialogue, in addition to being one of the first consultants on Islamic banking, having advised many governments and banks on the subject. Zaki was a visionary and proactively engaged in interfaith co-operation and dialogue with Christians, Jews, Sikhs, Hindus and Buddhists. He was the founder or chairman of dozens of civic and interfaith organisations including Vice Chair of World Congress of Faiths, Chair of The Abrahamic Forum and Chair of Forum Against Islamophobia and Racism.[25]

Despite being steeped in classical Islamic thought and scholarship, he was always open to new ideas, thoughts and solutions to challenges and difficulties facing Muslims, both in the West and in the Muslim world. He was truly a multi-dimensional scholar, reformer and academic who was well ahead of his time. In recognition of his contribution, Zaki was awarded an OBE in 1998 and an honorary knighthood in 2004, in addition to an honorary Doctor of Law Degree from the Glasgow Caledonian University in 2005. On a personal level, he was a pious, committed and energetic individual who considered all his deeds and actions to be nothing but devotion to God. However, his greatest legacies are the institutions he established and the hundreds of students, community activists and Imams he had trained and mentored in the United Kingdom over a period of a quarter of a century. He died and was buried in London at the age of 84.

# MALCOLM X

B. 1925 – D. 1965

UNITED STATES OF AMERICA

Malcolm Little, better known as Malcolm X, was born in Omaha in the American State of Nebraska. His father, Reverend Earl Little, was a Baptist Minister, and his mother, Louise, was a homemaker. However, the family struggled to overcome their social and economic difficulties, which often created tensions within his family, but Louise remained loyal to her husband. When Malcolm was six his father died (in disputed circumstances), and this again forced his family to experience more difficulties. Like his brothers and sisters, Malcolm was brought up in foster homes before he enrolled at Mason Junior High school in Lansing, where he completed the eighth grade. At school, his white teacher urged him to become a carpenter since becoming a lawyer, in his opinion, was an unrealistic aspiration for a black boy. Malcolm quit formal education in disgust.

Subsequently, he was sucked into the murky world of drugs, prostitution and crime, before becoming a seasoned street hustler and the leader of a gang of thieves, and thereby established his reputation as a fearsome leader of the local criminal fraternity. In due course, he was arrested and found guilty of armed robbery. Imprisoned for six years, he soon experienced a life-changing transformation. Reading widely enabled Malcolm to explore and understand the true nature and complexities of human life, culture and civilisation. So it was that, whilst still in prison, his brother introduced him to the teachings of Elijah Muhammad (1897-1975) and the Nation of Islam.

As expected, on his release from prison in 1952, Malcolm became an active member of the Nation. As an eloquent orator and great motivator of people, he took the message of the Nation directly to the people and of course his success won him much-needed recognition and acclaim from the Nation's hierarchy, including Elijah himself. His hard work, coupled with his indefatigable energy and commitment to his task, soon saw him rise from being an obscure assistant Minister of the Nation's Detroit Temple Number One, to its national spokesman within a short period. Most interestingly, when Malcolm first joined the Nation in the early 1950s, it had no more than several thousand followers but under his able leadership the Nation of Islam became a powerful mass-movement with more than a hundred thousand loyal followers. He regularly visited the black ghetto areas of Detroit, Boston and New York and urged the poor and disenfranchised black people to join the Nation and fight for their rights and liberty.

Thanks to Malcolm's efforts, the image of the Nation of Islam as a fringe fundamentalist group soon changed for good. Also, when his high-profile attacks on the root causes of economic inequality, social deprivation, political powerlessness and cultural ghettoisation of the African Americans struck a chord with the masses, his popularity hit an all-time high. His 'tell it as you see it' approach soon turned him into a cult figure within the black communities. By the same token, his frank and outspoken attack on the ruling classes began to anger the Establishment. It was not long before the right-wing American press began to brand him 'the angriest black man in America'. Even so, he soon became a voice for millions of voiceless African Americans who had been enduring economic hardship and social deprivation for many generations in the ghettos of Detroit, Boston, New York, Chicago, Philadelphia, Cleveland and Indianapolis.

As Malcolm's popularity continued to rise, Elijah Muhammad became concerned by the increasing politicisation of the Nation of Islam. Since he considered himself to be a religious leader rather than a politician, he was not too keen to get involved in politics and public affairs. And although Malcolm's loyalty to Elijah was absolute, the latter's apolitical stance on many important issues of the day dismayed him. During this period Malcolm became aware of Elijah's mismanagement of the Nation's finances, as well as his amoral sexual practices (such as his involvement in extramarital affairs), which of course shocked and horrified him. This prompted Malcolm to leave the Nation of Islam in 1964. After leaving the Nation, he and his supporters inaugurated two separate organisations, namely the Muslim Mosque, Inc., and the Organisation of Afro-American Unity (OAAU). The former was essentially a religious institution, while the latter became the political wing of the Muslim Mosque.

Thereafter, Malcolm travelled across Africa and the Middle East, and also performed the sacred *hajj* (pilgrimage to Makkah) where he experienced yet another life- changing transformation. He came into contact with mainstream Muslims and his experience of the universal brotherhood of man championed by Islam captured his imagination. In response, he openly renounced Elijah's distorted and racialistic interpretation of Islam and became an orthodox Muslim; from then on he became known by his new Muslim name, al-Hajj Malik al-Shabazz. From Makkah, he wrote scores of letters wherein he explained the reasons why he had had a change of heart and clearly spelled out his new thoughts and ideas on race relations, human rights, cultural co-existence and socio-political issues. On his return to America, he began to champion mainstream Islam and advocated the need for both racial and cultural tolerance and understanding across all sectors of American society.

He also developed an internationalist approach to human rights and Third World politics, and became an advocate of social equality, economic justice, political independence and freedom for the world's poor and dispossessed people – especially his fellow African Americans. Unfortunately, he did not live long enough to develop his thoughts on these issues in a systematic way, as he fell prey to an assassin's bullet on 21 February, 1965 three months short of his fortieth birthday (although according to another source, he was assassinated on his fortieth birthday).

Thankfully, just before his death, Malcolm had completed his autobiography with the assistance of Alex Haley. Published immediately after his death, *The Autobiography of Malcolm X*, provided a detailed and vivid account of his life and thought in his unique style.

By all accounts, Malcolm X was a truly revolutionary leader who championed the rights of America's poor and disadvantaged black people, and did so by the sheer force of his extraordinary character and personality.[26] Widely considered to be one of the founding fathers of the anti-racist movement, he was also one of the most influential Western Muslim leaders of the twentieth century (see my *The Muslim 100* [2008] for a detailed entry on Malcolm X).

# KHURRAM MURAD

B. 1932 – D. 1996

UNITED KINGDOM

Khurram Jah Murad, better known as Ustadh Khurram Murad, was born into a respected Muslim family in Bhopal, British India. He attended his village schools where he proved to be a talented student and successfully completed primary and secondary education, in addition to learning the Qur'an at the local *maktab*. He was barely 15 years of age when Britain decided to leave India and partition the country into two separate nations, namely Pakistan (consisting of East and West Pakistan) and independent India. During the political, social and economic turmoil of that period, Khurram's family left India and moved to Pakistan where they were forced to rebuild their lives from scratch.

However, young Khurram excelled in mathematics and science at school, and that prompted him to pursue higher education in engineering. He soon joined the University of Karachi, Pakistan to study civil engineering before graduating with a Bachelors degree in 1952. Keen to pursue advanced training in the same subject, a few years later, he moved to the United States of America. He enrolled at the University of Minnesota where he studied for a Master's degree in civil engineering, graduating in 1958. After completing his formal education, Khurram initially worked as a trainee engineer before going on to become a consultant civil engineer. He worked in many parts of the world including Pakistan, present-day Bangladesh, Iran and Saudi Arabia. During his time in Arabia, he played an important role in the planning, expansion and improvement of the Sacred Mosque (*Masjid al-Haram*) in Makkah.

Since his student days, Khurram was actively involved in learning, preaching and promoting Islam. As a result, he became involved with the *Islami Jami'at Talaba*, which was the youth wing of Mawlana Sayyid Abul A'la Mawdudi's (1903–1979) *Jama'at-i-Islami* (The Islamic Organisation) and served as its president from 1951 to 1952. Recognising his talent, commitment and dedication to his tasks, his senior colleagues subsequently elected him on to the central executive committee of the organisation (1963–1977), in addition to serving as president of its East Pakistan branch (1963–1971). As an advocate of Muslim unity and solidarity, he opposed the break-up of Pakistan in 1971 but the tide of history had turned decisively against the supporters of Pakistan.

In addition to serving as the editor of *Tarjumanul Qur'an* (Interpreter of the Qur'an), a monthly Urdu journal, he played a pivotal role in the development and expansion of the activities of The Islamic Foundation in Leicestershire, United Kingdom. Established in 1973, Khurram became one of its Trustees and its Director General, as well as editor of its well-known quarterly journal, *The Muslim World Book Review*. It was also during this period that he became actively involved with the British Muslim youth through the activities of the UK Islamic Mission, Young Muslims UK and The Islamic Foundation, among others. Being fluent in English, Urdu and Bengali, he was a gifted communicator who delivered hundreds of lectures across the country and, in so doing, inspired thousands of young British Muslims, men and women, to remain true to their faith and culture. At the same time, he urged them to become loyal and productive British citizens.

However, Khurram is best known today for his literary contributions. As a prolific writer and translator, he published more than 50 books and pamphlets on aspects of Islam and the challenges facing Western Muslims, both in English and Urdu. Although he was not a classically-trained Islamic scholar, his ability to explain aspects of Islam in simple, clear and jargon-free language made him very popular as a writer and public speaker. Some of his best known works include *Way to the Qur'an* (1985), *In the Early Hours: Reflections on Spiritual and Self-Development* (2004) and *Inter-Personal Relations: An Islamic Perspective* (2005). He also authored a series of booklets for Muslim children, focusing on the life of the Prophet and his Companions, which proved to be very popular with the younger generation. After a life time devoted to the service of Islam and especially Western Muslims, Khurram Jah Murad died in Leicester, United Kingdom at the age of 64.

Ⓝ

1. S. M. Imamuddin, *A Political History of Muslim Spain*.

2. Philip K. Hitti, *History of the Arabs*.

3. David J. Wasserstein, *The Caliphate in the West: An Islamic Institution in the Iberian Peninsula*.

4. Claude Addas, *Quest for the Red Sulphur: The Life of Ibn Arabi*.

5. William C. Chittick, *Ibn Arabi: Heir to the Prophets*.

6. See *Encyclopaedia of Islam (New Edition)*.

7. Ibid.

8. Barbara B. Gallardo, 'Beyond the *Haram*: Ibn Al-Khatib and His Privileged Knowledge of Royal Nasrid Women', *Medieval Encounters*, vol. 20.

9. Stanford J. Shaw, *History of the Ottoman Empire and Modern Turkey*, vol. 1.

10. Csaba Bekes, *The 1956 Hungarian Revolution: A History in Documents*.

11. Brent D. Singleton (ed.), *The Convert's Passion: An Anthology of Islamic Poetry from Late Victorian and Edwardian Britain*.

12. Harry T. Norris, *Islam in the Balkans: Religion and Society between Europe and the Arab World*.

13. Lord Headley, *A Western Awakening to Islam*.

14. Mahmud Tahir, 'Rizaeddin Fahreddin' in *Central Asian Survey*, vol. 7, no. 1.

15. Hazrat Syed Mohammad Zauqi Shah, *Tarbiyatul Ushaq* (Nuturing for the Godly).

16. J. W. Lovegrove (Habeeb-Ullah), *What is Islam?*

17. Paul Chacornac, *The Simple Life of Rene Guenon* and Robin Waterfield, *Rene Guenon and the Future of the West*.

18. Abdal Hakim Murad, 'The Great Divide: the unusual life of William Williamson', see www.masud.co.uk

19. Sir Archibald Hamilton, 'Why I became a Muslim', *The Islamic Review*, vol. 12, no. 2.

20. Paul Baxter, 'Nostalgia: Selsey's Muslim baronet', *Bognor Regis Observer*, 2013.

21. Isabelle Eberhardt, *In the Shadow of Islam*, and Annette Kobak, *The Life of Isabelle Eberhardt*.

22. Quoted by Jamie Gilman, *Loyal Enemies: British Converts to Islam, 1850–1950*.

23. See 'Special Feature: Dr Hamidullah, A Scholar's Scholar', *Impact International*, vol. 33, no. 1, 2 and 3.

24. Murad Wilfried Hoffman, 'Reviewed Work: *Islam fur Europa: Neue Perspektiven einer altern Religion* by Smail Balic', *Islamic Studies*, vol. 41, no. 3.

25. See 'Shaykh Dr Zaki Badawi: 1922–2006', *Q-News*, no. 365.

26. Malcolm X and Alex Haley, *The Autobiography of Malcolm X*.

# CONCLUSION

In the summer of 1989, Francis Fukuyama, a notable American scholar and academic, published an article in *The National Interest* under the title of 'The End of History'. The article generated heated discussion and debate in the United States and elsewhere because its author argued that the dominance of the Capitalist economic paradigm and prevalence of Western lifestyle signalled 'the end of history'. He subsequently expanded his arguments in the form of a book, entitled *The End of History and The Last Man* (1992).

A few years later, Samuel Huntington, another American scholar and academic, published an article titled 'The Clash of Civilizations' in which he asserted that cultural and religious differences between people of competing civilisations are likely to be the main cause of regional and global conflicts in the post-Cold War period. Like Fukuyama, he also went on to expand his thesis in the form of a book titled *The Clash of Civilizations and the Remaking of World Order* (1996). Perhaps inspired by Fukuyama and Huntington's theses, some Western leaders subsequently began to single out the Muslim world as the main incubator of security threats to Western political, economic and cultural interests in the Islamic world as well as globally.

The tragic events of 11 September, 2001 not only served to reinforce the Western world's historical image of Islam as the 'Other', but the concomitant portrayal of the Muslim world as the epicentre of global violence, hatred and terrorism soon became widespread in mainstream Western media, both visual and print. Such a skewed, monolithic and slanted view of Islam and the Muslim world became so dominant that impartiality, balance and fair-play was, of course, sacrificed at the altar of ignorance, demagoguery and vilification. To their credit, however, several prominent Western scholars and academics spoke out against such distortion, caricature and misrepresentation, but their voices were often drowned out by those who were determined to portray Islam and Muslims in a very negative light, as if they were 'foreign' to the West. In the words of one author,

> In our age, one might be forgiven for simply assuming that Islam and the West are polar opposites. For anti-immigrant activists in the West, the potent symbols of headscarves, Islamic law, mosques, and even footbaths (used to ritually wash before Islamic prayers) can represent an invasion or encroachment of foreign culture on Western territory. In this contentious view of the world, contemporary Muslims are often framed as strangers who hold foreign values, and the word 'crisis' is used to describe their supposed lack of integration and assimilation. Indeed, some Muslims and non-Muslims – from al-Qaeda sympathizers to Western political demagogues – gin up the idea that Islam and the West are on an inevitable collision course, even locked in a struggle to the death.[1]

The lack of knowledge and understanding of Islam, coupled with fear of the unknown, as well as ignorance of the history of Muslim presence in the West has clearly contributed to the growing misunderstanding and misrepresentation of Islam's role in Western cultures and societies, spanning over more than 1400 years. Indeed, very few Westerners, both Muslims and non-Muslims, are actually aware of the fact that,

> Since 711, when Muslims conquered parts of what today is Spain, Muslims have lived in the lands that are referred to today as 'the West'. In 929, Abd al-Rahman III of Cordoba declared independence from Muslim authorities in the 'East', including the Fatimid dynasty in Cairo and the Abbasid dynasty in Baghdad, creating the first Western caliphate, a powerful Islamic political entity. By the time these Muslims disappeared in the wake of the Reconquista by King Ferdinand and Queen Isabella in 1492, other Muslims had already established communities in Eastern Europe. In the 1200s, the military conquests of the Golden Horde led to the development of long-lasting Muslim communities in Hungary, Bulgaria, and Poland, which became a favourite destination for further immigration of Tatar Muslims from the Crimean region. By 1631, there were 100,000 Tatars in Poland, and in 1795, they joined other patriots to fight for the independence of the nation. During the fourteenth and fifteenth centuries, the Ottoman Turkish conquest of southeast Europe also resulted in the making of European Muslim communities in Romania, Greece, Albania, and the former Yugoslavia. For more than a millennium, all these Muslims contributed to the making of Western civilizations, societies, nations, and cultures.[2]

Needless to say, researching and writing this book has been a journey of self-discovery and enlightenment for a number of reasons. Firstly, this volume completes a trilogy focusing on my own triple heritage and identity, namely being Muslim, Bengali and Western. As such, in *The Muslim 100* (2008), I have surveyed Islamic thought, culture and history through the lives, thoughts and achievements of a hundred influential Muslims from the Prophet Muhammad (peace be on him) to Muhammad Ali, the great American sportsman and philanthropist of the twentieth century.

Likewise, in *The Muslim Heritage of Bengal* (2013), I explored the lives and works of forty-two great luminaries covering more than 800 years of Muslim history and culture of Bengal, focusing on both present-day Bangladesh and the Indian State of West Bengal. In the same way, in this volume, I have attempted to highlight the pivotal role played by more than fifty outstanding Western Muslims in the development and progress of Western thought, culture and civilisation over a period of fourteen hundred years.

Secondly, I have attempted to show that faiths, cultures and civilisations are, ultimately, the products of multiple influences and shared efforts, skills and contributions. That is to say, there is not a single world religion, culture or civilisation that has not been influenced or enhanced as a result of its encounter with other global faiths, cultures and civilisations. In other words, all faiths and cultures are the products of intercultural and intercivilisational interaction and exchange. Lastly, this book is my own humble answer to those who argue that Islam is an alien faith and culture to the West. Far from being a 'foreign' presence in the Western hemisphere, I hope that I have been able to show that Islam has been an *integral* part of Western culture and civilisation, at least since the beginning of the eighth century.

Attempts to disentangle Islam from the West are akin to separating a mother from her baby and, needless to say, all such efforts are bound to fail in the long run. Why? Because Muslim contribution to mathematics, science, philosophy, arts and architecture dominated Europe for more than a millennium, leaving their indelible marks on Western thought, culture and heritage, even if standard textbooks on European history and culture all too often overlook and ignore this aspect of our shared Western heritage.

Unlike political, economic, social and military history, the focus of this book has of course been cultural history based on a survey of the lives, thoughts and achievements of some of Western Islam's most important and enduring personalities. Although the individuals who have been featured in this book hailed from diverse racial and ethnic backgrounds, they all had one thing in common, namely they were Muslims who lived and pursued most, if not all, of their careers in the Western world rather than in the Islamic East.

However, researching and writing this book has certainly not been an easy or straightforward task. Indeed, in his seminal work, *Islamic History: A Framework for Inquiry* (1991), the historian R. Stephen Humphreys wrote that studying 'Islamic history presents severe challenges even to an experienced specialist. Many of these are technical in nature – e.g. the multitude of languages needed to read both sources and modern scholarship, the vast number of major texts still in manuscript, the poor organization of libraries and archives. More important, however, is the difficulty of grasping the subject as a whole, of developing a clear sense of the broad themes and concepts through which this sprawling and underdeveloped field of study can be bound together.'[3]

Needless to say, very little has changed since Humphreys' book was published, and therefore, studying Islamic history, including the classical, medieval and modern periods, remains a daunting undertaking, compounded by lack of funding and institutional support that are necessary in order to carry out a thorough and comprehensive study of any aspect(s) of Muslim thought, culture and history.

Despite being ill-equipped and unprepared, in this book, I have highlighted the pivotal role played by Western Muslims in the development of Western civilisation. If this humble effort helps to raise awareness and understanding of the history of Islam in the Western hemisphere, as well as Muslims' contributions to their local cultures and societies, then I will feel my effort has not been in vain. I conclude this book with the following words of Norman Daniel, a historian and medievalist *par excellence*:

> We must learn about Islam from Muslims, and learn dispassionately...putting ourselves as much as we can outside our own traditions. Christians may expect in return the opportunity to teach. If we are to learn what Muslims have to say about themselves, we may impart what we have to say about ourselves...I think that Muslims in their lives generally submit with reverence to Providence better than we do, and are more aware of God's government in everyday things. We must not take such discoveries as this with patronizing approval, but with humility. We have to ask why, with the benefits of the whole truth and sacraments of grace, we are still inferior in observance....Those who are truly confident that they have the truth need not fear the ultimate result of imparting it. Conversion may not follow, but it cannot possibly precede, the day when prejudice and hatred on both sides have been dispelled.[4]

1.  Edward E. Curtis IV (ed.), *The Bloomsbury Reader on Islam in the West*.

2.  Ibid.

3.  R. Stephen Humphreys, *Islamic History: A Framework for Inquiry*.

4.  Norman Daniel, 'The Development of the Christian Attitude to Islam', *The Dublin Review*, Winter 1957.

# BRIEF CHRONOLOGY OF WESTERN ISLAM

*This is not an exhaustive chronology of the Islamic history of the West nor is it meant to be one. All the entries have been kept short and simple, and all complicated historical information has been omitted where it was possible to do so. The date of birth and death of all the personalities covered in this book has been highlighted for quick referencing. Dates have been provided according to both the Gregorian and Hijri (Islamic) calendars.*

570 CE (Common Era) – Birth of Prophet Muhammad (peace be on him) in Makkah, today located in Saudi Arabia

573 – Birth of Abu Bakr al-Siddiq

576 – Birth of Uthman ibn Affan

579 – Birth of Bilal ibn Rabah

581ca – Birth of Umar ibn al-Khattab

584 – Birth of Khalid ibn al-Walid

610ca – Muhammad becomes Prophet (peace be on him)

614 – Damascus falls to the Persians

615 – Persians capture Jerusalem

622/1 AH (After Hijrah) – 'Hijrah' (migration) of the Prophet Muhammad from Makkah to Yathrib (Madinah), first year of the Islamic Calendar.

623/2 AH –The 'Constitution of Madinah' is formulated

632/11 AH – Death of the Prophet Muhammad (peace be on him)

638/17 AH – Conquest of Jerusalem by Caliph Umar

639/18 AH – Beginning of the Arab conquest of Egypt

647/27 AH – Beginning of the Arab conquest of *Ifriqiya* (corresponding to the Roman province of North Africa), completed by about 705

648/28 AH – Muslims launch expedition against the island of Cyprus during Mu'awiyah's governorship of Syria.

653/33 AH – Muslim control of Armenia is consolidated

663/43 AH – Muslims launch raids against Sicily

670/50 AH – Uqba ibn Nafi occupies north-west Africa

661/41 AH – Ali is murdered, his son Hasan becomes Caliph. Mu'awiyah establishes Umayyad rule

680/61 AH – Death of Mu'awiyah, Yazid succeeds him. Umayyads gain control of Makkah/Madinah

683/64 AH – Death of Yazid I, Mu'awiyah II succeeds him. Ibn al-Zubayr proclaims himself Caliph

692/73 AH – Hajjaj ibn Yusuf recaptures Makkah

697/78 AH – High taxation causes unrest in Egypt

711/93 AH – Birth of Malik ibn Anas. Muslims march into Europe

712/94 AH – Musa ibn Nusayr crosses into al-Andalus

716/98 AH – Death of Musa ibn Nusayr

728/110 AH – Death of Hasan al-Basri, the great theologian and Sufi sage of the Umayyad period

**729/111 AH – Birth of Abd al-Rahman I**

744–750/127–133 AH – The third Civil War leads to the defeat of the Umayyads at the hands of the Abbasids. Constantine V captures Syria. Abbasid leader, Ibrahim al-Abbas, is captured. Abul Abbas al-Saffah is declared Caliph. Marwan II killed by Abbasid agents

750/133 AH – Foundation of the Abbasid caliphate. Establishment of Pala dynasty in Bengal.

756/139 AH – Islamic Kingdom established in Spain by Umayyad prince, Abd al-Rahman I

758/141 AH – Al-Mansur builds the city of Baghdad

762/145 AH – Baghdad becomes Abbasid capital. 'Muhammad the Pure Soul' leads rebellion

785/169 AH – Death of Caliph al-Mahdi; al-Hadi succeeds him as Caliph

**788/172 AH – Death of Abd al-Rahman I**

**789/173 AH – Birth of Ziryab**

**810/195 AH – Birth of Ibn Firnas**

813/198 AH – Use of Arabic numerals becomes widespread

823/208 AH – Al-Waqidi (compiler of the Prophet's military campaigns) dies

827/212 AH – Beginning of the Aghlabite conquest of Sicily (completed in 902)

836/222 AH – Abbasid capital transferred from Baghdad to Samarra

844/230 AH – The Normans attack Seville

846/232 AH – Arab incursions into Rome

**857/243 AH – Death of Ziryab**

859/245 AH – The Normans burn down the mosque in Algeciras

869/256 AH – Black Africans brought to Basrah to work in the plantations

870/257 AH – Muslim occupation of the island of Malta

874/261 AH – Twelfth Shi'a Imam goes into hiding; end of direct rule of Shi'a Imams. Death of Abu Yazid al-Bistami, a prominent Sufi master

877/264 AH – Construction of the famous Ibn Tulun Mosque in Cairo begins

**887/274 AH – Death of Ibn Firnas**

**891/278 AH – Birth of Abd al-Rahman III of Islamic Spain**

893/280 AH – Rise of the Ismaili Shi'as to prominence under Fatimid leadership

897/284 AH – Death of al-Yaqubi, a famous Muslim geographer and historian

900/287 AH – Abu Bakr al-Razi (Rhazes) identifies diagnosis for 'smallpox' at Baghdad hospital

909/297 AH – Fatimids oust their rivals, the Rustamids, from Western Algeria

910/298 AH – Founding in *Ifriqiya* of the Shi'ite Fatimid caliphate

**911/299 AH – Birth of al-Hakam II**

915/303 AH – Foundation of the Tunisian city of al-Mahdiyah

921/309 AH – The Fatimids capture Moroccan province of Fez

923/311 AH – Death of al-Tabari, the great historian and commentator of the Qur'an

925/313 AH – Al-Munis, a Turkish general, becomes *de facto* ruler of Baghdad, to the dismay of Caliph al-Muqtadir

929/317 AH – Abd al-Rahman III of Córdoba becomes Caliph in Islamic Spain

930/318 AH – Qarmatians attack Makkah and escape with the 'Black Stone'.

935/324 AH – Death of Ibn Mujahid, a celebrated Arabic linguist and grammarian

**936/325 AH – Birth of Abulcasis**

**938/327 AH – Birth of Almanzor**

941/330 AH – Death of Abul Hasan al-Ash'ari, founder of the Ash'arite school of Islamic theology

951/340 AH – The Qarmatians return the 'Black Stone' to the Ka'bah in Makkah

957/346 AH – Death of Abul Hasan al-Mas'udi, the famous Muslim historian and traveller

**961/350 AH – Death of Abd al-Rahman III;** he is succeeded by al-Hakam II in al-Andalus

966/356 AH – The Danes under Harald Blatand ('Bluetooth') attack Lisbon

969/359 AH – Fatimid commander, Jawhar, conquers Egypt

973/363 AH – Fatimids gain control of Makkah and Madinah

**976/366 AH – Death of al-Hakam II**

978/368 AH – Fatimids capture Damascus

980/370 AH – Birth of Ibn Sina, the great physician and philosopher

982/372 AH – Muslims defeat Otto II at Capo Colonna in Calabria

985 – 1003/375-394 AH – Repeated Muslim attacks against Barcelona

**987/396 AH – Birth of Ibn Hayyan**

990/380 AH – Abul Qasim al-Zahrawi completes his *Tasrif,* a famous medical encyclopaedia

**994/384 AH – Birth of Ibn Hazm**

**1001/392 AH – Birth of Wallada bint al-Mustakfi**

**1002/393 AH – Death of Almanzor**

1009/400 AH – Fatimid Caliph al-Hakim destroys the Church of the Holy Sepulchre in Jerusalem

**1013/404 AH – Death of Abulcasis**

1015/406 AH – Fatimids seize Aleppo

1031/423 AH – Al-Qaim succeeds al-Qadir as Caliph. Umayyad rule in Andalus comes to an end

1037/429 AH – Death of Ibn Sina

1055/447 AH – Tughrul Beg enters Baghdad and becomes Sultan

1060/452 AH – The Normans launch their first attack against Sicily

1062/454 AH – Foundation of Marrakesh

1063–4/456–7 AH – Barbastro's campaign in Aragon

**1064/457 AH – Death of Ibn Hazm,** the great jurist and theologian of Islamic Spain

1065/458 AH – A seven year famine begins in Egypt

1073/466 AH – The Seljuk general Atziis captures Jerusalem from the Fatimids

**1075/468 AH – Death of Ibn Hayyan**

1085/478 AH – Alfonso VI, King of Leon-Castile, captures Toledo

1086/479 AH – The Castilians are defeated by the Almoravids at Zallaqa

1087/480 AH – Expedition against al-Mahdiyah

**1091/484 AH – Death of Wallada bint al-Mustakfi**

**1094/487 AH – Birth of Avenzoar**

**1095/488 AH – Birth of Avempace**

1095–9/489–493 AH – Pope Urban II calls for Crusade against Islam at Council of Clermont. Jerusalem captured by Crusaders and Latin Kingdom is established

**1099/493 AH – Birth of Dreses**

**1101/495 AH – Birth of Abubacer**

1102/496 AH – The Almoravids occupy Valencia

1105/499 AH – al-Ghazali completes *Ihya Ulum al-Din* (The Revivification of Religious Sciences)

1108/502 AH – Alfonso VI of Leon is defeated by the Almoravids

**1126/520 AH – Birth of Averroes**

1131/526 AH – Death of Umar al-Khayyam, the famous poet, astronomer and mathematician

**1139/534 AH – Death of Avempace**

1143/538 AH – First translation of the Qur'an into Latin by Peter the Venerable

**1145/540 AH – Birth of Ibn Jubayr**

1145 – 1146/540–541 AH – Pope Eugenius III publishes, in two different phases, his encyclical regulating the conduct of the Crusades: *Quantum praedecessores*

1147–8/542–543 AH – Second Crusade in Syria-Palestine

1154/549 AH – Almohads seize Granada

1157/552 AH – The Almohads reconquer Almeria

**1161/557 AH – Death of Avenzoar. Death of Dreses**

1165/561 AH – Works of Islamic philosophy and sciences translated into Latin in Toledo

**1165/561 AH – Birth of Ibn al-Arabi**

1171/567 AH – Egypt conquered by Salah al-Din; Fatimid rule ends and Sunni rule restored

**1185/581 AH – Death of Abubacer**

1187/583 AH – Muslim victory at the Horns of Hattin; Salah al-Din recovers Jerusalem for Islam

1187–92/583–588 AH – Third Crusade. Richard I taken prisoner by Leopold of Austria

1195/592 AH – The Almohads defeat the Castilians at Alarcos

**1197/594 AH – Birth of Bitar**

**1198/595 AH – Death of Averroes**

1202/599 AH – Fourth Crusade authorised by Pope Innocent III

1203/600 AH – Muhammad of Ghur completes conquest of northern India

1207/604 AH – Birth of Jalal al-Din Rumi, the famous Sufi poet

1212/609 AH – Alfonso VIII of Castile defeats Spanish Muslims

**1214/611 AH – Birth of Al-Qurtubi**

**1217/614 AH – Death of Ibn Jubayr**

1218/615 AH – Genghis Khan destroys the Qarakhitai Empire. Pope Innocent III sanctions Fifth Crusade

1219/616 AH – Francis of Assisi attempts to convert Muslims to Christianity

1221/618 AH – Tolui Khan destroys Herat

1227/625 AH – Death of Genghis Khan

1228–9/626–627 AH – Frederick II leads Sixth Crusade; Jerusalem recovered by a diplomatic agreement with the Sultan of Egypt, al-Malik al-Kamil

1236/634 AH – Ferdinand III of Castile captures Cordova

1238/636 AH – James I of Aragon captures Valencia

**1240/638 AH – Death of Ibn al-Arabi**

**1248/646 AH – Death of Bitar.** Louis II of France launches Seventh Crusade. Ferdinand III of Castile conquers Seville

**1256/654 AH – Birth of Abu Hayyan al-Gharnati**

1258/657 AH – The Mongols conquer Baghdad; end of the Abbasid caliphate

1267/666 AH – Christian conquest of Portugal completed

1270/669 AH – Louis IX dies after proclaiming Eighth Crusade

**1273/672 AH – Death of al-Qurtubi**

1281/680 AH – The Mamluks inflict a crushing defeat on the Mongols at Hims

1295–1304/695–704 AH – Ghazan becomes the first Mongol Khan to convert to Islam. Ottoman Empire inaugurated.

**1313/713 AH – Birth of Ibn al-Khatib**

1320/720 AH – The Khaljis are overthrown by Tughlaqs in India. **Birth of Abu Ishaq al-Shatibi**

1326/727 AH – The Ottomans capture Bursa. The death of Uthman, the founder of the Ottoman dynasty; succeeded by Orhan

**1344/745 AH– Death of Abu Hayyan al-Gharnati**

1354//755 AH – The Ottomans capture Ankara

1366/768 AH – Pope Urban V announces a Crusade against the Ottomans

**1374/776 AH – Death of Ibn al-Khatib**

**1388/791 AH – Death of Abu Ishaq al-Shatibi**

1389/792 AH – The Ottomans defeat the Serbs at the Battle of Kosova

1390/793 AH – Franco-Genoese Crusade against al-Mahdiyah, led by Louis II, Duke of Bourbon

1396/ 799 AH – Battle of Nicopolis; Crusaders defeated

1413/816 AH – Tughlaq dynasty is overthrown and replaced by the Sayyid dynasty in India

1451/855 AH – The Lodis displace the Sayyids as rulers of Delhi

1453/857 AH - Ottoman Sultan Muhammad II captures Constantinople (Istanbul)

1463/868 AH – The Bosnians begin to embrace Islam, abandoning Greek Christianity and Bogomilism

1475/880 AH – The first coffee house opens in Istanbul

**1478/883 AH – Birth of Khayr al-Din Barbarossa.** Islamic conquest of Majapait Kingdom in Java

1479/884 AH – Treaty of Constantinople concluded

**1480/885 AH – Birth of Gazi Husrev Bey.** Exploiting divisions amongst Tartar leaders, Grand Prince Ivan III of Moscow suspends payment of tribute. The Turkish fleet attacks and conquers Otranto; start of the Spanish Inquisition

1481/886 AH – Death of Sultan Muhammad II 'al-Fatih'

1489/895 AH – Birth of Sinan, the great Ottoman architect

1492/898 AH – Granada, the last Spanish Muslim Kingdom, falls to Ferdinand and Isabella. Christopher Columbus 'discovers' America. Birth of Sultan Sulaiman

1502/908 AH – Ferdinand and Isabella outlaw Islam in Spain. **Birth of Roxelana**

1503/909 AH – Ottomans gain control of Greece

1508/914 AH – Shah Ismail establishes his rule over Iraq

1517/923 AH – Ottomans gain control of Egypt, Syria, Makkah and Madinah. Martin Luther posts his 95 Theses, start of Protestant Reformation

1520/927 – The reign of Sulaiman the Magnificent begins; the Ottoman Empire reaches its zenith during his rule

1525/932 AH – Thomas Cromwell helps suppress 29 monasteries

1526/933 AH – Death of King Louis II of France. Battle of Panipat and establishment of Mughal rule in the subcontinent

1529/936 AH – The Ottomans siege Vienna. Treaty of Cambrai, end of the war of the League of Cognac

1530/937 AH – Paginus Brixiensis prints the first Qur'an in Rome

1534/941 AH – The Ottomans occupy Baghdad

1535/942 AH – Henry VIII declares himself the head of the Church of England, not the Pope. Charles V's crusade against Tunis

1536/943 AH – Treaty between France and Turkey

1538/ 945 AH – The fleet of the Papal-Imperial-Venetian League is defeated by Khair al-Din  at Preveza, at the entrance to the Gulf of Arta. Sultan Sulaiman conquers Aden to prevent Portuguese penetration into the Indian Ocean

1540/947 AH –Venice makes a separate peace with Sultan Sulaiman and renounces her last foothold in the Peloponnese

**1541/948 AH – Death of Gazi Husrev Bey.** Failed attempt by Charles V to attack Algiers

1542/949 AH – Birth of Akbar the Great of Mughal India

**1544/951 AH – Birth of Hasan Kafi Prusac**

1545/952 AH – Sultan Sulaiman and Ferdinand of Austria sign treaty

**1546/953 AH – Death of Khayr al-Din Barbarossa**

**1550/957 AH – Birth of Safiye Sultan**

1551/958 AH – The Hospitallers of Tripoli surrender to the Turks; the sultan appoints Turghud Ali governor of Tripoli

1552/959 AH – Russian conquest of Khazan

1556/964 AH – Russian conquest of Astrakhan

**1558/966 AH – Death of Roxelana**

1558–1559/966–967 AH – Elizabeth's Religious Settlement (secured Protestantism, but allowed some Catholic traditions). Act of Supremacy, Elizabeth as Head of the Church in England.

1565/973 AH – The Turks unsuccessfully besiege the island of Malta. The Barbary corsairs invade Andalusia with the support of the *morisco* population of the area

1566/974 AH – Death of Sultan Sulaiman; Salim II succeeds him

1568/976 AH – Treaty of Adrianopolis between the Turks and the Holy Roman Empire. The revolt of the *moriscos* is crushed by the Spaniards

1569/977 AH – The Ottomans plan to build a canal between the Volga and the Don to link the Black Sea with the Caspian

1570–2/ 978–980 AH – War between the Turks and the Venetians in Cyprus.  Ex-communication of Elizabeth from the Roman Catholic Church, declaring her as a heretic. The Battle of Lepanto; the Europeans block Ottomans from the Mediterranean

**1575/983 AH – Birth of Koprulu Mehmed Pasha**

1578/986 AH – The Battle of the Three Kings takes place in Morocco

1583–7/991–996 AH – Beginning of diplomatic and trade relations between England and the Ottoman Empire

1593–1606/1002–1015 AH – War between Austria and Turkey ended by the treaty of Zsitva Török. The East India Company is founded in London by Royal Charter. Death of Akbar the Great; his son Jahangir succeeds as Mughal ruler. **Death of Safiye Sultan**

1608/1017 AH – Jahangir grants trading rights to the British

**1611/1020 AH – Birth of Evliya Celebi**

**1615/1024 AH– Death of Hasan Kafi Pruscak**

1622/1032 AH – The English, with Persian assistance, expel the Portuguese from the Gulf of Hormuz

1639/1049 AH – The borders of Iraq and Iran are established with the Treaty of Qasr Shirin

1647/1057 AH – A. du Ryer translates the Qur'an into French.

**1661/1972 AH – Death of Koprulu Mehmed Pasha**

1672–6/1083–1087 AH – War between Turkey and Poland

1677–81/1088–1092 AH – War between Russia and Turkey

1681–4/1092–1096 AH – War between France and the Bey of Algiers. The Ottoman and Austrian Empires slide into war. War between Turkey, Austria and Poland. The Turks besiege Vienna

**1685/1097 AH – Death of Evliya Celebi**

1686/1089 AH – East India Company begins to operate from Calicut

1691–8/1103–1110 AH – Latin translation and commentaries on the Qur'an published by Father Ludovico Marracci

**1701/1113 AH – Birth of Ayuba Sulaiman Diallo**

1711/1123 AH – Peace between Turkey and Russia: the tsar is forced to surrender the stronghold of Azoz

1729/1142 AH – First book published in Turkish by a printing press in Istanbul (closed in 1742 but reopened in 1784)

1734/1147 AH – George Sale translates the Qur'an into English

1736–9/1149–1152 AH – War between Austria, Turkey and Russia. Peace of Belgrade

1745/1158 AH – Beginning of 'Wahhabi' movement in Arabia

1768–74/1182–1188 AH – War between Russia and Turkey. **Death of Ayuba Sulaiman Diallo.** Treaty of Kuchuk Kainarji as the Russians seize the Black Sea from the Ottomans

1781/1196 AH – Treaty between Austria and Russia for the division of the sultan's empire

1789–1807/1204–1222 AH – Al-Sanusi of Libya establishes an Islamic State. Ottomans carry out internal reform. **Birth of Jozef Z. Bem.** The French occupy Egypt under Napoleon as Muhammad Ali Pasha comes to power

1812/1227 AH – Muhammad Ali Pasha massacres 480 leaders in Cairo at a banquet

**1827/1243 AH – Birth of Lord Henry Stanley of Alderley**

1830/1246 AH – French invade Algeria and Amir Abd al-Qadir leads resistance movement

1839/1255 AH – Sultan Abd al-Majid I proclaims the 'useful ordinances' (*tanzimat*) under pressure from the European powers. Aden comes under British rule; serves as a major refuelling port in 1869 when Suez Canal opens

**1843/1259 AH – Birth of Amherst D. Tyssen**

1844/1260 AH – Birth of Muhammad Ahmad, the Mahdi of Sudan and founder of the Islamic State

**1846/1262 AH – Birth of Alexander Russell Webb**

1849/1266 AH – Birth of Muhammad Abduh, the father of Islamic Modernism

**1850/1267 AH – Death of Jozef Z. Bem. Birth of Sami Frasheri**

**1851/1286 AH – Birth of Ismail Bey Gaspirali**

1853–6/1259–1273 AH – Crimean war. **Birth of Lord Headley. Birth of William Henry Quilliam.** Treaty of Paris and 'declaration of warranty': the ports of Turkey are opened to Paris

**1858/1275 AH – Birth of Rizaeddin bin Fakhreddin.** Beginning of British rule in India

1862/1279 AH – Ma Ba leads resistance against the French in Senegal

1864/1281 AH – Turkistan annexed by Russia

**1865/1282 AH – Birth of Philippe Grenier**

**1867/1284 AH – Birth of Lady Evelyn Cobbold**

**1867/1284 AH – Birth of J. W. Lovegrove**

**1869/1286 AH – Birth of Ivan Agueli**

**1870/1287 AH – Birth of Mehmed Dzemaludin Causevic**

**1872/1289 AH – Birth of William Richard Williamson**

**1873/1290 AH – Birth of Hafiz Ali Korca**

**1874/1291 AH – Birth of John Yahya Parkinson**

**1875/1292 AH – Birth of Musa Jarullah. Birth of Marmaduke William Pickthall**

1876/1293 AH – Queen Victoria assumes the title of Empress of India. In Turkey, the 'Fundamental Law of the State', the sultan's first constitution, abolished immediately by Abd al-Hamid II. Birth of Muhammad Ali Jinnah, founder of Pakistan. **Birth of Sir Charles Archibald Hamilton**

**1877/1294 AH – Birth of Isabelle Eberhardt**

1878/1295 AH – Congress of Berlin and 'organisation' of the Balkans

**1879/1296 AH – Birth of Yusuf Ziyaeddin Ezheri**

1880/1297 AH – Birth of Abd al-Aziz ibn Saud, founder of modern Saudi Arabia

1881/1298 AH – Birth of Mustafa Kemal Ataturk, founder of the Turkish Republic. French conquest of Tunisia

**1884/1302 AH – Birth of Julius Germanus**

1885/1303 AH – Birth of Muhammad Ilyas, founder of the Tablighi Jama'at movement. **Birth of Harry St John Philby**

**1886/1304 AH – Birth of Rene Guenon**

**1888/1306 AH – Birth of Khalid Sheldrake**

1889/1307 AH – Sultan Abd al-Hamid II officially abolishes slavery

1897/1315 AH – The first Zionist Organisation is founded in Switzerland

1898/1316 AH – Political and diplomatic trip made by Kaiser Wilhelm II to the Ottoman Empire; talks in Damascus and visit to Jerusalem. The British defeat Mahdist State of Sudan

**1900/1318 AH – Birth of Leopold Weiss. Birth of Abdullah Ali al-Hakimi**

**1902/1320 AH – Birth of Knud Holmboe.** Birth of Ayatullah Khomeini, founder of the Islamic Republic of Iran

**1903/1321 AH – Death of Lord Henry Stanley of Alderley.** Construction of the Berlin to Baghdad Railway

**1904/1322 AH – Death of Sami Frasheri. Death of Isabelle Eberhardt**

1905/1323 AH – In India, formation of the province of Eastern Bengal with a Muslim majority

1906/1324 AH – Birth of Hasan al-Banna, founder of the Muslim Brotherhood in Egypt. Algeciras Conference: the Germans recognise the French 'position of pre-eminence' in Morocco. **Birth of Mehmed Handzic**

1907/1325 AH – Treaty of St Petersburg and division of Persia into areas of influence and interest, shared between England and Russia

**1908/1326 AH – Birth of Muhammad Hamidullah.** Young Turk Revolution takes place in Ottoman Turkey.

**1909/1327 AH – Birth of Martin Lings**

1911/1330 AH – African slave trade ended

1911–12/1330–1331 AH – War between Italy and Turkey over Tripolitania and Cyrenaica (Libya). **Birth of Husein Dozo**. Wars in the Balkans

**1914/1333 AH – Birth of Thomas Ballantine Irving. Birth of Noor Inayat Khan. Death of Ismail Bey Gaspirali.** First World War breaks out

**1916/1335 AH – Death of Alexander Russell Webb.** Sykes-Picot agreement: division of the Ottoman Empire's Arab territories between France and England

1917/1336 AH – **Death of Ivan Agueli.** Balfour Declaration, favouring the creation of a Jewish State in historic Palestine

1918/1337 AH – **Death of John Yahya Parkinson.** North Yemen gains independence

1919/1338 AH – **Birth of Knut Bernstrom.** Khilafat Movement in India supports the Ottoman Caliphate. King Abdullah is expelled from Saudi Arabia

1920/1339 AH – Constitution of the British Mandate over Palestine

1920–2/1339–1341 AH – Greek-Turkish war. Anglo-American-French crisis over the petrol fields of Mosul, partly resolved by the Conference of San Remo. **Birth of Smail Balic. Birth of Adil Zulfikarpasic.** Amir Faisal proclaimed King of Iraq; his brother Abdullah made Amir of Transjordania. **Birth of Zaki Badawi**

1924/1343 AH – Abolition of the Caliphate and dissolution of Islamic tribunals in Turkey. The creation of the secular Turkish Republic marks the end of Ottoman rule

1925/1344 AH– **Birth of Alija Izetbegovic and Malcolm X.**

1927/1346 AH – **Birth of Lois Ibsen al-Faruqi**

1928/1347 AH – In Egypt, Hasan al-Banna founds the 'Muslim Brotherhood' movement

1930/1349 AH – **Death of Amherst D. Tyssen.** The foundation of the Black Muslim movement in the United States. Iraq becomes an independent kingdom.

1931/1350 AH – Elijah Muhammad becomes leader of the Nation of Islam. **Death of Knud Holmboe**

1932/1351 AH – **Death of William Henry Quilliam. Birth of Khurram Murad.**

1933/1352 AH – **Birth of W. D. Muhammad**

1935/1354 AH – **Death of Lord Headley**

1936/1355 AH – **Death of Rizaeddin bin Fakhreddin.** Persia is officially renamed Iran by the Shah. **Death of Marmaduke William Pickthall**

1938/1357 AH – **Death of Mehmed Dzemaludin Causevic**

1939/1358 AH – **Death of Sir Charles Archibald Hamilton**

1940/1359 AH – **Death of J. W. Lovegrove**

1941/1360 AH – Sayyid Abul A'la Mawdudi establishes Jama'at-i-Islami in India

1942/1361 AH – **Birth of Muhammad Ali, the legendary American boxer**

1944/1363 AH – **Death of Noor Inayat Khan. Death of Philippe Grenier. Death of Mehmed Handzic**

1945/1364 AH – Abd al-Rahman Azzam founds the Arab League. The first meeting of the United Nations General Assembly takes place

1947/1366 AH – **Death of Khalid Sheldrake.** Britain's coal industry is nationalised. India gains independence from Britain and Pakistan is born

1948/1367 AH – National Health Service is established in Britain. Proclamation of the State of Israel in Palestine, and the first Arab-Israeli war

1949/ 1368 AH – Republic of Ireland comes into being. **Death of Musa Jarullah**

**1951/1370 AH – Death of Rene Guenon.** Conservatives, under Winston Churchill, win the general election in Britain

1952/1371 AH – Elizabeth II succeeds her father, George VI. Turkey becomes a member of NATO. Prince Husain becomes King of Jordan

1953/1372 AH – Watson and Crick publish their discovery of the structure of DNA

1954/1373 AH – Pan-Arabic agreement between Egypt, Syria and Saudi Arabia. **Death of Abdullah Ali al-Hakimi.** Algerian war of liberation begins

**1956/1375 AH – Death of Hafiz Ali Korca.** Passing of the Clean Air Act as a response to the severe London smog of 1952. Britain and France invade Egypt after dispute over the Suez Canal

1957/1376 AH – Ghana becomes the first British colony in Africa to gain independence. Britain tests its first hydrogen bomb

**1958/1377 AH – Death of William Richard Williamson**

1960/1379 AH – Organisation of Oil Producing Countries (OPEC) is founded in Baghdad. **Death of Harry St John Philby**

**1961/1380 AH – Death of Yusuf Ziyaeddin Ezheri**

1963/1382 AH – France vetoes Britain's entry to the European Common Market. **Death of Lady Evelyn Cobbold**

1964/1383 AH – The Palestine Liberation Organisation (PLO) is founded by Yasser Arafat. Muhammad Ali joins the Nation of Islam

1965/1384 AH – The Egyptian authorities crackdown on the Muslim Brotherhood in Egypt. **Death of Malcom X, assassinated**

1967/1386 AH – Formation of the People's Republic of Yemen, comprising Aden and former Protectorate of South Arabia. Seven Day War: the Israelis capture the whole area of Jerusalem, including the holy places of Islam

1969/1388 AH – King Faisal of Saudi Arabia calls for war against Israel after al-Aqsa Mosque is burnt. Organisation of the Islamic Conference (OIC) is founded. India: clashes between Hindus and Muslims in Ahmedabad

1971/1390 AH – Decimalised currency in Britain replaces 'pounds, shillings and pence'. Gulf States of Bahrain and Qatar gain independence from Britain. Indo-Pakistan war: East Pakistan becomes independent under the name of Bangladesh. Establishment of the Arab Emirates in the Persian Gulf

1973/1392 AH – Britain, Ireland and Denmark join the European Economic Community (EEC). In Libya, Gaddafi declares Islam to be 'the road to social revolution'

1974/1393 AH – Yasser Arafat addresses UN and calls for a Palestinian State

197–6/1394–1395 AH – Civil war between Christians and Muslims in Lebanon

1979/1400 AH – Signing of the peace treaty between Egypt and Israel. Conservative Margaret Thatcher becomes Britain's first female prime minister. **Death of Julius Germanus**. The Soviet Union invades Afghanistan

1980/1401 AH – Hizbullah (The Party of God) is founded in Lebanon. The State of Israel declares the annexation of the eastern part of Jerusalem

1982/1403 AH – Israel invades Lebanon for the second time and massacres take place in Sabra and Shatila. **Death of Husein Dozo**

**1986/1406 AH – Death of Lois Ibsen al-Faruqi**

1987/1407 AH – First Intifada takes place in Palestine. Shaykh Ahmad Yassin establishes HAMAS, the Palestinian Resistance Movement

1988/1408 AH – Benazir Bhutto becomes first female head of a Muslim country

1989/1409 – Soviet Union is defeated in Afghanistan

1990/1410 – Two Yemens united as Republic of Yemen

1990–1992/1410–1412 AH – First Gulf War. The demise of USSR. Civil War erupts in Yugoslavia. Channel Tunnel opens, linking London and Paris by rail. **Death of Leopold Weiss**

1993/1413 AH- Reciprocal declaration of recognition between the State of Israel and the Palestine Liberation Organisation; signing in Washington of the 'Declaration on the Principles of Independence of the Occupied Territories'.

1996/1416 AH – In Afghanistan, the integralist movement known as the Taliban seizes power. **Death of Khurram Murad.**

1997/1417 AH – Britain hands Hong Kong back to China after more than 150 years of British rule. Diana, Princess of Wales, dies in a car crash in Paris

1998/1418 AH – US embassies in Kenya and Tanzania are bombed

2000/1420 AH – Second Intifada breaks out in Palestine

2001/1421 AH – US Postal Service issues stamp to celebrate Eid, an Islamic festival. Terrorists hijack planes, destroying the twin towers of the World Trade Centre in New York and part of the Pentagon building in Washington. Pakistan becomes first Muslim nuclear power

2002/1422 AH – US and British invade Iraq to depose Saddam Hussein. **Death of Smail Balic. Death of Muhammad Hamidullah. Death of Thomas Ballantine Irving**

2003/1423 AH – Britain joins the US in a controversial invasion of Iraq, not backed by a United Nations mandate. **Death of Alija Izetbegovic**

2004/1424 AH – Ten new states, from eastern and southern Europe, join the European Union

2005/1425 AH – Kyoto Protocol on measures to control climate change comes into force. Suicide bombers kill 52 people on London Underground trains and a bus. Tony Blair re-elected British Prime Minister. **Death of Martin Lings**

**2006/1426 AH – Death of Zaki Badawi.** Israel invades Lebanon for the third time. Saddam Hussein, President of Iraq, hanged by American and British-backed Iraqi government. Three Muslim graves discovered in southern France dating back to the early eighth century.

2007/1427 AH – Palestinians form unity Government after conflict between Fatah and Hamas. Military-backed Caretaker Government in power in Bangladesh after months of political uncertainty and upheaval. Iran vows to continue with nuclear programme

**2008/1428 AH – Death of Adil Zulfikarpasic. Death of W. D. Muhammad**

**2009/1429 AH – Death of Knut Bernstrom**

2010/1430 AH – The National Assembly of France ban the burqa

2011/1431 AH – Tunisian government overthrown as Arab Spring spreads. Egyptian Revolution as President Hosni Mubarak resigns after 18 days of protests. Osama bin Laden, founder and leader of al-Qa'ida, killed in Pakistan by United States Navy SEAL. Riots across London due to the death of a local black man who was shot dead by police. Muammar Gaddafi, former leader of Libya, killed during the Battle of Sirte

2012/1432 AH – UK Government debt rises to about £1 trillion for the first time. Houla massacre as 108 civilians murdered by the Syrian Government.

2013/1433 AH – Pope Benedict XVI announces his resignation, the first Pope to do so in nearly 600 years. Death of Britain's first female prime minister, Margaret Thatcher. Death of Nelson Mandela, South Africa's first black president

2014/1434 AH – Scottish Independence Referendum; voted "No" by 55.3%

2015/1435 AH – Iran Nuclear Deal reached in Vienna between Iran and P5+1. Queen Elizabeth II becomes the longest-reigning British monarch

2016/1436 AH – **Muhammad Ali, the legendary American Muslim sportsman and philanthropist, dies**. Prime Minister, David Cameron, resigns in response to the UK's decision to leave the EU. Donald Trump is elected as America's 45th President. Conflict in Syria rages on.

# SELECTED
# BIBLIOGRAPHY

## A

Aasi, G. H., *Muslim Understanding of Other Religions: A Study of Ibn Hazm's Kitab al-Fasl fi al-Milal wa al-Ahwa wa al-Nihal*, New Delhi: Adam Publishers, 2007.

Abd-Allah, U. F., *A Muslim in Victorian America: The Life of Alexander Russell Webb*, New York: OUP, 2006.

Abu-Rabi, I. M., *Intellectual Origins of Islamic Resurgence in the Modern Arab World*, New York, SUNY, 1996.

Abun-Nasr, J. M., *A History of the Maghrib*, Cambridge: CUP, 1971.

Addas, C., *Quest for the Red Sulphur: The Life of Ibn Arabi*, Cambridge: The Islamic Text Society, 1993.

al-Ahari, M. (ed.), *Five Classic Muslim Slave Narratives*, Chicago: Magribine Press, 2006.

Ahmad, A., *A History of Islamic Sicily*, Edinburgh: Edinburgh University Press, 1975.

Ahmad, J., *Hundred Great Muslims*, Lahore: Ferozsons Ltd, 1984.

Ahmad, N., *Muslim Contribution to Geography*, Lahore: Muhammad Ashraf, 1972.

Ahmed, A. S., *Discovering Islam: Making Sense of Muslim History and Society*, London: Routledge, 1988.

Ahmed, L., *Women and Gender in Islam; Historical Roots of a Modern Debate*, New Haven: Yale University Press, 1992.

Ahmed, M. B. et al. (ed.), *Muslim Contributions to World Civilization*, Richmond: IIIT & AMSS, 2005.

Ahmed, N., *Forty Great Men and Women in Islam*, New Delhi: Adam Publishers, 1990.

Alam, Z., *Education in Early Islamic Period,* New Delhi: Markazi Maktaba Islami, 1991.

al-Alawi, J. D., *Matn al-Rushdi: Madkhal li-Qira'ah Jadiah*, Dar al-Bayda: Dar Tubqal, 1986.

Alder, L. and Dalby, R., *The Dervish of Windsor Castle*: The Life of Arminius Vambery, London: Bachman & Turner, 1979.

Ali. A., *Eminent Arab-Muslim Medical Scientists (622–1600)*, New Delhi: Kitab Bhavan, 2001.

Ali, A.Y., *The Meaning of the Holy Qur'an: New Edition with Revised Translation, Commentary and Index*, Maryland: Amana Publications, 2001.

Ali, M.M., *The Early Caliphate*, Lahore: Ahmadiyya Anjuman Isha'at Islam, 1983.

Ali, S.A., *A History of the Saracens*, New Delhi: Kitab Bhavan, 1994.

_____: *The Spirit of Islam*, New Delhi: Kutub Khana, no date.

_____: *Memoirs and Other Writings of Syed Ameer Ali* edited by Syed Razi Wasti, Lahore: People's Publishing House, 1968.

_____: *Muhammadan Law: Compiled from Authorities in the Original Arabic*, 2 vols, New Delhi: Kitab Bhavan, 2002.

_____: *A Critical Examination of the Life and Teachings of Mohammed*, London: Williams and Norgate, 1873.

_____: *Ethics of Islam*, Calcutta: Thacker, Spink and Co., 1893.

_____: *Islam*, London: Constable & Co., 1909.

Ali. M. S. et al. (ed.), *Muslim Contribution to Science and Technology*, Dhaka: Islamic Foundation, 1996.

Ali, M., *The Greatest: My Own Story*, USA: Graymalkin Media, 2015.

Allworth, E. (ed.), *Tatars of the Crimea*: Their Struggle for Survival, Durham: Duke University Press, 1988.

_____: *Muslim Communities Reemerge: Historical Perspectives on Nationality, Politics, and Opposition in the Former Soveity Union and Yugoslavia*, Durham: Duke University Press, 1994.

Amin, A., *Fajr al-Islam*, Beirut: Dar al-Kitab al-Arabi, 1969.

Andrabi, A. A., *Muhammad Asad: His Contribution to Islamic Learning*, New Delhi: Goodword Books, 2007.

Ansari, H., *The Infidel Within: Muslims in Britain since 1800*, London: Hurst and Co, 2004.

Ansari, M. A. H., *Sufism and Shari'ah: A Study of Shaykh Ahmad Sirhindi's Effort to Reform Sufism*, Leicester: The Islamic Foundation, 1986.

Arberry, A. J., *Revelation and Reason in Islam*, London: Allen & Unwin, 1957.

_____: *The Islamic Art of Persia*, New Delhi: Goodword Books, 2001.

_____: *Aspects of Islamic Civilization: As Depicted in the Original Texts*, London: Allen & Unwin, 1964.

_____: *Sufism: An Account of the Mystics of Islam*, London: Allen & Unwin, 1969.

Archer, N.P. (ed.), *The Sufi Mystery*, London: Octagon Press, 1988.

Arkoun, M., *Rethinking Islam: Common Questions, Uncommon Answers*, Oxford: Westview Press, 1994.

Armstrong, K., *A History of God*, London: Mandarin, 1994.

Arnold, T. W., *The Preaching of Islam*, Lahore: Muhammad Ashraf, 1979.

_____: *The Caliphate*, New Delhi: Adam Publishers, 1988.

_____: *The Islamic Art and Architecture*, New Delhi: Goodword Books, 2001.

Arsalan, A. S., *Our Decline and Its Causes*, Lahore: Muhammad Ashraf, 1990.

Asad, M., *The Message of the Qur'an*, Gibraltar: Dar al-Andalus, 1980.

_____: *The Road to Mecca*, Tangier: Dar al-Andalus, 1974.

_____: *Islam at the Crossroads*, Tangier: Dar al-Andalus, 1982.

_____: *Homecoming of the Heart (1932–1992)*, Lahore: Al Abbas International, 2016.

_____: *The Principle of State and Government in Islam*, CT: Martino Fine Books, 2016.

_____: *This Law of Ours and Other Essays*, Gibraltar: Dar al-Andalus, 1987.

Asceric-Todd, I., 'The Noble Traders: the Islamic Tradition of "Spiritual Chivalry" (*futuwwa*) in Bosnian Trade-guilds (16th – 19th centuries)', *The Muslim World*, vol. 97, No. 2.

Ashraf, S.A., *The Qur'anic Concept of History*, Leicester: The Islamic Foundation, 1980.

Atiya, A. S., *Crusades, Commerce and Culture*, New York: Wiley and Sons, 1966.

Attar, S., *The Vital Roots of European Enlightenment: Ibn Tufayl's Influence on Modern Western Thought*, MD: Lexington Books, 2010.

Attar, F., *Muslim Saints and Mystics*, translated by A.J. Arberry, London: Routledge and Keegan Paul, 1976.

Austin, A. D., *African Muslims in Antebellum America: A Source Book*, New York: Garland Publishers, 1984.

Ayoub, M. M., *The Crisis of Muslim History: Religion and Politics in Early Islam*, Oxford: Oneworld Publications, 2005.

Ayyubi, N. A., *Some Aspects of Islamic-Turkish Culture*, Aligarh: Aligarh Muslim University, 1988.

Azad, A.K., *Tarjuman al-Qur'an*, 2 vols, Lahore: Sind Sagar Academy, 1976.

Azami, M. M., *Studies in Hadith Methodology and Literature*, Indianapolis: American Trust Publications, 1977.

_____: *The History of the Qur'anic Text from Revelation to Compilation*, Leicester: UK Islamic Academy, 2003.

Azar, H., *The Sage of Seville: Ibn Zuhr, His Time, and His Medical Legacy*, Cairo: The American University in Cairo Press, 2008.

Azimabadi, B., *Great Personalities in Islam*, New Delhi: Adam Publishers, 1998.

Aziz, K. K., *Ameer Ali: His Life and Work*, Lahore: Publishers United, 1968.

## B

Badawi, M. A. Z., *Reformers of Egypt: A Critique of al-Afghani, Abduh and Ridha*, London: Routledge, 1980.

Bakar, O., *Classification of Knowledge in Islam*, Cambridge: Islamic Text Society, 1998.

_____: *The History and Philosophy of Islamic Science*, Cambridge: Islamic Text Society, 1999.

al-Baladhuri, *Kitab Futuh al-Buldan* (translated as 'The Origins of the Islamic State'), 2 vols, New Delhi: Cosmos Publications, 2010.

Baldock, J., *The Essence of Sufism*, Hertfordshire: Eagle Editions Ltd, 2004.

Baljon, J. M. S., *The Reforms and Religious Ideas of Sir Sayyid Ahmad Khan*, Lahore: Sheikh Muhammad Ashraf, reprinted 1970.

Barboza, S., *American Jihad: Islam after Malcolm X*, ebook published by Image, 2011.

Basu, S., *Spy Princess: The Life of Noor Inayat Khan*, Stroud: The History Press, 2008.

Bearman, P. J. et al. (ed.), *Encyclopaedia of Islam*, Second Edition, 12 vols, Leiden: Brill, 1960–2005.

Beg, M. A. J., *The Middle East in the Twentieth Century*, Cambridge: M. A. J. Beg, 2006.

Bennigsen, A. and Lemercier-Quelquejay, C., *Islam in the Soviet Union*, London: Pall Mall Press, 1967.

Bennigsen, A. and Wimbush, S. E., *Mystics and Commissars: Sufism in the Soviet Union*, London: Hurst & Company, 1985.

Berg, H., 'Elijah Muhammad and the Qur'an: The Evolution of His Tafsir', *The Muslim World*, vol. 89, No. 1.

Berlin, I., *The Proper Study of Mankind: An Anthology of Essays*, London: Pimlico, 1998.

Bianca, S., 'Titus Burckhardt (1908–1984): A Personal Recollection', *Sophia: The Journal of Traditional Studies*, vol. 5. No. 2.

Blanks, D. R. and Frassetto, M. (eds.), *Western Views of Islam in Medieval and Early Modern Europe: Perception of Other*, New York: St. Martin's Press, 1999.

Bloom, J. & Blair, S., *Islam: Empire of Faith*, London: BBC Worldwide Ltd, 2001.

Blunt, W., *Splendours of Islam*, London: Angus & Robertson, 1976.

Bossy, J., *Christianity in the West, 1400–1700*, Oxford: OUP, 1985.

Bosworth, C. E., *The Later Ghaznavids, Splendour and Decay: The Dynasty in Afghanistan and Northern India, 1040–1186*, New Delhi: Munshiram Manoharlal, 1992.

_____: *The New Islamic Dynasties*, New York: Columbia University Press, 1996.

Braudel, F., *A History of Civilizations*, London: Penguin, 1995.

Brotton, J., *This Orient Isle: Elizabethan England and the Islamic World*, London: Allen Lane, 2016.

al-Bukhari, *Sahih al-Bukhari* (Arabic text with English translation), 9 vols, New Delhi: Kitab Bhavan, 1987.

Bulliet, R., *The Case for Islamo-Christian Civilization*, New York: Columbia University Press, 2004.

Bullock, A. & Trombley, S. (eds.), *The New Fontana Dictionary of Modern Thought*, London: HarperCollins, 1999.

Burckhardt, T., *Introduction to Sufism*, London: Thorsons, 1995.

_____: *Sacred Art in East and West: Principles and Methods*, Bedfont: Perennial Books, 1986.

_____: *Mirror of the Intellect: Essays on Traditional Science and Sacred Art*, Cambridge: Quinta Essentia, 1987.

_____: *Fez: City of Islam*, Cambridge: Islamic Text Society, 1992.

_____: *Art of Islam: Language and Meaning*, Indiana: World Wisdom, 2009.

_____: *Essential Titus Buckhardt: Reflections on Sacred Art, Faiths, and Civilizations*, Indiana: World Wisdom Books, 2004.

_____: *Moorish Culture in Spain*, Lousville: Fons Vitae, 2001.

Burns, K., *Eastern Philosophy*, London: Arcturus Publishing, 2004.

Brockleman, C., *History of the Islamic Peoples*, London: Routledge and Keegan Paul, 1948.

Browne, E. G., *Arabian Medicine*, Lahore: Kazi Publications, no date.

_____: *A Literary History of Persia: From the Earliest Times to Firdawsi*, 4 vols, New Delhi: Goodword, 2002.


## C

Cain, P. J. & Hopkins, A. G., *British Imperialism: Innovation and Expansion 1688–1914*, Harlow: Longman Group, 1993.

Caksu, A. (ed.), *Proceeding of the Second International Symposium on Islamic civilisation in the Balkans*, Istanbul: IRCICA, 2006.

Carr, E. H., *What is History?* Basingstoke: Palgrave, 2001.

Castleden, R., *People Who Changed the World*, London: Time Warner Books, 2005.

Celebi, E., *An Ottoman Traveller: Selections from the Book of Travels of Evliya Celebi* (translated by Dankoff, R. and Sooyong, K.), London: Eland Publishing, 2010.

Chacornac, P., *The Simple Life of Rene Guenon*, New York: Sophia Perennis, 2005.

Chejne, A. G., *Ibn Hazm of Cordova and His Conception of the Sciences*, Chicago: Kazi, 1982.

Chittick, W. C., *Ibn Arabi: Heir to the Prophets*, Oxford: Oneworld, 2007.

Chowdhry, S.R., *al-Hajjaj ibn Yusuf: An Examination of His Works and Personality*, New Delhi: Kutub Khana, 1979.

Clark, K., *Civilization: A Personal View*, London: Book Club Associates, 1972.

Clark, P., *Marmaduke Pickthall: British Muslim*, London: Quartet Books, 1986.

Clot, A., *Suleiman the Magnificent*, London: Saqi, 2005.

_____: *Harun al-Rashid and the World of the Thousand and One Nights*, London: Saqi, 2005.

Cobbold, L. E., *Pilgrimage to Mecca*, London: Arabian Publishing, reprinted 2008.

_____: *Wayfarers in the Libyan Desert*, London: Arthur L. Humphreys, 1912.

_____: *Kenya: Land of Illusion*, London: John Murray, 1935.

Colville, J. (ed.), *Two Andalusian Philosophers: Abu Bakr Muhammad ibn Tufayl & Abul Walid Muhammad ibn Rushd*, London: Kegan Paul International, 1999.

Collingwood, R. G., *The Idea of History*, Oxford: OUP, 1994.

Cook, S.B., *Colonial Encounters in the Age of High Imperialism*, New York: HarperCollins, 1996.

Cook, M. A. (ed.), *A History of the Ottoman Empire to 1730*, Cambridge: CUP, 1976.

Cooper, J. et al. (ed.), *Islam and Modernity*, London: I.B.Tauris, 1998.

Cragg, K., *Counsels in Contemporary Islam*, Edinburgh: Edinburgh University Press, 1965.

Curtis IV, Edward E. (ed.), *The Bloomsbury Reader on Islam in the West*, London: Bloomsbury Academic, 2015.


## D

Daniel, N., *The Arabs and Mediaeval Europe*, Beirut: Librairie de Liban, 1975.

_____: *Islam and the West: The Making of an Image*, Oxford: Oneworld 1993.

_____: 'The Development of the Christian Attitude to Islam', *The Dublin Review*, Winter 1957.

Dankoff, R., *The Intimate Life of an Ottoman Statesman: Melek Ahmed Pasha (1588–1662)*, New York: SUNY, 1991.

Darwin, J., *After Tamerlane: The Global History of Empire*, London: Allen Lane, 2007.

Davies, N., *Europe: A History*, London: Pimlico, 1997.

Dawson, R. (ed.), *The Legacy of China*, London: Oxford University Press, 1964.

De Boer, T. J., *The History of Philosophy in Islam*, London: Luzac & Co, 1903.

De Bruijn, J. T. P., *Persian Sufi Poetry: An Introduction to the Mystical Use of Classical Poems*, Surrey: Curzon Press, 1997.

Dimond, D. S., *Islamic Painting*, publisher and date unknown.

Dozy, R., *Spanish Islam: A History of the Muslims in Spain*, New Delhi: Goodword Books, 2001.

Dunlop, D. M., *Arabic Science in the West*, Karachi: Pakistan Historical Society, 1958.

_____: *Arab Civilization to AD 1500*, Beirut: Librairie du Liban, 1971.


## E

Eberhardt, I., *The Passionate Nomad: The Diary of Isabelle Eberhardt*, London: Virago Press, 1987.

_____: *In the Shadow of Islam*, London: Peter Owen, 1993.

Ehrlich, E., *Nil Desperandum: A Dictionary of Latin Tags and Phrases*, London: Guild Publishing, 1987.

Enayat, H., *Modern Islamic Political Thought*, Kuala Lumpur: Islamic Book Trust, 2001.

d'Encause, H. C., *Islam and the Russian Empire: Reform and Revolution in Central Asia*, London: I. B. Tauris, 2009.

Eren, H. and Unay, S. (ed.), *Proceedings of the Third International Congress on Islamic Civilisation in the Balkans*, Istanbul: IRCICA, 2010.

Esposito, J.L. (ed.), *The Oxford Dictionary of Islam*, New York: Oxford Un

_____: (ed.), *Islam in Asia: Religion, Politics & Society*, New York: Oxford University Press, 1987.

_____: *The Oxford Encyclopaedia of the Modern Islamic World*, 4 vols, Oxford: Oxford University Press, 1995.

Esposito, J. and Voll, J. O. (ed.), *Makers of Contemporary Islam*, New York: OUP, 2001.

Essa, A. and Ali, O., *Studies in Islamic Civilization: The Muslim Conribution to the Renaissance*, Herndon: IIIT, 2011.

Euben, R. L., *Journeys to the Other Shore: Muslim and Western Travelers in Search of Knowledge*, New Jersey: Princeton University Press, 2008.


# F

Faivre, A. and Needleman, J. (ed.), *Modern Esoteric Spirituality*, London: SCM Press, 1993.

Fakhry, M., *Islamic Philosophy, Theology and Mysticism*, Oxford: Oneworld Publications, 2000.

_____: *A History of Islamic Philosophy*, New York: Columbia University Press, 1970.

_____: *Al-Farab, Founder of Islamic Neoplatonism: His Life, Works and Influence*, Oxford: Oneworld, 2002.

_____: *Averroes: His Life, Work and Influence*, Oxford: Oneworld, 2014.

Farmer, H. G., *A History of Arabian Music*, New Delhi: Goodword Books, 2001.

Faruqi, B. A., *The Mujjaddid's Conception of Tawhid*, Lahore: Muhammad Ashraf, 1979.

al-Faruqi, I., *Islam and Other Faiths*, Leicester: The Islamic Foundation, 1998.

_____: *Tawhid: Its Implication for Thought and Life*, IIIT, 1982.

al-Faruqi, I. R. and al-Faruqi, L., *The Cultural Atlas of Islam*, New York: Macmillan, 1986.

al-Faruqi, L., *Women, Muslim Society and Islam*, Illinois: American Trust Publications, 1988.

_____: *The Qur'an and the Sunnah*, London: IIIT, 2014.

_____: 'Artistic Acculturation and Diffusion among Muslims of the United States', *Essays in Islamic and Comparative Studies*, IIIT: 1982.

_____: 'Tartil al-Qur'an al-Karim', *Islamic Perspectives: Studies in Honour of Sayyid Abul Ala Mawdudi*, Leicester: The Islamic Foundation, 1979.

_____: 'Unity and Variety in the Music of Islamic Culture', *The Islamic Impact*, New York: Syracuse University Press, 1984.

Ferguson, N., *Civilization: The West and the Rest*, London: Penguin, 2011.

_____: *Empire: How Britain Made the Modern World*, London: Allen Lane, 2003.

Fierro, M., *Abd al-Rahman III*, Oxford: Oneworld, 2005.

Finkel, C., *Osman's Dream: The Story of the Ottoman Empire 1300–1923*, New York: Basic Books, 2007.

Finley, M. I., *The Use and Abuse of History*, London: Pimlico, 2000.

Fitzgerald, E., *The Rubaiyat of Omar Khayyam*, New York: Dover Publications, 1990.

Fletcher, R., *The Cross and the Crescent: Christianity and Islam from Muhammad to the Reformation*, London: Allen Lane, 2003.

Frazer, J., *The Golden Bough: A Study in Magic and Religion*, Hertfordshire: Wordsworth Editions, 1993.

Fuller, G. E., *A World without Islam*, New York: Back Bay Books, 2010.

Fremantle, A., *Loyal Enemy*, London: Hutchinson & Co, 1938.

Freeman-Grenville, G. S. P., *The Muslim and Christian Calendars*, London: OUP, 1963.

Frye, R. N., *The Golden Age of Persia*, London: Phoenix Press, 2000.

Fukuyama, F., *The End of History and the Last Man*, New York: Free Press, 1992.


## G

Gai Eaton, C., *The Richest Vein: Eastern Tradition and Modern Thought*, Lahore: Suhail Academy, 2004.

_____: *Islam and the Destiny of Man*, London: George Allen & Unwin, 1985.

_____: *Remembering God: Reflections on Islam*, Chicago: ABC International, 2000.

_____: *King of the Castle: Choice and Responsibility in the Modern World*, London, Bodley Head, 1977.

_____: *A Bad Beginning and the Path to Islam*, Cambridge: Archetype, 2010.

_____: *The Concept of God in Islam*, London: The Islamic Cultural Centre, no date.

Gandhi, R., *Understanding the Muslim Mind*, London: Penguin, 1987.

Garcia, H., *Islam and the English Enlightenment 1670–1840*, Baltimore: The John Hopkins University Press, 2012.

Geaves, R., *Islam in Victorian Britain: The Life and Times of Abdullah Quilliam*, Leicester: Kube Publishing, 2010.

_____: 'The Life and Times of Abdullah Quilliam: British Foreign Policy, Muslim Loyalties and Contemporary Resonances', *Arches Quarterly*, vol. 4, No. 8.

Geaves, R. and Gabriel, T., *Sufism in Britain*, London: Bloomsbury Academic, 2015.

Ghadanfar, M. A., *Great Women of Islam*, Riyadh: Darussalam, 2001.

GhaneaBassiri, K., 'Writing Histories of Western Muslims', *Review of Middle East Studies*, vol. 46, No. 2.

al-Ghazzali, *The Alchemy of Happiness*, translated by Claud Field, London: Octagon Press, 1983.

_____: *The Confessions of Al-Ghazzali*, translated by Claud Field, New Delhi: Kitab Bhavan, 1992.

_____: *Ihya Uloom al-Din* (translated as 'The Revival of Religious Learning'), 4 vols, Lahore: Muhammad Ashraf, 2000.

al-Ghazali, M., *The Socio-Political Thought of Shah Waliallah*, New Delhi: Adam Publishers, 2004.

Gibb, H. A. R. & Kramers, J.H. (ed.), *Shorter Encyclopaedia of Islam*, London: Luzac & Co., 1961.

_____: *The Travels of Ibn Battuta*, New Delhi: Goodword Books, 2001.

Giddens, A., *Modernity and Self-Identity*, Cambridge: Polity Press, 1991.

Gilbert, A. D., *The Making of Post-Christian Britain: A History of the Secularization of Modern Society*, Harlow: Logman, 1980.

Gilham, J., *Loyal Enemies: British Converts to Islam, 1850–1950*, London: Hurst & Co., 2014.

_____: 'Britain's First Muslim Peer of the Realm: Henry, Lord Stanley of Alderley and Islam in Victorian Britain', *Journal of Muslim Minority Affairs*, vol. 33, no. 1.

Gillat-Ray, S., *Muslims in Britain: An Introduction*, Cambridge: CUP, 2010.

Glasse, C., *The Concise Encyclopaedia of Islam*, London: Stacey International, 1989.

Glubb, J. B., *The Great Arab Conquests*, London: Hodder & Stoughton, 1963.

Goff, R. et al. (ed.), *The Twentieth Century: A Brief Global History*, New York: McGraw-Hill, 1998.

Goldstein, A., *Muhammad Ali: The Story of a Boxing Legend*, London: Carlton Books, 2014.

Goldziher, I., *Muslim Studies*, New Jersey: Transaction Publishers, 2006.

Green, N., *The Love of Strangers: What Six Muslim Students Learned in Jane Austen's London*, New Jersey: Princeton University Press, 2016.

Grunebaum, G. E., *Classical Islam: A History, 600–1258*, New York: Barnes and Noble, 1997.

_____: *Medieval Islam: A Vital Study of Islam at its Zenith*, Chicago: University of Chicago, 1954.

_____: *Unity and Variety in Muslim Civilization*, Chicago: University of Chicago Press, 1955.

Guenon, R., *The Crisis of the Modern World*, Varanasi: Indica 2007.

_____: *The Reign of Quantity and the Signs of the Times*, New York: Sophia Perennis, 2001.

_____: *The Symbolism of the Cross*, New York: Sophia Perennis, 2002.

_____: *The Multiple States of the Being*, New York: Sophia Perennis, 2002.

_____: *King of the World*, New York: Sophia Perennis, 2001.

_____: *Spiritual Authority and Temporal Power*, New York: Sophia Perennis, 2001.

_____: 'Islamic Esoterism', *Sophia: The Journal of Traditional Studies*, Vol. 5, no. 1.

Gunny, A., *Perceptions of Islam in European Writings*, Leicester: The Islamic Foundation, 2004.

## H

Haddad, Y. Y. et al., *Muslim Women in America: The Challenges of Islamic Identity Today*, New York: OUP, 2006.

Haddad, Y. Y. and Esposito, J. L., *Muslims on the Americanization Path?* New York: OUP, 1998.

Haddad, Y. Y. (ed.), *The Muslims of America*, New York: OUP, 1991.

Haig, W., *Comparative Tables of Islamic and Christian Dates*, New Delhi: Kitab Bhavan, 1981.

Hajnoczy, R., *Fire of Bengal*, Dhaka: University Press Ltd, 1993.

Halberstam, G., *Noor Inayat Khan: Muslim Pacifist. British Spy. National Hero.*, London: A & C Black, 2013.

Hale, W. and Bagis, A. I., *Four Centuries of Turco-British Relations*, Beverley: Eothen Press, 1984.

Hamidullah, M., *The Emergence of Islam*, New Delhi: Adam Publishers, 1995.

_____: *The First Written Constitution in the World*, Lahore: Muhammad Ashraf, 1981.

_____: *Le Prophete de l'Islam: Sa vie, son oeuvre* (translated as ' The Life and Work of the Prophet of Islam'), New Delhi: Adam Publishers, 2004.

_____: *Battlefields of the Prophet Muhammad*, New Delhi: Kitab Bhavan, 1992.

_____: *The Muslim Conduct of State*, Selangor: Islamic Book Trust, 2013.

_____: *Le Saint Coran: Traduction et Commentaire*, Paris: Club Francais du Livre, 1989.

_____: (ed.), *The Earliest Codification of the Hadith*, New Delhi: Adam Publishers, 2004.

Hasan, M., *History of Islam*, 2 vols, Lahore: Islamic Publications Ltd, 1992

al-Hassani, S.T.S. (ed.), *1001 Inventions: Muslim Heritage in Our World*, Manchester: FSTC, 2006.

Hattstein, M. & Delius, P. (ed.), *Islam: Art and Architecture*, Konigswinter: Konemann, 2004.

Hauser, T., *Muhammad Ali: His Life and Times*, London: Robson Books, 2004.

Haykal, M. H., *The Life of Muhammad*, translated by I.R. al-Faruqi, Indiana: The North American Islamic Trust, 1976.

Headley, L., *A Western Awakening to Islam*, London: J. S. Phillips, 1914.

_____: *Three Great Prophets of the World: Moses, Jesus and Muhammad*, Woking: The Islamic Review, 1923.

Herlihy, J., *Essential Rene Guenon: Metaphysical Principles, Traditional Doctrines, and the Crisis of Modernity*, Indiana: World Wisdom Books, 2009.

Hitti, P. K., *History of the Arabs: From the Earliest Times to the Present*, Basingstoke: Palgrave Macmillan, 2002.

_____: *Islam and the West: A Historical Cultural Survey*, New Jersey: Van Nostrand, 1962.

_____: *Makers of Arab History*, London: Macmillan, 1969.

Hoare, M. A., *The Bosnian Muslims in the Second World War: A History*, London: Hurst & Co., 2013.

_____: *The History of Bosnia: From the Middle Ages to the Present Day*, London, Saqi, 2007.

Hobsbawm, E. J., *The Age of Empire, 1875–1914*, London: Abacus, 1994.

Hodgson, M. G. S., *The Venture of Islam: Conscience and History in a World Civilization*, 3 vols, Chicago: Chicago University Press, 1974.

_____: *Rethinking World History: Essays on Europe, Islam, and World History*, Cambridge: CUP, 1993.

Holmboe, K., *Desert Encounter*, London: The Quilliam Press, 1994.

Holt, P.M. et al. (ed.), *The Cambridge History of Islam*, 4 vols, Cambridge: Cambridge University Press, 1970.

Holt, P. M., *The Age of the Crusades: The Near East from the Eleventh Century to 1517*, Harlow: Longman, 1986.

Horne, A. (ed.), *Telling Lives: From W. B. Yeats to Bruce Chatwin*, London: Mcmillan, 2000.

Houben, H., *Roger II of Sicily: A Ruler between East and West*, Cambridge: CUP, 2007.

Hourani, A., *Europe and the Middle East*, London: Macmillan Press, 1980.

_____: *Arabic Thought in the Liberal Age 1798–1939*, Cambrideg: CUP, 1984.

_____: *Islam in European Thought*, Cambridge: CUP, 1992.

_____: *A History of the Arab People*, London: Faber and Faber, 2005.

Hourani, G., *Arab Sea-faring in the Indian Ocean in Ancient and Early Medieval Times*, Beirut: Khayats, 1963.

Howarth, D., *The Desert King: A Life of Ibn Saud*, London: Collins, 1964.

al-Hujwiri, *Kashf al-Mahjub*, translated by Reynold A. Nicholson, Karachi: Darul Isha'at, 1990.

Humphreys, R. S., *Islamic History: A Framework for Inquiry*, Cairo: The American University in Cairo Press, 1992.

Huntington, S. P., *The Clash of Civilizations and the Remaking of World Order*, New York: Simon and Schuster, 1996.

Husain, S. S., *Civilization and Society*, Dhaka: Bangladesh Institute of Islamic Thought, 2002.

Husain, S. S. and Ashraf, S. A., *Crisis in Muslim Education*, London: Hodder and Stoughton, 1979.


I

Ibn al-Athir, *al-Kamil fi Ta'rikh*, 13 vols, Beirut: Dar Sadir, 1995.

Ibn Battutah, *Travels of Ibn Battutah, A.D. 1325–1352.* 5 vols, London: Hakluyt Society: Syndics of the Cambridge University Press, 1956.

Ibn Hazm, *Tawq al-Hamamah al-Hub fi'l Andalus* (translated as 'The Ring of the Dove'), CT: Martino Fine Books, 2014.

_____: *Akhlaq wa'l Siyar* (translated as 'In Pursuit of Virtue'), London: Ta Ha Publishers, 1990.

Ibn Ishaq, M., *Sirat Rasul Allah* (translated as 'The Life of Muhammad'), Karachi: Oxford University Press, 1990.

Ibn Jubayr, *The Travels of Ibn Jubayr*, New Delhi, Goodword Books, 2004.

Ibn Khaldun, *The Muqaddimah: An Introduction to History*, 3 vols, translated by F. Rosenthal, New Jersey: Princeton University Press, 1967.

Ibn Khallikan, *Kitab Wafayat al-A'yan* (translated as 'Biographical Dictionary'), 4 vols, New York: Johnson Reprint Corporation, 1961.

Ibn Rushd, *Tahafut al-Tahafut* (translated as 'Incoherence of the Incoherence'), 2 vols, Cambridge: Gibb Memorial Trust, 2008.

_____: *Faith and Reason in Islam: Averroes' Exposition of Religious Arguments*, Oxford: Oneworld, 2001.

Ibn al-Sa'i, *Consorts of the Caliphs: Women and the Court of Baghdad*, New York: New York University Press, 2015.

Ibn Taymiyyah, *A Muslim Theologian's Response to Christianity: Ibn Taymiyya's al-Jawab al-Sahih*, translated by T. F. Michel, New York: Caravan Books, 1984.

Ibn Tufayl, *Hayy ibn Yaqzan* (translated by Lenn Gooman), Chicago: University of Chicago Press, 2009.

Ibrahim, D., *The Islamization of Central Asia*, Leicester: The Islamic Foundation, 1993.

Ihsanoglu, E. (ed.), *Cultural Contacts in Building a Universal Civilisation: Islamic Contributions*, Istanbul: IRCICA, 2005.

Imamuddin, S. M., *Arabic Writing and Arab Libraries*, London: TaHa Publishers, 1983.

_____: *A Political History of Muslim Spain*, Dacca: Najmah Sons, 1969.

Inalcik, H., *The Ottoman Empire: The Classical Age 1300–1600*, London: Phoenix, 2000.

Iqbal, A., *Culture of Islam*, Lahore: Institute of Islamic Culture, 1974.

_____: *Life and Work of Muhammad Jalal-ud-Din Rumi*, New Delhi: Kitab Bhavan, 1999.

Iqbal, M., *The Reconstruction of Religious Thought in Islam*, Lahore: Muhammad Ashraf, 1982.

Irving, T. B., *The Falcon of Spain: A Study of Eighth-Century Spain with Special Emphasis upon the Life of the Umayyad Ruler Abdurrahman I*, Lahore: Shaikh Muhammad Ashraf, 1973.

_____: *Islam Resurgent: The Islamic World Today*, Lagos: Islamic Publications Bureau, 1979.

_____: *The Tide of Islam*, Cedar Rapids: Igram Press, 1982.

_____: *The Qur'an: Selections from the Noble Reading*, Cedar Rapids: Laurence Press, 1980.

_____: *The Qur'an: Basic Teachings*, Leicester: The Islamic Foundation, 1979.

_____: *Religion and Social Responsibility*, Lahore: Kazi Publications, 1979.

_____: *The Qur'an: Text, Translation and Commentary*, Tehran: Suhrawardi Research and Publication Center, 1998.

_____: *The Noble Qur'an: Arabic Text and English Translation*, Vermont: Amana Books, 1992.

_____: 'Teaching Arabic and Islam to English-speaking Muslims', *Impact International*, October 1973.

_____: *Dates, Names and Places: The End of Islamic Spain*, Iowa: Mother Mosque Foundation, 1990.

Irwin, R., *For Lust of Knowing: The Orientalists and their Enemies*, London: Penguin, 2007.

Ishaq, M., *India's Contribution to the Study of Hadith Literature*, Dhaka: Islamic Foundation Bangladesh, 1955 (reprinted 1995).

Izetbegovic, A. A., *Islam between East and West*, Indiana: American Trust Publications, 1993.

_____: *Inescapable Questions: Autobiographical Notes*, Leicester: The Islamic Foundation, 2003.

## J

Jackson, R., *Fifty Key Figures in Islam*, London: Routledge, 2006.

Jalbani, G. N., *Teachings of Shah Waliyullah of Delhi*, New Delhi: Islamic Book Service, 1998.

Jawad, H. A., *Towards Building a British Islam: New Muslims' Perspectives*, London: Continuum, 2012.

Johns. J., *Arabic Administration in Norman Sicily: The Royal Diwan*, Cambridge: CUP, 2002.

Jones, L. (ed.), *Encyclopaedia of Religion*, 14 vols, New York: Thomson Gale, 2005.

# K

Kairanawi, R., *Izhar al-Haq*, 4 vols, London: Ta Ha Publishers, 1990.

Kaldy-Nagy, G. (ed.), *The Muslim East: Studies in Honour of Julius Germanus*, Budapest: Lorand Eotvos University, 1974.

Kamali, M. H., *Principles of Islamic Jurisprudence*, Cambridge: Islamic Text Society, 1991.

Kanlidere, A., *Reform within Islam: The Tajdid and Jadid Movement among the Kazan Tatars 1809–1917*, Istanbul: Middle East and Balkan Studies Series, 1997.

Karamustafa, A. T., *Sufism: The Formative Period*, Edinburgh: Edinburgh University Press, 2007.

Karcic, F., *The Other European Muslims: A Bosnian Experience*, Sarajevo: Centre for Advanced Studies, 2015.

Karic, E., *Essays (on behalf) of Bosnia*, Sarajevo: El-Kalem, 1999.

_____: *Contribution to Twentieth Century Islamic Thought in Bosnia and Herzegovina*, vol. 1, Sarajevo: El-Kalem, 2011.

Karic, E. and Filandra, S., *The Bosniac Idea*, Zagreb: Nakladni Zavd Globus, 2004.

Karim, M. A., *Islam's Contribution to Science and Civilisation*, Foreword by Rabindranath Tagore, New Delhi: Goodword, 2001.

Karim, M. F., *Al-Hadis: Translation and Commentary of Mishkat ul-Masabih*, 4 vols, Lahore: The Book House, no date.

Keddie, N. R., *An Islamic Response to Imperialism: Political and Religious Writings of Sayyid Jamal ad-Din "al-Afghani"*, Berkeley: UCP, 1983.

_____: *Sayyid Jamal ad-Din "Al-Afghani": A Political Biography*, Berkeley: UCP, 1972.

Keilani, R. et al. (ed.), *Proceedings of the International Symposium on Islamic Civilisation in the Balkans*, Istanbul: IRCICA, 2000.

Kennedy, H., *The Prophet and the Age of the Caliphates*, Harlow: Pearson Education Ltd, 1986.

_____: *The Courts of the Caliphs: The Rise and Fall of Islam's Greatest Dynasty*, London: Weidenfeld & Nicolson, 2004.

_____: *The Great Arab Conquests: How the Spread of Islam Changed the World We Live In*, London: Phoenix, 2008.

Khalid, A., *The Politics of Muslim Cultural Reform: Jadidism in Central Asia*, Berkeley: UCP, 1998.

Khan, M. M., *The Muslim 100: The Lives, Thoughts and Achievements of the Most Influential Muslims in History*, Leicester: Kube Publishing, 2008.

_____: *The Muslim Heritage of Bengal*, Leciester: Kube Publishing, 2013.

_____: 'The Pioneers of Islam in Bengal: Early Muslim Preachers and Their Contributions', *Nazimuddin Ahmed Commemoration Volume*, Dhaka: Islamic Arts Organisation, 2011.

Khan, M. A. H., *A Persian at the Court of King George 1809–10*, London: Barrie & Jenkins, 1988.

Khan, N. I., *Twenty Jataka Tales*, Rochester: Inner Traditions, 1985.

Khan, M. M.A., *Mustafa Charit*, Dhaka: Kakali Prakashani, 2005.

Khandhlawi, M. Y., *Hayat-us Sahabah*, 3 vols, New Delhi: Idarat Isha'at-i-Diniyat, 1989.

Khulusi, S. A. (ed.), *Islam Our Choice*, Woking: The Woking Muslim Mission and Literary Trust, 1963.

Kinross, L., *The Ottoman Centuries: The Rise and Fall of the Turkish Empire*, New York: Morrow Quill, 1979.

Kobak, A., *Isabelle: The Life of Isabelle Eberhardt*, New York: Alfred A. Knopf, 1989.

Kurzman, C., *Modernist Islam, 1840–1940: A Sourcebook*, New York: OUP, 2002.

_____: *Liberal Islam: A Sourcebook*, New York: OUP, 1998.


## L

Lane-Poole, S., *The Muslims in Spain*, New Delhi: Goodword Books, no date.

Leaman, O. (ed.), *The Biography Encyclopaedia of Islamic Philosophy*, London: Bloomsbury Academic, 2006.

Lewis, B., *The Muslim Discovery of Europe*, London: Phoenix Press, 2000.

_____: *Islam and the West*, New York: OUP, 1993.

_____: *Istanbul and the Civilization of the Ottoman Empire*, Oklahoma: University of Oklahoma Press, 1982.

Lings, M., *Muhammad: His Life Based on the Earliest Sources*, Lahore: Suhail Academy, 1987.

_____: *What is Sufism?* London: Unwin Paperbacks, 1981.

_____: *A Return to the Spirit*, Louisville: Fons Vitae, 2005.

_____: *Shakespeare's Window into the Soul: The Mystical Wisdom in Shakespeare's Characters*, Rochester: Inner Traditions, 2006.

_____: *Ancient Beliefs and Modern Superstitions*, Lahore: Suhail Academy, 1999.

_____: *Enduring Utterances: Collected Lectures 1993–2001*, London: The Matheson Trust, 2014.

_____: 'Frithjof Schuon and Rene Guenon', *Sophia: The Journal of Traditional Studies*, vol. 5. No. 2.

_____: *A Sufi Saint of the Twentieth Century: Shaikh Ahmad al-Alawi*, Cambridge: Islamic Text Society, 1993.

_____: *The Secret of Shakespeare: His Greatest Plays Seen in the Light of Sacred Art*, Cambridge: Quinta Essentia, 1996.

Lovegrove, J. W., *What is Islam?*, Woking: The Woking Mosque, no date.

Ljubovic, A., *The Works in Logic by Bosniac Authors in Arabic*, Leiden: Brill, 2008.


## M

Madelung, W., *The Succession to Muhammad: A Study of the Early Caliphate*, Cambridge: Cambridge University Press, 1997.

Mahdi, M., *Ibn Khaldun's Philosophy of History*, London: Allen & Unwin, 1957.

Makdisi, G., *The Rise of Humanism in Classical Islam and the Christian West: With Special Reference to Scholasticism*, Edinburgh: Edinburgh University Press, 1990.

_____: *The Rise of Colleges: Institutions of Learning in Islam and the West*, Edinburgh: Edinburgh University Press, 1981.

Malcolm X, *The Autobiography of Malcolm X*, London: Penguin, 2007.

Malcolm, N., *Bosnia: A Short History*, London: Pan Books, 2002.

_____: *Kosovo: A Short History*, London: Pan Books, 2002.

Maalouf, A., *The Crusades through Arab Eyes*, London Saqi, 2006.

Maan, B. *The Thistle and the Crescent*, Argyle: Argyle Publishing, 2008.

al-Maqqari, *Kitab Nafh al-Tib min Ghusn al-Andalus al-Ratib*, 8 vols, Beirut: Dar Sadir, 1968 (abridged and translated as 'The History of the Mohammedan Dynasties in Spain'), London: Royal Asiatic Society Books, 2002.

Marsh, C. E., *From Black Muslims to Muslims: The Transition from Separatism to Islam, 1930–1980*, New Jersey: The Scarecrow Press, 1984.

Martin, R. C. (ed.), *Encyclopaedia of Islam and the Muslim World*, 2 vols, New York: Thomson Gale, 2004.

Martin, R. C. & Woodward, M. R., *Defenders of Reason in Islam: Mu'tazilism from Medieval School to Modern Symbol*, Oxford: Oneworld, 1997.

Marwick, A., *The Nature of History*, London: Macmillan Press, 1976.

Masud, M. K., *Shatibi's Philosophy of Islamic Law*, Delhi: Adam Publishers, 1997.

al-Mas'udi, *Muruj al-Dhahab wa Ma'adin al-Jawahir* translated as 'The Meadows of Gold' by P. Lunde & C. Stone, London: Keegan Paul International, 1989.

Matar, N., *Islam in Britain, 1558–1685*, Cambridge: CUP, 1998.

_____: *Turks, Moors and Englishmen in the Age of Discovery*, New York: Columbia University Press, 2000.

_____: *Europe through Arab Eyes, 1578–1728*, New York: Columbia University Press, 2008.

_____: *Henry Stubbe and the Beginnings of Islam: The Originall and Progress of Mahometanism*, New York: Columbia University Press, 2014.

_____: 'The Journeys of Hayy ibn Yaqzan', *Arches Quarterly*, vol. 4, No. 8.

al-Maturidi, *Ta'wilat Ahl al-Sunnah*, 10 vols, Beirut: Dar al-Kutub al-Ilmiyyah, 2005.

Mawdudi, S. A. A., *Tajdid-o-Ihya-i-Din* translated as 'A Short History of the Revivalist Movement in Islam', Lahore: Islamic Publications, 1986.

Mazrui, A. A., *Cultural Forces in World Politics*, London: James Currey, 1990. Books, 2002.

McNeill, W. H., *The Rise of the West: A History of the Human Community*, Chicago: University of Chicago Press, 1991.

Meggitt, J. J., *Early Quakers and Islam: Slavery, Apocalyptic and Christian-Muslim Encounters in the Seventeenth Century*, Eugene: Wipf and Stock Publishers, 2013.

Menocal, M. R., *The Ornament of the World: How Muslims, Jews, and Christians Created a Culture of Tolerance in Medieval Spain*, New York: Back Bay Books, 2002.

Merdjanova, I., *Rediscovering the Umma: Muslims in the Balkans between Nationalism and Transnationalism*, New York: OUP, 2013.

Metcalf, B. D., *Islamic Revival in British India*, Delhi: OUP, 2004.

Michon, J. L., 'In the Intimacy of Shaykh Abdul-Wahid – Rene Guenon – in Cairo (1947-1949)', *Sophia: A Journal of Traditional Studies*, vol. 3. No. 2.

_____: 'Titus Burckhardt and the Sense of Beauty: Why and How he Loved and served Morocco', *Sophia: The Journal of Traditional Studies*, vol. 5. No. 2.

Mishra, P., *From the Ruins of Empire: The Revolt Against the West and the Remaking of Asia*, London: Penguin, 2013.

Mirza, M. R. et al. (ed.), *Muslim Contribution to Science*, Lahore: Kazi Publications, 1986.

Moazzam, A., *Jamal al-Din al-Afghani: A Muslim Intellectual,* New Delhi: Concept Publishing, 1984.

Monroe, E., *Philby of Arabia*, Reading: Garnet Publishing, 1998.

Montefiore, S. S., *Heroes: History's Greatest Men and Women*, London: Quercus, 2009.

_____: *Monsters: History's Most Evil Men and Women*, London: Quercus, 2009.

Muhammad, E., *Message to the Blackman in America*, PA: House of Knowledge Publications, 1965.

Murad, K., *Way to the Qur'an*, Leicester: The Islamic Foundation, 1985.

_____: *In the Early Hours: Reflections on Spiritual and Self-Development*, Leicester: Revival Publications, 2007.

_____: *Inter-Personal Relations: An Islamic Perspective*, Leicester: The Islamic Foundation, 2005.

Murad, A. H., *Muslim Songs of the British Isles*, London: The Quilliam Press, 2005.

_____: 'Marmaduke Pickthall: a brief biography', see www.masud.co.uk

_____: 'The Unusual Life of William Williamson', see www.masud.co.uk

Muzaffar, A., *The Language of Political Islam: India 1200–1800*, London: C. Hurst & Co, 2004.


## N

Nadvi, A. S. S., *Hazrat Aisha Siddiqa: Her Life and Works*, Kuwait: Islamic Book Publishers, 1986.

_____: *Heroic Deeds of Muslim Women*, New Delhi: Adam Publishers, 1985.

_____: *Ard ul-Qur'an (A Geographical History of the Qur'an)* translated by S. M. Nadvi, Lahore: Muhammad Ashraf, 1974.

_____: *The Arab Navigation*, New Delhi: Adam Publishers, 2006.

Nadwi, A. H. A., *The Glory of Iqbal*, Lucknow: Academy of Islamic Research and Publications, 1979.

_____: *Islam and the Earliest Muslims: Two Conflicting Portraits*, Lucknow: Academy of Islamic Research & Publications, 1985.

_____: *Saviours of Islamic Spirit*, 4 vols, Karachi: Darul Isha'at, 1994.

_____: *Islamic Studies, Orientalists and Muslim Scholars*, Lucknow: Academy of Islamic Research & Publications, 1983.

Nash, G., *From Empire to Orient: Travellers to the Middle East 1830–1926*, London: I. B. Tauris, 2005.

Nasr, S. H. (ed.), *Islamic Spirituality*, 2 vols, London: SCM Press, 1989.

_____: (ed.), *The Study Qur'an: A New Translation and Commentary*, New York: HarperOne, 2015.

_____: *Science and Civilization in Islam*, Cambridge: Islamic Text Society, 1987.

_____: *Three Muslim Sages*, Cambridge: Harvard University Press, 1964.

_____: *Islamic Science: An Illustrated Study*, London: World of Islam Festival Publishing Company, 1976.

Nasr, S. H. and O'Brien, K., *In the Quest of the Sacred: The Modern World in the Light of Tradition*, Oakton: The Foundation for Traditional Studies, 1994.

Newman, A., *Safavid Iran*, London: I.B.Tauris, 2005.

Nicholson, R. A., *The Mystics of Islam*, London: Arkana, 1989.

_____: *A Literary History of the Arabs*, Cambridge: CUP, 1969.

Nielsen, J. S., *Muslims in Western Europe*, Edinburgh: Edinburgh University Press, 2001.

van Nieuwkerk, K. (ed.), *Women Embracing Islam: Gender and Conversion in the West*, Austin: University of Texas, 2006.

Norris, H. T., *Islam in the Balkans: Religion and Society between Europe and the Arab World*, London: Hurst & Company, 1993.


## O

O'Leary, D., *How Greek Science Passed to the Arabs*, Delhi: Goodword Books, 2001.

Ortayli, I., *Discovering the Ottomans*, Leicester: Kube Publishing, 2009.

Ozyurek, E., *Being German, Becoming Muslim: Race, Religion, and Conversion in the New Europe*, New Jersey: Princeton University Press, 2015.


## P

Parkinson, J. Y., *Essays on Islamic Philosophy*, Rangoon: British Burma Press, 1909.

_____: *Muslim Chivalry*, Rangoon: British Burma Press, 1909.

Philby, H. S. B., *The Heart of Arabia: A Record of Travel Exploration*, 2 vols, London: Constable and Company, 1922.

_____: *Arabian Oil Ventures*, Washington, D. C.: The Middle East Institute, 1964.

Pickthall, M. M., *The Cultural Side of Islam*, Lahore: Muhammad Ashraf, 1979.

_____: *Oriental Encounters*, London: Travellers Library, 1929.

_____: *The Meaning of the Koran: An Explanatory Translation*, New York: Dorset Press, no date.

_____: *The House of Islam*, New York: D. Appleton and Company, 1906.

_____: *Said the Fisherman*, London: Methuen and Co., 1910.

_____: *With the Turk in Wartime*, London: J. M. Dent & Sons, 1914.

Plumb, J. H., *The Death of the Past*, London: Macmillan Press, 1978.

_____: *The Pelican Book of the Renaissance*, Middlesex: Penguin, 1982.

## Q

Quraishi, M. T., *Ismail al-Faruqi: An Enduring Legacy*, Indiana: MSA, 1987.

Qureshi, S. A., *Letters of the Holy Prophet*, New Delhi: Noor Publishing House, 1986.

al-Qurtubi, *al-Jami li-Akham al-Qur'an*, 24 vols, Beirut: Al-Risalah, 2006.

## R

Rahim, A., *Principles of Muhammadan Jurisprudence*, Madras: S. P. C. Press, 1911.

Rahman, F., *Revival and Reform in Islam*, Oxford: Oneworld Publishers, 2000.

_____: *Islam*, New York: Holt, Rinehart and Winston, 1966.

_____: *Major Themes of the Qur'an*, Chicago: University of Chicago Press, 2009.

_____: *Islam and Modernity: Transformation of an Intellectual Tradition*, Chicago: University of Chicago Press, 1982.

Rahman, M. & Rahman, G., *Geography of the Muslim World*, Chicago: Iqra, 1997.

Rahnema, A., *Pioneers of Islamic Revival*, London: Zed Books, 2005.

Ramadan, T., *Muslims in France: The Way towards Coexistence*, Leicester: The Islamic Foundation, 1999.

Rashid, S., 'Islamic Influence in America: Struggle, Flight, Community', *Journal of Muslim Minority Affairs*, vol. 19, no. 1.

al-Raysuni, A., *Imam al-Shatibi's Theory of the Higher Objectives and Intents of Islamic Law*, Herndon: IIIT, 2011.

Reeves, M., *Muhammad in Europe: A Thousand Years of Western Myth-Making*, 2000.

Remnick, D., *King of the World: Muhammad Ali and Rise of an American Hero*, London: Picador, 2000.

Renier, G. J., *History: Its Purpose and Method*, London: George Allen & Unwin, 1950.

Rietbergen, P., *Europe: A Cultural History*, London: Routledge, 1998.

Roberts, J. M., *The Triumph of the West: The Origin, rise, and Legacy of Western Civilization*, London: Phoenix Press, 2001.

_____: *A History of Europe*, Oxford: Helicon Publishing, 1996.

Robertson, B. A., 'Islam and Europe: An Enigma or a Myth?' *The Middle East Journal*, vol. 48, No. 2.

Robinson, C. F. et al. (ed.), *The New Cambridge History of Islam*, 6 vols, Cambridge: CUP, 2010.

Robinson, F. (ed.), *Cambridge Illustrated History of the Islamic World*, Cambridge: Cambridge University Press, 1996.

Rosenthal, F., *The Classical Heritage in Islam*, London: Routledge & Keegan Paul, 1975.

Rumi, J., *The Mathnawi of Jalaluddin Rumi*, translated by R.A. Nicholson, 3 vols, Lahore: Islamic Book Service, 1989.

Ruthven, M., *Islam in the World*, London: Penguin, 2000.

Russell, B., *A History of Western Philosophy*, London: Unwin Hyman, 1979.

## S

as-Salabi, *The Biography of Shaikh Umar al-Mukhtar*, London: al-Firdous, 2011.

Sacks, J., *To Heal a Fractured World: The Ethics of Responsibility*, London: Continuum, 2005.

Sa'di, M., *The Bustan of Sa'di*, translated by A.H. Edwards, New Delhi: Kitab Bhavan, 2000.

Said, E.W., *Orientalism: Western Conceptions of the Orient*, London: Penguin, 1995.

Schacht, J. & Bosworth, C. E. (ed.), *The Legacy of Islam*, Oxford: Clarendon Press, 1974.

Schimmel, A., *And Muhammad is His Messenger: The Veneration of the Prophet in Islamic Piety*, Chapel Hill: University of North Carolina Press, 1985.

Schuon, F., *The Transcendent Unity of Religions*, Wheaton: Theosophical Publishing House, 1993.

_____: *Understanding Islam*, Indiana: World Wisdom, 2011.

_____: *The Essential Frithjof Schuon*, Indiana, World Wisdom Books, 2006.

_____: *Logic and Transcendence*, Indiana: World Wisdom Books, 2009.

_____: *From the Divine to Human*, Indiana: World Wisdom Books, 2013.

_____: *Sufism: Veil and Quintessence*, Indiana: World Wisdom Books, 2006.

_____: *Islam and Perennial Philosophy*, London: World of Islam Festival Publishing Company, 1976.

Seddon, M. S., *The Last of the Lascars*, Leicester: Kube Publishing, 2014.

Shaban, M. A., *Islamic History: A New Interpretation*, 2 vols, Cambridge: CUP, 1994.

Shah, I., *Thinkers of the East*, London: Penguin, 1974.

Shah-Kazemi, R., 'A Tribute to Martin Lings on the Occasion of his 90th Birthday', *Sophia: The Journal of Traditional Studies*, vol. 5. No. 2.

Shafiq, M., *Growth of Islamic Thought in North America*, Maryland: Amana Publications, 1994.

Sharif, M. M. (ed.), *A History of Muslim Philosophy*, 2 vols, Delhi: Adam Publishers, 2001.

Shaw, S. J., *History of the Ottoman Empire and Modern Turkey*, 2 vols, Cambridge: CUP, 2010.

Sherif, M. A., *Searching for Solace: A Biography of Abdullah Yusuf Ali*, Malaysia: Islamic Book Trust, 1994.

_____: *Brave Hearts: Pickthall and Philby: Two English Muslims in a Changing World*, Selangor: IBT, 2011.

_____: *Why an Islamic State: The Life Projects of two Great European Muslims*, Selangor: IBT, 2009.

Shushud, H., *Masters of Wisdom of Central Asia*, Moorcote: Coombe Springs Press, 1983.

Siddiqi, M. I., *Asharah Mubashsharah*, New Delhi: Idara Isha'at-i-Diniyat, 1990.

Siddiqi, M. Z., *Hadith Literature: Its Origin, Development and Special Features*, Cambridge: Islamic Text Society, 1993.

Siddiqi, M., *The Qur'anic Concept of History*, Islamabad: Islamic Research Institute, 1984.

_____: *Modern Reformist Thought in the Muslim World*, New Delhi: Adam Publishers, 1993.

Singleton, B. D. (ed.), *The Convert's Passion: An Anthology of Islamic Poetry from Late Victorian and Edwardian Britain*, Maryland: The Borgo Press, 2009.

_____: 'Brothers at Odds: Rival Islamic Movements in Late Nineteenth Century New York City', *Journal of Muslim Minority Affairs*, vol. 27, No. 3.

_____: *Yankee Muslim: Mohammed Alexander Russell Webb*, Maryland: The Borgo Press, 2007.

Smith, J. I., *Islam in America*, New York: Columbia University Press, 1999.

Smith, M., *Rabia the Mystic and Her Fellow Saints in Islam*, Cambridge: Press Syndicate, 1984.

Smith, J. Z., *The HarperCollins Dictionary of Religion*, London: HarperSanFrancisco, 1996.

Sonyel, S. R., *The Muslims of Bosnia: Genocide of a People*, Leicester: The Islamic Foundation, 1994.

Spengler, O., *The Decline of the West*, New York: OUP, 1991.

Suceska, A., 'The Position of the Bosnian Moslems in the Ottoman Empire', *International Journal of Turkish Studies*, vol. 1, No. 2.

Suvorova, A., *Muslim Saints of South Asia: The Eleventh to Fifteenth Centuries*, London: Routledge, 2004.

Stierlin, H., *Islamic Art and Architecture: From Isfahan to Taj Mahal*, London: Thames and Hudson, 2002.

Stulrajterova, K., 'Convivenza, Convenienza and Conversion: Islam in Medieval Hungary (1000–1400 CE)', *Journal of Islamic Studies*, vol. 24, issue 2.


**T**

al-Tabari, *Tarikh al-Rusul wal Muluk* (translated as 'The History of al-Tabari'), 38 vols, edited by Y. Yarshater, Albany: State University of New York Press, 1985–2000.

Tarnas, R., *The Passion of the Western Mind: Understanding the Ideas that have Shaped our World View*, London: Pimlico, 1996.

Taylor, J. A., *Muslims in Medieval Italy*, Oxford: Lexington Books, 2003.

Thompson, M. J. (ed.), *Islam and the West: Critical Perspectives on Modernity*, Maryland: Rowman & Littelfield, 2003.

Toynbee, A. J., *A Study of History*, 12 vols, Oxford: OUP, 1934–1961.

Tottoli, R. (ed.), *Routledge Handbook of Islam in the West*, London: Routledge, 2015.

Trimingham, S., *The Sufi Orders in Islam*, Oxford: Oxford University Press, 1971.

Troll, C.W., *Sayyid Ahmad Khan: A Reinterpretation of Muslim Theology*, New Delhi: Vikas Publishing, 1978.


**U**

al-Umuri, U. S., ''Abdullah Philby: Hayatuhu wa Asruhu', *Ad-Darah: Periodic Quarterly*, vol. 25, No. 3.


**W**

Waardenburg, J. (ed.), *Muslim Perceptions of Other Religions: A Historical Survey*, New York: OUP, 1999.

al-Wahhab, M. A., *Kitab al-Tawhid*, Kuwait: IIFSO, 1979.

Walker, D., *Islam and the Search for African-American Nationhood*, Atlanta: Clarity Press, 2005.

Walker, C. J., *Islam and the West: A Dissonant Harmony of Civilisations*, Stroud: Sutton Publishing, 2005.

Waliullah, S., *Sufism and the Islamic Tradition*, translated by G.N. Jalbani, London: Octagon Press, 1980.

_____: *Hujjat Allah al-Balighah*, Dhaka: Rashid Book House, 1992.

Walther, W., *Women in Islam: From Medieval to Modern Times*, New Jersey: Markus Wiener Publishing, 1993.

Warren, J., *History and the Historians*, Oxon: Bookpoint Ltd, 2004.

Wasserstein, D. J., *The Caliphate in the West: An Islamic Political Institution in the Iberian Peninsula*, Oxford: Clarendon Press, 1993.

Waterfield, R., *Rene Guenon and the Future of the West*, New York: Sophia Perennis, 2002.

Watt, W. M., *The Formative Period of Islamic Thought*, Oxford: Oneworld Publications, 1998.

Webb, M. A. R., *The Moslem World and Voice of Islam*, Marston Gate: Amazon.co.uk

Wheatcroft, A., *The Ottomans: Dissolving Images*, London: Penguin, 1995.

Williams, R., *Keywords: A vocabulary of culture and society*, London: Fontana Press, 1988.

Wolfe, M. (ed.), *One Thousand Roads to Mecca: Ten Centuries of Travelers Writing about the Muslim Pilgrimage*, New York: Grove Press, 1997.

Wood, S. A., *Christian Criticism, Islamic Proofs: Rashid Rida's Modernist Defence of Islam*, Oxford: Oneworld, 2012.


## Y

Yermolenko, G., 'Roxolana: "The Greatest Empress of the East"', *The Muslim World*, vol. 95, No. 2_____ (ed.), *Roxolana in European Literature, History and Culture*, Abingdon: Routledge, 2016.

Yusuf, I. (ed.), *Islam and Knowledge: Al-Faruqi's Conception of Religion in Islamic Thought*, New York: I. B. Tauris and IIIT, 2012.

Yusuf, S. M., *Studies in Islamic History and Culture*, Delhi: Adam Publishers, 1992.


## Z

Zaydan, J., *History of Islamic Civilization*, New Delhi: Kitab Bhavan, 1994.

_____: *Ta'rikh al-Tamaddun al-Islami*, 5 vols, Cairo, 1902.

Zekaj, R., *The Development of the Islamic Culture among Albanians during the 20$^{th}$ Century*, Tirane: AIITC, 1997.

Zulfikarpasic, A., *The Bosniak*, London: Hurst & Company, 1998.

# INDEX